THIRD EDITION

International Law

CLASSIC AND CONTEMPORARY READINGS

THIRD EDITION

International Law

CLASSIC AND CONTEMPORARY READINGS

EDITED BY

Charlotte Ku and Paul F. Diehl

New Delhi | Mumbai | Chennai | Kolkata | Bangalore | Hyderabad | Kochi | Guwahati

First Indian Edition 2010

VIVA BOOKS PRIVATE LIMITED

- 4737/23 Ansari Road, Daryaganj, New Delhi 110 002
  E-mail: vivadelhi@vivagroupindia.net, Tel. 42242200
- Plot No. 76, Service Industries, Shirvane, Sector 1, Nerul, Navi Mumbai 400 706
  E-mail: vivamumbai@vivagroupindia.net, Tel. 27721273, 27721274
- Jamals Fazal Chambers, 26 Greams Road, Chennai 600 006
  E-mail: vivachennai@vivagroupindia.net, Tel. 28290304, 28294241
- B-103, Jindal Towers, 21/1A/3 Darga Road, Kolkata 700 017
  E-mail: vivakolkata@vivagroupindia.net, Tel. 22836381, 22816713
- 7, Sovereign Park Apartments, 56-58, K. R. Road, Basavanagudi, Bangalore 560 004
  E-mail: vivabangalore@vivagroupindia.net, Tel. 26607409, 26607410
- 101-102 Mughal Marc Aptt., 3-4-637 to 641, Narayanguda, Hyderabad 500 029
  E-mail: vivahyderabad@vivagroupindia.net, Tel. 27564481, 27564482
- First Floor, Beevi Towers, SRM Road, Kaloor, Kochi 682 018, Kerala
  E-mail: vivakochi@vivagroupindia.net, Tel: 0484-2403055, 2403056
- 232, GNB Road, Beside UCO Bank, Silpukhuri, Guwahati 781 003
  E-mail: vivaguwahati@vivagroupindia.net, Tel: 0361-2666386

Published by arrangement with

Lynne Rienner Publishers Inc.
1800 30th Street, Boulder,
Colorado 80301
USA

ISBN 978-81-309-1219-6

Published by Vinod Vasishtha for Viva Books Private Limited, 4737/23, Ansari Road, New Delhi - 110 002. Printed and bound by Anand Sons, Delhi - 110 092.

Contents

1 International Law as Operating and Normative Systems: An Overview, *Charlotte Ku and Paul F. Diehl* 1

Part 1 International Law as Operating System

Sources of International Law

2 Hard and Soft Law in International Governance, *Kenneth Abbott and Duncan Snidal* 21

3 Traditional and Modern Approaches to Customary International Law: A Reconciliation, *Anthea Roberts* 49

4 Normative Hierarchy in International Law, *Dinah Shelton* 77

Participants in the International Legal Process

5 The New Treaty Makers, *Jose E. Alvarez* 101

6 Nongovernmental Organizations and International Law, *Steve Charnovitz* 117

Implementation and Compliance with International Law

7 Compliance with International Agreements, *Beth Simmons* 143

8 Filling In the Gaps: Extrasystemic Mechanisms for Addressing Imbalances Between the International Legal Operating and Normative Systems, *Charlotte Ku and Paul F. Diehl* 163

9 Princeton Principles on Universal Jurisdiction, *The Princeton Project* 185

International Legal Structures

10 A Babel of Judicial Voices? Ruminations from the Bench, *Rosalyn Higgins* 205

11 The Place of the WTO and Its Law in the International Legal Order, *Pascal Lamy* 219

12 The Role of the International Criminal Court in Enforcing International Criminal Law, *Philippe Kirsch* 237

Part 2 International Law as Normative System

To Regulate the Use of Force

13 "Jus ad Bellum," "Jus in Bello" . . . "Jus post Bellum"?—Rethinking the Conception of the Law of Armed Force, *Carsten Stahn* 247

14 Legal Control of International Terrorism: A Policy Oriented Assessment, *M. Cherif Bassiouni* 269

For the Protection of Individual Rights

15 The Evolving International Human Rights System, *Thomas Buergenthal* 289

16 The Responsibility to Protect: Humanitarian Concern and the Lawfulness of Armed Intervention, *Christopher C. Joyner* 319

For the Protection of the Environment

17 International Environmental Agreements: A Survey of Their Features, Formation, and Effects, *Ronald Mitchell* 341

18 Responsibility for Biological Diversity Conservation Under International Law, *Catherine Tinker* 371

Managing the Commons

19 The Territorial Temptation: A Siren Song at Sea, *Bernard Oxman* 401

20 Towards a New Regime for the Protection of Outer Space as a Province of All Mankind, *David Tan* 421

Part 3 The Future of International Law

21 The Yahoo Case and Conflict of Laws in the Cyberage,
Mathias Reimann 457

22 The Future of International Law Is Domestic
(or, The European Way of Law),
Anne-Marie Slaughter and William Burke-White 465

Index 491
About the Book 507

CHAPTER 1

International Law as Operating and Normative Systems: An Overview

Charlotte Ku and Paul F. Diehl

THE END OF THE COLD WAR IN 1989 HERALDED THE ADVENT of a new international order including a renewed emphasis and concern with international law. The US president at the time, George H. W. Bush, and others identified international relations "governed by the rule of law" as the defining feature of the emerging world order. Yet acts of genocide in Bosnia and Rwanda, together with the failure of the United Nations (UN) to meet renewed expectations, have left us with a world in which rules and norms are not always clearly defined or carefully observed.

In this collection, we consider international law from a fresh perspective, seeking to move beyond esoteric descriptions of the law prevalent in scholarly legal treatments, by examining international law's influence on political behavior, something largely ignored in standard analyses of international relations. There are several unique features of this effort. First, this book is perhaps the only collection that focuses on the politics of international law and does so by covering the main topics of the subject (e.g., sources, participants, courts, dispute settlement, jurisdiction, and sovereignty). Second, it is contemporary, reflecting the major changes in international relations after the Cold War and covering emerging topics in the subject such as human rights and the environment. Third, it attempts to draw a bridge between the purely legal and purely political consideration of public international law. Finally, this book offers an organizational scheme for considering international law, drawing the distinction between elements of international law that function as an operating system for international relations (e.g., courts, jurisdiction, etc.) and those that present a normative system that seeks to direct behavior in the international system (e.g., human rights, environmental prescriptions).

We begin by addressing the most basic of questions: What is international law? We then move to develop our conception of international law as a dual system for regulating interactions, both generally and within specific areas.

What Is International Law?

The basic question that we ask here—What is international law?—is straightforward enough, and it seems simple enough to answer. After all, we have a general image of what the *law* is, and the meaning of the word *international* seems self-evident. Yet when we put the two words together, we find ourselves faced with other questions that stem from our understanding of their meanings. In Western democracies, the word *law* immediately conjures up images of legislatures, police, and courts that create law, enforce it, and punish those who violate it. *International* brings up images not only of the United Nations but also of wide-ranging global differences—economic, cultural, and political. How can these two images come together? How can one imagine a structured and developed legal system functioning in a political environment that is diffuse, disparate, unregulated, and conventionally described as anarchic?

The basic question "What is international law?" embodies several other questions that need to be answered in order to understand what we are examining: (1) What does international law do? (2) How does it work? (3) Is it effective in what it does? And ultimately (4) What can we expect from it?

The first three questions necessarily deal with the diffusion and lack of regulation that exist in a political system consisting of multiple sovereign actors. As the principal possessors of coercive means in international relations, states seem to have their own exclusive recourse to the resolution of disputes. How can states be restrained? What can possibly modify their behavior? Yet behavior is restrained, and anarchy is not always the dominant mode of international politics. States also do not have a monopoly on international intercourse. International organizations, nongovernmental organizations (NGOs), multinational corporations, and even private individuals have come to play an increasing role in international relations, and accordingly international legal rules have evolved to engage these new actors.

This leads to the last of the four questions: If international law is a factor in state behavior, then what can we expect it to do? First, we expect it to facilitate and to support the daily business of international relations and politics. It does so principally by allocating decisionmaking power within the international system, thereby providing an alternative to unregulated competition. The structure and process of international law prevent the pursuit of multiple national or private interests from dissolving into anarchy. It also allows for the coexistence of multiple political units and their interaction. It provides a framework for the international system to *operate* effectively. Second, international law advances particular values—the regulation of the use of force, the protection of individual rights, and the management of the commons are prominent examples of such values. In this area, international law promotes the creation of a *normative* consensus on international behavior.

The Dual Character of International Law

International law provides both an operating system and a normative system for international relations. Conceptualizing international law as an operating system considers, in a broad sense, how it sets the general procedures and institutions for the conduct of international relations. As an operating system, international law provides the framework for establishing rules and norms, outlines the parameters of interaction, and provides the procedures and forums for resolving disputes among those taking part in these interactions. In contrast, international law as a normative system provides direction for international relations by identifying the substantive values and goals to be pursued. If the operating system designates the "structures" (in a loose sense) that help channel international politics, then the normative element gives form to the aspirations and values of the participants of the system. As a normative system, law is a product of the structures and processes that make up the operating system. The operating system is based on state consensus as expressed through widespread practice over time; the normative system must build a base of support for each if its undertakings. As an operating system, international law adopts a few of the functions that constitutions perform in some domestic legal systems by setting out the consensus of its constituent actors (states) on distribution of authority, responsibilities in governing, and the units that will carry out specific functions. We chose the word *operating* as one would conceive of a computer's operating system. It is the basic platform upon which a system will operate. When a computer's operating system (e.g., Microsoft Windows) functions to allow the use of specific word-processing programs, spreadsheets, and communications software, there is little direct consideration given to that system by the user. Similarly, the operating system of international law provides the signals and commands that make multiple functions and modes possible and when functioning often requires little conscious effort. As a normative system, international law takes on a principally legislative character by mandating particular values and directing specific changes in state behavior.

Below we outline our conceptions of the operating and normative systems and discuss their similarities and differences with related conceptions. We also briefly identify some trends in the evolution of the two systems. Integrated into these analyses are descriptions of the remaining chapters in the collection.

Operating System

The dual character of international law results from its Westphalian legacy in which law functions between, rather than above, states and in which the state carries out the legislative, judicial, and executive functions that in domestic legal systems are frequently assigned by constitutions to separate institutions. Constitutions also provide legal capacity by allocating power and by recognizing rights and duties. Constitutions further condition the environment in which power is to be used and rights and duties to be exercised.

In order for the operating system to maintain vibrancy and resiliency, and to assure the stability necessary for orderly behavior, it must provide for a dynamic normative system that facilitates the competition of values, views, and actors. It does so by applying the constitutional functions as described above when including new actors, new issues, new structures, and new norms. Who, for example, are the authorized decisionmakers in international law? Whose actions can bind not only the parties involved but also others? How do we know that an authoritative decision has taken place? When does the resolution of a conflict or a dispute give rise to new law? These are the questions that the operating system answers. Note, in particular, that the operating system may be associated with formal structures, but not all operating system elements are institutional. For example, the Vienna Convention on Treaties entails no institutional mechanisms, but it does specify various operational rules about treaties and therefore the parameters of lawmaking.

The operating system has a number of dimensions or components that are typically covered in international law textbooks but largely unconnected to one another. Some of the primary components include:

1. Sources of Law: These include the system rules for defining the process through which law is formed, the criteria for determining when legal obligations exist, and which actors are bound (or not) by that law. This element of the operating system also specifies a hierarchy of different legal sources. For example, the operating system defines whether UN resolutions are legally binding (generally not) and what role they play in the legal process (possible evidence of customary law).

2. Actors: This dimension includes determining which actors are eligible to have rights and obligations under the law. The operating system also determines how and the degree to which those actors might exercise those rights internationally. For example, individuals and multinational corporations may enjoy certain international legal protections, but those rights might be asserted in international forums only by their home states.

3. Jurisdiction: These rules define the rights of actors and institutions to deal with legal problems and violations. An important element is defining what problems or situations will be handled through national legal systems as opposed to international forums. For example, the 1985 Convention on Torture allows states to prosecute perpetrators in their custody, regardless of the location of the offense and the nationality of the perpetrator or victim, affirming the principle of universal jurisdiction.

4. Courts or Institutions: These elements create forums and accompanying rules under which international legal disputes might be heard or decisions enforced. Thus, for example, the Statute of the International Court of Justice provides for the creation of the institution, sets general rules of decisionmaking, identifies the processes and scope under which cases are heard, specifies the composition of the court, and details decisionmaking procedures (to name a few).

Our conception of an operating system clearly overlaps with some prior formulations but is different in some fundamental ways. Regime theory[1] refers to decisionmaking procedures as practices for making and implementing collective choice, similar to "regulative norms,"[2] that lessen transaction costs of collective action. Although these may be encompassed by the international law operating system, our conception of the latter is broader. The operating system is not necessarily issue-specific but may deal equally well (or poorly) with multiple issues—note that the International Court of Justice may adjudicate disputes involving airspace as well as war crimes. Regime decisionmaking procedures are also thought to reflect norms, rules, and principles without much independent standing.

H. L. A. Hart developed the notion of "secondary rules" to refer to the ways in which primary rules might be "conclusively ascertained, introduced, eliminated, varied, and the fact of their violation conclusively determined."[3] This comports in many ways with our conception of an international legal operating system. Yet Hart views secondary rules (his choice of the term *secondary* is illuminating) as "parasitic" to the primary ones. This suggests that secondary rules follow in time the development of primary rules, especially in primitive legal systems (which international law is sometimes compared to). Furthermore, secondary rules are believed to service normative ones, solving the problems of uncertainty, stasis, and inefficiency inherently found with normative rules.

Our conception of an international legal operating system is somewhat different. For us, the operating system is usually independent of any single norm or regime and, therefore, is greater than the sum of any parts derived from individual norms and regimes. The operating system in many cases, past its origin point, may precede the development of parts of the normative system rather than merely reacting to it. In this conception, the operating system is not a mere servant to the normative system, but the former can actually shape the development of the latter. For example, established rules on jurisdiction may restrict the development of new normative rules on what kinds of behaviors might be labeled as international crimes. Neither is the operating system as reflective of the normative system as Hart implies it is. The operating system may develop some of its configurations autonomously from specific norms, thereby serving political as well as legal needs (e.g., the creation of an international organization that also performs monitoring functions). In the relatively anarchic world of international relations, we argue that this is more likely than in the domestic legal systems on which Hart primarily based his analysis.

Indeed, this may explain why, in many cases, the operating system for international law is far more developed than its normative counterpart; for example, we have extensive rules and agreements on treaties but relatively few dealing with the use of force. Furthermore, the operating system has a greater stickiness than might be implied in Hart's formulations. The operating system may be more resistant to change and not always responsive to alterations in the normative system or the primary rules. This is not merely a matter of moving from a primitive legal system to a more advanced one (as Hart would argue) but rather considering how adaptive the two systems are to each other. Finally, our formulation sees effective norm development as dependent on the operating system or the structural dimension. A failure to understand this dependence may stall or obstruct a norm's effectiveness. Again, the metaphor of a computer's operating system may be useful, as the failure of the operating system to support adequately a software application will slow down or render inoperable features of that application for the user.

The evolution of the operating system in all of the areas enumerated above has been toward expansion—in the number of actors, in the forms of decisionmaking, and in the forums and modes of implementation. Although international law remains principally a body of rules and practices to regulate state behavior in the conduct of interstate relations, much of international law now also regulates the conduct of governments and the behavior of individuals within states and may address issues that require ongoing transnational cooperation. Human rights law is an example of the normative system regulating behavior within states. Such human rights law, however, may configure elements of the operating system in that the human rights granted may convey legal personality to individuals, thereby rendering them capable of holding or exercising legal rights. Activities such as the follow-up conferences to the Helsinki Accords or the periodic meetings of the parties to the Framework Convention on Climate Change are specific examples of the operating system designed to give such norms effect.

Because international law lacks the institutional trappings and hierarchical character of domestic law, its organizing principles and how they work are important to identify. These are the elements of the operating system. First, one must know where to find international law. Because the international legal system has no single legislative body, it is sometimes difficult knowing where to start. One begins with state behavior and examines the sources of international law to interpret state behavior and to identify when such behavior takes on an obligatory character. The sources of international law further provide guidance on how to find the substance of international law by highlighting key moments in the lawmaking process. Sources help us to locate the products of the lawmaking process by identifying its form. For example, international agreements are generally to be found in written texts. Law created by custom, however, will require locating patterns of state behavior over time and assessing whether this behavior is compelled by any sense of legal obligation.

There has been an expansion in the forms of law. This has led to thinking about law as a continuum "ranging from the traditional international legal forms to soft law instruments."[4] This continuum includes resolutions of the UN General Assembly, standards of private organizations such as the International Standards Organization, as well as codes of conduct developed in international organizations. An example is the adoption of a code of conduct on the distribution and use of pesticides by the Food and Agriculture Organization in 1985. The concept of a continuum is useful because these modes are likely not to operate in isolation but rather interact with and build on each other. Chapter 2, the first selection in Part 1 of this book, contrasts hard and soft international law. States may choose one form of law over the other, and Kenneth Abbott and Duncan Snidal explore some of the rationales for this; for example, hard law provides for more credible commitments than softer legal instruments. The two scholars thus reveal that international law is not inherently weak or strong, nor necessarily precise or imprecise. Rather, the configuration of law in the international system comes from explicit choice, and, whatever the form, advantages and disadvantages are attendant to it.

Customary practice and conventions work in tandem to regulate state behavior. The law applicable to the continental shelf is an example of this, as customary practice became codified in a subsequent convention. Traditional conceptions of international law sources have focused on custom and treaty-making between states. Framed in this way, traditional custom may be seen in steep decline relative to the international community of states' preference for more formal arrangements. In Chapter 3, Anthea Roberts challenges that notion by reconceptualizing the bases of customary behavior. She contends that even though traditional views of custom emphasized consistent state practice over time, we now analyze key statements of leaders and decisionmakers rather than state action. Thus, the balance of modern custom has shifted away from state practice and more toward the perception of a legal obligation *(opinio juris)* by those partaking in international relations activities. Such a conception provides for more numerous instances of customary law and lessens its decline in importance vis-à-vis formal international agreements.

There are many sources of hard international law, but at the top of the hierarchy is *jus cogens* or preemptory norms. No international law can violate or supersede such standards, but it is not clear what those norms are or how they come about. In Chapter 4, Dinah Shelton discusses the historical development of these elusive standards, such as the prohibition against slavery. She also covers how they are interpreted and what role they might play in the future of international law.

A second element of the international law operating system includes the participants or actors in the process who create the law and are the subjects of its precepts. This is central because international law is a system that relies largely on self-regulation by the system's units. The number of participants will affect the character of the political process of creating law by determining the number of interests that need to be taken into account, the available resources, and the modes of implementation. The substance of international law will reflect the participants' interests and capacities in the international system. Issues of how, where, and with what effect the law is implemented depend on the economic, political, and other circumstances of participants.

In part because of the expansion in the forms of international law, participants in the international legal process today include more than 190 states and governments, international institutions created by states, and elements of the private sector—multinational corporations and financial institutions, networks of individuals, and NGOs. Not all participants carry the same level of authority in the legal process, but they are recognized either in fact or in practice as playing a role in identifying and promoting particular values.[5] The partnership struck between NGOs and the government of Canada to promote a convention to ban the use of antipersonnel landmines is an example of the collaboration that various actors have undertaken in the international legal process, thereby giving new actors a role in the lawmaking and the subsequent implementation process.

It is in the steady increase in both the number and type of participants in the international legal process that we see some of the most tangible changes in international law. This increase is a critical change, because who is included and who is allowed a voice in the process both affects how the law operates and determines the content of the law. As Jose Alvarez illustrates in detail in Chapter 5, the prevalence of states negotiating bilateral treaties has been replaced with multilateral negotiating forums, often under the auspices of international organizations and involving significant input from NGOs and various other private actors that comprise part of civil society.

The increase in participants began with the end of the Thirty Years' War in 1648 and the acceptance of participation by Protestant princes within the same system as Catholic princes in Europe. The next increase resulted from the empire-building activities of the European powers, which brought non-European states into the international legal process. Most recently, the move has been to include individuals and NGOs, including multinational corporations, into the process. Each addition of participants increases the complexity of the lawmaking process. At the same time, many of the issues in international law today require multiple layers of cooperative and coordinated activity crossing public and private sectors for effective regulation and implementation. Complexity, therefore, cannot be avoided and, indeed, may now be required for the effective operation of international law.

Among the most dramatic changes in international law over the past few decades has been the emergence of NGOs as central players in the legal process. In Chapter 6, Steve Charnovitz details the legal status of NGOs and how they have changed international law. Most international organizations now include provisions for participation of NGOs. The author stops short of claiming that an international duty to consult such entities exists, but he suggests that the international community is moving in that direction.

A third element of the international law operating system is the process under which law is implemented and actors comply (or fail to do so) with international law. Although the number of international agreements has increased and the requirements are more elaborated, surprisingly little is known about what induces compliance with international obligations. The absence of an international police force and other traditional coercive mechanisms for compliance add to the puzzle of why states obey international law (and, in fact, we know they do so most of the time). Beth Simmons (Chapter 7) reviews different explanations for state compliance. These include those based on realpolitik formulations, those based on rationalist ideas, and those that emphasize more normative and less utilitarian considerations. In various ways, she finds each of these lacking in understanding the puzzle.

The enforcement of international law through the operating system is not always efficient or effective. Rather, ensuring compliance often requires reliance on mechanisms outside the formal operating system. Charlotte Ku and Paul Diehl (Chapter 8) identify four processes by which gaps in the operating system are filled: (1) NGOs and transnational networks, (2) internalization of international law, (3) domestic legal and political processes, and (4) soft law mechanisms. Although these mechanisms do not ensure a fully functioning legal system, they are in some cases superior to operating system components designed to fulfill the same functions.

Another aspect of creating an effective international law operating system is determining how remedies for wrongful acts or grievances will work. This requires an understanding of what the wrongful act or grievance is, who the aggrieved party is, who might be responsible for the act, and the applicable law for the situation. The applicable law will then determine the relevant forum or procedure for examining the grievance and will identify available remedies. Among the most critical of those operating rules concern jurisdiction: Which states are allowed to use their own national courts to prosecute individuals for which crimes? Perhaps the most controversial jurisdiction principle has been universal jurisdiction, which allows any state the right to try the accused, provided they have that person in custody. This principle was central in Spanish attempts to try General Augusto Pinochet for actions he took in Chile, as well as aborted attempts to prosecute Israeli prime minister Ariel Sharon in Belgium for acts committed in Lebanon. The Princeton Project (Chapter 9) has developed a set of guidelines, presented here, for how universal jurisdiction should be applied. This commentary on new principles for universal jurisdiction reveals the various disputes and competing interests that arise in constructing such operating system rules.

The forums and modes for implementation have also expanded. Although international law still relies on domestic legal and political structures for implementation, the international community has also created new international institutions and recognized transnational legal processes that have over time become recognized forums in which to engage in decision-making, interpretation, and recently even the prosecution of individuals on the basis of violations of international law.[6] Not only do representatives of states continue to meet to make law; they also meet routinely in international settings to ensure its implementation and compliance (e.g., meetings of UN organs or the Conference on Security and Cooperation in Europe follow-up meetings after the Helsinki Accords in 1975).

Two developments are particularly noteworthy. One is the emerging systematic understanding of how international norms or rules of behavior are actually being given effect and implemented through domestic legal systems. The other is the creation of international courts adding to the institutional underpinnings of international law. Both developments are additions to the capacity of the international legal system to meet its objectives.

The first development is evidenced by studies on transnational law, transnational legal process, and transnational networks. In his classic *Transnational Law,* Philip Jessup coined this term in order to capture the "complex interrelated world community which may be described as beginning with the individual and reaching up to the so-called 'family of nations' or 'society of states.'"[7] Harold Hongju Koh puts a contemporary gloss on this by describing a

> transnational legal process . . . whereby an international law rule is interpreted through the interaction of transnational actors in a variety of law declaring fora, then internalized into a nation's domestic legal system. Through this three-part process of interaction, interpretation, and internalization, international legal rules become integrated into national law and assume the status of internally binding domestic legal obligations.[8]

Anne-Marie Slaughter adds a political-science dimension to her contribution by recognizing a diffusion of state power and functions that makes possible the emergence of transnational networks of government regulators and administrators who can set standards and effectively make law.[9]

On the international level, the most notable operating system development is the creation of international courts to interpret and to implement the law. Standing permanent courts with impartial judges and a published jurisprudence are important building blocks in any legal system as means for not only settling disputes but also interpreting and elaborating existing law. When the decisions made are published, state behavior can be modified by setting a range of acceptable conduct and interpretation in particular areas. One of the most significant developments in building international legal institutions was the establishment of the International Court of Justice, a permanent tribunal with judges elected to serve in their individual capacities to settle disputes between states. Nevertheless, the nearly ninety years of the operation of the Permanent Court of International Justice and its successor (the International Court of Justice) demonstrate that the existence of a standing court has replaced neither the use of force nor other non-judicial methods to resolve international disputes.

Since the early 1990s, however, there has been an explosion of new international legal institutions and the increased use of extant courts. Rosalyn Higgins, a justice on the International Court of Justice (ICJ), reviews some of the potential problems that arise when multiple tribunals—for example the International Criminal Court and the ICJ—deal with the same issues or aspects of the same cases (Chapter 10). She then reviews several solutions to the difficulties that arise. Following Higgins's contribution, we include examinations of two of the most prominent and controversial judicial mechanisms: the World Trade Organization (WTO) dispute resolution process and the International Criminal Court (ICC).

A key element of the General Agreement on Tariffs and Trade, the landmark economic treaty concluded in April 1994, was the establishment of a WTO that has legal authority to monitor and adjudicate trade disputes between states. Pascal Lamy (Chapter 11) first describes what makes the WTO mechanism unique and a break with past arrangements under the General Agreement on Tariffs and Trade (GATT) system. He then discusses how the WTO legal system is linked with those of other international organizations. The ICC is one of the few international courts in which individuals, rather than states, may be parties to the proceedings. In Chapter 12, Philippe Kirsch provides some of the background for the ICC as well as identifying some of the key provisions of the ICC statute. It becomes clear that many of the provisions reflect the necessity of finding a middle ground between the ideals of punishing international crimes and the realities of diplomatic compromise between states with different political and cultural agendas. The effectiveness of the ICC is something that will have to be evaluated in future decades, but its mere creation represents a major divergence from past international legal practice.

Overall, the operating system provides the framework within which international law is created and implemented, and it defines the roles of different actors and also provides mechanisms for the protection of rights and the settlement of disputes. The materials presented in Part 1 demonstrate that even though key elements of the operating system are settled, they do not remain static. Pressures for change are ongoing and will succeed when changes are required to keep the operating system appropriate and effective in supporting contemporary international politics. The elements of the operating system must continuously pass a test of functionality: if they fail to perform, the elements will be replaced by others that serve the broad and general interest of allocating power and of ensuring reasonable order in the conduct of international relations. Competing demands and interests among the operating elements help to identify areas in which adjustments are needed so that when the political circumstances dictate change, international law is ready to respond.

The Normative System

We choose the word *normative* to describe the directive aspects of international law because this area of law functions to create norms out of particular values or policies. Using a different set of analogies, we could imagine normative processes as quasilegislative in character by mandating particular values and directing specific changes in state and other actors' behaviors. Use of the terms *norm* and *norms* abound in the study of international relations, and it is not always clear what meaning is conveyed by a particular construction. In the regimes literature, norms and principles (e.g., orthodox versus embedded liberalism in trade) are broader philosophies of how states and other actors should behave. Although they tend to be issue-specific (e.g., trade, human rights), regime norms are not generally defined at the micro level (e.g., precise changes in rules governing certain human rights violations). In this sense, they are similar to what Michael Barnett refers to as "constitutive norms."[10] Our conception of norms in one sense is narrower and more precise. We focus only on normative elements that have a legally binding character, analogous to the idea of rules in the regime literature. Because we are interested in the international legal system, we are not concerned with acts of "comity," which might be appropriate subjects for a broader inquiry of international norms. In another sense, we have a deeper conception for norms that goes beyond broad general principles to include specific elements about behavior. That is, our normative system is concerned with particular prescriptions and proscriptions, such as limitations on child labor.

Our conception of a normative system is similar to what Hart defines as primary rules that impose duties on actors to perform or abstain from actions.[11] But there is an important difference: Hart sees primary rules as the basic building blocks of a legal system, logically and naturally coming before the development of what we define as the operating system components. For Hart, a primitive legal system can be one with developed rules but without substantial structures to interpret or enforce those rules. We see a more developed international legal system in which norms may exist without specific reference to the operating system yet cannot function without using the operating system's mechanisms. Nevertheless, the normative system may remain somewhat autonomous from the operating system and may even lag behind in its development.

In defining the normative system, the participants in the international legal process engage in a political and legislative exercise that defines the substance and scope of the law. Normative change may occur slowly with evolution of customary practices, a traditional source of international law. Yet in recent historical periods, normative change has been precipitated by new treaties (e.g., the Nuclear Non-Proliferation Treaty) or by a series of actions by international organizations (e.g., the activities of the first team of UN weapons inspectors in Iraq).[12] Nevertheless, the establishment of international legal norms still is less precise and structured than in domestic legal systems where formal deliberative bodies enact legislation.

In contrast to the general terms associated with topics of the operating system (e.g., jurisdiction or actors), the topics of the normative system are issue-specific, and many components of the system refer to subtopics within issue areas (e.g., the status of women within the broader topic area of human rights). Many of these issues have long been on the agenda of international law. Proscriptions on the use of military force have their roots in natural law and early Christian teachings on just war. Many normative rules concerning the law of the sea (e.g., seizure of commercial vessels during wartime) also have long pedigrees in customary practice. Yet recent trends in the evolution of the normative system represent expansions in its scope and depth. Some current issue areas of international legal concern, most notably with respect to human rights and the environment, have developed almost exclusively during the latter half of the twentieth century. Furthermore, within issue areas, legal norms have sought to regulate a wider range of behaviors; for example, international law on the environment has evolved beyond simple concerns of riparian states to include concerns with ozone depletion, water pollution, and other problems.

The range of agreement on the normative content in particular issue areas varies and is not necessarily a function of the length of time that the issue has been on the international legal agenda. For example, in the area of the use of force, the United Nations Charter prohibits its use other than in self-defense. Yet empirically, the use of force in international relations has not been eliminated. Nevertheless, efforts to regulate its use have changed state behavior at least in its initial use and in the response of others to its use. Despite the legal standards and the institutional structures to support these standards, debates continue on the appropriate levels of force and on the appropriate responses to situations that may require stepping over the principle of nonintervention in the internal affairs of states. In the area of human rights, the normative content of human rights is unsettled.[13] The United States, for example, promotes items included in the Covenant on Political and Civil Rights but eschews involvement with the Covenant on Economic and Social Rights. The place of democracy in the panoply of rights is not automatically accepted. Debates surrounding the universal versus culture-based character of human rights are another indication that the normative content of international human rights law is still under development.

In summary, the normative system of international law defines the acceptable standards for behavior in the international system. These are issue-specific prescriptions and proscriptions, with some variation in the consensus surrounding them among the international community of states. The normative system of international law has undergone explosive growth, in scope and specificity, over the past half-century or so, although it remains underdeveloped relative to its domestic counterparts.[14]

The effectiveness of the normative system, however, depends largely on the operating system—the mechanisms and processes that are designed to ensure orderly compliance with norms—and they will change if problems signal a need for change. The normative system may facilitate compliance in isolation from the operating system by "compliance pull."[15] Compliance pull is induced through legitimacy, which is powered by the quality of the rule and/or the rulemaking institution. Still, "primary rules, if they lack adherence to a system of validating secondary rules, are mere *ad hoc* reciprocal arrangements."[16] Compliance pull may exist under such circumstances, but it will be considerably weaker than if secondary rules (related to the operating system) are present. Note that we are speaking of more than compliance concerns in dealing with norms. Regime theory has typically assumed that it is the desire to improve the efficiency of interstate interactions (e.g., reduce transaction costs) that drives the adoption of normative rules. Our view is that states adopt normative rules in order largely to promote shared values in the international system. Rule adoption and institution creation (largely operating system changes) may be helpful in implementation and in reducing transaction costs, but they are not a necessary element or purpose of normative change.

Prominent activity in the normative system of international law has been in the regulation of the use of force, the protection of human rights, the protection of the environment, and the management of the commons. In each of the four normative areas we have selected, the political bases of international law can be seen as states struggle to ensure the goals of peace, justice, and prosperity while not fully negating the rights accorded to them under national sovereignty. We find that many of these areas require the balancing or reconciling of inconsistencies as international law searches for generally applicable standards against a background of economic disparity and historic exploitation that stemmed from political and technological weakness.

The oldest segment of the international normative system concerns the use of force. Paradoxically, at the same time it is the most developed and also the least restrictive on state behavior. Carsten Stahn (Chapter 13) notes that the traditional distinction between states of war and states of peace, which have defined international law for centuries, no longer apply well to modern problems. In an era of peacebuilding and other involvement in the aftermath of war, the author outlines a series of principles for "postconflict" law, a situation not envisioned in traditional legal distinctions between war and peace. Terrorist attacks provide another significant challenge for international legal prescriptions given that such attacks are generally precipitated by individuals or groups (not states) and do not take traditional military forms. Accordingly, most international legal provisions for dealing with aggression seem to fit poorly with this form of conflict. In Chapter 14, M. Cherif Bassiouni reviews the current legal provisions for dealing with terrorism, revealing a broader set of laws than might be first evident, but still indicating an underdeveloped normative system in this area.

The piercing of the shell of state sovereignty is perhaps most dramatic in the area of human rights, where states no longer have full rein over actions within their borders. Thomas Buergenthal (Chapter 15) provides a historical overview of human rights norms and the institutions that are designed to ensure their observance. Unlike the international law on the use of force, which has a long history, human rights provisions in international law are far more recent, dating primarily to the UN Charter and thereafter.

The protection of human rights involves more than setting standards that states and other actors must meet. International law also conditions the actions of states and international organizations that wish to redress violations of human rights law. Traditional notions of state sovereignty limited the ability of others to intervene directly in the affairs of states, at least without the permission of that host state. Yet there has been a slow erosion of support for this concept of so-called hard-shell sovereignty. One key idea is that states or collectivities of states may have the right to intervene in other countries in order to respond to emergencies. Christopher Joyner (Chapter 16) examines "the responsibility to protect" and how this principle comports with legal provisions on humanitarian intervention, UN Charter rules on the use of force, sovereignty, and human rights norms such as that against genocide. The responsibility to protect has been cited by advocates of intervention in Darfur to stop mass killings and in Myanmar to ensure relief supplies in the aftermath of natural disaster.

Environmental protection is relatively new on the international legal agenda. Yet since the 1980s, states have increasingly regulated their own behavior by signing agreements establishing strict environmental standards and controls. The Rio summit of 1992 is only a recent example of how prominent the environmental issue has become in international relations. In Chapter 17, Ronald Mitchell identifies and describes the characteristics of the thousands of bilateral and multilateral treaties that deal with environmental issues. He also offers a tentative evaluation of their effectiveness, with an eye to determining the components that make for success in global environmental protection. Catherine Tinker (Chapter 18) adds a post-Rio overview in the area of protection of biological diversity. The environmental area challenges international law to address changing situations that render regulation through specific legal standards and obligations difficult. This has moved lawmaking into creating frameworks for cooperation and coordination in addition to creating specific legal obligations.

Closely related to international environmental efforts are normative constraints designed to preserve the benefits and riches of the global commons for all. Global commons law has generally developed in accordance with technological development and need; thus, the law of the sea is the oldest segment of law in this issue area but even there issues such as seabed mining have appeared only recently In Chapter 19, Bernard Oxman looks at the evolution of the law of the sea, from its early days to the present. He devotes significant attention to new innovations, such as the creation of the Exclusive Econonic Zone (EEZ). He also raises some doubts about the stability of the current arrangements as states seek to expand their territorial control and new mineral resources are discovered off shore. David Tan (Chapter 20) provides a summary of current international law on space as well as some proposals for how that law might further develop.

In Part 3, the concluding section of this book, we take a look into the future. The development of the internet and cyberspace raises dramatically new and different questions for international law, which is traditionally based on state sovereignty over conventional land, sea, and air spaces. Who can and should regulate cyberspace? Mathias Reimann, in Chapter 21, reviews a case against Yahoo! Inc. in a French court and identifies several "first generation" issues associated with regulating cyberspace, namely who should regulate it, whether existing conflict of laws provisions can handle such concerns, and how free speech might be protected in this new environment. He then notes that technology development has created a new set of concerns that will need to be addressed in the future. One might speculate that cyberspace will be one of the most prominent areas for international legal development in the coming decades, although it will be difficult for international law to keep up with technological advances.

Finally, Anne-Marie Slaughter and William Burke-White peek into the future and see the dividing lines between domestic and international law eroding. They see three functions of international law vis-à-vis domestic law as essential to promoting the normative values of the international community: strengthening domestic institutions, backstopping them, and compelling them to act. The authors regard the European Union as the prototype for how these arrangements might be achieved.

To address new challenges effectively will require adjustments to the operating system. Like much else in contemporary life, international law will be expected to make more complicated adjustments more rapidly and more frequently than at any other period of its development. This makes the study of this subject a richly rewarding exercise. It makes the practice of international law a daunting, but richly creative, exercise as new legal ground is broken to address changing circumstances. It further affirms the symbiotic relationship between the operating system and the normative system in which the capacity to sustain the operating system will increasingly depend on how well the international community can address its normative concerns.

Notes

1. Stephen Krasner, "Structural Causes and Regime Consequences: Regimes as Intervening Variables," in *International Regimes*, edited by Stephen Krasner (Ithaca, NY: Cornell University Press, 1982), pp. 1–2.
2. Michael Barnett, "The United Nations and Global Security: The Norm Is Mightier than the Sword," *Ethics and International Affairs* 9 (1995): 37–54.
3. H.L.A. Hart, *The Concept of Law*, 2nd ed. (Oxford, UK: Clarendon, 1994), p. 94.
4. Christine Chinkin, "The Challenge of Soft Law: Development and Change in International Law," *International and Comparative Law Quarterly* 38 (1989): 850–866; see also Prosper Weil, "Toward Relative Normativity in International Law," *American Journal of International Law* 77 (1983): 413–442.
5. Rosalyn Higgins, *Problems and Process: International Law and How We Use It* (Oxford, UK: Clarendon, 1994).
6. See Charlotte Ku and Christopher Borgen, "American Lawyers and International Competence," *Dickinson Journal of International Law* 18(3) (2000).
7. Philip C. Jessup, *Transnational Law* (New Haven, CT: Yale University Press, 1956), p. 1.
8. Harold Hongju Koh, "Transnational Legal Process," *Nebraska Law Review* 75 (1996): 181.
9. Anne Marie Slaughter, "The Real World Order," *Foreign Affairs* 76 (1997): 103.
10. Barnett, "The United Nations and Global Security."

11. Hart, *The Concept of Law*.

12. We do, of course, recognize that even with the trend toward treaties as the primary source of new international law, many treaties in recent decades have largely codified existing customary practice (e.g., significant portions of the Law of the Sea Conventions).

13. See, for example, Louis Henkin and John Lawrence Hargrove, *Human Rights: An Agenda for the Next Century* (Washington, DC: American Society of International Law, 1994).

14. See Christian Wiktor, *Multilateral Treaty Calendar, 1648–1995* (Dordrecht, Netherlands: Martinus Nijhoff, 1998), which contains 6,000 treaties.

15. Thomas M. Franck, *The Power of Legitimacy Among Nations* (New York: Oxford University Press, 1990).

16. Ibid., p. 184.

PART 1.1

International Law as Operating System: Sources of International Law

CHAPTER 2

Hard and Soft Law in International Governance

Kenneth Abbott and Duncan Snidal

CONTEMPORARY INTERNATIONAL RELATIONS ARE LEGALIZED to impressive extent, yet international legalization displays great variety. A few international institutions and issue-areas approach the theoretical ideal of hard legalization, but most international law is "soft" in distinctive ways. Here we explore the reasons for the widespread legalization of international governance and for this great variety in the degrees and forms of legalization.[1] We argue that international actors choose to order their relations through international law and design treaties and other legal arrangements to solve specific substantive and political problems. We further argue that international actors choose softer forms of legalized governance when those forms offer superior institutional solutions. We analyze the benefits and costs of different types of legalization and suggest hypotheses regarding the circumstances that lead actors to select specific forms. . . .

We begin by examining the advantages of hard legalization. The term *hard law* as used in this special issue refers to legally binding obligations that are precise (or can be made precise through adjudication or the issuance of detailed regulations) and that delegate authority for interpreting and implementing the law. Although hard law is not the typical international legal arrangement, a close look at this institutional form provides a baseline for understanding the benefits and costs of all types of legalization. By using hard law to order their relations, international actors reduce transactions costs, strengthen the credibility of their commitments, expand their available political strategies, and resolve problems of incomplete contract-

---

Excerpt from Kenneth W. Abbott and Duncan Snidal, "Hard and Soft Law in International Governance," *International Organization* 54:3 (Summer 2000), pp. 421–456.

ing. Doing so, however, also entails significant costs: hard law restricts actors' behavior and even their sovereignty.

While we emphasize the benefits and costs of legalization from a rational perspective focused on interests, law simultaneously engages normative considerations. In addition to requiring commitment to a background set of legal norms[2]—including engagement in established legal processes and discourse—legalization provides actors with a means to instantiate normative values. Legalization has effect through normative standards and processes as well as self-interested calculation, and both interests and values are constraints on the success of law. We consider law as both "contract" and "covenant" to capture these distinct but not incompatible characteristics. Indeed, we reject vigorously the insistence of many international relations specialists that one type of understanding is antithetical to the other.

The realm of "soft law" begins once legal arrangements are weakened along one or more of the dimensions of obligation, precision, and delegation. This softening can occur in varying degrees along each dimension and in different combinations across dimensions. We use the shorthand term soft law to distinguish this broad class of deviation from hard law—and, at the other extreme, from purely political arrangements in which legalization is largely absent. But bear in mind that soft law comes in many varieties; the choice between hard law and soft law is not a binary one.

Soft law has been widely criticized and even dismissed as a factor in international affairs. Realists, of course, focus on the absence of an independent judiciary with supporting enforcement powers to conclude that all international law is soft—and therefore only window dressing. But some international lawyers dismiss soft international law from a more normative perspective. Prosper Weil, for example, argues that increasing use of soft law "might destabilize the whole international normative system and turn it into an instrument that can no longer serve its purpose."[3] Others justify soft law only as an interim step toward harder and therefore more satisfactory legislation. The implication is that soft law—law that "falls short" on one or more of the three dimensions of legislation—is a failure.

We argue, in contrast, that international actors often deliberately choose softer forms of legalization as a superior institutional arrangement. To be sure, soft law is sometimes designed as a way station to harder legalization, but often it is preferable on its own terms. Soft law offers many of the advantages of hard law, avoids some of the costs of hard law, and has certain independent advantages of its own.[4] Importantly because one or more of the elements of legalization can be relaxed, softer legalization is often easier to achieve than hard legalization. This is especially true when the actors are states that are jealous of their autonomy and when the issue at hand challenges state sovereignty. Soft legalization also provides certain benefits not available under hard legalization. It offers more effective ways to deal with uncertainty, especially when it initiates processes that allow actors to learn about the impact of agreements over time.[5] In addition, soft law facilitates compromise, and thus mutually beneficial cooperation, between actors with different interests and values, different time horizons and discount rates, and different degrees of power.

The specific forms of soft law chosen reflect the particular problems actors are trying to solve. While our analysis focuses on softness in general, different forms of softness may be more acceptable or more efficacious in different circumstances. We suggest a number of variables—including transaction costs, uncertainty, implications for national sovereignty, divergence of preferences, and power differentials—that influence which forms of soft law, which combinations of obligation, precision, and delegation, are likely to be selected in specific circumstances. . . .

We employ a range of examples, to illustrate the wide variety of international legal arrangements. Although these examples do not provide a true empirical test of our arguments, they do provide evidence for their plausibility. To characterize our examples economically along the hard law/soft law continuum, we use the notation [O,P,D]. The elements of each triplet refer to the level of obligation, precision, and delegation, respectively. Variations along each dimension are indicated by capital letters for high levels (for example, O), small letters for moderate levels (for example, o), and dashes for low levels (-). Thus [O,P,D] indicates an arrangement that is highly legalized on all three dimensions and therefore constitutes "hard law"; [o,P,-] indicates an issue that has a moderate level of legal obligation coupled with high precision but very limited delegation; and [O,-,-] indicates an issue with high legal obligation but very low precision and very limited delegation. Although this tripartite categorization remains somewhat coarse, it suggests the continuous gradations of hardness and softness that are blurred when the hard law/soft law distinction is incorrectly taken as binary.

Rationales for Hard Law

Credible Commitments

The difficulty states have in credibly committing themselves to future behavior is widely viewed as a characteristic feature of international "anarchy" and an impediment to welfare-enhancing cooperation. In contracting theory, credible commitments are crucial when one party to an agreement must carry out its side of the bargain before other parties are required to perform, or more generally when some parties must make relation-specific investments in reliance on future performance by others. . . .[6]

Other assurance issues appear when one begins to disaggregate the state. For one thing, relation-specific investments can be political as well as material: a government offering economic or political concessions in return for human rights pledges, for example, would suffer domestic political costs if the other party reneged; it would therefore demand credible assurances. The government making those pledges might also wish to enhance credibility for internal purposes; to bind its successors in office or other branches of government, or to strengthen its citizens' incentives to adjust their practices and attitudes. . . .

In domestic societies, legal commitments are credible because aggrieved parties can enforce them, with the power of the state if necessary. Even "hard" international law falls short of this standard: international regimes do not even attempt to establish legal obligations centrally enforceable against states.[7] Yet it is erroneous to conclude that the "formal legal status" of international agreements is therefore meaningless. Legalizatlon is one of the principal methods by which states can increase the credibility of their commitments.[8]

One way legalization enhances credibility is by constraining self-serving auto-interpretation. Precision of individual commitments, coherence between individual commitments and broader legal principles, and accepted modes of legal discourse and argument all help limit such opportunistic behavior. Granting interpretive authority to courts or other legal institutions further constrains auto-interpretation.[9] Another way legalization enhances credibility is by increasing the costs of reneging. Regime scholars argue that agreements are strengthened when they are linked to a broader regime: violating an agreement that is part of a regime entails disproportionate costs, because the reputational costs of reneging apply throughout the regime. Legal commitments benefit from similar effects, but they involve international law as a whole in addition to any specific regime.

When a commitment is cast as hard law, the reputational effects of a violation can be generalized to all agreements subject to international law, that is, to most international agreements.[10] There are few alternatives to legalization when states wish to identify undertakings as reliable commitments. Alternatives like bonding and escrow are much more costly. In addition, international law provides the very foundations of statehood: principles of sovereignty, recognition, territorial competence, nonintervention, and so on. Violations weaken the international legal system and are self-defeating, at least over time.

More concretely, legalization enhances (albeit modestly) the capacity for enforcement. First, hard legal commitments, [O,P,D] or [O,p,D], are interpreted and applied by arbitral or judicial institutions, like those associated with the European Union (EU), the European human rights regime or the World Trade Organization (WTO). (Softer commitments may be invoked in political institutions.) Because legal review allows allegations and defenses to be tested under accepted standards and procedures, it increases reputational costs if a violation is found. The EU may currently be experiencing such aggravated costs as a result of the repeated negative legal rulings by WTO dispute settlement bodies in litigation over European restrictions on imports of hormone-treated beef (for which the EU was unable to demonstrate a legitimate scientific justification) and bananas.

Second, the law of state responsibility fixes consequences for legal violations. In particular, like some legalized regimes (such as the WTO), it authorizes proportional "countermeasures" where other remedies are unavailable. This legitimizes retaliation and clarifies its intent, reducing the costs and risks of self-help. Third, even international law can draw on some forms of centralized enforcement, through institutions like the UN Security Council and the international financial institutions.

Other interest-based costs of legal violations arise because international legal commitments often become part of domestic law. As John K. Setear points out, for example, Congress has provided that violations of the Whaling Convention and the Convention on International Trade in Endangered Species (CITES) constitute violations of U.S. law, carrying criminal penalties.[11] Ellen L. Lutz and Kathryn Sikkink further describe how international rules condemning torture and other atrocities have been characterized as customary international law and applied by U.S. courts.[12] When international commitments are incorporated into domestic law, the level of delegation associated with them rises dramatically (though it evokes weaker concern for national sovereignty): the commitments can now be applied by well-established systems of courts and administrative agencies; private actors can often initiate legal proceedings; and lawyers have incentives to invoke the rules. When supranational bodies like the European Court of Justice (ECJ) have also been granted legal authority, they can nurture "partnerships" with their domestic counterparts, strengthening both institutions.[13]

Domesticated commitments can more easily be enforced against private persons and their assets. A striking example is the litigation against General Pinochet, which was initiated by a Spanish magistrate enforcing international conventions banning torture and other atrocities that had become part of Spanish law. Although the British House of Lords ruled that Pinochet could not be held responsible for most of the charges against him, it did hold him answerable for acts committed after the torture convention had been incorporated into British law.

Legal commitments mobilize legally oriented interest and advocacy groups, such as the organized bar, and legitimize their participation in domestic decision making. They also expand the role of legal bureaucracies within foreign offices and other government agencies. Finally, so long as domestic actors understand legal agreements to be serious undertakings, they will modify their plans and actions in reliance on such commitments, increasing the audience costs of violations.

Legalization also increases the costs of violation through normative channels. Violation of a legal commitment entails reputational costs—again generalizable to all legal commitments—that reflect distaste for breaking the law. International law reinforces this effect through its strong emphasis on compliance (*pacta sum servanda* and the principle of good faith).[14] To the extent that states (or certain states) see themselves as members of an international society structured by international law, reputational effects may be even broader.[15] Law observance is even more highly valued in most domestic societies; efforts to justify international violations thus create cognitive dissonance and increase domestic audience costs.

Legal obligations are widely perceived as having particular legitimacy. In Thomas Franck's words, legitimacy creates an independent "compliance pull."[16] Individuals, government agencies, and other organizations internalize rules so that the advantages and disadvantages of compliance need not be recalculated each time they are invoked. Franck argues that the legitimacy of rules varies according to certain substantive qualities—determinacy and coherence, among other properties—and the procedures by which they were approved. Legal rules are often strong on these dimensions: relatively precise, internally consistent, and adopted through formalized and often elaborate procedures.

Legalization entails a specific form of discourse, requiring justification and persuasion in terms of applicable rules and pertinent facts, and emphasizing factors such as text, precedents, analogies, and practice. Legal discourse largely disqualifies arguments based solely on interests and preferences. The nature of this discourse affords legal professionals a prominent role. When authority is delegated to adjudicative institutions, proceedings can be highly formalized. Even without strong delegation, however, this discourse imposes some constraint on state action: governments will incur reputational costs within the legal community, and often beyond, if they act without a defensible position or without reasonable efforts to justify their conduct in legal terms.

Certain hypotheses regarding the independent variables that lead states to use hard law can be distilled from this analysis. First, states should use hard legal commitments as assurance devices when the benefits of cooperation are great but the potential for opportunism and its costs are high. These conditions are most likely in "contracts," such as trade or investment agreements, that include reciprocal commitments and nonsimultaneous performance. But they may also appear in "covenants"—such as environmental or labor agreements—when violations would impose significant externalities on others. Opportunism is less significant in coordination situations, where agreements are largely self-enforcing.[17] Indeed, international coordination standards are often voluntary, [-,P,d], and are created through institutions in which private actors have a significant role. Opportunism, and thus international legalization, is also less significant in settings where national actions have few external effects.[18]

Second, states should use hard legalization to increase the credibility of commitments when noncompliance is difficult to detect, as in most arms control situations. Legal arrangements often include centralized or decentralized monitoring provisions as an aspect of delegation. Even apart from these, however, legal commitments compensate in part for the reduced likelihood of detection by increasing the costs of detected violations.

Third, states should find hard law of special value when forming "clubs" of sincerely committed states, like the EU and NATO. Here legalization functions as an *ex ante* sorting device: because hard legal commitments impose greater costs on violators, a willingness to make them identifies one as having a low propensity to defect. Conversely, hard legalization is less significant in looser groupings like the Asia-Pacific Economic Cooperation forum (APEC), described by Miles Kahler that are not pursuing deep cooperation and thus do not require *ex ante* evidence of a sincere commitment from members.[19]

Fourth, looking within the state, executive officials should look to hard international law to commit other domestic agencies (especially legislatures) or political groups when those officials are able to make international agreements with little interference or control, and when their preferences differ significantly from those of competing power centers. In this perspective, domestic politics and constitutional law are significant explanatory variables.

Finally, as a secondary hypothesis, legal commitments should be more credible when made by states with particular characteristics. Externally, participation in other international legal regimes should enhance credibility: it exposes states to greater reputational costs and makes them more vulnerable to countermeasures. Internally, strong domestic legal institutions and traditions should enhance credibility. Many of the special costs of violating legal commitments stem from these characteristics.

Reducing Transactions Costs

On balance, at least, hard legalization reduces the transactions costs of subsequent interactions.[20] Two types of interactions are especially relevant: one is the "managerial" process of applying and elaborating agreed rules; the other is the more adversarial process of enforcing commitments. The role of international regimes in reducing transactions costs—especially the costs of negotiating supplementary agreements—has been extensively analyzed.[21]

That literature has not, however, distinguished legalization from other institutional forms.[22]

Consider the need to "manage" the application and evolution of agreements. With virtually all agreements, even those that are quite precise, provisions must be interpreted, applied to specific fact situations, and elaborated to resolve ambiguities and address new and related issues. Delegation to courts and other legal institutions is one important way states address these problems; we discuss delegation later in connection with incomplete contracts. Even where delegation is weak—for example, [O,p,d] or [O,p,-]—legalization facilitates interpretation, application, and elaboration by setting relatively clear bounds on dispute resolution and negotiation. Substantively, legalization implies that proposals for resolving disputes and for new or expanded rules must be integrated with existing norms. They should be compatible with settled rules if possible, so that bargains need not be reopened. In any case they should be compatible with the basic principles of the relevant regime, so that legal coherence is maintained.

Procedurally, hard law constrains the techniques of dispute settlement and negotiation when delegation is relatively low, legalization implies that most disputes and questions of interpretation should be addressed through specialized procedures, operated primarily by legal professionals using professional modes of discourse. Even when directly negotiated solutions are permitted, the existence of legal institutions means that states will bargain "in the shadow" of anticipated legal decisions. When legal rules are in effect, moreover, unauthorized coercive behavior is generally seen as illegitimate. It is no coincidence that legalization in the WTO was explicitly tied to a requirement that member states resolve their trade disputes through the new dispute settlement procedures, not through unilateral determinations and responses—a provision aimed directly at the coercive tactics of the United States under Section 301. Even hard international law is not foolproof, of course; the principles discussed here may be ignored in practice, especially by powerful states. Nonetheless, on the whole legalization remains an effective device for organizing ongoing interactions.

Consider next the need to "enforce" commitments. The previous section examined how legalization helps states increase the credibility of their own commitments. But legalization is also significant from the perspective of the states (and other actors) that have worked to obtain commitments from others, often in the face of strong resistance. We refer to such parties as "demandeurs." Whenever there are incentives for noncompliance with international commitments, demandeurs will seek ways to forestall or respond to violations by others.

As discussed earlier, hard legalization offers a rich assortment of international and domestic institutions and procedures and normative and reputational arguments for actors in this position. Compared to alternatives like frequent renegotiation, persuasion, or coercion, it materially reduces the costs of enforcement. Other things being equal, assuming in particular that the substance of an agreement is acceptable, demandeurs should prefer hard legalization, especially in the form [O,P,D].[23] Of course, other things being equal, states that resist agreement or desire greater flexibility should resist hard legalization, or at least strive for [O,p,D] commitments, for these very reasons. The compromises and tradeoffs that result are discussed in the following section.

Many of the hypotheses in the previous subsection can be reformulated from the demandeur's perspective. Demandeurs should seek hard legalization (1) when the likelihood of opportunism and its costs are high, and noncompliance is difficult to detect; (2) when they wish to limit participation to those strongly committed to an agreement; and (3) when executive officials in other states have preferences compatible with those of the demandeurs, but other elites within those states have divergent preferences. Finally, demandeurs should place greatest reliance on commitments by states that participate actively in legal regimes and have strong legal institutions, professions, and traditions.

Modifying Political Strategies

As proponents of legal process theory make clear, hard legalization allows states (and other actors) to pursue different political strategies as they work to extend and enforce (or to weaken or escape) international agreements.[24] Indeed, those strategies are often unavoidable. Both demandeurs and resisters may be as concerned with these tactical attributes as with the strategic issues of credibility and enforceability.

As defined in this issue, hard law includes specialized legal institutions. Regimes of the form [O,P,D] and [O,p,D] include judicial or arbitral organs that offer the specialized procedures and techniques for addressing disputes, questions of interpretation, and instances of noncompliance. Nonjudicial institutions, as in [O,p,d] regimes, are often authorized to interpret governing instruments, issue regulations or recommendations, draft proposed conventions, and the like. . . .

Hard legal commitments are sometimes incorporated directly into the internal law of participating states; even more frequently international agreements require states to enact implementing legislation, and sometimes to establish particular implementing institutions. Domestic litigation then becomes part of the international toolkit. There may, however, be jurisdictional obstacles to litigation by state claimants. In those situations, states must engage in the subtle process of identifying, encouraging, and supporting private litigants who will advance their interests.[25] Recent scholarship analyzes the strategies that supranational judges pursue to encourage actions by private litigants and national courts that will strengthen international law.[26] National governments presumably follow parallel strategies.

We hypothesize broadly that states will be more likely to seek hard legalization when the political strategies it offers are advantageous to them. Mundane issues such as the availability of resources and trained personnel can be quite significant; the United States and other advanced industrial nations with large legal staffs should be more amenable to legalization than countries with few trained specialists. States should also favor hard legalization when they can be confident that agreements will track their preferences, for legal procedures will allow them to implement those preferences efficiently and at low political cost. This suggests that powerful states have a significant and often overlooked stake in hard legalization. And states that seek to minimize political conflict in relations with other states or in particular issue-areas should favor hard legalization, for it sublimates such conflict into legal argument.

Handling Problems of Incomplete Contracting

States sometimes attempt to write detailed agreements to constrain auto-interpretation, reduce transactions costs, and increase enforceability. But though precision has great value, it also has several problems. It may be wasteful, forcing states to plan for highly unlikely events; it may be counterproductive, introducing opaque and inconsistent provisions; it may lead to undesirable rigidity; and it may prevent agreement altogether.

In any case, writing complete contracts is extremely difficult.[27] The principal-agent literature demonstrates that asymmetric information typically makes it impossible to write an optimal contract if the agent is risk-averse. Yet even this literature assumes that one could in principle write a contract complete with respect to all possible future states of the world. In fact, given bounded rationality and the pervasive uncertainty in which states operate, they can never construct agreements that anticipate every contingency. This problem invites opportunistic behavior and discourages both relation-specific investments and value-enhancing agreements.

Delegation is often the best way to deal with incomplete contracting problems. Regimes of the form [O,p,D] are clearly designed with this purpose in mind: they utilize administrative and judicial institutions to interpret and extend broad legal principles. The Treaty of Rome, for example, authorizes the ECJ and the European Community's legislative institutions to elaborate and apply general principles of competition law, such as "concerted practices" and "distortion of competition," through individual cases and general regulations. Even [O,P,D] regimes grant significant powers to administrative organs and judicial or arbitral bodies. Although many provisions of the European Convention on Human Rights, for example, are quite detailed, the European Court of Human Rights must still apply general standards—such as "inhuman and degrading treatment" and "respect for . . . private and family life"—in situations that could not have been anticipated when the convention was drafted.

Softer regimes often include nonjudicial procedures for filling out incomplete contracts, though these normally require state consent. Hard legal regimes, in contrast, grant greater independence to judicial or arbitral bodies but require them to follow agreed upon principles and to act only on specific disputes and requests. This combination of attributes, along with the background rules and expectations of international law, simultaneously constrains and legitimates delegated authority. One can hypothesize that states will grant such authority when the anticipated gains from cooperation are large and there is reasonable consensus on general principles, but specific applications are difficult to anticipate.

The Advantages of Soft Legalization

Hard law facilitates international interactions in the many ways already discussed, but it has significant costs and limitations. In this section, we explore how softer forms of legalization provide alternative and often more desirable means to manage many interactions by providing some of the benefits of hard law at lower cost. We emphasize both rationalist concerns, such as contracting costs, and the special role soft legal rules and institutions play in promoting learning and normative processes.

Contracting Costs

A major advantage of softer forms of legalization is their lower contracting costs. Hard legalization reduces the post-agreement costs of managing and enforcing commitments, but adoption of a highly legalized agreement entails significant contracting costs.[28] Any agreement entails some negotiating costs—coming together, learning about the issue, bargaining, and so forth—especially when issues are unfamiliar or complex. But these costs are greater for legalized agreements. States normally exercise special care in negotiating and drafting legal agreements, since the costs of violation are higher. Legal specialists must be consulted; bureaucratic reviews are often lengthy. Different legal traditions across states complicate the exercise. Approval and ratification processes, typically involving legislative authorization, are more complex than for purely political agreements. . . .

The costs of hard legalization are magnified by the circumstances of international politics. States, jealous of their sovereign autonomy, are reluctant to limit it through legalized commitments. Security concerns intensify the distributional issues that accompany any agreement, especially ones of greater magnitude or involving greater uncertainty. Negotiations are often multilateral. The scope of bargaining is often not clearly delimited, since the issues themselves are ill defined (for example, is free trade in magazines an economic issue or a cultural one?). Finally, the thinness of the international institutional context (including the low prevailing level of legalization) does little to lower the costs of agreement.

Soft legalization mitigates these costs as well. For example, states can dampen security and distributional concerns by opting for escape clauses, [o,P,d]; imprecise commitments, [O,p,d]; or "political" forms of delegation that allow them to maintain future control if adverse circumstances arise, [O,p,-]. These institutional devices protect state sovereignty and reduce the costs and risks of agreement while providing some of the advantages of legalization. Furthermore, soft legalization offers states an opportunity to learn about the consequences of their agreement. In many cases such learning processes will lower the perceived costs of subsequent moves to harder legalization.

The international nuclear regime illustrates these advantages.[29] Although fundamental nonproliferation obligations are set out in the Nuclear Non-Proliferation Treaty and other legally binding agreements, [O,P,d], many sensitive issues—such as the protection of nuclear materials—are regulated predominantly through recommendations from the International Atomic Energy Agency (IAEA), [-P,d]. Recommendations deal with technical matters, such as inventory control and transportation, at a level of detail that would be intractable in treaty negotiations. They also address issues of domestic policy, such as the organization of national regulatory agencies and the supervision of private actors, that states might regard as too sensitive for treaty regulation. When a high level of consensus forms around an IAEA recommendation, member states may incorporate its provisions into a binding treaty—as occurred with rules on the management of spent nuclear fuel and radioactive waste—but even these treaties must usually be supplemented by recommendations on technical issues. . . .

In sum, we argue that states face tradeoffs in choosing levels of legalization. Hard agreements reduce the costs of operating within a legal framework—by strengthening commitments, reducing transactions costs, and the like—but they are hard to reach. Soft agreements cannot yield all these benefits, but they lower the costs of achieving (some) legalization in the first place. Choices along this continuum of tradeoffs determine the "hardness" of legalization, both initially and over time.

In general, we hypothesize that softer forms of legalization will be more attractive to states as contracting costs increase. This proposition should be true both for relatively mechanical costs—such as those created by large numbers of actors and rigorous national ratification procedures—

and for more intensely political costs like those prevailing in negotiations with potentially strong distributional effects. In the remainder of this section, we explore the hard law/soft law tradeoff in terms of several key independent variables, each of which increases the costs of international agreement. These variables include sovereignty costs, uncertainty, divergence among national preferences, differences in time horizons and discount rates, and power differentials among major actors.

Sovereignty Costs

The nature of sovereignty costs. Accepting a binding legal obligation, especially when it entails delegating authority to a supranational body, is costly to states. The costs involved can range from simple differences in outcome on particular issues, to authority over decision making in an issue-area, to more fundamental encroachments on state sovereignty. While we recognize that the concept of "sovereignty" is broad and highly contested,[30] we use "sovereignty costs" as a covering term for all three categories of costs to emphasize the high stakes states often face in accepting international agreements. The potential for inferior outcomes, loss of authority, and diminution of sovereignty makes states reluctant to accept hard legalization—especially when it includes significant levels of delegation.

Sovereignty costs are relatively low when states simply make international legal commitments that limit their behavior in particular circumstances. States typically accept these costs in order to achieve better collective outcomes. . . . Such agreements are undoubtedly exercises of legal sovereignty. Nevertheless, even they may limit the ability of states to regulate their borders (for example, by requiring them to allow goods, capital, or people to pass freely) and to implement important domestic policies (as when free trade impinges on labor, safety, or environmental regulations), thus encroaching on other aspects of sovereignty.

Greater sovereignty costs emerge when states accept external authority over significant decisions. International agreements may implicitly or explicitly insert international actors (who are neither elected nor otherwise subject to domestic scrutiny) into national decision procedures. These arrangements may limit the ability of states to govern whole classes of issues—such as social subsidies or industrial policy—or require states to change domestic laws or governance structures. Nevertheless, the impact of such arrangements is tempered by states' ability to withdraw from international agreements—although processes of enmeshment may make it increasingly costly for them to do so.

Sovereignty costs are at their highest when international arrangements impinge on the relations between a state and its citizens or territory, the traditional hallmarks of (Westphalian) sovereignty. Of course, ordinary restrictions on domestic policies can have such effects in contemporary welfare states, but these are heightened and generalized when, for example, an international human rights regime circumscribes a state's ability to regulate its citizens. Similarly, the United States has correctly been concerned that an International Criminal Court might claim jurisdiction over U.S. soldiers participating in international peacekeeping activities or other foreign endeavors. Agreements such as the Law of the Sea Convention both redefine national territory (for example, by delineating jurisdiction over a territorial sea, exclusive economic zone, and continental shelf) and limit the capacity of states to restrict its use (for example, by establishing rights of innocent passage). Here, too, individual states retain the capacity to withdraw, but doing so may actually diminish their (legal) sovereignty, risking loss of recognition as members in good standing of the international community.

Legalization can lead to further, often unanticipated sovereignty costs over time. Even if rules are written precisely to narrow their range, or softened by including escape clauses or limiting delegation, states cannot anticipate or limit all of the possible effects.

Delegation provides the greatest source of unanticipated sovereignty costs. As Charles Lindblom points out, a grant of "authority always becomes to a degree uncontrollable."[31] Even nonjudicial organizations like the IMF or World Bank exert their independence in ways that go beyond the initial intentions or anticipations of the contracting states.[32]

The delegation of legal authority to independent domestic courts and agencies can create similar unexpected consequences. However, states generally feel they have ultimate control over domestic courts—they appoint the judges and control the justice departments that bring criminal actions—and so they find, in general, that domestic delegation has lower sovereignty costs.

Even the most powerful states recognize that legalization will circumscribe their autonomy. U.S. opposition to autonomous international institutions, whether the Enterprise in the Law of the Sea Convention, the International Criminal Court, or the UN more generally, reflects the special concern that delegation raises.[33] Even in NAFTA, where its political influence is paramount, the United States resisted delegating authority to supranational dispute settlement bodies for interstate disputes; only the Chapter 19 procedure for reviewing antidumping and countervailing duty ruling creates significant delegated authority. Congress also explicitly provided that the agreement would not be self-executing in domestic law, limiting delegation to national courts. More recently, concern that highly legalized WTO dispute settlement institutions might expand the meaning of the Uruguay Round agreements led Congress to provide for an early review of the costs and benefits of WTO membership, including the results of legal proceedings, tied to a fast-track procedure for withdrawal from the organization. Conversely, the willingness of the United States and other countries to subscribe to more constrained institutions indicates that their benefits outweigh their sovereignty costs—at least up to a point.

The notion of sovereignty costs is more complicated when competing domestic and transnational interests affect the development of international legalization. Certain domestic groups may perceive negative sovereignty costs from international agreements that provide them with more favorable outcomes than national policy. Examples include free-trade coalitions that prefer their states' trade policies to be bound by WTO rulings rather than open to the vagaries of individual legislatures, and environmental groups that believe they can gain more from an international accord than from domestic politics. For similar reasons, although a government that anticipates staying in power may be reluctant to limit its control over an issue, a government less certain of its longevity may seek to bind its successors through international legal commitments.[34] We discuss such domestic variations in the following section.

Sovereignty costs may also be negative for external reasons, as where participation in international arrangements enhances a state's international and domestic position.[35] Key aspects of sovereignty have been codified in a variety of legal instruments, including the 1933 Montevideo Convention on the Rights and Duties of States, Article 2 of the UN Charter, and the UN General Assembly Declaration on Principles of International Law Concerning Friendly Relations Among States. Regional legal arrangements like the Organization of American States (OAS) provide much-needed support for state sovereignty. Chapter IV of the OAS Charter promotes the independence and sovereign equality of member states regardless of power differentials and protects internal sovereignty through principles of nonintervention.

Although negative sovereignty costs are an important exception, positive sovereignty costs are the more standard (and more difficult) case for international legalization. Hard legalization—especially the classic legal model with centralized judicial institutions capable of amplifying the terms of agreements in the course of resolving disputes—imposes high sovereignty costs. Thus states face tradeoffs between the benefits and sovereignty costs of different forms of legalization.

States can limit sovereignty costs through arrangements that are nonbinding or imprecise or do not delegate extensive powers. Most often, states protect themselves by adopting less precise rules and weaker legal institutions, as in the Council of Europe's framework Convention for the Protection of National Minorities, [O,p,d]. They frequently provide that member states must adhere to a special treaty protocol before a court or quasi-judicial body can assert jurisdiction over them, as in the inter-

American human rights system, or that all parties to a particular dispute must consent before the case can be litigated. Still weaker forms of delegation—such as the consultation arrangements characteristic of arms control agreements, [O,P,-]—limit sovereignty costs even more, coupling legal obligations with political mechanisms of control and defense. Thus soft legalization offers a variety of means—none of them perfect—by which states can limit sovereignty costs. . . .

Soft law provides a means to lessen sovereignty costs by expanding the range of available institutional arrangements along a more extensive and finely differentiated tradeoff curve. How states evaluate these tradeoffs—and thus determine their preferences for different forms of legalization—depends on their own characteristics and the circumstances of particular issue-areas.

Sovereignty costs and issue type. Viewing constraints on national autonomy and sovereignty as costs that vary across issues, we hypothesize that states will prefer different forms of legalization in different issue-areas. At one extreme, sovereign costs are especially high in areas related to national security. Adversaries are extremely sensitive to unanticipated risks of agreement for the standard reasons advanced by realists, including relative gains. Even allies facing common external threats are reluctant to surrender autonomy over their security affairs. Therefore it is unsurprising that even in NATO, the most institutionalized alliance ever, delegation is moderate, [O,p,d], or that security arrangements have lagged behind other institutional developments in the EU. Similarly, bilateral arms control agreements like SALT can be very precise in specifying missile numbers and types and are unquestionably binding but are only minimally institutionalized, [O,P,-].

Political economy issues display a wide range of sovereignty costs and hence of legalization. At one extreme lie technical matters on which state interests are closely aligned, such as international transportation or food standards. Here sovereignty costs are low and the incidence of legalized agreements is correspondingly high. One even sees a significant level of delegation—including to organizations in which private actors play major roles, such as the International Organization for Standardization (ISO)—where sovereignty costs are low and technical complexity makes it hard to adapt agreements rapidly without some coordinating authority. Political economy issues like investment policy, money laundering, and security-related export controls, however, remain sensitive and have not been legalized to nearly the same extent. Similarly, tax policy, which lies at the core of all state functions but increasingly requires international coordination, is characterized by many bilateral treaties but displays little overall institutionalization.

Trade issues range between these extremes—sovereignty costs are significant but are frequently outweighed by the perceived benefits of legalized agreements. This is due partly to lesser conflicts of interest among states and partly to strong domestic support from beneficiaries of legalization. Consequently, even on a given issue, sovereignty costs can vary across states and over time. For example, the sovereignty costs of agricultural agreements are typically greater for less-developed states where the sector is larger and politically central; they have gradually decreased in OECD countries along with the relative importance of agriculture.

Finally, the most highly institutionalized arrangements, such as the EU, occur where there is a strong commitment to reducing sovereignty, or where a long process of legalized cooperation has led to institutionalization even against state resistance. The history of trade institutionalization is again instructive. In many respects, the WTO today is a stronger institution than the proposed International Trade Organization. Continued success in expanding trade under GATT changed domestic political balances and lowered the costs of further legalization. Moreover, states "learned" that harder legalization (such as a stronger dispute settlement mechanism) can produce greater benefits; they may also have been reassured regarding the dangers of enmeshment. Nevertheless, vigorous continuing disputes over the future of the WTO reflect states' continued wariness of sacrificing autonomy.

Uncertainty

Many international issues are new and complex. The underlying problems may not be well understood, so states cannot anticipate all possible consequences of a legalized arrangement. One way to deal with such problems is to delegate authority to a central party (for example, a court or international organization) to implement, interpret, and adapt the agreement as circumstances unfold. This approach avoids the costs of having no agreement, or of having to (re)negotiate continuously, but it typically entails unacceptably high sovereignty costs. Soft legalization provides a number of more attractive alternatives for dealing with uncertainty.

First, states can reduce the precision of their commitments: [O,p,d]. Of course, if they do not know the relevant contingencies, they cannot achieve the precision of hard law even if they wish to do so, except as to better-understood aspects of the problem. Thus an arms control agreement can precisely control known technologies and can even limit research into technologies whose results can reasonably be anticipated (such as testing antiballistic missile systems). But it cannot govern technologies whose military impact cannot be foreseen. And blanket limitations on all research with potential military implications would unacceptably impair the development of beneficial civilian technologies.

But uncertainty makes precision less desirable as well as less attainable. The classic distinction between risk and uncertainty is significant here. When risk is the central concern—that is, when actors cannot predict the outcome of an agreement but know the probability distribution of possible outcomes, conditional on agreement terms—precise agreements offer a way to manage and optimize risk-sharing.[36] But when circumstances are fundamentally uncertain—that is, when even the range for distribution of possible outcomes is unknown—a more precise agreement may not be desirable. In particular, if actors are "ambiguity-averse,"[37] they will prefer to leave agreements imprecise rather than face the possibility of being caught in unfavorable commitments. Unfamiliar environmental conditions like global warming provide good illustrations: because the nature, the severity, even the very existence of these threats—as well as the costs of responding to them—are highly uncertain, the imprecise commitments found in environmental "framework" agreements may be the optimal response.

A second way to deal with uncertainty is through arrangements that are precise but not legally binding, such as Agenda 21, the Forest Principles, and other hortatory instruments adopted at the 1992 Rio Conference on Environment and Development [-,P,-]. These allow states to see the impact of rules in practice and to gain their benefits, while retaining flexibility to avoid any unpleasant surprises the rules might hold. Sometimes precision is actually used to limit the binding character of obligations, as with carefully drawn exceptions or escape clauses. These also protect the parties in case the agreement turns out to have hidden costs or unforeseen contingencies, so that states are not locked into commitments they regret.

Third, although strong delegation can aggravate the uncertainty of agreements, moderate delegation—typically involving political and administrative bodies where states retain significant control—provides another way to manage uncertainty. UN specialized agencies and other international organizations, [-,p,d], play restricted administrative roles across a wide variety of issues, and a small number of (mainly financial) organizations have more significant autonomy.[38] These organizations have the capacity to provide information (and thus reduce uncertainty) and some capacity to modify and adapt rules or to initiate standards.[39] In general, however, even this level of delegation appears only in areas with low sovereignty costs, such as technical coordination. More fundamental elaboration of arrangements is typically accomplished through direct political processes. Thus arms control agreements are precise and binding but limit delegation to forums that promote political bargaining, not independent third-party decision making, [O,P,-].

Viewed dynamically, these forms of soft legalization offer strategies for individual and collective learning.[40] Consider the case where states are legally bound but in an imprecise way, as under the original Vienna Ozone Convention, [O,p,-]. These obligations offer flexibility and protection for states to work out problems over time through negotiations shaped by normative guidelines, rather than constrained by precise rules. Hortatory rules, for example, [-,p,d], similarly provide general standards against which behavior can be assessed and support learning processes that reduce uncertainty over time. Some emerging arrangements on the rights of women and children fit this model. Agreements that are precise but nonbinding, like the Helsinki Final Act, [-,P,d], often include institutional devices such as conferences and review sessions where states can potentially deepen their commitments as they resolve uncertainties about the issue.

Indeed, moderate delegation—including international organizations that provide support for decentralized bargaining, expertise, and capacities for collecting information—may be more appropriate than adjudicative procedures (domestic or international) for adapting rules as circumstances are better understood. Examples include the numerous international agencies that recommend (often in conjunction with private actors) international standards on a range of issues, including technology, transportation, and health. Although not binding, their recommendations provide precise and compelling coordination points to which states and private actors usually adhere. In other cases, consultative committees or formal international organizations may be empowered to make rules more precise as learning occurs. Effective institutions of this sort require a certain autonomy that states may be reluctant to grant over truly important issues. . . .

In this section we have argued that soft legalization provides a rational adaptation to uncertainty. It allows states to capture the "easy" gains they can recognize with incomplete knowledge, without allowing differences or uncertainties about the situation to impede completion of the bargain. Soft legalization further provides a framework within which states can adapt their arrangement as circumstances change and can pursue "harder" gains through further negotiation. Soft law avoids the sovereignty costs associated with centralized adjudication or other strong delegation and is less costly than repeated renegotiation in light of new information.

Our discussion also suggests hypotheses as to when different forms of legalization are most likely to be used. Consider the four possible high/low combinations of uncertainty and sovereignty costs, two of the major independent variables in analysis. Where both variables are low, states will be inclined toward hard legal arrangements to efficiently manage their interactions, [O,P,D]. When sovereignty costs are high and uncertainty is low, states will be reluctant to delegate but will remain open to precise and/or binding arrangements, [O,P,-]. Conversely, if sovereignty costs are low and uncertainty is high, states will be willing to accept binding obligation and at least moderate delegation but will resist precise rules, [O,p,d]. Finally, when both uncertainty and sovereignty costs are high, legalization will focus on the statement of flexible or hortatory obligations that are neither precise nor highly institutionalized, [o,p,-] or [-,p,-]. In all these cases, legalization provides a framework with which states can work to resolve their uncertainty, making harder legalization more attractive.

Soft Law as a Tool of Compromise

Compromise at a point in time. Soft law can ease bargaining problems among states even as it opens up opportunities for achieving mutually preferred compromises. Negotiating a hard, highly elaborated agreement among heterogeneous states is a costly and protracted process. It is often more practical to negotiate a softer agreement that establishes general goals but with less precision and perhaps with limited delegation.

Soft legalization allows states to adapt their commitments to their particular situations rather than trying to accommodate divergent national circumstances within a single text. This provides for flexibility in implementation, helping states deal with the domestic political and economic consequences of an agreement and thus increasing the efficiency with which it is carried out. Accordingly, soft law should be attractive in proportion to the degree of divergence among the preferences and capacities of states, a condition that increases almost automatically as one moves from bilateral through regional to multilateral negotiations.

Flexibility is especially important when uncertainty or one sticky problem threatens to upset a larger "package deal." Rather than hold up the overall agreement, states can incorporate hortatory or imprecise provisions to deal with the difficult issues, allowing them to proceed with the rest of the bargain. The labor and environmental side agreements to NAFTA are suggestive on this point.

Softness also accommodates states with different degrees of readiness for legalization. Those whose institutions, laws, and personnel permit them to carry out hard commitments can enter agreements of that kind; those whose weaknesses in these areas prevent them from implementing hard legal commitments can accept softer forms of agreement, perhaps through exceptions, reservations, or phase-in periods. Many treaties make such special provisions for developing countries, transitional economies, and other categories of states. States may prefer such an arrangement to either a softer agreement among all or a harder agreement with limited membership. Over time, if the soft arrangements are successful and without adverse consequences, the initially reluctant states may accept harder legalization. . . .

Advantages of flexibility do not come without cost. Soft law compromises make it hard to determine whether a state is living up to its commitments and therefore create opportunities to shirk. They also weaken the ability of government to undo the agreement. Again, states face a tradeoff between the advantages of flexibility in achieving agreement and its disadvantages in ensuring performance.

States can design different elements of an agreement with different combinations of hardness to fine-tune this tradeoff on different issues. Alternative forms of delegation can be used to limit the tendencies to shirk. In some cases, international reporting requirements may be sufficient to determine whether states are meeting their commitments. Elsewhere, requirements for domestic implementation, including domestic legalization, may empower private actors like firms or NGOs to enforce the agreement.

Compromise over time. Because even soft legal agreements commit states to characterize forms of discourse and procedure, soft law provides a way of achieving compromise over time. Consider a patient state (low discount rate) that is seeking a concession but is unwilling to offer enough immediately (for example, in linkage to other issues) to induce an impatient state to offer the concession. The patient state may nevertheless be willing to make a (smaller) current payoff in return for a soft legal agreement that has some prospect of enmeshing the impatient state in a process that will deliver the concession down the road. Insofar as states find it progressively costly to extricate themselves from legal processes, soft law helps remedy the commitment problem that looms large in international relations. . . .

The longer-term consequences of soft law, including processes of learning, do mean that legal agreements have an inevitable life cycle from softer toward harder legalization. Hard law is probably more likely to evolve from soft law than from (utopian) plans to create hard law full-blown. But this does not imply that all soft legalization is a way station to hard(er) legalization, or that hard legalization is the optimal form. The contracting difficulties noted earlier may never be resolved in some issue-areas; here, the attainable soft legalization will be superior to hard law that cannot be achieved. In these cases, continuing movement toward greater legalization is neither inevitable nor necessarily desirable. . . .

States may learn from experience that even soft forms of legalization can have powerful effects over time. As states internalize this lesson, they will be more alert to the possibilities of enmeshment and evolutionary growth in other negotiations. It would not be surprising, for example, if the Helsinki experience were still informing China's position on (even soft) human rights commitments. Impatient states may be forced to accept soft legalization in order to obtain current payoffs, but they may demand a higher price.

Compromise between the weak and the strong. Soft legalization facilitates compromise between weak and powerful states. The traditional legal view is that law operates as a shield for the weak, whereas the traditional international relations view is that law acts as an instrument of the powerful. These seemingly contradictory views can be reconciled by understanding how (soft) law helps both types of states achieve their differing goals.

Whatever their views on soft law, traditional legal scholars generally agree that legalization aids weak states. Weil, a severe critic of soft law, writes that "it is [hard] law with its rigor that comes between the weak and the mighty to protect and deliver."[41] Michael Reisman, more favorable toward soft law, agrees that law advantages the weak.[42] These views echo analyses of constitutionalism as a movement to create a government of laws, not of men (or states), in order to constrain the powerful.[43] At the international level, rules ranging from general principles of nonintervention to agreements like the Nuclear Non-Proliferation Treaty can be seen as bounding the struggle for power.

For just these reasons, small and dependent states often seek hard legalization. To the extent it is effective, hard law offers protection and reduces uncertainty by demarcating the likely behavior of powerful states. Lutz and Sikkink argue that Latin American states have long seen international law as providing them with exactly this type of protection from the United States.[44] Since they have less direct control over their own fates, small states also incur lower sovereignty costs from hard legalization. Indeed hard law may entail negative sovereignty costs, enhancing international standing and offering at least formal equality. Widespread African support for postcolonial boundaries, which make little sense on ethnic, political, or economic grounds, provides a striking illustration of the value of legal arrangements to weak states.

In contrast, many international relations scholars (and some critical legal scholars) hold the more skeptical view that international law is wholly beholden to international power. Powerful states have greater control over international outcomes, are less in need of protection, and face higher sovereignty costs. They have less need for legalization and more reason to resist it, even though their adherence is crucial to its success.

For these reasons, realists see international law largely as epiphenomenal, merely reflecting the distribution of power. Institutionalists also treat power (for example, hegemony and/or a capacity for decentralized retaliation) as a primary source of order and rules in the international system. Unlike realists, however, they argue that institutions have real effects, resulting in a disjuncture between the distribution of power and benefits in the system.

These perspectives can to some extent be reconciled by understanding legalization, especially soft legalization, as furthering the goals of both classes of states. Most importantly, legally binding and relatively precise rules allow strong and weak states to regularize their asymmetric relations. Because the continual, overt exercise of power is costly, powerful states gain by embodying their advantage in settled rules. Because weaker states are at a constant disadvantage in bargaining, they benefit from the certainty and credibility of legalized commitments. The result is not unlike an insurance contract, where a weaker party gladly pays a premium to a stronger one in return for the latter bearing, or in this case reducing, certain risks. In addition, both sides benefit by reducing the transactions costs of continual bargaining.

Of course, stronger states have disproportionate influence over the substance of agreed upon rules. But even the most powerful states cannot simply dictate the outcome of every negotiation because of the high costs of coercion. Instead, strong states must typically make the substantive content of legalized arrangements (just) attractive enough to encourage broad participation at an acceptable cost. Reduced bargaining costs normally provide ample room for such concessions.

Powerful states are most concerned with delegation, the major source of unanticipated costs. As a result, forms of legalization that involve limited delegation, for example [O,p,-] or [O,p,d], provide the crucial basis for cooperation between the weak and the strong. Lower levels of delegation prevent unexpected intrusions into the sovereign preserves of powerful countries while allowing them significant influence over decision making. Delegation to administrative bodies rather than judicial organs allows powerful states to retain control over ongoing issue management. The structure and decision-making rules of those bodies, including formal voting procedures, provide further means of balancing members' interests.

Soft legalization provides other important grounds for cooperation as well. We described earlier how legalization helps states solve commitment problems. This point becomes relevant when powerful states want small states to take actions that would leave them vulnerable. Powerful states can induce cooperation in such cases by agreeing to operate within a framework of legally binding rules and procedures, credibly constraining themselves from opportunistic behavior; with low levels of delegation, though, they can maintain predominant influence over decision making. For example, the United States ran its Gulf War operation through the UN Security Council, [O,p,d], even though doing so was burdensome, because this helped it to mobilize valuable support from weaker states, including bases in Saudi Arabia and financing from Japan. Involving the Security Council also allowed the supporting states to monitor and influence the scope of U.S. activities, notwithstanding the U.S. veto.

Finally, even without an external commitment problem, governments of weak states may find it domestically costly to be perceived as following the dictates of a powerful state. Organizing international arrangements in a legalized way, and delegating [modest supervisory authority to international agencies can mitigate these costs] without unduly interfering with the outcomes desired by the powerful state. We have elsewhere described the role of formal international organization as vehicles for this type of "laundering."[45] . . .

The Nuclear Non-Proliferation Treaty reflected an explicit bargain: weaker states accepted the existing nuclear oligopoly: powerful states agree to pursue weapons restraints and technology transfer. Obligation was high, though limited by escape clauses and the twenty-five-year renegotiation clause. Precision was high in limiting the transfer of military technology, but lower with regards to commercial technology transfers. Delegation to the IAEA has been largely controlled by the major powers (who monopolize the necessary expertise).

An understanding of soft legalization helps reconcile the seemingly contradictory views of the effect of law. Viewed as a process, legalization is a form of political bargaining where powerful states are advantaged. However, the efficiency gains of legalization for the powerful—cynically, providing an efficient means to extract benefits from the weak—depend on their offering the weak sufficiently satisfactory terms to induce their participation. Viewed as an outcome, legalization appears less political, since even powerful states must accept the constraints of legal principles and discourses to take advantage of legalized arrangements. Yet powerful states have the greatest influence on the substantive legal rules, and the institutions associated with (soft) international legalization are frequently constructed to ensure them a leading voice.

Conclusion

We have analyzed the spectrum of international legalization from soft informal agreements through intermediate blends of obligation, precision, and delegation to hard legal arrangements. Although even hard international law does not approach stereotypical conceptions of law based on advanced domestic legal systems, international legalization nevertheless represents a distinctive form of institutionalization. Ultimately, we can only understand the inclination of actors to cast their relations in legal form, and the variety of ways in which they do so, in terms of the value those institutional forms provide for them. Put plainly, international legalization is a diverse phenomenon because it helps a diverse universe of states and other actors resolve diverse problems.

Legalization reflects a series of tradeoffs. States are typically torn between the benefits of hard legalization—for example, mitigating commitment and incomplete contracting problems—and the sovereignty costs it entails. For their part, private actors generally seek hard legal arrangements that reflect their particular interests and values, but these demands often conflict with those of the other private actors or of governments. In settings like these, soft legalization helps balance competing considerations, offering techniques for compromise among states, among private actors, and between states and private actors. In addition, soft law helps actors handle the exigencies of uncertainty and accommodate power differentials.

Notes

1. We have profited from the insights in Keohane, Moravcsik, and Slaughter 1997, which was prepared in connection with this project.

2. The international legal system has developed over several centuries. International law includes secondary norms prescribing how primary rules are to be made, interpreted, and applied, as well as institutions through which both kinds of rules are implemented. The background legal system shapes many international interactions—indeed, it helps define the very notion of an international actor.

3. Weil 1983, 423.

4. For a related discussion of the benefits and costs of informal agreements, see Lipson 1991.

5. We draw on Koremenos's insightful work on how states structure treaties to enable mutual learning. Koremenos 1999.

6. Williamson 1989.

7. Keohane 1984, 88–89.

8. A more extreme way to address commitment problems, analogous to the merger of firms in business relationships that raise assurance problems, is to integrate separate sovereignties into a single political unit, such as a federal state. Integration can be partial as well as complete, as the EU illustrates. Even full integration, though, cannot solve commitment and other contracting problems among the many political, economic, and other interests within and across societies.

9. Deconstructionists, of course, would contest these statements. In practice, however, even observers of this bent see law as constraining interpretation. Koskenniemi 1999.

10. Keohane observes that states can reduce the force of reputational effects by distinguishing the circumstances of a violation from those surrounding other agreements. Keohane 1995. In the nineteenth century, the United States sought in this way to distinguish its treaties with "savage" Indian tribes, which it frequently violated, from agreements with European countries. The effort devoted to making this distinction, however, suggests that reputational effects would otherwise have spread across all legal agreements.

11. Setear 1999.

12. Lutz and Sikkink 2000.

13. See Burley and Mattli 1993; and Helfer and Slaughter 1997.

14. The rule of *pacta sunt servanda* is to some extent weakened by exceptions and defenses, notably the broad change-of-circumstances defense known as *rebus sic stantibus*. Yet these doctrines introduce needed flexibility; when they are found inapplicable, the normative force of the basic rule is enhanced.

15. See Wight 1977; Bull 1977; Hurrell 1993; and Buzan 1993.

16. Franck 1990.

17. Coordination agreements may not be self-enforcing when the benefits of moving the group to a new equilibrium are high. In these situations, especially when the gains to certain parties are large enough to make sure attempts are feasible, hard law may be useful as an assurance device.

18. Abbott and Snidal 1998.

19. Kahler 1988.

20. As discussed later, the costs of reaching a fully legalized agreement are often relatively high, leading actors to adopt softer forms of legalization.

21. Keohane 1984.

22. Compare Abbott and Snidal 1998.

23. We consider later the specific forms of legalization preferred by powerful and weak states.

24. Koh 1997.

25. This reverses the process associated with more traditional institutions like the Iran-U.S. Claims Tribunal where private actors encourage governments to initiate proceedings and provide support and encouragement to government litigators.

26. See Burley and Mattli 1993; Helfer and Slaughter 1997; Alter 1998b; Garrett, Kelemen, and Schulz 1998; and Mattli and Slaughter 1998b.

27. Incomplete contracting problems arise when any agreement is negotiated under conditions of incomplete or asymmetric information, risk, and uncertainty. For a recent overview, see Hart 1995.

28. The regimes literature does not always distinguish between the costs of transacting within regimes and the costs of creating regimes. In early work, regimes are seen as the legacy of hegemony, so that their creation is not directly addressed.

29. Kellman 1998.

30. Krasner offers four meanings or categories of sovereignty: domestic sovereignty (the organization of authority and control within the state), interdependence sovereignty (the ability to control flows across borders), international legal sovereignty (establishing the status of a political entity in the international system), and Westphalian sovereignty (preventing external actors from influencing or determining domestic authority structures). Krasner 1999. These categories overlap and do not covary in any necessary pattern.

Krasner argues that sovereignty has never been immutable, although legal sovereignty has tended to be more respected than Westphalian or other types of sovereignty. Indeed, some legal purists see sovereignty as a fundamental and inviolable legal concept relating to state supremacy in making and withdrawing from international treaties. But recent legal theorists argue that such a view is untenable given ongoing developments in international legalization; they conclude that "it is time to slowly ease the term out of polite language in international relations, surely in law." See Henkin et al. 1999, 19. We skirt these conceptual debates, focusing instead on the fact that states often perceive international legalization as infringing on their sovereignty, broadly construed.

31. Lindblom 1977, 24.

32. Abbott and Snidal 1998.

33. Shapiro takes the extreme view that such developments are an inevitable part of the development of any legal system. Shapiro 1981. Our view is that the advantages of legalization exert a powerful pull in this direction but that sovereignty costs provide significant resistance; we should expect a mixed level and international legalization according to the characteristics of issues and states, at least in the foreseeable future.

34. Colombatto and Macey offer a related view in arguing that governmental agencies seek international legalization in order to protect their administrative positions at a cost to domestic groups. Colombatto and Macy 1996.

35. In Krasner's terminology, these constitute international legal and Westphalian sovereignty, respectively.

36. See Knight 1921; and Ellsberg 1963.

37. Ambiguity aversion means that actors prefer known outcomes (including the status quo) to unknown ones. When actors know the possible outcomes but do not know which of two alternative probability distributions governs them, Ellsberg characterizes ambiguity aversion as assuming that an act leads to the minimum possible expected outcome. Ellsberg 1963. In this case, agents prefer incomplete to complete contracts even at zero contracting costs. See Mukerji 1998.

38. Abbott and Snidal 1998.
39. Gold 1983.
40. For a rational approach to learning, see Morrow 1994; and Koremenos 1999. For a more constructivist approach, see Finnemore 1996. Our view is that both learning as acquiring information and learning as changing preferences or identity are relevant (and compatible) aspects of legalization.
41. Weil 1983, 442.
42. Reisman 1988, 377.
43. Lindblom 1977.
44. Lutz and Sikkink 2000.
45. Abbott and Snidal 1998.

Bibliography

Abbott, Kenneth W., and Duncan Snidal. 1998. Why States Use Formal International Organizations. *Journal of Conflict Resolution* 42 (1): 3–32.

Alter, Karen J. 1998b. Who Are the Masters of the Treaty? European Governments and the European Court of Justice. *International Organization* 52 (1):121–47.

———. 2000. International Standards and International Governance. Unpublished manuscript, University of Chicago, Chicago, Illinois.

Bull, Hedley. 1977. *The Anarchical Society: A Study of Order in World Politics*. New York: Columbia University Press.

Burley, Anne-Marie, and Walter Mattli. 1993. Europe Before the Court: A Political Theory of Legal Integration. *International Organization* 47 (1): 41–76.

Buzan, Barry. 1993. From International System to International Society: Structural Realism and Regime Theory Meet the English School. *International Organization* 47: 327–52.

Colombatto, Enrico, and Jonathan R. Macey. 1996. A Public Choice Model of International Economic Cooperation and the Decline of the Nation State. *Cardozo Law Review* 18: 925–56.

Ellsberg, Daniel. 1963. Risk, Ambiguity, and the Savage Axioms. *Quarterly Journal of Economics* 75 (4): 643–69.

Finnemore, Martha. 1996. *National Interests in International Society*. Ithaca, N.Y.: Cornell University Press.

Franck, Thomas M. 1990. *Power of Legitimacy Among Nations*. New York: Oxford University Press.

Garret, Geoffrey, R. Daniel Kelemen, and Heiner Schulz. 1998. The European Court of Justice, National Governments, and Legal Integration in the European Union. *International Organization* 52 (1): 149–76.

Gold, Joseph. 1983. Strengthening the Soft International Law of Exchange Arrangements. *American Journal of International Law* 77: 443–89.

Hart, Oliver. 1995. *Firms, Contracts, and Financial Structure*. Oxford: Oxford University Press.

Helfer, Laurence, and Anne-Marie Slaughter. 1997. Toward a Theory of Effective Supranational Adjudication. *Yale Law Journal* 107 (2): 273–391.

Henkin, Louis, Gerald L. Neuman, Diane F. Orentlicher, and David W. Leebron. 1999. *Human Rights*. New York: Foundation Press.

Hurrell, Andrew. 1993. International Society and the Study of Regimes: A Reflective Approach. In *Regime Theory and International Relations*, edited by Volker Rittberger, 49–72. Oxford: Oxford University Press.

Kahler, Miles. 1988. Organizing the Pacific. In *Pacific-Asian Economic Policies and Regional Interdependence*, edited by Robert A. Scalapino, Seizaburo Sato, Jusuf Wanandi, and Sung-joo Han, 329–50. Berkeley: Institute of Asian Studies.

Kellman, Barry. 1998. Protection of Nuclear Materials. Paper prepared for meeting of American Society of Law Project on Compliance with Soft Law, 8–10 October, Baltimore, Md.

Keohane, Robert O. 1984. *After Hegemony: Cooperation and Discord in the World Political Economy*. Princeton, N.J.: Princeton University Press.

———. 1995. Contested Commitments and Commitment Pathways: United States Foreign Policy, 1783–1989. Paper presented at annual meeting of International Studies Association, 21–25 February, Chicago.

Keohane, Robert O., Andrew Moravcsik, and Anne-Marie Slaughter. 1997. Toward a Theory of Legalization. Paper presented at the Conference on International Law and Domestic Politics, 4–7 June, St. Helena, Calif.

Knight, Frank H. 1921. *Risk, Uncertainty, and Profit*. Boston: Houghton Mifflin.

Koh, Harold Hongju. 1997. Why Do Nations Obey International Law? *Yale Law Journal* 106: 2598–2659.

Koremenos, Barbara. 1999. On the Duration and Renegotiation of International Agreements. Ph.D. diss., University of Chicago.

Koskenniemi, Martti. 1999. Letters to the Editors of the Symposium (Symposium on Method in International Law). *American Journal of International Law* 93: 351–61.

Krasner, Stephen D. 1999. *Sovereignty: Organized Hypocrisy*. Princeton, N.J.: Princeton University Press.

Lindblom, Charles E. 1977. *Politics and Markets: The World's Political-Economic Systems*. New York: Basic Books.

Lipson, Charles. 1991. Why Are Some International Agreements Informal? *International Organization* 45 (4): 495–538.

Lutz, Ellen L, and Kathryn Sikkink. 2000. International Human Rights Law and Practice in Latin America. *International Organization* 54 (3): 633–659.

Mattli, Walter, and Anne-Marie Slaughter. 1998b. Revisiting the European Court of Justice. *International Organization* 52 (1): 177–209.

Morrow, James D. 1994. Modeling the Forms of International Cooperation: Distribution Versus Information. *International Organization* 48 (3): 387–423.

Mukerji, Sujoy. 1998. Ambiguity Aversion and the Incompleteness of Contractual Form. *American Economic Review* 88 (5): 1207–31.

Reisman, W. Michael. 1988. Remarks. *Proceedings of the 82nd Annual Meeting of the American Society of International Law* 22: 373–377.

Setear, Johm K. 1999. Whaling and Legalization. Unpublished manuscript, University of Virginia, Charlottesville, Virginia.

Shapiro, Martin. 1981. *Courts: A Comparative and Political Analysis*. Chicago: University of Chicago Press.

Weil, Prosper. 1983. Towards Relative Normativity in International Law? *American Journal of International Law* 77: 413–42.

Wight, Martin. 1977. *Systems of States*. Leicester: Leicester University Press.

Williamson, Oliver. 1989. Transaction Cost Economics. In *Handbook of Industrial Organization*, edited by R. Schmalensee and R.D. Willig, 135–182. Amsterdam: North Holland.

CHAPTER 3

Traditional and Modern Approaches to Customary International Law: A Reconciliation

Anthea Roberts

The Problem of Traditional and Modern Custom

The demise of custom as a source of international law has been widely forecasted.[1] This is because both the nature and the relative importance of custom's constituent elements are contentious. At the same time, custom has become an increasingly significant source of law in important areas such as human rights obligations.[2] Codification conventions, academic commentary, and the case law of the International Court of Justice (the Court) have also contributed to a contemporary resurrection of custom.[3] These developments have resulted in two apparently opposing approaches, which I term "traditional custom" and "modern custom." The renaissance of custom requires the articulation of a coherent theory that can accommodate its classic foundations and contemporary developments. This article seeks to provide an enriched theoretical account of custom that incorporates both the traditional and the modern approaches rather than advocating one approach over the other.

The Statute of the International Court of justice describes custom as "evidence of a general practice accepted as law."[4] Custom is generally considered to have two elements: state practice and *opinio juris*.[5] State practice refers to general and consistent practice by states, while *opinio juris* means that the practice is followed out of a belief of legal obligation.[6] This distinction is problematic because it is difficult to determine what states believe as opposed to what they say. Whether treaties and declarations constitute state practice or *opinio juris* is also controversial. For the sake of clarity, this article adopts Anthony D'Amato's distinction between action (state practice) and statements *(opinio juris)*.[7] Thus, actions can form custom only if

---

accompanied by an articulation of the legality of the action.[8] *Opinio juris* concerns statements of belief rather than actual beliefs.[9] Further, treaties and declarations represent *opinio juris* because they are statements about the legality of action, rather than examples of that action. As will be demonstrated below, traditional custom and modern custom are generally assumed to be alternatives because the former emphasizes state practice, whereas the latter emphasizes *opinio juris*.[10]

What I have termed traditional custom results from general and consistent practice followed by states from a sense of legal obligation.[11] It focuses primarily on state practice in the form of interstate interaction and acquiescence. *Opinio juris* is a secondary consideration invoked to distinguish between legal and nonlegal obligations.[12] Traditional custom is evolutionary[13] and is identified through an inductive process in which a general custom is derived from specific instances of state practice.[14] This approach is evident in *S.S. Lotus*,[15] where the Permanent Court of International Justice inferred a general custom about objective territorial jurisdiction over ships on the high seas from previous instances of state action and acquiescence.[16]

By contrast, modern custom is derived by a *deductive* process that begins with general statements of rules rather than particular instances of practice.[17] This approach emphasizes *opinio juris* rather than state practice because it relies primarily on statements rather than actions.[18] Modern custom can develop quickly because it is deduced from multilateral treaties and declarations by international fora such as the General Assembly, which can declare existing customs, crystallize emerging customs, and generate new customs.[19] Whether these texts become custom depends on factors such as whether they are phrased in declaratory terms, supported by a widespread and representative body of states, and confirmed by state practice.[20] A good example of the deductive approach is the Merits decision in *Military and Paramilitary Activities in and Against Nicaragua*.[21] The Court paid lip service to the traditional test for custom but derived customs of non-use of force and nonintervention from statements such as General Assembly resolutions.[22] The Court did not make a serious inquiry into state practice, holding that it was sufficient for conduct to be generally consistent with statements of rules, provided that instances of inconsistent practice had been treated as breaches of the rule concerned rather than as generating a new rule.[23]

The tests and justifications for traditional and modern custom appear to differ because the former develops slowly through state practice, while the latter can arise rapidly based on *opinio juris*.[24] This difference has spurred considerable discussion over two related issues. First, the legitimacy of traditional and modern custom has been debated at length.[25] David Fidler characterizes the various approaches to this issue as the dinosaur, dynamo, and dangerous perspectives.[26] The dinosaur approach focuses on traditional custom and argues that massive changes in the international system have rendered it an anachronism. For example, Jonathan Charney claims that the increasing number and diversity of states, as well as the emergence of global problems that are addressed in international fora, makes traditional custom an inappropriate means for developing law.[27] The dynamo perspective concentrates on modern custom and embraces it as a progressive source of law that can respond to moral issues and global challenges. For example, Theodor Meron, Richard Lillich, and Lori Bruun argue that modern custom based on declarations by international fora provides an important source of law for human rights obligations.[28] Finally, the dangerous perspective views modern custom as a departure from the traditional approach that has created an opportunity for legal and political abuse. Thus, Michael Reisman characterizes the increased dependence on custom as a "great leap backwards" designed to serve the interests of powerful states.[29] Similarly, Arthur Weisburd holds that modern custom often lacks the legitimacy of state consent because it is formed despite little, or conflicting, state practice.[30]

Second, the divergence between traditional and modern custom has been criticized as undermining the integrity of custom as a source of law. Patrick Kelly argues that custom is an indeterminate and malleable source of law, simply a "matter of taste."[31] According to D'Amato, the modern approach trashes the theoretical foundations of custom by inverting the traditional priority of state practice over *opinio juris*.[32] Sir Robert Jennings insists that "most of what we perversely persist in calling customary international law is not only *not* customary law: it does not even faintly resemble a customary law."[33] The phrases "modern," "new,"[34] "contemporary,"[35] and "instant"[36] custom appear inherently contradictory and obscure the real basis for forming this law. Hilary Charlesworth contends that modern custom can be rationalized only by dispensing with the traditional rhetoric of custom.[37] Bruno Simma and Philip Alston argue that the modern approach has created an "identity crisis"[38] for custom and would be better understood as a general principle of international law.[39] Likewise, Charney, Daniel Bodansky, and Hiram Chodosh conclude that modern custom is really a new species of universal declaratory law because it is based on authoritative statements about practice rather than observable regularities of behavior.[40]

Both the legitimacy and the integrity of traditional and modern custom have received considerable attention and polarized positions are evident. However, few commentators have transcended these debates by attempting to provide an overall theory of custom. Frederic Kirgis rationalizes the divergence in custom by analyzing the requirements of state practice and *opinio juris* on a sliding scale.[41] At one end, highly consistent state practice can establish a customary rule without requiring *opinio juris*. However, as the frequency and consistency of state practice decline, a stronger showing of *opinio juris* will be required. Kirgis argues that the exact trade-off between state practice and *opinio juris* will depend on the importance of the activity in question and the reasonableness of the rule involved.[42] Simma and Alston claim that this approach reinterprets the concept of custom so as to produce the "right" answers.[43] However, John Tasioulas argues that the sliding scale can be rationalized on the basis of Ronald Dworkin's interpretive theory of law, which balances a description of what the law has been with normative considerations about what the law should be. This perspective shows why the Court may be less exacting in requiring state practice and *opinio juris* in cases that deal with important moral issues.

This article builds on the work of Kirgis and Tasioulas and offers a defense of custom by seeking to reconcile the traditional and modern approaches. The second part analyzes the competing values of descriptive accuracy and normative appeal that are used to justify international law. These values characterize traditional and modern custom, respectively, because of their inductive and deductive methodologies and facilitative and moral content. The third part examines custom on a sliding scale and rejects this interpretive approach because it does not accurately describe the process of finding custom and would create customs that are apologies for power or utopian and unachievable.[44] The fourth part presents an alternative vision of Dworkin's interpretive theory of law applied to custom, which incorporates the justifications of descriptive accuracy and normative appeal and seeks to balance them in a Rawlsian reflective equilibrium.[45] The fifth part outlines the advantages of the reflective interpretive approach over the sliding-scale methodology. Rearticulating the theoretical foundations of custom in this more principled and flexible fashion will provide international actors with a coherent theory for applying custom. It will also help to justify the traditional and modern approaches to custom as two aspects of a single source of law, rather than characterize one approach as illegitimate and the choice between them as undermining the integrity of custom.

The Descriptive and Normative Approaches to Custom

Descriptive Accuracy and Normative Appeal

The values of descriptive accuracy and normative appeal provide important, and sometimes competing, justifications for international law. Descriptive accuracy (which focuses on what the practice has been) is valuable in justifying the content of international law because laws should correspond to reality.[46] Laws must bear some relation to practice if they are to regulate conduct effectively, because laws that set unrealistic standards are likely to be disobeyed and ultimately forgotten. This consideration particularly applies to decentralized systems of law, such as international law, where traditional enforcement mechanisms are unavailable or underdeveloped.[47] Descriptive accuracy is also essential to predictive power[48] because a theory that accurately describes practice enables more reliable predictions of future state behavior.[49]

The alternative justification for international law provided by normative appeal (which focuses on what the practice *ought to be*) involves procedural and substantive aspects. First, procedural normativity requires that the process for forming laws be transparent, so that states are aware of the real basis for forming customs and can regulate their actions accordingly.[50] It also entails an opportunity for states to participate in law formation and have their positions considered.[51] Legal rules are more likely to engender respect in a decentralized system, possibly even when the outcome is less favorable, if they result from a process perceived as legitimate.[52] Second, substantive normativity requires that laws be coherent and that their content be morally good or at least neutral, depending on their subject matter. Claims about "morality" are contentious because it remains unclear whether morality is objective or culturally relative. By morality, I am referring to commonly held subjective values about actions that are right and wrong, which a representative majority of states has recognized in treaties and declarations.[53]

Facilitative and Moral Customs

The best balance between the justifications of descriptive accuracy and normative appeal depends on the facilitative or moral content of the custom involved. International laws are ranged on a spectrum between facilitative and moral rules.[54] At one extreme, there are completely facilitative rules, which promote coexistence and cooperation but do not deal with substantive moral issues (such as that ships must pass on the left). Next come primarily facilitative rules that regulate interaction but also give rise to some moral considerations (such as the fair distribution of resources in a continental shelf). Moving to the middle, one finds rules that involve important facilitative and moral considerations (such as environmental rules). Toward the other extreme, the laws are primarily moral rather than facilitative (such as some human rights obligations) and peremptory rules that prohibit actions whether or not they affect coexistence and cooperation (such as *jus cogens* laws prohibiting genocide). While it is possible for a law to facilitate interaction between states and also have a strong moral content (such as the prohibition on the use of force), laws often tend more toward one or the other end of the spectrum.

Facilitative customs are more descriptive than normative because they turn a *description of actual practice* into a prescriptive requirement for future action.[55] Moral customs are more normative than descriptive because they prescribe future action based on *normative evaluations of ideal practice.* Traditional customs primarily facilitate coexistence and cooperation between sovereign states without having a peremptory moral character; for example, the law on diplomatic immunity.[56] State practice is dominant in establishing traditional facilitative customs because these rules turn empirical descriptions of past practice into prescriptive requirements for future practice.[57] However, international law has expanded since 1945 to include many moral issues such as human rights,[58] the use of force,[59] and environmental protection.[60] Louis Henkin characterizes this development as a move from state values to human values, and from a liberal state system to a welfare system.[61] State practice is less important in forming modern customs because these customs prescribe ideal standards of conduct rather than describe existing practice.[62] For example, the customary prohibition on torture expresses a moral abhorrence of torture rather than an accurate description of state practice.[63]

The moral content of modern custom explains the strong tendency to discount the importance of contrary state practice in the modern approach. Irregularities in description can undermine a descriptive law, but a normative law may be broken and remain a law because it is not premised on descriptive accuracy. For example, *jus cogens* norms prohibit fundamentally immoral conduct and cannot be undermined by treaty arrangement or inconsistent state practice.[64] Since the subject matter of modern customs is not morally neutral, the international community is not willing to accept any norm established by state practice.[65] Modern custom involves an almost teleological approach, whereby some examples of state practice are used to justify a chosen norm, rather than deriving norms from state practice. As noted above, this approach was evident in the *Nicaragua* case, where the Court held it sufficient for the conduct of states to be generally consistent with statements of rules, provided that contrary state practice had generally been "treated as breaches of that rule, not as indications of the recognition of a new rule."[66] Thus, the importance of descriptive accuracy varies according to the facilitative or moral content of the rule involved. . . .

The relative importance of substantive and procedural normativity links to criticisms of modern custom as creating quasi legislation on the basis of declarations and treaties.[67] Declarations of international fora are formally nonbinding, while states can determine whether, and to what extent, they wish to be bound by treaties.[68] By contrast, custom is generally binding except for the limited and contentious persistent objector rule.[69] Transforming declarations and treaties into custom changes their nature because customs can bind non-parties to treaties and declarations[70] and are not affected by reservations[71] or denunciation.[72] Thus, Prosper Weil argues that the requirements of treaties have "not been frontally assaulted but cunningly outflanked."[73] However, the emphasis on community consensus over individual state consent in modern custom reflects the priority of substantive normativity over procedural normativity in important moral issues. Modern custom evinces a desire to create general international laws that can bind all states on important moral issues.[74] According to Kirgis, "The alternative would be an international legal order containing ominous silences—where treaty commitments cannot be found—concerning the ways in which states impose their wills on other states or on individuals."[75] The international community discounts the importance of dissenting states and contrary state practice because it is not prepared to recognize exceptions to the maintenance of certain fundamental values. Recognizing exceptions to such rules would "shock the conscience of mankind"[76] and be contrary to "elementary considerations of humanity."[77] The substantive normativity of modern custom can therefore be used to justify a reduced focus on procedural normativity and descriptive accuracy.

The importance of descriptive accuracy and normative appeal, and procedural and substantive normativity, varies according to the facilitative and moral content of traditional and modern custom. The reduced focus on state practice in the modern approach is explained by its use to create generally binding laws on important moral issues.

Apology and Utopia

Descriptive accuracy and normative appeal provide important bases for justifying international law. While facilitative and moral rules respectively tend more toward descriptive accuracy and normative appeal, neither value is sufficient to justify all international laws. According to Koskenniemi, international law mediates between the competing tendencies of apology (description) and utopia (normativity).

> A law which would lack distance from State behaviour, will or interest would amount to a non-normative apology, a mere sociological description. A law which would base itself on principles which are unrelated to State behaviour, will or interest would seem utopian, incapable of demonstrating its own content in any reliable way.[78]

The conflicting values of description and normativity, and their respective risks of being an apology for power or utopian and unachievable, represent the fundamental tension in legal argument.[79] Theorists oscillate between these two extremes and each position remains open to challenge from the opposite perspective.[80] Thus, international legal argument is always dynamic. David Kennedy argues that "[e]ither international law has been too far from politics and must move closer to become effective, or it has become dangerously intermingled with politics and must assert its autonomy to remain potent."[81] The dynamic between description and normativity represents the "deep doctrinal schizophrenia" of law[82] or a "disciplinary hamster wheel" from which theorists appear unable to escape.[83]

While the justifications for traditional and modern custom mainly align with descriptive accuracy and normative appeal, neither approach is completely descriptive or normative because both recognize the importance of state practice and *opinio juris* to varying degrees. However, as the two approaches to custom tend toward opposite ends of the theoretical spectrum, the strongest criticisms of each come from the counterstandpoint. Traditional custom embodies the value of descriptive accuracy but the risk of apologism, so that one of the main criticisms of traditional custom is that it lacks democratic legitimacy (a normative criticism). By contrast, modern custom is normatively appealing but risks creating utopian rules, so it is criticized for producing norms that are divorced from reality (a descriptive criticism). The critiques of traditional and modern custom rest on this basis.

The advantages and disadvantages of traditional and modern custom are "dynamic" because criticisms of traditional custom tend to correspond to advantages of modern custom and vice versa. An improvement in normative appeal will often correspond to a decline in descriptive accuracy, while an enhancement of descriptive accuracy will often result in a deterioration of normative appeal. Whereas some rules are descriptively accurate and normatively appealing, the two justifications often have a relationship of inverse proportionality. For example, relying on declarations by international fora is potentially more democratic than relying on the actions of powerful states (a normative improvement in modern custom)—but since these declarations are supported by a majority of states rather than a predominance of power, they are less likely to be enforced in practice (a descriptive deterioration from traditional custom).[84] Similarly, the relationship between procedural and substantive normativity is also dynamic. For example, one could bind all states on important moral issues (a substantive normative advantage), but doing so would bind some states without their consent (a procedural normative problem).[85] Thus, the values of description and normativity represent the fundamental tension in legal argument[86] and both approaches remain open to challenge from the opposite perspective.[87] As seen, international law reveals a dynamic tension between descriptive accuracy and normative appeal. Traditional custom has descriptive strengths but lacks democratic legitimacy, while modern custom deals with substantive moral issues but produces laws that do not reflect reality. This tension leads to the issue of whether the two approaches can be reconciled in a single interpretive theory.

Custom on an Interpretive Sliding Scale

The divergence between the traditional and modern approaches to custom has been criticized as making custom indeterminate and malleable.[88] This part analyzes one attempt at reconciling them by applying Dworkin's interpretive theory of law to custom on a sliding scale.

Law as Interpretation: Dworkin

Dworkin argues that legal decisions aim at reformulating past decisions and practice in the most coherent and morally attractive way, consistent with the facts of legal history. Dworkin outlines three steps in the interpretive process: preinterpretation, interpretation, and post-interpretation.[89] In the preinterpretive stage, the rules and facts that form the practice to be interpreted are identified. The term preinterpretation is somewhat misleading because the collection of data is theory dependent.[90] Consequently, this stage requires a high degree of consensus to provide a common focus for interpretation.[91]

In the interpretive stage, the interpreter formulates a general explanation for the main elements of the practice. This explanation is called the "dimension of fit" and it imposes a rough threshold requirement that accepts an interpretation as eligible only if the raw data of legal practice adequately support it.[92] There can be three outcomes at this stage: no eligible interpretations, if every possible interpretation is inconsistent with the bulk of raw material available; easy cases, when there is only one eligible interpretation; and hard cases, where a range of eligible interpretations result because the tests are unsettled or the practice conflicting.

Postinterpretation only becomes relevant in hard cases, where interpreters must choose the best eligible interpretation according to the "dimension of substance."[93] The best interpretation is the one that makes the practice appear in the best light, judged according to the substantive aspirations of the legal system. This criterion involves consideration of moral and political ideals, as well as higher-order convictions about how these ideals should be prioritized when they conflict.[94]

The interpretive stage is backward looking and descriptive, while the postinterpretive stage is forward looking and normative. Dworkin's interpretive theory of law combines a descriptive historical investigation about what the law has been (fit) with a normative moral inquiry about what it should be (substance).[95] According to Dworkin: "propositions of law are not simply descriptive of legal history in a straightforward way, nor are they simply evaluative in some way divorced from legal history. They are interpretive of legal history, which combines elements of both description and evaluation but is different from both."[96]

What, however, is the relationship between fit and substance? Dworkin originally proposed a lexical ordering between them,[97] but in *Law's Empire* he revised the relationship. Fit provides a rough threshold criterion.[98] Interpretations need not fit every aspect of the existing practice, but they must fit enough for the interpreter to be "interpreting that practice, not inventing a new one."[99] On the other hand, if there are multiple eligible interpretations, then fit and substance must be balanced against each other.[100] Thus, any inadequacies of fit will count against an interpretation at the substantive stage because "an interpretation is *pro tanto* more satisfactory if it shows less damage to integrity than its rival."[101] Similarly, "defects of fit may be compensated . . . if the principles of that interpretation are particularly attractive."[102] The interpreter must therefore balance the relative strengths of fit and substance in different interpretations to determine the best interpretation. Dworkin likens this process to multiple authors writing consecutive chapters in a chain novel. Each author must contribute a chapter that provides sufficient continuity with the earlier chapters (fit) and develops the book in the best way (substance).[103] However, Dworkin details no method for weighing fit and substance other than the metaphor *balance.*[104] Hence, anyone using Dworkin's interpretive theory must correctly identify fit and substance and develop a working theory about how to balance them.

Custom on a Sliding Scale: Kirgis and Tasioulas

The international legal system is decentralized, resulting in multiple interpreters of custom. The existence and content of custom is usually determined by states and academics, though the Court remains the ultimate arbiter in some cases.[105] These interpreters are meant to determine customs on the basis of state practice and *opinio juris.*[106] However, the traditional and modern forms of custom both appear to emphasize one element at the expense of the other. Kirgis argues that the two approaches can be understood by viewing state practice and *opinio juris* as interchangeable along a sliding scale:[107]

> On the sliding scale, very frequent, consistent state practice establishes a customary rule without much (or any) affirmative showing of an *opinio juris,* so long as it is not negated by evidence of non-normative intent. As the frequency and consistency of the practice decline in any series of cases, a stronger showing of an *opinio juris* is required. At the other end of the scale, a clearly demonstrated *opinio juris* establishes a customary rule without much (or any) affirmative showing [of state practice].[108]

Yet when will a custom be formed on the basis only of state practice or *opinio juris,* instead of requiring both elements? According to Kirgis, the answer depends on the importance of the activity in question and the reasonableness of the rule involved. If an activity is not very destructive, then the Court will be more exacting in requiring both state practice and *opinio juris* to form a custom. By contrast, Kirgis states, "[t]he more destabilizing or morally distasteful the activity—for example, the offensive use of force or the deprivation of fundamental human rights—the more readily international decision makers will substitute one element for the other, provided that the asserted restrictive rule seems reasonable."[109]

Custom as a Reflective Interpretive Concept

Dworkin's interpretive theory of law incorporates the values of fit (description) and substance (normativity) but does not provide a mechanism for balancing them. Analyzing custom on a sliding scale is flawed because it misconceives the nature of fit and substance and risks creating customs that are apologies for power or utopian and unachievable. This part presents an alternative vision of Dworkin's interpretive theory as applied to custom, which re-conceptualizes the nature of fit and substance and balances them in a Rawlsian reflective equilibrium. . . .

Balancing Fit and Substance: A Reflective Methodology

Applying Dworkin's interpretive theory to custom is useful because it incorporates description (fit) and normativity (substance) into a single approach. If there are multiple eligible interpretations, the best interpretation is the one that most coherently explains the dimensions of fit and substance.[110] Coherence, which Dworkin calls integrity, is an important value in international law.[111] Interpretations should aim for coherence by mediating between fit and substance in the same way as Rawls mediates between intuitions and moral principles in ethical theories.[112] Instead of prioritizing one value above the other, Rawls advocates revising our interpretation of practice and principles, back and forth, until we have done everything possible to render our interpretation coherent and justified from both ends.[113] Rawls calls this a "reflective equilibrium. . . ."[114]

While custom and moral theories involve very different considerations, a Rawlsian reflective approach can be used more generally to reconcile the inductive and deductive methodologies that are common to both.[115] The dimension of fit and the theory of moral intuitionism are both inductive because they seek to infer a general rule from particular instances of practice. The dimension of substance is similar to moral principles because both deduce norms about practice from abstract statements of principles. Instead of prioritizing one value above the other, we should revise our interpretation of practice and principles until the two approaches are coherent and justified from both ends in a reflective equilibrium. While Dworkin argues that the best interpretation is objectively determinable,[116] I believe that subjectivity is inherent in interpreting raw data. However, the reflective process provides some guidelines for reconciling practice and principles rather than allowing one element to override the other. It also explains why the best interpretation of practice and principles will change over time in light of new data or theories.

Practical Application of the Reflective Interpretive Concept

A reflective equilibrium requires revising our interpretations of practice (fit) and principles (substance) to find the most coherent explanation of both dimensions in the case of multiple eligible interpretations. This section explores how the reflective interpretive approach applies to two practical problems in custom, first, by applying it to the spectrum of facilitative and modern customs, and second, by using it to explain the fluid nature of custom. This analysis demonstrates that the reflective interpretive approach is dynamic, varying over time and according to the nature of the custom involved.

The best balance between fit and substance will depend on the relative strength of the practice and principles in the custom involved. This is because the best interpretation of a custom usually leans toward the stronger element (practice or principles) as providing the greatest consistency with both elements. Traditional facilitative customs will result in a more descriptive equilibrium because they do not involve strong issues of principle. By contrast, modern customs with a strong moral content require a more normative equilibrium because they involve important issues of principle. Other customs, such as environmental protection, may involve strong normative and descriptive considerations, requiring a more even balance of fit and substance. Thus, traditional and modern customs exist on a facilitative-moral spectrum, which explains the asymmetrical application of fit and substance to them. . . .

The Fluid Nature of Custom

Customs can generally change and harden over time because custom is a fluid source of law. The content of custom is not fixed; it can develop and change in light of new circumstances. The formation and modification of custom is an uncertain process because international law lacks an authoritative guide as to the amount, duration, frequency, and repetition of state practice required to develop or change a custom.[117] Using Hart's terminology, custom would be a primitive source of law because it lacks clear rules of change. Instead, custom develops through a "slow process of growth, whereby courses of conduct once thought optional become first habitual or usual, and then obligatory, and the converse process of decay, when deviations, once severely dealt with, are first tolerated and then pass unnoticed."[118]

One reason for the difficulty of identifying the formation and change of custom is the radical decentralization of the international system. States are both legislators and subjects of international law, which explains why D'Amato argues that every breach of a customary law contains the seed for a new legality.[119] In one sense, the action is a breach because the state is judged as a subject of international law; in another sense, the action is a seed for a new law because the state acts as a legislator of international law.[120] However, whether a custom develops or changes depends not only on the actions of some states but also on the reactions of other states. This is because states are also both legislators and enforcers of international law. Thus, a breach will effectively repeal or modify an existing custom only if other states emulate the breach or acquiesce in its legality.[121]

The reflective interpretive approach is useful in explaining the fluid nature of custom. Just as customs can develop and change in light of new circumstances, so a reflective equilibrium is not stable because the best explanation of practice and principles must be reevaluated in light of new state practice, *opinio juris,* and moral considerations.[122] The best balance between practice and principles must be regularly reassessed. Consequently, conflicting data should never he discounted as irrelevant because they may significantly affect future interpretations. What is now an exception to, or a breach of, an accepted rule may later become integral to the explanation of a new general rule. According to D'Amato:

> When a state violates an existing rule of customary international law, it undoubtedly is "guilty" of an illegal act, but the illegal act itself becomes a disconfirmatory instance of the underlying rule. The next state will find it somewhat easier to disobey the rule, until eventually a new line of conduct will replace the original rule by a new rule.[123]

The number of disconfirmatory acts that are required before the breach of an old rule will constitute the basis for a new rule depends on the extent of previous practice and the importance of the moral principles involved. Moral customs, and in particular *jus cogens* norms, are unlikely to be undermined by contrary practice. Furthermore, well-established customs will demonstrate relative resistance to change because new state practice or *opinio juris* must be weighed against a wealth of previous contrary practice.[124] However, a custom can change quickly in the face of very strong state practice or *opinio juris,* particularly if the rule was uncertain or still developing.[125] Recent practice may also carry proportionately greater weight than past practice in determining the present or future state of custom. Customs can develop or change in light of the recognition of new moral considerations in international law. For example, the customary prohibition against genocide stemmed from the recognition of human rights as a substantive aim of international law after World War II. Likewise, currently nonbinding aspirations may harden into legally binding custom in the future. For example, D'Amato and Sudhir Chopra have argued that whales may have an emerging right to life under customary international law.[126] Thus, the content of custom can change in view of new practice and principles in international law.

The fluidity of custom is demonstrated by the debate over whether NATO's intervention in Kosovo has formed the basis for an emerging customary right to unilateral humanitarian intervention. In the *Nicaragua* case, the Court found a general customary prohibition on intervention in other states but held that "[r]eliance by a State on a novel right or an unprecedented exception to the principle might, if shared in principle by other States, tend towards a modification of customary international law."[127] Whether states have successfully created an exception to the general custom of non-intervention will depend in part on whether they "justified their conduct by reference to a new right of intervention or a new exception to the principle of its prohibition."[128] It will also depend on whether the action provokes protest by other states or is emulated or met with acquiescence. However, if a state *prima facie* breaches a custom but "defends its conduct by appealing to exceptions or justification contained within the rule itself, then whether or not the State's conduct is in fact justifiable on that basis, the significance of that attitude is to confirm rather than to weaken the rule."[129]

Most commentators have concluded that NATO's intervention in Kosovo was illegal under existing international law.[130] For example, Charney finds it indisputable that NATO's intervention violated the United Nations Charter and international law.[131] However, the precedential status of the intervention is more contentious. Simma argues that NATO's intervention should not become a precedent because of the exceptional factual circumstances in Kosovo, the insistence by participating states such as France and Germany that the intervention did not form a precedent, and the detrimental impact of allowing an isolated breach of collective security to become a general rule for unilateral action.[132] By contrast, Antonio Cassese argues that NATO's action may support an emerging custom allowing the use of forcible countermeasures to impede a state from committing large-scale atrocities within its own territory, in circumstances where the Security Council is incapable of responding to the crisis.[133] I submit that these conflicting arguments can he understood by employing a reflective interpretive approach.

To determine eligible interpretations of fit, one must primarily consider the state practice respecting unilateral humanitarian intervention.

Opponents of the norm focus on the lack of explicit authorization of NATO's action by the Security Council and the likelihood that China or Russia would have vetoed any resolution supporting intervention. The intervention also provoked significant protests by China, India, Namibia, Belarus, and the Russian Federation,[134] which undermines its ability to form a custom. Prominent members of NATO, including France and Germany, insisted that the intervention did not constitute a precedent for a general right to unilateral humanitarian intervention.[135] In pleadings for the case brought by the Federal Republic of Yugoslavia against ten NATO members in 1999, only Belgium expressly mentioned humanitarian intervention as a possible legal justification for action.[136] Thus, the intervening states did not attempt to justify their intervention on the basis of a new exception to the general prohibition on intervention.[137]

States have also repeatedly abstained from invoking the right of humanitarian intervention where there were grounds for doing so, including India's intervention in East Pakistan in 1971, Vietnam's invasion of Kampuchea in 1978, and Tanzania's intervention in Uganda in 1979.[138] These states justified their interventions on other grounds, such as self-defense, which suggests that they did not believe that unilateral humanitarian intervention was accepted in international law.[139] However, states will generally resort to factual or legal exceptions rather than openly admit they have breached a law, even if they wish to change it.[140] The absence of intervention in potentially analogous situations involving, for example, the Kurds in Turkey, the Chechens in Russia, and the Tibetans in China may also suggest that states did not believe that unilateral humanitarian intervention was permitted under international law.

By contrast, proponents of an emerging norm argue that NATO had authority to act because the Security Council had defined the situation in Kosovo as a "threat to peace and security in the region."[141] The lack of condemnation of NATO's intervention by the Security Council and most other states also indicates a general acquiescence in its legality. For example, a draft resolution condemning NATO's use of force was rejected by a vote of 12 to 3 in the Security Council,[142] and no state requested an immediate meeting of the General Assembly to condemn the intervention. Precedents can also be found for humanitarian intervention without explicit authorization by the Security Council, such as the action by the United States, France, and Great Britain in Iraq in 1991. Moreover, the interventions in Iraq and Kosovo provide more modern, and thus potentially more weighty, precedents than the counterexamples from the 1970s. Contrary examples of states seeking Security Council approval before intervening in other situations could represent a politically prudent course of action, rather than a necessary element of legality. Further, the failure of states to intervene in previous humanitarian crises represents discretionary nonaction, rather than obligatory negative practice or acquiescence, because a custom allowing intervention is a permissive right rather than an obligatory duty.[143]

The range of eligible interpretations brings the dimension of substance into play to help determine the best interpretation in light of the substantive aims of international law. Unilateral humanitarian intervention involves the conflicting substantive considerations of state sovereignty (which would support a duty of nonintervention) and humanitarian aims (which would support a right to intervention). Prohibitions on intervention and the use of force appear to be peremptory norms of international law.[144] Some humanitarian considerations, such as the prohibition on genocide, have also achieved *jus cogens* status.[145] The dimension of substance must include consideration of how the substantive aims of international law should be prioritized when they conflict. While state sovereignty has traditionally been accorded primary importance in international law, arguably the international community is increasingly recognizing exceptions to this principle in extreme humanitarian crises.[146] Thus, which principle will prevail when the two conflict depends on the extremity of the humanitarian crisis in question.

The dimension of substance also requires consideration of the procedural normativity of unilateral intervention. Critics of unilateral intervention argue that it is open to abuse and likely to result in selective and self-interested action.[147] Proponents argue that selective application is inherent in the concept of rights rather than duties, that selective intervention may be better than no intervention, and that it is unrealistic to expect states to intervene only when they are completely disinterested.[148] Some of the objections may also be met by clearly identifying the conditions for intervention so as to provide safeguards against abuse, rather than creating a blanket prohibition on intervention. Further, the alternatives to unilateral intervention, which are no intervention and collective intervention,[149] should be taken into account. Collective intervention, approved by the Security Council, is arguably less partisan and less open to abuse than unilateral intervention. However, the legitimacy of the Security Council itself is questionable because it comprises only fifteen states and the five permanent members all have the power of veto. Thus, collective action may not enjoy the advantages of procedural normativity. Collective action may also not be possible even in the face of extreme violations of human rights such as genocide. In such cases, unilateral intervention may be justified on the basis that the importance of the substantive moral issues involved outweighs deficiencies in procedural normativity.[150]

In applying the reflective equilibrium, we need to consider which explanation most coherently explains the competing conceptions of practice and principles outlined above. There are two eligible interpretations of custom, one prohibiting unilateral humanitarian intervention and one permitting it. Since the first interpretation more adequately explains the raw data of practice to date, the second interpretation would only be preferred if supported by a strong dimension of substance. Substantively, the principles of state sovereignty and nonintervention generally prevail, except in cases of extreme human rights violations such as genocide. From a procedural perspective, collective intervention is usually preferable to unilateral intervention, though the latter may be justified if the Security Council is paralyzed by the veto power. Thus, the dimension of substance provides equivocal support for both interpretations, which varies according to the circumstances of the case. The present state of practice and principles probably leads to the conclusion that unilateral humanitarian intervention is not currently recognized as an exception to the principle of nonintervention. However, a narrow right to unilateral humanitarian intervention may be emerging in exceptional circumstances where there are gross violations of human rights, peaceful avenues for settling the dispute have been exhausted, the veto power has rendered the Security Council incapable of taking coercive action, the action is undertaken by a group of states with the support (or at least the nonopposition) of the majority of states, and the armed force is used exclusively to stop the violations.[151] Whether this emerging norm is transformed into a binding custom will depend on future developments in the practice and principles of international law. Thus, the reflective interpretive approach can be used to demonstrate the fluid nature of custom as a source of law.

The Advantages of a Reflective Interpretive Approach

The contemporary interest in custom as a source of international law poses a challenge to articulate a coherent theory of custom. This is a difficult exercise because the traditional and modern approaches to custom appear to be opposed, with traditional custom emphasizing state practice and modern custom emphasizing *opinio juris.* The divergence between the descriptive and normative approaches of traditional and modern custom causes problems because the tests and justifications for traditional custom do not apply to modern custom and vice versa. Instead of advocating the rival merits and legitimacy of either approach, this article has sought to build an enriched theoretical account of custom that analyzes the competing justifications for traditional and modern custom and accommodates both approaches in a consistent interpretive theory.

This reconciliation provides a methodology for assessing asserted customs. After gathering evidence of state practice and *opinio juris,* one must apply the threshold criterion of fit to determine if there are any eligible interpretations that adequately explain the raw data of practice. Fit provides continuity and descriptive accuracy, so that state practice will assume primary importance at this stage. However, state practice is open to interpretation and should include intrastate action and inaction, not just interstate interaction and acquiescence. Some articulation of legality is needed to differentiate between legal custom and social practice. If there is no eligible interpretation, then there is no custom. If there is one eligible interpretation, then the custom is clear. If there are multiple eligible interpretations, then one must weigh the dimensions of fit and substance to determine the best interpretation.

Strong statements of *opinio juris* become relevant at this third stage because they represent normative considerations about what the law should be. The best interpretation is the one that most *coherently* explains fit and substance, which varies according to the facilitative or moral content of the custom involved. Primarily facilitative customs do not involve strong substantive considerations and thus will be determined principally by fit. Primarily moral customs give rise to strong procedural and substantive normative considerations, which must be balanced against deficiencies in fit. Custom is also a fluid source of law, which causes the point of equilibrium to vary over time in light of new state practice, *opinio juris*, and moral considerations. Consequently, the reflective interpretive approach results in a more sophisticated understanding of fit and substance and constitutes a more nuanced method for reconciling them than the sliding scale in various ways.

First, the reflective interpretive approach recognizes that the role of the dimension of fit is to provide descriptive accuracy. Questions of fit and descriptive accuracy are both backward looking because they focus on whether a custom is supported by past practice. Tasioulas claims that strong statements of *opinio juris* can form the basis of eligible interpretations at the dimension of fit. Similarly, Michael Akehurst has argued that state practice should include paper practice in the form of statements, declarations, and resolutions.[152] I have demonstrated that this approach is not feasible because statements often fuse *lex lata* and *lex ferenda* and thus lack descriptive accuracy. However, one can still form eligible interpretations of traditional and modern custom by considering the open-textured nature of practice. State practice should also include consideration of intrastate action (not just interstate interaction), obligations being observed (not just obligations being breached), and reasons for a lack of protest over breaches (other than acquiescence in the legality of those breaches). These forms of practice reflect the changing subject matter of international law to include intrastate issues and are descriptively accurate because they focus on action and inaction.

Second, I have outlined a dimension of substance that embodies both substantive and procedural normativity. Kirgis refers to strong moral issues but does not provide a theory for determining them. Tasioulas deliberately limits his discussion of the substantive aims of international law to coexistence and cooperation. By contrast, my approach provides a more expansive understanding of the substantive aims of international law, which includes recognized moral aims (such as the protection of human rights) that do not necessarily affect coexistence and cooperation. Substantive aims are frequently criticized as being subjective value judgments that serve as a vehicle for normative chauvinism. For this reason, I have defined moral issues as commonly held subjective values about right and wrong that have been adopted by a representative majority of states in treaties and declarations. This approach has several advantages. Focusing on commonly held, or intersubjective, values avoids the need to consider whether moral values can be objectively determined and it explains why these values can change over time. It also denotes an agreed set of values rather than requiring interpreters to determine what they believe the substantive aims of international law should be. It builds the concept of procedural normativity into the dimension of substance because these values have been accepted by a majority of states, which helps prevent accusations of Western ideological bias. Finally, while these statements may include *lex lata* and *lex ferenda*, the dimension of fit already provides a threshold test to determine if a custom is adequately supported by practice.

Third, I have suggested a more nuanced approach to balancing fit and substance than the crude sliding scale. Finding traditional custom on the strength of state practice and fit alone allows it to become an apology for state power.[153] Similarly, deducing modern custom purely from *opinio juris* and substance can create utopian laws that cannot regulate reality. Thus, the sliding scale can allow one element completely to outweigh the other. While a reflective equilibrium will lean toward the stronger value, it avoids extremes of apology and utopia. The strength of fit and state practice in traditional customs must still be balanced against their substantive deficiencies, such as a lack of procedural normativity. Similarly, modern customs must be supported by state practice because they must pass the threshold of it and deficiencies in their fit may still outweigh their moral content.[154] A lower standard of practice may be tolerated for customs with a strong moral content because violations of ideal standards are expected.[155] However, while occasional breaches may not nullify their legal character, massive, grave, and persistent violations will.[156] The only exceptions are *jus cogens* norms, which by definition cannot be undermined by contrary practice unless that practice creates another rule of *jus cogens*.[157]

Fourth, Kirgis and Tasioulas argue that the more morally distasteful an activity, the more readily the Court will substitute *opinio juris* for state practice and vice versa. However, I have explained that substantive considerations apply asymmetrically to traditional and modern customs because of their facilitative and moral content. This reasoning results in a better explanation of when, and on what basis, traditional and modern customs will be formed. It also means that, to the extent that the reflective equilibrium can still be criticized for apology and utopia, these criticisms are less compelling because they apply to facilitative and moral customs, respectively. Criticizing a facilitative custom for being an exercise of power is not problematic because it does not concern substantive moral issues. Instead, these customs are akin to domestic traffic rules. If developing states wish to challenge a traditional custom, they can enact declarations in international fora, as they did on whether there should be an international minimum standard of compensation for expropriation[158] or a national treatment standard.[159] Similarly, modern customs that set up ideal standards about moral issues are expected to be somewhat utopian. Meron argues that the international community is willing to accept gradual or partial compliance as fulfilling the requirements for forming moral customs.[160] Alasdair MacIntyre argues that the charge of utopianism is made by "the deliberately shortsighted who congratulate themselves upon the limits of their vision."[161] While hard law that is always enforced may be preferable to soft law, the choice in areas such as human rights is often between soft law and no law.[162] Giving these aspirations some legal force may be preferable to giving them no legal status, because they can be enforced in extreme situations such as apartheid in South Africa[163] and their legal status may harden over time.[164]

Finally, the reflective equilibrium can be used to explain the fluid nature of customary international law. The sliding scale assumes that state practice and *opinio juris* are fixed and irreconcilable quantities that must be traded off against each other to form eligible interpretations of custom. However, I have demonstrated that state practice is open textured and capable of being interpreted in various ways. For example, contrary state practice can be analyzed as a breach of an old rule or as the seed of a new rule. Finding the best interpretation of practice and principles requires one to determine the most coherent explanation of state practice and *opinio juris*, rather than simply giving preference to one and discounting the other. For this reason, conflicting state practice should never he discounted as irrelevant to interpretation, because it may contain the seed for a new custom. It also clarifies how customs change over time in light of new state practice, *opinio juris*, and moral considerations.

The reflective interpretive approach rearticulates the theoretical foundations of custom in a more principled and flexible fashion. Instead of debating the relative merits and legitimacy of traditional and modern custom, this interpretive theory seeks to justify and reconcile the two approaches and, in so doing, offers a coherent theory of custom that helps to defend its integrity as a source of international law.

Notes

1. *E.g.*, N. C. H. Dunbar, *The Myth of Customary International Law*, 1983 Austl. YB. Int'l. L. J. Patrick Kelly, *The Twilight of Customary International Law*, 40 Va. J. Int'l L. 449 (2000).

2. Theodor Meron, Human Rights and Humanitarian Norms as Customary Law (1989) [hereinafter Human Rights and Humanitarian Norms as Customary Law].

3. Eduardo Jimenez de Arechaga, *Custom*, in Change and Stability in International Law-Making 1, 2973 (Antonio Cassese & Joseph H. H. Weiler eds., 1988) [hereinafter Change and Stability]; W. Michael Reisman, *The Cult of Custom in the Late 20th Century*, 17 CAL. W. Int'l. L. J. 133 (1987).

4. International Court of Justice Statute Art. 38(1) (b) [hereinafter ICJ Statute].

5. North Sea Continental Shelf (FRG/Den.; FRG/Neth.), 1969 ICJ Rep. 3, 44 (Feb. 20).

6. Restatement (Third) of the Foreign Relations Law of the United States sec. 102(2) (1987) [hereinafter Restatement]; Ian Brownlie, Principles of Public International Law 497il (5th ed. 1998); Michael Byers, Custom, Power, and the Power of Rules, at 130 (1999) [hereinafter Custom, Power, and the Power of Rules].

7. Anthony D'Amato, The Concept of Custom in International Law at 89–90,160 [hereinafter The Concept of Custom].

8. D'Amato, The Concept of Custom at 74–75.

9. D'Amato at 35–39; Michael Akehurst, *Custom as a Source of International Law* (1974–75) at 36–37.

10. *E.g.*, Ted Stein, Remarks [on customs and treaties], in Change and Stability at 12,13.

11. North Sea Continental Shelf, 1969 ICJ Rep. at 44. . . .

12. North Sea Continental Shelf, 1969 ICJ Rep. at 44; Right of Passage over Indian Territory (Port. v. India), Merits, 1960 ICJ Rep. 6, 42–43 (Apr. 12); Asylum (Colom./Peru), 1950 ICJ Rep. 266, 276–77 (Nov. 20); S.S. "Lotus" (Fr. v. Turk.), 1927 PCIJ (Ser. A) No. 10, at 28 (Sept. 7).

13. The Paquete Habana, 175 U.S. 677, 686 (1900). . . .

14. Delimitation of the Maritime Boundary in the Gulf of Maine Area (Can. v. U.S.), 1984 ICJ Rep. 246, 299 (Oct. 12). . . .

15. S.S. "Lotus," 1927 PCIJ (ser. A) No. 10, at 18, 29; *see also* Nottebohm (Liech. v. Goat.), Second Phase, 1955 ICJ Rep. 4, 22 (Apr. 6); S.S. Wimbledon, 1923 PCIJ (Ser. A) No. 1, at 25 (Aug. 17).

16. Hiram Chodosh, *Neither Treaty nor Custom. The Emergence of Declarative International Law*, 26 Tex. Int'l. L. J. 87, 102 n.70 (1991).

17. Bruno Simma & Philip Alston, *The Sources of Human Rights Law: Custom, Jus Cogens, and General Principles*, 1988–89 Austl. YB. Int'l. L. 82 [hereinafter *The Sources of Human Rights Law*].

18. Bin Cheng, *United Nations Resolutions on Outer Space: "Instant" International Customary Law?* 5 Indiana J. Int'l. L. 23 (1965), reprinted in International Law: Teaching and Practice 237 (Bin Cheng ed., 1982).

19. North Sea Continental Shelf, 1969 ICJ Rep. at 44; Eduardo Jimenez de Arechaga, Remarks [on general principles and General Assembly resolutions], in Change and Stability at 48.

20. Akehurst, *Custom as a Source* at 6977; Jonathan I. Charney, *Universal International Law*, 87 AJIL 529, 544–45 (1993).

21. Military and Paramilitary Activities in and Against Nicaragua (Nicar. v. U.S.), Merits, 1986 ICJ Rep. 14 (June 27) [hereinafter *Nicaragua*]; see also Western Sahara, Advisory Opinion, 1975 ICJ Rep. 12, 30–37 (Oct. 16); Legal Consequences for States of the Continued Presence of South Africa in Namibia (South West Africa) Notwithstanding Security Council Resolution 276 (1970), Advisory Opinion, 1971 ICJ Rep. 16, 31–32 (June 21) [hereinafter Namibia Advisory Opinion].

22. *E.g.*, Declaration on Principles of International Law Concerning Friendly Relations and Co-operation Among States in Accordance with the Charter of the United Nations, GA Res. 2625, UN GAOR, 25th Sess., Supp. No. 28, at 121, UN Doc. A/8028 (1970); Conference on Security and Co-operation in Europe, Final Act, Aug. 1, 1975, 73 Dept St. Bull. 323 (1975), reprinted in 14 ILM 1292 (1975) [hereinafter Helsinki Accord].

23. *Nicaragua,* 1986 ICJ Rep. at 98, para. 186.

24. Georges Abi-Saab, Remarks [on custom and treaties], in Change and Stability at 9; Louis Henkin, *Human Rights and State "Sovereignty,"* 25 GA J. Int'l. L. 37 (1995/96) [hereinafter *Human Rights and State "Sovereignty"*]; Simma & Alston, *Twilight of Customary International Law* at 90; Ted Stein, *The Approach of a Different Drummer. The Principle of the Persistent Objector in International Law,* 26 Harv. Int'l. L. J. 457, 457 (1985) [hereinafter *The Approach of a Different Drummer*].

25. Consider, for example, the strong and conflicting responses to the *Nicaragua* case. Symposium, *Appraisals of the ICJ's Decision: Nicaragua.* United States *(Merits),* 81 AJIL 77 (1987).

26. David Fidler, *Challenging the Classical Concept of Custom,* 1996 Ger. Y. B. Int'l L. 198, 216–31 [hereinafter *Challenging the Classical Concept of Custom*].

27. Charney, *Universal International Law* at 543.

28. Meron, Human Rights and Humanitarian Norms; Lori Bruun, *Beyond the 1948 Convention—Emerging Principles of Genocide in Customary International Law,* 17 MD. J. Int'l. L. & Trade 193, 2169717 (1993) [hereinafter *Beyond the 1948 Convention*]; Richard B. Lillich, *The Growing Importance of Customary International Human Rights Law,* 25 GA. J. Int'l. & Comp. L. 1, 8 (1995/96) [hereinafter *The Growing Importance of Customary International Human Rights Law*].

29. Reisman, *The Cult of Custom* at 135.

30. Arthur A. Weisburd, *Customary International Law: The Problem of Treaties,* 21 Vand. J. Transnational L. 1 (1988) [hereinafter Weisburd, *Customary IL*].

31. Kelly, *The Twilight of Customary International Law* at 451.

32. Anthony A. D'Amato, *Trashing Customary International Law,* 81 AJIL 101 (1987).

33. Robert Y. Jennings, *The Identification of International Law,* in International Law Teaching at 3, 5.

34. Curtis A. Bradley & Jack L. Goldsmith, *Customary International Law as Federal Common Law: A Critique of the Modern Position,* 110 Harv. L. Rev. 815, 838 (1997); Kelly, *The Twilight of International Law* at 454 n.20, 484.

35. Stein, *Remarks [on customs and treaties]* in Change and Stability at 12.

36. Bin Cheng, in International Law at 249.

37. Hilary C. M. Charlesworth, *Customary International Law and the* Nicaragua *Case,* 1984–87 Austl. YB. Int'l. L. [hereinafter *Customary International Law and the* Nicaragua *Case*].

38. Simma & Alston, *The Sources of Human Rights Law* at 88, 96.

39. Id. at 102–06.

40. Daniel Bodansky, *Customary (and Not So Customary) International Environmental Law,* 3 IND.J. Global Legal Stud. 105, 116–19 (1995) [hereinafter *Customary (and Not So Customary) International Environmental Law*].

41. Frederic L. Kirgis Jr., *Custom on a Sliding Scale,* 81 AJIL 146 (1987) [hereinafter *Custom on a Sliding Scale*]; John Tasioulas, *In Defense of Relative Normativity: Communitarian Values and the* Nicaragua *Case,* 16 Oxford J. Legal Stud. 85 (1996) [hereinafter *In Defense of Relative Normativity*].

42. Kirgis, *Custom on a Sliding Scale* at 149.

43. Simma & Alston, *The Sources of Human Rights Law* at 83.

44. For an explanation of the phrases "apology for power" and "utopian and unachievable," see Martti Koskenniemi, From Apology to Utopia: The Structure of International Legal Argument 2 (1989).

45. Ronald Dworkin, Law's Empire (1986); John Rawls, A Theory of Justice 20 (1972).

46. Bin Cheng, *Custom: The Future of General State Practice in a Divided World,* in The Structure and Process of International Law: Essays in Legal Philosophy, Doctrine, and Theory 513, 539 (Ronald St. J. Macdonald & Douglas M. Johnston eds., 1983).

47. Bodansky, *Customary (and not so Customary) International Environmental Law* at 116–19.

48. Jerome Frank, *Law and the Modern Mind,* in Lloyd's Introduction to Jurisprudence (Michael Freeman ed., 6th ed. 1994); Oliver Wendell Holmes, *The Path of Law,* 10 Harv. L. Rev. 457, 457 (1896–97); Karl Llewellyn, *Some Realism About Realism,* 44 Harv. L. Rev. 1222 (1931).

49. Simma & Alston, *The Sources of Human Rights* at 89.

50. Bin Cheng, *Custom: The Future of General State Practice in a Divided World* at 539; Charlesworth, *Customary International Law and the* Nicaragua *Case* at 27.

51. Thomas R. Tyler, Why People Obey the Law 170–73 (1990). . . .

52. Tyler, Why People Obey the Law at 163, 170–73, 175–78; Thomas M. Franck, *Legitimacy in the International System,* 82 AJIL 705. . . .

53. These values are intersubjective, i.e., values commonly held by a group of subjects, in this case states. Jan Narveson, *Inter-subjective,* in The Oxford Companion to Philosophy (Ted Honderich ed., 1995) [hereinafter Oxford Companion].

54. H. L. A. Hart, The Concept of Law at 225.

55. Hans Kelsen, Principles of International Law 307–08, 418 (1952).

56. Kelly, *The Twilight of Customary Law,* at 479–80.

57. Simma & Alston, *The Sources of Human Rights Law,* at 89.

58. Bruun, *Beyond the 1948 Convention* at 2169717; Lillich, *The Growing Importance of Customary International Human Rights Law* at 8.

59. *E.g., Nicaragua,* 1986 ICJ Rep. 14.

60. Bodansky, *Customary (and Not So Customary) International Environmental Law.*

61. Henkin, *Human Rights and State "Sovereignty"* at 34–35.

62. Schacter, *supra* note 15, at 11; Fernando R. Teson, Humanitarian Intervention: An Inquiry Into Law and Morality 14 (1988); Theodor Meron, *On a Hierarchy of International Human Rights,* 80 AJIL 1, 199720 (1986); Oscar Schachter, *Entangled Treaty and Custom,* in International Law at a Time of Perplexity 717, 733–34 (Yoram Dinstein ed., 1989).

63. Restatement, sec. 102.

64. Vienna Convention on the Law of Treaties, *opened for signature* May 23, 1969, Art. 53, 1155 UNTS 331; *see also* Restatement, sec. 102; David Harris, Cases and Materials on International Law 42, 835 (5th ed. 1998); H. W. A. Thirlway, International Customary Law and Codification 110 (1972); Charlesworth, *Customary International Law and the* Nicaragua *Case* at 4; H.W.A. Thirlway, International Customary Law and Codification (1989); Antonio Cassese, International Law in a Divided World 179 (1989).

65. Schachter, International Law in Theory and Practice (1995) at 11; see also Schachter, *Entangled Treaty and Custom,* in International Law at a Time of Perplexity (Yoram Dinstein ed., 1989), at 733–34 [hereinafter *Entangled Treaty and Custom*].

66. *Nicaragua,* 1986 ICJ Rep. at 98, para. 186.

67. Henkin, *Human Rights and State "Sovereignty"* at 37; Fred L. Morrison, *Legal Issues in the* Nicaragua *Opinion,* 8 AJIL 160, 162 (1987).

68. Vienna Convention on the Law of Treaties, Art. 26; Schachter, *Entangled Treaty and Custom* at 727–28.

69. According to the persistent objector rule, states that have persistently objected during the emergence of a custom are not bound by it. Gerald Fitzmaurice, *The General Principles of International Law Considered from the Standpoint of the Rules of Law,* 92 Recueil Des Cours 1, 49–50 (1957); Stein, *The Approach of a Different Drummer* at 457. However, the International Court of Justice has endorsed the persistent objector rule only twice, and arguably both times in *obiter dicta.* Fisheries case (UK v. Nor.), 1951 ICJ Rep. 16, 131 (Dec. 18); Asylum (Colom./Peru), 1950 ICJ Rep. 266, 2779778 (Nov. 20); *see also* Nuclear Tests (Austl. v. Fr.), 1974 ICJ Rep. 253, 286–93 (Dec. 20) (Gross, J., sep. op.). Further, a state cannot be a persistent objector to *jus cogens* rules and theorists have generally concluded that the practical application of the rule is limited. Byers, Custom, Power, and the Power of Rules at 181; Anthony A. D'Amato, The Concept of Custom in International Law (1971) at 187–99, 233–63 [hereinafter The Concept of Custom in International Law]; Jonathan I. Charney, *The Persistent Objector Rule and the Development of Customary International Law,* 1986 Brit, YB. Int'l. L. 1, 11–16.

70. It may also discourage states from voting for aspirational instruments. Thomas M. Franck, *Some Observations on the ICJs Procedural and Substantive Innovations,* 81 AJIL 116, 119 (1987).

71. *Nicaragua,* 1986 ICJ Rep. at 113–14, paras. 217–18; Meron, Human Rights and Humanitarian Norms as Customary Law at 6–7, 27; Pierre Imbert, *Reservations and Human Rights Conventions,* 6 Hum. Rts. Rev. 28 (1981); Schachter, *Entangled Treaty and Custom* at 727–28.

72. Vienna Convention on the Law of Treaties, art. 43.

73. Prosper Weil, *Towards Relative Normativity in International Law?* 77 AJIL 413, 438 (1983).

74. Cassese, International Law in a Divided World at 31, 110, 398; Charlesworth, *Customary International Law and the* Nicaragua *Case* at 1973; Tasioulas, *In Defense of Relative Normativity* at 116–17.

75. Kirgis, *Custom on a Sliding Scale* at 148.

76. Reservations to the Convention on the Prevention and Punishment of the Crime of Genocide, Advisory Opinion, 1951 ICJ Rep. 15, 23 (May 28).

77. Corfu Channel case (UK v. Alb.), Merits, 1949 ICJ Rep. 4, 22 (Apr. 9).

78. Koskenniemi, From Apology to Utopia at 2.

79. Byers, Custom, Power, and the Power of Rules at 49.

80. Koskenniemi, From Apology to Utopia at 42.

81. David Kennedy, *When Renewal Repeals: Thinking Against the Box*, 32 N.Y.U. J. Int'l. L. & Pol. 335, 355 (2000) [hereinafter *When Renewal Repeals*].
82. Dworkin, Law's Empire at 271.
83. Kennedy, *When Renewal Repeals* at 407.
84. Mohammed Bedjaoui, Towards a New International Economic Order (1979) at 141–44 [hereinafter Towards a New International Economic Order].
85. Fidler, *Challenging the Classical Concept of Custom* at 220–22, 224–25.
86. Byers, Custom, Power and the Power of Rules at 49.
87. Koskenniemi, From Apology to Utopia at 42.
88. Kelly, *The Twilight of Customary International Law* at 451.
89. Dworkin, Law's Empire at 66.
90. Id.
91. Id. at 65–66.
92. Id. at 255.
93. Id. at 256.
94. Id.
95. Ronald Dworkin, *Law and Morals*, *Natural Law*, and *Legal Positivism*, in Oxford Companion, at 473, 473–74, 606, 606–07, and 476, 476–77, respectively; Ronald Dworkin, *Law as Interpretation*, 60 Tex. L. Rev. 527, 528 (1982) [hereinafter Dworkin, *Interpretation*].
96. Dworkin, *Interpretation* at 528.
97. Ronald Dworkin, Taking Rights Seriously 340–41 (3d ed. 1981); Ronald Dworkin, *Is There Really No Right Answer in Hard Cases?* in A Matter of Principle 143 (1985).
98. Dworkin, Law's Empire at 255–57.
99. Id. at 66.
100. John Finnis, *On Reason and Authority* in Law's Empire, 6 Law & Phil. 357, 373–74 (1987) [hereinafter *On Reason and Authority*].
101. Dworkin, Law's Empire at 246–47.
102. Id. at 257.
103. Id. at 228–32.
104. Finnis, *On Reason and Authority* at 374.
105. Bodansky, *Customary (and Not So Customary) International Environmental Law*.
106. ICJ Statute Art. 38(1) (b); North Sea Continental Shelf (FRG/Den.; FRG/Neth.), 1969 ICJ Rep. 3, 44 (Feb. 20).
107. *See Nicaragua*, 1986 ICJ Rep. 14; Namibia Advisory Opinion, 1971 ICJ Rep. 16; Corfu Channel case (UK v. Alb.), Merits, 1949 ICJ Rep. 4, 34 (Apr. 9).
108. Kirgis, *Custom on a Sliding Scale* at 149.
109. Id.
110. *See also* "coherentism" in epistemology. Nicholas Everitt & Alec Fisher, Modern Epistemology 102–07 (1995).
111. Thomas M. Franck, Fairness in International Law and Institutions (1995); Thomas M. Franck, The Power of Legitimacy Among Nations (1990); Franck, *Legitimacy in the International System* at 735–36.
112. Rawls, A Theory of Justice (1972) at 20; John Rawls, *Outline of a Decision Procedure for Ethics*, 60 Phil. Rev. 177 (1951); *see also* Dworkin, Law's Empire. I am not arguing that the international system is akin to Rawls's concept of the original position; rather, that his notion of a reflective equilibrium can be used more generally to reconcile inductive and deductive methodologies.
113. Rawls, A Theory of Justice at 21.

114. Id. at 19–20.

115. Rawls, A Theory of Justice at 20 n.7; *see also* Nelson Goodman, Fact, Fiction, and Forecast 65–68 (4th ed. 1983).

116. Dworkin, Law's Empire at 239–40.

117. Byers, Custom, Power, and the Power of Rules at 156–62; D'Amato, The Concept of Custom at 56–66.

118. Hart, The Concept of Law at 90.

119. D'Amato, The Concept of Custom at 97–98.

120. Weisburd, *Customary IL* at 30–31.

121. North Sea Continental Shelf (FRG/Den.; FRG/Neth.), 1969 ICJ Rep. 3, 44 (Feb. 20); id. at 230–31 (Lachs, J., dissenting); Akehurst, The Concept of Custom at 37; Weisburd, *Customary IL* at 107.

122. Rawls, A Theory of Justice at 20.

123. D'Amato, The Concept of Custom at 97.

124. Byers, Custom, Power, and the Power of Rules at 157–59.

125. Bin Cheng, in International Law at 249.

126. Anthony A. D'Amato & Sudhir K. Chopra, *Whales: Their Emerging Right to Life,* 85 AJIL 21 (1991).

127. *Nicaragua,* 1986 ICJ Rep. at 109, para. 207.

128. Id.

129. Id. at 98, para. 186.

130. *E.g.,* Charney, *supra* note 124, at 834; Louis Henkin, *Kosovo and the Law of Humanitarian Intervention,* 93 AJIL 824, 824–25 (1999).

131. Charney, *Anticipatory Humanitarian Intervention in Kosovo* at 834.

132. Bruno Simma, *NATO, The UN and the Use of Force: Legal Aspects,* 10 Eur. J. Int'l. L. 1 (1999), at <http://www.ejil.org/journal/index.html> (visited Oct. 1, 2001) [hereinafter *NATO, The UN and the Use of Force*].

133. Cassese, Ex iniuria ius oritur: *Are We Moving Towards International Legitimation of Forcible Humanitarian Countermeasures in the World Community?* 10 EUR. J. INT'L. L. 23 (1999).

134. The draft resolution condemning NATO's use of force, UN Doc. S/I 999/328, was sponsored by Belarus, India, and the Russian Federation and supported by China, Namibia, and the Russian Federation in the Security Council.

135. For example, German Foreign Minister Kinkel stated, "The decision of NATO [on air strikes against the Federal Republic of Yugoslavia] must not become a precedent." Deutscher Bundesug, Plenarprotokoll 13/248, at 23, 129 (Oct. 16, 1998), quoted in Simma, *NATO, the UN and the Use of Force.*

136. Some states focused exclusively on the preliminary issue of jurisdiction; others, including Germany, argued that the intervention represented a justifiable exception to the normal rules. The United States focused on the humanitarian catastrophe, the acute threat to security of neighboring states, the serious violation of humanitarian law, and the resolutions of the Security Council but did not expressly argue for a right to unilateral humanitarian intervention. Oral pleadings (Yugo. v. U.S. et al.), 1999 ICJ Pleadings (Legality of Use of Force), at http://www.icj.cij.org.

137. Charney, *Anticipatory Humanitarian Intervention in Kosovo* at 836–39.

138. C. Gray, *After the Ceasefire: Iraq, the Security Council and the Use of Force,* 1994 Brit. Y.B. Int'l L. 135, 162; Dino Kritsiotis, *Reappraising Policy Objections to Humanitarian Intervention,* 19 Mich. J. Int'l. L. 1005, 1014 (1998).

139. Charney, *Anticipatory Humanitarian Intervention in Kosovo* at 836–37.

140. Cassese, Violence and Law in the Modern Age 35–39; Meron, Human Rights and Humanitarian Norms as Customary at 60; Henkin, How Nations Behave at 70; Charlesworth, *Customary International Law and the* Nicaragua *Case* at 21.

141. SC Res 1203 (Oct. 24, 1998); see also SC Res. 1199 (Sept. 23, 1998); SC Res. 1160 (Mar. 31, 1998).

142. *See* UN Doc. S/1999/328.

143. This distinction is made by D'Amato, The Concept of Custom at 61–63, though not with respect to unilateral humanitarian intervention.

144. Brownlie, Principles of Public International Law at 515; Cassese, International Law in a Divided World at 147.

145. Brownlie, Principles of Public International Law at 515; Shaw, *Genocide in International Law* in International Law in a Time of Perplexity.

146. Kritsiotis, *Reappraising Policy Operations in Humanitarian Intervention* at 1040–46.

147. Christine M. Chinkin, *Kosovo: A "Good" or "Bad" War?* 93 AJIL 841, 847 (1999).

148. Kritsiotis, *Reappraising Policy Operations in Humanitarian Intervention* at 1040–46.

149. Henkin, *Kosovo and the Law of "Humanitarian Intervention"* at 824–25.

150. Ruth Wedgwood, *NATO's Campaign in Yugoslavia,* 93 AJIL 828, 833 (1999).

151. Cassese, Ex iniuria ius oritur; Charney, *Anticipatory Humanitarian Intervention in Kosovo* at 836–39; Wedgwood, *NATO's Campaign in Yugoslavia* at 828.

152. Akehurst, *Custom as a Source of International Law* at 53.

153. Koskenniemi, From Apology to Utopia at 2.

154. Meron, Human Rights and Humanitarian Norms as Customary Law at 44–45.

155. Id. at 44; Schachter, *New Custom: Power,* Opinio Juris *and Contrary Practice* at 539; Schachter, *Entangled Treaty and Custom* at 735.

156. Meron, Human Rights and Humanitarian Norms as Customary Law 58.

157. Vienna Convention on the Law of Treaties, art. 53.

158. Supported by Resolution on Permanent Sovereignty over Natural Resources, GA Res. 1803, UN GAOR, 17th Sess., Supp. No. 17, at 15, UN Doc A/5217 (1962). *See also* Brownlie, Principles of Public International Law at 527–29, 535–38.

159. Supported by Charter of Economic Rights and Duties of States, GA Res. 3281, UN GAOR, 29th Sess., Supp. No. 30, at 50, UN Doc. A/9030 (1974). See also Brownlie, Principles of Public International Law, at 526–27, 538.

160. Meron, Human Rights and Humanitarian Norms as Customary Law 44.

161. Alasdair Macintyre, Three Rival Versions of Moral Enquiry: Encyclopaedia, Genealogy, and Tradition 234 (1990); see also Tasioulas, *In Defense of Relative Normativity* at 127.

162. Condorelli, Remarks [on *lex lata* and *lex ferenda*] at 81; Pellet, *The Normative Dilemma* at 47.

163. D'Amato, The Concept of Custom at 89; Henkin, *Human Rights and State "Sovereignty"* at 39, 42.

164. Chinkin, *The Challenge of Soft Law* at 857–858.

CHAPTER 4

Normative Hierarchy in International Law

Dinah Shelton

SYSTEMS OF LAW USUALLY ESTABLISH A HIERARCHY OF NORMS based on the particular source from which the norms derive. In national legal systems, it is commonplace for the fundamental values of society to be given constitutional status and afforded precedence in the event of a conflict with norms enacted by legislation or adopted by administrative regulation; administrative rules themselves must conform to legislative mandates, while written law usually takes precedence over unwritten law and legal norms prevail over nonlegal (political or moral) rules. Norms of equal status must be balanced and reconciled to the extent possible. The mode of legal reasoning applied in practice is thus naturally hierarchical, establishing relationships and order between normative statements and levels of authority.[1]

In the international legal system, the question of hierarchy of norms involves the fundamental nature and structure of international law and the rules of recognition by which law is distinguished from norms that are not legally binding. Scholars in recent years have debated this issue more frequently than their predecessors did during the first decades of the twentieth century, when participants in the international legal system, the matters of international concern, and international institutions were far fewer in number.

This essay examines the extensive debate over hierarchy of norms and sources in international law. It focuses on assertions about the upper extreme, that there exist superior norms (*jus cogens* or peremptory norms), overriding other norms and binding all states, including objecting states.[2] The essay examines theoretical approaches to *jus cogens* and shows that while the concept is widely supported in the literature, sometimes to an abusive extent, state practice and judicial opinions have been slow to recognize

---

or give legal effect to assertions of such norms. At the same time, a perceptible trend toward discovering peremptory norms has emerged in international and national tribunals, raising a new set of problems about the consequences of such recognition.

A review of the literature as well as the jurisprudence reveals confusion over the rationale for *jus cogens* norms and their source, content, and impact, as well as the interface of such norms with obligations *erga omnes* and international crimes. Although it may be appropriate today to recognize fundamental norms deriving from an international public order, the extensive assertions of peremptory norms made by some writers and international tribunals, without presenting any evidence to support the claimed superior status of the norms under consideration, pose risks for the international legal order and the credibility of the authors and tribunals.

[Another issue] not examined in depth in this essay, pertains more to choice of law between conflicting norms of equivalent status, although one obvious means of resolving a conflict is to designate one norm or subject matter as hierarchically superior to others.[3] The problem of conflict has grown with the "fragmentation of international law"[4] over time. As international law has expanded into new subject areas over the past century, with a corresponding proliferation of international treaties and institutions, conflicts have increasingly arisen between substantive norms or procedures within a given subject area or across subject areas, necessitating means to reconcile or rank the competing rules. States are finding it appropriate to designate preferences between norms within treaties or between different treaties, or to develop choice-of-law principles. Conceptual problems abound because almost every purported principle of precedence (e.g., *lex specialis derogate lex generali*) has exceptions and no rule establishes when to apply the principle and when to apply the exception.

Apart from treaty provisions, claims of primacy may be made by those involved in promoting or ensuring respect for a particular body of international law. Some human rights institutions, for example, have asserted the priority of human rights guarantees in general over other international law, without necessarily claiming that the entire body of law constitutes *jus cogens*. The UN Committee on Economic, Social and Cultural Rights, in a 1998 statement on globalization and economic, social, and cultural rights,[5] declared that the realms of trade, finance, and investment are in no way exempt from human rights obligations. The Committee's concerns were raised a second time in a statement urging members of the World Trade Organization (WTO) to adopt a human rights approach to trade matters, asserting that the "promotion and protection of human rights is the first responsibility of Governments."[6]

The asserted primacy of all human rights law has not been reflected in state practice. If eventually accepted, it will reject the notion of *lex specialis* for trade or other fields where states can claim to be free from human rights obligations. It could also profoundly affect the work of all international organizations, which commonly claim to be governed only by their constituting legal instruments and the mandate therein conferred.

In addressing normative hierarchy as well as choice of law, there is apparently a focus on process, because the identification of legal norms and their relative normativity is achieved by considering the procedural norms that allow recognition of substantive rules. State agreement on the means to identify binding international obligations was formulated initially in the Statute of the Permanent Court of International Justice (PCIJ) and iterated in the Statute of the International Court of Justice. These texts direct that international disputes be resolved primarily through the application of international conventions and international custom.[7] They make no reference to hierarchy, except by listing doctrine and judicial decisions as "subsidiary" and evidentiary sources of law. Although the ICJ Statute is directed at the Court, it remains today the only general text in which states have acknowledged the authoritative procedures by which they agree to be legally bound to an international norm. It remains for proponents to demonstrate the existence of an accepted hierarchy in practice or other means of creating legal norms.

Jus Cogens

In Theory

The theory of *jus cogens* or peremptory norms[8] posits the existence of rules of international law that admit of no derogation and that can be amended only by a new general norm of international law of the same value. It is a concept that lacks both an agreed content and consensus in state practice. In most instances it is also an unnecessary concept because, as discussed further below, the derogating act violates treaty or custom and thus contravenes international law without the need to label the norm peremptory.

Development of jus cogens. The notion of *jus cogens* originated solely as a limitation on international freedom of contract. It was discussed at length for the first time by Verdross in 1937.[9] Even prior to this, however, Quincy Wright had noted the problem of "illegal" treaties, based on a 1916 judgment[10] of the Central American Court of Justice denying the capacity of Nicaragua to conclude the 1914 Bryan-Chamorro Treaty with the United States.[11] The Court held that Article 2 of the Treaty, which gave the United States a ninety-nine-year lease on a naval station on Nicaraguan territory in the Gulf of Fonseca, could not be applied because it derogated from the customary international law rights of El Salvador and Honduras to condominium in the gulf. The Court also agreed with Costa Rica that Article 1 of the Treaty conflicted with an 1858 treaty between Costa Rica and Nicaragua that protected boundary waters. The decision in favor of Costa Rica upheld the earlier treaty. In his commentary Wright appears to agree with de Visscher that custom and treaties may create "objective" rules of international law that are of universal and permanent applicability, but he notes that the treaty was affecting the rights of nonsignatories and finds this fact a proper ground for the Court's decision. Judge Schucking's well-known dissent in the PCIJ's *Chinn* case, in which he argued that the Court should refuse to enforce an agreement contrary to international public policy, was also influential and specifically cited by Verdross.[12]

Verdross's article was written in response to a report on the law of treaties[13] that had failed to discuss the problem of a treaty in conflict with general international law. According to Verdross, freedom to conclude treaties could be limited only if general international law contained rules that have the character of *jus cogens*. He took a practical approach to the question: finding nothing in theory to preclude the possibility of such rules, he looked to see whether international law had established such rules in practice. He concluded that compulsory norms of customary international law, such as freedom of the high seas, would work to invalidate any agreement in which two or more states sought to exclude other states from the use of the high seas.[14] It is not clear, however, why a doctrine of *jus cogens* is necessary to refuse enforcement of treaties of this type. The law of treaties has long held that states cannot by treaty affect the rights of third states without their consent, a rule now codified in VCLT Articles 34–35.

Verdross's other category of *jus cogens* consisted of general principles of morality or public policy "common to the juridical orders of all civilized states,"[15] a concept more in keeping with later writings on the topic. He grounded recourse to these ethical standards in the reference to general principles of law recognized by civilized nations in the Statute of the PCIJ. He acknowledged the difficulty of finding common ethical rules among members of the international community, but found an "unequivocal" common principle in the decisions of national courts that everywhere regard treaties as invalid if they "restrict the liberty of one contracting party in an excessive or unworthy manner or . . . endanger its most important rights."[16] To ascertain which international treaties are immoral, Verdross sought to determine the moral tasks states must accomplish, to seek the ethical minimum. He listed maintenance of law and order within the state, defense against external attack, care for the bodily and spiritual welfare of citizens at home, and protection of citizens abroad. Any treaty that would prevent a state from fulfilling one of these essential tasks would be regarded as immoral.[17]

In the considerable literature that has materialized since the appearance of Verdross's article, the concept of *jus cogens* has received widespread support, without any agreement or clarity about its source, content, or impact.

Sources of peremptory norms. Verdross viewed the source of peremptory norms as residing in general principles of law recognized by all legal systems. Others believe peremptory norms arise from consent, natural law *(jus necessarium pro omnium),* international public order, or constitutional principles. A strictly voluntarist view of international law rejects the notion that a state may be bound by an international legal rule without its consent and thus does not recognize a collective interest that is capable of overriding the will of an individual member of the society. States are deemed to construct the corpus of international law either through agreements or through repeated practice out of a sense of legal obligation.[18] Indeed, international law has traditionally been defined as a system of equal and sovereign states whose actions are limited only by rules freely accepted as legally binding. The PCIJ, in one of its early decisions, stated that "[t]he rules of law binding upon States . . . emanate from their own free will as expressed in conventions or by usages generally accepted as expressing principles of law."[19] As recently as 1986, the ICJ reaffirmed this approach with respect to the acquisition of weaponry by states. In the *Nicaragua* Judgment the Court stated: "[I]n international law there are no rules, other than such rules as may be accepted by the State concerned, by treaty or otherwise, whereby the level of armaments of a sovereign State can be limited, and this principle is valid for all States without exception."[20]

The only references to peremptory norms in international texts are found in the Vienna conventions on the law of treaties and they can be read largely to support a voluntarist basis for *jus cogens*. An early rapporteur on the law of treaties of the International Law Commission proposed that the ILC draft convention on the law of treaties include a provision voiding treaties contrary to fundamental principles of international law.[21] This proposal clearly took a nonconsensual approach, as it constituted a challenge to the view that states have the right *inter se* to opt out of any norm of general international law. At the same time, it did not identify the basis for creating or determining "fundamental principles of international law." The proposal represented "progressive development" of international law rather than codification of existing state practice.

The provisions eventually adopted at the Vienna Conference on the Law of Treaties limited the ability of states to escape fundamental norms, but they also established state consent as the foundation for such rules. Article 53 of the 1969 VCLT, concerning treaties between states, provides that a treaty will be void "if, at the time of its conclusion, it conflicts with a peremptory norm of general international law." Such a norm is defined by the VCLT as one "accepted and recognized by the international community of states as a whole as a norm from which no derogation is permitted and which can be modified only by a subsequent norm of general international law having the same character." Article 64 adds that the emergence of a new peremptory norm of general international law will void any existing treaty in conflict with the norm. Thus, Article 53 demands that there first be established a norm of general international law and, second, that the *international community of states as a whole* agree that it is a norm from which no derogation is permitted. While this definition precludes an individual state from vetoing the emergence of a peremptory norm, it sets a high threshold for identifying such a norm and bases the identification squarely in state consent.

Even so limited, the concept was controversial from the start and divided the Vienna Conference on the Law of Treaties. Strong support came from the Soviet bloc and from newly independent states, which saw it as a means of escaping colonial-era agreements. Western countries were less positive and several expressed opposition to the notion of peremptory norms, voting against the provision and withholding ratification of the treaty because of persisting objections to the concept. To date, the VCLT has garnered 108 ratifications, a little over half the countries of the world.

Various scholars have convincingly argued that the language of VCLT Article 53 establishes a purely consensual regime for the creation of peremptory norms and that as a progressive development in international law the provision binds only states parties to the Vienna Convention.[22] Some authors have gone further to argue that as a result of the progressive nature of the provision and its consensual formulation, neither nonparties to the VCLT nor new states are bound by peremptory norms to which they object,[23] which seems incompatible with the objective of creating norms from which no derogation is possible. Eric Suy has proposed perhaps the most plausible and creative solution to this issue, reconciling the consensual approach of the VCLT and the less positivistic approach discussed in the next few paragraphs. Suy distinguishes public order norms from *jus cogens* norms. In his view, no society, international or otherwise, can live without at least a minimum of fundamental principles that exert a higher value in the legal system, but *jus cogens* has a place only in the law of treaties. What exists outside treaty law is the international public order, consisting of principles and rules whose enforcement is of such vital importance to the international community as a whole that any unilateral action, or any agreement that contravenes such a principle, can have no legal force. Any breach of such a public order norm would fall in the realm of state responsibility.[24]

Many scholars have long objected that the source of international obligation cannot lie in consent, but must be based on a prior, fundamental norm that imposes a duty to comply with obligations freely accepted.[25] Without a source of this norm outside consent, there is an unavoidable circularity of reasoning.[26] It is certainly rational to accept that such a framework has become necessary in the light of global problems threatening human survival in an unprecedented fashion. The emergence of global resource crises, such as the widespread depletion of commercial fish stocks, the destruction of the stratospheric ozone layer, and anthropogenic climate change, has produced growing concern about the "free rider," the holdout state that benefits from legal regulation accepted by others while enhancing its own profits through continued utilization of the resource or ongoing production and sale of banned substances. Recalcitrant states not only profit by rejecting regulatory regimes adopted by the overwhelming majority of states, they threaten the effectiveness of such regimes and pose risks to all humanity. The traditional consent-based international legal regime lacks a legislature to override the will of dissenting states, but efforts to affect their behavior are being made, first, through the doctrine of peremptory norms or universal law applicable to all states, and, second, through expanding the concept of international law to include soft law. The same approach may be taken toward states seeking to denounce, or acting to violate, multilateral agreements that reflect widely and deeply held values, such as those guaranteeing human rights or expressing humanitarian law.

In sum, the source of peremptory norms has been variously attributed to state consent, natural law, necessity, international public order, and the development of constitutional principles. The different theories lead to considerably different content for *jus cogens* norms and consequences for their breach.

***The content of* jus cogens.** Neither the International Law Commission nor the Vienna Conference on the Law of Treaties developed an accepted list of peremptory norms, although both made reference in commentaries and discussion to the norms against genocide, slave trading, and use of force other than in self-defense. Some developing countries referred to permanent sovereignty over natural resources as a peremptory norm.[27] The different theories as to the source of peremptory norms affect the contents; those who adhere to the voluntarist approach generally see the content as limited to a few rules that states have recognized as not being subject to derogation, reservation, or denunciation. Natural law proponents would subscribe to an even stricter list of immutable principles of justice. In contrast, theories based on community values result in a longer list of evolving norms. Eduardo Jiménez de Aréchaga posits that "[t]he substantive contents of *jus cogens* are likely to be constantly changing in accordance with the progress and development of international law and international morality."[28]

Since the adoption of the Vienna Convention, the literature has abounded in claims that additional international norms constitute *jus cogens*. Proponents have argued for the inclusion of all human rights, all humanitarian norms (human rights and the laws of war), or singly, the duty not to cause transboundary environmental harm, freedom from torture, the duty to assassinate dictators, the right to life of animals, self-determination, the right to development, free trade, and territorial sovereignty (despite legions of treaties transferring territory from one state to another). During the Cold War, Soviet writers asserted the invalidity of treaties that conflicted with the "basic principles and concepts" of international law, defined to include universal peace and security of nations; respect for sovereignty and territorial integrity; noninterference in internal affairs; equality and mutual benefit between nations; and *pacta sunt servanda*. Examples of invalid agreements included the NATO pact, the peace treaty between the United States and Japan, the SEATO agreement, and the U.S.-UK agreement on establishing air bases.[29] In most instances, little evidence has been presented to demonstrate how and why the preferred norm has become *jus cogens*. Wladyslaw Czapliński correctly comments that "the trend to abuse the notion of *jus cogens* is always present among international lawyers."[30]

The legal consequences of **jus cogens.** In Manhattan, along one of the major crosstown streets, the curb in front of a bus stop is painted red, which is known throughout the United States to denote a no-parking zone. On a street lamp next to the bus stop is a sign reading "No Parking." Above that, a second sign reads "Absolutely no parking." On top, a third sign dictates "Don't even *think* of parking here." If signs one and two can be taken to stand for treaty and custom, the question must be asked: what does the third sign add in practice other than visual shoe pounding? Does it make the law against parking in the bus zone more binding? Clearly not. Does it indicate that the sanctions are more severe? Possibly, but nothing on the signs reveals this to be the case. Does it mean that the police will pass more frequently to enforce the parking ban? This is also a possible consequence, although not one that is clear from the sign itself. The questions provoked by the signs may also be asked about the category of *jus cogens*.

According to VCLT Article 53, a peremptory norm operates to void any treaty entered into contrary to the norm. Yet it is hard to accept the practical import of the VCLT: if one assumes that two states enter into an agreement, for example to commit genocide, slave trading, or aggression, Article 71 would dictate that the parties should then eliminate the consequences of any illegal act performed in reliance on the treaty and bring their relations into conformity with the peremptory norm. Since the treaties and acts mentioned would also be likely to constitute breaches of UN Charter Article 103, it would seem unnecessary to resort to *jus cogens*. Erika de Wet, using torture as an example and citing the *Furundžija* case,[31] posits several other specific consequences for states breaching a peremptory norm: delegitimizing any legislative, administrative, or judicial act authorizing the prohibited act; overriding domestic amnesty; allowing victims to file in international tribunals to hold national measures internationally unlawful; obtaining civil damages from courts in any jurisdiction; allowing universal jurisdiction for criminal investigation, prosecution, and punishment; and excluding application of political offense exceptions or statutes of limitations. Yet most of these consequences could seemingly result from the enforcement of treaty and customary norms without the necessity of *jus cogens* designation. National laws and policies do not excuse the breach of an international obligation and the procedures for enforcement may be developed independently of a *jus cogens* designation. In fact, perhaps the only real impact of *jus cogens* would be on a state, if any, that did not adhere to a single one of the many treaties banning torture and persistently claimed the right to commit torture, as the norm banning the practice emerged into customary international law.

Indeed, although the idea of *jus cogens* originated solely as a limitation on the treaty-making power of states, today an assertion that a norm is *jus cogens* seems more often intended to override the will of persistent objectors to the emergence of the norm as customary international law. If *jus cogens* is "a norm from which no derogation is possible" and its creation by "the international community as a whole" means anything less than unanimity, then the issue of dissenting states arises.

In reality, the problem is likely to arise rarely because those norms most often identified as *jus cogens* are clearly accepted as customary international law and there are no persistent objectors. In addition, the obligations deemed basic to the international community—to refrain from the use of force against another state, to settle disputes peacefully, and to respect human rights, fundamental freedoms, and self-determination—are conventional obligations contained in the UN Charter, to which all member states have consented. Nearly all states have also accepted the humanitarian conventions on the laws of war, expressions of customary international law to which there are no persistent objectors. The multilateral regimes for the oceans, outer space, and key components of the environment (climate change, protection of the ozone layer, and biological diversity) are widely accepted. Thus, in most cases the problem is one of ensuring compliance by states that have freely consented to the obligations in question and not one of imposing obligations on dissenting states. Under these circumstances, the value added by labeling norms as peremptory is certainly open to question.

According to those who find the source of *jus cogens* in state consent, the consequence is limited to the law of treaties, pursuant to the provisions of the VCLT. Those provisions preclude states from concluding valid treaties contrary to peremptory norms because such treaties would be illegal and void *ab initio*. There are no other consequences under the most stringent consensual approach, although some writers admit that if treaties violating peremptory norms are illegal, there may then be consequences in the law of state responsibility.

Those who accept a less consensual source for peremptory norms, whether based in natural law or implicit acceptance of "necessary" legal rules, agree that the consequences are much broader. *Jus cogens* in this perspective overrides contrary international and domestic law, whether the state in question accepts or dissents from the asserted peremptory norm.

In Practice

The concept of *jus cogens* has been invoked largely outside its original context in the law of treaties and with only limited impact. At the International Court of Justice, until early 2006, the term appeared only in separate or dissenting opinions or when the Court was quoting other sources.[32] Previously, states rarely raised the issue,[33] and when they did the Court seemed to take pains to avoid any pronouncement on it.[34]

The 1986 *Nicaragua* decision, most often cited for the Court's recognition of *jus cogens,* did not in fact approve either the concept or the content of such norms.[35] In the subsequent advisory opinion on nuclear weapons, the ICJ utilized descriptive phrases that could be taken to refer to peremptory norms, although the language is unclear. The Court called some rules of international humanitarian law so fundamental to respect for the human person and "elementary considerations of humanity" that "they constitute intransgressible principles of international customary law."[36] Whether "intransgressible" means the rules are peremptory or was used simply to emphasize the binding nature of the customary norms is uncertain, but the former reading may be more plausible.

The first occasion on which the International Court gave support to the existence of *jus cogens* was in the February 3, 2006, Judgment on Preliminary Objections in *Armed Activities on the Territory of the Congo*.[37] The Democratic Republic of the Congo (DRC or the Congo) alleged violations of human rights and humanitarian law resulting from acts of armed aggression committed by Rwanda in the DRC. Three bases of jurisdiction asserted by the Congo involved claimed breaches of peremptory norms. First, the DRC alleged breaches of the Genocide Convention and contended that Rwanda's reservation withholding jurisdiction from the ICJ was invalid because it sought to prevent the Court from safeguarding the peremptory norms manifest in the Convention. Second, the DRC accused Rwanda of filing an invalid reservation to the Racial Discrimination Convention, which according to the DRC also contains peremptory norms. Third, the DRC invoked Article 66 of the Vienna Convention on the Law of Treaties, to assert that the Court has jurisdiction to settle all disputes arising from the violation of peremptory norms.

The Court for the first time explicitly and overwhelmingly recognized the existence of *jus cogens* in its analysis of the validity of Rwanda's reservations to the Genocide and Racial Discrimination Conventions. With respect to the Genocide Convention, the Court reaffirmed that the rights and obligations contained therein are rights and obligations *erga omnes*,[38] then pronounced the prohibition of genocide to be "assuredly" a peremptory norm of general international law. In making this straightforward statement, the Court did not offer any reference, evidence, or analysis that might help to establish criteria for identifying other peremptory norms or the consequences of such a characterization.

As in most other cases where peremptory norms have been recognized, the legal consequences of this classification were essentially imperceptible. The Court held by 15-2[39] that it lacked jurisdiction over the dispute, reaffirming that "[u]nder the Court's Statute that jurisdiction is always based on the consent of the parties."[40] Concerning the Rwandan reservations, the Court held that a reservation to ICJ jurisdiction cannot be judged invalid on the ground that it withholds jurisdiction over *jus cogens* violations. Thus, "[w]hen a compromissory clause in a treaty provides for the Court's jurisdiction, that jurisdiction exists only in respect of the parties to the treaty who are bound by that clause and within the limits set out therein."[41] As for the Genocide Convention, the Court characterized Rwanda's reservation to Article IX precluding the Court's jurisdiction as one "meant to exclude a particular method of settling a dispute relating to the interpretation, application or fulfillment of the Convention" and not one affecting substantive obligations relating to acts of genocide themselves.[42] It was therefore valid, there being no peremptory norm of international law requiring a state to consent to ICJ jurisdiction in a case involving genocide.

The Court took the same approach to the DRC's argument against the validity of Rwanda's reservation to the dispute settlement provision of the Racial Discrimination Convention, but the Judgment leaves unclear whether or not the Court accepted the DRC's claim that the prohibition of racial discrimination is a *jus cogens* norm. The Court simply referred back to its reasoning on the Genocide Convention and reaffirmed the nonexistence of a peremptory norm requiring states to consent to ICJ jurisdiction, leaving open its characterization of the substantive norms in the treaty.

Finally, the Court assessed whether or not Article 66 of the Vienna Convention provides a basis for ruling on alleged *jus cogens* violations.[43] The Court found no basis for jurisdiction, accepting Rwanda's argument that the Vienna Convention is not retroactive. Therefore, it would not apply to the treaties in question, unless Article 66 could be found to codify customary international law, which the Court held it does not do. In sum, according to the ICJ, neither the *erga omnes* nor the peremptory character of a norm of itself gives the Court jurisdiction to decide a dispute, which always depends on the consent of the parties. No peremptory norm requires a state to consent to jurisdiction where compliance with a peremptory norm is the issue before the Court.

In its own jurisprudence, the Inter-American Commission on Human Rights has referred to the concept of *jus cogens* several times, suggesting natural law as an additional source of obligation. The Commission has declared the right to life, for example, to be a norm of *jus cogens*

> derived from a higher order of norms established in ancient times and which cannot be contravened by the laws of man or of nations. The norms of jus cogens have been described by public law specialists as those which encompass public international order . . . accepted . . . as necessary to protect the public interest of the society of nations or to maintain levels of public morality recognized by them.[44]

In an opinion on the application of the death penalty to juvenile offenders in the United States, the Commission gave a more detailed account of its methodology for finding *jus cogens* norms.[45] According to the Commission, developments in the corpus of international human rights law relevant to interpreting and applying the American Declaration on the Rights and Duties of Man may be drawn from various sources of international law, including the provisions of other international and regional human rights instruments and customary international law, which covers those customary norms considered to form a part of *jus cogens*. The Commission reiterated that the concept of *jus cogens* derives from ancient law concepts of a "superior order of legal norms, which the laws of man or nations may not contravene," "rules which have been accepted, either expressly by treaty or tacitly by custom, as being necessary to protect the public morality recognized by them."[46] The Commission saw the principal distinguishing feature of these norms as their "relative indelibility," in that they constitute rules of customary law that "cannot be set aside by treaty or acquiescence but only by the formation of a subsequent customary rule of contrary effect.[47] More particularly, norms of *jus cogens* cannot be avoided by being a persistent objector. These rules represent fundamental values such that violations are considered to shock the conscience of humankind; they therefore bind the international community as a whole, irrespective of protest, recognition, or acquiescence.

The Commission proceeded to list the "[c]ommonly cited examples of rules of customary law that have attained the status of *jus cogens* norms": the prohibitions of genocide, slavery, forced disappearances, and torture or other cruel, inhuman, or degrading treatment or punishment. The Commission added without comment: "It has been suggested that a reliable starting point in identifying those international legal proscriptions that have achieved *jus cogens* status is the list of rights that international human rights treaties render non-derogable."[48] In specific cases, the Commission would look for evidence of recognition of the indelibility of the norm by the international community as a whole. "This can occur where there is acceptance and recognition by a large majority of states, even if over dissent by a small number of states."[49] On the precise issues before it,

> [t]he Commission considers that . . . broad hemispheric adherence to the American Convention, including Article 4 (5) thereof, constitutes compelling evidence of a regional norm repudiating the application of the death penalty to persons under 18 years of age even amongst those states such as Guatemala, Jamaica and Grenada that, like the United States, have retained the death penalty.[50]

The International Criminal Tribunal for the Former Yugoslavia (ICTY), the first tribunal to discuss *jus cogens,* supports the existence of such norms and has declared the prohibition of torture as one of them:

> Because of the importance of the values it protects, [the prohibition against torture] has evolved into a peremptory norm or jus cogens, that is, a norm that enjoys a higher rank in the international hierarchy than treaty law and even "ordinary" customary rules. The most conspicuous consequence of this higher rank is that the principle at issue cannot be derogated from by States through international treaties or local or special customs or even general customary rules not endowed with the same normative force. . . . Clearly, the jus cogens nature of the prohibition against torture articulates the notion that the prohibition has now become one of the most fundamental standards of the international community.[51]

The Human Rights Committee addressed *jus cogens* in its General Comment No. 29 on states of emergency, issued on August 31, 2001.[52] According to the Committee, the list of nonderogable rights in Article 4(2) of the Covenant on Civil and Political Rights is related to, but not identical with, the content of peremptory human rights norms because, while some nonderogable rights are included in Article 4 "partly as recognition of the[ir] peremptory nature," other rights not included also figure among peremptory norms.[53] The Committee insisted that

> States parties may in no circumstances invoke article 4 of the Covenant as justification for acting in violation of humanitarian law or peremptory norms of international law, for instance by taking hostages, by imposing collective punishments, through arbitrary deprivations of liberty or by deviating from fundamental principles of fair trial, including the presumption of innocence.[54]

While this statement may appear to be adding new conditions to Article 4, in fact paragraph 1 explicitly provides that any measures taken by states in derogation of Covenant rights must not be "inconsistent with their other obligations under international law."[55] Thus, the Committee asserted that one test of the legitimacy of measures in derogation of Covenant rights can be found in the definition of certain violations as crimes against humanity.

The concept of *jus cogens* norms has been pressed most strongly in the domestic courts of the United States, initially in an effort to avoid U.S. constitutional doctrine that considers treaties and custom equivalent to other federal law, allowing the president and Congress to enact U.S. law inconsistent with international law. *Jus cogens* obligations were asserted first in an effort to enforce the 1986 ICJ Judgment against the United States in the *Nicaragua* case.[56] Lawyers argued that the constitutional precedents do not apply to norms of *jus cogens*, which have a higher status that binds even the president and Congress. The Court accepted the theory *arguendo*, but held that compliance with a decision of the ICJ is not a *jus cogens* requirement.

Other domestic court cases involving *jus cogens* fall into one of two categories. First are cases in which sovereign immunity has acted to shield defendants from civil lawsuits for damages. The issue has arisen most often in courts of the United States and the United Kingdom. In both forums lawyers argued that the foreign sovereign immunity law must be interpreted to include an implied exception to sovereign immunity for violations of *jus cogens* norms. The argument relies on the idea of implied waiver, positing that state agreement to elevate a norm to *jus cogens* status inherently results in an implied waiver of sovereign immunity. Every court in these two systems thus far has rejected the argument and upheld immunity, although some judicial panels have split on the issue.[57]

In the case of former Chilean leader Augusto Pinochet Ugarte, the issue of *jus cogens* arose in response to a claim of immunity from criminal prosecution. Among the many opinions in the case, the one by Lord Millett stated that "[i]nternational law cannot be supposed to have established a crime having the character of a *jus cogens* and at the same time to have provided an immunity which is co-extensive with the obligation it seeks to impose."[58] Ultimately, however, the judgment did not rely on *jus cogens* to determine the issue because treaty law as implemented by UK law controlled the matter.

Four recent cases from different national courts demonstrate the confusion over *jus cogens* and its relationship to issues of immunity. In all of the cases the courts held that the underlying violations constituted breaches of norms of *jus cogens*, two cases involved war crimes and two concerned torture—but the courts split evenly on whether a finding of *jus cogens* violations overrides immunity. In cases from Greece and Italy, the respective supreme courts held that German crimes committed during World War II were not protected by sovereign immunity.[59] In contrast, an Ontario court of appeal and an English appellate tribunal held that the *jus cogens* prohibition of torture does not override sovereign immunity.[60]

A second category of domestic law cases in which the nature of norms as *jus cogens* has been asserted concerns cases filed pursuant to the U.S. Alien Tort Statute (ATS).[61] Some of the plaintiffs have asserted violations of norms of *jus cogens*, often wrongly claiming that the landmark decision *Filartiga v. Pena-Irala*[62] held torture to violate a *jus cogens* norm. But the federal appellate court in that case held that official torture constitutes a violation of the law of nations and never mentioned the doctrine of *jus cogens* norms. In fact, no ATS case has turned on the character of the violated norm as *jus cogens* or "ordinary" custom.

The recently completed ILC articles on state responsibility and accompanying commentary take the position that peremptory norms exist, urging that the concept has been recognized in international practice and in the jurisprudence of international and national courts and tribunals.[63] The commentary notes that the issue of hierarchy of norms has been much debated, but finds support for *jus cogens* in the notion of *erga omnes* obligations and the inclusion of the concept of peremptory norms in the Vienna Convention on the Law of Treaties.

The articles propose a hierarchy of the consequences of various breaches of international law. Article 41 sets forth the particular consequences said to result from the commission of a serious breach of a peremptory norm. The text imposes positive and negative obligations upon all states. With respect to the first, "[w]hat is called for in the face of serious breaches is a joint and coordinated effort by all States to counteract the effects of these breaches."[64] The commentary concedes that the proposal "may reflect the progressive development of international law" in an effort to strengthen existing mechanisms of cooperation.[65] The core requirement, to abstain from recognizing consequences of the illegal acts, finds more support in state practice, with precedents including rejection of the unilateral declaration of independence by Rhodesia, the annexation of Kuwait by Iraq, and the South African presence in Namibia. Article 41 of the articles on state responsibility, however, extends the duty to combat and not condone illegal acts beyond the requirements of the UN Charter.

Toward the Future

The concerns raised by most proponents of *jus cogens* are serious and the rationale that emerges from the literature is one of necessity: the international community cannot rely upon a consensual regime to address many modern international problems. *Jus cogens* is needed because the modern interdependence of states demands an international order *public* containing rules that require strict compliance. The ILC commentary to the articles on state responsibility favors this position, asserting that peremptory rules exist to "prohibit what has come to be seen as intolerable because of the threat it presents to the survival of States and their peoples and the most basic human values."[66] The suggested urgent need to act fundamentally challenges the consensual framework of the international system by seeking to impose on dissenting states obligations that the "international community" deems fundamental. State practice has yet to catch up fully with this plea of necessity.

Nonetheless, the emergence of international criminal law has led some to see a strengthening in application of *jus cogens* norms. This possibility necessitates consideration of the nature of international crimes and the relationship of this body of law to doctrines of obligations of *jus cogens* and obligations *erga omnes*. The ICJ was the first to identify the category of obligations *erga omnes* in dicta in the *Barcelona Traction* case.[67] The characterization of an obligation as one owed the international community as a whole could derive from the fact that such obligations generally aim at regulating the internal behavior of a state, such as in the field of human rights, and thus no other state is likely to be materially affected by a breach. Consequently, the principle of effectiveness supports broad standing, because without it violations could not be challenged. However, the rationale stated by the ICJ for recognizing this category of obligations appears more substantive: that "[i]n view of the importance of the rights involved, all States can be held to have a legal interest in their protection."[68] This statement suggests that obligations *erga omnes* have specific and broad procedural consequences *because of* the substantive importance of the norms they enunciate. In addition, the fact that all states can complain of a breach may make it more likely that a complaint will be made following commission of a wrongful act, suggesting that a higher priority is accorded to these norms even if they are not considered substantively superior. The ICJ's examples of such obligations included the outlawing of aggression and genocide and protection from slavery and racial discrimination.

Like obligations *erga omnes,* international crimes are so designated because the prohibited acts are deemed of such importance to the international community that individual criminal responsibility should result from their commission.[69] Unlike obligations *erga omnes,* however, international criminal norms can pose problems of relative normativity. It has been clear since the Nuremberg trials that conforming to or carrying out domestic law is no excuse for breach of international criminal law; it would seem plausible as well, if unlikely to arise in practice, that a defense based on carrying out international legal obligations, such as those contained in a bilateral treaty, would fail if those obligations contradict the requirements of criminal law.[70] In this respect, norms of criminal law would be given supremacy over other international law in practice.

Other aspects of the interrelationship of these categories of norms and the sources that create them should be noted. First, neither the designation of international crimes nor that of obligations *erga omnes* involves a purported new source of law; crimes are created and defined through the conclusion of treaties and obligations *erga omnes* by treaty and customary international law. Both, however, may emerge from a global recognition of fundamental moral or ethical values. Second, it appears logical that all international crimes are obligations *erga omnes* because the international community as a whole identifies and may prosecute and punish the commission of such crimes. The reverse, however, is not the case. Not all obligations *erga omnes* have been designated as international crimes. Racial discrimination, for example, is cited as an obligation *erga omnes* but is not included among international crimes.

Among those acts designated as international crimes, there appears to be no hierarchy. The ICTY declared in the *Tadiç* judgment that "there is in law no distinction between the seriousness of a crime against humanity and that of a war crime."[71]

Conclusion

The growing complexity of the international legal system is reflected in the increasing variety of forms of commitment adopted to regulate state behavior in regard to an ever-growing number of transnational problems. The various international actors create and implement a range of international commitments, some of which are in legal form, some of which are claimed to have supremacy over other norms, and some of which are contained in nonbinding instruments.

In practice, conflicts between norms and their interpretation are probably inevitable in the present, largely decentralized international legal system where each state is entitled initially and equally to interpret for itself the scope of its obligations and the implementation those obligations require. The interpretations or determinations of applicable rules may vary considerably, making all international law somewhat relative, in the absence of institutions competent to render authoritative interpretations binding on all states.

There are also dangers of relative normativity alluded to by Professor Weil in 1983 and other hazards that have surfaced since that time. Many authors and litigators have exhibited a pronounced inflationary tendency: nonlaw becomes soft law, soft law becomes hard law, and various customary and treaty norms become *jus cogens*. It is even possible, according to some, that nonbinding instruments, such as General Assembly resolutions, can identify the supreme norms of *jus cogens*. Resolutions of international organizations are treated in a variable manner, depending more on their content than on their form and process of adoption. At the other end of the spectrum, the notion of *jus cogens* has been invoked to such a point in publications and litigation in the United States that it risks devaluing "ordinary" customary international law. Notably, in some pleadings in Alien Tort Claims cases defendants and even the United States government asserted that a claim could not lie under the law of nations unless it was considered *jus cogens*. Fortunately, this misconstruction of the term "law of nations" was not adopted by the United States Supreme Court in *Sosa v. Alvarez-Machain*.[72]

The extent to which the system has moved, and may still move, toward the imposition of global public policy on nonconsenting states remains highly debated, but the need for limits on states' freedom of action seems to be increasingly recognized. International legal instruments and doctrine now often refer to the "common interest of humanity"[73] or "common con cern of mankind" to identify broad concerns that could form part of international public policy. References are also more frequently made to "the international community" as an entity or authority of collective action. In addition, multilateral agreements increasingly contain provisions that affect nonparty states, either by providing incentives to adhere to the norms, or by allowing parties to take coercive measures that in practice require conforming behavior of states that do not adhere to the treaty. The UN Charter itself contains a list of fundamental principles[74] and in Article 2(6) asserts that these may be imposed on nonparties if necessary to ensure international peace and security. Perhaps the most significant positive aspect of this trend toward normative hierarchy is its reaffirmation of the link between law and ethics, in which law is one means to achieve the fundamental values of an international society. It remains to be determined, however, who will identify the fundamental values and by what process.

Notes

1. Martti Koskenniemi, *Hierarchy in International Law: A Sketch,* 8 EUR. J. INT'L L. 566 (1997).

2. *See, e.g.,* LAURI HANNIKAINEN, PEREMPTORY NORMS *(JUS COGENS)* IN INTERNATIONAL LAW (1988); Gennady M. Danilenko, *International* Jus Cogens: *Issues of Law-making,* 2 EUR. J. INT'L L. 42(1991); Antonio Gómez Robledo, *Le* Jus Cogens *International: Sa Genese, Sa Nature, Ses Fonctions,* 172 RECUEIL DES COURS 9 (1981 III); Christian Tomuschat, *Obligations Arising for States Without or Against Their Will,* 241 RECUEIL DES COURS 195 (1993 IV). For a dissenting view, see Anthony D'Amato, *It's a Bird, It's a Plane, It's* Jus Cogens*!* 6 CONN.J. INT'LL. 1(1990).

3. The primacy of the United Nations Charter is set forth in Article 103, which provides that "[i]n the event of a conflict between the obligations of the Members of the United Nations under the present Charter and their obligations under any other international agreement, their obligations under the present Charter shall prevail." This "supremacy clause" has been taken to suggest that the aims and purposes of the United Nations—maintenance of peace and security, and promotion

and protection of human rights—constitute an international public order to which other treaty regimes and the international organizations giving effect to them must conform.

4. The phrase has been used by the International Law Commission, which took up the topic on the basis of a feasibility study entitled "Risks Ensuing from Fragmentation of International Law," which was presented at its fifty-second session in 2000.

5. UN Comm. on Economic, Social and Cultural Rights, Statement on Globalization, para. 5 (May 11, 1998), 6 INT'L HUM. RTS. REP. 1176 (1999), *available at* <http://www.globalpolicy.org/globalize/define/unstate.htm>.

6. UN Comm. on Economic, Social and Cultural Rights, Statement to the Third Ministerial Conference of the World Trade Organization (Nov. 26, 1999), UN Doc. E/C.12/1999/9, para. 6.

7. General principles of law are a third, more rarely used, source of international law, and judicial decisions and teachings of highly qualified publicists provide evidence of the existence of a norm. *See* ICJ Statute Art. 38.

8. The terms *jus cogens* and peremptory norms are used interchangeably.

9. Alfred von Verdross, *Forbidden Treaties in International Law,* 31 AJIL 571(1937). Verdross returned to this subject three decades later as the Vienna Convention on the Law of Treaties was being negotiated. Alfred Verdross, Jus Dispositivum and Jus Cogens *in International Law,* 60 AJIL 55 (1966) [hereinafter Verdross, Jus Dispositivum].

10. Costa Rica v. Nicaragua (Central Am. Ct. Justice Sept. 30, 1916, *translated and reprinted in* 11 AJIL 181 (1917).

11. Quincy Wright, *Conflicts Between International Law and Treaties,* 11 AJIL 566 (1917).

12. Oscar Chinn, 1934 PCIJ (ser. A/B) No. 63, at 149–50 (Schucking, J. dissenting). For a discussion, see H. Arthur Steiner, *Fundamental Conceptions of International Law in the Jurisprudence of the Permanent Court of International Justice,* 30 AJIL 414, 417–19 (1936).

13. *The Law of Treaties,* Harvard Research in International Law, 29 AJIL Supp. 655 (1935)

14. Quincy Wright would probably have responded that it is unnecessary to have recourse to *jus cogens* when a treaty purports to deny third parties their rights under customary international law because those affected would not have given their consent to the "new rule" and thus the agreement would not be enforced against them.

15. Verdross, *supra* note 11, at 572.

16. *Id.* at 574. Verdross may well have had in mind the Austrian capitulation to Nazi Germany.

17. Writing during the Great Depression, Verdross made reference specifically to the immorality of an obligation to pay foreign debts to the point that essential public services were affected within a state. *Id.* at 575.

18. Louis Henkin, *International Law: Politics, Values and Functions,* 216 RECUEIL DES COURS 9,45 (1989 IV); I.I. Lukashuk, *ThePrinciple* Pacta Sunt Servanda *and the Nature of Obligation Under International Law,* 83 AJIL 513 (1989).

19. S.S. Lotus (Fr, v. Turk.), 1927 PCIJ (ser. A) No. 10, at 18 (Sept. 7).

20. Military and Paramilitary Activities in and Against Nicaragua (Nicar. v. U.S.), Merits, 1986 ICJ REP. 14, 135, para. 269 (June 27).

21. Sir Humphrey Waldock proposed the concept and three categories of *jus cogens:* (1) illegal use of force, (2) international crimes, and (3) acts or omissions

whose suppression is required by international law. The categories were dropped by the ILC, because each garnered opposition from at least two-thirds of the Commission. *See* SZTUCKI, *supra* note 47; Richard D. Kearney & Robert E. Dalton, *The Treaty on Treaties,* 64 AJ1L 495, 535, (1970).

22. Wladyslaw Czapliński, *Concept of* Jus Cogens *and Obligations* Erga Omnes *in International Law,* 1997–1998 POLISH Y.B. INT'L L. 87, notes the objections made during the *travaux préparatoires* of the VCLT and the claims of several states that the proposal on *jus cogens* constituted a progressive development (Argentina, Mali, and Sierra Leone). He concludes: "It seems manifest that *jus cogens* did not constitute part of customary law before the concluding of the Vienna Convention and it binds exclusively parties to the Convention." *Id.* at 88. He adds: "Generally speaking, states are not particularly wishing to invalidate their international obligations because of their hypothetical non-conformity with *jus cogens.*" *Id.* at 89.

23. FARHAD MALEKIAN, THE SYSTEM OF INTERNATIONAL LAW: FORMATION, TREATIES, RESPONSIBILITY, sec. 2.2.1.2 (1987).

24. Eric Suy, Remarks, *in* CHANGE AND STABILITY IN INTERNATIONAL LAW-MAKING 97 (Antonio Cassese & Joseph H. H. Weiler eds., 1988).

25. HANS KELSEN, THE PURE THEORY OF LAW 214–17 (Max Knight trans., 2d rev. ed. 1967) (1937). Oscar Schachter identified thirteen theories about the origin of obligation in international law. Oscar Schachter, *Towards a Theory of International Obligation,* 8 VA. J. INT'L L 300 (1968).

26. A natural-law origin of international obligation was the dominant theory among scholars until the nineteenth century, when positivism and an emphasis on the sovereignty of states emerged in theory and practice.

27. The judgment of March 24,1982, of the arbitral tribunal in the *Aminoil v. Kuwait* case rejected the claim that permanent sovereignty over natural resources constitutes a principle of *jus cogens.* Kuwait and Am. Independent Oil Co., 21 ILM 976 (1982) (Reuter, Sultan, & Fitzmaurice arbs., 1982).

28. E. Jiménez de Aréchiaga, *General Course in Public International Law,* 159 RECUEIL DES COURS 9,67 (1978 I).

29. Jan F. Triska & Robert M. Slusser, *Treaties and Other Sources of Order in International Relations: The Soviet View,* 52 AJIL 699, 710, 717–18 (1958). Grigorii Tunkin proclaimed in 1974 that the Brezhnev doctrine, which he called proletarian internationalism, was a *jus cogens* norm. C. I. TUNKIN, THEORY OF INTERNATIONAL LAW 444 (William E. Butler trans., 1974).

30. Czapliński, *supra* note 24, at 88.

31. Prosecutor v. Furundžija, No. IT-95-17/1-T10 (Dec. 10,1998), *available at* <http://www.un.org/icty>.

32. *See, e.g.,* Right of Passage over Indian Territory (Port. v. India), Menu, 1960 ICJ REP. 6, at 135, 139–140 (Apr. 12) (Renandes, J. *ad hoc,* dissenting); South West Africa, Second Phase (Eth. v. S. Afr.; Liber. v. S. Afr.), 1966 ICJ REP. 6, 298 (July 18) (Tanaka, J., dissenting).

33. Gabăíkovo-Nagymaros Project (Hung./Slovk.), 1997 ICJ REP. 7, para. 112 (Sept.25) (noting that neither side had contended that new peremptory norms of environmental law had emerged).

34. *See* North Sea Continental Shelf (FRG/Den.; FRG/Neth.), 1969 ICJ REP. 3, para. 72 (Feb. 20) (declining to enter into or pronounce upon any issue concerning *jus cogens).*

35. Military and Paramilitary Activities in and Against Nicaragua (Nicar. v. U.S.), Merits, 1986 ICJ REP. 14, 100, para. 190 (June 27) (citing the ILC assertion

that the norm against aggression is a peremptory norm as evidence that it is an obligation under customary international law).

36. Legality of the Threat or Use of Nuclear Weapons, Advisory Opinion, 1996 ICJ REP. 226, para. 79 (July 8).

37. Armed Activities on the Territory of the Congo (New Application: 2002) (Dem. Rep. Congo v. Rwanda), Jurisdiction and Admissibility (Int'l Ct. Justice Feb. 3, 2006) [hereinafter Congo v. Rwanda Judgment].

38. Congo v. Rwanda Judgment, para. 64 (citing Application of the Convention on the Prevention and Punishment of the Crime of Genocide (Bosn. & Herz. v. Yugo.), Preliminary Objections, 1996 ICJ REP. 595, 616 (July 11)).

39. Neither of the dissenting judges contested the existence of *jus cogens;* they would have found jurisdiction on other bases.

40. Congo v. Rwanda Judgment, para. 64.

41. *Id.,* para. 65 (citing Armed Activities on the Territory of the Congo (New Application: 2002) (Dem. Rep. Congo v. Rwanda), Provisional Measures, 2002 ICJ REP. 245 (July 10)). Even if the reservation had been held invalid, it is not clear that the result would have been in favor of jurisdiction. The consequences of an invalid reservation set forth in the Vienna Convention on the Law of Treaties do not include ignoring the reservation and treating the party as if the reservation had not been made. *See* VCLT, Arts. 20, 21.

42. Congo v. Rwanda Judgment, para. 67. The Court so noted its previous advisory opinion finding that the Genocide Convention permits reservations, pointed out that it had given effect to Article IX reservations in prior cases, and noted that the DRC had failed to object to Rwanda's reservation when it was made. *Id.,* paras. 66, 68.

43. Article 66(a) provides that "any one of the parties to a dispute concerning the application or the interpretation of Article 53 or 64 [the provisions concerning *jus cogens*] may, by a written application, submit it to the International Court of Justice for a decision unless the parties by common consent agree to submit the dispute to arbitration."

44. Victims of the Tugboat "13 de Marzo" v. Cuba, Case 11.436, Inter-Am. C.H.R., Report No. 47/96, OEA/ Ser.L/V/II.95, doc. 7 rev. ¶79 (1996).

45. Michael Domingues (United States), Case 12.285, Inter-Am. C.H.R., Report No. 62/02, OEA/Ser.L/V/11.117, doc.1, rev.1 (2003).

46. *Id.,* para. 49 (quoting Roach & Pinkerton v. United States, Case 9647, Inter-Am. C.H.R., Res. No. 3/87, OEA/Ser.L/V/II.71 (1987)).

47. *Id.*

48. *Id.*

49. *Id.,* para. 50.

50. *Id.,* para. 64.

51. Prosecutor v Furundžija, No IT-95-17/1-T, ¶¶ 153–54 (Dec. 10, 1998).

52. UN Human Rights Comm., General Comment No. 29, States of Emergency (Article 4), UN Doc. CCPR/ C/21/Rev.1/Add.11 (2001).

53. *Id.,* para. 11.

54. *Id.*

55. ICCPR, *supra* note 13, Art. 4 (1).

56. Comm. of U.S. Citizens Living in Nicar. v. Reagan, 859 F.2d 929, 940 (D.C. Cir. 1988).

57. *See, e.g.,* Siderman de Blake v. Republic of Arg., 965 F.2d 699 (9th Cir. 1992), *cert. denied,* 507 U.S. 1017 (1993); Ye v. Zemin, 383 F.3d 620 (7th Cir. 2004), *cert. denied,* 2005 U.S. LEXIS 3351 (Apr. 18,2005); Sampson v. Fed.

Republic of Germany, 250 F.3d 1145 (7th Cir. 2000; Hwang Geum Joo v. Japan, 332 F.3d 679 (D.C. Cir. 2003); Princz v. Fed. Republic of Germany, 26 F.3d 1166 (D.C. Cir. 1994); Kane v. Winn, 319 F.Supp.2d 162, 199 (D. Mass. 2004).

58. Regina v. Bow Street Metro. Stipendiary Magistrate, *Ex parte* Pinochet (No. 3), [1992] 2 All E.R. 97, 179, [2000] 1 A.C. 147 (H.L).

59. Prefecture of Voiotia v. Fed. Republic of Germany, Areios Pagos [Supreme Court] 11/2000 (Greece); Ferrini v. Fed. Republic of Germany, Cass., sez. un., 6 Nov. 2003, n.5044, 87 RI VISTA DI DIRITTO INTERNAZIONALE 539 (2004). The Italian case is discussed in Pasquale De Sena & Francesca De Vittor, *State Immunity and Human Rights: The Italian Supreme Court Decision on the* Ferrini *Case,* 16 EUR. J. INT'L L. 112 (2005).

60. Bouzari v. Iran, C38295, [2004] O.J. 2800 (Ont. Ct. App. June 30, 2004); Jones v. Saudi Arabia, [2004] EWCA (Civ) 1394, [1].

61. 28 U.S.C. §1350 (2000) ("The [federal] district courts shall have original jurisdiction of any civil action by an alien for a tort only, committed in violation of the law of nations or a treaty of the United States."). The ATS is part of the Judiciary Act of 1789, ch. 20, §9(b).

62. Filartiga v. Peña-Irala, 630 F.2d 876 (2d Cir. 1980). The only U.S. Supreme Court decision to consider issues arising under the ATS, *Sosa v. Alvarez -Machain,* 542 U.S. 692 (2004), also failed to mention *jus cogens.*

63. Articles on Responsibility of States for Internationally Wrongful Acts, *in* Report of the International Law Commission on the Work of Its Fifty-third Session, UN GAOR, 56th Sess., Supp. No. 10, at 43, 282, 287, Arts. 40, 41, UN Doc. A/56/10 (2001) [hereinafter State Responsibility Articles], Art. 40 Commentary, para. 2.

64. *Id.* at 287, Art. 41 Commentary, para. 3.

65. *Id.*

66. State Responsibility Articles, *supra* note 63, at 283, Air. 40 Commentary, para. 3.

67. BarcelonaTraction, Light & Power Co. (Belg. v. Spain), Second Phase, 1970 ICJ REP. 3, para. 33 (Feb. 5).

68. *Id;* see also East Timor (Port. v. Austl.), 1995 ICJ REP. 90, para. 29 (June 30); Application of the Convention on the Prevention and Punishment of the Crime of Genocide (Bosn. & Herz. v. Yugo.), Preliminary Objections, 1996 IC REP. 595, para. 31 (July11).

69. The collective nature of the state as subject of international law makes imposition of state criminal responsibility problematic. Although the International Law Commission included a provision on state crimes in early versions of its articles on state responsibility, the provision was eventually excluded.

70. The treaty itself might be considered void as a violation of peremptory norms if it required or authorized the commission of an international crime.

71. Prosecutor v. Tadiç, Judgment in Sentencing Appeals, No. IT-94-1-A, ¶69 (Jan.26, 2000). For a criticism of this view and discussion of the conflicting practice of the ICTY, see Allison Marston Danner, *Constructing a Hierarchy of Crimes in International Criminal Law Sentencing,* 87 VA, L. REV. 415(2001).

72. Sosa v. Alvarez-Machain, 542 U.S. 692 (2004).

73. *See* LOS Convention, *supra* note 16, An. 137(2); Treaty on Principles Governing the Activities of States in the Exploration and Use of Outer Space, Including the Moon and Other Celestial Bodies, Jan. 27, 1967, pmbl., para. 2, 18 UST 2410, 610 UNTS 205.

74. UN Charter Art. 2.

PART 1.2

International Law as Operating System: Participants in the International Legal Process

CHAPTER 5

The New Treaty Makers

Jose E. Alvarez

The Proliferation of Treaties

. . . There is little doubt that recent decades have witnessed a striking proliferation in treaties, including multilateral agreements of ambitious substantive scope that aspire to universal participation. Since the establishment of the U.N., treaties have attempted to codify both traditional topics of international law (e.g., the law of the sea, diplomatic and consular relations, the law of treaties, the law of war, or international humanitarian law) as well as newer subjects not previously regarded as amenable to or suitable for international regulation (such as trade, intellectual property, investment, and international criminal law). From 1970 through 1997, the number of international treaties more than tripled.[1] Even that ostensible unilateralist, the United States, has not been immune from being drawn into this dense treaty network. In the 1990s the United States concluded 3,106 treaties, after 3,690 in the 1980s, 3,212 in the 1970s, and 2,438 in the 1960s.[2] We often suggest that the primary explanation for international legalization is functionalism. In other words, states are driven to regulate at the international level by ever-rising movements of people, goods, and capital across borders, along with positive and negative externalities emerging from such flows—from the rise in a common house rights ideal to emerging threats to the global commons. But we should not lose sight of the fact that the proliferation of treaties is aided and abetted by the concomitant rise in intergovernmental organizations.[3] The age of global compacts is not incidentally also the age of IOs.

As of 1995, of some 1,500 multilateral treaties in existence, nearly half were attributable to U.N. system organizations, and the rate of production of new treaties undertaken within the auspices of international organization appears to be steadily increasing.[4] A substantial number of the approximately 3,500 meetings undertaken annually within the U.N. involve some kind of treaty-making activity and that organization alone has been involved in the conclusion of some 300 multilateral agreements.[5] The U.N. and other comparable institutions have helped to create a "gigantic treaty network . . . regulating all major international activities."[6] Some international organizations—such as the U.N. itself, the International Labour Organization (ILO), and the WTO—were intended to be what they have become: virtual treaty machines. Whole areas of modern international law, including human rights, would be unimaginable absent treaties concluded under IO auspices.[7]

The Role of International Organization

How have IOs changed the realities of treaty making to bring about multilateral regimes that are both decried and praised for eroding sovereignty?

In the 19th century, the fundamental mechanism for multilateral treaty making was the ad hoc conference. Before the advent of multilateral treaty making required the initiative of a state sufficiently aroused about an issue that it was willing to devote scarce diplomatic resources to motivate others and to convene such a conference on its territory. Usually, the initiator state determined which states to invite and the negotiating agenda. Once convened, the success or failure of such conferences turned on the acumen and leverage exercised by the government representatives present. In accordance with the principle of sovereign equality, decisions were usually taken on the basis of unanimity. The governments present determined whether there would be subsequent efforts to complete the treaty or, if the treaty concluded, whether there would be any procedures for follow-up. In the usual case, enforcement was left to reciprocal action by the individual state parties. Except in unusual circumstances, each multilateral treaty negotiation was a freestanding and entirely ad hoc undertaking, with no necessary connection to any other treaty arrangement.

The shortcomings of such conferences are, in retrospect, obvious.[8] Since they were dependent on the willingness of a particular state host, treaty making was haphazard and proposals for negotiations on such compacts usually came long after the need for international regulation had become acute. Even when treaty conferences were convened, there were no guarantees that all states needed to resolve the underlying problem or that would be affected by any proposed solution would be present. Complications could ensue due to the failure either to include all relevant state parties or all interests not being adequately represented by state delegations. Those invited and present at those conferences could not be sure that the full dimensions of an issue, much less related questions that might be of interest only to some states, would be aired—especially if such issues were deemed outside the scope of the host state's agenda or would raise prickly issues for the gracious host. Since preparations for such conferences were typically left to each state that managed to send a delegation, there was no assurance that negotiations would be based on all available technical or factual data or that all states would have equal access to any such information or to applicable legal precedents. Individuals at such negotiations may have met for the first time at the negotiating site and, given the absence of instantaneous communications, were relatively cut-off from their national capitals during the negotiation period. All of these factors led to rigidities in states' negotiating positions. All of them dampened the likelihood of success.[9]

In game theoretic terms, the ad hoc conferences of the 19th century resembled single play prisoners' dilemmas, lacking the benefits that we might achieve with repeated play or long term association, including reductions in transactions costs and uncertainty, and mutual reliance on long term reputation over short-term calculations of interest. There were few sunk costs involved in such forms of treaty making. No international civil servants existed to serve as repositories of knowledge, to transmit information or to propose compromise formulations; without international institutions, there were fewer mechanisms to enable states to pool their resources. There were few established rules of bureaucratic procedure that could be relied upon at the international level to encourage what economists and others have called "path dependencies."[10]

Further, multilateral treaties were, in the 19th century at least, not very multilateral. If a treaty was, despite evident deficiencies, concluded, the state designated as the state of registry was in a position to deny attempts to ratify by governments that it did not wish to associate with, thereby discouraging actual universal participation. Nor was this an entirely academic concern: this was a time, after all, when many states of the world were considered to be beneath the notice of "civilized states." Worse still, in the absence of on-going mechanisms for follow-up, treaty regimes failed to deepen and could even become obsolete due to changing needs or technology.

The establishment of organizations aspiring to universal or nearly universal membership corrected many of these shortcomings and have made the ad hoc treaty conference unconnected to an established IO a less preferred venue for treaty making. Most multilateral treaty regimes of any depth today are the product of one or more of the following four organizational patterns for treaty making: (1) IO (especially U.N. sponsored) treaty-making conferences; (2) expert treaty-making bodies; (3) "managerial" forms of treaty making; or what some have called institutional mechanisms for "treaty making with strings attached." Each will be briefly described below.

U.N. treaty-making conferences—such as the massive 1998 negotiations at Rome to establish an International Criminal Court (ICC) involving approximately 160 states, 33 intergovernmental organizations, over 200 NGOs, and over 400 journalists on site—usually occur after a canvassing of views, occasionally exhaustive, and often convene with a draft text in hand. Modern treaty-making conferences operate on the basis of flexible determinations of consensus rather than rigid unanimity rules. They follow established organizational patterns, such as division between a plenary and more specialized bodies and formal versus informal sessions. They rely as well on reasonably clear rules procedure that avoid the need to reinvent the wheel on such topics as the credentials of delegates or rules for submitting proposals or quorums.[11] Often they rely upon familiar groupings of states seen elsewhere in the U.N.—associations that encourage issue linkage package deals. They use IO secretariats to conduct advance preparations (such as circulating detailed questionnaires among participants) to formulate manageable work plans, and to encourage reliance on final standard clauses as with respect to reservations and entry into force. IO staff also serve as legitimating conduits for proposals made by unpopular or isolated states. Members of the international civil service even on occasion assist in drafting compromise language.

The second organizational pattern relies on experts—as with respect to public international law (such as the International Law Commission [ILC]), international economic law (such as the United Nations Commission on International Trade Law [UNCITRAL]), or more specialized topics (such as the International Civil Aviation Organizations [ICAO] delineated), predictable procedures that produce large volumes of information, as with respect to the current practices and opinions of states. Usually working in tandem with U.N. conferences, these institutionalized experts produce drafts that, at their best, achieve technocratic legitimacy because of their source and quality. For example, ILC commentaries and draft provisions for proposed treaties that have yet to be concluded have sometimes been relied upon by states and others as reliable accounts of existing custom.

Managerial forms of treaty making, in areas such as trade, the environment, and human rights, attempt to secure the benefits of institutionalization on an on-going basis and not only when treaties are initially concluded. They establish entities that are authorized to elaborate standards, as well as monitoring bodies charged with enforcement and interpretation, including, in the cases of regional human rights and trade, binding forms of dispute settlement. Thus, environmental framework conventions establish committees of the parties and other working groups for on-going norm elaboration, interpretation, and "soft" enforcement, such as consideration of states reports of implementation. These framework conventions establish "living" treaty regimes without recourse, in the usual case, to formal international organizations with distinct legal personality or substantial secretariats. Whether or not they resort to harder forms of enforcement such as binding dispute settlement, several of these managerial regimes have deepened over time and all offer "the prospect of a virtually continuous legislative enterprise"[12] capable of responding to changes in technology or to the needs of the parties. The success of these modern treaty regimes can no longer be judged the way we judged the 19th century compact—through a snapshot frozen at a single moment in time. The success of these living treaties is now best measured through a modern motion picture, which is able to record their evolutionary development across time. The twelve protocols of the European system of Human Rights, the 1987 Montreal Protocol on Substances that Deplete the Ozone Layer, and the Uruguay Round are all products of managerial regimes and are characteristic of how they function.

Finally, there is treaty making that is constitutionally sanctioned, even mandated, under the charter of a formal full-fledged IO that tries to pressure its members to ratify the treaties produced by the regime. The clearest manifestation of such "treaty making with strings attached" is the ILO. The ILO's Constitution incorporates a highly structured, relatively rigid set of procedures that produce, at predictable intervals, treaty instruments—at last count over 1,170 of them. The ILO's Constitution ties "strings" to its instruments, requiring ILO members to bring the conventions to the attention of their legislatures and requiring periodic follow-up reports on implementation. A variety of ILO expert bodies thereafter engage in monitoring and dispute settlement, though not clearly with binding effect. The ILO attempts, with mixed success, something of an end-run around sovereign consent. The reporting and other obligations imposed under the ILO's Charter mobilize shame on behalf of treaty ratification.

Of course, these four organizational patterns for treaty making are not invariably successful. Some organizational venues have delegitimized treaty negotiation efforts. During the bad old days of the New International Economic Order (NIEO), for example, endorsement of an economic treaty by the General Assembly was the kiss of death—at least among western business constituencies. IO bureaucracies like bureaucracies elsewhere, may also prove inefficient or ineffective at encouraging agreement; they may develop their own agendas at the expense of the state principals they ostensibly serve. Ritualized institutional precedents may sometimes limit negotiators' field of vision; path dependencies, such as an infatuation with decisions by "consensus" however cosmetic, may lock negotiations onto the wrong historical path or result in meaningless lowest common denominator solutions. Modern international law is strewn with the wreckage of package deals that fail to secure the rates of ratification expected within a reasonable time—even when these result from the efforts of experts as in the ILO. And there is no guarantee that even when IOs promulgate widely ratified treaties, what IOs produce are any better at taking care of the underlying problems sought to be solved. As with respect to domestic law, more law or more treaties is not necessarily a good thing. Quantity should not be confused with quality.

But, these four organizational patterns have changed the landscape of treaty making in at least *five* respects that are essential to understanding both the nature of globalization as well as perceived erosions of sovereignty.

First, IOs have dramatically expanded the diversity of actors involved in treaty making. The winners have been less powerful governments, NGOs and other interest groups, the international civil service and experts, including public international law scholars. Due to the use of IOs as venues, it is now far more likely that even small less powerful states will be able to make an impact on the types of issues that are subject to treaty negotiations, as well as with respect to the substance of what is ultimately concluded. Thanks to such venues less powerful governments are more likely to be able to secure the benefits of a treaty obligation with powerful states. Without IOs, powerful states would be freer to engage bilaterally or multilaterally only with those states with whom they have an interest in contracting. IOs, even if only by making the neutral U.N. and not a host state the depository of treaty ratifications, have made modern multilateral treaties more truly multilateral, thereby democratizing treaty making.

Structural aspects of IOs, including provisions for access to documents and for observer or other forms of non-voting status, have in addition provided entry points for NGOs' growing participation in various forms of interstate diplomacy, including treaty making. They permit domestic interest groups, along with relevant domestic government agencies, to direct their lobbying efforts on those IOs that are the most promising venues for their concerns. Thus, business groups in the United States whose competitive interests were threatened by the United States' Foreign Corrupt Practices Act sought to multilateralize the regulation of bribery—and thereby level the playing field—in the forum most likely to reach their main European and Japanese competitors, namely the Organization for Economic Cooperation and Development (OECD). Similarly, a transnational alliance of business leaders anxious to secure enforceable intellectual property rights, dissatisfied with World Intellectual Property Organization's (WIPO) efforts, were able to frame this issue as a proper matter for the WTO.[13]

In addition, the conception of an international civil service as a breed apart, distinct from the governments from which these individuals emerge, has legitimized the participation of IO secretariats in treaty making. The power of such individuals to become active in treaty making, only sometimes explicitly conferred—as in a resolution inviting secretariat participation in the compiling of state views or in drafting an initial negotiating text—has been generally assumed to be part of a secretariat's "implied powers."

Expert treaty-drafting bodies have opened the door to yet other type of non-state actor: the individual legitimized by their expertise and claim to independence. In other organizations, such as the ILO, the participation of distinct constituencies—namely employers and labor unions—is built into the constitutional structure of treaty making. In these respects as well the involvement of IOs in treaty making has "democratized" the process. The wider diversity of state and non-state actors helps to explain the wider diversity of treaties concluded in the age of IOs, as well as the variety of pressures that are brought to bear on those governmental representatives who are still, in most respects, at least formally in charge of the initiation of treaty making, as well as formal ratification.

Second, IOs have either multiplied the options for treaty initiators or complicated their lives depending on one's point of view. Today, the initiation of a multilateral treaty negotiation requires, as a key and crucial decision, the matter of organizational venue. Those in on negotiating modern international compacts need to decide just between whether to convene a special ad hoc conference or resort to a standing international organization. They also need to decide which international organization and which organs within them ought to be involved. In recent years, the international community has confronted a number of such choices. Treaty efforts on bribery have involved regional IOs such as the OECD, the European Union, the OAS, and the Council of Europe, as well as international financial organizations and the U.N. General Assembly.[14] Nuclear proliferation issues have involved choices as between the IAEA or the U.N. General Assembly, while foreign investment, initially considered in the OECD (and in regional treaties), may yet be folded into the WTO.

Determining which organization and which sub-organ ought to be the venue in which to initiate a treaty process may determine whether the process will involve time-consuming and exhaustive analysis of the current state of the law by general legal experts,[15] more superficial examination of the need for a treaty by those attentive to the political desires of states,[16] or thorough examination of the need for a treaty relegated to technical experts in relatively narrow specialties.[17] Alternatively, treaty initiators may opt for processes that contain elements of all of these, such as the ILO. Organizational venues may also determine whether negotiators will be able to take advantage of credible dispute settlement process[18] or other supervisory procedures, be able to engage in a gradualist strategy that relies initially on soft law and soft enforcement, or be able to secure efficacious regional credibility.[19] The choice of organizational venue may determine whether treaty negotiations will be more or less transparent since distinct IOs have different traditions in this respect. Given this range of choices, the ability to choose among organizational venues implicitly forces treaty initiators to consider matters relating to the substance of the proposed treaty even before formal negotiations begin.

The choice of organizational venue speaks volumes concerning the intent of principal treaty backers. Those who attempt to insert a new issue in a WTO trade round, for example, would appear to be suggesting that the issue has an implicit link to trade, since that is the WTO's domain, and that it is an issue that can be appropriately made the subject of WTO dispute settlement as well as WTO-sanctioned trade retaliation if necessary, since these remedies have, at least since the Uruguay Round, been assumed to be applicable to all or most matters within the WTO. Anticipation that both the linkage to trade and enforcement issues will need to be addressed casts a shadow—a positive and a negative—over the prospect of initiating negotiations within the WTO.[20] While it might be assumed that the prospective binding dispute settlement would tend to discourage adding new issues to the trade regime, it would appear that in at least some cases such organizational realities may enhance the attractiveness of the WTO. Certainly the pressure to link some issues to the trade regime such as labor rights or environmental concerns, stems in part from penance-envy:[21] the perception, accurate or not, that WTO dispute settlement constitutes the most effective enforcement tool available at the global level and that such a potentially effective tool ought to be made applicable to these other concerns. At the same time, IOs develop distinct institutional cultures that may hinder attempts to use them as negotiating venues in some cases. The WTO's tradition of including issues in trade rounds only if these can be the basis of reciprocal concessions, for example, may make it difficult to build into regime treaty commitments less amenable to such trades.[22]

Third, because IOs increase the number of actors involved as well as the options available to treaty makers, they have a third impact; they alter the role of state power. The involvement of IOs may decrease the salience of traditional state power. Unlike in the 19th century, a serious multilateral treaty negotiation today does not require a hegemonic prime mover. Suggestions for such negotiations may be and are made even by the least powerful state representatives to an international organization, as in the U.N. General Assembly or comparable plenary bodies where the formal rules for voting (one state/one vote), can secure majority support for proposed treaty making over the opposition of a minority of powerful states. The 1990 action by the General Assembly that ultimately led to the successful conclusion of the Rome Statute for the ICC on July 17, 1998, stemmed from a 1989 initiative by Trinidad and Tobago, for example. Thanks to IOs, smaller or less powerful states are also more likely to find allies in a common cause, thereby permitting some leverage to be asserted even as against powerful states.

The access rights given to NGOs also increase the proportionate power of these purported representatives of international civil society over treaty-making decisions. Intense and successful NGO lobbying efforts on behalf of some treaties—as with respect to land-mines or to establish an individual complaints mechanism for the Convention of the Elimination of Discrimination Against Women (CEDAW)—are the predictable result.[23] The increasing attention given to the power NGOs misses part of the picture if it fails to acknowledge that intergovernmental organizations are often the conduit for the growing clout of NGOs.[24]

The verv existence of IOs conditions the traditional use of state power. In theory, governments retain the option of starting treaty negotiations the old-fashioned way, namely through a diplomatic approach to select states and invitations to a special ad hoc conference to conclude a stand-alone treaty. In practice, while such ad hoc conferences continue to be used for some treaty negotiations, many modern multilateral treaty negotiations have been authorized by an IO, such as the U.N. General Assembly, and many of these treaties establish bodies that function much like IOs even after a text is concluded, as in environmental regimes. The reasons are straightforward: most treaty initiators want to secure the advantages of an organizational setting, and even when key players do not, there may be considerable political pressure brought to bear to secure the endorsement of the organizational body whose established competence appears most directly relevant. Today, even a powerful state would find it difficult to attempt a major multilateral treaty-making effort regarding international civil aviation, for example, without at least attempting to involve ICAO or presenting credible reasons why that institution's involvement would be inappropriate. In addition, should the relevant organs of ICAO, including the expert bodies normally involved in such efforts, reject such a proposal, the prospects for a successful negotiation involving a credible number of participants are considerably diminished. Where an IO exists with jurisdiction over a matter that is proposed for treaty making, its mere existence affects the decision of whether, when, and where to initiate such a negotiation.

At the same time, IOs remain vehicles for the assertion of power. The choice among organizational venues is often influenced not to say determined, by the continuing realities of relative power. It was important in the now comparatively innocent 1960s and 1970s when airline hijackings first dominated the headlines, for example, for the primary movers of anti-terrorism conventions, like the United States, to have these negotiations initiated in the relatively efficient confines of ICAO rather than in the U.N. General Assembly. Western preferences have also prevailed with respect to other choices of venue—as respect to the trade regime (over WIPO) for intellectual property; the International Atomic Energy Agency (IAEA) (over the General Assembly) for certain proliferation conventions; and OECD (over the WTO) for the aborted Multilateral Agreement Investment (MAI). Power still matters to modern treaty making but it is often exercised to a distinct end: to favor one organizational forum for negotiations over another.[25]

Even when powerful states prevail in their choice of organizational venue, that choice may constrain them. Particular organizational venues often constrain even the powerful. The United States paid a price for the various anti-terrorism conventions that it successfully and speedily concluded under ICAO auspices some thirty years ago. While the United States would have preferred a comprehensive treaty regime leading to the suppression of the most serious acts of terrorist violence regardless of setting, the ICAO setting for such negotiations, while far preferable to the U.S. standpoint than the General Assembly, compelled a narrower and more piecemeal approach. It virtually ensured criminalization only for acts directly relating to civil aviation, namely violence on board aircraft, the target of aircraft for destruction, aircraft hijacking, and offenses at international airports.[26] In addition, while the United States initially wanted a regime that would permit joint enforcement action such as an international civil aviation boycott against a state that failed to honor its obligations to extradite terrorists, it quickly abandoned this goal when negotiators realized that such a hard sanction was a non-starter in an organization with an ethos that identifies the right to engage in civil aviation as a fundamental sovereign right.[27] Today, in the wake of September 11th, the United States appears to be scrambling back to an organization that it sought to avoid in the 1970s, namely the U.N., since that organization now offers the better prospect for achieving broader anti-terrorism goals, including treaties that fill gaps remaining in the wake of ICAO's efforts.

In addition, since states rightly assume that the choice of organizational forum matters, they expend considerable resources to make sure the right one is chosen. Strenuous and diplomatically costly efforts were necessary to make sure that, for example, foreign investment negotiations were initiated in the OECD, and not the WTO. In that instance, while the United States and many of the other leading exporters of capital would have preferred a regime for foreign investment with global reach, the decision to negotiate the MAI within an organization with a more limited membership was a calculated, ultimately unsuccessful, gamble to forego geographical reach in favor of presumptive depth of obligation.

Fourth, international organizations have vastly increased the amount of information available to treaty initiators. The information supplied by organizational venues may encourage the initiation of treaty making directly, as through proposals made by IOs, or indirectly, by inspiring certain governments to act. Many have contended that the negotiations leading to the 1987 Montreal Protocol would never have been initiated, for example, but for the level of scientific data concerning ozone depletion generated by the various entities established by the preceding Vienna Convention for the Protection of the Ozone Layer.[28] The supply of information may alter not only the decision of whether to initiate treaty making, but how and where to do so. Today, decisions to pursue particular topics in a distinct organizational setting are likely to be taken with full awareness of the prior history of that forum with respect to the topic in question and may reflect an intention to affect the substantive result on many matters—and not merely enforcement method, as in the WTO example above. A decision to attempt to initiate today the subject of foreign investment in the next WTO trade round, for example, would appear tantamount to a decision to give up on certain investment protections. This would certainly be the implication a prospective treaty initiation would take from the WTO's extensive reports on its diverse membership's views on the subject, as well as the organization's prior efforts, as in connection with Trade Related Investment Measures (TRIMs) or the General Agreement on Trade in Services (GATS).[29] Those who, desiring a successful conclusion to such a negotiation, propose adding investment issues to the next WTO Round would presumably be doing so because they want investment guarantees to extend to the WTO's global membership, because even the "lesser" investor rights, and possible duties, would presumably be subject to binding WTO dispute settlement open only to GATT parties (and not directly to investors themselves as under bilateral investment treaties [BITs] and NAFTA's Chapter 11) because the failure of the OECD's prior efforts leaves no other credible organizational option, or because of some other presumed benefit, such as possible trade offs with respect to other issues anticipated within the same trade round. As this suggests, organizational venues and the information they produce considerably enhance the likelihood of "nesting" issues in a broader context so that the "fabric of one provides the foundation of another"[30] as well as with respect to making links between issues that facilitate package deals. It is also important to recognize that information produced by one organizational venue in the course of one treaty negotiation, such as the lengthy negotiations to conclude the U.N. Convention on the Law of the Sea, have had important spillover effects on other negotiations, as with respect to later dealings with respect to environmental accords; such effects are increasingly anticipated, thereby influencing interstate reactions in both the earlier and later sets of negotiations.

A decision to pursue negotiations in a particular organization might also be tantamount to a decision *not* to conclude a full-scale multilateral treaty on the subject but some other kind of instrument. Thus, decisions to initiate discussions in, for example, UNCITRAL, are taken with the full knowledge that, given the practices of that body, this may be tantamount to deciding in favor of either a "model law" that can inspire the harmonization of domestic laws or nonbinding "guidelines" instead of a binding treaty.[31] Certain organizational settings are suited to regulatory or recommendatory action and not the initiation of a binding treaty instrument—and prove themselves attractive negotiating sites precisely for that reason. Indeed, we are becoming increasingly aware that IOs are dramatically changing the other primary source of international obligation—custom—as well as treaties. The new treaty makers are also generating new custom that differs markedly from the slow, laborious accumulation of bilateral practices and expressions of *opinio juris* that characterized traditional customary international law.[32]

As this suggests, international organizations may occasionally have an adverse impact on the possibility that particular multilateral negotiations will be initiated. Judging from the large number of multilateral efforts sponsored annually under their auspices, however, it would appear that the existence of permanent organizational venues for such negotiations has generally made states more amenable to multilateral treaty making—or at least made it more likely that a shrewd initiator will be able to find a forum that favors treaty negotiations.

This implies a fifth and final change from 19th century treaty-making efforts: particularly to the extent anticipated treaty negotiations are to take place within established organizational fora and not through the convening of a special ad hoc conference, support for initiating treaty negotiations may emerge much more easily and quickly than in an earlier age when states were required to mobilize and devote substantial diplomatic and other resources for such efforts. Treaty negotiations are, in short, more likely when they can take advantage of organizational venues whose "sunk costs" have already been absorbed by their members. Voting in favor (or, more common, merely refusing to disturb consensus) of a resolution that directs that international civil servants ought to study "topic x" with respect to the "propriety of concluding an international convention" on said topic is often seen as an anodyne or a relatively cost free decision. Even when a state's delegate to the IO in question realizes that such decision is not really cost free and that it may begin a process whose momentum may prove difficult to stop, it is usually less painful politically to join consensus in favor of initiating treaty negotiations than resist. In addition, to the extent organizational venues with a diverse membership tend to expand the potential negotiating agenda and increase the potential for nesting and package deals, these realities increase the numbers of states willing to engage in negotiations or to whom such negotiations are of interest.

Notes

1. Stewart Patrick, *Multilateralism and its Discontents: The Causes and Consequences of U.S. Ambivalence*, in *Multilateralism and U.S. Foreign Policy* 10 (Stewart Patrick & Shepard Forman eds., 2002).

2. *United States Senate, Treaties and Other International Agreements: The Role of the United States Senate—A Study Prepared for the Committee on Foreign Relations*, S. Doc. No. 106–71, 106th Cong., 2d Sess. 39 (2001). A study of the treaty practices of the United States in the most recent period, after its rise to the status of sole superpower, finds traditional U.S. ambivalence towards adherence to treaties only "slightly more marked" than in prior periods. See Nico Krisch, *Weak as a Constraint, Strong as a Tool: The Place of International Law in U.S. Foreign Policy*, in *Unilateralism and U.S. Foreign Policy* (David Malone & Yuen Foong Khong eds., 2003).

3. At present, there are more than 250 conventional international governmental organizations, roughly another 5,200 intergovernmental bodies of various kinds, and over 1,500 non-governmental organizations registered with the U.N. See Charlotte Ku, *Global Governance and the Changing Face of International Law*, 2 AUNS Rep. And Papers 5, 24 (2001). While these numbers are impressive, it is important to recognize that international institutions have life cycles and occasionally die. The growth in these institutions "occasionally plateau[s] following periodic organizing burst." Id. at 22 (quoting Shanks, Jacobson, and Kaplan).

4. Paul Szasz, *General Law-Making Processes*, in 35 United Nations Legal Order 59 (Oscar Schachter & Christopher C. Joyner eds., 1995). While, according to one study, there were only eighty-six multilateral treaties concluded in the 100 years between 1751–1850, there were more than 2,000 concluded for the twenty-five year period between 1951–1975. Ku, *supra* note 10, at 5. This is not to suggest, however, either that the number of multilateral treaties has been rising in predictable or steady fashion over recent years or that even greater numbers of traditional intergovernmental organizations on the model of the U.N. are being established by such treaties. Neither is true. That study reveals a drop-off in the number of new multilateral treaties being concluded in the 1976–1995 period compared to the period of 1951–1976, along with a decrease in the number of treaties that create conventional intergovernmental organizations in the model of the U.N. Id. at 5–23. That study also indicates that multilateral treaties intended for general participation by all states still constitute a minority of all treaties concluded annually and that the bulk of treaty making remains on a bilateral basis. Id. at 5. But note that the absence of growth in traditional intergovernmental organizations does not signify a withdrawal of commitment from other forms of institutionalization considered here, including the rise in unconventional forms of institutions. For a survey of these in one specified field, see for example, Paul C. Szasz, *The Proliferation of Arms Control Organizations*, in *Proliferation of International Organizations* 135 (N. M. Blokker & H. G. Schermers eds., 2001); see also Philippe Sands & Pierre Klein, *Bowett's Law of International Institutions* 121–28 (5th ed. 2001) (discussing environmental accords).

5. Roy Lee, *Multilateral Treaty-Making and Negotiation Techniques: An Appraisal*, in *Contemporary Problems of International Law: Essays in Honour of Georg Schwarzenberger on His Eightieth Birthday* 157 (Bin Chang & Edward Brown eds., 1998).

6. Id. at 158.

7. See id. at 177–216.

8. See, e.g., Sands & Klein, *supra* note 11, at 1–4. This is not to deny the impact, over the long term, of conferences such as the First Hague Peace Conference in 1899 which, in the views of some, helped to usher in the modern period devoted to building international institutions culminating in the establishment of the League of Nations. See, e.g., Ku, *supra* note 10, at 14–15.

9. See, e.g., Sands & Klein, *supra* note 11, at 3–4.

10. For a survey and critique of path dependency theory, see S. J. Liebowitz & Stephen E. Margolis, *Path Dependence, Lock-in, and History*, 11 J. L. Econ. & Org. 205 (1995). For consideration of the relevance of path dependency to the evolution of the common law, see Oona A. Hathaway, *Path Dependence in the Law: The Course and Pattern of Legal Change in a Common Law System*, 86 Iowa L. Rev. 601, 622–30 (2001).

11. Robbie Sabel, *A Study of the Rules of Procedure for Conferences and Assemblies of International Intergovernmental Organizations* (1997).

12. Gunter Handl, *Environmental Security and Global Change: The Challenge of International Law* in *Environmental Protection and International Law* 199 (W. Lang et al. eds., 1991).

13. See Kenneth W. Abbott, *Rule-Making in the WTO: Lessons from the Case of Bribery and Corruption*, 4 J. Int'l. Econ. L. 275, 282–83 (2001). Abbott goes on to explain that business interests did not pursue their interests in transnational regulation on bribery within the WTO because leveling the playing field against the smaller non-OECD competitors "was not a sufficiently high priority." Id. at 282.

14. Id.

15. Such as the ILC.

16. E.g., in the assemblies of various IOs representing the full membership.

17. Such as in ICAOs Legal Committee.

18. As in the WTO.

19. See, e.g., id. at 289–90 (noting how the U.S.'s strategy with respect to the regulation of bribery was highly congenial to the OECD given that organization's tendency to act through a variety of both hard and soft instruments, as well as reliance on peer review and public pressure rather than litigation).

20. Id.

21. I owe this colorful turn of phrase to Joel Trachtman.

22. See, e.g., Abbott, *supra* note 20, at 286, 291. Abbott contends that the WTO's culture of focusing on market access to the exclusion of more normative dimensions as well as emphasis on hard law rather than softer obligations, made it an unlikely forum for focusing on the normative aspects of the bribery and corruption issue in the ways that the OECD was able to do. Id. at 286–291.

23. For a discussion of the early evolution of an Operational Protocol to CEDAW, and the impact of U.N.-sponsored human rights conferences at Vienna (1993) and Beijing (1995), see Lilly Sharipa-Behrmann, *An Optimal Protocol to CEDAW: A Further Step Towards Strengthening of Women's Human Rights*, in *Liber Amicorum: Professor Ignaz Siedl Honhenveldern in Honour of His 80th Birthday* 683 (Gerhard Hafner et al. eds., 1998). For a critical view of the significant role played by NGOs with respect to the landmines convention, see Kenneth Anderson, *The Ottawa Convention Banning Landmines, the Role of International Non-governmental Organizations and the Idea of International Civil Society*, 11 Eur. J. Int'l. L. 91 (2000).

24. Indeed, some believe that international society has entered a new post-institutional period dominated by international civil society. See, e.g., Ku, *supra* note 10 at 26–34 (noting the larger rise in the numbers of NGOs relative to the more modest increase in the numbers of traditional intergovernmental organizations).

25. Nor, of course, does power cease to be relevant once negotiations begin or a treaty is concluded. As ICAO's anti-terrorism conventions remind us, use of an organizational venue for purposes of negotiation does not ensure that organizational mechanisms will be used for enforcement. Those conventions avoid the use of established ICAO fora, including the methods of dispute settlement within ICAO's con-

stitution (resort to the ICAO Council and to the ICJ). Instead, the extradition and prosecution regime effectively puts the onus of enforcement back on state parties, thereby giving powerful states, capable of exerting leverage on others, considerable free rein.

26. See Tokyo Convention on Offenses and Certain Other Acts Committed on Board Aircraft, Sept. 14, 1963, 20 U.S.T. 2941, 704 U.N.T.S. 219; Hague Convention for the Suppression of Unlawful Seizures of Aircraft, Dec. 16, 1970, 22 U.S.T. 1641, 860 U.N.T.S. 105; Montreal Convention for the Suppression of Unlawful Acts Against the Safety of Civil Aviation, Sept. 23, 1971, 24 U.S.T. 565; Protocol for the Suppression of Unlawful Acts of Violence at Airports Serving International Civil Aviation, Feb. 24, 1988, ICAO Doc. 9518, 27 I.L.M. 627.

27. See Geoffrey M. Levitt, *Democracies Against Terror* 10–11 (1988) (discussing history of the 1970 Hague Convention for the Suppression of Unlawful Seizure of Aircraft).

28. See, e.g., Robin R. Churchill & Geir Ulfstein, *Autonomous Institutional Arrangements in Multilateral Environmental Agreements: A Little-Noticed Phenomenon in International Law,* 94 AM. J. Int'l. L. 623 (2000). For a more critical view of managerial regimes, see George W. Downs et al., *The Transformative Model of International Regime Design: Triumph of Hope or Experience?* Colum. J. Transnat'l L. 465 (2000).

29. See General Agreement on Trade in Services, Apr. 15, 1974, Marrakesh Agreement Establishing the World Trade Organization, Annex 1B, *Legal Instruments—Results of the Uruguay Round,* 33 I.L.M. 1167 (1994) [hereinafter GATS]; Agreement on Trade Related Investment Measures, Apr. 15, 1994, Marrakesh Agreement Establishing the World Trade Organization, Annex 1A, *Legal Instruments—Results of the Uruguay Round* 33 I.L.M. 81 (1994) [hereinafter TRIMS]; see also *International Trade Law Handbook* 387–531 (Raj Bhala ed., 2001). These Agreements are also available on the WTO web site at http://www.wto.org (last visited Feb. 21, 2002).

30. For a description of nesting, see Duncan Snidal, *The Game Theory of International Politics,* 58 World Pol. 25, 45 (1985).

31. For a recent report of UNCITRAL's efforts, see *Report of the United Nations Commission on International Trade Law on the Works of its Thirty-Second Session,* U.N. GAOR, 54th Sess., Supp. No. 17, U.N. Doc. A/54/17 (1999).

32. New custom may emerge from consciously created norms applicable even with respect to non-parties to a widely ratified convention; it may also result from information generated in plenary organizational fora such as the U.N. General Assembly. See Jonathan I. Charney, *Universal International Law,* 87 AM. J. Int'l. L. 529, 536–42 (1995).

CHAPTER 6

Nongovernmental Organizations and International Law

Steve Charnovitz

NONGOVERNMENTAL ORGANIZATIONS (NGOs) HAVE EXERTED a profound influence on the scope and dictates of international law. NGOs have fostered treaties, promoted the creation of new international organizations (IOs), and lobbied in national capitals to gain consent to stronger international rules. A decade ago, Antonio Donini, writing about the United Nations, declared that "the Temple of States would be a rather dull place without nongovernmental organisations."[1] His observation was apt and is suggestive of a more general thesis: had NGOs never existed, international law would have a less vital role in human progress.

Often it has been crusading NGOs that led the way for states to see the international dimension of what was previously regarded as a purely domestic matter. As new issues arose in international affairs, interested NGOs formed federations or networks with organizations in different countries. This transnationalism has served as a source of strength for NGOs in their various interactions with governments. NGOs act as a solvent against the strictures of sovereignty.

The contribution of NGOs to the vibrancy of international law is a puzzle because, doctrinally, international law is understood to be a product of state positivism. The key to the puzzle lies in the nature of NGOs. Like the state, the NGO is composed of individuals, but unlike the state, the NGO enjoys a relationship with the individual that is voluntary. Individuals join and support an NGO out of commitment to its purpose. That purpose plus organization gives NGOs whatever "authority" they have, and it will be moral authority rather than legal authority.

The self-actuated nature of NGOs distinguishes them from typical IOs,

---

whose mandates are agreed to and limited by states. NGOs do not gain their influence from delegation by states. Rather, whatever influence they have is achieved through the attractiveness of their ideas and values. No NGO is guaranteed influence, not even the most venerable of NGOs, the Red Cross movement. Influence must constantly be earned.

NGOs can change the behavior of states, but very often NGOs fail to do so.[2] Measuring NGO success has become more complicated because for many important issues, competing NGOs have been positioned on all sides of any debate. Years ago, the most involved NGOs were reliable advocates of a stronger world public order. Today, overwhelming NGO support for the international rule of law can no longer be assumed. NGOs follow their own stars.

An appreciation of Simeon E. Baldwin, Wilhelm Kaufmann, and Elihu Root is an appropriate way to begin an analytical survey of international NGO activism spanning the past one hundred years. Earlier than others, Baldwin saw how new modes of transnational "individual action" could change the behavior of states. As the public congresses matured into IOs, the private groups developed more direct forms of advocacy than holding their own assemblies and drafting resolutions for governments. Instead, they found ways to attach themselves to IOs and to be present at international negotiations in order to lobby for manifold causes.

One fairly new aspect of NGOs is their geographic range. Thirty years ago, many countries lacked significant NGO activity. The range of activity was even smaller 145 years ago when Francis Lieber wrote about the role of associations and found that "all-pervading associative spirit" only in England and America.[3] Today, the associative spirit is nearly universal.

I. Who NGOs Are and What They Do

The Identity of NGOs

The NGOs that are the subject of this article are groups of persons or of societies, freely created by private initiative, that pursue an interest in matters that cross or transcend national borders and are not profit seeking.[4] Such NGOs are usually international in the sense of drawing members from more than one country. Although profit-seeking business entities are not NGOs, associations of business entities can be, such as the International Chamber of Commerce.[5]

Everything about nongovernmental organizations is contested, including the meaning of the term. In his 1963 treatise on NGOs, J. J. Lador-Lederer observed that the semantic negation neglects the most significant part of the organizations, which is that their strength comes from "their capacity at continuous existence and development."[6]

The UN system continues to use the term "NGO," and the chief reason for doing so may be because Article 71 of the UN Charter states, "The Economic and Social Council may make suitable arrangements for consultation with non-governmental organizations which are concerned with matters within its competence."[7] The Charter, however, does not define NGO.

Although commentators sometimes suggest that the term "nongovernmental organization" originated during the 1930s or in 1945,[8] it actually goes back to just after World War I. In his 1919 book on international cooperation, Dwight W. Morrow contrasted "non-governmental organizations" with organizations composed of sovereign states.[9] In 1920 Sophy Sanger employed the term "non-government organisation" in her account of how such organizations had not been able to participate in 1906 in the first multilateral negotiations to conclude labor treaties.[10] The label "nongovernmental organization" was apparently not used in the League of Nations. Instead, the NGOs of that era were called unofficial, nonpublic, voluntary, or private organizations. By 1943, if not earlier, scholars of international law had begun to use "non-governmental organization."[11]

Although NGOs are by definition nongovernmental, NGO membership can cover a broader range than just private individuals. A leading example is the IUCN/World Conservation Union, with its variegated membership of 82 states, 111 governmental agencies, and over 800 NGOs. Some NGOs, such as Parliamentarians for Global Action, are composed of individuals who are public officials. Other NGOs, such as United Cities and Local Governments, are composed of subnational governments. That organization harks back to 1913, and today has members in more than 100 countries.

The traditional distinction between an NGO and an IO is that IOs are established by intergovernmental agreements and NGOs via cooperation of individuals. That distinction holds even when IOs provide formal institutional roles for NGOs. For example, the treaties establishing the International Labour Organization (ILO) and the World Tourism Organization provide for nongovernmental roles in organizational governance. So do the charters of the Joint United Nations Programme on HIV/AIDS (UNAIDS) and the Arctic Council.[12]

NGO Functions in International Law

NGOs contribute to the development, interpretation, judicial application, and enforcement of international law.[13]

NGOs may be most prolific when new fields of law are initiated or new treaties drafted. An early example concerns the rights of women. In 1928, after women's groups journeyed to the sixth Pan-American Conference, the governments agreed to hold a plenary session to hear the women's representatives, and accepted their proposal to create the Inter-American Commission of Women.[14] Another major milestone occurred when NGOs advanced language on human rights for the UN Charter and then aided the diplomats drafting the Universal Declaration of Human Rights.[15] Advocacy by NGOs and indigenous groups has been similarly instrumental in achieving new international protections for indigenous peoples. In recent years, networks of NGOs worked to inspirit negotiations for the International Criminal Court.[16]

Another function engaged in by NGOs is the interpretation of international law. For example, NGOs helped to develop the "Siracusa Principles" in 1984, on the meaning and scope of the derogation and limitation provisions of the International Covenant on Civil and Political Rights.[17] Theodor Meron has noted that by championing a broad construction of the Fourth Geneva Convention, the International Committee of the Red Cross (ICRC) clarified that rape is a crime under international humanitarian law.[18]

NGOs seek to contribute to international adjudication by making friend-of-the-court submissions to tribunals. Typically, an NGO initiates action by requesting leave from a court to submit a brief.[19] In an authoritative study of NGO participation, Dinah Shelton found that major international tribunals, except the International Court of Justice (ICJ), had developed procedures to enable NGOs to submit information or statements on pending cases.[20] Since the publication of Shelton's study in 1994, the trends she documented have continued apace.[21] For example, organs of the International Criminal Tribunal for the Former Yugoslavia and the International Criminal Tribunal for Rwanda have requested amicus submissions in some cases and received them from individual jurists and NGOs.[22] On the other hand, NGOs have not yet sought to submit an amicus brief to the International Tribunal for the Law of the Sea.[23]

Although the ICJ remains closed to NGO participation, a useful step toward greater openness was taken in 2004.[24] The ICJ adopted Practice Direction XII, which provides that, in an advisory proceeding, when an international NGO submits a statement or document on its own initiative, it will be placed in a designated location in the Peace Palace.[25] The paper will not be considered part of the case file but will be treated as a readily available publication and may be referred to by states and IOs in the same manner as publications in the public domain.

Over the past decade, amicus curiae briefs have been admitted into trade and investment adjudication. Although no explicit provision in the Agreement Establishing the World Trade Organization (WTO) permits amicus briefs, the Appellate Body ruled in 1998 that WTO panels had discretion to accept unsolicited briefs, and it ruled in 2000 that it could accept such briefs.[26] That development appeared to influence investor-state arbitration under the North American Free Trade Agreement (NAFTA) where, to the surprise of many observers, in 2001 the tribunal in *Methanex* held that it had the power to accept written amicus submissions.[27] Thereafter, the intergovernmental NAFTA Free Trade Commission issued a statement officially recommending a procedure that investor-state tribunals could adopt to guide such private submissions.[28] When the *Methanex* tribunal issued its final award in August 2005, the decision contained a reference to the "carefully reasoned Amicus submission."[29] Following *Methanex*, two other investment arbitration tribunals ruled that they had the power to accept amicus briefs.[30] These developments are significant because amicus submissions in investment arbitration were unknown before 2001.

Despite the initial fanfare regarding NGO opportunities at the WTO, neither the Appellate Body nor the panels have made substantive use of the information in amicus curiae submissions.[31]

In contrast to their participation as amici, the ability of NGOs to initiate cases is less extensive. One tribunal that has been open to NGOs is the African Commission on Human and Peoples' Rights, which has allowed states, individuals, and NGOs with observer status to submit communications alleging a violation of the African Charter.[32] The European Court of Human Rights permits an NGO to bring a case if the NGO itself claims to be a victim. Other opportunities present themselves in international administrative entities that permit NGOs to bring complaints. For example, the World Bank Inspection Panel entertains requests for inspection from an organization, association, society, or other grouping of two or more individuals that believes it is likely to be adversely affected as a result of the Bank's violation of its own policies and procedures.[33]

NGOs are now often engaged in the review and promotion of state compliance with international obligations. Oscar Schachter, a keen observer, detected this budding development in 1960,[34] and in the following decades, the NGO role flowered in the monitoring of human rights, humanitarian, and environmental law.[35] In their 1995 book *The New Sovereignty*, Abram Chayes and Antonia Chayes devoted a chapter to the impact of NGOs on treaty compliance, and pointed out that, "[i]n a real sense, [NGOs] supply the personnel and resources for managing compliance that states have become increasingly reluctant to provide."[36] In the decade since that book was published, the NGO role has continued to expand. For example, the parties to the Aarhus Convention agreed to allow NGOs with observer status to nominate candidates for the Convention's Compliance Committee.[37] NGOs can also play an important role within a domestic political system in pressing the government to meet its obligations under a ratified treaty.

The last NGO function to be noted is assistance to collective enforcement efforts. For example, in a 1992 resolution regarding the former Yugoslavia, the UN Security Council called on states "and, as appropriate, international humanitarian organizations to collate substantiated information" relating to violations of humanitarian law.[38] In a 2003 resolution regarding Sierra Leone, the Security Council called on "States, international organizations and non-governmental organizations to continue to support the National Recovery Strategy of the Government of Sierra Leone."[39]

II. Legal Status of NGOs

The analysis in this part examines the legal status of NGOs in two senses—their legal personality and the special capacity they can gain to take part in intergovernmental decision making.

NGO Personality

Legal personality is a key factor in determining the rights and immunities of an NGO and its standing before courts. In general, an NGO enjoys legal personality only in municipal law, not in international law.[40] Yet because NGOs so often operate in more than one country, they face potential problems of being subject to conflicting laws and of inability to carry their legal status from one country to another.[41]

Transnational NGOs have learned how to maneuver without formal international personality. In some instances, the crucial role that an NGO plays has led governments to accord rights to it that are typically granted only to IOs. For example, the ICRC and the International Federation of Red Cross and Red Crescent Societies have signed headquarters agreements with numerous states that provide for certain privileges and immunities.[42]

Over the years, the efforts to achieve an international legal personality for NGOs have exposed some unresolved tensions. On the one hand, providing such recognition may help prevent interstate conflicts and, in the words of the 1923 draft convention, may further "the general interest of the international community to encourage the development of non-profit-making international associations."[43] On the other hand, states have worried that granting international recognition to NGOs may reduce governmental control over them, and NGOs have worried that such recognition might entail a loss of autonomy. With the increased attention to NGO (mis)behavior in recent years, a new treaty would more likely impose regulation on NGOs than facilitate freedom of association.[44]

NGOs as Consultation Partners

In the absence of international NGO law as such, Article 71 of the UN Charter has served de facto as a charter for NGO activities. The legal capacity of the NGO under Article 71 might be termed a consultation partner. Although Article 71 establishes consultative opportunities for the NGOs granted status by the UN Economic and Social Council (ECOSOC), an individual NGO does not have a treaty-based right to be consulted in a particular situation.

Article 71, written in 1945, reflected established IO consultative practices regarding NGOs.[45] The first treaty to provide for NGO input was the 1905 convention creating the International Institute of Agriculture. One of the duties of the institute was to

> [s]ubmit to the approval of the governments, if there is occasion for it, measures for the protection of the common interests of farmers and for the improvement of their condition, after having utilized all the necessary sources of information, such as the wishes expressed by international or other agricultural congresses or congresses of sciences applied to agriculture, agricultural societies, academies, learned bodies, etc.[46]

Thus, the congresses and societies were designated as sources of information for intergovernmental decision making. When participating governments drafted the Covenant of the League of Nations in 1919, they included Article 25, which stated that "[t]he Members of the League agree to encourage and promote the establishment and co-operation of duly authorised voluntary national Red Cross organisations."[47] That article was inserted at the suggestion of the League of Red Cross Societies, and led to extensive cooperation between the League of Nations and the Red Cross movement.

By the early 1920s, active collaboration between the League of Nations and unofficial organizations was an established practice and would continue throughout the life of the League.[48] For example, the League of Nations spearheaded the creation of the International Relief Union, whose founding convention provided a "consultative capacity" for relief organizations and other qualified organizations and called for "free co-operation" between the union and "other official or non-official organisations."[49] The League of Red Cross Societies played an important role in drafting the convention and presenting it to governments.[50]

Just as the Red Cross societies in 1919 sought to gain a textual foothold in the League of Nations Covenant, a rainbow of NGOs in 1945 sought to gain such a foothold in the UN Charter. The major commentaries on the Charter miss[51] the entrepreneurial role of the NGOs at the San Francisco Conference in lobbying for and securing Article 71 so as to endow themselves with an official status.[52] In view of the longtime pre-1945 practice of a consultative role for NGOs in IOs, the legislating of Article 71 was more incremental than transformational.

Nevertheless, Article 71 soon took on an importance far broader than its own text and, for that reason, the status attained by NGOs through Article 71 became a foundation stone for their efforts to strengthen international law. Even though Article 71 refers only to ECOSOC, a consultative role for NGOs gradually became an established practice throughout the UN system. [53]

Although many of these ECOSOC rules have remained constant, some have changed significantly. First, the 1950 NGO Rule required that an NGO be of "recognized standing" *and* that it "represent a substantial proportion of the organized persons within the particular field in which it operates."[54] By contrast, the 1996 Rule dispenses with this two-part requirement. Now the NGO must "be of recognized standing within the particular field of its competence or of a representative character."[55] Second, the preference in the 1950 Rule for international, rather than national, NGOs has now been eliminated.[56] Third, the 1996 Rule adds a requirement that an NGO given status "have a democratically adopted constitution" and that it "have a representative structure and possess appropriate mechanisms of accountability to its members, who shall exercise effective control over its policies and actions through the exercise of voting rights or other appropriate democratic and transparent decision-making processes."[57] This attention to internal NGO governance reflects the growing concerns in the early 1990s about the legitimacy and accountability of NGOs.

The 1996 NGO Rule codified the existing practice of suspending or withdrawing consultative status from NGOs that no longer meet the eligibility requirements or that misbehave as perceived by ECOSOC's Committee on Non-governmental Organizations. For example, engaging in "unsubstantiated or politically motivated acts" against UN member states can be grounds for losing status.[58] An NGO challenged by the government-only ECOSOC committee is to be given written reasons and accorded an opportunity to present its response.[59]

The work of the committee in granting and reviewing accreditation of NGOs has been criticized for overpoliticization and lack of due process.[60] At present, no judicial review is available for a refusal by ECOSOC to grant an NGO consultative status. In my view, ECOSOC could increase the committee's credibility by permitting some NGOs to serve as members.

The consultation norms underlying Article 71 have influenced institutional developments outside the United Nations. For example, in 1999 the Organization of American States (OAS) adopted the Guidelines for the Participation of Civil Society Organizations in OAS Activities.[61] In 2001 the Constitutive Act of the African Union called for the establishment of an advisory Economic, Social and Cultural Council composed of different social and professional groups of the member states.[62] Another example of mimesis is the Antarctic Treaty consultative process where designated NGOs, such as the International Association of Antarctica Tour Operators, are permitted to participate.

III. How NGOs Changed International Law

In a recent study, José Alvarez observed: "Although the impact of NGOs on legal development ebbs and flows, no one questions today the fact that international law—both its content and its impact—has been forever changed by the empowerment of NGOs."[63] Indeed, an extensive body of scholarship now attests to the importance of NGOs to developments in international law.[64] With the rise of NGOs in international policymaking, thoughtful writers have seen the increasing tensions between reality and international law orthodoxy. For instance, in 1932 political scientist Stanley H. Bailey wrote that "[t]he interposition of the fiction of the personified state conceals the reality that the greater part of the world-order is built out of the innumerable associations of individuals and groups which have not directly entered the sphere of governmental relations."[65]

In a lecture delivered a decade ago, Judge Higgins pointed to NGO demands as one phenomenon in "the reformation in international law."[66] An aspect of that reformation is a change in "the concept of international law" and, in particular, "in our notions of" the identity of the users and beneficiaries of international law.[67] Thus, in taking note of NGOs as players in UN conferences, Higgins wrote that "[t]he interest of NGOs, and indeed their entitlement to be present at these gatherings, has been an important matter for them and for governments alike."[68]

The reformation of international law extends both to content and to process. The vastly expanded content of international law has been stimulated by NGOs, particularly in human rights, humanitarian, and environmental law. Through their focus on the rights of individuals, rather than the rights (and sovereignty) of states, leading NGOs surely deserve credit for helping to humanize modern international law, both treaty and customary.[69]

NGOs helped to transform the processes of international law as they learned how to mobilize states and leverage public opinion. As the mode of diplomacy changed from bilateral contracts to plurilateral law, NGOs invited themselves to the constitutive events, first as petitioners and later as accredited observers. The Congress of Vienna of 1814–1815 was the first intergovernmental conference to feature extensive lobbying by private actors.[70] The Hague Peace Conference of 1899 attracted a mélange of voluntary associations, and inaugurated the idea of the NGO parallel conference.[71] The League Conference of 1923 to draft the Convention Relating to the Simplification of Customs Formalities may have been the earliest intergovernmental negotiation in which an NGO—the International Chamber of Commerce—was specifically accredited to participate.[72]

NGOs as Competitors

What made international law susceptible to being influenced by NGOs? One of the earliest insights was the NGO advantage in being independent. NGOs can be more creative than government officials because NGOs are not burdened with the need to champion a particular national or governmental interest.

Another factor that may explain the influence of NGOs has been their ability to construct and encourage new norms for an interdependent world. In 1902 Pierre Kazansky perceived that the activities of international societies and associations were leading to the development of "international social interests."[73] This result contributed to what Kazansky called "international administration," which is "activity of states, international societies and their organs" directed to the "goal of protecting international social interests."[74] During the past decade, scholars looking at NGO and other nonstate participation have employed the terms "transnational advocacy networks," "transnational norm entrepreneurs," "nongovernmental norm entrepreneurs," and "transnational moral entrepreneurs."[75] As these terms indicate, the NGO seeks to sell its norms to authoritative decision makers and the public.

The concept of the entrepreneurial NGO animates theories about states and IOs. In an article about why NGOs should be able to participate in the WTO, Daniel Esty contended that nongovernmental "competition" could lead to a richer WTO politics, which could help improve the effectiveness of the WTO.[76] In his Hague Academy lecture, Judge Raymond Ranjeva analyzed the NGO as a "competitor" important to the implementation of international law.[77] The role of NGOs as norm entrepreneurs has also been incorporated into theories of why states obey international law.[78]

Successful NGOs have gained advantage through innovation and adaptation. Nobel Prize co-winner Jody Williams famously remarked about the importance of the Internet, electronic mail, and facsimile communication to the land mines campaign. Yet that same story of utilizing technology for publicity can be told about many NGO campaigns—for example, the use of the slide show by the Congo Reform movement in the early 1900s. NGO mobility is another advantage. Being autonomous and nimble, NGOs can travel to trouble spots where governments or IOs fear to go or are slow to reach.

Assessing the NGO contribution to the reformation of international law requires special attention to the IO. NGOs were key proponents of establishing some of the earliest IOs. Once an IO is set up, interested NGOs will typically seek information about its activities and access to observe and influence decision making in the IO. Such acts of NGO self-interest need no explanation.

Less obvious is why governments agree to give access to NGOs. Over the years, many rational-choice explanations have been offered for this phenomenon, including that NGOs provide needed expertise, enhance public support for the IO, and assist in the domestic internalization of norms developed in the IO. Analysts have explored "the symbiotic relationship between IOs and NGOs" with the two sides offering mutual legitimation.[79] This relationship is carried out openly. For example, UN secretary-general Kofi

Annan has declared: "I see a United Nations which recognizes that the NGO revolution—the new global people-power—is the best thing that has happened to our Organization in a long time."[80]

Some scholars have emphasized the symmetry of the IOs and the international-minded NGOs in that both are nonstate actors pursuing international goals.[81] Although that model is valid, a better model for analysis may be to consider the IO not as an actor to which authority has been delegated but, rather, as a designated arena where various governmental and nongovernmental participants compete and cooperate."[82] Appreciating the sites of international decision making as arenas in which NGOs compete for public support avoids a more problematic interpretation of the NGO role, namely, that NGOs represent the public.

The international arena with the thickest nongovernmental participation is the ILO. Over the years, many analysts have suggested applying the ILO's method of NGO participation to other intergovernmental bodies,[83] but this has not happened. The tripartism of the ILO worked because in 1919 the workers, employers, and governments were the principal stakeholders. In the postindustrial world, however, few important international employment issues involve only three principal stakeholders. Indeed, as Virginia Leary pointed out, the ILO's tripartism may impede it from offering adequate participatory opportunities to other NGOs, such as human rights groups."[84] Beyond the ILO, a tripartite government-business-NGO formula for IOs is imaginable, but surely too compartmentalized for the plethora of market and nonmarket interests in play today.

IV. The Legitimacy of NGO Participation

The question whether the tripartism of the ILO was legitimate did not generate much attention in 1919 in the negotiations that established the ILO. Yet today the legitimacy of milder forms of NGO participation is under attack.

In the 1996 ICJ *Nuclear Weapons* cases, Judges Gilbert Guillaume and Shigeru Oda separately expressed concerns about the propriety of NGO influence on governments. Judge Guillaume, while agreeing to comply with the request by the UN General Assembly, issued a separate opinion saying that the Court could have dismissed that request (as well as the request by the World Health Organization) as inadmissible because it had originated in a campaign conducted by associations and groups.[85]

Kenneth Anderson and David Rieff have offered a more detailed analysis of the legitimacy of NGO advocacy.[86] In part, they object to the inflated rhetoric asserting that internationally active NGOs make up "global civil society" and that, as such, speak for the people(s) of the world.

In my view, an NGO cannot justify its own activist role on the claim that it represents the public. So Anderson and Rieff are right to criticize the pretentious assertions of some NGOs.[87] Nevertheless, their argument misses the possibility that more open and inclusive processes of decision making can help to overcome the allegedly attenuated democratic legitimacy of international governance.

Throughout the twentieth century, many commentators have examined nongovernmental participation in IOs and reflected on what that might mean for democracy. For example, in 1927 Georges Scelle chronicled the role of professional interests and private organizations in the ILO and the League of Nations, and saw in that practice an evolution "toward the gradual creation of an international 'democracy'."[88] A few years ago, James Crawford and Susan Marks observed that "the vastly enhanced participation in recent years of non-governmental organizations at the international level is one indication of the pressures and possibilities for democracy in global decision-making."[89] And Menno Kamminga has written that by contributing the views of civil society, NGOs "confer badly needed legitimacy on the international system."[90] A common thread in this stream of scholarship is that the nation-state does not constitute the highest level attainable by democracy.

Intergovernmental consultations with NGOs can enhance the legitimacy of international decision making, but it is the consultation itself that makes the contribution, not the quantity of NGO support obtained.

As Florentino Feliciano pointed out several decades ago, our world is "a graduated series of community contexts—each exhibiting a public order system—of varying territorial scope."[91] Every territorial context can be relevant and legitimate for use by an NGO motivated by an international mission. Indeed, the most successful NGOs operate at many levels in localities, national capitals, and international arenas. They play multilevel games.

How is legitimacy attained? A study by Daniel Bodansky, focusing on international environmental law, posits three bases of legitimacy—state consent, procedural fairness, and the substantive outcomes achieved.[92] A study by Robert O. Keohane and Joseph S. Nye Jr., focusing on the WTO, suggests that legitimacy at the international level depends on both the procedures followed ("inputs") and the results obtained ("outputs").[93] Keohane and Nye call attention to existing mechanisms for "nonelectoral accountability" through a "communicative environment" that may involve "global publics" such as NGOs, even when there is no "global community."[94] They conclude that "some form of NGO representation in the institutions involved in multilateral governance. . . could help to maintain their legitimacy."[95] In a more recent study on the sources of normative legitimacy of multilateral decision making, Keohane contends that in the twenty-first century, only democratic principles, appropriately adopted, can confer legitimacy.[96]

Whether NGO participation adds to, or detracts from, the legitimacy of international decision making can be explored through an analysis of inputs and outputs. The input is the process of decision making. The output is the effectiveness of the decisions reached.

NGOs facilitate input legitimacy in several ways. One is to promote accountability by monitoring what government delegates say and do in the IO and to communicate that information to elected officials and the public. Another is to help assure that decision makers are aware of the sympathies and interests of the people who will be affected by intergovernmental decisions.[97]

The contribution of NGOs to input legitimacy may depend on several factors. One is the independence and integrity of the NGO. During the past decade, many analysts have pointed to the need for NGOs to be transparent and accountable.[98] Another factor is whether a consultation process assures a fair balance of NGOs from different parts of the world.[99] Over the past twenty years, NGOs have joined together more often in large coalitions, a practice that can overcome narrow-minded perspectives.

NGOs can contribute to output legitimacy in several ways. One is to offer their specialized expertise to enable more informed decisions. NGOs can often be sources of information that governments may not have. Another is to raise the quality of policy deliberations so that the choices available are better understood.[100]

Of course, NGO participation does not necessarily improve the outputs from IOs or multilateral negotiations. Consultation with NGOs takes time, which can exact a cost. Moreover, while inviting the NGOs in makes the entire process more transparent to the public, such transparency can lead to different results than would ensue if governments arrived at agreements behind closed doors. Sometimes the involvement of NGOs in negotiations has led governments to formulate impractical agreements.

V. Toward a Duty to Consult NGOs

The practice of consulting with NGOs is widespread and continues to expand. For most of its existence, the UN Security Council appeared to be off-limits for NGOs, but that insularity ended in 1997 when NGOs began to brief groups of Council members and then, in 2004, the Council itself.[101] NGOs have occasionally addressed special sessions of the UN General Assembly and, in September 2005, two NGO leaders made short presentations to the World Summit.[102] During the 1990s, NGOs gained some limited opportunities to provide input within the World Bank, and to a lesser extent, the International Monetary Fund. The international financial institution for the environment, the Global Environment Facility (GEF), provides for five

NGOs to participate in GEF Council meetings and these NGOs are chosen by the GEF's NGO network.

Only a few multilateral agencies continue to resist adopting an NGO consultation process. In 2006 the most notable holdout is the WTO. The ostensible reason was given in a WTO decision enacted in 1996, which noted "the special character of the WTO, which is both a legally binding intergovernmental treaty of rights and obligations among its Members and a forum for negotiations."[103] The decision went on to state that "there is currently a broadly held view that it would not be possible for NGOs to be directly involved in the work of the WTO or its meetings."[104] A decade later, that view remains strongly held—even though international NGOs are now exerting more influence on high-profile trade issues, such as maintaining access to pharmaceuticals and reducing trade-distorting agricultural subsidies.

Another (embarrassing) footdragger is the International Law Commission (ILC), which does not provide opportunities for NGO.[105] Yet it seems only a matter of time until a more progressive approach to codification flowers there, too. The ILC already has authority in its Statute to "consult with any international or national organizations, official or non-official, on any subject entrusted to it if it believes that such a procedure might aid it in the performance of its functions."[106] A good first step for the ILC would be to hold a one-day public hearing during its annual session.

In view of this breadth of practice on consulting NGOs, the question whether states or IOs have a duty to consult NGOs is an interesting one. The answer appears to be no at this time, but a review of the sources of law can be instructive.

The main human rights treaties do contain some important language on point. The International Covenant on Civil and Political Rights states that "[e]veryone shall have the right to freedom of expression; this right shall include freedom to seek, receive and impart information and ideas of all kinds, *regardless of frontiers*."[107] The American Declaration of the Rights and Duties of Man states that "[e]very person has the right to submit respectful petitions to any competent authority, for reasons of either general or private interest, and the right to obtain a prompt decision thereon."[108] Yet those provisions may be too general to demonstrate a duty to consult.

A review of specialized treaties shows an incorporation of NGO consultation processes, but the treaties typically do not enthrone a duty. Aside from the special case of the ILO, where employer and worker delegates serve as group representatives on the Governing Body, the usual practice in international regimes is that participation of NGOs is permissive rather than mandatory. For example, the convention on land mines lists relevant NGOs among the entities that *may* be invited to attend meetings of states parties, review conferences, or amendment conferences.[109]

Yet there is one important exception: The environment regime has given NGO participation legal mooring. Several multilateral environmental agreements call for the automatic admission of NGO observers. The first to do so was the Convention on International Trade in Endangered Species of Wild Fauna and Flora (CITES) of 1973.

After CITES, other major environmental agreements were written using similar language except for "may be admitted" rather than "shall be admitted."[110] Nevertheless, such provisions still maintain a presumption for granting observer status to NGOs.

One objection to a claim of an international duty to consult is that there is not yet a binding international norm obliging states to consult with NGOs in domestic legislative, executive, or judicial decision making. That would be a powerful argument, on the assumption that a norm regarding the international level must move up from the national level. Yet that assumption may be unjustified. For example, according to Lyman White, a leading scholar on NGOs in the mid–twentieth century, ECOSOC's implementation of Article 71 culminating in the 1950 Rule "went further in extending to Non-Governmental Organizations opportunities for the presentation of their views than have ever been extended to nongovernmental groups by any national government."[111] The general point is that IOs are not limited to being the lowest common denominator of the states composing them.

The views of publicists should also be examined in ascertaining whether there is a duty to consult. Over the past several years, several commentators have suggested that international decision makers have an obligation to provide consultative opportunities for private groups, or contended that NGOs have a right to render advice.[112]

Writing in different centuries, Immanuel Kant and Nathan Feinberg propounded a similar thesis that states have an obligation to listen to nongovernmental opinion and to take it into account when making decisions affecting other nations. What Kant and Feinberg recognized in their times has become a clearer reality in our time.

Looking to the future in 1971, Louis Sohn took note of the fact that UN bodies were assigning a slightly bigger role to NGOs, and suggested that "[i]f this continues over a number of years, their role may become very important."[113] Sohn's prediction was so much on target that in recent years, some commentators have worried about the possibility that government consultation with NGOs has become sufficiently extensive to have an adverse effect on international decision making. One such concern is that too much of a good thing leads to NGO congestion. Another of these concerns is that the exertion of pressure on negotiations by single-interest NGOs makes it harder to formulate a genuine common interest.

The concern that the NGO pursuit of a solitary interest can lead to a counterproductive outcome may have some validity, but significant benefits are gained from the robust debate that ensues. For example, whatever the faults of the environment NGOs and development NGOs that criticized international economic policy in the 1990s, they succeeded in exposing the dangers of insularity in the WTO and the Bretton Woods institutions. That experience points to a practical benefit of NGOs, which is that they can help to cross-fertilize norms among IOs. In addition, the traditional political economy concern about partial and special interests will have less applicability to NGOs that espouse process-based causes (e.g., Transparency International).

The pursuit of individual interests by NGOs leaves open the question of how to reconcile competing interests. In a paper presented to the 1939 annual meeting of the American Society of International Law, Roscoe Pound noted the rise of associations and institutions, and identified a need for "[a] theory of interests" to assist in the recognition, classification, comparison, and valuing of "competing interests."[114] That intellectual task remains. In Pound's view, a law governing international relations would have to deal effectively with the claims, demands, and desires being asserted, and he pondered whether one should think of world society as an institution "englobing" states.[115] Looking ahead, I predict that NGOs will continue to inject competing facts and sentiments into public debate, and that intergovernmental consultations with NGOs will help to achieve more englobing international law in the twenty-first century.

Notes

1. Antonio Donini, The Bureaucracy and the Free Spirits: Stagnation and Innovation in the Relationship Between the UN and NGOs, 16 THIRD WORLD Q. 421 (1995).

2. See Russel Lawrence Barsh & Nadia Khattak, *Non-governmental Organisations in Global Governance: Great Expectations, Inconclusive Results*, in JUSTICE PENDING: INDIGENOUS PEOPLES AND OTHER GOOD CAUSES. ESSAYS IN HONOUR OF ERICA-IRENE DAES 15, 23–26 (Gudmundur Alfredsson & Maria Stavropoulou eds., 2002) (noting a lack of data for demonstrating NGO effectiveness).

3. FRANCIS LIEBER, ON CIVIL LIBERTY AND SELF-GOVERNMENT 129 (enlarged ed. 1859).

4. This definition draws from Article 2 of Professor Suzanne Bastid's resolution cited *infra* note 58, which sought to establish an international status of associations.

5. Unlike other analysts, I do not reserve the term "NGO" for organizations that pursue a "public interest," and I do not exclude from the definition of an NGO the labor unions, professional associations, or other organizations that pursue a "single interest" or a "special interest." In my view, it is not always easy to distinguish a public interest from a special interest or a public benefit from a mutual benefit. Furthermore, a policy organization typically pursues both a membership interest and the organization's conception of the public interest.

6. J. J. LADOR-LEDERER, INTERNATIONAL NON-GOVERNMENTAL

ORGANIZATIONS AND ECONOMIC ENTITIES: A STUDY IN AUTONOMOUS ORGANIZATION AND *IUS GENTIUM* 13 (1963). He suggests an alternative term, "International Autonomous Entities." *Id.*

7. UN Charter Art. 71.

8. For example, Jeremy Rabkin has contended that the term "nongovernmental organization" is "a Stalinist concept" originating in a defense by the Soviet Union of its delegation to the ILO. Jeremy Rabkin, Why the Left Dominates NGO Advocacy Networks, written version of paper delivered at conference entitled "Nongovernmental Organizations: The Growing Power of an Unelected Few," American Enterprise Institute (June 11, 2003), *at* <http://www.aei.org/events/eventID.329,filter.all/event_detail.asp>.

9. DWIGHT W. MORROW, THE SOCIETY OF FREE STATES 81(1919). Morrow was later to serve as a U.S. ambassador and U.S. senator.

10. Sophy Sanger, *Practical Problems of International Labour Legislation, in* LABOUR AS AN INTERNATIONAL PROBLEM 135, 136 (E. John Solano ed., 1920). Sanger was one of the drafters of the provisions on labor in the Treaty of Versailles.

11. See Harold D. Lasswell & Myres S. McDougal, *Legal Education and Public Policy: Professional Training in the Public Interest,* 52 YALE L. J. 203, 221–22 (1943) (using that term).

12. On the UNAIDS Programme Coordinating Board, there are five NGOs, including associations of people living with HIV/AIDS. The Arctic Council includes six permanent participants from organizations of Arctic indigenous persons.

13. See LUNG-CHU CHEN, AN INTRODUCTION TO CONTEMPORARY INTERNATIONAL LAW, ch. 4 (2d ed. 2000) (giving examples of NGO functional activities in intelligence, promoting, prescribing, invoking, applying, terminating, and appraising).

14. James Brown Scott, *Inter-American Commission of Women,* 24 AJIL 757, 759–60 (1930); George A. Finch, *James Brown Scott, 1866–1943,* 38 AJIL 183, 210 (1944) (noting Scott's own role in getting the women heard).

15. See, e.g., ANTONIO CASSESE, HUMAN RIGHTS IN A CHANGING WORLD 173 (1990); WILLIAM KOREY, NGOS AND THE UNIVERSAL DECLARATION OF HUMAN RIGHTS: A CURIOUS GRAPEVINE 29–50 (1998); PAUL GORDON LAUREN, THE EVOLUTION OF INTERNATIONAL HUMAN RIGHTS: VISIONS SEEN 183, 188–89 (1998); W. Michael Reisman, *Private International Declaration Initiatives, in* LA DÉCLARATION UNIVERSELLE DES DROITS DE L'HOMME 1948–98, at 79 (1998); Louis B. Sohn, *The United Nations at Fifty: How American International Lawyers Prepared for the San Francisco Bill of Rights,* 89 AJIL 540 (1995).

16. See, e.g., Mahnoush H. Arsanjani, *The Rome Statute of the International Criminal Court,* 93 AJIL 22, 23–39 (1999).

17. Theo van Boven, *The Role of Non-governmental Organizations in International Human Rights Standard-Setting: A Prerequisite of Democracy,* 20 CAL. W. INT'L. L. J. 207, 219–20 (1990). The NGOs were the International Commission of Jurists, the International Association of Penal Law, and the Urban Morgan Institute of Human Rights.

18. Theodor Meron, *Rape as a Crime Under International Humanitarian Law,* 87 AJIL 424, 426 (1993).

19. Ruth Mackenzie, *The* Amicus Curiae *in International Courts: Towards Common Procedural Approaches? in* CIVIL SOCIETY, INTERNATIONAL COURTS AND COMPLIANCE BODIES 295, 302–04 (Tullio Treves et al. eds., 2005) (discussing filtering mechanisms).

20. Dinah Shelton, *The Participation of Nongovernmental Organizations in International Judicial Proceedings,* 88 AJIL 611, 641–42 (1994). Her study dealt extensively with the Inter-American Court of Human Rights and the European Court of Human Rights.

21. See, e.g., Hervé Ascensio, L'amicus curiae devant les juridictions internationales, 105 REVUE GÉNÉRALE DE DROIT INTERNATIONAL PUBLIC [RGDIP] 897 (2001).

22. Christine Chinkin & Ruth Mackenzie, Intergovernmental Organizations as "Friends of the Court," in INTERNATIONAL ORGANIZATIONS AND INTERNATIONAL DISPUTE SETTLEMENT: TRENDS AND PROSPECTS 135, 148–49 (Laurence Boisson de Chazournes, Cesare P. R. Romano, & Ruth Mackenzie eds., 2002); Patrizia De Cesari, *NGOs and the Activities of the* Ad Hoc *Criminal Tribunals for Former Yugoslavia and Rwanda, in* CIVIL SOCIETY, INTERNATIONAL COURTS AND COMPLIANCE BODIES, *supra* note 19, at 113.

23. Philippe Gautier, *NGOs and Law of the Sea Disputes, in* CIVIL SOCIETY, INTERNATIONAL COURTS AND COMPLIANCE BODIES, *supra* note 19, at 233, 242.

24. Lance Bartholomeusz, *The* Amicus Curiae *Before International Courts and Tribunals,* 5 NON-STATE ACTORS & INT'L L. 209, 212 (2005) ("Although the Court was initially open to NGO participation in its advisory jurisdiction, in 1971 it locked the door, let some materials slip under the door in 1996, and then since 2004 left it slightly ajar.").

25. ICJ, Practice Direction XII (July 30, 2004), available at <http://www.icj-cij.org>.

26. Laurence Boisson de Chazournes & Makane Moïse Mbengue, *The* Amici Curiae *and the WTO Dispute Settlement System: The Doors Are Open,* 2 L. & PRAC. INT'L CTS. & TRIBUNALS 205 (2003).

27. Methanex Corp. and United States, Decision on Petitions from Third Persons to Intervene as "Amici Curiae," paras. 33, 53 (NAFTA Ch. 11 Arb. Trib. Jan. 15, 2001), *available at* <http://www.state.gov/documents/organization/6039.pdf>.

28. Sean D. Murphy, Contemporary Practice of the United States, 98 AJIL 841 (2004).

29. *Methanex,* Final Award on Jurisdiction and Merits, para. 27 (NAFTA Ch. 11 Arb. Trib. Aug. 3, 2005), *available at* <http://www.state.gov/s/l/c5818.htm>.

30. Bartholomeusz, *supra* note 34, at 265–72, 285. One was a case under NAFTA using UNCITRAL rules (the *UPS* case), and the other a case under a bilateral investment treaty between France and Argentina using ICSID rules (the *Aguas argentinas* case).

31. See Jeffrey L. Dunoff, *Border Patrol at the World Trade Organization,* 1998 Y.B. INT'L ENVTL. L. 20, 22–23 (predicting that the openness to amicus briefs would be illusory).

32. Nsongurua J. Udombana, *So Far, So Fair: The Local Remedies Rule in the Jurisprudence of the African Commission on Human and Peoples' Rights,* 97 AJIL 1, 2 (2003); Dean Zagorac, *International Courts and Compliance Bodies: The Experience of Amnesty International in* CIVIL SOCIETY, INTERNATIONAL COURTS AND COMPLIANCE BODIES, *supra* note 19, at 11, 34–37.

33. Ellen Hey, *The World Bank Inspection Panel: Towards the Recognition of a New Legally Relevant Relationship to International Law,* 2 HOFSTRA L. & POL'Y SYMP. 61, 66 (1997).

34. *Role of Non-governmental Groups in the Development of International Law,* 54 ASIL PROC. 194, 220, 221 (1960) (comments of Oscar Schachter).

35. *See, e.g.*, David P. Forsythe, *Who Guards the Guardians: Third Parties and the Law of Armed Conflict*, 70 AJIL 41, 44–46 (1976) (discussing the Formal role of the ICRC); Harold K. Jacobson & Edith Brown Weiss, *Assessing the Record and Designing Strategies to Engage Countries*, *in* ENGAGING COUNTRIES: STRENGTHENING COMPLIANCE WITH INTERNATIONAL ENVIRONMENTAL ACCORDS 511,527,529,533 (Edith Brown Weiss & Harold K. Jacobson eds., 1998); Maya Prasad, *The Role of Non-governmental Organizations in the New United Nations Procedures for Human Rights Complaints*, 5 DENV. J. INT'L L. & POL'Y 441 (1975).

36. ABRAM CHAYES & ANTONIA HANDLER CHAYES, THE NEW SOVEREIGNTY: COMPLIANCE WITH INTERNATIONAL REGULATORY AGREEMENTS, ch. 11, at 250, 251 (1995).

37. First Meeting of the Parties to the Aarhus Convention, Decision I/7, UN Doc. ECE/MP.PP/2/Add.8, annex, para. 4(2004). NGOs can also submit communications alleging noncompliance by a party to the Convention. See Report of the Compliance Committee, UN Doc. ECE/MP.PP/2005/13, paras. 24–27. The Aarhus Convention is the Convention on Access to Information, Public Participation in Decision-Making and Access to Justice in Environmental Matters, June 25, 1998, 38 ILM 517 (1999).

38. SC Res. 771, para. 5 (Aug. 13, 1992).

39. Res. 1470, para. 8 (Mar. 28, 2003).

40. *See generally* Kerstin Martens, *Examining the (Non-)Status of NGOs in International Law*, IND. J. GLOBAL LEGAL STUD., Summer 2003, at 1; Karsten Nowrot, *Legal Consequences of Globalization: The Status of Non-governmental Organizations Under International Law*, 6 IND. J, GLOBAL LEGAL STUD. 579 (1999).

41. This problem was recognized by the late nineteenth century. For example, Pasquale Fiore wrote that societies (which are "the result of freedom of association for a common interest") are granted rights by the sovereignty of a state, and thus that such societies "may not as of right exercise their functions in foreign countries." PASQUALE FIORE, INTERNATIONAL LAW CODIFIED AND ITS LEGAL SANCTION 34–35 n. 1 (Edwin M. Borchard trans., 1918).

42. Menno T. Kamminga, *The Evolving Status of NGOs Under International Law: A Threat to the Inter-State System? in* NON-STATE ACTORS AND HUMAN RIGHTS, *see e.g.*, Ralph G. Steinhardt, *Corporate Responsibility and the International Law of Human Rights: The New* "Lex Mercatoria," *in* NON-STATE ACTORS AND HUMAN RIGHTS at 93, 98–99. In addition, the ICRC and the federation were granted observer status in the UN General Assembly in the early 1990s. Note that the ICRC claims to be an entity other than an IO or NGO. ICRC, DISCOVER THE ICRC 6 (2005).

43. 1 UNION OF INTERNATIONAL ASSOCIATIONS, INTERNATIONAL ASSOCIATION STATUTE SERIES, app. 4.1 (1988). Institut de droit international, Draft Convention Relating to the Legal Position of International Associations (1923), *reprinted in* UNION OF INTERNATIONAL ASSOCIATIONS, [hereinafter Draft Convention]. This and the other documents noted here from the UIA Statute Series are available online at <http:// www.uia.be/legal/>. The predecessor organization to the UIA was founded in 1907.

44. *See* Emanuele Rebasti, Workshop Report, A Legal Status for NGOs in Contemporary International Law? (Eur. Univ. Inst. Workshop Report, Nov. 2002), at <http://users.unimi.it/sociv/documenti/report.doc> (remarks of Pierre-Marie Dupuy).

45. RUTH B. RUSSELL (assisted by Jeannete E. Muther), A HISTORY OF

THE UNITED NATIONS CHARTER 800–01 (1958) (stating that Article 71 "formalized a normal practice under the League of Nations of consulting with interested nongovernmental organizations concerned with pertinent economic and social activities"). Of course, consultations with NGOs had declined in the period preceding 1945.

46. Convention on the International Institute of Agriculture, June 7, 1905, Art. 9(f), 35 Stat. 1918, 1 Bevans 436. Unofficial international agricultural congresses had begun in 1878.

47. League of Nations Covenant Art. 25; Chandler P. Anderson, *The International Red Cross Organization,* 14 AJIL 210, 214 (1920).

48. *See, e.g.,* 29 INTERNATIONAL LAW ASSOCIATION, CONFERENCE REPORT 363–65 (1920) (remarks of Wyndham A. Bewes); Manley O. Hudson, *The First Conference for the Codification of International Law,* 24 AJIL 447, 451(1930) (noting that organizations of women sent representatives to the conference at The Hague and that a conference committee devoted a session to hearing statements from the organizations).

49. Convention and Statute Establishing an International Relief Union, July 12, 1927; Convention Art. 5(2), Statute Art. 1, 135 LNTS 248. The International Relief Union was the first IO to have a provision in its charter providing for a consultative capacity for NGOs.

50. LYMAN CROMWELL WHITE (assisted by Marie Ragonetti Zocca), INTERNATIONAL NON-GOVERNMENTAL ORGANIZATIONS: THEIR PURPOSES, METHODS, AND ACCOMPLISHMENTS 246–47 (1951).

51. Article 71, in 2 THE CHARTER Of THE UNITED NATIONS: A COMMENTARY 1069, 1070 (Bruno Simma ed., 2d ed. 2002) (making no mention of the lobbying by NGOs at the conference); LELAND M. GOODRICH, EDVARD HAMBRO, & ANNE PATRICIA SIMONS, CHARTER OF THE UNITED NATIONS: COMMENTARY AND DOCUMENTS 444 (3d & rev. ed. 1969) (mentioning the NGOs but not the active role they played).

52. *See Democratic Processes: The Non-governmental Organizations,* 1951 ANN. REV. UN AFF. 165, 182 (remarks of Waldo Chamberlin); DOROTHY B. ROBINS, EXPERIMENT IN DEMOCRACY: THE STORY OF U.S. CITIZEN ORGANIZATIONS IN FORGING THE CHARTER OF THE UNITED NATIONS 122–28 (1971) (noting the catalytic role of James T. Shotwell). Robins and Chamberlin were both present at the San Francisco Conference. *See also* E. Suy, *The Status of Observers in International Organizations,* 160 RECUEIL DES COURS 75, 102 (1978 II) (noting the pressure brought by the NGOs on the drafters of the Charter).

53. H. LAUTERPACHT, INTERNATIONAL LAW AND HUMAN RIGHTS 24–26, 63–64 (1950); Dianne Otto, *Nongovernmental Organizations in the United Nations System: The Emerging Role of International Civil Society,* 18 HUM. RTS Q. 107, 127 (1996). For a survey of current UN practices by agency, see UN NON-GOVERNMENTAL LIAISON SERVICE, UN SYSTEM ENGAGEMENT WITH NGOs, CIVIL SOCIETY, THE PRIVATE SECTOR, AND OTHER ACTORS: A COMPENDIUM (2005), available at <http://www.un-ngls.org/publications.htm>.

54. 1950 NGO Rule, Review of Consultative Arrangements with Non-governmental Organizations, ESC Res. 288 (X), para. 8 (Feb. 27, 1950), *reprinted in* LADOR-LEDERER, *supra* note 6, para. 5.

55. 1996 NGO Rule, *supra* note 54, para. 9 (emphasis added).

56. *Compare* 1950 NGO Rule, *supra* note 54, paras. 8–9, *with* 1996 NGO Rule, *supra* note 72, paras. 4–5.

57. 1996 NGO Rule, *supra* note 54, paras. 10, 12.

58. *Id.*, para. 57(a).

59. *Id.*, para. 56.

60. *See, e.g.*, Jurij Daniel Aston, *The United Nations Committee on Non-governmental Organizations: Guarding the Entrance to a Politically Divided House*, 12 EUR. J. INT'L L. 943 (2001). The recent Report of the Panel of Eminent Persons on United Nations-Civil Society Relations (Cardoso Report) stated that "it is essential to depoliticize the accreditation process." We the Peoples: Civil Society, the United Nations and Global Governance, UN Doc. A/58/817, at 54, para. 127 (2004).

61. OAS Permanent Council, CP/Res. 759 (1217/99) (1999).

62. Corinne A. A. Packer & Donald Rukare, *The New African Union and Its Constitutive Act*, 96 AJIL 365, 375(2002).

63. JOSÉ E. ALVAREZ, INTERNATIONAL ORGANIZATIONS AS LAW-MAKERS 611 (2005); *see also* Eibe Riedel, *The Development of International Law: Alternatives to Treaty-Making? International Organizations and Non-State Actors*, *in* DEVELOPMENTS OF INTERNATIONAL LAW IN TREATY MAKING 301,317 (Rüdiger Wolfrum & Volker Röben eds., 2005) (stating that NGO involvement in all processes of IO activities has been crucial and indispensable).

64. *See, e.g.*, CONSTRUCTING WORLD CULTURE: INTERNATIONAL-NONGOVERNMENTAL ORGANIZATIONS SINCE 1875 (John Boli & George M. Thomas eds., 1999); "THE CONSCIENCE OF THE WORLD": THE INFLUENCE OF NON-GOVERNMENTAL ORGANISATIONS IN THE UN SYSTEM (Peter Willetts ed., 1996); Tom Farer, *New Players in the Old Game: The De Facto Expansion of Standing to Participate in Global Security Negotiations*, 38 AM. BEHAVIORAL. SCIENTIST 842 (1995); Anne-Marie Slaughter, *International Law and International Relations*, 285 RECUEIL DES COURS 9, 96–151 (2000) (constituting chapter 3, The Role of NGOs in International Lawmaking); *The Growing Role of Nongovernmental Organizations*, 89 ASIL PROC. 413 (1995); P. J. Simmons, *Learning to Live with NGOs*, FOREIGN POL'Y, Fall 1998, at 82.

65. S. H. BAILEY, THE FRAMEWORK OF INTERNATIONAL SOCIETY 81(1932).

66. Rosalyn Higgins, *The Reformation in International Law*, *in* LAW, SOCIETY AND ECONOMY 207, 211–15 (Richard Rawlings ed., 1997).

67. *Id.* at 212, 215.

68. *Id.* at 215.

69. On customary international law, see John King Gamble & Charlotte Ku, *International Law—New Actors and New Technologies: Center Stage for NGOs?* 31 LAW & POL'Y INT'L Bus. 221, 244(2000); Stephan Hobe, *The Role of Non-State Actors, in Particular of NGOs, in Non-contractual Law-making and the Development of Customary International Law*, *in* DEVELOPMENTS OF INTERNATIONAL LAW IN TREATY MAKING, *supra* note 84, at 319, 328.

70. The issues in play were the slave trade, religious freedom, and intellectual property. Max J. Kohler, Jewish Rights at International Congresses, AM. JEWISH Y.B. 5678, at 106, 109–10 (1917); LAUREN, *supra* note 15, at 40; HAROLD NICOLSON, THE CONGRESS OF VIENNA: A STUDY IN ALLIED UNITY: 1812–1822, at 132 (1946).

71. *See* David D. Caron, *War and International Adjudication: Reflections on the 1899 Peace Conference*, 94 AJIL 4, 15 (2000). In 1908, in his Nobel Peace Prize lecture, Fredrik Bajer likened the "organization of peace" to a "house – of three stories," including on the first story the peace associations; on the second story, the interparliamentary conferences; and on the third story, the intergovernmental Hague

Peace conferences. Fredrik Bajer, The Organization of the Peace Movement (May 18, 1908), at <http://nobelprize.org/peace/laureates/1908/bajer-lecture.html>.

72. International Conference on Customs and Other Similar Formalities: Official Instruments Approved by the Conference, League of Nations Doc. C.D.I.96(1). 1923, at 25; GEORGE L. RIDGEWAY, MERCHANTS OF PEACE 212–13 (1938).

73. Pierre Kazansky, Théorie de l'adminissration internationale, 9 RGDIP 353,354,357(1902) (trans. by author).

74. *Id.* at 361.

75. *See, e.g.*, MARGARET E. KECK & KATHRYN SIKKINK, ACTIVISTS BEYOND BORDERS 1 (1997); Harold Hongju Koh, *Bringing International Law Home,* 35 HOUS. L. REV. 623, 646,647 (1998); Ethan A. Nadelmann, *Global Prohibition Regimes: The Evolution of Norms in International Society,* 44 INT'L ORG. 479, 482 (1990).

76. Daniel C. Esty, *Non-governmental Organizations at the World Trade Organization: Cooperation, Competition, or Exclusion,* 1 J. INT'L ECON. L. 123, 135–37 (1998).

77. Raymond Ranjeva, *Les organisations non gouvernementales et la mise en oeuvre du droit international,* 270 RECUEIL DES COURS 9, 23, 100 (1997).

78. *See, e.g.*, Harold Hongju Koh, *Transnational Legal Process,* 75 NEB. L. REV. 181, 203–04 (1996).

79. *See* ALVAREZ, *supra* note 63, at 287, 610, 612.

80. UN Press Release SG/SM/7318, Partnership with Civil Society Necessity in Addressing Global Agenda, Says Secretary-General in Wellington, New Zealand Remarks (Feb. 29, 2000).

81. *See, e.g.*, Malgosia Fitzmaurice, *Actors and Factors in the Evolution of Treaty Norms,* 4 AUSTRIAN REV. INT'L & EUR. L. 1 (1999); Volker Röben, *Proliferation of Actors, in* DEVELOPMENTS OF INTERNATIONAL LAW IN TREATY MAKING, *supra* note 84, at 511, 512. The earliest textbooks on international organization gave attention to NGOs. *See, e.g.*, FREDERICK CHARLES HICKS, THE NEW WORLD ORDER, ch. 20 (1920); PITMAN B. POTTER, AN INTRODUCTION TO THE STUDY OF INTERNATIONAL ORGANIZATION, ch. 18 (rev. ed. 1922).

82. David Bederman has suggested that IOs be visualized as "communities." David J. Bedernian, The Souls of International Organizations: Legal Personality and the Lighthouse at Cape Spartel 36 VA. J. INT'L L. 275, 371–72 (1996).

83. *See, e.g.*, Geoffrey Palmer, New Ways to Make International Environmental Law, 86 AJIL 259, 280–83 (1992).

84. Virginia A. Leary, *Lessons from the Experience of the International Labour Organisation, in* THE UNITED NATIONS AND HUMAN RIGHTS 580, 585 (Philip Alston ed., 1992).

85. Legality of the Threat or Use of Nuclear Weapons, Advisory Opinion, 1996 ICJ REP. 226, 287–88, para. 2 (July 8) (Guillaume, J., sep. op.). He suggested "piercing the veil" of the IOs. *Id.* In its opinion, the Court stated "that the political nature of the motives which may be said to have inspired the request and the political implications that the opinion given might have are of no relevance in the establishment of its jurisdiction to give such an opinion." 1996 ICJ REP. at 234, para. 13.

86. Kenneth Anderson & David Rieff, *"Global Civil Society": A Sceptical View, in* GLOBAL CIVIL SOCIETY 2004/5, at 26, 37 (Helmut Anheier et al. eds., 2004).

87. Note that the idea of NGOs as serving a representative function at the United Nations goes back to how UN member governments implemented Article 71

in 1950 in calling for an accredited NGO to "represent a substantial proportion of the organized persons within the particular field in which it operates." *See* text at note 54 *supra*.

88. GEORGES SCELLE, UNE CRISE DE LA SOCIETE DES NATIONS 144–46 (1927) (trans. by author). Scelle's term for NGOs was extra-state societies. GEORGES SCELLE, PRECIS DE DROIT DES GENS 288 (1932).

89. James Crawford & Susan Marks, *The Global Democracy Deficit: An Essay in International Law and Its Limits*, *in* RE-IMAGINING POLITICAL COMMUNITY: STUDIES IN COSMOPOLITAN DEMOCRACY 72, 83 (Daniele Archibugi, David Held & Martin Kohlet eds., 1998).

90. Kamminga, *supra* note 42, at 110.

91. Florentino P. Feliciano, Book Review, 68 YALE L.J. 1039, 1047 (1959) (reviewing C. WILFRED JENKS, THE COMMON LAW OF MANKIND (1958)).

92. Daniel Bodansky, *The Legitimacy of International Governance: A Coming Challenge for International Environmental Law?* 93 AJIL 596, 612 (1999).

93. Robert O. Keohane & Joseph S. Nye Jr., The Club Model of Multilateral Cooperation and Problems of Democratic Legitimacy, in EFFICIENCY, EQUITY, AND LEGITIMACY: THE MULTILATERAL TRADING SYSTEM AT THE MILLENNIUM 264, 282 (Roger B. Porter et al. eds., 2001).

94. *Id.* at 283–84.

95. *Id.* at 289–90.

96. Robert O. Keohane, The Contingent Legitimacy of Multilateralism, in MULTILATERALISM UNDER CHALLENGE? POWER, INTERNATIONAL ORDER, AND STRUCTURAL CHANGE (Edward Newman, Ramesh Thakur & John Tirman eds., 2006).

97. *See* Frederick S. Dunn, *The International Rights of Individuals*, 35 ASIL PROC. 14, 18(1941)

98. *See, e.g.*, MICHAEL EDWARDS, NGO RIGHTS AND RESPONSIBILITIES (2000); August Reinisch, *The Changing International Legal Framework for Dealing with Non-State Actors*, *in* NON-STATE ACTORS AND HUMAN RIGHTS, *supra* note 10, at 37, 48–49; Peter J. Spiro, *Accounting for NGOs*, 3 CHI. J. INT'L. L. 161(2002); Eric Stein, *International Integration and Democracy: No Love at First Sight*, 95 AJIL 489, 533 (2001).

99. Christine Chinkin, *Human Rights and the Politics of Representation: Is There a Role for International Law?* *in* THE ROLE OF LAW IN INTERNATIONAL POLITICS: ESSAYS IN INTERNATIONAL RELATIONS AND INTERNATIONAL LAW 131, 144 (Michael Byers ed., 2000).

100. *See* CHIANG PEI-HENG, NON-GOVERNMENTAL ORGANIZATIONS AT THE UNITED NATIONS 5 (1981) (suggesting that the most important function of NGOs is "providing alternative programs and ideas, and views in opposition to or critical of official policies and opinions").

101. At the 2004 meeting, CARE International and the International Center for Transitional Justice briefed Council members on the role of civil society in postconflict peace building. Arria and Other Special Meetings Between NGOs and Security Council Members, June 22, 2004, *available at* http://www.globalpolicy.org/security/mtgsetc/brieindx.htm.

102. Before the summit, the president of the General Assembly presided over informal interactive hearings with NGOs and the private sector.

103. Guidelines for Arrangements on Relations with Non-governmental Organizations, Doc. WT/L/1 62, para. VI (1996). Once a year, the WTO Secretariat sponsors a symposium in which invited NGOs participate in panel sessions along

with business leaders, government officials, and academics. In addition, NGOs are invited to attend WTO ministerial conferences as silent observers. For example, in December 2005, over eight hundred NGOs attended the Hong Kong ministerial conference.

104. *Id.*

105. Christine Chinkin, *Enhancing the International Law Commission's Relationships with Other Law-making Bodies and Relevant Academic and Professional Institutions, in* MAKING BETTER INTERNATIONAL LAW: THE INTERNATIONAL LAW COMMISSION AT 50, at 333, 339–41, UN Sales No. E/F.98.V.5 (1998); HILARY CHARLESWORTH & CHRISTINE CHINKIN, THE BOUNDARIES OF INTERNATIONAL LAW: A FEMINIST ANALYSIS 101 (2000).

106. Statute of the International Law Commission, Art. 26(1).

107. International Covenant on Civil and Political Rights, Dec. 16, 1966, Art. 19(2), 999 UNTS 331 (emphasis added).

108. 3 American Declaration of the Rights and Duties of Man, May 2, 1948, Art. XXIV, 43 AJIL Supp. 133(1949).

109. Convention on the Prohibition of the Use, Stockpiling, Production and Transfer of Anti-personnel Mines and on Their Destruction, Sept. 18, 1997, Arts. 11.4, 12.3, 13.2, 36 ILM 1507 (1997).

110. That language occurs in conventions regarding the ozone layer, hazardous waste, climate change, biodiversity, desertification, hazardous chemicals, and persistent organic pollutants. In sonic meetings, NGOs are invited to make oral statements at the invitation of the chair.

111. Lyman White, *Non-governmental Organizations and Their Relations with the United Nations,* 1951 ANN. REV. UNAFF. 165, 166–67. At the time that he made this observation, White was a UN staff official working on NGO affairs.

112. JANNE ELISABETH NIJMAN, THE CONCEPT OF INTERNATIONAL LEGAL PERSONALITY 469 (2004); Laurence Boisson de Chazournes & Philippe Sands, *Introduction* to INTERNATIONAL LAW, THE INTERNATIONAL COURT OF JUSTICE AND NUCLEAR WEAPONS 1, 10 (Laurence Boisson de Chazournes & Philippe Sands eds., 1999); Peter Willetts, *From "Consultative Arrangements" to "Partnership": The Changing Status of NGOs in Diplomacy at the UN.* 6 GLOBAL GOVERNANCE 191,205(2000).

113. Louis B. Sohn, Remarks on the role of lawyers and legal resourcefulness, *in* THE EFFECTIVENESS OF INTERNATIONAL DECISIONS: PAPERS OF A CONFERENCE OF THE AMERICAN SOCIETY OF INTERNATIONAL LAW AND THE PROCEEDINGS OF THE CONFERENCE 488, 291 (Stephen M. Schwebel ed., 1971).

114. Roscoe Pound, *The Idea of Law in International Relations,* 33 ASIL PROC. 10, 18 (1939).

115. *Id.* at 21. Pound says that he borrowed the term "englobing" from the French jurists of the International school.

PART 1.3

International Law as Operating System: Implementation and Compliance with International Law

CHAPTER 7

Compliance with International Agreements

Beth Simmons

A CENTRAL THEME IN MUCH RECENT INTERNATIONAL RELAtions scholarship is the growing role of formal international agreements and supranational authority in the ordering of relations among sovereign states. The growing range of authoritative commitments is evidenced by the movement since World War II to codify customary practices into explicit international legal instruments. The range of international agreements has grown rapidly over the past 40 years with the development of rules that regulate economic, social, communications, environmental, and human rights behavior. Evidence of the growth in supranational authority includes not only the number of international organizations that have mushroomed in the postwar years, but also, most strikingly, the growth and development of legally binding forms of third-party dispute settlement: The evolution of the dispute-settlement procedures of the General Agreement on Tariffs and Trade (GATT) into the more formal and less discretionary structure of the World Trade Organization (WTO), the 1996 inauguration of the International Maritime Court in Hamburg to handle disputes arising from the United Nations' Law of the Seas, the growing activism of the European Court of Justice, and the recent flurry of contentious case activity at the International Court of Justice[1] are all examples of states agreeing voluntarily to give up a portion of the most basic aspect of their sovereignty—the authority to act as the final judge of one's own actions—to authoritative international institutions.

These developments are a puzzle for the study of international relations, the traditional assumption of which has been that national governments generally desire to preserve their legal sovereignty, particularly the sole authority to judge the acceptability of their policies in the international

---

sphere. According to much mainline theorizing, states make commitments—especially formal legal commitments—either cautiously or cynically, and are reluctant to delegate decision making to supranational bodies. Over the past two decades, a good deal of theoretical and empirical work has been devoted to explaining why states have entered into this vast web of agreements voluntarily. Much of this work has examined issues relating to international economic and social interactions among states (the primary focus of this essay). Explanations have focused on the functional need for agreements due to the rising level of interdependence (Keohane 1984), the desire for greater regularity and predictability in actors' mutual relations (Brierly 1963), and growing state responsibility in the economic and social realm (Röling 1960, Friedmann 1964). Dominant international-relations paradigms generally hold that governments agree to sacrifice a degree of their legal freedom of action in order to secure policy changes from others or to gain influence over other states' policies (Keohane 1993).

Until recently, far less attention has been devoted to understanding why governments actually comply with such agreements, given that they can be costly in the short term and are not likely to be centrally enforced. Four broad approaches to this question are reviewed here: realist theory, rational functionalism, domestic regime–based explanations, and normative approaches. These perspectives are not mutually exclusive, and the less one is willing to straw-man the arguments of the major proponents, the clearer become the numerous points of overlap. For example, although realist theory has rarely been articulated in such as way as to take international legal constraints seriously, some of its major proponents would admit that international law compliance is fairly widespread (Morgenthau 1985). Similarly, scholars who focus on normative convergence as a source of compliance hardly rule out coercive processes to encourage such convergence (Bull 1977). Approaches that link domestic regime type with international rule compliance often tap into a deeper set of factors relating to the role of liberal principles and beliefs in securing international behavior consistent with the rule of law (Dixon 1993). Some functionalist arguments point to domestic regime characteristics as a source of "market failure" that make international agreements all the more necessary. Nonetheless, these four broad approaches diverge in important respects and provide a useful way to arrange the growing literature on compliance with international agreements.

Despite the recent interest in issues surrounding compliance, and more generally the effects of rules on international politics, the effort to link theory with evidence is still in its infancy. This is partly due to conceptual difficulties in identifying compliance itself. Another obstacle has been methodological: Difficulties in demonstrating causation remain, along with problems of selection bias in the use of cases and the analysis of data. Because the endeavor to understand compliance has been interdisciplinary, involving legal scholars and sociologists as well as political scientists, differing methods of analysis, reasoning, and standards of proof pervade the literature. Although these differences are enriching and have narrowed through scholarly cooperation, they do help account for the disparate nature of much of the relevant literature.

The first section discusses the concept of compliance and presents strategies for its measurement. The second section reviews four strands of international relations theory (inserting legal scholarship where arguments are compatible, even if the authors are not self-consciously writing within the tradition under examination) and culls from them a range of explanations and empirical findings regarding international legal commitments and compliance. The third section of this essay draws some conclusions about our knowledge of compliance with international agreements and suggests directions for future research.

The Meaning and Measurement of Compliance

In his groundbreaking study on compliance with international public authority, Oran Young (1979) suggested: "Compliance can be said to occur when the actual behavior of a given subject conforms to prescribed behavior, and non-compliance or violation occurs when actual behavior departs significantly from prescribed behavior." This definition distinguishes compliance behavior from treaty implementation (the adoption of domestic rules or regulations that are meant to facilitate, but do not in themselves constitute, compliance with international agreements). It also distinguishes compliance from effectiveness; a poorly designed agreement could achieve high levels of compliance without much impact on the phenomenon of concern (pollution levels for example). While compliance may be necessary for effectiveness, there is no reason to consider it sufficient. The literature reviewed here is almost exclusively concerned with the conformity of behavior to rules, rather than the ultimate outcome of such conformity (Jacobson & Weiss 1995, 1997).

Furthermore, most of the literature reviewed discusses compliance with explicit rules or agreements, often of a legal character or of normative import, and not "compliance" with the demands of an adversary or the requests of an ally. The concern is typically with obligations that flow from authoritative agreements, widely held normative prescriptions, or authoritative interpretations of proper behavior, rather than acquiescence to unilateral political demands based on the exercise of power alone. In practice, of course, agreements among asymmetrically endowed actors are rarely perfectly voluntary, and the decision to "conform to prescribed behavior" might rest on an amalgam of obligation and felt coercion. Fisher (1981) has drawn an important distinction between "first order" and "second order" compliance. The former refers to compliance with standing, substantive rules often embodied in treaty arrangements (Downs & Rocke 1995, Chayes & Chayes 1995). Second-order compliance is compliance with the authoritative decision of a third party, such as a panel of the World Trade Organization, the United Nations Human Rights Committee, or the International Court of Justice (Bulterman & Kuijer 1996, Fisher 1981). The study of first-order compliance encounters difficulties in establishing an underlying "rate" of compliance, as it is far from clear how one could conceptualize a denominator for such a rate. As a result, researchers looking at the same set of behaviors can disagree vehemently over whether "most" foreign policy actions are effectively governed by law, rules, and agreements, or whether such considerations have little effect on state behavior (Henkin 1979). Studies of second-order compliance can often more convincingly establish such a rate and can narrow the range of behavior that would constitute compliance by focusing on a particular, often precisely rendered, decision (Fisher 1981). Unfortunately, rulings represent only the tip of the iceberg of the larger compliance problem, and are likely to represent a biased set of observations, especially since only governments willing to make concessions are likely to submit to authoritative decision-making processes (Coplin 1968).

Finally, most researchers admit it is difficult to judge whether a particular policy constitutes compliance at all (Jacobson & Weiss 1997). Often international agreements are written so as to permit a range of interpretations regarding the parties' obligations. Furthermore, compliance is rarely a transparent, binary choice. Actors' behavior is often intentionally ambiguous, dilatory, or confusing, and frequently takes place under conditions in which verification of compliance is difficult (Young 1979). In other contexts, actors may make good faith efforts to comply that nonetheless fall short of an agreement's prescribed behavior. Some researchers have dealt with these ambiguities by making such assessments in the context of generally prevailing expectations (Chayes & Chayes 1995). Going further, constructivist approaches assume that standards of compliance are socially constructed and must not be imposed by the analyst, making each assessment highly context-specific.

International Relations Theory and the Problem of Compliance

Compliance and the Realist Tradition

For realists, power, rather than law, has traditionally been the primary determinant of the course of interstate relations. Most realists—theoreticians and practitioners—tend to be highly skeptical that treaties or formal agreements significantly influence state actions (Boyle 1980, Bork 1989/90). Although Hans Morgenthau (1985) admitted that "during the four hundred years of its existence international law ha[d] in most instances been scrupulously observed," he thought that this could be attributed either to convergent interests or prevailing power relations. Governments make legal commitments cynically and "are always anxious to shake off the restraining influence that international law might have upon their foreign policies, to use international law instead for the promotion of their national interests" (Morgenthau 1985). Similarly, Hoffmann (1956) described the nation state as "a legally sovereign unit in a tenuous net of breakable obligations." In this formulation, what governments are legally bound to do or refrain from doing has little bearing on their actual behavior, except as provided by a coincidence of law and national interest. Aron (1981) put it succinctly: "International law can merely ratify the fate of arms and the arbitration of force."

To realists, the decentralized nature of the international legal system is its prime defect. International agreements lack restraining power, especially since governments generally retain the right to interpret and apply the provisions of international agreements selectively (Morgenthau 1985). Realists view the activities of major powers and the pursuit of important interests as highly unlikely to be constrained by legal authority or prior agreement.

In short, realists typically assume that international law is merely an epiphenomenon of interests or is only made effective through the balance of power (Oppenheim 1912). Aron and other realists have admitted that "the domain of legalized interstate relations is increasingly large" but argued that "one does not judge international law by peaceful periods and secondary problems" (Aron 1981). In the realm of high politics, realists have been especially skeptical about the rule of law and legal processes in international relations (see for example Diehl 1996, Fisher 1981, Bulterman & Kuijer 1996). For the most part, realist perspectives focus on the fundamental variables of power and interest, rarely inquiring further into states' compliance with international agreements.

Compliance and Rational Functionalism

A different set of expectations is suggested by a rational functional approach to the study of international institutions. Functionalist approaches view international agreements as a way to address a perceived need: International legal agreements are made because states want to solve common problems that they have difficulties solving any other way, e.g., unilaterally or through political means alone (Bilder 1989). Rational functionalism shares realists' concern with states' incentives to comply with or disregard international agreements, but is less likely to denigrate the cooperative problems that pervaded the realm of so-called low politics. By the mid 1980s it was increasingly difficult to relegate economic, social, and environmental issues to the status of "secondary problems," given the robustness of the postwar peace among developed countries. Unlike realist theorists, those taking a functional approach did not assume that these issues posed trivial problems for compliance. The initial assumption of rational functionalism is not that states cynically manipulate their legal environment, but that they "engineer" it in what are taken to be sincere efforts to affect an otherwise suboptimal outcome.

Both realism and rational functionalism are interest-driven approaches in which incentives play a crucial role.[2] The latter, however, views the particular agreements and even the international legal system in toto as a collective good, from which states collectively can benefit, but to which none wants to contribute disproportionately and by which none wants to be disadvantaged consistently. Rational functionalist analysis focuses on the perceived benefits of a system of rule-based behavior and on the individual incentives for states to contribute to, or detract from, such a system. Because they are often crucial to solutions, agreements are taken seriously. Therefore, in the absence of severe, unresolved collective-action problems or overwhelming, unaddressed incentives to defect, obligations are likely to be carried out.

Though functionalist theories concentrate on why states obligate themselves rather than why they comply with their obligations, theorists in this vein have suggested a number of mechanisms that potentially influence compliance behavior. The central mechanism for securing compliance is related to reputation: States anticipate paying a higher cost in the long run for breaking agreements in an effort to achieve immediate gain (Keohane 1984, Schachter 1991). Indeed, one function of international agreements is to enhance the reputational consequences of noncompliant behavior by providing mechanisms that increase transparency and therefore improve information regarding other states' behavior (Keohane 1984, Milgrom et al. 1990, Mitchell 1994). Some authors have argued that reputational explanations for compliance are especially relevant for new and developing countries, which have an interest in developing a reputation as "rule of law" countries (Shihata 1965). Greater transparency and opportunities for reciprocity also enhance compliance where there is repeated play within a small group, for example in the European Union (EU) or among the large countries in the WTO. Functionalist accounts often emphasize the crucial role of international institutions in providing a focal point for acceptable behavior (Garrett & Weingast 1993). These institutions facilitate the convergence of expectations and reduce uncertainty about other states' future behavior.

Like proponents of the normative research agenda discussed below, some functionalists point out that the standards or "focal points" created by international agreements or institutions can gain a high degree of legitimacy both internationally and domestically (Franck 1990, Peck 1996, Tacsan 1992). This legitimacy in turn can have important political consequences (Claude 1966). In this view, the search for a legitimate rule is a rational response to the need for a stable solution to an otherwise costly, intractable problem or dispute.

The starting point for functionalist explanations of international agreements and compliance is the inability of states to solve a problem without the institutional device. Like realist approaches, most functionalist approaches to international politics begin with the premise that states delegate sovereignty begrudgingly. Despite states' strong preference for solving international controversies through political means, even unilaterally if necessary, functional theories recognize that this may not be possible. Most functional theorizing has been systemic, focusing on international market failure and problems of collective action (Keohane 1984). Relatively little attention has been given to the domestic political reasons why international agreement may be impossible without an international institution, but in principle, the source of the "suboptimality" in functional theory could be either domestic or systemic.

One important exception to the systemic focus of most functional accounts of compliance is a theoretical study of the GATT rules by Downs & Rocke (1995). This work indicates that uncertainty regarding domestic politics and interest-group demands has a tremendous influence on the nature of international agreements undertaken, the severity of sanctions required, and hence the degree of compliance to be expected from participants in the GATT regime. Downs & Rocke argue that GATT's weak enforcement norm is a result of uncertainty about the future demands of interest groups: Most states do not want aggressive enforcement of the GATT because domestic conditions may arise under which they themselves will be compelled to violate GATT obligations (Downs & Rocke 1995). This uncertainty tilts preferences toward shorter and less stringent punishments, reducing the cooperative demands of the treaty agreement (as the costs of defection rise, a highly cooperative treaty becomes too risky to be practical). In this model, reached deductively through a game-theoretical representation, domestic uncertainty makes rule violation harder to punish, which makes compliance harder to secure. The expectation of these difficulties endogenizes the treaty commitment itself by contributing to a watering down of the initial agreement.

Other studies that locate the source of suboptimality at the domestic level have focused less on the implications for sanctioning and more on the role of international agreements or authoritative interpretations of obligations in creating constraints that resonate in domestic politics. This approach begins with the observation that domestic institutions can obstruct the realization of benefits for society as a whole: Preference outliers can capture domestic institutions and thus hold policies hostage to their demands; well-organized interests can exert particularistic influences on policy, decreasing overall welfare; decision makers can have time-inconsistent preferences that cause them to pursue short-term interests at the expense of longer-term gains; political polarization can lead to suboptimal outcomes or decisional paralysis at the domestic level. Under these circumstances, actors may have incentives not only to make international agreements (e.g., to freer trade, fixed exchange rates, convergent macroeconomic policies), but also to comply with them in order to solve an intractable domestic problem. In this view, international agreements place a desired constraint on policy where domestic politics alone has proved socially suboptimal. Furthermore, authoritative external decisions may reduce the domestic political costs of particular courses of action—an argument regularly invoked to explain compliance with the European Monetary Union (EMU) and the International Monetary Fund (IMF), for example. Those who have examined bargaining in the context of legal-dispute settlement have argued that concessions tend to be easier to make, from a domestic political point of view, when legally required by an authoritative third party (Fischer 1982, Merrills 1969). Thus the value of compliance flows as much or more from its domestic political benefits as from the benefits of securing changes in the behavior of other states in the system.

Finally, a large and growing literature has focused on one of the most tangible sources of suboptimal social behavior: domestic administrative or technical incapacities. A host of studies, many relating to compliance with environmental accords, point to the inability (as distinct from unwillingness) of governments to comply with their international obligations. A consortium of scholars headed by Jacobson & Brown Weiss (1995, 1997), comparing the compliance performance of nine countries across five environmental accords in the past ten years, concludes that administrative capacity has been a crucial variable. A country's administrative capacity includes the knowledge and training of personnel responsible for environmental policy, adequate financial resources, the appropriate domestic legal mandate/authority to accomplish program implementation, and access to relevant information. Lacking such administrative or technical capacities, rule-consistent behavior may simply not be within a signatory's choice set. Outside agencies can help countries develop such capacities; the function of international agreements, in this case, is not only to specify obligations but to facilitate their attainment for certain classes of signatories deemed unable, without external resources, to meet particular standards of behavior (Haas et al. 1993).

Compliance and the Nature of the Domestic Regime

Another approach receiving attention in the study of interstate disputes, and more recently in legal circles, may be termed democratic legalism. (This appellation is not used by proponents of this approach but is convenient for the purposes of this article.) In this formulation, regime type is crucial to understanding the role of law in interstate relations (Slaughter 1995). While the domestically formulated functionalist literature focuses on the range of domestic conditions that can contribute to or detract from compliance, democratic legalism looks at the distinctive features of democratic regimes that tend to bind them into a "zone of law" in the conduct of their foreign relations.

The thrust of this literature is that democracies are more likely to comply with international legal obligations. One line of reasoning advanced to sustain this argument suggests that because liberal democratic regimes share an affinity with prevalent international legal processes and institutions, they tend to be more willing to depend on the rule of law for their external affairs as well. This argument depends on the notion that norms regarding limited government, respect for judicial processes, and regard for constitutional constraints carry over into the realm of international politics (Dixon 1993). Thus, countries with independent judiciaries are more likely to trust and respect international judicial processes than those lacking domestic experience with such institutions. Political leaders accustomed to constitutional constraints on their power in a domestic context are more likely to accept principled legal limits on their international behavior; therefore, governments with strong constitutional traditions, particularly those in which intragovernmental relations are rule governed, are more likely to accept rule-based constraints on their international behavior. This reasoning dovetails with a growing argument that liberal democracies are more likely than are other regime types to revere law, promote compromise, and respect processes of adjudication (Doyle 1986, Dixon 1993, Raymond 1994).

A specific mechanism that might tighten the link between the domestic rule of law and international behavior is the absorption of the latter into the corpus of domestic regulation itself. Assuming a close correlation between regime type and meaningful domestic legal restraints on the public exercise of authority, "[O]ne of the best ways of causing respect for international law is to make it indistinguishable from domestic law" (Fisher 1981). This parallels Keohane's 1992 notion of the "enmeshment" of international commitments into domestic politics and political institutions. One example of such absorption can be found in military manuals: Both Britain and the United States have imported international law concerning war fighting into their military handbooks. The idea is to make the two sets of law incentive compatible, such that "[p]atriotism and national loyalty will be aligned on the side of compliance" (Fisher 1981, p. 147). However, replication of international rules at the domestic level is no guarantee of their potency. Where international law is easily absorbed into the domestic system of rules one can wonder if behavior would have been much different in its absence; where international rules do not comport well with indigenous legal culture, expectations for compliance should not be high.

A second, distinct mechanism also supports the importance of democracy for law compliance. It rests on the observation that the leader of a liberal democracy may be constrained by the influence of international legal obligations on domestic groups, who are likely to cite such rules or rulings to influence their own government's policy. In one version of this argument, the mechanism of the compliance pull is domestic interest groups, who may have an interest in or preference for compliant behavior (Young 1979, Schachter 1991). Studies of compliance with environmental accords, for example, found that democracies provide more freedom for nongovernmental organizations (NGOs) to operate, allowing the formation and strengthening of transnational coalitions to influence government compliance efforts (Jacobson & Brown Weiss 1997). NGOs have been similarly crucial in the human rights area, and countries that have embarked on a transition to democracy have been influenced by their presence (Sikkink 1993). The weight of an international obligation or an authoritative legal forum may be vital in convincing domestic audiences actively to oppose a government policy, raising the political costs of noncompliance. Fisher (1981) has argued that these costs are likely to be especially heavy in the case of second-order compliance involving violation of an international authority's specific decision against a government, rather than a standing rule about which the government is likely to argue.

There is an affinity between this strand of democratic legalism and various kinds of functional reasoning that view international institutions as essential in influencing the domestic political debate surrounding a controversial foreign policy choice. The distinctive contribution of democratic legalism is its expectation of systematic differences between liberal democracies and nondemocracies: Domestic political constraints encouraging law-abiding behavior are assumed to be much stronger in democracies. Therefore, democratic countries are expected to be more willing to use legal institutions to regulate international behavior and settle disputes, and to comply more readily with these agreements once they are made.

Normative Approaches to Compliance

Normative considerations are present to some degree in the observation that democratic norms relating to the rule of law may influence governments' attitudes toward international law compliance. But a growing school of research places normative considerations at the center of its analysis of state behavior. This approach accepts that normative concerns are capable of driving perceptions of interest, and that the best way to understand normative influences is through a subjective rather than an analytically imposed framework of meaning. In this view, normative standards of appropriate conduct are socially constructed reference points against which state behavior can be gauged.

Normative influences have a long tradition in the study of international law compliance. At the turn of the century, for instance, Root (1908) cited "moral force" as a reason for compliance with the decisions of arbitration panels. The predominance of realist theory in the study of international relations after World War II edged aside such arguments as naive, until a more subtle understanding of the relationship between international power and international society was articulated. Bull (1977) provided an early antecedent to what loosely can be termed a more constructivist approach to the problem of international law compliance. Although he believed in the ultimate importance of the balance of power in international politics, Bull's work emphasized the critical importance of international society (shared norms and beliefs) to the effective functioning of international law. Parting with such realist skeptics as Aron, Bull thought international law existed because actors in international relations assume that the rules under which they act are legal rules. This did not, however, justify "our treating them as a substantial factor at work in international politics" (1977, p. 137). Bull did not cite behavioral evidence, but drew on the discourse with which diplomats described, justified, and excused their actions: "What is a clearer sign of the inefficacy of a set of rules is the case where there is not merely a lack of conformity as between actual and prescribed behavior, but a failure to accept the validity or binding quality of the obligations themselves—as indicated by a reasoned appeal to different and conflicting principles, or by an unreasoned disregard of the rules."

Bull's work opened the way for a more interpretive, contextual approach to the understanding of compliance than that of his realist predecessors, with whom he shared a healthy respect for the balance of power. He believed that the primary function of international law is to help mobilize compliance with the rules of what he termed international society, but he remained skeptical that law could impose serious restraints on international behavior. Law could influence compliance only in the presence of a social system marked by shared norms and beliefs (Bull 1977).

Bull's central insight was that actor behavior alone was inadequate to convey intersubjective meaning and hence was an insufficient indicator of the role of rules, norms and agreements in international politics. This insight was explicated by international regimes[3] theorists working in the constructivist mode in the 1980s, most brilliantly by Kratochwil & Ruggie

(1986). Rather than look to the violation of norms as the entire rule-compliance story, these scholars argued that analysts needed to understand state behavior as interpreted by other states and as intended by the actors themselves. Agreeing with Bull, they noted it was important to research how states justified their actions, and whether the international community responded to proffered rationales. "Indeed, such communicative dynamics may tell us far more about how robust a regime is than overt behavior alone" (Kratochwil & Ruggie 1986). In this view, even divergent practices of actors could express principled reasoning and shared understanding. What constitutes a breach of obligation is therefore not simply an objective description of a fact but an intersubjective appraisal. These observations comport well with the distinguishing features of social constructivism: its concern with the nature, origins, and functioning of social facts, the understanding of which is limited by more utilitarian approaches.

The implications for theory and research are profound. Kratochwil & Ruggie suggested that the emphasis on "rational institutional design"—a primary interest of the functionalist approaches discussed above—was fundamentally misplaced. Whereas such scholars as Downs & Rocke argued that relative incentives, rather than such concepts as fairness, drove the compliance decision, the more subjective, normative approach suggested that "rational institutions" can be undermined if their legitimacy is questioned (Kratochwil & Ruggie 1986). This assertion dovetailed with legal and sociological attempts to understand voluntary law compliance for individuals, groups, and organizations as a function of the perceived legitimacy of the law and legal processes themselves. (At the individual level, see Tyler 1990. With reference to collective organizations, see Knoke & Wood 1981.) The thrust of this literature is that perceived legitimacy of a legal rule or authority heightens the sense of obligation to bring behavior into compliance with the rule.

But if legitimacy is central to voluntary compliance, how can one explore this relationship in a non-tautological way? One approach is to locate the compliance pull of international norms in the nature of the norm itself. Franck (1990) has argued that the legitimacy of a rule—its ability to exert a pull toward voluntary compliance—should be examined in light of its ability to communicate, which in turn is influenced by the rule's determinacy and its degree of coherence. Similarly, Legro (1997) has proposed rule attributes such as specificity, durability, and concordance as one way to consider the effect of norms on outcomes. In his view, the clearer, more durable, and more widely endorsed a prescription, the greater will be its impact on compliance behavior.

Others have focused on the substance of the rule as underpinning its moral force and legitimacy. For example, Fisher (1981) asserted that rules will be better complied with when they follow commonly held notions of fairness and morality; for example, proscribing killing rather than informing on friends, or prescribing reciprocal rather than uni-obligational behavior. He holds that the more "elemental" the rule—the more it reflects *malum in se* rather than *malum in prohibitum*—the more first-order compliance should be expected. Similar arguments have been advanced in the area of human rights compliance. Keck & Sikkink (1998) argue that among the wide array of human rights standards embodied in international agreements, two kinds of prohibitions are most likely to be accepted as legitimate transnationally and cross-culturally: norms involving bodily integrity and the prevention of bodily harm for vulnerable or innocent groups, and norms involving legal equality of opportunity. These norms, they argue, transcend culturally specific belief systems and resonate with basic ideas of human dignity common to most cultures, enhancing their legitimacy as behavioral prescriptions.

International, transnational, and nongovernmental organizations play a significant role in normative processes described in some of this literature. While the rational functionalist literature acknowledges that such entities can provide focal points that narrow the range of equilibrium outcomes, scholars in the normative vein would go much further: International institutions and organizations legitimate particular rules, enhancing their effectiveness through a heightened sense of obligation rather than through their mere instrumental value as a convenient point of convergence (Claude 1965, Peck 1996). Tacsan (1992) for example, has written that the International Court of Justice (ICJ), as a producer and disseminator of new and consensual knowledge, can establish a point where normative expectations converge through an interactive bargaining process. He argued that the ICJ's redefinition of self-determination, non-intervention, collective self-defense, and regional use of force determined the normative expectations that ultimately prevailed in Central America's peace settlement. The normative approach values authoritative institutions that review states' policies for consistency with their international agreements, not because they have the formal power of sanction, but because such procedures legitimate the attempt to find a gap between governments' commitments (formal stances) and their actions. Some have argued that this is why NGOs favored creating a Sustainable Development Commission at the 1992 UNCED in Rio de Janeiro—not because it would have the formal power of sanction, which realist and some functionalist perspectives would point out as a major weakness, but because it would legitimate the process of holding governments accountable for their behavior and its relationship to their stated positions.

In short, normative approaches to the problem of compliance focus on the force of ideas, beliefs, and standards of appropriate behavior as major influences on governments' willingness to comply with international agreements. The hallmarks of this research are its departure from the radically individualized methodology of some variants of realist and functionalist approaches and its embrace of international obligations as social constructs that must be understood and analyzed in an intersubjective framework of meaning. Scholars have attempted to marshal positive methodologies in the study of normative influences; Kacowicz (1994) looked at normative convergence as reflected in substantive treaty provisions and its effect on the prospects for peaceful territorial change, and Kegley & Raymond (1981) used "quasi-authoritative treatises" to draw correlations between prevailing legal norms and states' use of force. However, the intersubjective formulation of the problem has largely resisted such approaches. Scholars who have studied the social ideational influences on international politics submit that such factors as aspirations, legitimacy, and the notion of rights are reasons for actions, which are not the same as causes of actions (Ruggie 1998). Moreover, its explicitly inductive and high-contextual methodology distinguishes this approach from the (neo)realist and functionalist literature.

Conclusions

Research on compliance with international agreements encompasses a wide range of approaches to the study of international relations and crosses over into the disciplines of law and sociology. Yet despite an apparently sprawling literature, the empirical work that might link theory with observed behavior (or subjective understandings of such behavior, as constructivists would have it) has only begun to accumulate in recent years.

Part of the difficulty in the empirical study of compliance has been methodological. If the central analytical issue is to understand the conditions under which states behave in accordance with rules to which they have committed themselves or, more broadly, in accordance with prevailing norms of international behavior, then it is important to isolate the impact of those rules and norms. Several studies have tried to demonstrate a correlation between legal standards and state behavior, sometimes employing large databases and statistical techniques, but most are unconvincing in demonstrating causation, or even in providing an explanatory link between actions taken and the existence of agreements or normative considerations. It has been shown that much international behavior is consistent with international law, even in the conduct of hostilities between states (see for example Kegley & Raymond 1981, Tillema & Van Wingen 1982). It has been far more difficult, however, to show any causal link between legal commitments and behavior.

Establishing causation has been complicated by problems of selection bias and endogeneity. As realists have noted, selection bias proliferates rules in issue areas with minimal problems of strategic cooperation. From

Aron's 1981 complaint that it is no test of international law merely to look at "secondary" problems, to Downs et al.'s (1996) observation that compliance is not very interesting if international agreements are mere "flight control" agreements from which no one has much interest in defecting, there are good reasons to expect that the problem of compliance with treaties will be easier to resolve than the problem of international cooperation in general. This difference is due to the fact that treaty negotiation is endogenous: Governments are more prone to make agreements that comport with the kinds of activities they were willing to engage in anyway, and from which they foresee little incentive to defect. The endogeneity of treaty agreements also weakens the standards of behavior within agreements, which might be expected to improve compliance, but only because the rules are lax.

As a result, it is difficult to show that a rule, commitment, or norm per se influenced governments to take particular positions that represent compliance. In his account of compliance with the partial test ban treaty, Young (1979) gives away the reasons for compliance in the absence of enforcement mechanisms by admitting that the states involved had only extremely weak incentives to go against the agreement. It has been difficult to construct research around crucial case studies showing that agreements have created new and powerful incentives or have altered actors' perceptions of their interests.

The problem of selection bias creates inferential obstacles for the study of second-order compliance as well. Where significant national interests are involved, governments are arguably likely to resist or ignore international jurisdiction (Fischer 1982). As a result, cases in which third parties render authoritative rulings with which the parties are legally bound to comply are likely to be "easy" cases involving parties eager to settle their dispute and therefore willing to make concessions anyway (Coplin 1968, Schwarzenberger 1945), cases involving countries that tend to be law-abiding, or perhaps cases involving small countries whose weak negotiating position gives them little to lose by going through legal processes. However, the nature of the selection bias may differ across issue areas depending on the nature of the dispute-settlement mechanism in place. In the human rights area, the requirement of the "exhaustion of domestic remedies" might have the opposite effect on the pool of litigated cases: States with good domestic rules are not likely to produce many internationally reviewed cases. With respect to trade disputes under the GATT and now the WTO, incentives exist to sue the largest traders, as such suits offer much greater payoffs than going after small markets. In some issue areas, third parties themselves may act strategically, altering the nature of cases brought before them; for example, they may avoid taking jurisdiction for cases in which they anticipate a lack of compliance. The point is that in any given issue area the "litigation pool" is unlikely to be typical of the international community of states. The impact of these biases will influence our ability to draw inferences regarding compliance with authoritative third-party decisions. In some cases, adjudication or arbitration may complement what states would have done anyway; in other issue areas, its impact may vary.

Little has been done to determine whether selection bias is truly pervasive. For example, it should be possible to produce evidence that countries or country pairs that agree voluntarily to third-party arbitration or other judicial processes for settling their disputes are systematically different from a random sample of countries. Endogeneity of substantive agreements poses more difficulty and may require another strategy. One is to select cases in which there is evidence of a shift in state interests over time, rendering a previous commitment inconvenient or even costly to maintain, at least in the short run. The endogeneity problem would be minimized to the extent that compliance with earlier agreements is delinked from obvious explanations of strong, narrow, and immediate "interest-based" reasons to comply.

There are other ways to address the endogeneity of treaties themselves. One is to view the negotiation phase as an integral aspect of the compliance process. Scholars emphasizing the persuasive functions of legal agreements and discourse have also been interested in the contribution of participatory negotiation to eventual compliance. Taking a more constructivist approach to compliance, rather than worry about controlling for endogenous effects of treaty negotiation, one might incorporate its discursive elements into a fuller story of the compliance process. Governments persuade and become convinced of the value or appropriateness of particular standards of behavior over the months, years, and even decades they spend in their formulation. This research agenda might even call for an examination of the discourse used by participants as such negotiations unfold; attitudes toward compliance are shaped by and reflected in this discourse. This strategy uses the negotiation process as data on attitudes toward compliance, rather than viewing it as a source of bias in making inferences.

Despite the conceptual and methodological difficulties, research into the question of compliance with international agreements represents a substantial advance in the study of international law and institutions as important influences on international politics. Realism's assumption that such effects were marginal discouraged empirical investigation and broader theoretical innovations that might have addressed the variations that patently existed across issue areas, among nations, and over time. The current emphasis on the effects of rules on behavior has gone well beyond the functionalist studies of the 1980s, which were primarily concerned with the phenomena of rule creation and evolution rather than their behavioral effects. Nonetheless, we are a long way theoretically and empirically from an understanding of the conditions under which governments comply with international agreements. Pockets of progress mark particular issue areas, such as the environment and human rights, but more effort is needed to subject these findings to the broader concerns of international politics.

Notes

1. During the Cold War, the Court decided only one contentious case on average per year; in 1995, however, the Court had a record number of 13 cases before it.

2. The two approaches differ significantly regarding the role of sanctions versus the use of incentives to "manage" the process of compliance. Chayes & Chayes (1995) emphasize the persuasive function of international law. To enhance compliance, scholars and practitioners should move from an enforcement model that focuses on sanctions and punishments to a management model that focuses on positive incentives and negotiation. Critics respond that such a "managerial approach" to compliance will only go so far, arguing that deep cooperation—compliance with agreements proscribing behavior that is truly difficult to forswear or prescribing behavior that is costly in the short term—will require some form of enforcement (Downs et al. 1996). The distinction between enforcement and management approaches is often made in the context of domestic law enforcement (Hawkins & Thomas 1984, Snavely 1990).

3. "International regimes" were not conceived as isomorphic with international law, but the overlap is significant. International regimes were defined by Stephen Krasner (1983) as "principles, norms, rules, and decisionmaking procedures around which actor expectations converge in a given issue area.

References

Aron R. 1981. *Peace and War: A Theory of International Relations*. Malabar, FL: Robert E. Krieger. pp. 820.

Bilder R. B. 1989. International third party dispute settlement. *Denver J. Int. Law Policy*. 17(3):471–503.

Bork R. H. 1989/90. The limits of "international law." *Natl. Interest* 18:3–10.

Boyle F. A. 1980. The irrelevance of international law. *Calif. West. Int. Law J.* p. 10.

Brierly J. L. 1963. *The Law of Nations*. London: Sir Humphrey Waldock. 6th ed. p. 442.

Bull H. 1977. *The Anarchical Society: A Study of Order in World Politics*. New York: Columbia Univ. Press. p. 335.

Bulterman M. K., Kuijer M. 1996. *Compliance with Judgments of International Courts*. The Hague: Martinus Nijhoff. p. 172.

Chayes A., Chayes A. H. 1995. *The New Sovereignty: Compliance with International Regulatory Agreements*. Cambridge, MA: Harvard Univ. Press. p. 417.

Claude I. L. 1966. Collective legitimization as a political function of the United Nations. *Int. Organ.* 20(3):367–79.

Coplin W. D. 1968. The World Court in the international bargaining process. In *The United Nations and its Functions*, ed. R. W. Gregg, M. Barkin, pp. 313–31. Princeton, NJ: Princeton Univ. Press.

Diehl P. F. 1996. The United Nations and Peacekeeping. In *Coping with Conflict After the Cold War*, ed. E. Kolodziej, R. Kanet, pp. 147–65. Baltimore: Johns Hopkins Univ. Press.

Dixon W. J. 1993. Democracy and the management of international conflict. *J. Confl. Resol.* 37(1):42–68.

Downs G. W., Rocke D. M. 1995. *Optimal Imperfection? Domestic Uncertainty and Institutions in International Relations*. Princeton, NJ: Princeton Univ. Press. p. 159.

Downs G. W., Rocke D. M., Barsoom P. N. 1996. Is the good news about compliance good news about cooperation? *Int. Organ.* 50(3):379–406.

Doyle M. W. 1986. Liberalism and world politics. *Am. Polit. Sci. Rev.* 80:1151–69.

Fischer D. D. 1982. Decisions to use the international court of justice: four recent cases. *Int. Stud. Q.* 26(2):251–77.

Fisher R. 1981. *Improving Compliance with International Law*. Charlottesville: Univ. Virginia Press. p. 370.

Franck T. M. 1990. *The Power of Legitimacy Among Nations*. New York: Oxford Univ. Press. p. 303.

Friedmann W. 1964. *The Changing Structure of International Law*. London: Stevens & Sons. p. 410.

Garrett G., Weingast B. R. 1993. Ideas, interests, and institutions: constructing the EC's internal market. In *Ideas and Foreign Policy*, ed. J. Goldstein, R. O. Keohane, pp. 173–206. Ithaca, NY: Cornell Univ. Press.

Haas P. M., Keohane R. O., Levy M. A. 1993. *Institutions for the Earth: Sources of International Environmental Protection*. Cambridge, MA: MIT Press. p. 448.

Hawkins K., Thomas J. M. 1984. *Enforcing Regulation*. The Hague: Kluwer Nijhoff. 198 pp.

Henkin L. 1979. *How Nations Behave: Law and Foreign Policy*. New York: Columbia Univ. Press and Counc. For. Relat. 2nd ed. p. 400.

Hoffmann S. 1956. The role of international organization: limits and possibilities. *Int. Organ.* 10(3):357–72.

Jacobson H. K., Weiss E. B. 1995. Compliance with international environmental accords. *Global Governance* 1:119–48.

Jacobson H. K., Weiss E. B. 1997. Compliance with international environmental accords: achievements and strategies. Presented at Harvard Univ. Sem. Law Int. Relat. Feb. 5.

Kacowicz A. M. 1994. The problem of peaceful territorial change. *Int. Stud. Q.* 38:219–54.

Keck M., Sikkink K. 1998. *Activists Beyond Borders: Advocacy Networks in International Politics*. Ithaca, NY: Cornell Univ. Press. p. 240.

Kegley C. W. Jr., Raymond G. A. 1981. International legal norms and the preservation of peace, 1820–1964: some evidence and bivariate relationships. *Int. Interact.* 8(3):171–87.

Keohane R. O. 1984. *After Hegemony: Cooperation and Discord in the World Political Economy*. Princeton, NJ: Princeton Univ. Press. p. 290.

Keohane R. O. 1992. Compliance with international commitments: politics within a framework of law. *Am. Soc. Int. Law Proc.* 86:176.

Keohane R. O. 1993. Sovereignty, interdependence, and international institutions. In *Ideas and Ideals: Essays on Politics in Honor of Stanley Hoffmann*, ed. L. B. Miller, M. J. Smith, pp. 91–107. Boulder, CO: Westview.

Knoke D., Woods J. R. 1981. *Organized for Action: Commitment in Voluntary Associations*. New Brunswick, NJ: Rutgers Univ. Press. p. 263.

Krasner S. D. 1983. Structural causes and regime consequences: regimes as intervening variables. In *International Regimes*, ed. S. D. Krasner, pp. 1–21. Ithaca, NY: Cornell Univ. Press.

Kratochwil F. V., Ruggie J. G. 1986. International organization: a state of the art on an art of the state. *Int. Organ.* 40(4):753–75.

Legro J. W. 1997. Which norms matter? Revisiting the "failure" of internationalism. *Int. Organ.* 51(1):31–63.

Merrills J. G. 1969. The justiciability of international disputes. *Can. Bar Rev.* 47:241–69.

Milgrom P. R., North D. C., Weingast B. R. 1990. The role of institutions in the revival of trade: the law merchant, private judges, and the champagne fairs. *Econ. Polit.* 2(1):1–23.

Mitchell R. B. 1994. Regime design matters: intentional oil pollution and treaty compliance. *Int. Organ.* 48(3):425–58.

Morgenthau H. J. 1985. *Politics Among Nations: The Struggle for Power and Peace*. New York: Knopf. 6th ed. p. 688.

Oppenheim, L. 1912. *International Law*. London: Longmans, Green. 2nd ed.

Peck C. 1996. *The United Nations as a Dispute Settlement System*. The Hague: Kluwer Law Int. 301 pp.

Raymond G. A. 1994. Democracies, disputes, and third-party intermediaries. *J. Confl. Resol.* 38(1):24–42.

Röling B. V. A. 1960. *International Law in an Expanded World*. Amsterdam: Djambatan. p. 126.

Root E. 1908. The sanction of international law. *Proc. Am. Soc. Int. Law* 2:14–17.

Ruggie J. G. 1998. *Constructing the World Polity: Essays on International Institutionalization*. New York: Routledge.

Schachter O. 1991. *International Law in Theory and Practice*. Dordrecht, Netherlands: Martinus Nijhoff. 431 pp.

Schwarzenberger G. 1945. *International Law*. London: Stevens & Sons.

Shihata I. F. I. 1965. The attitude of new states toward the International Court of Justice. *Int. Organ.* 19(2):203–22.

Sikkink K. 1993. Human rights, principled issue-networks, and sovereignty in Latin America. *Int. Organ.* 47(3):411–441.

Slaughter A. M. 1995. International law in a world of liberal states. *Eur. J. Int. Law* 6:503–38.

Snavely K. 1990. Governmental policies to reduce tax evasion: coerced behavior versus services and values development. *Policy Sci.* 23:57–72.

Tacsan J. 1992. *The Dynamics of International Law in Conflict Resolution*. Dordrecht, Netherlands: Martinus Nijhoff.

Tillema H. K., Van Wingen J. R. 1982. Law and power in military intervention. *Int. Stud. Q.* 26(2):220–50.

Tyler T. 1990. *Why People Obey the Law*. New Haven: Yale Univ. Press. p. 273.

Young O. R. 1979. *Compliance and Public Authority*. Baltimore: Johns Hopkins Univ. Press. p. 172.

CHAPTER 8

Filling In the Gaps: Extrasystemic Mechanisms for Addressing Imbalances Between the International Legal Operating and Normative Systems

Charlotte Ku and Paul F. Diehl

DEBATES OVER THE LEGALITY AND LEGITIMACY OF THE USE OF force in Iraq in 2003 are but one of the more recent examples in which the norms of international law and the system charged with implementing those norms seemed irreconcilable. This, in fact, reveals a more general problem in international law in which norms and the capacity to implement those norms may not be consonant. Until the international system provides adequate capacity, states and other actors will seek ad hoc and sometimes extrasystemic means to accomplish their ends. By doing so, they may foster more enduring, system-wide change.

Among the most visible changes in any legal system are the adoption of new rules or norms of behavior for its members.[1] In the international legal system, these norms are often specific to a particular problem area. For example, the Convention on Torture reflected the international community's consensus on outlawing certain human rights violations. Similarly, the global trade agreement emerging from the Doha Round of negotiations may include provisions to limit the use of national agricultural subsidies. The Kyoto Protocol sets limits for the emission of greenhouse gases. Each of these is a component of what we have referred to elsewhere as the "normative system,"[2] or the part of international legal system that is quasi-legislative in character by mandating particular values and directing specific changes in state and other actors' behaviors. In effect, the normative system prescribes, and more often proscribes, certain behaviors for the subjects of international law.

The mere specification of behavioral norms does not guarantee that the

---

Reprinted from *Global Governance: A Review of Multilateralism and International Organizations*, vol. 12, no. 2.

normative system will function efficiently. It cannot ensure that those precepts will be observed even when the political will to do so exists. There must be the appropriate processes and structures in place to give effect to the norms. We refer to this as the "operating system." As an operating system, international law functions as a constitution does in a domestic legal system by setting out the consensus of its constituent actors (states) on distribution of authority, responsibilities in governing, and the units which will carry out specific functions; conventionally, these are classified under sources, actors, jurisdiction, and institutions. We chose the word operating as one would in characterizing a computer's operating system. It is the basic platform upon which a system will operate. When the computer operating system (e.g., Microsoft Windows) functions to allow the use of specific word processing programs, spreadsheets, or communications software, there is little direct consideration given to that system by the user. Similarly, the operating system of international law provides the signals and commands that make multiple functions and modes possible, and when functioning often requires little conscious effort.

In the ideal conception, there is symmetry between the normative and operating systems: the latter is designed, and perfectly so, to serve the needs of the former. Indeed, this is largely Hart's conception in which secondary rules serve to give effect to primary rules.[3] In practice, we argue that this is not always the case. Norms are often created in the legal system, but there are not always corresponding provisions in the operating system to give them full effect. For example, the Genocide Convention does not include provisions for universal jurisdiction and until the creation of ad hoc tribunals and the International Criminal Court (ICC), there were no international courts to prosecute individuals accused of genocide. The new norm may be incompatible with the operating system or the norm may be de novo, leaving the operating system incapable of ensuring its application. The imbalance goes beyond international law's centuries-old lack of centralized enforcement mechanisms. It also includes limitations with respect to actors' abilities to assert rights (e.g., individuals and international organizations), law-making procedures, and jurisdictional rules in the operating system. We have argued further that the operating system does not always adapt to changes in the normative system, leading to a suboptimal imbalance between the two systems.[4]

What happens when there is an imbalance between the operating and normative systems? One obvious outcome is nothing; the imbalance remains, and the norms of the system are not given full effect. For example, human rights provisions abound but can be widely ignored in the absence of enforcement mechanisms. In this article, however, we identify several other possibilities. Our contention is that adaptations occur that compensate for, or at least mitigate, the effects of the operating-normative systems imbalance and may over time lead to operating system change. Specifically, we explore four kinds of extrasystemic[5] adaptations: (1) actions by NGOs and transnational networks, (2) internalization of international law, (3) domestic legal and political processes, and (4) "soft law" mechanisms. Our contention is that the international legal system is partly kept functioning by such adaptations even though they technically fall outside the framework of the international legal system. In making this argument, we hope to shed light on the international legal process as well as add to the dialogue in the four areas noted above.

The Operating-Normative System Imbalance

The development of a new legal norm (or the extensive modification of an existing one) may produce changes in the international operating system. Yet the latter is far from guaranteed. First, the extant operating system may be able to accommodate the new norm with no changes required. For example, a new global trade agreement may comport well with existing World Trade Organization mechanisms, including its forum for dispute resolution. In this way, new norms do not upset the equilibrium between normative and operating systems.

Of central concern to this analysis is a second scenario. A new norm may arise that necessitates a change in the operating system in order to give the former full effect, but such a change does not occur. In earlier work, we specified the conditions under which operating system change would follow from a normative change.[6] We argued that the operating system only responds to normative changes when a response is "necessary." The operating system must be incompatible, ineffective, or insufficient to give the new norm effect. For example, holding individuals responsible for torture or other crimes (Convention on Torture) created new norms, but is incompatible with operational rules on sovereign immunity; the Spanish case against General Pinochet is indicative of this tension. Exceptions to foreign sovereign immunity may need to be created in order for the operating system to be consonant with these new agreements and the legal norms embedded in them.

Yet necessity is not a sufficient condition for operating system change. Operating system change must also be roughly coterminous with a dramatic change in the political environment (i.e., "political shock"). There is inherent inertia in any political system, and international law has been characterized as changing more glacially than other legal systems. Accordingly, we posit that some significant impetus must be present before the operating system adjusts to the normative change. That impetus must come from a significant political shock. Political shocks can be discrete events, such as world wars, acts of terrorism, natural disasters, pandemics, or horrific human rights abuses. Shocks might also appear as significant processes, such as global democratization or technological revolution, that extend over a period of time and only have an impact when a critical threshold is reached.

Political shocks may have the effect of changing the normative and operating system simultaneously or sequentially. That is, an initial political shock may prompt a normative change (e.g., restrictions on the use of military force after World War I), and this may include corresponding changes in the operating system (e.g., the creation of the League of Nations and its provisions for dealing with aggression). In contrast, the operating system change may not result from the same shock as that which prompted the initial normative change. Thus, it may take another shock, potentially many years later, for the operating system to be altered.

Even when necessity and political shocks are present, opposition from leading states and domestic political factors might serve to block or limit such operating system change. Change will likely not occur in the operating system, or be incomplete, when such an alteration threatens the self-interest of the dominant states and/or is actively opposed by one or more of those states. If this change occurs without the acquiescence of dominant states, it may prove to be sufficiently minimal and ineffective so as not to challenge their interests. This differs from normative system change that may proceed even if dominant states object. The necessity of consent from the dominant state(s) can, therefore, be seen as an obstacle that needs to be achieved prior to any effective operating system change taking place. This limitation is not a component of the operating system per se, defined by international legal rules, but rather is an exogenous constraint reflective of power relationships in the international legal system.

The above summary illustrates that operating system change, although needed, may not occur. Even when alterations in the operating system take place, they may do so years after the need emerged from the original normative change. In either case, there is a significant imbalance between the operating and normative systems, with the net result being that certain norms will not have effect in the system; that is, they will not be implemented, observed, or enforced in an efficient manner. What is likely to happen as a result of this imbalance? Most obvious is nothing: the system remains out of equilibrium, and new international legal norms have limited or no effect on behavior. Yet, another possibility exists. In the remaining part of this essay, we detail four different adaptations by which the operating-normative system imbalance is redressed—all outside the formal international legal system. Over time, such adaptations may also provide the mode for operating system change.

Extrasystemic Mechanisms for Adaptation

Impetuses for Adaptation

Although disequilibrium may persist, extrasystemic mechanisms may arise to address some or all of the gaps in the operating system. Unlike biological systems, which may be inherently adaptive, the international legal system requires some agency to achieve change. That is, actors outside (e.g., non-governmental organizations) or inside (e.g., states) of the legal operating system must observe the imbalance and have incentives to redress it; such incentives may be strategic and self-interested or they may be altruistic. There are several broad reasons why agents may seek to provide solutions to the operating-normative system imbalance.

First, actors may want to include interested parties, heretofore excluded from the operating system in a particular issue area. Most often, these interested parties are the ones who are willing to supply the monitoring or enforcement capabilities needed to ensure norm compliance. This is most evident in the human rights area in which private organizations, such as Human Rights Watch, carve out roles for themselves in reporting on human right violations. Actors may involve such parties for a number of reasons. Actors may already have good working relationships with interested parties (e.g, certain NGOs), and thereby feel more comfortable with those entities playing important roles in implementation rather than relying on traditional actors such as government or other public entitles in the international legal operating system. Some actors (e.g., weaker states) may regard themselves as incapable (in terms of power, resources, or expertise) to fill in the gaps, and thereby seek third parties who can fill the roles required. Interested parties may desire to participate for altruistic reasons because they believe that their efforts are superior to extant operating system procedures or just because such organizations want to enhance their roles, task expansion behavior characteristics of organizations of all varieties.

Second, the intervention of other actors may be to ensure that some issues not automatically part of the existing structures and processes are included. Actors may desire that issues concerning indigenous peoples, for example, be included as part of the monitoring of environmental accords. Extrasystemic mechanisms may ensure that such concerns are reflected in the implementation of the norm, something that would not occur under present operating system mechanisms.

Third, actors, especially individual states, may desire greater control over the implementation of norms. Accordingly, they create structures and processes outside of the international legal operating system, perhaps even blocking efforts at operating system change. Regulation of norms may then be left to domestic legal systems or powerful actors, who then have some discretion (and national sovereignty) over the norm as it affects those actors. This is important in that it shows that actors are not always motivated by achieving greater compliance with international norms when they create mechanisms to supplement or replace international legal procedures.

Below, we identify four different adaptations by which the operating-normative system imbalance is redressed. We should note that the outcomes of all these processes are not necessarily a fully functioning and effective system of norm implementation. Extrasystemic adaptations may still leave holes in the operating system unfilled and even when gaps are addressed, the adaptations may be inefficient or ineffective. Still, most adaptations have the effect of improving norm implementation and the effect of the normative system. Several of these also have the effect of skirting the barriers imposed by opposition to the operating system change presented by the leading states in the international system.

NGOs and Transnational Networks

Traditionally, nongovernmental organizations (NGOs) were involved only in the process of norm creation. Most notably, they raised the salience of global problems, and helped mold treaty language, albeit usually working through national delegations. The prominence of women's issues on the international agenda today and the adoption of treaties such as the Landmines Convention and the Statute for an International Criminal Court, are examples of strategic NGO-state alliances that resulted from highly effective political lobbying.[7] Increasingly, however, NGOs are also assisting with elements of the operating system, particularly with the monitoring and implementation of legal instruments.[8] As treaties increasingly provide frameworks rather than static statements of norms, NGOs have a wider range of opportunities to influence the development of both the normative and operating systems.

Contemporary circumstances have created opportunities for nongovernmental organizations (NGOs) to play more roles as a supplement or substitute to the international law operating system. This stems, in part, from international law's shift in focus from concerns of the state to those of the individual. Also, the technical character of many issues now facing policymakers continues to make them, as they have been for decades, receptive to expert information. "New technology and the increasingly complex and technical nature of issues of global concern not only increase decision makers' uncertainty about their policy environment but also contribute to the diffusion of power, information, and values among states, thereby creating a hospitable environment for epistemic communities."[9] Technology has also "broken governments' monopoly on the collection and management of large amounts of information."[10] Events leading up to the signing of the convention to ban the use of antipersonnel landmines (Ottawa Convention, 1997) provided an example of the new power that individuals linked by technology, organized into a political network, and working in alliance with governments can wield.[11] Thus, some NGOs are well positioned to assume roles in the implementation of norms, especially in those areas in which specialized expertise is required.[12]

Beyond expertise, NGOs have been directly called up to perform operating system functions heretofore carried out by other actors. Intergovernmental organizations (IGOs) have specifically contributed to the prominence of NGOs as they have sought to circumvent governments. As governments seem less able or willing to meet the financial needs of norm monitoring and compliance, IGOs have tapped the vast private wealth available through the intermediation of NGOs. Thus, as national governments have been less willing to carry out the duties of the operating system or support international institutions that will perform those functions, NGOs have been called up to fill the gap, often as "subcontractors" to broader IGO efforts. Perhaps most famously, the International Committee of the Red Cross (ICRC) is charged with monitoring compliance with international humanitarian law as it relates to prisoners of war. NGOs can also supplement government and international governmental organization capacity in helping to keep abreast of specific issues areas. This is important where even the most well-staffed government agencies can rarely dedicate full-time staffs to the many issues which now comprise international affairs.

NGOs have been especially instrumental in filling operating system gaps in human rights and the environment, issue areas in which states needed political support and capacity "on the ground." Private organizations have an advantage in pursuing these activities within countries that no foreign government could. Furthermore, the political power and experience gained in promoting various norms continued beyond the enactment of specific obligations to monitoring their ongoing development and implementation. Given their familiarity with the issues and the players, NGOs may in fact be more expert at monitoring and overseeing development of norms than the formal organizations created to do so on an official basis. Keohane and Nye observed that in addition to the formal governance provided by states and the intergovernmental organizations that they created, governance now also takes place through networks of agents that can be both public and private and that derive credibility from their flexibility and dynamism to address new issues with fewer start-up costs.[13]

This bottom up approach runs counter to the classical image of international law as the product of an international conference of diplomats. Yet, it has evolved as an important source of international law as more private activity from trade to child custody issues move across international borders. The bottom up approach is not grassroots, but relies on networks of practitioners whose practice and behavior affect the content and form of certain rules because they are the very individuals who are key to that particular practice. This is similar to the kind of transgovernmental network to which Slaughter refers.[14] The structure of an influential group can be informal, but the group wields influence because it is cohesive and recognized by those who are key to the work in a specific area. The bottom up approach recognizes that such informal arrangements can exist outside of the government sphere and can also have important regulatory or normative effect because the behavior will be consistent among all who are in the network.

One example of such nongovernmental law-making can be found in the letter of credit practices used by commercial banks called the Uniform Customs and Practice for Documentary Credits. Though not law, US courts and courts elsewhere have used this standard to resolve letter of credit disputes. Another example is in the area of export credit insurance where the International Union of Credit and Investment Insurers adopted standards that ultimately found their way into more formal international agreement. These are narrow and technical areas, but if we think back to the origins of much of the UN specialized agency system we have today, perhaps we can appreciate the importance and potential power of such privately generated best practices and standards.[15]

Another example is when civil society groups ally with intergovernmental organizations to set standards and pursue initiatives that subsequently are embraced by national governments, but are first pursued or articulated by private groups. There are an increasing number of examples of this occurring, and private organizations remain active in the implementation of an international convention:

- Framework Convention for Tobacco Control: two NGO alliances are closely identified with efforts to prepare and adopt the Framework Convention—the Framework Convention Alliance with more than 200 NGOs in 91 countries and the Tobacco Transnationals made up of 75 groups in 50 countries
- Landmines Convention and the celebrated network that won organizer Jody Williams the Nobel Peace Prize
- The Statute of the International Criminal Court
- Driftnet Fishing
- Corporate social responsibility standards employing techniques of international standard-setting and litigation through domestic channels, for example, use of the U.S. Alien Tort Claims Act with regard to UNOCAL in Myanmar and Shell in Nigeria.[16] Such steps indicate movement away from voluntary standards of corporate social responsibility to international obligations that carry legal liability and accountability.[17]

The drawback to the bottom up approach is that it assumes a developed legal and political system that is adequately mature and specialized to participate in the global network in a particular area. It further assumes that resources would be available to move towards common objectives. The bottom up approach puts a premium on participation. As such, it can disadvantage national legal systems that are not part of existing networks. The bottom up approach at the international level, however, may be advanced by the decentralization and privatization of public services such as health, and a global economy that can outpace national governments' abilities to regulate.

In addition to NGOs, we see that voluntary, transnational networks have demonstrated their power to contribute to the operating system, especially to influence states in the monitoring of state conduct in the treatment of their own citizens. "Principled issue networks," as agents for change in state behavior and even in international standards, have emerged from the increased level of private transnational activity. Made possible through resources provided by foundations, spurred on by the commitment of individuals, and held together by new technologies, these transnationally-linked organizations have had some notable achievements particularly in the protection of human rights.[18] Even decades ago, the kind of "people power" generated by Helsinki Watch, Charter 77, Solidarity, and other groups eventually created pressures for human rights and an end to the cold war from within the Warsaw Pact countries themselves. Yet, while it seems clear that the public sector can no longer function effectively without the cooperation and participation of the private sector and the involvement of individual citizens, it remains true that the private sector cannot solve all problems without the infrastructure and coordination that states and international institutions provide.

The importance of NGOs and private transnational networks functioning as part of civil society caused UN Secretary-General Annan to note that: "We must also adapt international institutions, through which states govern together, to the realities of the new era. We must form coalitions for change, often with partners well beyond the precincts of officialdom."[19] As Kaldor observes, the elements of civil society—voluntary associations, movements, parties, and unions for example, enable individuals "to act publicly."[20]

We note that some transnational networks are built not exclusively between private actors, but are actually bridges connecting officials in different governments. Such official, albeit informal, networks can play key roles in ensuring the effectiveness of international standards. A prominent current example is in the global effort to fight terrorism. Slaughter notes that "Public attention has focused on military cooperation, but the networks of financial regulators working to identify and freeze terrorist assets, of law enforcement officials sharing vital information on terrorist suspects, and of intelligence operatives working to preempt the next attack have been equally important. Networked threats require a networked response."[21] One might expect such networks to become even more prominent as globalized problems proliferate and traditional mechanisms prove inadequate for regulating behavior.

Yet there are concerns about whether the international legal operating system can rely on these informal arrangements. First, the ad hoc and selective character of these partnerships have caused concern about the effectiveness and reliability of such arrangements as durable pillars of global governance. Second is an exaggerated perception of the ability of NGOs and transnational networks to carry out a wide range of operating system activities. The potential fragmentation in information, resources, and decision-making may, in the long run, be a serious threat to the order and authority that are requisite to civil society.

Despite these concerns, most scholars acknowledge the positive influence NGOs and transnational networks have had on contemporary international law in areas such as the well being of individuals, human rights, gender and race equality, environmental protection, sustainable development, indigenous rights, nonviolent conflict resolution, participatory democracy, social diversity, and social and economic justice.[22] In the broadest sense, we may be moving towards the point where effective and sustained attention to these issues requires the political and financial mobilization of resources at all levels from local to global. This is where the voluntary, local, and issue specific character of NGOs and transnational networks make them a useful link between the sub-national community and national and international communities and institutions. By providing a link, NGOs supplement the human and financial resources of governments and intergovernmental organizations.

Legal Internalization

Traditional conceptions of the international legal operating system rely on international institutions and processes to supervise norms. Yet, one of the adaptations to inadequacies in this system is to rely on domestic legal mechanisms to pick up the slack. This is described well by the third component of Koh's view of transnational legal process: internalization: "Legal internalization occurs when an international norm is incorporated into the domestic legal system through executive action, judicial interpretation, legislative action, or some combination of the three. . . . Judicial internalization can occur when domestic litigation provokes judicial incorporation of human rights norms either implicitly, by construing existing statutes consistently with international human rights norms, or explicitly, through what I have elsewhere called 'transnational public law litigation.'"[23]

Some internalization is provided for within the confines of the international legal operating system. When a treaty explicitly requires national executing legislation to give norms effect domestically (e.g., rules on endangered species), then this can be considered an element of the operating system. Still, unique features of national legal systems leave much of the incorporation of international law to domestic legal rules and processes, thus technically placing such adaptations outside of the rules of the international operating system. Furthermore, in other stances, internalization happens independently of treaty provisions and is stimulated by domestic political actors.

Legal internalization redresses problems with implementation or enforcement in which some states are unwilling to follow the international norm. The problem may take place for a variety of legal, political, social, or economic reasons. One response is legislative internalization, when domestic lobbying embeds international law norms into binding domestic legislation or even constitutional law that officials of a non-complying government must then obey as part of the domestic legal fabric. Local actors then attain standing to press claims and seek redress in domestic courts.

More recently, with the case of Osbaldo Torres v. the State of Oklahoma before the Oklahoma Court of Criminal Appeals, we see the effort of domestic legal institutions to give effect to the decision of the International Court of Justice in the case of Avena and other Mexican Nationals.[24] In its decision, one of the Oklahoma Court's judges acknowledged that the U.S. was bound by treaties,[25] in this case, the Statute of the International Court of Justice and the Vienna Convention on Consular Relations, and that the court was therefore bound to abide by the opinion in the Avena case.[26]

The European Union represents a special case and one in which internalization has gradually become more systematic. Slaughter and Mattli described the process whereby European states have incorporated EU law into their own legal system: "Until 1963 the enforcement of the Rome treaty [the constituent treaty of the European Union], like that of any other international treaty, depended entirely on action by the national legislatures of the member states of the community. By 1965, a citizen of a community country could ask a national court to invalidate any provision of domestic law found to conflict with certain directly applicable provisions of the treaty. By 1975, a citizen of an EC country could seek the invalidation of national law found to conflict with self-executing provisions of community secondary legislation, the 'directives' to national governments passed by the EC Council of Ministers. And by 1990, community citizens could ask their national courts to interpret national legislation consistently with community legislation in the face of undue delay in passing directives on the part of national legislatures."[27]

The pioneering work in the development of a regional human rights system that the jurisprudence of the European Court of Human Rights represents is a further important example of the interactions between extranational and national systems of law. One of the more sweeping recent examples is that of the British incorporation of the European Convention on Human Rights into its domestic law that "marks a dramatic shift in how individual rights are conceptualized under British law. . . . The Human Rights Act, which puts courts and other public authorities under a positive duty to 'give effect' to the rights enumerated in the European Convention in their day-to-day activities, marks a shift in the perception of civil liberties from residual freedoms to positive rights."[28]

The incorporation of international norms into domestic legal processes has several advantages. Among the most notable is that the monitoring and enforcement of the law is invested in national legal operating systems, all or most of which are more developed and better resourced than the international system. This means that norms violations are more likely to be detected, and most importantly there are established mechanisms for dealing with such violations. Although there has been a significant increase over the last decade in the creation of international tribunals, the international court system is still quite weak and structurally limited when compared to its domestic counterparts. Indeed, one might argue that legal internalization may, in some cases, be superior to international operating system equivalents.

Legal internalization, however, is not without its flaws or limitations. First, internalization is probably most effective in monist legal systems in which national and international law are part of the same system. In addition, the adaptation is strongest in systems in which some international laws may supercede national laws (e.g., Germany) as opposed to those in which the national and international law are considered co-equals (e.g., United States). Second, legal internalization as an adaptation to operating system inadequacy is likely to be incomplete when viewed from a global perspective. For internalization to be effective fully, it must take place in almost 200 different states. This is unlikely, as some states will resist such actions and there is no assurance that such internalizations will be consistent with the objects and purposes of the international norms.

Even if it were to occur universally, the lack of democratic processes and legal mechanisms in many states will prevent international norms from influencing the behavior of government officials. Authoritarian states may be characterized by the lack of independent interest groups to press for norm compliance or the ability of state officials to subvert the legal process in order to avoid being held accountable for norm violations. There are instances, however, of states allowing access to their national courts to hear claims that may have occurred outside the boundaries of that state. Belgium has enacted universal jurisdiction provisions that might allow it to prosecute Israeli Prime Minister Ariel Sharon for actions during the 1982 invasion of

Lebanon, although Belgium has recently limited its application. Furthermore, foreign plaintiffs have relied on a 200+ year old US law, the Alien Tort Claims Act, to make claims for actions that did not occur in the United States and did not involve any US citizens.[29] Thus, there are even adaptations for other failed adaptations to inadequacies in the international operating system. Third, legal internalization may be ill-suited or irrelevant for international norms that deal exclusively with the interactions between states, absent an internal component. Thus, while in some sense, these adaptations are the ideal response to operating system failures, in practice they are likely to be only a partial solution or a step to more permanent operating system change.

Domestic Legal and Political Processes

National safeguards are not a substitute for international regulation or legal internalization, but when the latter fail or prove inadequate, regulation can and does move to the national level. National safeguards further come in two forms—the formal and the informal. Formal safeguards are found in constitutions and national institutions such as legislatures, courts, and budgets.[30] These institutions and their underlying processes may provide disincentives or prohibitions against norm violations that are independent of international influences, but nevertheless effective. For example, prohibitions against certain human rights violations may be embedded in national law, and these may have been present even before the development of a concomitant international norm.

Informal safeguards operate through political culture and public opinion.[31] The effectiveness of these safeguards varies widely depending on the strength of the domestic political system, including whether it is democratic and how open it is to public debate or not. To the extent that international norms are shared by domestic audiences and/or are encased in national cultures, there will be informal, but powerful, constraints on government officials to adhere to those norms. This may occur even if national legal constraints are absent. Domestic constituencies may play a critical role in the willingness of governments to comply with international agreements.[32] Governments will be especially responsive to such influences when those constituencies can exercise electoral leverage on leading political officials (e.g., they are significant parts of the government's "selectorate" or coalition) and/or they can provide extensive information about their own state's compliance. European state compliance with the Long Range Transboundary Air Pollution Convention can largely be attributed to these elements.[33]

National political and legal processes may also take on more prominent roles in cases when international law appears inadequate to address particular circumstances. When existing international standards and structures are under stress, national debate and political process may help to fill the gap and set the criteria for action as well as the limits for such operations.[34] For example, the closer the use of military force gets to war, the more national systems play a role in the decision to take part in such operations and in overseeing them. This process, in turn, contributes to shaping both the practice and scope of international action. As the Panel on UN Peace Operations concluded in 2001: "[T]he United Nations does not wage war. Where enforcement action is required, it has consistently been entrusted to coalitions of willing States, with the authorization of the Security Council acting under Chapter VII of the Charter."[35]

The interactions of international and domestic decision-making processes have been well recognized by international organization scholars like Cox and Jacobson who concluded in their classic study of decision-making, *The Anatomy of Influence,* that the significance of international organizations is better judged "not as how independent they are of states, but how far they involve the effective policy-making process of governments."[36] What debates over the 2003 war in Iraq now tell us is that involving the effective policy-making processes of national governments is no longer adequate in all cases. National decision-making processes require certain levels of legitimacy that may now include appropriate international authorization and standards.

As with other adaptations to international operating system gaps, reliance on domestic political and legal processes is far from foolproof. Similar to internalization, there will be considerable variance across states with respect to national laws that serve to monitor and protect international norms. In addition, we recognize that domestic audiences and culture may not always be supportive of international norms; note the divergence between international norms on the status of women and cultural views on female genital mutilation. Furthermore, government officials may choose to ignore or circumvent domestic law or public opinion in foreign policy. The rule of national law and the ability of domestic audiences to sanction violators (at election time) is much greater in democracies than in states that lack an independent judiciary and mechanisms for public input into policy formulation.

Despite its limitations, relying on domestic legal and political processes as substitutes for the international operating system has some very attractive features. Most notably is that if international norms are already protected in national legal systems and well ensconced in national culture and attitudes, international law may be almost self-enforcing. Whether it has been providing the definitive interpretations of humanitarian intervention or preemptive action, the UN Charter system dealing with the use of force has come under increasing stress since the end of the Cold War in 1989.[37] Yet if the current structure of international institutions does not effectively address these questions, does this necessarily mean the return to a self-judging and unregulated international security system? Implicit in that question is the assumption that without international regulation by international institutions, state behavior is essentially unregulated. Such a conclusion would overlook the considerable number of national safeguards that can exist at the state level to protect against the wanton loss of lives and resources through military operations that do not serve a state's interests. In some cases, there may be little need for international operating system provisions, and therefore little concern if such mechanisms are absent or deficient. Perhaps one of the most serious inadequacies of the present international operating system is in the area of the use of force.

"Soft Law" Mechanisms

Finally, but far from least important, are so-called "soft law" mechanisms for ensuring norm compliance. Chinkin points out that the term soft law encompasses a wide range, but also that it is an increasingly used tool:

> There is a wide diversity in the instruments of so-called soft law which makes the generic term a misleading simplification. Even a cursory examination of these diverse instruments inevitably exposes their many variables in form, language, subject matter, participants, addressees, purposes, follow up and monitoring procedures. These variables, coupled with the inherent contradictions in any concept of soft law, highlight the challenges presented to the structure and substance of the traditional legal order by the increasing use of soft law forms.[38]

Despite the ambiguity, soft law mechanisms are broadly those that do not involve a formal legal obligation or legal processes, but nevertheless represent a shared understanding or consensus about procedure or behavior among the parties. In the context of the operating system, informal or soft mechanisms for resolving jurisdictional disagreements (e.g., how to resolve disputes when overlapping jurisdiction is present) or disputes over substance (e.g., what diplomatic solutions are legitimized) represent soft law adaptations to inadequacies in "hard law" provisions. A growing body of empirical work shows that such informal mechanisms influence behavior.[39]

As noted above, soft law mechanisms have multiple forms and purposes and we cannot describe all those variations here. Nevertheless, for illustration purposes, we describe a few of the ways in which soft law fills the gaps left by its hard law counterparts. Soft law may provide for both norms and their implementation when formal agreements are not possible or involve issues that are heretofore considered domestic concerns. For example, commodity agreements or marketing specific products, such as breast milk substitutes, provide a way to monitor and regulate behavior of international concern without resort to a treaty.[40] Similarly, soft law is a vehicle to link international law to private entities regulated principally by domestic law, such as individuals and transnational corporations.[41] Soft law may also function as a supplement or follow-up to traditional operating system mechanisms. Indeed, as in the case of international environmental law, a treaty may provide for a framework convention that can be followed by protocols that generate soft law or practice to supplement the original text. Dinah Shelton explained that: "Typically, the framework convention establishes a structure for further co-operation between the parties through monitoring and implementation procedures, exchanging data, and facilitating regulation."[42]

Soft law fills in some gaps left by the formal operating system, but why would actors choose to rely on the former, which are sometime ambiguous and may create multiple regimes? Kenneth Abbott and Duncan Snidal identify a number of advantages of soft law.[43] These include lower contracting or negotiating costs, especially in comparison to long and detailed legal agreements such as those concerning trade negotiated under the auspices of the World Trade Organization. Soft law also entails fewer sovereignty costs, something that states may reluctantly bear when signing hard legal agreements. States may also adopt soft law provisions for norms in relatively new areas of international law (e.g., Forest Principles), whose implementation effects cannot be easily foreseen or for which rapid changes might be on the horizon (e.g., areas of environmental law). Soft law provides greater flexibility as states do not risk creating operating system institutions that may be difficult to adapt or eliminate over time.[44] Finally, soft law institutions and processes may be the product of compromises when states desire a particular international norm, but are reluctant to create the necessary operating system mechanisms that ensure its effect.

Despite the challenges, Chinkin observed that soft law is also a phenomenon that is here to stay because international affairs have outpaced the ability of the traditional law-making machinery "through international organizations, specialized agencies, programmes, and private bodies that do not fit the paradigm of Article 38(1) of the Statute of the ICJ."[45] We may also find that over time, soft law may harden through practice or through implementation by international or national institutions.

Conclusion

We began with a classification of the international legal system into two component parts: normative and operating systems respectively. The former refers to the often issue-specific prescriptions for behavior in international law (e.g., good neighbor principle in environmental law). The latter includes the mechanisms (e.g., jurisdiction rules, courts) designed to ensure that the norms are implemented and observed. We noted that a problem occurs when the operating system is unable to promote (or is inefficient in promoting) the efficacy of certain norms. The international legal system may persist in a state of suboptimality. The major portion of this paper was dedicated to identifying extrasystemic adaptations that have emerged to respond to the operating-normative system imbalance.

We see at least four different adaptations or governance mechanisms, formally outside the international legal system, that supplement or substitute for the operating component of that system. These are (1) NGOs and transnational networks, (2) internalization of international law, (3) domestic legal and political processes, and (4) soft law mechanisms. An implicit assumption in some analyses is that such adaptations, while valuable or even essential, are less desirable than a fully functioning operating system composed of purely international structures and processes. There is some truth to that assumption, but it is too simplistic.

Extrasystemic adaptations do not fill all the gaps of the operating system and cannot always substitute for effective international operating system components. Our analysis indicates that none of the four adaptations alone is sufficient to ensure that international norms are adopted and actors continue to adhere to their prescriptions. Even in combination, a number of holes remain. Furthermore, because some of the adaptations are ad hoc, there is a tendency for periods of imbalance to persist until actors react. In addition, such ad hoc measures are not well suited for addressing new concerns or sudden changes in the international legal system. Finally, adaptations tend to be unevenly distributed across state members of the international legal system. Rarely will certain adaptations (i.e., internalization) spread to all 190 plus states in the world, leaving more of a patchwork of international norm compliance rather than blanket coverage. One might presume that legal systems in developed and democratic countries are more amenable to some adaptations than poorer and authoritarian governments. Still, it may not be necessary for the operating system or the extra-system adaptations to function perfectly; indeed it is probably unrealistic to expect this. It may be enough to achieve "acceptable" levels of compliance[46] in order to achieve most of the goals of the normative system.

Despite their limitations, we also concluded that such adaptations may be superior to operating system mechanisms in a number of instances. For example, soft law mechanisms offered flexibility and greater acceptability advantages for states and this may make normative provisions more likely to be adopted in the first place. Furthermore, reliance on domestic legal and political institutions that are stronger and more developed than international structures allows greater access for a range of actors and more effective compliance mechanisms to ensure implementation of the norms. In areas in which international agreement is of a framework or guiding principle character or in which the shape of an international legal obligation is still in formation, such extralegal mechanisms may be useful precursors to more specific international standards and obligations.

Slaughter concluded that the international governance model of a multipurpose international institution like the United Nations at its center had built-in limits because "it requires a centralized rule-making authority, a hierarchy of institutions, and universal membership."[47] In place of this, she observes that governance has moved into a transgovernmental order of "courts, regulatory agencies, executives, and even legislatures . . . networking with their counterparts abroad, creating a dense web of relations. . . ."[48] Drawing on examples from various sectors in her book, *A New World Order*, Slaughter argues that a transgovernmental order can provide a much more expandable and flexible system of governance than is available through the classic system of states and intergovernmental organizations.[49] Our analysis of the international legal operating and normative systems suggest something quite similar. To understand fully how international law functions today, one must look beyond traditional state-to-state or government-to-government legal institutions, processes, and mechanisms.

Notes

1. In this essay, we use the terms "norms" and "rules" interchangeably to signify the existence of a binding international legal obligation.

2. Charolotte Ku and Paul F. Diehl, *International Law* (Boulder: Lynne Rienner Publishers, 2003), pp. 1–19.

3. H.L.A. Hart, *The Concept of Law* (Oxford: Oxford University Press, 1994).

4. Paul F. Diehl, *et al.*, "The Dynamics of International Law: The Interaction of Normative and Operating Systems," *International Organization* 57, no.1 (Winter 2003): 43–75.

5. By extrasystemic, we refer to mechanisms outside of the traditional, state-centric *international* legal system as defined by extant treaty and customary law. Extrasystemic adaptations would include, for example, actions by nongovernmental organizations (NGOs) in lobbying governments or organizations as well as changes in *national* law that have an international effect. Extrasystemic adaptations, however, would *not* include NGO activity authorized within the system, such as the role of the International Committee of the Red Cross specified in the Geneva Conventions.

6. Diehl, *et al.*, "The Dynamics of International Law: The Interaction of Normative and Operating Systems."

7. Charlotte Ku and John K. Gamble, "International Law—New Actors and New Technologies: Center Stage for NGOs?" *Law and Policy in International Business* 32, no. 2 (2000): 221–262.

8. *See* Cynthia Price Cohen, "The Role of Nongovernmental Organizations in the Drafting of the Convention on the Rights of the Child," *Human Rights Quarterly* 12, no. 1 (1990): 137–147.

9. Emanuel Adler and Peter M. Haas, "Conclusion: Epistemic Communities, World Order, and the Creation of a Reflective Research Program," *International Organization* 46 (1992): 367, 387.

10. Jessica T. Mathews, "Power Shift," *Foreign Affairs* 76, no. 1 (January/February 1997).

11. See Stephen Greene, "A Campaign to Sweep Away Danger," *Chronicle of Philanthropy* 60 (October 1997). See also Richard Price, "Transnational Civil Society Targets Land Mines," *International Organization* 52 (1998): 613–644.

12. See, for example, Janet Koven Levit, "A Bottom-Up Approach to International Lawmaking: The Tale of Three Trade Finance Instruments," *The Yale Journal of International Law* 30 (Winter 2005): 125–209.

13. Robert Keohane and Joseph F. Nye, Jr., "Introduction" in Joseph F. Nye, Jr., and John D. Donohue, eds., *Governance in a Globalizing World* (Brookings Institution Press, 2000), pp. 18–20.

14. Anne-Marie Slaughter, *A New World Order* (Princeton: Princeton University Press, 2004).

15. See Janet Koven Levit, "A Bottom-Up Approach to International Lawmaking: The Tale of Three Trade Finance Instruments," *The Yale Journal of International Law* 30 (Winter 2005): 125–209.

16. See John De, et al., v. Unocal Corporation, 2002 WL 31063976 (U.S. Court of Appeals for the Ninth Circuit, 2002) and Wiwa v. Royal Dutch Petroleum Co, 226 F.3d88 (U.S. Court of Appeals for the Second Circuit, 2000).

17. See Isabella Bunn, "Global Advocacy for Corporate Accountability: Transatlantic Perspectives from the NGO Community," *American University International Law Review* 19, no. 6 (2004): 1265–1306.

18. Kathryn A. Sikkink, "Human Rights, Principled Issue-Networks, and Sovereignty in Latin America" *International Organization* 47, no. 3 (1993): 411–441.

19. UN Secretary-General Kofi A. Annan's Report, "*We the Peoples": The Role of the United Nations in the 21st Century* (April 3, 2000).

20. Mary Kaldor, "The Idea of Global Civil Society," *International Affairs* 79, no. 3 (2003): 585.

21. Slaughter, *A New World Order*.

22. See, e.g., Dianne Otto, "Nongovernmental Organizations in the United Nations System: The Emerging Role of International Civil Society," *Human Rights Quarterly* 18, no. 1 (1996): 140–141.

23. Harold H. Koh, "Why Do Nations Obey International Law?" *The Yale Law Journal* 106 (1997): 2599–2659.

24. International Court of Justice, Judgment, *Case Concerning Avena and Other Mexican Nationals (Mexico v. United States of America)*, No. 128, (March 31, 2004).

25. Oklahoma Court of Criminal Appeals: *Osbaldo Torres v. the State of Oklahoma* (No. PCD-04-442) [May 13, 2004]. See also Lori Damrosch, Brief of International Law Experts and Former Diplomats as *Amici Curiae* in Support of Petitioner, Appeal from the District Court of Oklahoma, County, State of Oklahoma Case No. CF-1993-4302 (April 30, 2004).

26. See also Carlos Manuel Vazquez, "*Breard* and the Federal Power to Require Compliance with ICJ Orders of Provisional Measures," *American Journal of International Law* 92 (October 1998): 683–691.

27. Anne-Marie Burley (Slaughter) and Walter Mattli, "Europe Before the Court: A Political Theory of Legal Integration," *International Organization* 47, no. 1 (Winter 1993): 42.

28. Douglas Vick, "The Human Rights Act and the British Constitution," *Texas International Law Journal* 37 (2002): 330.

29. Anne-Marie Slaughter and David Bosco, "Plaintiff's Diplomacy," *Foreign Affairs* 79, no. 5 (2002): 102–117.

30. For examples of constitutional restraints, see Lori Damrosch, "The Interface of National Constitutional Systems with International Law and Institutions on Using Military Forces: Changing Trends in Executive and Legislative Powers," in Charlotte Ku and Harold K. Jacobson, eds., *Democratic Accountability and the Use of Force in International Law* (Cambridge University Press 2003), pp. 39–60.

31. For examples of such political factors, see Karen Mingst, "Domestic political factors and decisions of use military forces" in Ku and Jacobson eds., *Democratic Accountability and the Use of Force in International Law,* pp. 61–80.

32. Xinyuan Dai, "Why Comply?: The Domestic Constituency Mechanism," *International Organization* 59, no. 2 (2005): 363.

33. Ibid.

34. See Adam Roberts, "NATO's "Humanitarian War,"' *Survival* 3 (1999):107.

35. UN Report of the Panel on United Nations Peace Operations A/55/305 (August 21, 2000).

36. Richard W. Cox and Harold K. Jacobson, *The Anatomy of Influence: Decision Making in International Organization* (New Haven: Yale University Press 1973), p. 428.

37. Boutros-Ghali, *An Agenda for Peace 1995* (1995).

38. Christine Chinkin, "The Challenge of Soft Law: Development and Change in International Law," *International and Comparative Law Quarterly* 38 (1989): 850.

39. See Dinah Shelton, ed., *Commitment and Compliance: The Role of Non-Binding Norms in the International Legal System* (Oxford University Press 2000); Abram Chayes and Antonia Handler Chayes, *The New Sovereignty: Compliance with International Regulatory Agreements* (Harvard University Press, 1996); Edith Brown Weiss and Harold K. Jacobson, *Engaging Countries: Strengthening Compliance with International Environmental Accords* (The MIT Press 1998). See also Duane Windwor and Kathleen A. Getz, "Multilateral Cooperation to Combat Corruption: Normative Regimes Despite Mixed Motives and Diverse Values," *Cornell International Law Journal* 33, no. 3 (2000); Alhaji B.M. Marong, "Toward a Normative Consensus Against Corruption: Legal Effects of the Principles to Combat Corruption in Africa," *Denver Journal of International Law and Policy* 30, no. 2 (Spring 2002): 99–129; Andreanna M. Truelove, "Oil, Diamonds, and Sunlight: Fostering Human Rights Through Transparency in Revenues from Natural Resources," *Georgetown Journal of International Law* 35 (Spring 2004): 207; Alfred C. Aman, Jr., "Ceding Public Power to Private Actions: Globalization, Democracy, and the Need for a New Administrative Law," *UCLA Law Review* 49 (August 2002); Kal Raustiala, "The Architechture of International Cooperation: Transgovernmental Networks and the Future of International Law," *Virginia Journal of International Law* 43 (Fall 2002): 1–92; Daniel L. Feldman, "Conflict Diamonds, International Trade Regulations, and the Nature of Law," *University of Pennsylvania Journal of International Economic Law* 24, no 4 (Winter 2003): 835–874.

40. Chinkin, "The Challenge of Soft Law: Development and Change in International Law."

41. *Ibid.*

42. Christine Chinkin, "Normative Development in the International Legal System," in Dinah Shelton, ed., *Commitment and Compliance: The Role of Non-*

Binding Norms in the International Legal System (Oxford University Press 2000), p. 27.

43. Kenneth W. Abbott and Duncan Snidal, "Hard and Soft Law in International Governance," *International Organization* 54, no. 3 (2000): 421–456.

44. See also Charles Lipson, "Why Are Some International Agreements Informal?" *International Organization* 45, no. 4 (1991): 495.

45. Chinkin, *"Normative Development in the International Legal System."*

46. Abram Chayes and Antonia Handler Chayes, "On Compliance," *International Organization* 47, no. 2 (Spring 1993): 175.

47. Anne-Marie Slaughter, "The Real New World Order," *Foreign Affairs* 76 (September/October 1997): 183.

48. *Ibid.*, p. 184.

49. See Slaughter, *A New World Order.*

CHAPTER 9

Princeton Principles on Universal Jurisdiction

The Princeton Project

The Challenge

During the last century millions of human beings perished as a result of genocide, crimes against humanity, war crimes, and other serious crimes under international law. Perpetrators deserving of prosecution have only rarely been held accountable. To stop this cycle of violence and to promote justice, impunity for the commission of serious crimes must yield to accountability. But how can this be done, and what will be the respective roles of national courts and international tribunals?

National courts administer systems of criminal law designed to provide justice for victims and due process for accused persons. A nation's courts exercise jurisdiction over crimes committed in its territory and proceed against those crimes committed abroad by its nationals, or against its nationals, or against its national interests. When these and other connections are absent, national courts may nevertheless exercise jurisdiction under international law over crimes of such exceptional gravity that they affect the fundamental interests of the international community as a whole. This is universal jurisdiction: it is jurisdiction based solely on the nature of the crime. National courts can exercise universal jurisdiction to prosecute and punish, and thereby deter, heinous acts recognized as serious crimes under international law. When national courts exercise universal jurisdiction appropriately, in accordance with internationally recognized standards of due process, they act to vindicate not merely their own interests and values but the basic interests and values common to the international community.

Universal jurisdiction holds out the promise of greater justice, but the jurisprudence of universal jurisdiction is disparate, disjointed, and poorly

---

Reprinted with permission of The Princeton Project.

understood. So long as that is so, this weapon against impunity is potentially beset by incoherence, confusion, and, at times, uneven justice.

International criminal tribunals also have a vital role to play in combating impunity as a complement to national courts. In the wake of mass atrocities and of oppressive rule, national judicial systems have often been unable or unwilling to prosecute serious crimes under international law, so international criminal tribunals have been established. Treaties entered into in the aftermath of World War II have strengthened international institutions, and have given greater clarity and force to international criminal law. A signal achievement of this long historic process occurred at a United Nations Conference in July 1998 when the Rome Statute of the International Criminal Court was adopted. . . . The jurisdiction of the International Criminal Court will, however, be available only if justice cannot be done at the national level. The primary burden of prosecuting the alleged perpetrators of these crimes will continue to reside with national legal systems.

Enhancing the proper exercise of universal jurisdiction by national courts will help close the gap in law enforcement that has favored perpetrators of serious crimes under international law. Fashioning clearer and sounder principles to guide the exercise of universal jurisdiction by national courts should help to punish, and thereby to deter and prevent, the commission of these heinous crimes. Nevertheless, the aim of sound principles cannot be simply to facilitate the speediest exercise of criminal jurisdiction, always and everywhere, and irrespective of circumstances. Improper exercises of criminal jurisdiction, including universal jurisdiction, may be used merely to harass political opponents, or for aims extraneous to criminal justice. Moreover, the imprudent or untimely exercise of universal jurisdiction could disrupt the quest for peace and national reconciliation in nations struggling to recover from violent conflict or political oppression. Prudence and good judgment are required here, as elsewhere in politics and law.

What is needed are principles to guide, as well as to give greater coherence and legitimacy to, the exercise of universal jurisdiction. These principles should promote greater accountability for perpetrators of serious crimes under international law, in ways consistent with a prudent concern for the abuse of power and a reasonable solicitude for the quest for peace.

The Princeton Project

The Princeton Project on Universal Jurisdiction has been formed to contribute to the ongoing development of universal jurisdiction. The Project is sponsored by Princeton University's Program in Law and Public Affairs and the Woodrow Wilson School of Public and International Affairs, the International Commission of Jurists, the American Association for the

International Commission of Jurists, the Urban Morgan Institute for Human Rights, and the Netherlands Institute of Human Rights. The Project convened at Princeton University in January 2001 an assembly of scholars and jurists from around the world, serving in their personal capacities, to develop consensus principles on universal jurisdiction.

This assembly of scholars and jurists represented a diversity of viewpoints and a variety of legal systems. They are, however, united in their desire to promote greater legal accountability for those accused of committing serious crimes under international law.

The Princeton Principles on Universal Jurisdiction

The participants in the Princeton Project on Universal Jurisdiction propose the following principles for the purposes of advancing the continued evolution of international law and the application of international law in national legal systems.

Principle 1: Fundamentals of Universal Jurisdiction

1. For purposes of these Principles, universal jurisdiction is criminal jurisdiction based solely on the nature of the crime, without regard to where the crime was committed, the nationality of the alleged or convicted perpetrator, the nationality of the victim, or any other connection to the state exercising such jurisdiction.

2. Universal jurisdiction may be exercised by a competent and ordinary judicial body of any state in order to try a person duly accused of committing serious crimes under international law as specified in Principle 2(1), provided the person is present before such judicial body.

3. A state may rely on universal jurisdiction as a basis for seeking the extradition of a person accused or convicted of committing a serious crime under international law as specified in Principle 2(1), provided that it has established a prima facie case of the person's guilt and that the person sought to be extradited will be tried or the punishment carried out in accordance with international norms and standards on the protection of human rights in the context of criminal proceedings.

4. In exercising universal jurisdiction or in relying upon universal jurisdiction as a basis for seeking extradition, a state and its judicial organs shall observe international due process norms including but not limited to those involving the rights of the accused and victims, the fairness of the proceedings, and the independence and impartiality of the judiciary (hereinafter referred to as "international due process norms").

5. A state shall exercise universal jurisdiction in good faith and in accordance with its rights and obligations under international law.

Principle 2: Serious Crimes Under International Law

1. For purposes of these Principles, serious crimes under international law include: (1) piracy; (2) slavery; (3) war crimes; (4) crimes against peace; (5) crimes against humanity; (6) genocide; and (7) torture.

2. The application of universal jurisdiction to the crimes listed in paragraph 1 is without prejudice to the application of universal jurisdiction to other crimes under international law.

Principle 3: Reliance on Universal Jurisdiction in the Absence of National Legislation

With respect to serious crimes under international law as specified in Principle 2(1), national judicial organs may rely on universal jurisdiction even if their national legislation does not specifically provide for it.

Principle 4: Obligation to Support Accountability

1. A state shall comply with all international obligations that are applicable to: prosecuting or extraditing persons accused or convicted of crimes under international law in accordance with a legal process that complies with international due process norms, providing other states investigating or prosecuting such crimes with all available means of administrative and judicial assistance, and undertaking such other necessary and appropriate measures as are consistent with international norms and standards.

2. A state, in the exercise of universal jurisdiction, may, for purposes of prosecution, seek judicial assistance to obtain evidence from another state, provided that the requesting state has a good faith basis and that the evidence sought will be used in accordance with international due process norms.

Principle 5: Immunities

With respect to serious crimes under international law as specified in Principle 2(1), the official position of any accused person, whether as head of state or government or as a responsible government official, shall not relieve such person of criminal responsibility nor mitigate punishment.

Principle 6: Statutes of Limitations

Statutes of limitations or other forms of prescription shall not apply to serious crimes under international law as specified in Principle 2(1).

Principle 7: Amnesties

1. Amnesties are generally inconsistent with the obligation of states to provide accountability for serious crimes under international law as specified in Principle 2(1).

2. The exercise of universal jurisdiction with respect to serious crimes under international law as specified in Principle 2(1) shall not be precluded by amnesties which are incompatible with the international legal obligations of the granting state.

Principle 8: Resolution of Competing National Jurisdictions

Where more than one state has or may assert jurisdiction over a person and where the state that has custody of the person has no basis for jurisdiction other than the principle of universality, that state or its judicial organs shall, in deciding whether to prosecute or extradite, base their decision on an aggregate balance of the following criteria:

a. multilateral or bilateral treaty obligations;

b. the place of commission of the crime;

c. the nationality connection of the alleged perpetrator to the requesting state;

d. the nationality connection of the victim to the requesting state;

e. any other connection between the requesting state and the alleged perpetrator, the crime, or the victim;

f. the likelihood, good faith, and effectiveness of the prosecution in the requesting state;

g. the fairness and impartiality of the proceedings in the requesting state;

h. convenience to the parties and witnesses, as well as the availability of evidence in the requesting state; and

i. the interests of justice.

Principle 9: Non Bis In Idem *Double Jeopardy*

1. In the exercise of universal jurisdiction, a state or its judicial organs shall ensure that a person who is subject to criminal proceedings shall not be exposed to multiple prosecutions or punishment for the same criminal conduct where the prior criminal proceedings or other accountability proceedings have been conducted in good faith and in accordance with international norms and standards. Sham prosecutions or derisory punishment resulting from a conviction or other accountability proceedings shall not be recognized as falling within the scope of this Principle.

2. A state shall recognize the validity of a proper exercise of universal

jurisdiction by another state and shall recognize the final judgment of a competent and ordinary national judicial body or a competent international judicial body exercising such jurisdiction in accordance with international due process norms.

3. Any person tried or convicted by a state exercising universal jurisdiction for serious crimes under international law as specified in Principle 2(1) shall have the right and legal standing to raise before any national or international judicial body the claim of *non bis in idem* in opposition to any further criminal proceedings.

Principle 10: Grounds for Refusal of Extradition

1. A state or its judicial organs shall refuse to entertain a request for extradition based on universal jurisdiction if the person sought is likely to face a death penalty sentence or to be subjected to torture or any other cruel, degrading, or inhuman punishment or treatment, or if it is likely that the person sought will be subjected to sham proceedings in which international due process norms will be violated and no satisfactory assurances to the contrary are provided.

2. A state which refuses to extradite on the basis of this Principle shall, when permitted by international law, prosecute the individual accused of a serious crime under international law as specified in Principle 2(1) or extradite such person to another state where this can be done without exposing him or her to the risks referred to in paragraph 1.

Principle 11: Adoption of National Legislation

A state shall, where necessary, enact national legislation to enable the exercise of universal jurisdiction and the enforcement of these Principles.

Principle 12: Inclusion of Universal Jurisdiction in Future Treaties

In all future treaties, and in protocols to existing treaties, concerned with serious crimes under international law as specified in Principle 2(1), states shall include provisions for universal jurisdiction.

Principle 13: Strengthening Accountability and Universal Jurisdiction

1. National judicial organs shall construe national law in a manner that is consistent with these Principles.

2. Nothing in these Principles shall be construed to limit the rights and

obligations of a state to prevent or punish, by lawful means recognized under international law, the commission of crimes under international law.

3. These Principles shall not be construed as limiting the continued development of universal jurisdiction in international law.

Principle 14: Settlement of Disputes

1. Consistent with international law and the Charter of the United Nations states should settle their disputes arising out of the exercise of universal jurisdiction by all available means of peaceful settlement of disputes and in particular by submitting the dispute to the International Court of Justice.

Pending the determination of the issue in dispute, a state seeking to exercise universal jurisdiction shall not detain the accused person nor seek to have that person detained by another state unless there is a reasonable risk of flight and no other reasonable means can be found to ensure that person's eventual appearance before the judicial organs of the state seeking to exercise its jurisdiction.

Commentary on the Princeton Principles

Why Principles? Why Now?

The Princeton Principles on Universal Jurisdiction (Principles) are a progressive restatement of international law on the subject of universal jurisdiction. The Principles contain elements of both *lex lata* (the law as it is) and *de lege ferenda* (the law as it ought to be), but they should not be understood to limit the future evolution of universal jurisdiction. The Principles are intended to help guide national legislative bodies seeking to enact implementing legislation; judges who may be required to construe universal jurisdiction in applying domestic law or in making extradition decisions; governments that must decide whether to prosecute or extradite, or otherwise to assist in promoting international criminal accountability; and all those in civil society concerned with bringing to justice perpetrators of serious international crimes.

Participants in the Princeton Project discussed several difficult threshold questions concerning universal jurisdiction. How firmly is universal jurisdiction established in international law? It is of course recognized in treaties, national legislation, judicial opinions, and the writings of scholars, but not everyone draws the same conclusions from these sources. Commentators even disagree on how to ascertain whether universal jurisdiction is well established in customary international law: for some, the acceptance by states that a practice is obligatory *(opinio juris)* is enough; for others, the consistent practice of states is required.

When it is agreed that an obligation has been created in a treaty, legal systems differ in how they incorporate international obligations into domestic law. In many legal systems, the national judiciary cannot apply universal jurisdiction in the absence of national legislation. In other systems it is possible for the judiciary to rely directly on treaties and customary international law without waiting for implementing legislation. Accordingly, Principle 3 encourages courts to rely on universal jurisdiction in the absence of national legislation, so long as their legal systems permit them to do so. Principle 11 calls upon legislatures to enact laws enabling the exercise of universal jurisdiction. Principle 12 calls for states to provide for universal jurisdiction in future treaties and protocols to existing treaties.

Participants in the Princeton Project also carefully considered whether the time is ripe to bring greater clarity to universal jurisdiction. While it has been with us for centuries, universal jurisdiction seems only now to be coming into its own as a systematic means for promoting legal accountability. Universal jurisdiction was given great prominence by the proceedings in London involving former Chilean leader General Augusto Pinochet, and now courts around the world are seriously considering indictments involving universal jurisdiction.

In light of current dynamics in international criminal law, some supporters of universal jurisdiction question whether now is the time to clarify the principles that should guide its exercise. Might it not be better to wait to allow for unpredictable, and perhaps surprisingly progressive, developments? Is there a danger of stunting the development of universal jurisdiction by articulating guiding principles prematurely? . . . Our aim is to help guide those who believe that national courts have a vital role to play in combating impunity even when traditional jurisdictional connections are absent. These Principles should help clarify the legal bases for the responsible and reasoned exercise of universal jurisdiction. Insofar as universal jurisdiction is exercised, and seen to be exercised, in a reasoned, lawful, and orderly manner, it will gain wider acceptance. Mindful of the need to encourage continued progress in international law, these Principles have been drafted so as to invite rather than hinder the continued development of universal jurisdiction.

The Principles are written so as to both clarify the current law of universal jurisdiction and encourage its further development. As already noted, the Principles are addressed sometimes to the legislative, executive, or judicial branches of government, and sometimes to a combination of these.[1] The Principles are intended for a variety of actors in divergent legal systems who will properly draw on them in different ways. We acknowledge, for example, that in some legal systems, and according to some legal theories, judges are constrained in their ability to interpret existing law in light of aspirations to greater justice, or other principled aims. Nevertheless, judges on international and regional tribunals, and judges on national constitutional and supreme courts, often have greater interpretive latitude. Our hope is that these Principles might inform and shape the practice of those judges and other officials who can act to promote greater justice and legal accountability consistent with the constraints of their offices. We also offer these Principles to help guide and inform citizens, leaders of organizations in civil society, and public officials of all sorts: all of these different actors could benefit from a clearer common understanding of what universal jurisdiction is and when and how it may reasonably be exercised.

When and How to Prosecute Based on Universality?

In defining universal jurisdiction, participants focused on the case of "pure" universal jurisdiction, namely, where the nature of the crime is the sole basis for subject matter jurisdiction. There has been some scholarly confusion on the role of universal jurisdiction in famous prosecutions, such as the trial in Jerusalem of Adolph Eichmann.[2] In addition, it is important to recall that simply because certain offenses are universally condemned does not mean that a state may exercise universal jurisdiction over them.

Participants in the Princeton Project debated whether states should in general be encouraged to exercise universal jurisdiction based solely on the seriousness of the alleged crime, without traditional connecting links to the victims or perpetrators of serious crimes under international law. On the one hand, the whole point of universal jurisdiction would seem to be to permit or even encourage prosecution when states find within their territory a noncitizen accused of serious crimes under international law. In this way, universal jurisdiction maximizes accountability and minimizes impunity. The very essence of universal jurisdiction would seem, therefore, to be that national courts should prosecute alleged criminals absent any connecting factors (for example, even if the crimes were not committed against the enforcing states' citizens, or by its citizens).

There is, nevertheless, great concern that particular states will abuse universal jurisdiction to pursue politically motivated prosecutions. Mercenary governments and rogue prosecutors could seek to indict the heads of state or other senior public officials in countries with which they have political disagreements. Powerful states may try to exempt their own leaders from accountability while seeking to prosecute others, defying the basic proposition that equals should be treated equally. Members of peacekeeping forces might be harassed with unjustified prosecutions, and this might deter peacekeeping operations.

Should the Principles insist at least that the accused is physically present in the territory of the enforcing state? Should other connecting links also be required? Participants decided not to include an explicit requirement of a territorial link in Principle 1(1)'s definition. This was done partly to allow for further discussion, partly to avoid stifling the evolution of universal jurisdiction, and partly out of deference to pending litigation in the International Court of Justice.[3] Nevertheless, subsection (2) of Principle 1 holds that a "competent and ordinary" judicial body may try accused persons on the basis of universal jurisdiction "provided the person is present before such judicial body." The language of Principle 1(2) does not prevent a state from initiating the criminal process, conducting an investigation, issuing an indictment, or requesting extradition, when the accused is not present.

The Principles contain a number of provisions describing the standards that legal systems and particular prosecutions would have to meet in order to exercise universal jurisdiction responsibly and legitimately. Subsections (3) and (4) of Principle 1 insist that a state may seek to extradite persons accused or convicted on the basis of universal jurisdiction "provided that it has established a *prima facie* case of the person's guilt" and provided that trials and punishments will take place in accordance with "international due process norms" relevant human rights standards, and the independence and impartiality of the judiciary. Later Principles contain additional safeguards against prosecutorial abuses: Principle 9, for example, guards against repeated prosecutions for the same crime in violation of the principle of *non bis in idem*, or the prohibition on double jeopardy.[4] Principle 10 allows states to refuse requests for extradition if the person sought "is likely to face a death penalty sentence or to be subjected to torture" or cruel or inhuman treatment or sham proceedings in violation of international due process norms. The Principles reinforce proper legal standards for courts and should help guide executive officers considering extradition requests.

Of course, effective legal processes require the active cooperation of different government agencies, including courts and prosecutors. The establishment of international networks of cooperation will be especially important to the effective development of universal jurisdiction. Therefore, Principle 4 calls upon states to comply with their international obligations to either prosecute or extradite those accused or convicted of crimes under international law, so long as these legal processes comply with "international due process norms." Universal jurisdiction can only work if different states provide each other with active judicial and prosecutorial assistance, and all participating states will need to insure that due process norms are being complied with.

All legal powers can be abused by willfully malicious individuals. The Princeton Principles do all that principles can do to guard against such abuses: they specify the considerations that conscientious international actors can and should act upon.

Which Crimes Are Covered?

The choice of which crimes to include as "serious crimes under international law" was discussed at length in Princeton.[5] The ordering of the list of "serious crimes" was settled by historical progression rather than an attempt to rank crimes based upon their gravity.

• "Piracy" is a crime that paradigmatically is subject to prosecution by any nation based on principles of universality, and it is crucial to the origins of universal jurisdiction, so it comes first.[6]

• "Slavery" was included in part because its historical ties to piracy reach back to the Declaration of the Congress of Vienna in 1815. There are but a few conventional provisions, however, authorizing the exercise of universal jurisdiction for slavery and slave-related practices.[7] The phrase "slavery and slave-related practices" was considered but rejected by the Princeton Assembly as being too technical in nature. However, it was agreed that the term "slavery" was intended to include those practices prohibited in the Supplementary Convention on the Abolition of Slavery, the Slave Trade, and Institutions and Practices Similar to Slavery.[8]

• "War crimes" were initially restricted to "serious war crimes," namely "grave breaches" of the 1949 Geneva Conventions and Protocol I, in order to avoid the potential for numerous prosecutions based upon less serious violations.[9] The participants, however, did not want to give the impression that some war crimes are not serious, and thus opted not to include the word "serious." The assembly agreed, though, that it would be inappropriate to invoke universal jurisdiction for the prosecution of minor transgressions of the 1949 Geneva Conventions and Protocol I.

• "Crimes against peace" were also discussed at length. While many argue that aggression constitutes the most serious international crime, others contend that defining the crime of "aggression" is in practice extremely difficult and divisive. In the end, "crimes against peace" were included, despite some disagreement, in part in order to recall the wording of Article 6(a) of the Nuremberg Charter.[10]

• "Crimes against humanity" were included without objection, and these crimes have now been authoritatively defined by Article 7 of the Rome Statute of the International Criminal Court.[11] There is not presently any conventional law that provides for the exercise of universal jurisdiction over crimes against humanity.

• "Genocide" was included without objection. Article 6 of the Genocide Convention provides that a person accused of genocide shall be tried in a court of "the State in the territory of which the act was committed."[12] However, Article 6 does not preclude the use of universal jurisdiction by an international penal tribunal, in the event that such a tribunal is established.

• "Torture" was included without objection though some noted that there are some disagreements as to what constitutes torture. "Torture" is intended to include the "other cruel, inhuman, or degrading treatment or punishment" as defined in the Convention Against Torture and Other Cruel, Inhuman or Degrading Treatment or Punishment.[13] Moreover, the Torture Convention implicitly provides for the exercise of universal jurisdiction over prohibited conduct.[14]

Apartheid, terrorism, and drug crimes were raised as candidates for inclusion. It should be carefully noted that the list of serious crimes is explicitly illustrative, not exhaustive. Principle 2(1) leaves open the possibility that, in the future, other crimes may be deemed of such a heinous nature as to warrant the application of universal jurisdiction.

When and Against Whom Should Universal Jurisdiction Be Exercised?

Among the most difficult questions discussed in the Princeton Project was the enforcement of universal jurisdiction, and the question of when if ever to honor immunities and amnesties with respect to the commission of serious crimes under international law. Especially difficult moral, political, and legal issues surround immunities for former or current heads of state, diplomats, and other officials (see Principle 5). Immunity from international criminal prosecution for sitting heads of state is established by customary international law, and immunity for diplomats is established by treaty. There is an extremely important distinction, however, between "substantive" and "procedural" immunity. A substantive immunity from prosecution would provide heads of state, diplomats, and other officials with exoneration from criminal responsibility for the commission of serious crimes under international law when these crimes are committed in an official capacity. Principle 5 rejects this substantive immunity ("the official position of any accused person, whether as head of state or government or as a responsible government official, shall not relieve such person of criminal responsibility nor mitigate punishment"). Nevertheless, in proceedings before national tribunals, procedural immunity remains in effect during a head of state's or other official's tenure in office, or during the period in which a diplomat is accredited to a host state. Under international law as it exists, sitting heads of state, accredited diplomats, and other officials cannot be prosecuted while in office for acts committed in their official capacities.

The Princeton Principles' rejection of substantive immunity keeps faith with the Nuremberg Charter, which proclaims: "The official position of defendants, whether as Heads of State or responsible officials in Government Departments, shall not be considered as freeing them from responsibility or mitigating punishment."[15] More recently, the Statutes of the International Criminal Tribunal for the Former Yugoslavia (ICTY) and that of the International Criminal Tribunal for Rwanda (ICTR) removed substantive immunity for war crimes, genocide, and crimes against humanity.[16] Principle 5 in fact tracks the language of these statutes, which, in turn, were fashioned from Article 7 of the Nuremberg Charter.[17]

None of these statutes addresses the issue of procedural immunity. Customary international law, however, is quite clear on the subject: heads of state enjoy unqualified "act of state" immunity during their term of office. Similarly, diplomats accredited to a host state enjoy unqualified *ex officio* immunity during the performance of their official duties.[18] A head of state, diplomat, or other official may, therefore, be immune from prosecution while in office, but once they step down any claim of immunity becomes ineffective, and they are then subject to the possibility of prosecution.

The Principles do not purport to revoke the protections afforded by procedural immunity, but neither do they affirm procedural immunities as a matter of principle. In the future, procedural immunities for sitting heads of state, diplomats, and other officials may be called increasingly into question, a possibility prefigured by the ICTY's indictment of Slobodan Milosevic while still a sitting head of state.[19] Whether this unprecedented action will become the source of a new regime in international law remains to be seen. Participants in the Princeton Project opted not to try and settle on principles governing procedural immunity in order to leave space for future developments.

Another possible limit on the prosecution of "serious crimes under international law" are statutes of limitations.[20] Principle 6 reaffirms that statutes of limitations do not apply to crimes covered by universal jurisdiction. Conventional international law supports this position, at least as concerns war crimes and crimes against humanity.[21] Admittedly, the practice of states leaves something to be desired, here as elsewhere. Subsection (1) of Principle 13 provides that national judicial organs shall construe their own law in a manner "consistent with these Principles." If a nation's law is silent as to a limitations period with respect to a certain serious crime under international law, for example genocide, a local judge could draw on this subsection and legitimately *refuse* to apply by analogy another statute of limitations for a crime that was codified, e.g., murder. Because the laws of many nations include limitations periods, a number of participants suggested that the Principles should exhort states to eliminate statutes of limitations for serious crimes under international law; Principle 11 does this.

Another significant discussion took place on the topics of amnesties and other pardons that might be granted by a state or by virtue of a treaty to individuals or categories of individuals. Some participants were very strongly against the inclusion of any principle that recognized an amnesty for "serious crimes under international law." Others felt that certain types of amnesties, coupled with accountability mechanisms other than criminal prosecution, were acceptable in some cases: at least in difficult periods of political transition, as a second best alternative to criminal prosecution. Much controversy surrounds accountability mechanisms such as South Africa's Truth and Reconciliation Commission. We considered trying to specify the minimum prerequisites that should have to be satisfied in order for accountability mechanisms to be deemed legitimate (including such features as individualized accountability), but in the end those assembled at Princeton decided not to try and provide general criteria. Accordingly, Principle 7 expresses only a presumption that amnesties are inconsistent with a state's obligations to prevent impunity.[22] Subsection (2) recognizes that if a state grants amnesties that are inconsistent with obligations to hold perpetrators of serious international crimes accountable, other states may still seek to exercise universal jurisdiction.

Who Should Prosecute?

Principle 8 seeks to specify factors that should be considered when making judgments about whether to prosecute or extradite in the face of competing national claims. The list of factors is not intended to be exhaustive.[23] This Principle is designed to provide states with guidelines for the resolution of conflicts in situations in which the state with custody over a person accused of serious international crimes can base its jurisdiction solely on universality, and one or more other states have asserted or are in a position to exercise jurisdiction.

Originally, the drafters expressed a preference for ranking the different bases of jurisdiction so as to indicate which should receive priority in the case of a conflict. Almost without exception, the territorial principle was thought to deserve precedence. This was in part because of the longstanding conviction that a criminal defendant should be tried by his "natural judge." Many participants expressed the view that societies that have been victimized by political crimes should have the opportunity to bring the perpetrators to justice, provided their judiciaries are able and willing to do so.

Although it was decided not to rank jurisdictional claims, the Principles do not deny that some traditional jurisdictional claims will often be especially weighty. For example, the exercise of territorial jurisdiction will often also satisfy several of the other factors enumerated in Principle 8, such as the convenience to the parties and witnesses, as well as the availability of evidence.

What Protections for the Accused?

If universal jurisdiction is to be a tool for promoting greater justice, the rights of the accused must be protected. Principle 9 protects accused persons against multiple prosecutions for the same crime. There was no objection among the participants as to desirability of such safeguards. Several of the participants, however, questioned whether the prohibition on double jeopardy—*non bis in idem*—was a recognized principle of international law. Under regional human rights agreements, *non bis in idem* has been interpreted to apply within a state, but not between states. It was noted, however, that the importance of the doctrine of *non bis in idem* is recognized in almost all legal systems: it qualifies as a general principle of law and, as such, could be said to apply under international law.[24] Subsection (3) specifically grants an accused the right "and legal standing" to invoke the claim of *non bis in idem* as a defense to further criminal proceedings. This provision is designed to allow a defendant to independently raise this defense in jurisdictions that would otherwise only permit the requested state, in its discretion, to invoke the double jeopardy principle on an accused person's behalf.

Subsection (1) of Principle 10 requires that an extradition request predicated upon universality be refused if the accused is likely to face the death penalty, torture, or "other cruel, degrading, or inhuman punishment or treatment." This latter phraseology should be construed in accord with its usage as described in the Torture Convention.[25]

There was also some discussion about whether to include a provision on trials *in absentia* in the Principles. Although generally considered anathema in common law countries, such trials are traditional in certain civil law nations, such as France, and serve a valuable function with respect to the preservation of evidence. In the end it was decided not to refer to such trials in the Principles.

Conclusion: Promoting Accountability Through International Law

Several of the remaining principles have already been mentioned, and their import should be clear. Principles 11 and 12 call upon states both to adopt legislation to enable the exercise of universal jurisdiction and to include provisions for universal jurisdiction in all future treaties. The first sentence of Principle 13 was included by the drafters to memorialize their intention that nothing in the Principles should be construed as altering the existing obligations of any state under terrorism conventions. Subsection (1) of Principle 14 calls for states to peacefully settle disputes arising out of the application of universal jurisdiction.

Universal jurisdiction is one means to achieve accountability and to deny impunity to those accused of serious international crimes. It reflects the maxim embedded in so many treaties: *aut dedere autjudicare,* the duty to extradite or prosecute. All of the participants in the Princeton Project felt it important that the Principles not be construed to limit the development of universal jurisdiction or to constrain the evolution of accountability for crimes under international law, and this conviction is made explicit in Principle 13.

National courts exercising universal jurisdiction have a vital role to play in bringing perpetrators of international crimes to justice: they form part of the web of legal instruments which can and should be deployed to combat impunity. The Princeton Principles do not purport to define the proper use of universal jurisdiction in any final way. Our hope is that these Principles can bring greater clarity and order to the exercise of universal jurisdiction, and thereby encourage its reasonable and responsible use.

Notes

1. *See, e.g.,* Principle 3 which encourages judicial organs to rely on universal jurisdiction, Principle 11 which calls upon legislatures to enact laws enabling the exercise of universal jurisdiction, and Principle 12 which exhorts governments to include provisions for universal jurisdiction in new treaties and protocols to existing treaties.

2. *See Attorney General of Israel v. Eichmann,* 36 I.L.R. 5 (Isr. D.C., Jerusalem, 12 Dec. 1961), aff'd, 36 I.L.R. 277 (Isr. S. Ct., 29 May 1962), which is often cited as representing the exercise of universal jurisdiction by Israel, although many argue that the decision was more fundamentally predicated upon the passive personality doctrine and the protective principle under a unique Israeli statute passed by the Knesset in 1950. See Bass, *supra* note 3.

3. *See* the International Court of Justice's order in the case of *Arrest Warrant of 11 April 2000* (Congo v. Belg.) (8 Dec. 2000), in which these issues feature prominently. In a recent development, on 20 March 2001, the Senegalese Cour de Cassation held that Hissene Habre, the former president of Chad, could not be tried on torture charges in Senegal. *See* Marks, *supra* note 3.

4. *See* Principle 9. Note also that the drafters intended the international due process norms in Principle 1(4) to be illustrative and not exhaustive. The right to reasonable bail (Cf. Principle 14[2]) and the right to counsel were also referred to as being included among the essential due process guarantees. *See also* Universal Declaration of Human Rights, 10 Dec. 1948, arts. 10,11, G.A. Res. 217A (III), U.N. Doc. A1810 (1948); International Covenant on Civil and Political Rights, 19 Dec. 1966, arts. 14, 15,999 U.N.T.S. 171 [hereinafter ICCPR].

5. *See* Principle 2(1).

6. *See, e.g.,* Convention on the High Seas, 29 Apr. 1938, art. 19,450 U.N.T.S. 82, 13 U.S.T. 2312 ("On the high seas, or in any other place outside the jurisdiction of any state, every state may seize a pirate ship or aircraft, or a ship taken by piracy and under the control of pirates, and arrest the persons and seize the property on board."); United Nations Convention on the Law of the Sea, 10 Dec. 1982, art. 105, U.N. A/CONE62/122, 21 I.L.M. 1261.

7. *Cf* Convention for the Suppression of the Traffic in Persons and of the Exploitation of the Prostitution of Others, 21 Mar. 1950, art. 11,96 U.N.T.S. 271 ("Nothing in the present Convention shall be interpreted as determining the attitude of a Party towards the general question of the limits of criminal jurisdiction under

international law."); Convention Relative to the Slave Trade and Importation into Africa of Firearms, Ammunition, and Spiritous Liquors, 2 July 1890, art. 5,27 Stat. 886,17 Martens Nouveau Recucil (ser. 2) 345; Treaty for the Suppression of the African Slave Trade, 20 Dec. 1841, arts. 6,7,10, and annex B, Pt. 5,2 Martens Nouveau Recuell (ser. 1) 392.

8. 7 Sept. 1956, 266 U.N.T.S. 3,18 UST. 3201.

9. *See* Geneva Convention for the Amelioration of the Condition of the Wounded and Sick in Armed Forces in the Field, 12 Aug. 1949, art. 50,75 U.N.T.S. 31,6 U.S.T. 3114, T.I.A.S. No. 3362; Geneva Convention for the Amelioration of the Condition of Wounded, Sick and Shipwrecked Members of Armed Forces at Sea, 12 Aug. 1949, art. 51,75 U.N.T.S. 85, 6 U.S.T. 3217, T.I.A.S. No. 3363; Geneva Convention Relative to the Treatment of Prisoners of War, 12 Aug. 1949, art. 130,75 U.N.T.S. 135,6 U.S.T. No. 3316, T.I.A.S. No. 3364; Geneva Convention Relative to the Protection of Civilian Persons in Time of War, 12 Aug. 1949, art. 147,75 U.N.T.S. 287,6 U.S.T 3516, T.I.A.S. No. 3365; Protocol I Additional to the Geneva Conventions of 12 August 1949, 12 Dec. 1977, art. 85, U.N. Doc. A/32/144, Annex I.

10. *See* Charter of the International Military Tribunal, 8 Aug. 1945, art. 6(a), 82 U.N.T.S. 284,59 Stat. 1546 [hereinafter Nuremberg Charter], annexed to Agreement for the Prosecution and Punishment of the Major War Criminals of the European Axis, 8 Aug. 1945, 82 U.N.T.S. 279, 59 Stat. 1544.

11. 17 July 1998, art. 7, U.N. Doc. AICONF.183/9, 37 I.L.M. 999 [hereinafter ICC Statute].

12. Convention on the Prevention and Punishment of the Crime of Genocide, 9 Dec. 1948, art. 6, 78 U.N.T.S. 277.

13. G.A. Res. 39/46, Annex, U.N. GAOR, 39th Sess., Supp. No. 51, U.N. Doc. A/39/51 (1984), entered into force 26 June 1987 [hereinafter Torture Convention], draft reprinted in 23 I.L.M. 1027, modified 24 I.L.M. 535.

14. Id. arts. 5,7(1).

15. Nuremberg Charter, *supra* note 10, art. 7.

16. *See* Statute of the International Criminal Tribunal for the Former Yugoslavia, art. 7(2), S.C. Res. 808, U.N. SCOR, 48th Sess., 3175th mtg., U.N. Doc. S/RE51808 (1993), annexed to *Report of the Secretary-General Pursuant to Paragraph 2 of UN. Security Council Resolution* 808 (1993), U.N. Doc. S/25704 & Add.1 (1993) [hereinafter ICTY Statute]; Statute of the International Criminal Tribunal for Rwanda, art. 6(2), S.C. Res. 955, U.N. SCOR, 49th Sess., 3453d mtg., Annex, U.N. Doc. S/RES/955 (1994) [hereinafter ICTR Statute].

17. *See* ICTY Statute, *supra* note 16, art. 7(2); ICTR Statute, *supra* note 16, art. 6(2). Article 27 of the ICC Statute similarly provides: 1. This Statute shall apply equally to all persons without any distinction based on official capacity. In particular, official capacity as a Head of State or Government, a member of a Government or parliament, an elected representative or a government official shall in no case exempt a person from criminal responsibility under this Statute, nor shall it, in and of itself, constitute a ground for reduction of sentence. 2. Immunities or special procedural rules which may attach to the official capacity of a person, whether under national or international law, shall not bar the Court from exercising its jurisdiction over such a person.

ICC Statute, *supra* note 11, art, 27.

Article 98 of the ICC Statute, however, yields to the primacy of other multilateral treaties in assessing immunity:

1. The Court may not proceed with a request for surrender or assistance which would require the requested State to act inconsistently with its obli-

gations under international law with respect to the State or diplomatic immunity of a person or property of a third State, unless the Court can first obtain the cooperation of that third State for the waiver of the immunity.

2. The Court may not proceed with a request for surrender which would require the requested State to act inconsistently with its obligations under international agreements pursuant to which the consent of a sending State is required to surrender a person of that State to the Court, unless the Court can first obtain the cooperation of the sending State for the giving of consent for the surrender.

Id. art. 98.

Note that Article 27 is located in Part III of the ICC Statute; while Article 98 is contained in Part IX of the Statute, which contains no prohibitions on immunities, and thus seems to permit a head of state, diplomat, or other official to invoke procedural immunity, where applicable.

18. *See* Vienna Convention on Diplomatic Relations, 18 Apr. 1961, 500 U.N.T.S. 95, 23 U.S.T. 3227; *see also* United States Diplomatic and Consular staff in Tehran (U.S. v. Iran), 1980 I.C.J. 3 (May 24). These temporary immunities are not revoked by this subsection. Such doctrines, however, may be in the process of erosion. *See infra* note 25 and accompanying text.

19. Prosecutor v. Milosevic (Indictment) (24 May 1999), at http://www.un.org/icty/indictment!english/mil-ii990524e.htm.

20. *See* Principle 6.

21. *See* Convention on the Non-Applicability of Statutory Limitations to War Crimes and Crimes Against Humanity, 26 Nov. 1968, 754 U.N.T.S. 73; European Convention on Non-Applicability of Statutory Limitations to Crimes Against Humanity and War Crimes (Inter-European), 25 Jan. 1974, Europ. T.S. No. 82.

22. *See* Principle 7(1).

23. This method of listing relevant factors has been employed in other similar contexts, such as in determining jurisdictional priority over extraterritorial crime, *see* Restatement (Third) of Foreign Relations Law of the United States at 403 (1987), and in resolving conflict of laws problems, see Restatement (Second) of Conflict of 6 (1971).

24. It is also included in the ICCPR, *supra* note 9, art. 14(7), and the American Convention on Human Rights, 22 Nov. 1969, art. 8(4), 1144 U.N.T.S. 123, O.A.S. T.S. No.36.

25. *See* Torture Convention, *supra* note 13, art. 1.

PART 1.4

International Law as Operating System: International Legal Structures

CHAPTER 10

A Babel of Judicial Voices? Ruminations from the Bench

Rosalyn Higgins

THE COURT [INTERNATIONAL COURT OF JUSTICE] IS IN THE thick of real life overlapping jurisdiction issues. We are currently hearing the *Bosnia and Herzegovina v Serbia and Montenegro Genocide Convention Case:*[1] Bosnia and Herzegovina is currently pleading. For both evidence as to facts and claims as to law, Bosnia and Herzegovina relies very much on the ICTY. Serbia and Montenegro is taking a different route, calling witnesses of their own to testify. There has in fact been only one genocide conviction to date in the ICTY[2] Are *dicta* of other tribunals on genocide (when the legal determination relates to a different crime) a relevant source of law for the ICJ? In what circumstances can a tribunal rely on findings of fact of another? We gave our judgment in *Congo v Uganda.*[3] We made findings of fact and law that are surely going to be relevant to the case that is now pending in the ICC: they have evidence teams out "on the ground."

How much difference in the application of legal findings of facts does it make that the ICTY and the ICC are dealing with crimes of individuals, while we are dealing with the responsibility of States? In particular, is the concept of "intent" (a requisite to the crime of genocide) the same for individuals as for States?

This "intermingling" of legal regimes is in fact going on all around us. The intellectual debate began with expressed concerns about fragmentation arising from the now many judicial institutions, and what the less reverent may have perceived as "judicial turf wars."

But really, the issue is not only "*who* decides?" and, if there are over-

---

Reprinted with permission from Rosalyn Higgins, "A Babel of Judicial Voices? Ruminations from the Bench," *International and Comparative Law Quarterly* 55 (October 2006): 791–804.

lapping subject-matter jurisdictions, "whose view prevails?" It is also how does any given court decide which of the many norms now developed are applicable? What happens if different tribunals see things differently? Can these bodies function in isolation from each other? Are there good solutions to problems that may be engendered by the multiplying of institutions and the deepening of international law?

Let me go back to some of the issues I see emerging:

1. The widening and thickening of the context of international law has meant that even within a given court or tribunal there is often an issue as to choice of applicable law. This is not entirely a matter of *lex specialis*. Rather it is a matter of locating the corpus of law at the heart of a difficult issue. Thus the Court in its Advisory Opinion of 1996[4] declined the suggestion that the legality of nuclear weapons could be answered by reference to the right to life provision (Article 6) in the International Covenant on Civil and Political Rights,[5] or by principles of environmental law.[6] The Court did not see these as being "displaced" by a *lex specialis* consisting of Charter law and *jus in bello*. Rather, it was that these areas of law, while important, were not at the heart of the matter.

2. This example can be contrasted with the situation where alternative plausible applicable norms could in fact lead to different solutions. If you share the perception of law as choices between competing norms, rather than the automatic application of a single rule, then you will recognize this as a longstanding phenomenon: do you, the decision-maker, decide in the instant case that the use of force is prohibited or that self defence is allowed? Do you decide that jurisdiction is territorial or that the protective principle is established? The deepening and widening of contemporary international law has surely made this reality—that law is more than "bright rules" that simply need to be applied—ever more apparent. My point can be illustrated by two recent examples.

There is a desire to ensure that the most heinous crimes do not escape justice, even when no special international tribunals may yet be established to ensure this: this is the underlying purpose of the principle of universal jurisdiction. And there is a generally perceived understanding that persons representing States at the highest levels must be allowed to have free contact with each other, protected from physical harm: this is what is guaranteed by the law on State and diplomatic immunities. There is a clear tension between these norms as they may fall to be applied in a particular case. Of course, if States agree as to which shall prevail under a particular treaty being drafted, the matter is resolved. Thus immunity is excluded under the Statutes of the new criminal courts[7] and under the International Convention Against Torture. But under general international law the matter is not so clear. The matter can really only be resolved by deciding which of these alternative plausible norms is to prevail on the facts of a particular case. The applicable law relied on by the International Court of Justice in the *Arrest Warrant* case was the law of immunities.[8] Its "choice" was made easier by the decision of Belgium not to press its initial arguments relating to universal jurisdiction.

The European Court of Human Rights was faced with a similar choice of norms in the *Al-Adsani* case, where a right guaranteed by the specific treaty of that Court (the European Convention on Human Rights)—the right of access to a court—was pitted against immunity from suit under general international law.[9] Employing the well established choice-making technique under that Convention, the European Court found that state immunity was "generally accepted by the community of nations" and that accordingly the denial to the applicant of access to the court was not disproportionate.[10] (In the ESA cases the Court had also found that the function of immunities necessary to an international organization was not disproportionate as regards a limitation to the right of access to court of an applicant: it thus here, too, "chose" to apply the immunity norm in the particular context.)[11]

This "competition of norms" becomes more controversial when the background is a claim of a grave offence. This was the case both in the *Arrest Warrant* case and the *Al-Adsani* case, where incitement to racially based extermination, and torture, respectively, had been alleged.

3. Two tribunals interpret the same norm differently. The example of fragmentation most frequently cited is that of the test for control of irregular forces for purposes of responsibility adopted by the ICTY in the *Tadiç* case.[12] The Appeals Chamber of the ICTY decided not to follow the "effective control" test that had been elaborated by the International Court of Justice in the *Nicaragua v USA* case, choosing instead to create an "overall control" test that required a lower threshold.[13] My own view is that we should not exaggerate problems allegedly presented by *Tadiç*. First, we should acknowledge that the ICJ's test in *Nicaragua* has not been without its critics. Second, the Appeals Chamber sought to minimize any bifurcation by explaining that it was operating within the framework of international humanitarian law, and this corpus of rules and principles may itself suggest legal criteria for determining when armed forces in an armed conflict are fighting on behalf of a foreign power.[14] Accordingly, the Appeals Chamber turned its attention first to Article 4A of the Third Geneva Convention of 1949, which lists the requirements for being considered "lawful combatants."[15] This Article was perceived by the Appeals Chamber as implicitly referring to its own test of control over irregulars and paramilitary units that might be fighting on behalf of belligerent States, with the key being the notion of effectiveness and the aim of deterring deviation from its standards

to the maximum extent possible. Of course, this still raises the spectre of "special regimes," distinct from general international law. Or is it really a question of context as to which test should be applied? Interestingly, the same issue is being raised again in *Bosnia and Herzegovina v Serbia and Montenegro*, where Bosnia has suggested to us that we might not want to apply the *Nicaragua v USA* control test because the Genocide Convention itself, it is argued, suggests its own "control test," relevant for responsibility over paramilitaries.

Sometimes, of course, interpretative options are led by practical needs. It is easy to understand why the Appeals Chamber *needed* to establish that the former Federal Republic of Yugoslavia had "overall control" over the Bosnian Serb Army (the VRS) of Republika Srpska. In order for Article 2 of the Statute of the ICTY—which deals with "Grave Breaches of the Geneva Conventions of 1949"—to apply, the nature of the conflict must be international. Specifically, the Appeals Chamber needed to find that after 19 May 1992, when the Yugoslav Army withdrew from Bosnia and Herzegovina, the conflict continued to be international because the Bosnian Serb Army, operating within the territory of Bosnia and Herzegovina, was being controlled by the former Federal Republic of Yugoslavia. Again, context was controlling.

In the meantime, the Court has very recently affirmed its control test as articulated in *Nicaragua v USA* in the *Congo v Uganda* case.[16] It explained that although Uganda acknowledged giving training and military support to the "Mouvement de liberation du Congo," there was no probative and credible evidence that Uganda controlled, or could control, the manner in which such assistance was used. Accordingly, citing the pertinent paragraphs of *Nicaragua*, as well as Articles 5 and 8 of the ILC Articles on State Responsibility, the Court concluded that the requisite tests for sufficiency of control of paramilitaries had not been met with regards to the relationship between Uganda and the "Mouvement de liberation du Congo."[17]

Thus some differences of perception between the ICJ and the ICTY do remain on this control test for purposes of responsibility, but given the different relevant contexts, they hardly constitute a drama.

It is also interesting to see the different reactions of different tribunals, whose jurisdiction relates to acts of States within their jurisdiction, as to whether that includes acts performed overseas by those in public authority. For the European Court of Human Rights in Bankoviç,[18] the concept of "the legal space of the European Convention" was critical. Analysing Article 1 of the European Convention on Human Rights, which states that "The High Contracting Parties shall secure to everyone within their jurisdiction the rights and freedoms defined in Section I of this Convention," the Strasbourg Court concluded that there was no jurisdictional link between the

Convention and the extra-territorial acts that had taken place in the territory of the Federal Republic of Yugoslavia that was beyond the legal space of the Convention. These answers given by the Strasbourg Court were more cautious than the jurisdictional formulation preferred by the Human Rights Committee in the face of the comparable question. The Committee explained that Article 2 of the International Covenant on Civil and Political Rights, which states that "Each State Party to the present Covenant undertakes to respect and to ensure to all individuals within its territory and subject to its jurisdiction the rights recognized in the present Covenant," meant that a State Party must respect and ensure the Covenant rights to anyone within the power or effective control of that State Party, even if not situated within the territory of the State Party.[19]

I want to make it crystal clear that a State will of course be responsible for the acts attributable to it, even when those occur outside of its own jurisdiction. That underlies, for example, the ICJ's recent findings about the unauthorized conduct of Ugandan forces in the Congo. But that is a different matter from that of establishing a jurisdictional link prior to any consideration of substance.

An interesting issue under this heading (application of the same norm by different courts) arose for the International Court of Justice in the *LaGrand*[20] and *Avena*[21] cases. There, it will be recalled, the Court determined that Article 36, paragraph 1, of the Vienna Convention on Consular Relations contained individual rights. It was proposed by Germany in *LaGrand* to categorize these individual rights further as human rights.[22] Cited in support of this proposition was Advisory Opinion OC-16/99 by the Inter-American Court, which had had occasion to pronounce on the very same clause.[23] Just as the jurisdiction of the ICTY in *Tadiç* depended upon a certain finding as regards control of irregular groups, so the jurisdiction of the Inter-American Court was dependent upon Article 36, paragraph 1, of the Vienna Convention being a human right. In its *dispositif,* the Inter-American Court of Human Rights unanimously held that Article 36 of the Vienna Convention on Consular Relations concerns the protection of the rights of a national of the sending State and is part of the body of international human rights law.[24] Consequently, the Court had competence *ratione materiae* to address the other questions raised by Mexico that pertained to Article 36, paragraph 1(b), of the Convention. In the *LaGrand* case, the International Court limited itself to finding that Article 36, paragraph 1, was an individual right. It made no response to the claim that it was also a human right.[25]

The issue came back again in the *Avena* case, where it was Mexico that now contended that Article 36, paragraph 1, of the Vienna Convention was to be classified as a human right, again citing the Inter-American Court.[26] The Court again made no determination on this point. But it did state, *obiter,* that neither the text nor the object and purpose of the Convention, nor any indication in the *travaux préparatoires* appeared to support the conclusion that Mexico drew from its contention in that regard.[27]

It may be thought that as no determination of this issue was necessary for the ICJ to make its substantive findings under the Consular Convention, unity among tribunals might have been better served by maintaining its prior silence on the issue.

At the same time, we should not exaggerate the phenomenon of fragmentation.

Courts Usually Seek Common Approaches

Much has been made of the virtually sole example of a relatively recent court deliberately deciding an issue of general international law differently from how the same point had already been decided by the International Court of Justice. What is little commented on, but is in my view of significantly more importance, is the tremendous efforts that courts and tribunals make, both to be consistent inter se and to follow the International Court of Justice.

A few years ago, I gave the Gordon Slynn Lecture on "2 Courts in Europe"—in fact, it was really about three courts, as my survey of the handling of general international law concerned Strasbourg as well as Luxembourg.[28] The efforts at compliance with general international law of these courts, even within the context of specialized institutional treaties, was striking. I am sure that a further analysis of the case-law, directed at the last five years, would show the same reality. The rules of treaty interpretation, as articulated by the International Court of Justice continue very much to be in view. Whether one agrees with the finding or not, the European Court on Human Rights has, in the *Al-Adsani* case, purported to locate the rights protected under the convention within general international law. The Luxembourg Court of First Instance has recently issued several judgments with general international law at their heart.

A learned paper on the European Court of Justice and the Vienna Convention was given only a few weeks ago at Lincoln's Inn by Sir Francis Jacobs. And the Strasbourg Court has in terms found the International Court's reasoning in *LaGrand* on the binding nature of interim measures to be useful for a comparable finding as regards a non-identical convention.[29] As has rightly been observed by a commentator, the International Court's own findings were based on an understanding of the character of courts generally going beyond the limits of the mere text of the Statute.[30]

There is also a striking similarity of approach across the various courts and tribunals as to the temporal issue in treaty interpretation. The concept of critical date retains its importance in identifying the moment at which a dispute crystallizes, and facts subsequent to it are to be treated as "coloured" or without legal pertinence. But there are circumstances in which the intention of the original parties as the key to interpretation may no longer be paramount. The notion of "original intention" has long been qualified by the idea that the parties themselves, because of the nature of the treaty that they agreed to, just have assumed that matters would evolve. This has long been the case so far as human rights treaties are concerned. The European Court of Human Rights has consistently held that uncertain provisions are to be interpreted in the light of contemporary morals and ideas.[31] This idea is now more widely applied. In the recent *Iron Rhine* case, for example, the Arbitral Tribunal adopted what it termed the "evolutive approach," saying that the Iron Rhine Treaty was one where the parties must have supposed that there would be profound commercial developments in the future.[32] Accordingly, the treaty was to be read so as to breathe future economic life into the sparse textual provisions. This same trend is discernable across courts, tribunals and arbitration tribunals.

Some courts work consciously to coordinate their approaches. Professor Trindade, a past president of the Inter-American Court of Human Rights, is surely right when he says of his Court and the European Court of Human Rights that the two courts have a common understanding that, for example, "human rights treaties . . . have a normative character, of *ordre public*"; "that in their application one ought to ensure an effective protection *(effet utile)* of the guaranteed rights"; "and that permissible restrictions by States on human rights in the form of reservations and limitations are to be restrictively interpreted."[33] He suggests that this coordination, built out of mutual respect, is a model to other courts.

What Should We Do About Any Babel That Does Exist?

Institutional Hierarchy?

One school of thought urgently proposes that a judicial hierarchy be established within our horizontal international legal order. The leading proponent is Judge Gilbert Guillaume, former President of the International Court of Justice, who has advanced this idea in a series of speeches at the United Nations and articles in various journals.[34] Overlapping jurisdictions means that plaintiffs can "forum shop" to their advantage. Applicants will take into consideration factors such as court access, applicable procedure, court composition, the court's case-law and its capacity to issue urgent orders when deciding which specific forum to choose. Judge Guillaume thus worries that a market-driven desire to be "popular" will result in a decline in quality of judicial decisions of the various competing tribunals. Furthermore, overlapping jurisdictions heighten the risk of inconsistent or contradictory judgments being rendered.

Judge Guillaume concludes that relations between courts need to be institutionalized to ensure harmony both procedurally (which tribunal should be seized of the case and development of principles such as *res judicata*) and substantively (consistency of rendered decisions). He argues that the ICJ should occupy a privileged position in the international judicial hierarchy for a variety of reasons: (1) It is the only court with a universal general jurisdiction; (2) it is the "principal judicial organ of the United Nations"; and (3) its age and length of duration give it special authority. However, Judge Guillaume is unclear about how precisely to institutionalize this privileged position of the ICJ. He does not believe that there is sufficient political will actually to formalize the position of the ICJ as a supreme appellate body that has the capacity to review judgments rendered by other international bodies. Alternatively, he posits that a version of the preliminary reference procedure available under Article 234 of the EC Treaty in European Community law should be institutionalized so that Courts can refer new questions of general international law to the International Court of Justice.

My own views on these issues have been somewhat different.[35] My starting point has been that the multiplication of intended legal institutions has resulted in a de facto decentralization of some subject-matter which the ICJ could in principle deal with *ratione materiae*. When one compares the tribunals established to deal with specialized areas of international law with the ICJ, one readily sees that the tribunals are more open to non-State actors, can respond more quickly, and are composed of experts in complex subject-matter. I can see no reason why States who have deliberately chosen such new bodies to respond to their real-life needs should support the slowing down of the work of these specialist tribunals to allow some form of reference to the ICJ. And I find it ironic that the proponents of "unity" in international law should think it possible for a specialist tribunal to retain full powers in "specialist" areas of law while referring over to the ICJ the issues of "general" international law. Are the particular and the general so easy to distinguish and slice up? And do we really want to do so?

Further, many of these specialist tribunals have what comes close to compulsory jurisdiction. There are not the same opportunities for non-participation in the judicial process, or the fashioning of reservations thereto, as there are under the International Court's Statute. Why should States who have declined to submit to the jurisdiction of the International Court of Justice agree to a reworking of the international system so that matters they have agreed to submit to particular specialized tribunals may in part still finish up with the ICJ? In sum, I have always regarded the "hierarchical" approach to the risks of Babel as unworkable.

The Koskenniemi Approach

The International Law Commission, with Marti Koskenniemi as leader of a special study group, has embarked upon a most interesting project, where the theme is resolutely *not* the relations between the expanding courts and tribunals. Rather, it is an analysis of whether international law itself—and, in particular, certain provisions of the Vienna Convention on the Law of Treaties—does not provide the medicine to heal such fragmentation as is proving painful. We may think of this as the gene therapy approach to fragmentation. I greatly welcome this study, and the interesting reports produced by Professor Koskenniemi thus far. It has laid particular emphasis on the *lex specialis* regime and self-contained regimes: time prevents any comment on these aspects of the matter. The International Law Commission Study also has given special attention, as "problem solvers," to the application of successive treaties relating to the same subject-matter (Article 30 of the Vienna Convention) and the modification of multilateral treaties between certain of the parties only (Article 41 of the Vienna Convention). I shall leave others to make such observations as they choose on these. What has specially caught my attention is the work of the International Law Commission Study Group on two other "solutions" to the question of fragmentation: (i) Norms and provisions that, unusually for international law, seek to establish some hierarchy and (ii) Article 31(3)(c) of the Vienna Convention on the Law of Treaties. As the Report observes, there is no hierarchy as such between sources of international law, but the special character of certain specific norms may result in them "having a special or privileged status because of their content, effort, scope of application, or on the basis of consent between the parties."[36]

Hierarchy of Norms

In the *Democratic Republic of the Congo v Rwanda* Judgment of 3 February 2006, the Court confirmed that the prohibition of genocide was a norm having the character of *jus cogens*.[37] But it then reaffirmed its longstanding position that its jurisdiction under the Statute can only be established through consent; it went on to confirm the fact that a party contends that a *jus cogens* norm has been violated does not of itself establish a basis for jurisdiction.[38]

So far as more substantive matters relating to *jus cogens* are concerned, there always remains the problem of exactly what norms have the character *jus cogens*, so as to establish a clear hierarchy in the case of a conflict of substantive applicable norms. The examples are likely, in my view, to be very, very few in number. In the *Oil Platforms* case, some judges viewed the application of norms relating to the use of force as having this special character, and for this reason among others, displacing the more obvious applicable law. It seems to me self-evident that the use of force, when it is prohibited in the circumstances of Article 2 (4) of the Charter, but permitted in the circumstances of Article 51 of the Charter, is not a *jus cogens* provision that without more sets aside a different specific, applicable law.

As for Article 103 of the United Nations Charter, its primacy is incontestable, although it might at first be thought that its invocation will be so exceptional as to not greatly add to our problem-solving devices. That being said, recent judgments of the Luxembourg Court of First Instance have suggested that this provision may have its role to play in reconciling potential diverse legal orders. In litigation arising out of Security Council sanctions directed at the Taliban, the European Court had "to consider . . . the relationship between the international legal order under the United Nations and the domestic or community legal order, and also the extent to which the exercise by the Community and its Member States of their powers is bound by resolutions of the Security Council adopted under Chapter VII of the Charter of the United Nations."[39] The Court looked to what it termed the principles of customary international law[40] to establish the rule of primacy. Interestingly, it cited in that context Article 27 of the Vienna Convention and Article 103 of the Charter, together with a determination of the International Court of Justice in 1984 in the *Nicaragua* case that "all the regional, bilateral and even multilateral arrangements . . . must always be made subject to the provision of Article 103 of the Charter of the United Nations."[41] As the Court of First Instance put it, by concluding a treaty between them, they could not transfer to the Community more powers than they possessed under the UN Charter. The International Court of Justice's *Lockerbie* judgment was also invoked to extend that primacy to Security Council resolutions carried out under Article 25 of the Charter.[42] The *Yusuf* case thus found, building on the opinion of Advocate General Jacobs in *Bosphorus* in 1996, that because Chapter VII Security Council resolutions are binding on Member States of the Community, they must take other measures necessary to ensure these resolutions are put into effect.[43]

The stepping stones were thus laid to a finding of immense importance: that Member States must leave unapplied any provision of Community law that raises any impediment to the proper performance of obligations under the UN Charter.

Interestingly, and perhaps more controversially, the Luxembourg Court of First Instance reserved to itself a power of judicial review to ensure that the primacy of UN binding resolutions under Article 103 of the Charter was not negated by "a failure of the resolutions to observe the fundamental preempting provisions of *jus cogens*."[44] Comparable findings were made in the Judgment issued on the same day in the *Kadi* case.[45] This raises a whole series of different issues, including whether it is the Luxembourg Court that holds any power of judicial review of Security Council resolutions, if such power indeed exists.

Might the answer lie in Article 31(3)(c) of the Vienna Convention, a provision on which Professor Koskenniemi places considerable store? The 2003 judgment of the International Court of Justice in the *Oil Platforms* case suggests that invocation of this provision is likely to bring its own attendant problems.[46] It may be recalled that in that case the Court had found the United States not to be in violation of Article X, paragraph 1, of the US-Iran Treaty of Amity concerning freedom of commerce and navigation between the parties.[47] In proceeding nonetheless to examine another clause of that Treaty, which the United States had as a precaution invoked as a defence to any such violation, the Court noted that it was faced with another question of treaty interpretation. The issue was whether the "measures" permitted under that other clause (Article XX(1)(A)) could be understood as including recourse to force. Turning to Article 31(3)(c) of the Vienna Convention for assistance, the Court noted that it was there specified that interpretation must take into account "any relevant rules of international law applicable in the relations between the parties."[48] This led it in turn to Article 2, paragraph 4, of the Charter, and through this route to certain findings of law as to the impermissibility of the United States military action in the Gulf.

Article 31(3)(c) was thus used to introduce the entirety the law of *jus ad bellum*, even though, in the jurisdictional phase of the case, the Court had stated that its competence was limited to pronouncing upon Article X(1) of the Treaty of Amity—freedom of commerce. Indeed, in the jurisdictional phase of the case, it had exactly excluded the same subject-matter as later became *reintroduced* by virtue of a reliance on Article 31(3)(c).

In the complex of facts in law globally referred to as the *Bosphorus* case, the issue of the UN sanction régime had worked its way through the courts of Ireland, the European Court of Justice, and then, in June 2005, the European Court of Human Rights sitting as a Grand Chamber (Article 1, Protocol 1 there being in issue).[49] After a survey of the law of the European Communities and UN sanctions resolutions, the Strasbourg Court turned to the Vienna Convention on the Law of Treaties, invoking in particular Article 31 (3)(c).[50] It referred to the need to interpret the Convention in the light of the relevant rules of international law. It further stated (invoking *Al-Adsani*) that "The Court has also long recognized the growing importance of international cooperation and of the consequent need to secure the proper functioning of international organizations."[51] Whether Article 31(3)(c) is needed to secure these ends can be debated.

The application of Article 31(3)(c) of course feeds into the issue of "special regimes," which are receiving particular attention in the International Law Commission study. Of course, in one sense every treaty is a "special regime"—particular arrangements are the very raison d'étre of treaties. But this concept has come to have a particular resonance in environmental law, and even more particularly in the WTO system. After early controversy it has now become accepted by the WTO panels and appellate body that WTO law does not exist in isolation from general international law. As Koskenniemi rightly observes: "a regime can receive (or fail to receive) legally binding force ('validity') only by reference to (valid or binding) rules or principles *outside* it."[52] The issue has been around a long time. This truism was recognized long ago in the context of petroleum concessions, which in the 1970s it was equally à la mode to perceive as special self-contained regimes. The change, through time, in the sorts of special regimes that attract our attention today does not alter the flaw in logic which suggests they can exist isolated from general international law.

Conclusion

I admire the work being done by the International Law Commission Study Group on Article 31 (3)(c), but because I suspect that invocation of this provision brings with it as many problems as it resolves, I am sceptical that it is the overall answer to systemic fragmentation.

What, then, is to be done? There are no simplistic answers. Neither suggestions of a judicial hierarchy nor suggestions that Article 31 of the Vienna Convention might be the solution seem to me persuasive.

We judges are going to have to learn how to live in this new, complex world, and to regard it as an opportunity rather than a problem:

- We must read each other's judgments.
- We must have respect for each other's judicial work.
- We must try to preserve unity among us unless context really prevents this.

Notes

1. *Application of the Convention on the Prevention and Punishment of the Crime of Genocide (Bosnia and Herzegovina v Serbia and Montenegro).*

2. *Prosecutor v Radislav Krstiç* Case No IT-98-33-A, Appeals Chamber, judgment of 19 Apr 2004.

3. *Armed Activities on the Territory of the Congo (Democratic Republic of the Congo v Uganda)* (judgment of 19 Dec 2005).

4. *Legality on the Threat or Use of Nuclear Weapons, Advisory Opinion* [1996] ICJ Rep 1996 226.

5. ibid [1996] ICJ Rep1996 240, para 25.

6. ibid 243, para 33.

7. See, eg, Art 27 of the Rome Statute of the International Criminal Court.

8. Arrest Warrant of 11 April 2000 *(Democratic Republic of the Congo v Belgium) (Judgment)* [2002] ICJ Rep 2002, 3 (in particular, paras 45 et seq).

9. *Al-Adsani v United Kingdom* No 35763/97, ECHR 2001-XI.

10. ibid para 56.

11. *Waite and Kennedy v Germany* No 26083/94, ECHR 1999-I, paras 72–4 and *Beer and Regan v Germany* [GC] No 26083/94, ECHR 1999-I, paras 62–4.

12. *Prosecutor v Tadiç* Case No IT-94-1-A, Appeals Chamber, judgment of 15 July 1999.

13. ibid para 137.

14. ibid para 90.

15. ibid para 92.

16. *Case concerning Armed Activities on the Territory of the Congo (Democratic Republic of the Congo v Uganda)* (judgment of 19 Dec 2005).

17. ibid para 160.

18. *Bankoviç v Belgium and 16 Other Contracting States* [GC] No 52207/99, ECHR.

19. *See* General Comment No 31 [80], *Nature of the General Legal Obligation Imposed on States Parties to the Covenant* CCPR/C/21/Rev1/Add 13, 26 May 2004.

20. *LaGrand (Germany v United States of America), Judgment*, 2001 ICJ Rep 2001 466.

21. *Avena and Other Mexican Nationals (Mexico v United States of America) (Judgment)* [2004] ICJ Rep 2004 12.

22. *LaGrand* (n) [2001] ICJ Rep 2001 494, para 78.

23. See *The Right to Information on Consular Assistance in the Framework of the Guarantees of the Due Process of Law,* Advisory Opinion OC-16/99 of 1 Oct 1999, Inter-American Court of Human Rights.

24. ibid para 141(2).

25. *LaGrand* (n) [2001] ICJ Rep 2001 494, paras 77–8.

26. *Avena* (n) [2004] ICJ Rep 2004 31–2, para 30.

27. ibid 60–1, para 124.

28. Rosalyn Higgins 'The ICJ, the ECJ and the Integrity of International Law' (2003) 52 ICLQ 1 (The text of the 2002 Lord Slynn European Law Foundation Lecture, given on 10 Apr 2002).

29. See, eg, *Mamatkulov and Abdurasulovic v Turkey* [GC] Nos 46827/99 and 46951/99, 2005, 4 Feb, paras 116–17.

30. Beate Rudolf 'Unity and Diversity of International Law in the Settlement of International Disputes' in Andreas Zimmermann and Rainer Hoffman (eds) *Proceedings of an International Symposium of the Kiel Walther Schucking Institute of International Law, November 4–7, 2004* (Duncker and Humblot Berlin 2006) 396.

31. See, eg, *Matthews v United Kingdom* [GC] No 24833/94, S 39, ECHR 1999-I.

32. *In the Arbitration Regarding the Iron Rhine ('Ijzeren Rijn') Railway (Belgium v Netherlands),* Arbitral Award of 24 May 2005, available at <www.pca-cpa.org/ENGLISH/RPC/BENL/BE-NL%20Award%20corrected%20200905.pdf> (last visited 28 Mar 2006) paras 80–5.

33. *Case of Caesar v Trinidad and Tobago* No 123, Series C, I/A Court H.R., judgment of 11 Mar 2005, Separate Opinion of Judge Cançado-Trindade, para 7.

34. See, eg, Speech by His Excellency Judge Gilbert Guillaume, President of the International Court of Justice, to the Sixth Committee of the General Assembly of the United Nations, 27 Oct 2000, available at <www.icjcij.org/icjwww/ipresscom/SPEECHES/iSpeechPresident_Guillaume_SixthCommittee_20001027.htm> (last visited 28 Mar 2006); see also Gilbert Guillaume 'The Future of International Judicial Institutions' (1995) 44 ICLQ 848 and 'Advantages and Risks of Proliferation: A Blueprint for Action' (2004) 2 Journal of Intl Criminal Justice 300.

35. See, eg Rosalyn Higgins 'The ICJ, the ECJ and the Integrity of International Law' (n 28) 17–20.

36. Chapter XI, 'Fragmentation of International Law: Difficulties Arising from the Diversification and Expansion of International Law' in Report of the fifty-seventh session of the International Law Commission (2005) GA Official Records, 60th Sess, Supp No 10 (A/60/10) 223, para 487.

37. *Case concerning Armed Activities on the Territory of the Congo (New Application: 2002) (Democratic Republic of the Congo v Rwanda), Judgment on Jurisdiction of the Court and Admissibility of the Application* [2006] ICJ Rep 2006 para 64.

38. ibid para 69.

39. *Yusuf and Al Barakaat International Foundation v Council and Commission* Case T 306/01, judgment of the Court of First Instance of 21 Sept 2005, para 228.

40. ibid para 232.

41. ibid para 233.

42. ibid para 234.

43. ibid para 239.

44. ibid para 277.

45. *Kadi v Council and Commission* Case T-315/01, judgment of the Court of First Instance of 21 Sept 2005.

46. *Case concerning Oil Platforms (Islamic Republic of Iran v United States of America) (Judgment)* [2003] ICJ Rep 2003 161.

47. ibid 218, para 125(1).

48. ibid 182, para 41.

49. *Bosphorus Hava Yollari Turizm ve Ticaret Antonim fiirketi (Bosphorus Airways) v* Ireland [GC] No 45036/98, ECHR 2005.

50. ibid para 100.

51. ibid para 150.

52. Chapter X, 'Fragmentation of International Law: Difficulties Arising from the Diversification and Expansion of International Law' in Report of the Firty-sixth Session of the International Law Commission, GA Official Records, 59th Sess, Supp No 10 (A/59/10), p 290, para 218.

CHAPTER 11

The Place of the WTO and Its Law in the International Legal Order

Pascal Lamy

TRADE IS TO BE FOUND AT THE ORIGIN OF ENTIRE SEGMENTS of public international law, and it accounts for one of its main sources: the treaty. Indeed, one of the first international legal instruments to leave a trace in history was the commercial treaty between Amenophis IV and the King of Alasia (Cyprus) in the 14th century BC. This treaty exempted Cypriot traders from customs duty in exchange for the importation of a certain quantity of copper and wood. Nothing has fundamentally changed since then: at the beginning of the 21st century we still have bilateral trade agreements. But they now have to be reported to the WTO, so that they may be checked for consistency with international trade rules.

The international legal order, on the other hand, has evolved dramatically. The great empires have disappeared into the annals of history. Philippe le Bel and Jean Bodin's jurists progressively conceptualized the notion of sovereignty; the treaties of Westphalia ushered in a society defined by the pre-eminence of sovereign states, the 1815 Congress of Vienna laid the foundations of multilateralism, and the 19th century saw the first international organizations come to light. With the creation of the League of Nations, followed by the United Nations system and, finally, with the disintegration of the Eastern Bloc, the 20th century witnessed the evolution from traditional international law between states towards a contemporary and universal international law open to new players, including international organizations and non-governmental organizations.

Thus, the international legal order has experienced a number of upheavals. But its evolution has been neither linear nor homogeneous—

Reprinted with permission from Pascal Lamy, "The Place of the WTO and Its Law in the International Legal Order," *European Journal of International Law* 17 (2006): 969–984.

which is why international society still bears the marks of several historical stages in the process.

As a metaphorical illustration, let us take the three physical states of matter: gas, liquids and, finally, solids. Today's international legal order is simultaneously composed of these three states. Gas is the coexistence of particles devoid of any hierarchical differentiation: the Westphalian order made up of sovereign states organized according to an essentially "horizontal" logic with a decentralized responsibility mechanism. The solid state is reflected in the European Union, the perfect example of an international integration organization which produces rules that it interprets "autonomously" and whose primacy and direct applicability is guaranteed through a system of judicial remedy. The judicialization of responsibility of Member States for violations of Community law is a cornerstone of this integrated legal order. Between the gaseous state and the solid state, there remains the liquid state. It is to this category that the World Trade Organization belongs. Neither entirely vertical nor entirely horizontal in essence, resembling an organization for intergovernmental cooperation in certain respects while being closer to an international integration organization in others, the WTO represents a unique legal order or system of law. At the risk of oversimplification, in fact, I will draw no distinction between a system of law, a legal system and a legal order. The reason why the international legal order exists in several physical states is that it is evolving; and the WTO is both a product and a vehicle of that evolution.

Indeed, the WTO is an international organization that brings together two concepts of international law. Leaving aside one or two specificities, it is a permanent negotiating forum between sovereign states and is therefore a cooperation organization akin to international conferences established under traditional international law. But it also comprises a sophisticated dispute settlement mechanism which makes it an integration organization, rooted in contemporary international law. In simple terms, the WTO's sophisticated dispute settlement mechanism makes it a distinctive organization.

Above all, the WTO comprises a true legal order. If we take up Professor Jean Salmon's definition, "a body of rules of law constituting a system and governing a particular society or grouping," we see that there exists, within the international legal order, a specific WTO legal order. The WTO system has two essential attributes: valid rules and enforcement mechanisms. But the fact that it is specific does not mean that it is insular or isolated. These are the two points that I will be discussing here in an effort to explain firstly how this legal system fits into the international legal order and, secondly, how it links in with the other legal systems.

Let us begin with the first point, and examine what makes the WTO a unique legal system within the international legal order.

The WTO is an international organization. This may seem obvious, and yet it took over 50 years to achieve that outcome. This protracted effort to acquire a legal existence has left its mark.

The GATT, which was replaced by the WTO in 1995, was a provisional agreement that entered into force in January 1948 and was to disappear with the treaty creating the International Trade Organization (ITO). Since that treaty never entered into force, the GATT remained, for a half a century, an agreement in simplified form which, in principle, did not provide for any institutional continuity. Thus, the GATT did not have "Members" but "contracting parties," a term which highlighted the purely contractual nature of the arrangement. Without an international organization in the strict sense of the term, and therefore without a separate international legal personality, the GATT could only operate through its contracting parties and, for its everyday work, with the support of the Interim Commission for the International Trade Organization (ICITO), a provisional commission responsible for establishing the ITO.

Thus, it was almost 50 years later, with the Marrakesh Agreement, that a truly international organization was finally created, i.e., according to the definition given by the International Law Commission in its draft articles on the responsibility of international organizations, "an organization established by a treaty or other instrument governed by international law and possessing its own international legal personality." In order to avoid any ambiguity, the Agreement Establishing the WTO states in Article VIII that the Organization shall have legal personality.

The implications of this status are numerous. The Marrakesh Agreement states that Members shall accord the WTO such privileges and immunities as are necessary for the exercise of its functions. Thus, its legal personality comprises an international facet, which enables it to act at the international level, and an internal personality, which enables it to conclude contracts for the purposes of its day-to-day operations and, among other things, to employ its 600 permanent staff members. As with all international organizations, the competencies of the WTO are limited by the principle of speciality. But alongside its subject-matter competence, which is explicitly provided for in its constituent instrument, the WTO also has implicit competencies. Thus, the main consequence of this status of international organization is that it enables the WTO to have its own will, which is expressed in a legislative output within the limits fixed by its constituent instrument, and to interact with other international players.

As a true international organization, the WTO now comprises an integrated and distinctive legal order: it produces a body of legal rules (1), making up a system (2), and governing a community (3).

1. A body of legal rules, first of all. The WTO is a treaty comprising some 500 pages of text accompanied by more than 2,000 pages of schedules

of commitments. Moreover, 50 years' worth of GATT practice and decisions—what is known as the "GATT *acquis*"—have been incorporated into what constitutes the new WTO treaty. WTO rules are regularly renegotiated. While it is true that the WTO Secretariat and the WTO bodies do not have any general power to adopt formally binding rules, the WTO bodies are able to adopt effective decisions that provide pragmatic responses to specific needs; and in that sense, they do produce a kind of secondary legislation. The system is no longer based solely on the principles of a certain diplomacy which often led, under the GATT, to the adoption of negotiated solutions that reflected the relative power of the states involved. The WTO does not produce equity, in the meaning given to the term by public international law—rather, it produces legality.

2. These legal rules form an integrated system. Indeed, the WTO agreements are integrated in a "single undertaking," which forms an entity that is meant to be coherent. A number of provisions recall this fact, in particular Article II:2, which states that the multilateral trade agreements "are integral parts" of the Agreement Establishing the WTO and are "binding on all Members." This is why they are annexed to the Agreement Establishing the WTO. In the *Indonesia–Autos* dispute, the panel which ruled in the first instance recalled that there was a presumption against conflict between the different provisions of the WTO treaty since they formed part of agreements having different scopes of application or whose application took place in different circumstances. On several occasions, the Dispute Settlement Body (DSB) reaffirmed that Members must comply with all of the WTO provisions, which must be interpreted harmoniously and applied cumulatively and simultaneously. Thus, the WTO treaty is in fact a "single agreement," which has established an "organized legal order."

3. WTO law governs a community, namely its Members. In *United States–Section 301,* the panel confirmed the existence of a GATT/WTO legal order and even seemed to suggest that this order was characterized by its "[i]ndirect impact on individuals." For, by contrast, "when an actual violation takes place . . . in a treaty the benefits of which depend in part on the activity of individual operators the legislation itself may be construed as a breach, since the mere existence of legislation could have an appreciable "chilling effect" on the economic activities of individuals." The qualification of nations as no longer only objects of WTO law, but also as subjects, is still disputed. Leaving that debate aside, I would say that the WTO rules above all effectively govern the community of its Members, since failure to comply is punishable in the framework of the DSB. In other words, they do form a new legal order as defined above.

However, this integrated legal system is not "clinically isolated": there is a presumption of validity in international law and the rules of its treaties must therefore be read in harmony with the principles of international law. Thus, the WTO legal order respects, *inter alia*, the sovereign equality of states, good faith, international cooperation, and the obligation to settle disputes peacefully, not to mention the rules of interpretation of conventions which the Appellate Body, for example, applies without hesitation. The WTO respects general international law, while at the same time adapting it to the realities of international trade. In joining the international legal order, the WTO has produced its own unique system of law.

Leaving aside the doctrinal debate on the autonomy of international economic law, it is clear that WTO law is largely a circumstantial application of international law in general. I shall illustrate this with two examples, two principles of general international law which the WTO has brought to life in its own manner and on which it has left a lasting imprint: the sovereign equality of states and the obligation to settle disputes peacefully.

The sovereign equality of states requires formal equality between states of different sizes and power. This principle is fully respected at the WTO. While most international economic organizations have a restricted body alongside their plenary body, the WTO is unusual in that the totality of its Members participate, as a matter of law, in all of its bodies—from the Ministerial Conference, which meets at least once every two years, to the General Counçil, which functions during the interim period, not to mention each of the councils and committees. All of the decisions are taken according to the principle "one government/one vote" and by consensus. While it is true that this rule of consensus is responsible for a certain sluggishness in the negotiations, it does enable all states, whatever their share in international trade, to express their views and to participate on an equal footing.

The principle of equality is also reflected concretely in the substantial rules of the WTO. For example, in the form of the principle of non-discrimination it can be found in the most-favoured-nation clause and the national treatment rule. It also underlies the principle of reciprocity, which is at the heart of the negotiating mechanism. Indeed, as recalled by the UN Secretary-General before the General Assembly in 2004, equality is a fundamental requirement:

> At the international level, all States—strong and weak, big and small—need a framework of fair rules, which each can be confident that others will obey. Fortunately, such a framework exists. From trade to terrorism, from the law of the sea to weapons of mass destruction, States have created an impressive body of norms and laws.[1]

But as Kofi Annan points out, these rules must also be fair—which is why the WTO goes beyond formal equality and seeks to establish real equality. True equality can only exist between equals. When it comes to trade, some of the less developed countries require certain flexibilities if trade and development are to continue to exist side by side, so the developing countries can enjoy non-reciprocal benefits, in particular special and differential treatment. This deviation from the GATT principles for the developing countries was made official in 1964, with the addition to the GATT text of Part IV, "Trade and Development."

Article XXXVI.8 states that "[t]he developed contracting parties do not expect reciprocity for commitments made by them in trade negotiations to reduce or remove tariffs and other barriers to the trade of less-developed contracting parties." And there is also the so-called Enabling Clause, which provides for the establishment of a "generalized system of preferences" that authorizes the developed countries to grant tariff advantages to the developing countries as an exception to the most-favoured-nation clause. These are positive discrimination mechanisms to ensure effective equality among Members. They are in no way inconsistent with the sovereign equality of states—on the contrary, precisely as in the case of domestic laws, where social legislation is an essential corollary to equal dignity of men and women, this adaptation of applicable rules to the real situation of states is a way of ensuring more genuine equality. You will probably recognize here the very pertinent remarks of my old friend Professor Alain Pellet.

The WTO, then, rests largely on the principle of sovereign equality of states. But this does not mean that it is incapable of showing the kind of pragmatism that befits the area of trade in applying the principles of traditional international law.

Let me add, with regard to the sovereignty of states, that, in principle, only sovereign states are equal. This is why, in principle, the traditional international organizations are made up of states only. It is true that the WTO remains an inter-state framework. However, once again it has been able to adapt to the evolution of international society and the emergence of new actors.

Members may be "customs territories," so that Chinese Taipei has been able to join the WTO, and Hong Kong has been able to continue participating as an autonomous Member following its return to China. Similarly, the participation of the European Community as a WTO Member is unique. In the 1970s, the Commission participated de facto in GATT meetings, substituting for the European Economic Community Members to express a common position. With the creation of the WTO, this practice was formalized. The Organization's constituent treaty provides that the number of votes of the European Communities and their Member States shall in no case exceed the number of their Member States. What is new here is above all the participation of the Community alongside its Member States.

Also worth mentioning in this respect is the growing participation of NGOs—a term which the WTO interprets in a very broad sense. Article V:2 of the Agreement Establishing the WTO stipulates that "[t]he General

Council may make appropriate arrangements for consultation and cooperation with non-governmental organizations concerned with matters related to those of the WTO." There has been no detailed arrangement to date, but the General Council adopted guidelines in 1996 specifying the nature and scope of relations between the WTO Secretariat and the NGOs. These new rules have served as the basis for a policy of greater transparency towards the NGOs. This does not mean, however, that they are allowed into the actual negotiating forum: the WTO remains an inter-state negotiating framework. Nor are the NGOs given access to the Dispute Settlement Body, although they have been allowed a growing role in the proceedings through *amicus curiae* briefs since the report of the Appellate Body in *United States–Shrimps*.

It is in fact necessary to preserve the inter-state framework of the WTO while keeping an ear open to the non-state actors that represent civil society. This balance aims to ensure that the WTO acts in the general interest which, in principle, is embodied in the state, while the NGOs defend—quite legitimately—interests that are often specific. Nevertheless, the WTO, in recognizing the role of NGOs, is contributing to their impact within the international legal order. Thus, the WTO has also acted as a vehicle in the evolution of international law towards its contemporary form, and indeed is a driving force in the progressive transformation of international society into an international community.

Let us turn to another example of the WTO respecting general international law while adapting it to the constraints of its own legal order: the principle of the obligation to settle disputes by peaceful means.

This obligation is a principle that lies at the heart of general international law and is enshrined in the United Nations Charter. Twenty-five years later, the General Assembly voted the famous Declaration on the seven principles of peaceful coexistence, which recalls that "States shall settle their international disputes by peaceful means in such a manner that international peace and security and justice are not endangered."[2] Thus, when they created the international organizations, the states ensured that their chief goal was to maintain peace through appeasement and prevention of international tensions. They then introduced the dispute settlement systems. In this context, the creation of a multilateral trading system was a means of ensuring both peace through law and peace through prosperity.

The implementation of the principle of the obligation to settle disputes by peaceful means, with bodies created to that end, is a way of institutionalizing international responsibility, the main characteristic of which, in traditional international law, is decentralization. It has now been established that states are responsible for any negative impact of their wrongful acts; but the determination of their responsibility and, above all, its implementation, remain essential to the effectiveness and efficiency of any legal system. One of the WTO's distinctive features is its sophisticated dispute settlement mechanism which, as I mentioned earlier, tends to make it more of an integration organization, "solid" rather than "liquid." Under Article 56 of the text of the International Law Commission on "Responsibility of States for Internationally Wrongful Acts," which appears as an annex to General Assembly Resolution 56/83, the WTO dispute settlement mechanism is a special system, or *lex specialis*. Consequently, the DSB can go beyond general international law on the road to communitizing WTO law—that is, consolidating its legal system in the wake of an institutionalization of international responsibility.

Although still influenced by its origins, when, in the words of Professor Canal-Forgues, it was more of a quasi-judicial conciliation mechanism, the WTO dispute settlement system introduced a new "jurisdiction" which ensures the enforcement of rulings and recommendations. At the same time, the procedure tends to preserve the fundamental requirements of fair trial. It is a compulsory jurisdiction that is broadly accessible to Members; it decides according to law; the procedure for adopting decisions is quasi-automatic; rulings are made by independent persons, and their implementation is subject to continuous multilateral monitoring until full satisfaction of the complainant where a violation has been found. Moreover, the Appellate Body functions more or less like a court of cassation, which hears only matters of law. This confirms the essentially legal nature of the system.

Above all, WTO jurisdiction is compulsory for all WTO Members. No Member may oppose the initiation of a dispute settlement procedure by another Member. In other words, that Member must submit to WTO law. Contrary to what may happen in other international forums, for example the International Court of Justice, all WTO Members have, by definition, accepted the compulsory and exclusive jurisdiction of the DSB for all matters relating to the WTO agreements.

In order to avoid fragmentation of the dispute settlement mechanisms that existed under the GATT regime, the Marrakesh Agreements also sought to preserve the unity of the system under the DSB. Thus, the settlement of all disputes relating to WTO rules has been placed under the auspices of a single institutional body, the Dispute Settlement Body, and is subject to a single body of rules and procedures contained in the Understanding. In other words, it is an integrated system.

An important, and in many ways innovative, feature of this system is the presumption of legal and economic interest in bringing proceedings, which confirms the hypothesis of a "communitization" of WTO law: each Member State can enforce WTO law whether or not it has a direct and personal interest—in the interests, so to speak, of the "community of states parties." This principle, which dates back to the GATT period, was revived by the Appellate Body in *EC–Bananas*, when it confirmed that the United

States had sufficient interest to bring proceedings against the European Community, even though, in practical terms, the Americans did not export bananas. In other words, any state may initiate dispute settlement procedures on the basis of a claim that another Member is not complying with its obligations under WTO law.

Everything is done to ensure that the complaint, if it is substantiated, is followed by concrete effects. After the adoption by the panel, and possibly the Appellate Body, of their "recommendations," WTO Members continue to monitor and to follow up on the implementation by the losing country of the conclusions of the case. Furthermore, if the conclusions are not fully implemented, the winning party that so requests may impose countermeasures in the form of trade sanctions.

What can we conclude from all of these mechanisms? First of all, they are the confirmation of a certain "communitization" that is under way at the WTO, with an institutionalization of international responsibility. The idea is essentially to ensure respect for the rule rather than reparation, a clear sign of the transformation of a society into a community. It is no longer the interest of the adversely affected party that counts, but the common interest. Indeed, violation of the law that applies to the community is in itself an infringement of the rights of all of the Member states, which are all entitled to feel that they have been adversely affected. In other words, responsibility is generated by an objective "fact": it is the result of non-compliance, whatever the consequences may be.

But what is interesting about the institutionalization of international responsibility by the DSB is that sovereign states ultimately retain a certain control over the result of the peaceful settlement of disputes. When it comes to enforcing the consequences of a DSB decision, we revert to law in its most traditional form, since the decision in fact authorizes the state that has won the case to exercise its right to countermeasures. The countermeasures are determined by the state itself, which is free within the limits of the treaty and subject to arbitration, to decide on their scope. These countermeasures (formerly "unarmed reprisals") are the product of international law in its most traditional form: the right of each state to take the law into its own hands. Thus, there is a margin of controlled freedom or sovereignty, a balance between the decentralized responsibility of traditional international law and the complete jurisdictionalization of the peaceful settlement of disputes. The WTO is one of the rare systems to have truly succeeded in regulating countermeasures applied by the powerful states by making their application contingent on the prior collective approval of Members.

In the final score, I share the view of Professor Ruiz-Fabri: to all intents and purposes the WTO is a true jurisdiction, since the political control that the DSB is able to exercise remains largely theoretical. The "reverse" consensus mechanism practically automatically requires the DSB to reach a decision as long as the complainant remains determined to pursue the case.

Thus, WTO law is a body of legal rules making up a system and governing a community. As such, the WTO incorporates an integrated and distinctive legal order. Bringing together traditional international law, which it respects, and contemporary international law, which it is helping to promote, the WTO has become a part of the international legal order as a *sui generis* legal system. But how does WTO law link to the legal systems of other international organizations within the international legal order?

This leads me to the second part, which will examine the link between the legal system of the WTO and the legal systems of other international organizations. The effectiveness and legitimacy of the WTO depend on how it relates to norms of other legal systems and on the nature and quality of its relationships with other international organizations. In order to address more specifically the place and the role of the WTO's legal system in the international legal order, I will briefly discuss how the WTO's provisions operate and treat other legal norms, including norms developed by other international organizations. I will first address this issue from a normative point of view, and then from an institutional perspective. I will show that the WTO, far from being hegemonic, as it is sometimes portrayed to be, recognizes its limited competence and the specialization of other international organizations. In this sense the WTO participates in the construction of international coherence and reinforces the international legal order. The WTO, its treaty provisions and their interpretation, confirms the absence of any hierarchy between WTO norms and those norms developed in other forums: WTO norms do not supersede or trump other international norms.

In fact, the GATT, and now the WTO, recognizes explicitly that trade is not the only policy consideration that Members can favour. The WTO contains various exception provisions referring to policy objectives other than trade, often under the responsibility of other international organizations. Our Appellate Body has managed to operationalize these exception provisions so as to provide Members with the necessary policy space to ensure, if they wish, that their actions in various forums are coherent.

Let me give a few examples of how our system deals with non-trade concerns and norms developed in other forums and you will see why I believe that the WTO has been pro-active in stimulating efforts of international coherence.

The WTO is of course a "trade" organization; it comprises provisions that favour trade opening and discipline trade restrictions. The basic philosophy of the WTO is that trade opening obligations are good, and even necessary, to increase people's standards of living and well-being. But, at the same time the GATT, and now the WTO, contains provisions of "exceptions" to these market access obligations. The old—but still in force—

Article XX of GATT provides that nothing prevents a Member from setting aside market access obligations when a Member decides, unilaterally, that considerations other than those of trade must prevail. This can happen when, for instance, a Member has made commitments in other forums, say on an environmental issue, when such an environmental commitment may lead to market access restrictions.

The revolution brought about by WTO jurisprudence was to offer a new teleological interpretation of the WTO that recognizes the place of trade in the overall scheme of states' actions and the necessary balance that ought to be maintained between all such policies.

How is this done within the WTO legal order? First, and very simply, the WTO treaty was considered and interpreted as a "treaty." In the very first WTO dispute, an environment-related dispute *(US–Gasoline)*, the Appellate Body concluded that the Panel had overlooked a fundamental rule of treaty interpretation, expressed in the Vienna Convention on the Law of Treaties (Vienna Convention). I am sure this sounds very obvious to international legal experts! The Appellate Body first recalled that this general rule on treaty interpretation had attained the status of a rule of customary or general international law. It was important to do so because, as you may know, neither the USA nor the EC have ratified the Vienna Convention on Treaties. Then, the Appellate Body made its first statement, now famous, on the nature of the relationship between the WTO and the international legal order: "the GATT is not to be read in clinical isolation from public international law."

Recalling that pursuant to Article 31 of the Vienna Convention, terms of treaties are to be given "their ordinary meaning, in their context and in the light of the Treaty's object and purpose," the Appellate Body noted that the Panel Report had failed to take adequate account of the different words actually used for each of the Article XX exceptions. This led to a reading that offered much more flexibility in the so-called environment exception and a categorical turnabout in 50 years of GATT jurisprudence.

In relying on the steps and principles of the Vienna Convention, panels as well as the Appellate Body have since often referred to the "context" of the WTO treaty and to non-WTO norms when relevant. I have been told that no other international dispute system is so attached to the Vienna Convention! In my view, this insistence on the use of the Vienna Convention is a clear confirmation that the WTO wants to see itself as being as fully integrated into the international legal order as possible.

The linkage between the WTO and other sets of international norms was also reinforced when the Appellate Body stated that in the WTO, exception provisions—referring to such non-trade concerns (environment, morality, religion, and so on)—are not to be interpreted narrowly: exceptions should be interpreted according to the ordinary meaning of the terms of such exceptions. In this context, our Appellate Body has insisted that exceptions cannot be interpreted and applied so narrowly that they have no relevant or effective application.

The Appellate Body further expanded the availability of WTO exceptions in the following manner. In the WTO, exceptions are subject to what we call a "necessity test," a test having features of a "proportionality" requirement. When assessing whether a measure is "necessary" for any non-WTO concern, a new and additional balancing test is to be used.

Such an assessment will have to balance (1) the "value" protected by such a measure—and the more important this "value," the easier it will be to prove the necessity (and the importance of the value will affect the entire balancing process); (2) the choice of the measure selected to implement such a non-trade concern—is it a complete or partial ban on trade? Is it a labelling requirement? Is it a discriminatory tax?; and, finally, (3) the trade impact of the restriction.

Once a measure prioritizing a non-trade value or standard is considered "necessary," there is always an assessment as to whether the measure is indeed applied in a non-protectionist manner, pursuant to the chapeau of Article XX. Here again the Appellate Body has said that when assessing whether a measure complies with Article XX, a "balance" between WTO market access obligations and a government's right to favour policies other than trade must always be kept.

Our jurisprudence has determined that the "control" exercised by the chapeau of Article XX of GATT, against disguised protectionist measures, is in fact an expression of the "good faith" general principle or an expression of the principle against the *"abus de droit."* I quote:

> the task of interpreting and applying the chapeau is, hence, essentially the delicate one of locating and marking out a line of equilibrium between the right of a Member to invoke an exception. . . and the rights of the other Members under varying substantive provisions. . . The location of the line of equilibrium . . . is not fixed and unchanging: the line moves as the kind and the shape of the measures at stake vary and as the facts making up specific cases differ.[3]

But let's not get dizzy or sea sick! Here again, faced with tensions between Members' market access obligations and the right to favour non-WTO considerations (and norms of other legal systems), the Appellate Body has introduced a form of "balancing test" or "proportionality test" between sets of values, or between sets of rights and obligations.

I hope it is now clear that WTO Members' trade restrictions imposed to implement non-trade considerations will be able to prevail over WTO market access obligations so long as they are not protectionist. In other words, the WTO provisions themselves recognize the existence of non-WTO norms and other legal orders and attempts to limit the scope of application of its own provisions, thereby nourishing sustainable coherence within the international legal order.

Another fundamental principle of the WTO is that Members can set national standards at the level they wish, as long as such Members are consistent and coherent. For example, in the dispute between Canada and the European Communities over the importation of asbestos-related material, the Appellate Body stated clearly that France was entitled to maintain its ban since it was based on authentic health risks and standards recognized in other forums and no alternative measures could guarantee zero risk as required by the EC regulation.

An additional feature of the WTO that confirms its integration into the international legal order, is the legal value and status it provides to international standards and norms developed in other forums. For instance, the Sanitary and Phytosanitary (SPS) Agreement states that Members' measures based on standards developed in Codex Alimentarius, the International Office of Epizootics and the International Plant Protection Convention are presumed to be compatible with the WTO. So, while Codex and others do not by any means legislate in the normal or full sense, the norms that they produce have a certain authority in creating a presumption of WTO compatibility when such international standards are respected. The SPS Agreement provisions thus provide important incentives for states to base their national standards on, or conform their national standards to, international standards. Therefore the WTO encourages Members to negotiate norms in other international forums, which they will then implement coherently in the context of the WTO.

I could give you further examples, but let me simply point to the preamble of the Marrakesh Agreement Establishing the WTO which, contrary to that of the GATT, explicitly refers to sustainable development as an objective of the WTO. While it is not yet clear whether sustainable development has crystallized into a general principle of law, the reference to such an important non-trade principle shows that the signatories of the WTO were, in 1994, fully aware of the importance and legitimacy of environmental protection as a goal of national and international policy.

In the famous *US–Shrimps* dispute, this preambular language was considered to indicate that further flexibility should be introduced when interpreting "natural resources" in the environment exception, and that it added, I quote: "colour, texture and shading to the rights and obligations" of WTO provisions. It also made explicit reference to the need to interpret WTO provisions—and especially the old GATT provisions—in an "evolutionary manner," taking into account the ordinary meaning of the terms of the WTO at the time of the dispute, rather than at the time of their drafting in 1947. This allowed the Appellate Body to consider contemporary treaties that define "natural resources" and to conclude that these definitions should also be used in the WTO so as to ensure some international coherence with respect to natural resources.

I agree therefore with Professor Abi-Saab, a member of our Appellate Body, that in using general principles of public international law in its interpretation of the WTO provisions, the Appellate Body has confirmed that the WTO is operating within the compound of the international legal order.

The WTO does, therefore, take into account other norms of international law. Absent protectionism, a WTO restriction based on non-WTO norms will trump WTO norms on market access. In so doing, it expands coherence between systems of norms or legal order. Moreover, I believe that in leaving Members with the necessary policy space to favour non-WTO concerns, the WTO also recognizes the specialization, expertise and importance of other international organizations. In sum, the WTO is well aware of the existence of other systems of norms and of the fact that it is not acting alone in the international sphere.

Existing relations between the WTO and other international organizations again reflect efforts of coherence within the international legal order. Now that the WTO is an authentic international organization with full legal personality, it has set up an important network of formal and de facto arrangements with other actors on the international scene. The greater the coherence within the international legal order, the stronger the international "community."

Let us look briefly at the actual interactions between the WTO and other international organizations. There are, for example, explicit WTO provisions on IMF/World Bank/WTO coherence with an explicit mandate to the Director General. There exists a series of inter-agency cooperation on technical assistance and capacity-building with several international organizations. Indeed the current Round of negotiations is to some extent premised on coherence, as we are suggesting a new "Aid-for-Trade programme" which brings together several multilateral organizations and regional development banks to assist developing countries in reaping the benefits of trade opening!

We also have formal cooperation agreements with other international organizations. For example, in the area of standard-setting, we now have a mechanism—the Standards and Trade Development Facility—involving the WTO, World Bank, Food and Agriculture Organization (FAO), World Health Organization and the World Organization for Animal Health. Some 75 international organizations have regular or ad hoc observer status in WTO bodies. The WTO also participates as an observer in many international organizations. Although the extent of such cooperation varies, coordination and coherence between the work of the WTO and that of other international organizations continue to evolve in a pragmatic manner. The WTO

Secretariat maintains working relations with almost 200 international organizations in activities ranging from statistics, research, standard-setting, to technical assistance training.

As I wrote in 2004,[4] I am a firm advocate of international coherence. I would not dare to say that "international coherence" is a general principle of international law! But I recall that international cooperation is one of the United Nations' objectives, as stated in Article 1 of the UN Charter. I believe that efforts towards international coherence are the only way to ensure the peaceful evolution of international relations and our international legal system. But international coherence is also crucial to ensuring the legitimacy of the WTO and the effectiveness of trade rules.

The WTO's mantra in favour of trade openness plays a vital role in Members' growth and development, but it is not a panacea for all the challenges of development; neither is it necessarily easy to accomplish, nor in many circumstances can it be effective unless it is embedded in a supportive economic, social and political context and a coherent multi-faceted policy framework. Trade opening can only be politically and economically sustainable if it is complemented by policies which address, at the same time, capacity problems (whether human, bureaucratic or structural); the challenges of distribution of the benefits created by freer trade; the need for a sustainable environment; respect for public morals, and so forth. This is also about international legal coherence.

All of these policies are intertwined with the other treaty obligations of WTO Members. Hence, further international coherence will only assist in getting the best out of the WTO! Since WTO norms are not hierarchically superior or inferior to any other norms (except *jus cogens*) states must find ways to coordinate all of these policies in a coherent manner. I believe that the WTO favours and encourages such coherence.

But this is not enough, and the description I just put forward is, to some extent, misleading. Although I personally believe in the need for more global governance, I am a "pragmatic practitioner." This brings me twice back down to earth! States often find themselves faced with opposite—even contradictory—sets of international obligations. Moreover, as treaties proliferate, so do dispute settlement systems as well as the potential for clashes with the WTO's compulsory and binding dispute settlement mechanism.

Let me give you one example and you will quickly see the "cracks" in the coherence of our international legal order. The *EC–Swordfish* dispute was concerned with the following situation. In 1999, Chile enacted swordfish conservation measures, by regulating gear and limiting the level of fishing through the denial of new permits. Chile effectively prohibited the utilization of its ports for landing and service to EC long liners and factory ships that disregarded minimum conservation standards. The EC challenged those measures as being contrary to its WTO transit. Chile demanded that the EC enact and enforce conservation measures for its fishing operations on the high seas, in accordance with the United Nations Convention on the Law of the Sea (UNCLOS). Chile responded to the EC's WTO challenge by initiating the dispute settlement provisions of UNCLOS and invited the EC to the International Tribunal on the Law of the Sea (ITLOS). The substantive issues before the WTO included the right of Chile to benefit from the application of Article XX of GATT on the conservation of natural resources, when acting pursuant to UNCLOS. The issue before UNCLOS could have included whether or not Chile was entitled to regulate and limit access to swordfish as part of a conservation programme.

In such a situation, it is conceivable that both instances would have examined whether UNCLOS effectively requires, authorizes or tolerates Chile's measures, and whether the Chilean measures were compatible with UNCLOS, an element that could influence a WTO panel in its decision as to whether or not Chile may benefit from the application of the exception provision on the environment. It is, therefore, conceivable that the two forums may reach different conclusions on the same facts or on the interpretation of the applicable law.

Fortunately, in that dispute, the parties reached an agreement to suspend both their disputes before ITLOS and before the WTO. But in the absence of a mutual agreement, the WTO panel would have proceeded much faster than that of ITLOS. Short of any agreement between the parties and in the absence of any international rule as to how these two different mechanisms should interact, many scenarios may emerge. In light of the quasi-automaticity of the compulsory and binding WTO dispute mechanism, it is unlikely that a WTO panel would decline jurisdiction because another dispute process—albeit more relevant and better equipped—has been seized for a similar or related dispute. And if both processes were triggered at the same time, it is quite probable that the WTO panel process would proceed much faster than any other process.

This is where part of the imbalance of our international legal order remains. Although the WTO, through its dispute settlement system, can show that it does take into account the norms of other legal orders, many still challenge the fact that it will be for the WTO judge to determine the balance, the "line of equilibrium" between trade norms and norms of other legal orders. Indeed, at present, if a measure has an impact on trade, the matter can always be taken to the WTO dispute settlement system fairly simply and quickly. The WTO adjudicating body will then have to determine whether the trade restriction can find justification in the exception provisions of the WTO. In assessing the invocation of such WTO exception justification, the WTO judge may in fact be deciding on the relative hierarchical value between two sets of norms.

Indeed, if a WTO Member invokes the environment exception to justify a trade restriction adopted pursuant to a multilateral environment agreement (MEA), in practice, it is the WTO judge who will determine whether, and the extent to which, compliance with such an MEA can provide a WTO justification for trade restriction. If, in support of its invocation of the WTO exception for public morals, a Member points to an International Labour Organization (ILO) resolution condemning a specific state for violation of core labour standards, it is the WTO judge who will finally decide on the legal value and impact of such an ILO resolution on international trade and its opposability to trade rules.

But I believe there is no reason to provide the WTO with the exclusive authority to operate the much-needed coherence between norms from different legal orders. The lack of coherence of our international legal system is amplified by the relative power of the WTO and in particular its dispute settlement mechanism. This shows the discrepancy between the WTO's very powerful enforcement mechanism and the traditional decentralized system of countermeasures still used in several legal orders. I do not think that the solution lies in weakening our dispute system. Many aspects of the WTO need to be improved, but I believe that the WTO dispute settlement system works well. The solution to the potential imbalance I have alluded to lies, I believe, in strengthening the enforcement (the effectiveness) of other legal orders so as to rebalance the relative power of the WTO in the international legal order.

This would not solve all our problems because we would then find ourselves with several powerful legal orders for which coordination would still be lacking! We also need to address the fragmentation of international law and the disorganized multiplication of international legal sub-systems. Until then, legal orders and legal systems will continue to co-exist and coherence will depend on ad hoc solutions based on the goodwill and interests of the jurisdictions concerned. Several unsatisfactory solutions have been suggested, including a referral to the International Court of Justice (ICJ) in situations of concurrent jurisdictions. A call for order has already been made by the ICJ against the dangers of fragmented and contradictory international law. The International Law Commission has undertaken important work in that direction.

Let me now conclude. Today's international legal order will be able to evolve peacefully only to the extent that the existing legal orders evolve through mutual respect. There is no exception to this rule, and the WTO is well aware of its importance.

The WTO has evolved from the GATT's closure. States signatories to the GATT wanted to reinforce the status of the international trading system and provided it with a formal international organization: the WTO. This international organization is now up and running well; it even produces effective norms of derivative law *(droit dérivé)*. The legal value and enforcement of those norms adopted by WTO bodies are matters for debate but the WTO normative capacity, including as a forum for permanent negotiations and its powerful but open dispute settlement mechanism, confirms the *sui generis* nature of its legal order.

In addition, the WTO makes full use of its international legal personality and is now collaborating actively with other international organizations. But there is more. In setting up a system whereby good faith norms developed in other forums are presumed to be WTO-consistent, the WTO not only gives due deference to other legal systems but it also stimulates negotiations in such other specialized forums and reinforces the coherence of our legal order. In this sense the WTO is an engine, a motor energizing the international legal order. This is, in my view, the place and role of the WTO and its legal order in the international legal order: a catalyst for international mutual respect towards international coherence and even for increased global governance, which I believe is needed if we want the world we live in to become less violent, be that social, political, economic or environmental violence.

Notes

1. Address by Kofi Annan at the opening of the general debate of the 59th Session of the General Assembly, New York, 21 Sept. 2004, available at http://www.un.org/Pubs/chronicle/2004/issue3/0304p4.asp.
2. Declaration on Principles of International Law Concerning Friendly Relations and co-operation among States in accordance with the Charter of the United Nations, GA Res. 2625, Annex, 25 UN GAOR, Supp. (No.28), UN Doc. A/5217 (1970), at 121.
3. Appellate Body Report on *US–Shrimp*, at para. 159.
4. P. Lamy, *La démocratie monde* (2004).

CHAPTER 12

The Role of the International Criminal Court in Enforcing International Criminal Law

Philippe Kirsch

The Need for an International Criminal Court

For experts on human rights it is clear that the protection of individuals from violations of human rights and humanitarian law requires appropriate mechanisms to enforce the law. For decades, international law lacked sufficient mechanisms to hold individuals accountable for the most serious international crimes. Naturally, like any other crimes, punishment for grave breaches of the Geneva Conventions or for violations of the Genocide Convention or the customary law of war crimes and crimes against humanity depended primarily on national courts. The problem is that it is precisely when the most serious crimes were committed that national courts were least willing or able to act because of widespread or systematic violence or because of involvement of agents of the State in the commission of crimes. If you look at the past to the best known historical events of that kind—Nazi Germany, Rwanda, the former Yugoslavia, Cambodia—the governments themselves or their agents were involved in the commission of those crimes. And so the failures of national courts in these contexts protected perpetrators with impunity. To prevent impunity in those situations, it is necessary to enforce international justice when national systems are unwilling or unable to act.

The first actions taken by the international community were to create ad hoc tribunals in such situations. The first tribunals were, of course, those of Nuremberg and Tokyo after World War II. Then, more recently, the United Nations set up tribunals for Rwanda and the former Yugoslavia. These tri-

---

Reprinted with permission from Philippe Kirsch, "The Role of the International Criminal Court in Enforcing International Criminal Law," *American University International Law Review* 22 (2007): 539–547.

bunals were extremely important. They were pioneers. They showed that international justice could work, but they all possessed several limitations.

One is that only a few States participated in their creation. The Nuremberg and Tokyo tribunals were set up by the victorious Allied powers after World War II, and the Rwanda and Yugoslavia tribunals were created by the Security Council. There are also other limitations. Ad hoc tribunals are limited to specific geographic locations. They respond primarily to events in the past. Their establishment involves extensive costs and delays. Last but not least, their creation depended, every time, on the political will of the international community at the time. And so in some cases there was action; in some cases there was nothing. As a result, their ability to punish perpetrators of international crimes and to deter future perpetrators has been limited. Eventually, a permanent truly international court was necessary to respond to the most serious international crimes and to overcome the limitations of the ad hoc tribunals.

In the summer of 1998, the U.N. General Assembly convened the Rome Conference to fill this essential need by establishing the ICC. In creating the ICC, States were particularly concerned with guaranteeing the Court's underlying legitimacy. Unlike the ad hoc tribunals, the ICC is the first and only tribunal that was created by an international treaty, which enabled all States to participate in its creation. All States were invited to participate in the negotiations of the statute and the vast majority—160—did so. There was a genuine effort to seek wide agreement among States without compromising the key values and objectives behind a fair and impartial court. Efforts towards universal acceptance were largely achieved. Eventually, on July 17, 1998, the Statute was approved by 120 States.

After the Rome Conference, a Preparatory Commission met for over three and a half years. It was charged with developing the Court's subsidiary instruments, notably, the Rules of Procedure and Evidence and the Elements of Crimes. It should be noted that the Rules of Procedure and Evidence for every other international criminal tribunal were developed by the judges in those tribunals. In the case of the ICC, they were developed by the States, again because States wanted to ensure that the system underlying the operation of the ICC would be as tight as possible. There was a very good reason for this; I will go back to that a little later. But it is clear that since the ICC would have prospective jurisdiction over then unknown situations, it was impossible for the States to know what exactly the ICC would deal with. Therefore it was absolutely vital for States to ensure that the ICC would be a purely judicial court.

Out of the desire I referred to earlier to ensure as wide acceptance as possible, all decisions taken by the Preparatory Commission were taken by consensus—by general agreement. That included the adoption of both the Rules of Procedure and Evidence and the Elements of Crimes. By this method of consensus, the Preparatory Commission contributed significantly to international support for the Court.

At the end of 2000, the deadline for signature of the Rome Statute, 139 States had signed the Statute, which was about twenty more than those that had voted for the Statute in 1998. To my knowledge, this is a unique case in the history of a treaty negotiation. Normally what happens is that you vote for an instrument at the time of the conference because it is easier and then forget about it because that is also easier. In the case of the ICC, the momentum to have a functioning Court in place was such that indeed, as I said, the number of signatures was higher than the number of votes at the conference.

In the eight years since the adoption of the Rome Statute, 102 countries representing broad geographical diversity have ratified or acceded to the Statute. I think it is a very good pace for a treaty establishing an international institution, in particular an international institution that requires considerable modifications in the legislation of States that have ratified the Statute.

The Features of the International Criminal Court

Having discussed the need for the Court, I turn now to the features of the Court. I would like, first of all, to dispel a common misperception about the Court. The ICC does not have universal jurisdiction. Its jurisdiction is limited to crimes committed on the territory of or by nationals of States which have voluntarily consented to its jurisdiction. These bases of jurisdiction—territory of the crime and the nationality of the perpetrator—are the most firmly established bases of criminal jurisdiction.

The Court's jurisdictional regime recognizes the special role of the Security Council in maintaining peace and security. Under the Statute, the Security Council may refer situations to the Court so that it no longer has to create ad hoc tribunals as it did for the former Yugoslavia and Rwanda. The Security Council has already used this power when it referred the situation in Darfur, Sudan, to the Court—Sudan not being a Party to the Rome Statute. The Security Council, acting under Chapter VII of the U.N. Charter, may also defer an investigation or a prosecution for a period of one year.

The Court's jurisdiction is also limited temporally. It has jurisdiction only over events since its Statute entered into force on July 1, 2002. No crime committed before that time can be dealt with by the ICC. The Court's subject matter jurisdiction covers the most serious international crimes. In that sense, although obviously the ICC deals with the most serious violations of human rights, it is not a human rights court in the traditional sense. It is a criminal court. It is a criminal court that is limited to genocide, crimes against humanity, and war crimes. The crimes contained in the Statute are well established in customary and conventional international law as well as national laws.

The Statute also provides that the Court has jurisdiction over the crime of aggression, but the Court will not exercise this jurisdiction until both a definition of aggression, and conditions for the exercise of jurisdiction are agreed upon. This has to happen through an amendment to the Statute, agreed to by the States Parties. Such amendment could occur at the earliest at a review conference to be held in 2009. Aggression was seen by many States as a symbolic crime—a crime that certainly was central to proceedings after World War II. It was a general view among States that if aggression were not committed, many other crimes would not be committed and therefore aggression had to be part of the Statute. However, there was no agreement on how aggression should be defined and there was certainly no agreement how to move from a declaration of aggression by States as an act covered by public international law to proceedings covering individuals having been involved in their crimes under international criminal law.

Even where the Court has jurisdiction, it will not necessarily act. This is the fundamental point that has to be understood about the ICC. The ICC is a court of last resort. It is intended to act only when national courts are unwilling or unable to carry out genuine proceedings. This is known as the principle of complementarity. Under this principle, a case will be inadmissible if it is being or has been investigated or prosecuted by a State with jurisdiction. In addition, a case will be inadmissible if it is not of sufficient gravity to justify action by the Court.

There is an exception under the principle of con plementarity where the Court may act. This is when the State is unwilling or unable genuinely to carry out the investigation or prosecution. For example, if proceedings were undertaken solely to shield a person from criminal responsibility—and that can take different forms, which are indeed spelled out in the Statute—or if the proceedings were carried out in a manner inconsistent with an intent to bring the person to justice.

It follows from what I said earlier, from the concern of States to ensure that the Court would be a purely judicial institution and would act in a purely judicial way, that the guarantee of a fair trial and protection of the rights of the accused have paramount importance before the ICC. The Statute incorporates the fundamental provisions of the rights of the accused or the rights of the accused and due process common to national and international legal systems.

A particular feature of the ICC, which is different again from ad hoc tribunals, is the treatment given to victims. Victims have of course participated in other international proceedings, but largely as witnesses for the prosecutor or for the defense. In the case of the ICC, victims may participate in proceedings even when not called as witnesses. The Court also has the power to order reparations to victims including restitution, compensation, and rehabilitation. The ICC has the obligation to take into account the particular interests of victims of violence against women and children.

The International Criminal Court Today

I would like to turn next to where the Court is today. Three States Parties have referred situations occurring on their own territories to the Court and in addition, as I mentioned earlier, the Security Council has referred the situation in Darfur, Sudan, a non–State Party. After analyzing the referrals for jurisdiction and admissibility, the Prosecutor began investigations in three situations: Uganda, the Democratic Republic of the Congo, and Darfur, Sudan. The Prosecutor is also monitoring five other situations.

In March this year, the first wanted person was surrendered to the Court. Mr. Thomas Lubanga Dyilo, a national of the Democratic Republic of the Congo, is alleged to have committed war crimes; namely, conscripting and enlisting children under the age of 15 and using them to participate actively in hostilities. The confirmation of charges against Mr. Lubanga is scheduled for September and if the charges are confirmed, the trial will begin thereafter.

Arrest warrants have also been issued in the situation in Uganda for five members of the Lord's Resistance Army, including its leader Joseph Kony. In that case, the alleged crimes against humanity and war crimes contained in the warrants include sexual enslavement, rape, intentionally attacking civilians, and the forced enlistment of child soldiers. The arrest warrants were initially issued under seal because of concerns about the security of victims and witnesses. The warrants were only made public once the Pre-Trial Chamber was satisfied that the Court had taken adequate measures to ensure security.

This illustrates a major difference between the ICC and other international tribunals, which by and large were dealing with crimes that had been committed in the past in the course of conflicts that were over. The ICC deals with crimes that continue to be committed in the course of conflicts that are ongoing. As a result, the ICC faces many challenges in particular in relation to its field activities and security.

The Future of the International Criminal Court

Finally, I would like to turn to what we can expect from the Court and from the wider system of international justice in the future. As investigations and trials proceed, the Court of course recognizes that it has the primary responsibility to demonstrate its credibility in practice through fair, impartial and efficient proceedings consistent with due process and proper administration of justice.

But the Court will never be able to end impunity alone. Its success will depend upon the support and commitment of States, international organizations, and civil society. The Court is complementary, as I said, to national jurisdictions and States will continue to have the primary responsibility to investigate and prosecute crimes—the Court being, as I said, only a court of last resort. There will be situations where national systems do not work properly or are unable to work. Because the Court's jurisdiction is limited to national and territories of States Parties, continued ratification of the Statute is essential to the Court having a truly global reach.

When the Court does act, it will require cooperation from States at all stages of the proceedings, such as by executing arrest warrants, providing evidence, and enforcing sentences of the convicted. Cooperation is absolutely crucial. For example, without sufficient support in arresting and surrendering persons, there can be no trials. Not only the States where crimes were committed or wanted persons are located can help, but all States in a position to provide cooperation can assist the Court. What States wanted when they created the ICC was a strong judicial institution, but not an institution that had at its disposal the normal tools of any national court. The ICC has no army. The ICC has no police. That's what States wanted, and—having wanted that system—now States need to cooperate with the Court to ensure that the system works. International organizations also provide critical support for the Court. The support of the United Nations is particularly important in this regard. The United Nations and the Court cooperate on a regular basis, both in our field activities and our institutional relations. In October, 2004, the Secretary General of the United Nations and I concluded a relationship agreement, which was later supplemented by an agreement with the U.N. Mission in the Democratic Republic of Congo.

The Court is also developing its cooperation with regional organizations. In April, the Court entered into a cooperation agreement with the European Union. We hope to do the same with the African Union in the near future. There is also a role for cooperation by the Organization of American States ("OAS"). The OAS has been a strong proponent of the Court. Court officials, including myself, have participated in a number of meetings of the OAS.

Then we come to non-governmental organizations ("NGOs") and civil society more broadly, which are also instrumental to the work of the Court. NGOs have played a large role in urging ratification of the Statute. They have assisted States in developing legislation implementing the Rome Statute. Local NGOs may possess knowledge which is directly relevant to the Court's work in the field. NGOs also continue to have a critical role in disseminating information about and building awareness of the ICC.

As I said at the outset, academic institutions such as this Academy have a particularly important role in relation to the Court. It is my experience, truly, that ignorance is one of the biggest obstacles to the success of the Court. Often, opposition to the Court is based on misconceptions which can be easily avoided. I believe that the more people understand the Court, the more it will be accepted. Of course, for that to happen there needs to be a dialogue. If there is no dialogue, the chances of mutual understanding are much lower.

In conclusion, I would say that the creation of the ICC was a truly historic achievement, more than fifty years in the making, but its creation was only the beginning. The Court now stands as a permanent institution capable of punishing perpetrators of the worst offenses known to humankind. Indeed, as early as 2004, the U.N. Secretary General stated that the Court "was already having an important impact by putting would-be violators on notice that impunity is not assured and serving as a catalyst for enacting national laws against the gravest international crimes."[1] Indeed, we at the Court who have a system of monitoring media reports on issues of international criminal justice and a fairly broad set of related issues do know how much notice is taken of the Court in many situations—some situations which are already under the jurisdiction of the Court and many other situations elsewhere.

To be fully effective, we must continue our efforts to ensure that the Court has the support necessary to dispense justice as fairly and efficiently as possible. If there is only one thing that you should retain from this piece, it is that the Court will do whatever it can to be as credible as possible, but that it will only succeed with concrete, tangible support.

Note

1. The Secretary-General, *Report of the Secretary-General on the Rule of Law and Transitional Justice in Conflict and Post-Conflict Societies*, ¶ 49, *delivered to the Security Council*, U.N. Doc. S/2004/616 (Aug. 3, 2004).

PART 2.1

International Law as Normative System: To Regulate the Use of Force

CHAPTER 13

"Jus ad Bellum," "Jus in Bello" . . . "Jus post Bellum"?—Rethinking the Conception of the Law of Armed Force

Carsten Stahn

SINCE *GROTIUS' DE JURE BELLI AC PACIS*, THE ARCHITECTURE of the international legal system has been founded upon a distinction between the states of war and peace. At the beginning of the 20th century, it was taken for granted that "the law recognizes a state of peace and a state of war, but that it knows nothing of an intermediate state which is neither one thing nor the other."[1] Today, this claim stands to be revisited.

Traces of the historic distinction between war and peace are still present in some distinct areas of law.[2] However, war and peace are no longer perceived as strict organizing frameworks for the categorization of rules of international law. The United Nations Charter has narrowed the grounds on which subjects of international law may legitimately resort to armed violence.[3] There are multiple situations in which (what was formerly called) "the law of war" and the "law of peace" apply simultaneously.[4] Moreover, the question of how to make peace in periods of transition following war has become one of the main preoccupations of international law and practice since 1945.[5] These developments raise some doubts as to whether some of the traditional understandings of international law still suffice to explain the complexities of contemporary international law.

Both the increase of interventions and the growing impact of international law on post-conflict peace make it particularly timely and pertinent to take a closer look at the architecture of the law of armed force. The current debate about the law of armed force is mostly focused on a discussion of the *status quo* of *jus ad bellum and jus in bello*[6] and the relationship between these two branches of law. This essay seeks to offer a different perspective

---

Reprinted with permission from Carsten Stahn, "Jus ad bellum," "jus in bello" . . . "jus post bellum"?—Rethinking the Conception of the Law of Armed Force," *European Journal of International Law* 17 (2006): 921–943.

on the contemporary law of armed force, by suggesting a systemic rethinking of the categories of the law. It argues that some of the dilemmas of contemporary interventions may be attenuated by a fresh look at the past, namely a (re)turn to a tripartite conception of armed force based on three categories: *"jus ad bellum," "jus in bello"* and *"jus post bellum."*

The Erosion of the Classical War—Peace Distinction

This exercise requires some reconsideration of formerly established groundwork. The starting point is the bipolar peace and war distinction. This classical distinction has its origin in 19th-century thinking when war and peace were conceived to be completely distinct legal regimes. War and peace were not only distinguished in temporal terms ("state of war"/"state of peace"), but were considered to be independent legal frameworks with mutually exclusive rules for wartime and peacetime.[7] This clear-cut distinction lost its *raison d'être* in the 20th century. Three changes may be observed, in particular:

The gradual outlawry of war as a legal institution in the 20th century has removed one fundamental prerequisite of the classical peace/war dichotomy, namely the recognition of war as a legitimate category of law. War is no longer treated as a legally accepted paradigm, but as a factual event regulated by (different bodies of) law. It has thus become uncommon to treat war and peace as separate and diametrically opposed legal institutions and to theorize the rules of international law on the basis of this dialectical relationship.

Second, there is no (longer a) clear dividing line between war and peace. The classical dichotomy of peace and war has lost part of its significance due to the shrinking number of inter-state wars after 1945 and the increasing preoccupation of international law with civil strife and internal armed violence.[8] International practice has dealt with multiple situations which are neither "declared wars" in the conventional sense, nor part of peacetime relations, such as threats to peace caused by repressive state policies. Moreover, international law comes into play in processes of transition from one stage to the other, namely in transitions from peace to war or in transitions from war to peace.[9] If one were to theorize this phenomenon, it would be more correct to speak of a tri-dimensional (rather than bipolar) system, covering the phases of conflict, peacetime relations and the transition from conflict to peace.

Third, it is becoming increasingly clear that some of the problems arising in the period of transition from conflict to peace cannot be addressed by a simple application of the "law of peace" or the "laws of war," but require "situation-specific" adjustments, such as organizing frameworks and principles which are specifically geared towards the management of situations of transition between conflict and peace.[10]

Revisiting the Dualist Conception of the Law of Armed Force

This transformation is only partially reflected in the contemporary conception of the law of armed force. This body of law is based on a dualist conception of armed force which distinguishes the law of recourse to force (*jus ad bellum*) from the law governing the conduct of hostilities (*jus in bello*).

The distinction between *jus ad bellum* and *jus in bello* has a long tradition in the theory of warfare. However, it found its place in positive law only at the time of the League of Nations, when the Kellogg-Briand Pact outlawed the absolute power to resort to war by its prohibition of aggressive war.[11]

The recognition of *jus ad bellum* and *jus in bello* as legal concepts has brought important conceptual innovations *vis-à-vis* the legal thinking of the 19th century. It has not only changed the perception of war, but reaffirmed the indiscriminate application of the obligations of warring parties in the conduct in hostilities. *Jus ad bellum* and *jus in bello* were declared to be distinct normative universes, in order to postulate the principle that all conflicts shall be fought humanely, irrespective of the cause of armed violence.

However, the current architecture of the law of force continues to be shaped by certain antinomies. Firstly, the distinction between the justification for the use of force and the *jus in bello* is not always as clear-cut and stringent as is sometimes claimed. While there is agreement that principles and entitlements under *jus in bello* (for instance, the requirements of necessity, proportionality and humanity and the privileges of combatants) should generally apply independently of the cause of armed conflict, there are cases in which findings under one body of law shape the applicability or interpretation of the other body of law.[12] Following the motivation of interventions in cases such as Iraq in 1991 and Kosovo in 1999, there has even been discussion whether there should be a new normative dispensation, according to which egregious violations of *jus in bello* could be regarded as the trigger for rights under the *jus ad bellum*.

Secondly, the dualist conception of the law of armed force carries an idea of exclusiveness which is increasingly anachronistic in the context of the growing diversification and application of international law in all spectrums of public life. The *jus ad bellum/jus in bello* narrative reflects, to some extent, the traditional dichotomy between war and peace. *Jus ad bellum* is traditionally perceived as the body of law which provides grounds justifying the transition from peace to armed force, while *jus in bello* is deemed to define "the conduct and responsibilities of belligerent nations, neutral nations and individuals engaged in armed conflict in relation to each other and to protected persons."[13] This understanding suggests that each of these two bodies of law contains its own specific and exclusive system of rules which comes into play in circumstances when the traditional rules of the "law of peace" cease to be of adequate guidance. Such an assumption is misleading, because it is premised on the idea that the underlying period in time is governed by a specific body of law,[14] rather than by a multiplicity of subject-specific legal regimes originating from different sources of law.

Moreover, this dualist system, with its strict focus on the period of armed hostilities, is increasingly artificial since it fails to reflect the growing interrelation between armed violence and restoration of peace. A dualist conception of armed conflict based on the division between *jus ad bellum* and *jus in bello* presents a simplified account of the sequencing and categorization of human conduct throughout armed hostilities. The operation of both systems of rules (governing armed force) is centred on a specific period, namely the period from the outbreak of hostilities to conflict termination. This centralization is open to criticism because it is often impossible to draw a clear-cut distinction between the (continued) conduct of armed hostilities and a post-conflict setting. It also fails to reflect the growing impact of international law on the restoration of peace after conflict.

These findings make it necessary to revisit the classical dualist construction of the law of armed force (*jus ad bellum/jus in bello*) and to think about a broader conception of conflict, including the recognition of principles governing peace-making after war.

Features of Jus ad Bellum *and* Jus in Bello

One of the main achievements of the modern law of armed force is that it provides more than a mere framework outlawing armed violence or setting limitations on the conduct of armed forces. Contemporary rules of armed force do not contain only prohibitions for states and armed forces; they channel armed violence and regulate the relations between different actors (military forces, civilians, ousted government) in situations of armed conflict. However, the classical concepts of *jus ad bellum* and *jus in bello* contain gaps with respect to the management of post-conflict relations.

Concepts such as individual criminal responsibility or the "humanization" of the conduct of warfare[15] were far less developed at the time, when the current rules of *jus ad bellum* and *jus in bello* were originally conceived. The traditional rules of *jus in bello* are therefore only partially equipped to address the problems arising in the context of peacemaking and the transition from armed conflict to peace. The classical rationale of *jus in bello* is to limit the consequences of armed conflicts on non-combatants (including vulnerable groups such as the wounded, women and children), property and the environment. Accordingly, *jus in bello* provides only a fraction of principles governing the process of conflict termination, including capitulations and armistices.[16] Similarly, the principle of international criminal responsibility for the commission of serious crimes is only partially covered by the Geneva Law.[17]

Furthermore, gaps and structural ambiguities exist on at least three other levels: the temporal scope of application of the norms of international humanitarian law, the continuing uncertainty about the feasible scope of application of rules of international humanitarian law, and the difficulty to conduct exercises in state- or nation-building under the auspices of the law of occupation.

The norms of international humanitarian law, by definition, apply only to a limited extent to the period following the cessation of hostilities. Additional Protocol I provides that the application of the Geneva Conventions and the Protocol will cease "on the general close of military operations."[18] This moment is usually deemed to occur "when the last shot has been fired."[19] Only selected provisions apply after the "cessation of active hostilities." A "post-conflict" duty, namely the obligation to repatriate, is activated in a classical "wartime" situation, namely before the close of military operations, which marks the date of the termination of "armed conflict." Moreover, parts of the "law of war," namely specific duties of the occupant under the laws of occupation, continue to apply in a "peacetime" situation, namely after the close of military operations.[20] The norms of international humanitarian law are therefore only to a limited extent relevant to the broader process of building peace after conflict.

Secondly, there are doubts as to the extent to which it is desirable and feasible to extend the applicability norms of "*jus in bello*" to the process of peace-making. Following the Bulletin of the Secretary-General on the observance of international humanitarian law by UN forces, there is widespread agreement that UN peacekeepers are bound to observe "fundamental principles and rules of international humanitarian law," although the UN is not a party to the Hague or Geneva Conventions.[21] However, it is unclear as to what extent international humanitarian law can and should be used to regulate civilian activities undertaken by such actors in the aftermath of the conflict, whether it be under the umbrella of occupation, the United Nations, or within the framework of a multinational administration. In these situations, the choices of international humanitarian law collide with other frameworks such as international human rights law, which offers, in many ways, a more modern and a more nuanced framework to address challenges of peace-building. International human rights law regulates public authority directly from the perspective of individual and group rights (human rights, minority rights, self-determination), whereas international humanitarian law continues to view public authority, at least partly, through the lens of competing state interests.[22]

The law of occupation, the only branch of the *jus in bello* which deals explicitly with post-conflict relations, is ill-suited to serve as a framework of administration.[23] Both the Hague and the Geneva law are conceived of as legal frameworks to address temporary power-vacuums after conflict. Their focus lies on the maintenance of public security and order and the protection of the interests of domestic actors. These requirements force occupying powers to exercise restraint in the shaping of the law and institutions of occupied territories.[24] The examples of post-war Germany and Japan have shown that the needs and dynamics of processes of post-conflict reconstruction are difficult to reconcile with the provisions of the law of occupation *stricto sensu*.

The limitations of the law of occupation again became apparent in the case of the occupation of Iraq. In this case, the Security Council invented a new model of multilateral occupation,[25] which merged the structures of belligerent occupation with elements of peace-making under Chapter VII, in order to facilitate reconstruction under the umbrella of collective security. This model produced more questions than answers. Security Council Resolution 1483 embodied some modern principles of international law into the framework of the occupation.[26] However, the reference of the Council to two parallel legal regimes, namely the continued application of the law of occupation on the one hand,[27] and principles of state-building on the other,[28] left the limits of reconstruction in a legal limbo.[29] Some measures of the Coalition Provisional Authority (CPA), such as the creation of the Iraqi Special Tribunal or the reform of the Iraqi private sector,[30] remained doubtful from a legal perspective.[31]

These examples confirm that the contemporary *jus ad bellum* and *jus in bello* are based on related, but partly distinct, rationales or foundations from the process of peacemaking.[32] It therefore makes some sense to argue that the period of transition from conflict deserves an autonomous legal space in the architecture of the law of armed force.

Inadequacies of a Dualist Conception of the Law of Armed Force

Logically, the argument in favour of an extension of the categories of the law of armed force could have been made in the 1930s. However, the claim for recognition of a third branch of the law of armed force is particularly compelling at a time when the restoration of peace and justice in the (post-) conflict stage is conceived as the other side of the coin of intervention.

Peacemaking as the other side of intervention. The case in favour of the regulation of peace-making is in part supported by a change of discourse about the justification of intervention. Traditionally, the use of military force was justified by the purpose of thwarting security threats or conquering foreign territories. The prohibition of the use of force and the revitalization of the collective security system have modified this picture. Today, interventions are often justified by a bundle of post-conflict oriented purposes, including, most notably, the defence of universal and communitarian values such as human rights, democracy or self-determination.[33] Increasingly, attempts are made to justify intervention on multiple grounds, which take into account the effects of the intervention on the post-conflict phase. In such circumstances, it is only logical that this phase be recognized in the equation of armed force.

This tendency is further reflected in contemporary practice. There are multiple initiatives to establish a link between the "pre-" and the "(post-) conflict" phase. The most far-reaching proposition has been made by the International Commission on Intervention and State Sovereignty. In its report, *The Responsibility to Protect*, the Commission suggested a new conception of responsibility following intervention ("responsibility to rebuild"), noting that modern interventions cannot end after the cessation of military activities, but require ongoing engagement to prevent conflict.[34] Subsequently, this idea was taken up in slightly moderated form in the High-Level Panel Report on Threats, Challenges and Change,[35] the Report of the Secretary-General entitled "In Larger Freedom: Towards Development, Security and Human Rights for All"[36] and in the Outcome Document of the 2005 World Summit[37] which lays down certain basic principles concerning the meaning and scope of the international "responsibility to protect."[38] It can also be found in the mandate of the Peacebuilding Commission, which was created to address the challenge of helping countries with the transition from war to lasting peace. These steps indicate a growing link between the use of force and the restoration of peace.

From morality to legality. Traditionally, this link has been explained in moral terms. Proponents of the just war theory have used moral justifications to argue that a "just war" requires "a just peace."[39] Similarly, *"jus post bellum"* was mostly theorized as a moral paradigm.[40] Recently, this line of reasoning was used in the context of modern interventions. It has been argued that humanitarian interventions create a certain moral responsibility to become engaged in reconstruction.[41] A similar argument has been made in the context of nation-building in Iraq.[42] Some scholars have taken the view that the coalition had an ethical responsibility to help rebuild Iraq, because it had been involved in promoting regime change. The collapse of law and order and domestic structures following the intervention, it is argued, created a moral duty for coalition members to stay in Iraq and a moral justification to exercise "temporary political authority as trustee on behalf of the people governed, in much the same way that an elected government does."[43] This experience has sparked calls for a better theorization of post-war justice "for the sake of a more complete theory of just war."[44]

These suggestions are useful, but they do not go far enough. A purely "morality-driven" justification of post-conflict engagement does not suffice to explain the reality of contemporary practice. There are some indications that there is a legal connection between the "pre-" and the "post-conflict" phase. In contemporary practice, it is not enough to establish that the motives which lead up to the recourse to force pursue a lawful and commonly accepted purpose. The acceptability of an intervention is equally measured by its effects and implications after the use of armed force.

A legal connection between the use of force and post-conflict engagements may be construed in at least two ways. The performance of post-conflict engagements may either be a building block of the legality of liberal interventions or a means to render the consequences of an unauthorized use of force more acceptable in the international legal system.

The first type of argument has been made in connection with liberal interventions ("humanitarian intervention," "democratic intervention") in general. Both humanitarian and democratic interventions are directly founded on the idea of peace-making through the restoration of human rights and standards of good governance.[45] It has therefore been argued that such interventions require states to take sustainable measures to implement the proclaimed goals of the use of force, including efforts to restore basic human rights and democratic governance in the post-intervention phase. This obligation is derived from the very requirements of liberal interventions and considerations of proportionality of the use of force.[46] Such uses of force, so goes the argument, are only permissible if the corresponding action is appropriate and capable of removing the threat that motivated the use of force ("*Verpflichtung zur Nachsorge*").[47] The novelty of this approach lies in the fact that it derives certain (post-) conflict responsibilities from the very requirements of intervention,[48] instead of deducing such duties from the concept of responsibility for internationally wrongful acts (reparation, compensation).[49]

It is more difficult to establish a link between the use of force and post-conflict engagement in the context of unauthorized interventions. There is some ground to argue that the issue of the legality of the use of force and the conduct after intervention should be kept entirely apart in such cases.[50] However, one may witness a certain tendency in practice to invoke post-conflict engagement as a factor to validate intervention or to respond benevolently to the status quo created by it.[51] Some interventions (Liberia, Sierra Leone, Kosovo, Afghanistan, Iraq) have drawn support from different scales of approval and legitimation, which vary according to the intent of the Security Council and the degree of UN engagement: *ex post facto* validation and mitigation.[52]

Both lines of thought confirm one common trend, namely a growing interweaving of the concepts of intervention and the restoration of peace. Some interventions appear to require subsequent (post-) conflict engagement, in order for their outcomes to be recognized as valid or acceptable. This finding lends support to the view that considerations of (post-) conflict peace should form part of the architecture of the law of armed force.

Historical Origins of a Tripartite Conception of Armed Force

Calls for an expanded conception of the law of armed force are by no means novel. The plea for a tripartite conception of rules of armed conflict has some precedents in legal history. Several proponents of the "just war" doctrine discussed post-conflict principles in their writings. Francisco Suarez, for example, argued in favour of extending the just war categories to a third period, namely the ending of justly declared and fought wars.[53] In his Disputation XIII on War (1621), Suarez distinguished three periods in his conception of a just war: "its inception; its prosecution, before victory is gained; and the period after victory." Furthermore, he formulated post-conflict principles based on necessity concerning war reparation, the fate of property rights after war and the treatment of the conquered state.[54]

A more refined account of the forms and conditions of conflict termination was given only four years later by Hugo Grotius, who secularized just war theory in his *De Jure Belli ac Pacis*.[55] Grotius placed war within the broader categories of justice and control. Book Three of his work incorporates not only concrete principles on the lawfulness of the waging of war and permissible conduct in hostilities, but also rules on surrender, calls for moderation in the acquisition of sovereignty, guidelines on good faith between enemies, rules for the interpretation of peace treaties and indications "in what manner the law of nations renders the property of subjects answerable for the debt of sovereigns." Grotius concluded his work with "admonitions on behalf of good faith and peace," postulating that even "in war peace should always be kept in view." However, overall, Grotius' work remained focused on the identification of principles concerning the period of hostilities itself.

Findings on the conduct of post-conflict relations may also be found in Vattel's *Droit des Gens, ou Principes de la Loi Naturelle* of 1758.[56] Vattel repudiated, in particular, Hobbes' conception of war as the natural state of man and dedicated Book IV of his law of nations to the restoration of peace "and the obligation to cultivate it," which he derived from natural law.[57] Chapter II of Book IV dealt exclusively with peace treaties. It set out general principles concerning the formation, the effect, and the execution of peace treaties, which were designed to serve as guidelines for the conduct of sovereign actors.

This thinking was later developed by Immanuel Kant, who may be counted as one of the conceptual founders of a tripartite conception of warfare. Kant introduced the notion of "right after war" ("*Recht nach dem Krieg*") in his philosophy of law (*Science of Right*), which formed part of *The Metaphysics of Morals*.[58] Kant expressly divided the "right of nations in relation to the state of war" into three different categories, namely "1. the right of going to war; 2. right during war; and 3. right after war, the object of which is to constrain the nations mutually to pass from this state of war and to found a common constitution establishing perpetual peace."[59] Kant's ideas were novel, because he linked the rules of war to the broader perspective of eternal peace. He developed this thought in Article 6 of the Articles for Perpetual Peace Among States. He established an express connection between the rules of *jus in bello* and perpetual peace, stating that "[n]o state shall during war, permit such acts of hostility which would make mutual confidence in the subsequent peace impossible," such as "the employment of assassins, prisoners, breach of capitulation, and incitement to treason in the opposing state."[60]

Kant's preoccupation with (just) war termination did not end here. Kant identified a number of parameters, according to which peace should be shaped. One of the central premises of his post-war theory, which may again be found in the "Articles for Perpetual Peace" is that "[n]o treaty of peace shall be considered valid as such, if it was made with a secret reservation of the material for a future war."[61] Furthermore, he argued that the victor is not entitled to punish the vanquished or to seek compensation merely because of its military superiority. Kant emphasized that peace settlements must respect the sovereignty of the vanquished state and the self-determination of its people, foreshadowing thereby some of the key features of modern peace-making.[62]

A Modern Framework for an Old Idea

This holistic understanding of the use of armed force gains new relevance in a modern context.

From "Jus post Bellum" to "Rules and Principles of (Post-)conflict Peace"

Of course, the classical conception of "justice after war" cannot simply be transposed to a modern setting. Certain adjustments must be made, if the idea of "*jus post bellum*" is translated from a moral principle into a legal notion.

First, the concept of a fair and just peace must be decoupled from the historical understanding which associated fairness with the idea of justice in favour of the party which had fought a just and lawful war (being a war which was waged for the right reasons) and fought in an appropriate manner. Today, considerations of fair and just peace must be deemed to apply equally to all parties to a conflict. Thus, the principal justification for distinguishing *jus ad bellum* and *jus in bello* applies equally with respect to the idea of "*jus post bellum*": parties must end a dispute in a fair and just fashion irrespective of the cause of the resort to force. At the same time, principles of conflict termination apply independently of violations in the conduct of armed force.[63] Such violations may even strengthen the need for fair and just peace-making (accountability, compensation, rehabilitation).

Second, the applicability of principles of post-conflict peace can no longer depend exclusively on moral considerations, such as righteousness of waging war. The concept of a fair and just peace must be framed by reference to certain objective rules and standards that regulate guidelines for peace-making in the interest of people and individuals affected by conflict.

Third, peace-making is not strictly aimed at a preservation or return to the legal *status quo ante*, but must take into account the idea of transforming the institutional and socio-economic conditions of polities under transition. In this sense, peace-making differs from the classical rationale of the law of occupation. The ultimate purpose of fair and just peace-making is to remove the causes of violence. This may require positive transformations of the domestic order of a society. In many cases, a fair and just peace settlement will ideally endeavour to achieve a higher level of human rights protection, accountability and good governance than in the period before the resort to armed force.

However, the classical rationale behind the notion of *jus post bellum*, namely the idea of regulating the ending of conflicts and easing the transition to peace through certain principles of behaviour, is highly relevant in the context of international law in the 21st century. It may be argued that the classical concepts of *jus ad bellum* and *jus in bello* are complemented by a specific set of rules and principles that seek to balance the interests of different stakeholders in transitions from conflict to peace. Under this construction, armed force must not only be lawful under the law on the recourse to force and in keeping with the rules of *jus in bello* but must also satisfy certain rules of (post-) conflict settlement.

The regulation of substantive components of peace-making is not merely determined by the discretion and contractual liberty of the warring factions, but is governed by certain norms and standards of international law derived from different fields of law and legal practice.

Just a few examples suffice to illustrate this argument here. The formation of peace settlements is governed by Article 52 of the Vienna Convention on the Law of Treaties and considerations of procedural fairness; the limits of territorial dispute resolution are defined by the prohibition of annexation and the law of self-determination; the consequences of an act of aggression are *inter alia* determined by parameters of the law of state responsibility, Charter-based considerations of proportionality and human rights–based limitations on reparations;[64] the exercise of foreign governance over territory is limited by the principle of territorial sovereignty; the prohibition of "trusteeship" (over UN members) under Article 78 of the Charter limits occupation law under the Fourth Geneva Convention, as well as the powers of the Security Council under the Charter; the law applicable in a territory in transition is determined by the law of state succession as well as certain provisions of human rights law (for instance, non-derogable human rights guarantees) and the laws of occupation; finally, the scope of individual criminal responsibility is defined by treaty-based and customary law-based prohibitions of international criminal law.

These norms may be said to be part of a broader regulatory framework ("post- conflict law"), which encompasses substantive legal rules and principles of procedural fairness governing transitions from conflict to peace. These norms are in many cases partly codified, but entangled with or superseded by subsequent international practice. Moreover, they are complemented by legal principles or "soft law," which are relevant to particular decisions or situations. Some norms (for instance, *jus cogens* prohibitions) constitute "hard" law ("rules").[65] They are applicable "in an all-or-nothing fashion."[66] Others are based on broader principles which may be balanced against each other, "taking into account the relative weight of each."[67]

Sketches of Post-conflict Law

It would go beyond the framework of this contribution to present a conclusive account of rules and principles of post-conflict peace. However, six organizing rules and principles may be presented here by way of an example. These principles share some parallels with the parameters of just peace under the just war theory (right intention, legitimate authority for a peace settlement; discrimination and proportionality of the terms of peace), without being identical to the latter. They may be derived from a comparative survey of international law and practice in the three major eras of peace settlements: namely 1919, 1945 and the post–Cold War era.

Fairness and inclusiveness of peace settlements. Firstly, there is some evidence that the establishment of sustainable peace requires a collective bargaining process, involving a fair hearing of the interests of all parties to the conflict at the negotiating table.

At the time of the Treaty of Versailles, the terms of peace were essentially set by a bargaining process amongst the victors over the rights and obligations of the vanquished. Today, such conduct would conflict with certain standards of peace-making. Article 34 of the Vienna Convention on the Law of Treaties posits that a peace treaty does not bind states that did not consent to its terms. Accordingly, no single state and no group of states may unilaterally make binding determinations for a third state. Moreover, modern practice points towards a neutralization of interests in the bargaining process. If the defeated entity is not present at the negotiation of the peace settlement itself, its interests should be determined by a collective forum with third-party input.

Similar considerations of fairness apply in favour of groups and minorities protected by international law by virtue of the right to self-determination and autonomy rights. These groups may be represented by state entities in treaty negotiations. However, they are entitled to an adequate representation of their collective interests in a constitutional settlement regulating their status.

The demise of the concept of punishment for aggression. Secondly, international practice since 1945 indicates the replacement of the harsh concept of territorial punishment for purposes of deterrence by the more moderate techniques of state responsibility, disarmament and institutional security arrangements.

International law has become hostile to the idea of "punishing" an aggressor through the imposition or dictate of territorial changes in the post-conflict phase.[68] Territorial mutilations or compulsory transfers of populations of the kind that took place at the end of the Second World War would be ruled out today under the UN Charter and the 1949 Geneva Conventions.[69] Peace-makers are required to respect the territorial integrity of the vanquished state and the rights of its people.[70]

The only organ which could theoretically take punitive measures against states that have placed themselves outside the community of peace-loving and law-abiding nations, is the Security Council. However, even the Council's authority under the Charter would hardly suffice to justify *permanent* transfers of territory against or without the will of a state for the purpose of deterring future aggression. Such action conflicts with the limits of the Security Council under Article 24 of the Charter, including the recognition of territorial integrity and the principle of self-determination. Moreover, less intrusive post-conflict measures, such as reparation, disarmament and adjudication of war crimes, are usually at hand and better suited to serve the purpose of peace-making which guides the exercise of powers by the Council under the Charter.

The humanization of reparations and sanctions. A similar trend towards moderation in the treatment of an aggressor may be traced in the area of reparations. Contemporary developments in international law point to the emergence of a rule that prohibits the indiscriminate punishment of a people through excessive reparation claims or sanctions.

Harsh financial loads may not only make a people accountable for misdeeds of an irresponsible regime, but amount to the collective punishment of an entire population. One of the lessons emerging from the practice of peace treaties is that reparation and compensation claims must be assessed in light of the economic potential of the wrongdoing state and its implications for the population of the targeted state.[71]

This conclusion was drawn by the former Article 43(3) of the 1996 Draft Articles on State Responsibility, which stated that reparation shall "in no case . . . result in depriving the population of a State of its own means of substance." This claim receives additional support from the move to targeted sanctions under the collective security regime and the rise of socio-economic human rights obligations preventing states or international actors from imposing economic liabilities on another state which would disable the latter in ensuring minimum socio-economic standards (food, health care) *vis-à-vis* its own population.[72]

The move from collective responsibility to individual responsibility. Similarly, there is a move from collective to individual responsibility. This move is reflected in the crystallization of the principle of individual criminal responsibility. This principle prohibits collective punishment, that is, punishment of persons not for what they have done, but for the acts of others; furthermore, it establishes the general rule that individuals are punished for their own wrongdoing, and not on behalf of the state.[73] This differentiation prevents a population from being held accountable for the misdeeds of its rulers and from being exposed to charges of collective guilt.

Towards a combined justice and reconciliation model. Fifthly, there is a trend towards accommodating post-conflict responsibility with the needs of peace in the area of criminal responsibility. This specific tension did not receive broad attention in historical peace settlements, partly because the concept of international criminal responsibility was less developed, and partly because peace settlements were less frequently dedicated to the resolution of the problems of civil wars. Today, it is at the heart of contemporary efforts of peace-making. Modern international practice, particularly in the context of United Nations peace-building, appears to move towards a model of targeted accountability in peace processes, which allows amnesties for less serious crimes and combines criminal justice with the establishment of truth and reconciliation mechanisms.[74]

People-centred governance. Lastly, there is a shift of focus from state-centred mechanisms of organizing public power to "people-based" (individual and/or group-based) techniques of political settlement. Peace-making, more than ever before, is tied to the ending of autocratic, undemocratic and oppressive regimes, and directed towards the ideal of "popular sovereignty" held by individuals instead of states or elites. A procedural legal basis for this claim may be found in Article 21 of the Universal Declaration of Human Rights and Article 25 of the International Covenant on Civil and Political Rights. Moreover, a broader notion of internal self-determination has emerged since World War II, which links the protection of a people under international law to the enjoyment of institutional rights (such as autonomy of federalist structures) in the domestic legal system. Finally, human rights guarantees and procedures for holding governments accountable are increasingly part of a treaty-based or "regional *acquis*," and therefore binding on successor states or regimes.[75]

These norms may be said to create, *inter alia*, a duty for domestic or international holders of public authority in situations of transition to institute political structures that embody mechanisms of accountability *vis-à-vis* the governed population and timelines to gradually transfer power from political elites to elected representatives.

Conclusion

These few examples indicate that there are certain macro-changes in the conception of peace-making. Modern practice displays a stark tendency to move from a statist and national-interest driven conception of conflict termination to a pluralist and problem-solving approach to peace-making, uniting affected parties, neutral actors and private stakeholders in their efforts to restore sustainable peace. This process lends new support to an old postulate, namely the idea of (re-)connecting the concepts of *jus ad bellum* and *jus in bello* to considerations of fair and just peace-making (the former "*jus post bellum*").

The recognition of a tripartite conception of the law of armed force would serve several purposes. It would fill, first of all, a certain normative gap. At present, there is a considerable degree of uncertainty about the applicable law, the interplay of different structural frameworks as well as the possible space for interaction between different legal orders and bodies of law (international law v. domestic law, human rights law v. law of occupation etc.) in a post-conflict environment. The articulation of a body of law after conflict would identify legal rules, which ought to be applied by international actors (unless an exception applies) and clarify specific legal principles, which serve as guidance in making legal policy choices in situations of transition.

Secondly, the revival of a tripartite conception of armed force has a certain systemic function. It would build a bridge between the "pre-" and the "post-"conflict phase, which is lacking in the contemporary architecture of the law of armed force. The recognition of rules and principles of post-conflict peace would establish a closer link between the requirements of the use of force and post-conflict responsibilities in the context of intervention. Under a tripartite conception of the law of armed force, international actors might be forced to consider to a broader extent the impact of their decisions on the post-conflict phase, including modalities and institutional frameworks for peace-making, before making a determination whether to use force.

Moreover, such rules and principles might allow a more nuanced assessment of the legality or legitimacy of the use of force. This argument is particularly compelling in the context of humanitarian and democratic interventions. Such interventions would be judged not only by their purported goals, but by their implications and effects. Post-conflict law might provide the necessary parameters and benchmarks to determine whether the respective goals have been implemented in a fair and effective manner and in accordance with the law.

Finally, the development of post-conflict law may have certain implications for the contemporary *jus in bello*. The move to a tripartite conception of the law of armed force would, in particular, avoid an overburdening of the obligations of the military and temper the concerns of those who argue that the contemporary *jus in bello* is not meant to serve as a surrogate framework for governance in peacetime situations, while preserving the interests of peace-making. Considerations of fair and just peace would be part of the equation of armed force, however not under *jus in bello* in the proper sense, but under the law after conflict. These principles would have an indirect impact on the phase of armed conflict itself. Parties to an armed conflict would operate under a general obligation to conduct hostilities in a manner which does not preclude a fair and just peace settlement in the post-conflict phase.

It is clear from this survey that some of the features of a tripartite conception of armed force (for instance, the interplay between *jus ad bellum, jus in bello* and *jus post bellum*) require further thought. However, one fact is becoming increasingly evident: the development of rules and principles of post-conflict peace should form part of the agenda and the table of contents of international law in the 21st century.

Notes

1. See House of Lords, Lord MacNaghten, *Janson v Driefontein Consolidated Mines Ltd.* [1902] AC 484. Lassa Oppenheim's classical treatise on international law divided the entirety of the rules of international law into the cate-

gories of peace and war. See H. Lauterpacht (ed), *Oppenheim's International Law* (6th edn., 1947), i (Peace) and ii ("War and Neutrality").

2. See, *inter alia,* the project of the ILC on the effects of armed conflict on the law of treaties. For a survey of the various reports of the Commission on this topic, see ILC, *Effects of armed conflicts on treaties,* available at http://untreaty.un.org/ilc/guide/1_10.htrn.

3. See S. Neff, *War and the Law of Nations* (2005), at 315–356.

4. A good example is the parallel applicability of human rights law and international humanitarian law. See ICJ, *Legal Consequences of the Construction of a Wall in the Occupied Palestinian Territory,* Advisory Opinion of 9 July 2004 [2004] ICJ Rep 136, para. 106.

5. Multi-dimensional peacekeeping operations and modern interventions have gradually led to a departure from the notion of peace in the mere absence of violence ("negative peace"). This is, *inter alia,* reflected in the concept of collective "responsibility to protect," which encompasses three dimensions of communitarian conflict management in cases of large-scale atrocities: preventive action, responsive action, and post-conflict engagement ("responsibility to prevent," "responsibility to react," and "responsibility to rebuild"). See paras. 138 and 139 of GA Res. 60/1 (2005 World Summit Outcome) of 24 Oct. 2005.

6. See among others Ratner, "Jus ad Bellum and Jus in Bello after September 11," 96 AJIL (2002) 905; Lietzau, "Old Laws, New Wars: Jus ad Bellum in an Age of Terrorism," 8 *Max Planck Yearbk* UN L (2005) 383.

7. War and peace were diametrically opposed concepts. It was assumed that a "state of war" excluded the applicability of the law of peace. For an insightful discussion see Neff, *supra* note 3. at 177–196.

8. See Human Security Report, *The Changing Face of Global Violence* (2005), at 18 ("[i]n the last decade, 95% of armed conflicts have taken place within states, not between them").

9. Principles of the traditional "law of peace" are increasingly applied to societies, which are not in a clear situation of war or peace, but are involved in a process of transition from conflict to peace (e.g. the gradual collapse of state structure).

10. There appears to be a growing awareness that to end hostilities requires not only measures to terminate conflict (conflict termination), but active steps to build peace (peacemaking). This type of engagement has facilitated the application of norms of international law to situations of transition from conflict to peace, such as standards for transitional justice, elections, and democratization as well as property claims mechanisms, compensation regimes, and individual human rights procedures in (post-)conflict societies. Some of the rules and procedures applicable in situations from conflict to peace require deviations from commonly established norms in order to accommodate the specific tensions of societies in transition. Standards of democratic governance may have to be adjusted to a polity in transition. Caretaker governments, e.g., may be allowed to exercise governing authority without being formally legitimated through the holding of elections. Criminal proceedings may have to be focused on the prosecution of the "most serious crimes" ("targeted accountability"). Property claims may have to be dealt with in specific mass claims procedures in order to facilitate a speedy reversion of the consequences of armed conflict and/or to facilitate minority returns.

11. It appears in legal writing in the 1920s. Enriques used the term *jus ad bellum* in 1928. See Enriques, "Considerazioni sulla teoria della guerra nel diritto internazionale," 20 *Rivista di diritto internazionale* (1928) 172. Later, Kunz took up the notion in an article pubished in 1934: see Kunz, "Plus de lois de guerre?," 41 *Revue*

Générale de Droit International Public (1934) 22. However, the breakthrough came only after the end of the Second World War, when the express distinction between *jus ad bellum* and *jus in bello* gained widespread acceptance in monographs: see. e.g., L. Kotzsch, *The Concept of War in Contemporary History and International Law* (1956), at 86 and 89.

12. The most prominent example of the nexus between *jus in bello* and *jus ad bellum* is the definition of armed conflict in Art. 1(4) of Additional Protocol I, which extends the applicability of the law governing international armed conflicts to "armed conflicts which people are fighting against colonial domination and alien occupation and against racist regimes in the exercise of their right of self-determination." It is occasionally argued that *jus in bello* and *jus ad bellum* constitute "sometimes competing, sometimes complementary" bodies of law. See Berman, "Privileging Combat? Contemporary Conflict and the Legal Construction of War," 43 Columbia J Transnat'l L (2004) 6.

13. See the definition of *jus in bello* in Wikipedia Encyclopedia, *Laws of War*, available at http://en.wikipedia. org/wiki/Jus_in._bello.

14. This understanding was reflected in the legal tradition of the 19th century according to which the presence of a state of war precluded the application of all rules applicable in peacetime. See Neff, *supra* note 3. at 178.

15. See Meron, "The Humanization of Humanitarian Law," 94 *AJIL* (2000) 239. For a human-rights-based interpretation of the laws of war see, e.g., Martin, "Using International Human Rights Law for Establishing a Unified Use of Force Rule in the Law of Armed Conflict," 64 Saskatchewan L Rev (2001) 347.

16. See Arts 35–41 of the 1907 Hague Convention (IV) Respecting the Laws and Customs of War on Land.

17. See, *inter alia*, the provisions on grave breaches of the Geneva Conventions. In its jurisprudence, the ICTY, found that crimes committed in non-international armed conflicts are punishable under customary international law, although "common Article 3 of the Geneva Conventions contains no explicit reference to criminal liability for violation of its provisions": see ICTY, *Prosecutor v Tadic*, Decision on Defence Motion for Interlocutory Appeal on Jurisdiction, 2 Oct. 1995, at paras 128–132.

18. See Additional Protocol I, Art. 3(b): See also Fourth Geneva Convention, Art. 6 which provides that the application of the convention shall cease "on the close of military operations."

19. See *Final Record of the Diplomatic Conference of Geneva of 1949* (Berne: Federal Political Department, 1949, repr. 2005), ii–A, at 815. However, the protracted nature of modern conflicts and the involvement of potentially numerous armed groups and factions make it often difficult to determine a definitive point in time at which the laws of war cease to operate: see Roberts, "The End of Occupation: Iraq 2004," 54 *ICLQ* (2005) 27, at 34.

20. See Art. 6 of the Fourth Geneva Convention.

21. See United Nations, Secretary-General's Bulletin, ST/SGB/1999/13, 6 Aug. 1999, at para. 1. This position has been defended by the Institut de Droit International since the early 1970s. See Institut de Droit International. "Resolution, Conditions of Application of Humanitarian Rules of Armed Conflict to Hostilities in which United Nations Forces may be Engaged," 54(II) *Annuaire Institut de Droit International* (1971)465. See also generally M. Zwanenburg, *Accountability of Peace Support Operations* (2005).

22. See Mégret and Hoffmann, "The UN as a Human Rights Violator? Some Reflections on the United Nations Changing Human Rights Responsibilities," 25 *Human Rights Quarterly* (2003) 314.

23. For a discussion see Bhuta, "The Antinomies of Transformative Occupation," 16 *EJIL* (2005) 740.

24. See Art. 43 of the Hague Regulations as well as Art. 47 of the Fourth Geneva Convention. Arts 64 and 65–71 of the Fourth Geneva Convention provide certain exceptions to the continuation of the previously applicable law.

25. See also Benvenisti, "The Security Council and the Law on Occupation: Resolution 1483 on Iraq in Historical Perspective," 1 *Israel Defense Forces L Rev* (2003) 23, sect. III.

26. The resolution reaffirmed, in particular, that post-war occupation does not entail a transfer of sovereignty or title over the territory, but rather a mandate to build or restore domestic self-determination or self-government. Furthermore, as occupying powers, the US and the UK were bound to promote the welfare of the local population, including ensuring equal rights and justice, while being subjected to a rudimentary form of public accountability via their duty to report to the Security Council: *ibid.*

27. SC Resolutions 1483 and 1511 recognized the occupation of Iraq but did not authorize it in a formal way. The Coalition Provisional Authority therefore remained bound by the Hague Regulations and the Geneva Conventions. This was set out in a letter dated 8 May 2003 in which the UK and the US stated that they would "strictly abide by their obligations under international law, including those relating to the essential humanitarian needs of the people of Iraq."

28. Several responsibilities mentioned in SC Resolution 1483 went beyond the ordinary framework of the maintenance of law and order under the laws of occupation ("effective administration of the territory"): "creation of conditions in which the Iraqi people can freely determine their own political future" (para. 4); establishment of "national and local institutions for representative governance" (para. 8.c).

29. See also Zwanenburg, "Existentialism in Iraq: Security Council Resolution 1483 and the Law of Occupation," 86 *Int'l Rev of the Red Cross* (2004) 745, at 765–766.

30. CPA Order No. 39 provided the basis for the privatization of the Iraqi economy, while permitting 100% foreign ownership in most sectors. Bids were limited to members of the "coalition of the willing."

31. For a critical survey of the practice of the Coalition Provisional Authority in Iraq see Sassòli, "Legislation and Maintenance of Public Order and Civil Life by Occupying Powers," 16 *EJIL* (2005) 694.

32. The need for an autonomous set of criteria for *jus post bellum* under the just war doctrine has been stressed by Michael Walzer with respect to occupations: see Walzer, "Just and Unjust Occupation," in M. Walzer, *Arguing About War* (2004), at 163.

33. This is partly a result of the ever-widening interpretation of the notion of "international peace and security" in the practice of the Security Council.

34. See Report of the International Commission on Intervention and State Sovereignty, *The Responsibility to Protect* (Dec. 2001), para. 5.1.

35. See Report of the UN High-level Panel on Threats, Challenges, and Change. *A More Secure World: Our Shared Responsibility* (2004), at paras 201–203.

36. See Secretary-General, *In Larger Freedom, Towards Development, Security and Human Rights for All,* 21 Mar. 2005, at para. 135. The UN Secretary-General emphasized a similar need in his report, *The Rule of Law and Transitional Justice in Conflict and Post-conflict Societies,* 23 Aug. 2004, at para. 2.

37. See GA Res. 60/1 (2005 World Summit Outcome) of 24 Oct. 2005.

38. See *ibid,* at paras. 138 and 139.

39. For a survey see M. Walzer, *Just and Unjust Wars: A Moral Argument with*

Historical Illustrations (3rd edn., 2000): see also B. Orend, *Michael Walzer on War and Justice* (2000) and Stanford Encyclopedia of Philosophy, *War*, available at http://plato.stanford.edu/entries/war/.

40. See Orend. "Justice After War." 16 *J Ethics & Int'l Affairs* (2002)43, at 44 ("a coherent set of plausible values to draw on while developing an account of just war settlement").

41. See Korhonen, "'Post' as Justification: International Law and Democracy-Building after Iraq," 4 *German LJ* (2003), No. 7. For a discussion of legality and morality in the context of Kosovo see also Krisch, "Legality, Morality and the Dilemma of Humanitarian Intervention After Kosovo," 33 *EJIL* (2003) 323.

42. See N. Feldman, *What We Owe Iraq: War and the Ethics of Nation-Building* (2004).

43. *Ibid.*, at 3.

44. See Bass, *supra* note 8, at 384. A similar argument is made by DiMeglio, *supra* note 8, at 162.

45. For arguments in this direction see Reka, "UNMIK as International Governance within Post-Conflict Societies," *New Balkan Politics*, Issue 7/8, available only at http://www.newbalkanpolitics.org.mk/ napis.asp?id=17&lang=English, sect. II ("[m]aybe the case of Kosovo could represent a contribution towards the new liberal doctrine for the 're-conceptualization of international law,' by which the 'transnational legal process thereby spurs internal acceptance of international human rights' principles").

46. The exercise of administering functions by UNMIK and KFOR in Kosovo has been regarded as a formal requirement of the legality of the humanitarian intervention itself, which is said to impose a post-conflict responsibility on the intervening actors *("Verpflichtung zur Nachsorge"):* see P. Zygojannis, *Die Staatengerneinschaft und das Kosovo* (2002) at 125 ("[d]ie Verpflichtung des Intervenienten zur Nachsorge als Rechtsfolge durchgeführter humanitärer Intervention").

47. *Ibid.*

48. Note that this argument has recently been used by the High-Level Panel on Threats, Challenges, and Change in its list of criteria for the authorization of interventions by the Security Council. The Report of the High-Level Panel on Threats, Challenges, and Change linked the legitimacy of interventions to their capacity to meet "the threat in question": see High-Level Panel, *supra* note 35, at para. 207.

49. See Arts 31 and 36 of the ILC Draft Articles on the Responsibility of States for Internationally Wrongful Acts, *Report of the ILC on the Work of its Fifty-third Session,* UN GAOR, 56th Sess., Supp. No. 10, at 43, UN Doc A/56/10 (2001).

50. In particular, a forcible regime change cannot be justified by the mere invocation of the law of occupation: see Chesterman, "Occupation as Liberation: International Humanitarian Law and Regime Change," 18 *Ethics & Int'l Affairs* (2004) 51, at 56.

51. For a broader examination see Franck, *Recourse to Force: State Action Against Threats and Armed Attacks* (2002), at 158–162. Such a technique was explicitly applied by the Council in the context of its retroactive endorsement of the unauthorized ECOMOG interventions in Liberia and Sierra Leone: see SC Res. 788 (1992) and SC Res. 1260 (1999).

52. Note that the Report of the High-Level Panel on Threats, Challenges, and Change establishes criteria not only for the authorization, but also for the endorsement of the use of military force: see High-Level Panel, *supra* note 35, at para. 207.

53. See Suarez, "The Three Theological Virtues, Disputation XIII," in J.B. Scott (ed.), *Classics of International Law* (1995), xx, at 836. See also Vitoria, *supra*

note 16, De Indis, iii, at 60 ("Third Canon: When victory has been won and the war is over, the victory should be utilized with moderation and Christian humility, and . . . so far as possible should involve the offending state in the least degree of calamity and misfortune, the offending individuals being chastised with lawful limits").

54. However, his findings were deeply shaped by the scholastic tradition. Suarez endorsed, *inter alia*, a victor's right to just punishment of the conquered state and the entitlement of the victorious power to deprive citizens of the opponent of their goods and their liberty, if necessary for complete satisfaction: see Suarez, *supra* note 53, at 840 and 843.

55. See H. Grotius, *De Jure Belli ac Pacis* (trans. F.W. Kelsey), in J.B. Scott (ed.). *Classics of International Law* (1995), ii. See on Grotius and Just War Theory P. Haggenmacher, *Grotius et la Doctrine de la Guerre Juste* (1983).

56. See E. de Vattel, *Le Droit des Gens, ou Principes de la Loi Naturelle, appliqués à la Conduite et aux Affaires des Nations et des Souverains* (1758), iii. English translation by C.G. Fenwick, "The Law of Nations or the Principles of Natural Law Applied to the Conduct and to the Affairs of Nations and of Sovereigns," in J. B. Scott (ed.), *Classics of International Law*, Vattel, Text of 1758. Books I–IV (1995), at 15.

57. See Vattel, *supra* note 56, Bk IV, chap. I, at 343.

58. Kant's *The Science of Right* was published in 1796, as the first part of his *Metaphysics of Morals (Die Metaphysik der Sitten)* (1797).

59. See I. Kant, *The Science of Right, supra* note 58, at 53 (Nature and Division of the Right of Nations).

60. See I. Kant, *Perpetual Peace* (1795), Sect. 1. Art. 6.

61. *Ibid.*, Sect.1, Art.1.

62. See Kant, *Science of Right, supra* note 58, at 58 (Right after War). A weakness of Kant's law after conflict is that he still relied on the notion of "conquest" and neglected the concept of individual criminal responsibility. Similarly, he did not rule out the possibility that an "unjust enemy" can be forced "to accept a new constitution of a nature that is unlikely to encourage their warlike inclinations."

63. Note also that *jus in bello* makes no distinction between lawful and unlawful combatants when determining duties under the law of occupation.

64. Note that the crime of aggression forms part of the jurisdiction of the International Criminal Court. However, the exercise of jurisdiction by the Court is contingent on the definition of the crime under Statute: see Art. 5(2) of the Rome Statute of the International Criminal Court, 17 July 1998.

65. Sometimes, different legal provisions may conflict or compete with each other (e.g., duty to prosecute *v* duty of a state to protect the security of its people: right of individual of access to the Court *v* immunity of international organizations). Such conflicts may be solved by way of a distinction between "rules" and "principles": see R. Dworkin, *Taking Rights Seriously* (1978), at 24 ff.

66. *Ibid.*

67. *Ibid.*

68. The Draft Articles of the International Law Commission on State Responsibility, supra note 49, refrain from approving any concept of punishment of a State for the commission of unlawful acts of force. They limit the consequences of internationally wrongful acts to the level of "civil responsibility," according to which a State can obtain restitution, compensation, and satisfaction only for the harm suffered.

69. Art. 49 of the Fourth Geneva Convention prohibits forcible transfers of population and deportation.

70. This may be derived from Art. 2(1) of the UN Charter and the prohibition of annexation under international law. See also GA Res. 2625 (XXV), Declaration on Principles of International Law concerning Friendly Relations and Co-operation among States in accordance with the Charter of the United Nations.

71. As noted by Professor Brownlie, "experience has shown that victors can hardly expect to exact "adequate compensation" in reparations for large-scale aggression without violating the principles of humanity and good policy": see I. Brownlie. *International Law and the Use of Force by States* (1963), 153.

72. See also the UK's comment on former Art. 43(3) of the ILC Draft Articles on State Responsibility, noting that reparation must not endanger international peace and security. See UN Doc A/CN.4/488.104.

73. The autonomy of individual responsibility from state responsibility is, in particular, expressed in the removal of official immunity from punishment for aggression, genocide, crimes against humanity, and war crimes. See Art. 27 of the Rome Statute, Art. 7(2) of the ICTY Statute, and Art. 6 of the ICTR Statute.

74. For a full discussion see Robinson, "Serving the Interests of Justice: Amnesties, Truth Commissions and the International Criminal Court," 14 *EJIL* (2003) 481; Stahn, "United Nations Peacebuilding, Amnesties and Alternative Forms of Justice: A Change in Practice?," 84 *Int'l Rev of the Red Cross* (2002), 191: *ibid.* "Complementarity, Amnesties and Alternative Forms of Justice—Some Interpretative Guidelines for the ICC," 3 *J Int'l Criminal Justice* (2005) 695.

75. See, e.g., Human Rights Committee, General Comment No. 26, which established the principle of automatic succession of States into obligations under human rights treaties.

CHAPTER 14

Legal Control of International Terrorism: A Policy Oriented Assessment

M. Cherif Bassiouni

TERRORISM HAS EXISTED, IN ONE FORM OR ANOTHER, IN MANY societies for as long as history has been recorded. The differences between its various manifestations, however, have been as to methods, means, and weapons. As the means available to inflict significant damage to society improve, the harmful impact of terrorism increases. And as weapons of mass destruction become more accessible, the dangers to the world community increase.

This essay assesses substantive international norms and their enforcement, and highlights the weaknesses of the international system's effectiveness in combating transnational crime generally, and terrorism in particular. It starts with defining the phenomenon of terrorism, before proceeding into a critical assessment of the modalities of interstate cooperation in penal matters and offering a few recommendations thereto. It is necessarily more a survey than an in-depth study of the questions addressed. . . .

Terrorism is a strategy of violence designed to instill terror in a segment of society in order to achieve a power-outcome, propagandize a cause, or inflict harm for vengeful political purposes. That strategy is resorted to by state actors either against their own population or against the population of another country. It is also used by non-state actors, such as insurgent or revolutionary groups acting within their own country or in another country. Lastly, it is used by ideologically motivated groups or individuals, acting either inside or outside their country of nationality, whose methods may vary according to their beliefs, goals, and means.

State and non-state actors who commit terrorist acts can be distinguished, *inter alia,* on the basis of their participants, their goals, their methods, and the means they have at their disposal. But these actors all resort to

---

a strategy of terror-violence in order to achieve goals that include a power-outcome. The quantum or level of violence employed by actors in each category will usually depend on their access to means of terror-inspiring effects, and on whether these effects are likely to cause consequences conducive to attaining the desired power-outcome.

The advent of globalization has helped terrorist groups such as Al Qaeda. Globalization is characterized by the elimination of time and distance barriers and the increased popular access to information, technology, and communications. These characteristics have been exploited by both legitimate and illegitimate enterprises. They have particularly benefited terrorist groups by allowing the groups' members and supporters to cross state borders, acquire and move equipment, obtain information, communicate with one another, and transfer funds transnationally with much greater ease, all the while relying on the worldwide media to broadcast both their message and the success of their operations. Globalization has also allowed terrorist groups to network with one another, permitting terrorist groups to develop strategic alliances with other groups engaged in transnational criminality in order to develop synergetic connections and to maximize respective capabilities and effectiveness. These networks have particularly developed between terrorist groups and organized crime; in Colombia, for example, the Revolutionary Armed Forces of Colombia (FARC) funds its rebellion by protecting the drug traffickers.[1] Terrorist groups also rely on techniques perfected by organized crime, particularly their methods of and sources for obtaining funding, arms, and military equipment on the illegal market. Because of economic globalization and the lack of international control of arms trafficking, terrorist groups seldom lack access to weapons and military equipment; the so-called "black market" is quite open and accessible to those with funds. For example, with arms purchased from funds obtained in the illegal diamond trade and laundered in European financial institutions, the Liberian and Sierra Leone rebels have terrorized their respective peoples for a decade, leaving an estimated 200,000 and 300,000 people dead, thousands of children mutilated, and thousands of women raped.[2] These rebels, particularly their leaders, have benefited from the loopholes in financial and criminal controls that have resulted from globalization.

The Weaknesses of Existing International Law in Addressing Terrorism

Non-Specific Conventional and Customary International Law Applicable to Terrorism

Given the advent of globalization and the development of international terrorism, the international community must establish effective means of punishing such international criminal acts. Currently, the conduct of state actors and insurgent or revolutionary groups is governed by the 1948 Genocide Convention,[3] customary international criminal law governing crimes against humanity (since there is no applicable international convention other than the 1998 Statute of the International Criminal Court), the 1984 Convention against Torture,[4] and the various norms against war crimes as reflected in the customary law of armed conflict, and the four 1949 Geneva Conventions and their two 1977 Protocols.[5]

There is significant overlap between conventions and custom within the international criminal framework. The Convention against Torture, the Genocide Conventions, and the prohibitions on crimes against humanity apply in times of war and peace. However, the customary law of armed conflict and the Geneva Conventions apply only in times of war or armed conflict, either of an international or non-international character. These norms, applicable in the context of armed conflict, while sufficient, are seldom enforced against state actors and even less often enforced against non-state actors.[6] Furthermore, none of them makes distinctions in criminal responsibility between decision-makers and senior executors and lesser-rank personnel.[7]

In addition, these conventions lack an enforcement mechanism to truly deter and punish criminal behavior on an international scale. Certain international attempts have been made in the course of the last decade to provide effective enforcement. The Security Council established the International Criminal Tribunal for the Former Yugoslavia (ICTY) in 1993 and the International Criminal Tribunal for Rwanda (ICTR) in 1994 to prosecute persons charged with the first three of these crimes (genocide, crimes against humanity, and war crimes), committed in the context of these two conflicts. In no other conflict since World War II has such a post-conflict justice mechanism been established. When the ICC enters into effect, it will in time become a universal accountability mechanism for these three crimes. The extent to which the existence of such a system of international criminal justice can be an effective deterrent is, however, to be seen. Further, universal jurisdiction of international conventions has spurred domestic attempts at enforcement of such laws against international crime.[8] Indeed, the Torture Convention may become more effectively enforced as the Pinochet experiment in the United Kingdom[9] provides the precedent for increased state use of universal jurisdiction for national prosecutions. Universal jurisdiction can also be relied upon by national legal systems to prosecute genocide, crimes against humanity, war crimes, and torture. However, as crimes against humanity are not yet posited in conventional international criminal law other than in the two *ad hoc* tribunals of the JCTY and JCTR, and in the ICC Statute, it would be useful to have a specialized international convention on crimes against humanity, which, like Article 7 of the ICC Statute, would include non-state actors. In that way, crimes against humanity would encompass certain forms of terrorism committed by an "organization" which, on the basis of a "policy," engages in "widespread" or "systematic" attack upon "a civilian population," by means of killing and other specified acts.[10] An international convention prohibiting such crimes would likely allow for universal jurisdiction of the acts committed and thus increase national prosecution of terrorist acts.

The lack of coordinated international control of other dangerous and international criminal conduct also prevents effective enforcement. There is a significant legal gap, for example, in the control of weapons of mass destruction, such as nuclear, chemical, and biological weapons. For instance, there are no conventions on the prohibition of the use of nuclear weapons, whether by state or non-state actors. In addition, the 1993 Chemical Weapons Convention[11] lacks effective enforcement provisions applicable to unlawful terrorist use, and the 1972 Bacteriological Convention[12] does not criminalize the use of such agents for terrorist attacks. The Bacteriological Convention had been in the process of being amended for years, only to have a final draft opposed by the United States in 2001 as a result of pressures from the chemical and pharmaceutical industries. Thus, progress toward adopting a new convention with effective criminal provisions has been forestalled.

There is, in short, no normative fabric to international criminal law, just bits and pieces of overlapping norms with significant gaps as to their coverage. Even those norms that could be enforced, are subject to the recurring problem of a lack of effective enforcement by states. When states are permitted to rely on universal jurisdiction to enforce such norms, through their national legal systems, they fail to do so, even though such enforcement is required by international humanitarian law and other norms. International criminal law, therefore, suffers from both substantive and enforcement deficiencies, leading to a substantial lack in deterrence.

Specific Treaty-Based International Law Applicable to Terrorism

Treaty-based international legal efforts to combat terrorism have suffered from similar problems in enforcement and deterrence, and are characterized in particular by the absence of a comprehensive convention governing the international dimensions of the fight against terrorism. Instead, the legislative international legal framework is comprised of thirteen international conventions,[13] adopted over a span of thirty-two years (1969–2001), that apply to different types of terrorist acts, including: airplane hijacking (4);[14] piracy on the high seas (2);[15] attacks or kidnappings of internationally protected persons, U.N. personnel, and diplomats (2);[16] attacks upon civilian maritime vessels;[17] attacks upon platforms on the high seas;[18] the taking of civilian hostages;[19] the use of bombings and explosives in terrorist acts;[20]

the financing of terrorism;[21] and nuclear terrorism (pending).[22] Several regional intergovernmental organizations have established anti-terrorism conventions as well, including the Organization of American States (1971);[23] the Council of Europe (1977);[24] the South Asian Association for Regional Cooperation (1987);[25] the League of Arab States (1998);[26] the Organization of African Unity (1999);[27] and the Organization of the Islamic Conference (2000).[28]

As mentioned earlier, there is no comprehensive convention on terrorism that even modestly integrates, much less incorporates into a single text, these thirteen conventions so as to eliminate their weaknesses. The logic of such a comprehensive convention on terrorism is compelling, as is the logic against the current piecemeal approach taken by the separate conventions. Nevertheless, the United States has consistently opposed such a convention since 1972, ostensibly so that it can pick and choose from these disparate norms those that it wishes to rely upon. Above all, the United States does not want to have an effective multilateral scheme that would presumably restrict its unfettered political power to act unilaterally.

International Institutions

International legal crime-fighting institutions, in place to facilitate prevention of transnational crime, have also been ineffective. The United Nations has a Centre for International Crime Prevention in Vienna whose mandate includes fighting terrorism;[29] but the Centre has historically been underfunded, understaffed, and bereft of political influence within the U.N. system. Furthermore, in recent years it has suffered from disastrous leadership, further reducing its effectiveness.[30] Therefore, not only does it need new leadership, staff, and resources, but it needs a new mandate that better incorporates the fight against terrorism in this globalization-induced era of increased international and transnational criminal activity. In October 2001, the Security Council established a committee to deal with terrorism, at the behest of the United States, following the adoption of Security Council Resolution 1373.[31] Because the Security Council deals only with international "peace and security" threats under its powers contained in Chapter VII of the U.N. Charter, the new committee's focus is necessarily confined to a limited set of terrorist acts (those that threaten international peace and security).[32] The ad hoc nature of this Committee also portends that it may not outlive its present usefulness.

The International Criminal Police Organization (INTERPOL) has been only marginally effective in combating terrorism because major powers, like the United States, do not fully trust it. Furthermore, INTERPOL is a police association and does not include intelligence agencies. It is self-evident that combating international terrorism cannot succeed while beholden to the same bureaucratic boundaries that exist between law enforcement and intelligence agencies in domestic contexts. In this sense, INTERPOL merely reflects a political and bureaucratic reality that exists in almost all countries of the world, and which inevitably reduces its effectiveness. In fact, until 1993, INTERPOL was effectively precluded from dealing with terrorism altogether because its Charter prohibited it from dealing with such "political" matters.[33] While INTERPOL has since changed, it remains ineffective for the reasons expressed above.

Certain regional intergovernmental organizations have bodies or committees that deal with transnational criminal activity, including terrorism;[34] but not one of these bodies has any intelligence or law enforcement function.[35] Instead, they essentially do research, develop policy recommendations, and prepare draft treaties—functions that only indirectly contribute to combating terrorism.

Interstate Cooperation in Penal Matters

There are presently 190+ member-states of the United Nations, with significant variation among them in intelligence, law enforcement, prosecutorial, and judicial capabilities. Thus, it is easy for groups that engage in transnational criminality, including terrorism, to find countries where they can seek refuge, obtain support, or operate without much concern of detection.

Experience in combating transnational criminal activity, including terrorism, reveals that the first and most important stage in interdiction is intelligence and law enforcement cooperation. Such cooperation serves primarily as a means of prevention and deterrence, and only ultimately as a means of bringing perpetrators to justice. National systems, however, distribute these functions between competing bureaucratic agencies, thus reducing their individual and combined effectiveness. Furthermore, each separate national agency tends to develop *ad hoc* relationships with its counterparts in a select number of countries; so whatever information that is shared between corresponding agencies of different countries runs into the same intra-national bureaucratic impediments to information sharing and cooperation.

There is so far no international treaty that governs interstate law enforcement and intelligence cooperation. Thus, the international cooperation that does exist takes place outside international and national legal scrutiny. Therefore, there exists no protection of citizens against abuse of power and invasion of privacy, leading to a greater risk that those who are the victims of mistaken identity will have fewer means of protection at their disposal. International criminal law has so far developed six modalities for international cooperation in penal matters. Agreements, in some form, exist covering extradition, legal assistance, transfer of criminal proceedings, recognition of foreign penal judgments, transfer of sentenced persons, and freezing and seizing of assets. These six modalities, however, are not contained in a single international convention that integrates them in a way that makes them more effective. Instead, they are scattered in the provisions of a number of multilateral regional conventions.[36] There are no U.N.-sponsored international conventions dealing with any of these areas.[37]

In dealing with cooperation in international criminal enforcement, states rely on a web of bilateral treaties, each dealing with a separate modality of interstate cooperation in penal matters. While multilateral conventions dealing with substantive international criminal law, such as the thirteen aforementioned conventions dealing with terrorism,[38] do contain provisions on extradition and mutual legal assistance, these provisions are not consistent from convention to convention, and are usually limited to a few lines.[39] Instead, the United States, for example, has 137 bilateral extradition treaties applicable to 103 states, and 34 bilateral treaties on mutual legal assistance.[40] Worldwide, there are hundreds of bilateral treaties on extradition and mutual legal assistance. Other modalities, such as recognition of foreign penal judgments and transfer of criminal proceedings are seldom the subject of such bilateral agreements, while others still, such as the freezing and seizing of assets, are used only by a few states. Even the most significant for combating terrorism, the freezing and seizing of assets, until now has seldom been used except in connection with drug trafficking, due to the financial incentives that governments have in seizing assets derived from drug sales and then distributing them among their prosecutorial and law enforcement agencies.

States also rely on domestic legislation to enact these six modalities of interstate cooperation into law; as stated above, with the exception of Austria, Germany, Italy, and Switzerland, all other states deal with each of these modalities separately, thus precluding the integration of these modalities in order to make them more effective. For instance, the United States only has statutory provisions that deal with extradition and transfer of sentenced persons.[41] The extradition statute was drafted in 1825 with some recent modification.[42] At present, however, the provision is ridden with gaps that treaties and court decisions attempt to fill with considerable variation, rendering enforcement cumbersome, lengthy, and costly.[43]

The absence of both multilateral and domestic enforcement regimes that integrate the six modalities mentioned above has resulted in making interstate cooperation in penal matters cumbersome, lengthy, and, more often than not, ineffective. Developing countries, in particular, lack not only the legislative resources to engage in these modalities of interstate cooperation, but also the required expertise in their ministries of justice, interior, and foreign affairs to deal adequately with these processes. The United Nations' efforts to train experts in these areas, for instance, through its Crime Prevention Centre in Vienna, have been few and far between.

Regional organizations such as the Council of Europe, the Organization of American States and the Commonwealth Secretariat, have been better about undertaking such efforts. But these actions, too, have been limited.

In sum, the international community has not undertaken the effort of codifying international criminal law, either in its substantive or procedural aspects. Academic efforts in this direction have been sporadic,[44] and have not received significant governmental attention. As a result, there is a substantial weakness in the normative and procedural framework that is necessary to provide the bases for international cooperation in penal matters. Even reliance on national legal systems, for both the reasons stated above and those left unaddressed, were proved weak and inefficient.

State Responsibility for the Sponsorship or Failure to Take Appropriate Preventative Measures of Terrorism

International law establishes a principle whereby states that breach their international obligations are held responsible for their breaches. That responsibility has historically been of a civil nature. The remedy for a state that is aggrieved by such a breach is to bring an action before the International Court of Justice, and to obtain damages or reparations. A breach based on omission occurs where a state's failure to take appropriate action to carry out its obligations, or to prevent harm from occurring to other states, can trigger liability.

Since the late 1970s, the International Law Commission, which had been working on the codification of the Principles of State Responsibility,[45] has also considered the concept of state criminal responsibility.[46] But the concept of state criminal responsibility has met with a great deal of opposition, as evidenced by the fact that the ICC Statute does not contain such international criminal responsibility. Nevertheless, in recent years the Security Council has imposed sanctions on both Libya[47] and Sudan[48] on the basis that these states have permitted terrorist organizations to operate from within their respective territories, but with the implication that these countries may have even been involved in more direct support for such organizations, both within and beyond their own territories. The imposition of sanctions, which have the effect of collective punishment on a given population, are certainly punitive. Consequently, even though state criminal responsibility has not been officially recognized, punitive consequences have been attached to states whenever the Security Council has determined that such state action constitutes a breach of peace under Chapter VII of the U.N. Charter.

International criminal law since the Nuremberg judgment has, however, recognized the concept of criminal responsibility for organizations such as the S.S. and S.A. of Nazi Germany.[49] The events of September 11 should raise the question of whether or not state responsibility should include the concept of state criminal responsibility, much in the same way as it includes breaches of other international obligations, including failure to act. Failure to act should encompass the failure to develop appropriate national legislation to prevent and suppress terrorism—and all other international crimes as well—and to enforce both international law and national legislation in connection with such crimes. The area of state criminal responsibility is an area of international law that has not so far been adequately developed, probably for the reason that international criminal law has not sufficiently evolved as a new discipline which bridges international and criminal law.

Old and New Concepts of Conflicts of a Non-International Character

Conflicts of a non-international character are regulated in conventional international humanitarian law by Common Article 3 of the four Geneva Conventions of August 12, 1949;[50] and further developed in Additional Protocol II of 1977.[51]

These norms were originally intended to give some protection to combatants and civilians in the context of wars of national liberation, which reached their height during the decolonization era of the 1950s to the 1970s. In turn, this period of national liberation insurgency was followed by a period of uprisings by revolutionary groups who fought their governments for regime-change. These insurgents and revolutionary groups[52] resorted to acts of terror-violence against colonizers/settlers and domestic regimes, acts which led to their being referred to as terrorists. While the term "terrorism" clashed with the legitimacy of such a right to engage in a war of national liberation or to topple dictatorial regimes, it properly described the means employed to those ends. This legitimacy-versus-means issue is still with us today.

The Geneva Conventions and Additional Protocols are based on the unarticulated premise that even legitimate ends do not justify certain means. Insurgents and revolutionaries, though not without right to resort to armed conflict, must nonetheless abide by the rules of armed conflict applicable to combatants and non-combatants in the context of non-international armed conflicts. The same applies to state forces fighting against such groups.[53] Violations by one side do not allow reprisals in kind by the other.[54] Thus, symmetry in legal obligations is established.

Insurgent and revolutionary groups, however, do not have the same military means and capabilities available to conventional state forces, and therefore feel that they cannot abide by the same rules if they are to succeed. They are reinforced in their disregard of these norms by the fact that state forces also seldom respect these rules. In addition, these groups are not professional combatants and have neither the command and control nor the training that regular and well-disciplined armed forces have. Additional Protocol II tried to take some of these factors into consideration by inducing compliance of insurgent and revolutionary groups with international humanitarian law through the relaxation of conditions for prisoner of war status under the 1949 Conventions.[55] This inducement—essentially one of status recognition—has naturally been met with considerable resistance on the part of states, who fear that this gives such groups misplaced legitimacy.

These problems were seldom resolved in the many conflicts of a non-international character that have occurred since World War II, where neither governments nor insurgent and revolutionary groups abided by either the terms of Common Article 3 or those of Additional Protocol 11.[56] In fact, there has almost always been a premium for insurgent and revolutionary groups to increase their violence, including terror-violence, to levels that will garner them recognition and legitimacy, and eventually political settlements.[57] The result is that in conflicts of a non-international character the norms exist but are neither followed nor enforced.

This situation of lawlessness in the non-international context still exists. Governments do not want to give legitimacy to insurgent and revolutionary groups, while the latter are unwilling to abide by international humanitarian law in view of the imbalance of power that exists between them and the states or regimes they are fighting against. They claim that legitimacy is on their side and that a double standard is used against them. Thus, they legitimize their terror-violence in their own perception.

With few exceptions, until September 11, conflicts of a non-international character occurred between an insurgent or revolutionary group and a state or regime. Probably the first conflict that at least began as one of a non-international character was the Vietnam conflict. The Viet Cong used Laos as a base and a travel route for operations in South Vietnam, which was deemed to be another country.[58] Another example is that of the U.S.-sponsored Nicaragua Contras whose base of operation was in Honduras. In the first case, the United States bombed Laos in violation of that state's sovereignty but the United States considered it an exercise of a legitimate right of self-defense. In the second case, the United States had no such legal justification.[59]

The operations of Al Qaeda against the interests of the United States, including both domestic[60] and foreign-based[61] actions, emanated from Afghanistan but with a support network in several countries. This raises novel questions in international humanitarian law. The first of these is whether a state can be at war with a group operating from another country (or from more than one country) with membership consisting of multiple nationalities. The second regards the legal implications of such an armed conflict.

The answer to the first question is in the negative, because only states can be at war. Clearly, however, a state can be engaged in an armed conflict with an insurgent or revolutionary group, irrespective of that group's legitimacy, and vice versa. This is reflected in Common Article 3 and Additional Protocol II.[62] The fact that, historically, such conflicts were confined to the territory of a given state does not alter the legal status of the participants in that conflict and the international humanitarian law applicable to them. The laws of armed conflict are not geographically bound. They relate to the conduct of combatants with clear limits and inderogable prohibitions with respect to what these norms refer to as "protected targets." Thus, under no circumstances can, *inter alia,* non-combatant civilians, POWs, the sick, the wounded, and the injured at land, at sea, and in hospitals, be attacked. The rationale is simply a humanitarian one and the prohibition is absolute. The only available exonerating circumstance is a reasonable mistake of fact. But no rule of military necessity exonerates those who commit such violations from criminal responsibility.[63] International humanitarian law opted for a neutral rule that protects certain targets, but by implication it favors state forces over insurgent or revolutionary forces in light of the balance of power. Regardless, however, the law is binding on both state and insurgent or revolutionary forces.[64]

Al Qaeda's attacks against the United States on September 11 and earlier fall within this paradigm: they are subject to the strictures of international humanitarian law, regardless of the legitimacy of their perpetrators' cause. If Al Qaeda violates such norms (as it has), those who committed such acts may properly be considered war criminals. Furthermore, a country such as Afghanistan that has given such a group a base of operation is also responsible for the actions of that group, and the United States is entitled to use force based on its "inherent right of self-defense" under Article 51 of the U.N. Charter. If combatants from that group are seized in the field, that is, in Afghanistan, they can be tried by a Military Commission established by the Commander of U.S. forces in the field. This is permissible under the customary law of armed conflict, and there certainly is precedent. The United States did so in the Far East after World War II, and one case reached the United States Supreme Court, *In re Yamashita.*[65]

With respect to combatants from a foreign state with which the United Stares is formally at war and who are caught within the United States, the only precedent for a Military Commission was in 1942 when President Roosevelt established one to try eight German saboteurs. The validity of such a Commission was recognized by the Supreme Court in *ex parte Quinn,*[66] even if its jurisdiction in this case applied to U.S. citizens.[67] But these combatants were also nationals of a state with which the United States was at war in accordance with a proper declaration of a state of war by Congress in accordance with Article I of the Constitution.

There is therefore a valid legal basis for the Presidential Military Order of November 13, 2001, with respect to Military Commissions in the field that are outside the United States, and for Military Commissions in the United States for Violations of the Laws and Customs of War.[68] Not so for jurisdiction over persons in the United States or outside the United States who do not fall within these categories. With respect to persons within the United States, other than those mentioned above, the Military Order violates the Constitutional doctrine of separation of powers, and in particular, Article 1, Section 8, Clause 4; Article III, Section 2; and the due process clauses of the Fourteenth and Fifth Amendments and the Fourth, Fifth, Sixth and Eighth Amendments. Regrettably, this type of legal analysis and resort to the norms of international humanitarian law have not been sufficiently aired in the post–September 11 context.

Finally, it should be noted that the attacks upon the United States of September 11 constitute "Crimes Against Humanity" as defined in Article 7 of the Statute of the International Criminal Court (ICC).[69] The provisions of the ICC Statute are not applicable to the United States, as the treaty establishing the ICC has not yet entered into effect and the United States has not ratified it. Further, the United States, unlike other countries, does not have a domestic statute on "Crimes Against Humanity," and the Uniform Code of Military Justice does not apply to acts committed by civilians in the United States.[70] This is an opportunity to pass appropriate legislation to include these crimes in Title 18 U.S.C. and make them subject to the jurisdiction of Federal Courts.[71]

Conclusion

"Terrorism" is a value-laden term. Consequently, it means different things to different people, a characteristic that perhaps is best expressed in the saying, "What is terrorism to some is heroism to others," and has never been satisfactorily defined. Yet the phenomenon is as old as history, even as its manifestations have changed as a result of new technology. Both state and non-state actors have resorted to the same approaches in terrorizing civilian populations, while using different weapons and techniques. For both, the goals of terror-violence are political. However, where non-state actors are often ideologically motivated, state actors, soldiers and police personnel who are either conscripts or persons seeking a career or temporary job in these bodies, are usually not.

The need for a comprehensive convention on terrorism that is, as much as possible, value-neutral, encompassing all actors, and covering all modalities and techniques of terror-violence, is self-evident. Such a convention, though, has been politically elusive. Governments understandably seek to exclude state actors from the definition of terrorism, and reject the notion that a causal connection even exists between state-sponsored acts of terror-violence and terror-violence committed by non-state actors. Since governments inevitably prevail in the international arena, the definition of terrorism has been limited to encompass unlawful conduct by non-state actors. Even with respect to this confined definition, however, governments have avoided developing an international legal régime to prevent, control, and suppress terrorism, preferring instead the hodgepodge of thirteen treaties that currently address its particular manifestations. The absence of a coherent international legislative policy on terrorism is consistent with the *ad hoc* and discretionary approach that governments have taken toward the development of effective international legal responses to terrorism. Thus, international legal norms governing terrorism rest essentially on the identification of certain types of conduct or means employed. To date, there is no international initiative to systematize, update, integrate, or even harmonize these international norms.

Interstate cooperation in penal matters is also limited due to this lack of a coherent and cohesive international legal regime. National legal systems are therefore left with whatever jurisdictional and resource means they have at their disposal, making them ineffective in dealing with terrorism's international manifestations. The exclusion of state actors' unlawful terror-violence acts from inclusion in the overall scheme of terrorism control highlights the double standard that non-state actors lament and use as a justification for their own transgressions. This disparity of treatment between state and non-state actors is plainly evident, and constitutes one of the reasons for the attraction of adherents to non-state terrorist groups.

Since the current renewed interest in the subject of terrorism is due to the tragic events of September 11, 2001, it may be useful to confront certain controversial questions. First, these attacks were not only criminal, but unconscionable as to their harmful consequences, both human and economic. Additionally, the incidents were a blow to the invulnerability of the world's only superpower. But in comparative terms, the estimated 3,000 casualties of September 11 pale in contrast to some 5,000–23,000 people killed by other forms of violence, and the 15,000 people killed by drunk driving in the United States every year.[72] The effect of the reaction on many throughout the Arab and Muslim world, which consists of 1.3 billion people worldwide is to ask why, applying the same legal and moral standards, is the U.S. sponsored embargo on Iraq, which has caused the deaths of an estimated five hundred thousand innocent children, acceptable? Of course, there are several valid distinctions between the embargo and the attacks upon the United States, but not in comparative human terms. In the end, the

United States bears an indirect responsibility for that outcome in Iraq. Similarly, a large segment of the world population asks why Israel's repression of the Palestinian people, which includes the commission of "grave breaches" of the Geneva Convention and what the customary law of armed conflict considers "war crimes," is deemed justified, while Palestinians' unlawful acts of targeting civilians are condemned? These are only some contemporary examples of the double standard that fuels terrorism. All these acts are unjustifiable, and one wrong does not make another right.

Terrorism springs our of despair and injustice; it is the weapon of the weak, not the coward; it is indiscriminate and a crime against its innocent victims. It must he addressed with effective and legitimate means by law enforcement and the national justice systems of all countries of the world. The control of its manifestations depends on international cooperation, but its prevention requires addressing its causes.

In 1961, President John F. Kennedy, addressing an Organization of American States heads of states meeting in Punta del Esre, Uruguay, said "those who make peaceful evolution impossible, make violent revolution inevitable."[73] If we want to put an end to the forms of violence that we call terrorism, then we need an effective international legal regime with enforcement capabilities that can, as Aristotle once said, apply the same law in Athens as in Rome.[74] This is the only alternative to Mao Tse-Tung's exhortation, to paraphrase, that truth comes out of the barrel of a gun.[75]

Notes

1. M. Cherif Bassiouni & Edoardo Vetere, *Organized Crime and Its Transnational Manifestations*, in International Criminal Law 883 (M. Cherif Bassiouni ed., 2d ed. 1999).

2. *See* Human Rights Watch, Sierra Leone: A Call For Justice, http://www.hrw.org/campaigns/sleone.

3. Genocide Convention, *supra* note 1.

4. Torture Convention, *supra* note 4.

5. Geneva Convention I, *supra* note 3; Geneva Convention II, *supra* note 3; Geneva Convention III, *supra* note 3; Geneva Convention IV, *supra* note 3. Note that only Additional Protocol I applies to conflicts of a non-international character, while Additional Protocol II applies to conflicts of a non-international character. *See* Additional Protocol I, *supra* note 3; Additional Protocol II, *supra* note 3.

6. There is an absence of criminal prosecutions after conflicts occur, as evidenced by the fact that the Security Council had to establish the ICTY and ICTR in order to bring about the prosecution of crimes committed in, respectively, the former Yugoslavia and Rwanda. See M. Cherif Bassiouni, *Searching for Peace and Achieving Justice: The Need for Accountability* 59 L. & Contem. Props. 1, 99728 (1996); Steven Ratner & Jason Abrams, Accountability for Human Right Atrocities in International Law: Beyond the Nuremberg (26 ed. 2001); Diane F. Orentlicher, *Settling Accounts: The Duty to Prosecute Human Rights Violations of a Prior Regime*, 100 Yale L. J. 2537 (1991).

7. *See* Bassiouni, *supra* note 2, at 369–446.

8. *See* International Law Association. Final Report on the Executive of University Jurisdiction in Respect of Gross Human Rights Offenses, 404 (2000); M. Cherif Bassiouni, *Universal Jurisdiction for International Crimes: Historical Perspectives and Contemporary Practice,* 42 VA. J. Int'l. L. (2001). *See also* Princeton University Progress in Law and Public Affairs, The Princeton Principles of Universal Jurisdiction (2001) (prescribing principles to govern the application of universal jurisdiction in light of its potential for abuse).

9. Regina v. Bow Sr. Metro. Stipendiary Magistrate, *parte* Pinochet Ugarte (No. 3), 1 A.C. 147 (2000); Christine M. Chinkin, *Congressional Decision, Regina v. Bow Street Stependiary Magistrate, Ex Parte Pinochet Ugarte (No. 3),* 93 Ass. J. Int'l. L. 703, 704 (1999).

10. ICC Statute, *supra* note 1, art. 7. *See also* M. Cherif Bassiouni, Crimes Against Humanity in International Law (2d rev. ed. 1999).

11. Convention on the Prohibition of the Development, Production, Stockpiling and Use of Chemical Weapons and on their Destruction, Jan. 13, 1993, S. Treaty Doc. No. 103–21, 1974 U.N.T.S. 3.

12. Convention on the Prohibition of the Development, Production and Stockpiling of Bacteriological (Biological) and Toxin Weapons and on their Destruction, Feb. 25, 1972, 26 U.S.T. 583, 1015 U.N.T.S.

13. *See* M. Cherif Bassiouni, International Terrorism: Multilateral Conventions 1937–2001 (2001).

14. Montreal Convention for the Suppression of Unlawful Acts Against the Safety of Civil Aviation, Sept. 23, 1971, 24 U.S.T. 564, 974 U.N.T.S. 17 Montreal Protocol for the Suppression of Unlawful Acts of Violence at Airports Serving Civil Aviation, Feb. 24, 1988, S. Treaty Doc. No. 100–19, 27 I.L.M. 627; Hague Convention for the Suppression of Unlawful Seizure of Aircrafts, Dec. 16, 1970, 22 U.S.T. 1641, 860 U.N.T.S. 105; Tokyo Convention on Offences and Certain Other Acts Committed on Board Aircraft, Sept. 14, 1963, 20 U.S.T. 2941, 704 U.N.T.S. 219.

15. Convention on the Law of the Sea, Dec. 10, 1982, 1833 U.N.T.S. 3; Convention on the High Seas, Apr. 29, 1958, 13 U.S.T. 2312, 430 U.N.T.S. 11.

16. Convention on the Safety of United Nations and Associated Personnel, Dec. 9, 1994, G.A. Res. 49/59, U.N. GAOR, 49th Sess., Supp. No. 49, at 299, U.N. Doc. A/49/49 (1994); Convention on the Prevention and Punishment of Crimes Against Internationally Protected Persons, Including Diplomatic Agents, Dec. 14, 1973, 28 U.S.T. 1975, 1035 U.N.T.S. 167.

17. Convention for the Suppression of Unlawful Acts Against the Safety of Maritime Navigation, Mar. 10, 1988, S. Treaty Doc. No. 101–1, 27 I.L.M. 668.

18. Protocol for the Suppression of Unlawful Acts Against the Safety of Fixed Platforms Located on the Continental Shelf, Mar. 10, 1988, S. Treaty Doc. No. 101–1, 27 I.L.M. 685.

19. Convention Against the Taking of Hostages, Dec. 17, 1979, T.I.A.S. No. 11,081, 1316 U.N.T.S. 205.

20. International Convention for the Suppression of Terrorist Bombings, Jan. 9, 1998, S. Treaty Doc. No. 106–6, 37 I.L.M. 251.

21. International Convention for the Suppression of the Financing of Terrorism, G.A. Res. 109, U.N. GAOR, 54th Sess., Supp. No. 49, Agenda Item 160, at 408, U.N. Doc. A/54/109 (1999).

22. Draft Convention on the Suppression of Acts of Nuclear Terrorism, Jan. 28, 1997, U.N. Doc. A/AC.252/L.3.

23. Organization of American States: Convention to Prevent and Punish Acts

of Terrorism Taking the Form of Crimes Against Persons and Related Extortion that Are of International Significance, Feb. 2, 1971, 27 U.S.T. 3949, 1986 U.N.T.S. 195.

24. European Convention on the Suppression of Terrorism, Jan. 27, 1977, Europ. No. 90, 1979 U.N.T.S. 94 [hereinafter European Terrorism convention].

25. South Asian Association for Regional Cooperation Convention on Suppression of Terrorism, U.N. GAOR, 44th Sess., U.N. Doc. A/S1/136 (1989).

26. The League of Arab States, The Council of Arab Interior and Justice Ministers: The Arab Convention on the Suppression of Terrorism, Apr. 22, 1998, http://www.leagueofarabstates.org/W..NewsAntiterrorism.asp.

27. Organization of African Unity: Convention on the Prevention and Combating of Terrorism, July 14, 1999. http://untreaty.un.org/English/Terrorism.asp.

28. Organization of the Islamic Conference: Convention of the Organization of the Islamic Conference on Combating International Terrorism, Oct. 11, 2000, *reprinted in* UN. Doc. A154/637, Annex, http://www.oic-un.orgi2fiicfmlc.html.

29. Operated within the United Nations' Office for Drug Control and Crime Prevention, the Center works closely with the United Nations' Terrorism Prevention Branch, also based in Vienna.

30. *See* Report of the Office of Internal Oversight Services, U.N. GAOR, 56th Sess., Agenda Item 130, U.N. Doc. A/56/381 (2001), http://www.un.org/Depcs/oios/reports/a5fi...38I.pdf. Report of the Office of Internal Oversight Services on the Inspection of Programme Management and Administrative Practices in the Office for Drug Control and Crime Prevention, U.N. GAOR, 56th Sess., Agenda Items 123, 124, 134, 143, U.N. Doc. A156/83 (2001), http://www.un.orgiDeprsloios/reports/a5&83.htm; Triennial Review of the Implementation of the Recommendations Made by the CPC at its Thirty-Eighth Session on the In-Depth Evaluation of the U.N. Crime Prevention and Criminal Justice, U.N. ESCOR, 41st Sess.

31. S.C. Res. 1373. U.N. SCOR, 56th Sess., 4385th mtg., U.N. Doc. S/Res/1373 (2001).

32. *See* id. 76.

33. *See* Interpol Const., art. 3, http://www.interpol.int/Publit/ICPO/LegalMaterialS/Constitution..asp ("It is strictly forbidden for the organization to undertake any Intervention or activities of a political, military, or religious or racial character."). However, the organization recognized the role it could play in combating international terrorism as early as 1985. *See* International Terrorism and Unlawful Interference with Civil Aviation, Interpol G.A. ass. No. AGN/54/RES/1 (1985), http://www.interpol.intipobiic/terrorism/default.55p. *See also, Mary Jo Grotenroth, Interpol's Role in International Law Enforcement* in Legal Responses To International Terrorism: U.S. Procedural Aspects 375, 381 (1988) (Interpol's resolution on terrorism); Nepore, *The Role of International Criminal Police (INTERPOL),* in A Treatise on International Criminal Law: Crimes and Punishment 676 (M. Cherif Bassiouni & Ved P. Nanda eds., 1973).

34. These organizations include the Commonwealth Secretariat, the Council of Europe, the European Union, the League of Arab States, and the Organization of American States.

35. *See* M. Cherif Bassiouni, *Policy Considerations on Interstate Cooperation in Criminal Matters,* in International Criminal Law, *supra* note 13, at 3.

36. *See, e.g.,* Inter-American Convention on Extradition, O.A.S. T.S. No. 60 (February 25, 1981), http://www.oas.org/iuridico/english/sigsfb..47 html; Inter-American Convention on Mutual Assistance in Criminal Matters, O.A.S. T.S. No. 75 (May 23, 1992); European Convention on Extradition, Dec. 13, 1957, 359 U.N.T.S. 273. *See also,* Ekrehart Moller-Rappard & M. Cherif Bassiouni, European Inter-State Co-operations in Criminal Matters: The Council of Europe's Legal Instruments (2d ed. 1991) (for a discussion on the Council of Europe's Conventions). The

League of Arab States also has a convention on extradition and one on mutual legal assistance.

37. *See* U.N. Model Treaty on Extradition, G.A. Res. 116, U.N. GAOR, 45th Sess., Annex, at 21197 15, U.N. Doc. A/RES/45/1 16 (1990); U.N. Model Treaty on Mutual Assistance in Criminal Matters, G.A. Res. 117, 45th Sess., Annex, at 21549, U.N. Doc. A/RES/117 (1990).

38. *See supra* notes 26–34 and accompanying text.

39. *See* M. Cherif Bassiouni & Edward M. Wise, Aut Dedere Aut Judicare: The Duty to Prosecute or Extradite in International Law 79719 (1995). *See also* M. Cherif Bassiouni, International Extradition in United States Law and Practice 295–382 (3d ed. 1996).

40. *See* 18 U.S.C. 3181–3196 for a listing of these treaties.

41. Id. 3181–3195.

42. Antiterrorism and Effective Death Penalty Act of 1996, Pub. L. No. 104–132, at 443(a), 110 Stat. 1280(1996).

43. A 1984 proposal for comprehensive revision of the statute was rejected because it was deemed to contain too many individual guarantees. *See also* M. Cherif Bassiouni, *Extradition Reform Legislation in the United States: 1981–1983*, 17 Akron L. Rev. 495 (1984); *United States and United Kingdom Supplementary Extradition Treaty: Hearings Before the Subcomm. on Foreign Relations, United States Senate*, 99th Cong. (1985).

44. *See* M. Cherif Bassiouni, A Draft International Criminal Code and a Draft Statute for an International Criminal Tribunal (1987).

45. The International Law Commission concluded its work in 2001. *See* International Law Commission, Report by the International Law Commission on the Work of its Fifty-Third Session, Apr. 23 to June 1 and July 2 to Aug. 10, 2001, U.N. GAOR, 53d Sess., Supp. No. 10, U.N. Doc. A/56/10 (2001).

46. *See* M. Cherif Bassiouni, *The Sources and Content of International Criminal Law: A Theoretical Framework*, in 1 Int'l. Crim. L. 3, *supra* note 13, at 27 (2d ed. 1999).

47. S.C. Res. 748, U.N. SCOR, 42d Sess., 3063d mtg., U.N. Doc. S/Res.f 748 (1992).

48. S.C. Res. 1054, U.N. SCOR, 4 Crh Sess., 3660th mtg., U.N. Doc. S/Rest 1054 (1996).

49. See Bassiouni, *supra* note 58, at 24.

50. *See* Geneva Convention I, *supra* note 3, art. 3; Geneva Convention II, *supra* note 3, art. 3; Geneva Convention III, *supra* note 3, art. 3; Geneva Convention IV, *supra* note 3, art. 3. *See also,* Documents on the Laws of War (Adam Roberts & Richard Gucif eds., 3d ed. 2000). With respect to the customary law of armed conflict, *see* International Committee for the Red Cross, International Law Concerning the Conduct of Hostilities (1996).

51. *See* Additional Protocol II, *supra* note 3.

52. The terms "insurgents" and "revolutionary groups" are just two of the terms used to describe groups of this type. *See* The International Law of Civil War (Richard Falk ed., 1971); Elizabeth Chadwick, Self-Determination, Terrorism, and the International Humanitarian Law of Armed Conflict (1996); Restructuring the Global Military Sector: New Wars (Mary Kaldot & Basket Vaske eds., 1997).

53. *See, e.g.,* Howard S. Levie, Terrorism in War: The Law of War Crimes (1993). *See also* Hans-Peter Gasser, *Prohibition of Terrorist Attacks in International Humanitarian Law,* 1985 Int'l. Rev. Red Cross 200, 203 (1985).

54. *See* Frits Kashoven & Liesbeth Zeoveld, Constraints on the Waging of War: An Introduction to International Humanitarian Law (3d ed. 2001).

55. *See* Additional Protocol II, *supra* note 3, art. 43. *See also,* Commentary on

the Protocols of 8 June 1977 to the Geneva Convention of 12 August 1949 (Yves Sandoz et al. eds., 1987).

56. The failure to resolve these problems has generated considerable harm in those conflicts. For a survey of such harm, see Jennifer Balint, *Conflict Victimization and Legal Redress*, 14 Nouvelles Etudes Penales 101 (1998).

57. This was the case with recent rebellions in Liberia and Sierra Leone, which resulted in approximately 200,000 and 300,000 victims, respectively, most of whom were innocent civilians, and many of whom had their limbs cut off or were raped.

58. North Vietnam and South Vietnam were legally deemed two different countries, but North Vietnam rejected that contention and argued that all of Vietnam was one country. *See* The Vietnam War and International Law (Richard Falk ed., 1976).

59. *See* Military and Paramilitary Activities in and Against Nicaragua (Nicar. v. U.S.) (1986) I.C.J. 14.

60. With respect to the September 11 attacks, both the hijacking and the subsequent destruction of the four airplanes occurred within the continental United States.

61. Foreign-based actions include attacks upon the U.S. Embassies in Kenya and Tanzania and against a U.S. naval vessel the *U.S.S. Cole,* in Yemen.

62. *See* George Aldrich, *The Laws of War on Land,* 94 Am. J. Int'l. L. 42 (2000).

63. *See, e.g.,* Christopher Greenwood, A Manual of International Law (1995); Leslie C. Green, Essays on the Modern Law of War (2d ed., 1999); The Law of War Crimes: National and International Approaches (Timothy L. H. McCormack & Gary J. Simpson eds., 1997) [hereinafter Law of War Crimes].

64. *See* Law of War Crimes, *supra* note 18.

65. 327 U.S. 1 (1946) (upholding the authority of Supreme Allied Commander General Douglas MacArthur to establish such Commissions). *See also* 327 U.S. 759 (1946) ("The motion for leave or file petition for writ of habeas corpus and writ of prohibition is denied and the petition for writ of certiorari is also denied on authority of Application of Yamashita, and Yamashita v. Styer"); Lawrence Taylor, A Trail of Generals: Homma, Yamashita, MacArthur (1981).

66. 317 U.S. 1 (1942).

67. Id. at 37.

68. Military Order, *Detention, Treatment and Trial of Certain Non-Citizens in the War Against Terrorism,* 66 Fed. Reg. 57, 833 (Nov. 13, 2001). *See* Jordan Paust, *After My Lai: The Case for War Crimes Jurisdiction over Civilians in Federal District Courts,* 50 Tex. L. Rev. 6 (1971).

69. *See* ICC Statute, *supra* note 1; Bassiouni, *supra* note 1; *International Criminal Court Ratification and National Implementing Legislation,* 71 Rev. Int'l. Detroit Penal (2000).

70. *See* 10 U.S.C. 801–946 (2000). *See also* Jordan Paust, M. Cherif Bassiouni et al., International Criminal Law: Cases and Materials (2d. rev. ed. 2000).

71. *See* Paust, *supra* note 80.

72. 23,040 cases in 1990, and 15,530 cases in 1999. See Federal Bureau of Investigation, Uniform Crime Reports: Crime in the United States 1999, Index of Crime, http://www.fbi.gov/urr/99cius.htm.

73. The Law of Dissent and Riots (M. Cherif Bassiouni ed., 1971).

74. *See* Aristotle, the Nicomachean Ethics (David Ross trans., Oxford Univ. Press, 1998).

75. Quotations from Chairman Mao Tse-Tung 33 (Stuart Schram ed., 1967) ("Every communist must grasp the truth, 'Political power grows out of the barrel of a gun.'").

PART 2.2

International Law as Normative System: For the Protection of Individual Rights

CHAPTER 15

The Evolving International Human Rights System

Thomas Buergenthal

FEW, IF ANY, BRANCHES OF INTERNATIONAL LAW HAVE UNDERgone such dramatic growth and evolution as international human rights. This branch of international law did not really come into its own until after World War II. Before then, what today we would broadly characterize as human rights law consisted of diffuse or unrelated legal principles and institutional arrangements that were in one way or another designed to protect certain categories or groups of human beings. Included in this mix prior to World War I were state responsibility for injuries to aliens, international humanitarian law (as we know it today), the protection of minorities, and humanitarian intervention.

The end of World War I and the establishment of the League of Nations produced the postwar treaties for the protection of minorities, whose application was limited to certain countries. The Covenant of the League of Nations provided for a mandates system, consisting of rudimentary normative and institutional processes for the protection of the indigenous populations of some former colonies. These developments, however, did not result in a comprehensive body of law that could be denominated international human rights law, although a few legal scholars promoted the concept.[1] Some of them even succeeded in having the Institute of International Law (Institut de droit international or Institute) adopt a "Declaration of the International Rights of Man" (Declaration) in 1929.[2] After emphasizing in its preamble that "the juridical conscience of the civilized world demands the recognition for the individual of rights preserved from all infringement on the part of the State," the Declaration asserted that it was the duty of states to recognize for all individuals, "without distinction as to nationality,

Reprinted with permission of The American Society of International Law.

sex, race, language, or religion," the right to life, liberty, and property; it further declared that states had the duty to recognize to all individuals the free exercise of religion and freedom to use the language of their choice.[3]

That the subject of human rights was still very much in its infancy is apparent from an Editorial Comment by Philip Marshall Brown that appeared in the *American Journal of International Law* in 1930, reporting on the 1929 meeting of the Institute and the adoption of its Declaration.[4] The author noted that the Declaration "aims not merely to assure individuals their *international* rights, but it aims also to impose on all nations a standard of conduct towards all men, *including their own nationals*."[5] Noting that the Declaration "thus repudiates the classic doctrine that states alone are subjects of international law," Brown continued: "Such a revolutionary document, while open to criticism in terminology and to the objection that it has no juridical value, cannot fail, however, to exert an influence on the evolution of international law."[6]

Even as late as 1937, Hersch Lauterpacht, as editor of the fifth edition of Oppenheim's *International Law*—his first edition of that work—left intact the book's section entitled "The Law of Nations and the Rights of Man," which denied that such rights existed, but commented in a footnote as follows:

> The principles of [the 1929] Declaration are not expressive of the law and practice of many States; neither is their non-observance treated by other States as a breach of International Law. But it is believed that the development of International Law in accordance with its true function is, in the last resort, bound up with the triumph of the spirit expressed in these principles.[7]

In dealing with the evolution of international human rights law, this essay focuses on the evolution of legal norms and institutional mechanisms for the protection of civil and political rights. Limitations of space did not permit me, except in passing, to deal with comparable norms and institutions applicable to economic, social, and cultural rights, or with so-called peoples' rights or other emerging substantive and institutional elements of contemporary international human rights law. This essay thus presents only one aspect, or part, of the burgeoning human rights revolution.

Early Institutional Developments

The regional human rights machinery in existence today, as well as the plethora of United Nations human rights bodies, traces its antecedents to League of Nations institutions that dealt with minorities' rights and mandated territories. After World War I, the Allied and Associated Powers concluded a series of treaties with Austria, Bulgaria, Czechoslovakia, Greece, Poland, Romania, Turkey, and Yugoslavia for the protection of the rights of the minorities living in those countries. The League agreed to become the guarantor of the obligations the states parties assumed in these treaties. It performed that function by developing special mechanisms, including so-called Committees of Three that reviewed petitions from minorities charging violations of their rights. Serious legal questions that grew out of these reviews were frequently submitted by the Council of the League to the Permanent Court of International justice, which produced an extensive jurisprudence on the subject.[8]

The League of Nations mandates system applied only to the former colonies of the states that were defeated in World War I. Under Article 22 of the League's Covenant, these colonies were transformed into mandates to be administered by some of the victorious powers in that war. Article 22 further provided that the mandatory states were to administer the mandated territories in accordance with "the principle that the well-being and development of [indigenous] peoples form a sacred trust of civilisation." These states also assumed the obligation to report annually to the League on the discharge of their responsibilities as mandatories. A Mandates Commission, established by the League, was charged with reviewing these reports. Had the League survived, the commission might have been able to transform itself over time into an effective mechanism capable of ensuring that the mandatory powers complied with their obligations. It might also have been able gradually to strengthen these obligations. Although the dissolution of the League of Nations put an end to the work of the commission, some of its functions devolved on the United Nations Trusteeship Council, which was entrusted with powers to supervise the administration of the remaining mandates and other non-self-governing territories. Once most of these territories acquired their independence, the Trusteeship Council itself was abolished.

The United Nations Charter

International human rights law, as we know it today, begins with the Charter of the United Nations. According to its Article 1(3), one of the purposes of the United Nations is the achievement of "international co-operation in . . . promoting and encouraging respect for human rights and for fundamental freedoms for all without distinction as to race, sex, language, or religion." That the UN Charter should have listed this subject among the Organization's purposes is not surprising, considering that it was drafted in the aftermath of World War II, the Holocaust, and the murder of millions of innocent human beings. But contrary to what might have been expected given this background, the Charter did not impose any concrete human rights obligations on the UN member states. Although a group of smaller countries and nongovernmental organizations (NGOs) attending the San Francisco Conference fought for the inclusion of an international bill of rights in the Charter,[9] these efforts failed, principally because they were opposed by the major powers.[10]

Instead of a bill of rights, the San Francisco Conference adopted some intentionally vague Charter provisions on human rights. The two major human rights provisions, in addition to Article 1(3) referred to above, are Articles 55 and 56. Article 55 reads in part as follows:

> With a view to the creation of conditions of stability and well-being which are necessary for peaceful and friendly relations among nations based on respect for the principle of equal rights and self-determination of peoples, the United Nations shall promote:
>
> (c) universal respect for, and observance of, human rights and fundamental freedoms for all without distinction as to race, sex, language, or religion.

Article 56 of the Charter provides, in turn, that "[a]ll Members pledge themselves to take joint and separate action in co-operation with the Organization for the achievement of the purposes set forth in Article 55."[11] The vagueness of these human rights provisions, read together with the non-intervention clause found in Article 2(7) of the Charter,[12] tended for years to hamper serious UN action in confronting human rights violations. State claims based on Article 2(7) were gradually rejected by a majority of the UN membership. But they continued to be regularly made in different UN organs by states that wanted, and in the early days frequently managed, to defeat, or at least weaken, some proposed human rights measures by arguing that how they treated their nationals essentially fell within their domestic jurisdiction, and hence was protected against UN intervention under Article 2(7).[13]

Despite their vagueness, however, the human rights provisions of the Charter did prove to have important consequences.[14] In time, the membership of the United Nations came to accept the proposition that the Charter had internationalized the concept of human rights. This did not mean that as soon as the Charter entered into force, all human rights issues were ipso facto no longer essentially within the domestic jurisdiction of states. It did mean, though, that states were deemed to have assumed some international obligations relating to human rights. Although the full scope of these rights remained to be defined, states could no longer validly claim that human rights as such were essentially domestic in character. Equally important, the obligation imposed by Article 56 on UN member states, which requires them to cooperate with the Organization in the promotion of human rights, provided the United Nations with the requisite legal authority to embark on what became a massive lawmaking effort to define and codify these rights. The centerpiece of this effort was the proclamation in 1948 of the Universal Declaration of Human Rights.[15] The adoption of a large number of human rights conventions followed, including the two International Covenants on Human Rights in 1966. These two treaties, together with the human rights provisions of the Charter and the Universal Declaration, constitute the International Bill of Rights. Although the Universal Declaration was adopted as a nonbinding UN General Assembly resolution and was intended, as its preamble indicates, to provide "a common understanding" of the human rights and fundamental freedoms mentioned in the Charter, it has come to be accepted as a normative instrument in its own right. Together with the Charter, the Universal Declaration is now considered to spell out the general human rights obligations of all UN member states.

UN Human Rights Law and Practice

UN human rights law has evolved over the past sixty years along two parallel paths, one based on the UN Charter, the other on the human rights treaties adopted by the Organization. The Charter-based system comprises the human rights principles and institutional mechanisms that different UN organs have developed in the exercise of their Charter powers. The treaty-based system consists of a large number of human rights treaties drafted under UN auspices that codify much of the international human rights law in existence today. Some of these treaties also establish institutional mechanisms to monitor compliance by the states parties with the obligations imposed by these instruments.

The Charter-Based System

The UN Human Rights Council,[16] the successor to the Human Rights Commission, lies at the center of the Charter-based system, followed by the Commission on the Status of Women and various subsidiary bodies of the Council, such as the Sub-Commission on the Promotion and Protection of Human Rights, formerly the Sub-Commission on the Prevention of Discrimination and Protection of Minorities. Although the Human Rights Commission took the position into the mid-1960s that it lacked the power to act on violations of human rights brought to its attention, that attitude began to change as more and more newly independent states joined the United Nations and campaigned for UN antiapartheid measures. They argued that the United Nations had the requisite authority to take such action because a state that practiced apartheid could not be said to be "promoting" human rights without discrimination, as required by Articles 55 and 56 of the

Charter. This argument gradually prevailed, prompting the General Assembly to call on South Africa to end apartheid and on Southern Rhodesia to do away with its racial discrimination policies. The Economic and Social Council followed up with a series of resolutions on the subject. In one of the earliest, ECOSOC authorized the Human Rights Commission "to make a thorough study of situations which reveal a consistent pattern of violations of human rights, as exemplified by the policy of apartheid as practised in the Republic of South Africa. . . , and racial discrimination as practised notably in Southern Rhodesia."[17] This narrow mandate was expanded a few years later when ECOSOC empowered the Commission and its subcommission to act on complaints from groups and individuals that revealed "a consistent pattern of gross and reliably attested violations of human rights."[18] This resolution opened the way for the Commission and subcommission to deal with gross violations of human rights in general, that is, whether or not they involved apartheid or racial discrimination.

These and related ECOSOC resolutions enabled the Human Rights Commission gradually to develop a growing number of UN Charter–based mechanisms for dealing with large-scale human rights violations. Today the system consists of mushrooming rapporteur and special-mission components, as well as the Office of the United Nations High Commissioner for Human Rights with its own bureaucracy.[19] (It is too early to say what changes in this practice, if any, the newly established Human Rights Council will adopt.) These institutions derive their normative legitimacy from the Charter itself and from the Universal Declaration of Human Rights.[20]

The Treaty-Based System

The treaty-based human rights system of the United Nations began with the adoption by the General Assembly of the Convention on the Prevention and Punishment of the Crime of Genocide on December 9, 1948, one day before the proclamation of the Universal Declaration of Human Rights. Since then the United Nations has adopted a large number of human rights treaties.[21] The most important of these are the International Convention on the Elimination of All Forms of Racial Discrimination; the International Covenant on Civil and Political Rights and the International Covenant on Economic, Social and Cultural Rights; the International Convention on the Elimination of All Forms of Discrimination Against Women; the Convention on the Rights of the Child; and the Convention Against Torture and Other Cruel, Inhuman or Degrading Treatment or Punishment. With the exception of the Genocide Convention and the Covenant on Economic, Social and Cultural Rights, each of the foregoing treaties provides for a so-called "treaty body," which consists of a committee of independent experts that monitors compliance by the states parties with the obligations they assumed by ratifying these conventions. Some years after the Covenant on Economic, Social and Cultural Rights entered into force, ECOSOC created a similar body for that Covenant by resolution.[22]

Although the six treaty bodies in existence today are not judicial institutions, they have had to interpret and apply their respective conventions in reviewing and commenting on the periodic reports the states parties must submit to them, and in dealing with the individual complaints that some treaty bodies are authorized to receive. This practice has produced a substantial body of international human rights law. While one can debate the question of the nature of this law and whether or not it is law at all, the fact remains that the normative findings of the treaty bodies have legal significance, as evidenced by references to them in international and domestic judicial decisions.[23]

Over the years numerous states have ratified the human rights treaties the United Nations and its specialized agencies have adopted. These conventions not only have internationalized the subject of human rights as between the parties to them, but also to the same extent have internationalized the individual human rights these treaties guarantee. Since some of these treaties have been very widely ratified by member states of the international community, they may be viewed as creating an entire body of customary international human rights law. Nonstates parties may therefore find it increasingly difficult to claim that the human rights guarantees these treaties proclaim, particularly those from which derogation is not permitted, impose no legal obligations on them.

The General Assembly and the Security Council

Even in the days when the power of the General Assembly to deal with charges that member states were engaging in large-scale violations of human rights gave rise to lengthy debates based on Article 2(7) of the Charter, the Assembly was nevertheless able to adopt some resolutions calling on at least some of the states to stop these practices. Its early resolutions, however, tended to be rather mild or timid. But as time went by and it relied increasingly on a more expansive reading of the human rights provisions of the Charter and the normative significance of the Universal Declaration, the General Assembly became more assertive and demanding in its resolutions. In the case of particularly egregious violations, such as those involving apartheid, the General Assembly even invited states to impose sanctions.[24]

The nonbinding character of General Assembly resolutions tended to diminish their effectiveness as a tool for putting an end to large-scale violations of human rights. For many years, the Security Council, while having the power under Chapter VII of the Charter to adopt binding resolutions and to order enforcement measures, including economic sanctions and military action, could rarely agree on taking such measures, even in cases involving egregious human rights violations that could readily be characterized as a threat to the peace within the meaning of Article 39 of the Charter. That situation changed to a large extent with the end of the Cold War, which had prevented unanimity among the Council's permanent members. With increasing frequency, the Security Council has exercised its powers under Chapter VII in situations involving massive violations of human rights. What we are seeing today, despite the Council's ambivalence in dealing forcefully with the human tragedy being played out in Darfur, is the gradual emergence of a modern version of collective humanitarian intervention. This development can be attributed to the convergence of two important factors: the growing assertion of power by the Security Council in the post–Cold War era and the expanding willingness of the international community to confront massive violations of human rights with economic sanctions or force, if necessary.[25]

Overall Achievement of the United Nations

The most important contribution of the United Nations to the protection of human rights consists of the many human rights instruments—resolutions, declarations, and conventions—it has adopted since it came into being. These instruments, together with the human rights provisions of the Charter, laid the normative foundation of the contemporary international human rights revolution. They inspired the lawmaking processes that created the European, inter-American, and African human rights systems. They have also influenced, in part at least, the contents of the legal norms under which international criminal tribunals operate today.

The six UN treaty bodies, which currently supervise the implementation of the major UN human rights conventions, have played an important role over the years in strengthening the international human rights system. Although their powers are limited, these bodies have been able gradually to examine ever more intrusively the human rights policies and practices of the states parties to these conventions. This process—the review of the periodic reports these states must submit to the treaty bodies—has required the states publicly to explain and defend their human rights policies every few years. The very knowledge that their human rights policies will be scrutinized in this fashion by one or the other treaty body puts pressure on states to reexamine these policies and may lead to an improvement in the human rights situation in some countries at a minimum. This entire process also makes those states that are not parties to these treaties aware of the progressive internationalization of almost all aspects of their national human rights policies. That, in turn, cannot but have beneficial consequences in at least some countries as far as their human rights situations are concerned.

It must be recognized, however, that the United Nations and its various human rights institutions are largely ineffectual in dealing with individual human rights violations. Here, the regional human rights systems, dealt with below, are more effective. Unfortunately, regional human rights systems have been established in only three regions of the world, even though they are needed in every one. The UN system is better equipped to deal with large-scale violations of human rights, for which it commands the necessary political, military, and public relations resources. The great weakness of the UN system, particularly its Charter-based system, is its susceptibility to politicization. Politicization has resulted in the frequent condemnation of certain violators of human rights while others, some even more blatant, escape criticism. The replacement of the UN Human Rights Commission with the new Human Rights Council was designed to address this problem but is unlikely to resolve it, if only because the United Nations is a political body whose actions are determined by political considerations.[26] The Organization can do only what a majority of its member states want it to do, and many states prefer to do as little as possible about human rights violations, particularly those committed by their friends or allies. This reality is frequently lost sight of when UN human rights action or inaction is criticized.

Regional Human Rights Systems

The European Convention on Human Rights ushered in the first regional system for the protection of human rights. It was followed by the inter-American and African systems. All three of the existing systems seek in one form or another to supplement the human rights efforts of the United Nations by providing protective mechanisms suited to their regions. In addition to guaranteeing many of the human rights that various UN instruments proclaim, each regional system also codifies those rights to which the region attaches particular importance because of its political and legal traditions, its history and culture.

The European Human Rights System

The European Convention for the Protection of Human Rights and Fundamental Freedoms established what has become the most effective international system for the protection of individual human rights to date. It has also served as a model for the two other regional human rights systems. The Convention traces its origin to the late 1940s, when the states constituting the Council of Europe, then a grouping of Western European states only, concluded that UN efforts to produce a treaty transforming the lofty principles proclaimed in the Universal Declaration of Human Rights into a binding international bill of rights would take many years to come to fruition. Rather than wait, they decided that the Council of Europe should proceed on its own. The justification for not waiting was expressed in the preamble to the European Convention,[27] which stated that the members of the Council of Europe were "resolved, as the Governments of European countries which are like-minded and have a common heritage of political traditions, ideals, freedom and the rule of law, to take the first steps for the collective enforcement of certain of the rights stated in the Universal Declaration."[28]

By 1953, the ten ratifications necessary to bring the Convention into force had been deposited, and a total of forty-six states are now parties to it. This dramatic increase in its membership is due in large measure to the geopolitical transformation of Europe that resulted from the demise of the Soviet Union and the end of the Cold War. Today most European states are members of the Council of Europe and states parties to the Convention, including Russia and some former Soviet Republics, as well as the United Kingdom, France, and Germany. In the meantime, the Convention itself and the system it established have also been significantly transformed.

When the European Convention entered into force, it guaranteed only a dozen basic civil and political rights.[29] The list of these rights has grown significantly over the years with the adoption of additional protocols that have expanded the Convention's catalog of rights. In the meantime, these rights have been extensively interpreted by the Convention institutions and the national courts of the member states. In the process, the meaning and scope of these rights also have increasingly come to reflect the contemporary needs of European society. The result is a modern body of human rights law to which other international, regional, and national institutions frequently look when interpreting and applying their own human rights instruments.

In addition, the institutions of the European Convention have undergone extensive changes. The original Convention machinery consisted of a European Commission and Court of Human Rights. The main function of the Commission was to pass on the admissibility of all applications, both interstate and individual.[30] Of the various admissibility requirements, the exhaustion of domestic remedies occupied much of the Commission's time. Because not all states parties to the Convention had been required to accept the jurisdiction of the Court when they ratified the Convention,[31] the Commission also had to deal with cases that were not or could not be referred to the Court. At that time, only states and the Commission had standing to bring cases to the Court; individuals did not.

The institutional structure of the European system was substantially changed with the adoption of Protocol No. 11 to the Convention, which entered into force in 1998. It abolished the Commission and gave individuals direct access to the Court. The Convention thus became the first human rights treaty to give individuals standing to file cases directly with the appropriate tribunal. Today the European Court numbers forty-six judges, that is, a judge for each member state of the Council of Europe. The Plenary Court, which consists of all judges, exercises mainly administrative functions. The judicial work of the Court is performed by three bodies of judges: Committees (three judges), Chambers (seven judges), and the Grand Chamber (seventeen judges). The Committees are authorized to reject, by unanimous vote, individual applications as inadmissible. Chambers deal with the remaining admissibility issues and the merits of most interstate and individual applications. The Grand Chamber has a dual function. Under certain circumstances, particularly when a Chamber is called upon to decide serious questions of interpretation of the Convention or its protocols, it may opt to relinquish its jurisdiction in favor of the Grand Chamber. In certain "exceptional cases," the Grand Chamber may also act as an appellate tribunal and hear cases already decided by a Chamber.

Over time, the European Court of Human Rights for all practical purposes has become Europe's constitutional court in matters of civil and political rights.[32] Its judgments are routinely followed by the national courts of the states parties to the Convention, their legislatures, and their national governments. The Convention itself has acquired the status of domestic law in most of the states parties and can be invoked as such in their courts.[33] While at times some of the newer states parties find it difficult to live up to their obligations under the Convention, a substantial majority of states applies the Convention faithfully and routinely.

The success of the European Convention system has brought with it a caseload for the Court that it has found more and more difficult to cope with.[34] To address this problem, in 2004 the Council of Europe adopted Protocol No. 14 to the Convention.[35] Once it enters into force, the Protocol should enable the Court to reduce its caseload substantially by a variety of methods, some of which have not escaped criticism because they are likely to result, so it is claimed, in the automatic rejection of many meritorious cases.[36] It cannot be doubted, however, that the current caseload has become unmanageable, seriously impeding the effective implementation of the Convention.[37]

The Inter-American Human Rights System

When the Charter of the Organization of American States (OAS) was adopted in Bogotá, Colombia, in 1948, it made only general reference to human rights. But the same Bogotá conference also proclaimed the American Declaration of the Rights and Duties of Man, though merely in the form of a nonbinding conference resolution. Before the American Convention on Human Rights entered into force in 1978, the human rights provisions of the OAS Charter, read together with the American Declaration, provided the sole, albeit rather weak, legal basis for the protection of human rights by the OAS.[38]

Until 1960, the OAS made no serious effort to create a mechanism for the enforcement of these rights. That year the Inter-American Commission on Human Rights was established. Composed of seven independent experts elected by the General Assembly of the OAS, the Commission was charged with the promotion of the rights proclaimed in the American Declaration. It was to perform this task by preparing country studies and by adopting resolutions of a general character only. Six years later, the Commission was authorized to establish a limited petition system that allowed it to receive individual communications, charging large-scale violations of a selected number of basic rights set out in the American Declaration, including the right to life, equality before the law, freedom of religion, freedom from arbitrary arrest, and the right to due process of law. During this period, the Commission was hampered in the exercise of its functions because, rather than being a Charter organ, it was designated an "autonomous entity" of the OAS, which denied it the requisite constitutional status to be taken seriously by the member states. This unsatisfactory state of affairs was remedied in 1970 with the entry into force of the Protocol of Buenos Aires. It amended the OAS Charter and transformed the Commission into a Charter organ whose "principal function shall be to promote the observance and protection of human rights and to serve as a consultative organ of the Organization in these matters."[39]

In the early years of its existence, both as autonomous entity and later as Charter organ, the Commission was kept busy preparing reports on human rights situations in various countries. These reports were grounded in on-site visits and information in petitions presented to it. The Commission adopted its first country reports in the early 1960s.[40] These dealt with the human rights situations in Cuba, Haiti, and the Dominican Republic. Only the Dominican Republic granted permission for a visit to the country, making it the first OAS member state to host a so-called *in loco* or on-site investigation by the Commission. During that on-site visit, the Commission criss-crossed the country, held hearings, and met with different groups of claimants. This modus operandi was subsequently adopted for on-site visits generally. The Commission's most dramatic on-site investigation took place in Argentina. There it verified the allegations of the massive forced disappearances that had occurred in that country during its "dirty war." The publication of its report on the Argentine situation had a highly beneficial impact on conditions in that country.[41] For many years, even after the entry into force of the American Convention on Human Rights, the Commission's *in loco* investigations occupied much of its time, primarily because in the 1960s, 1970s, and early 1980s many Latin American countries continued to be ruled by authoritarian regimes that engaged in widespread violations of human rights. Most of these states did not, of course, ratify the Convention until the installation of democratic regimes in their countries. The investigations and reports of the Commission provided the only means for pressuring these states to improve their human rights conditions.

The American Convention on Human Rights was concluded in San José, Costa Rica, in 1969 and came into force in 1978. Like the European Convention, the American Convention guarantees only civil and political rights.[42] While the list of rights the European Convention guarantees has grown with the adoption of further protocols, the drafters of the American Convention opted for a comprehensive instrument that drew heavily on the much more extensive catalog of rights enumerated in the International Covenant on Civil and Political Rights. However, not all the rights guaranteed in the American Convention are derived from the Civil and Political Covenant. Some of them reflect the historical and cultural traditions of the Americas, such as the provision that guarantees the right to life. It provides, inter alia, that this right "shall be protected by law and, in general, from the moment of conception."[43] Delegates from Latin America's overwhelmingly Catholic countries insisted on this provision during the drafting of the Convention.

The institutional structure of the American Convention is modeled on that of the European Convention as originally drafted, that is, before its Protocol No. 11 entered into force. The American Convention provides for a seven-member Inter-American Commission on Human Rights and an Inter-American Court of Human Rights of seven judges. Because the Commission established by the Convention retains the powers its predecessor exercised as an OAS Charter organ, all OAS member states have the right to nominate and elect the members of the Commission. But only the states parties to the Convention may nominate and elect the judges of the Court. Since to date not all OAS member states have ratified the Convention, the Commission continues to apply the human rights provisions of the Charter and the American Declaration of the Rights and Duties of Man to these states, besides acting as a Convention organ with regard to the states parties to that instrument. Importantly, this dual role of the Commission permits it to deal with massive violations of human rights that, though not within its jurisdiction as a Convention organ, it can address as a Charter organ regardless of whether or not the state in question is a party to the Convention. By contrast, the European Convention applies in principle only to individual human rights violations as such.

By ratifying the American Convention, states are automatically considered to have accepted the jurisdiction of the Commission to hear cases brought against them by individuals. Interstate complaints can be heard by the Commission only if the applicant and respondent states have each filed a separate declaration accepting the Commission's jurisdiction to receive such complaints. Until Protocol No. 11 to the European Convention on Human Rights entered into force, no other human rights instrument conferred on individuals the favorable status they enjoy under the American Convention. The Inter-American Commission passes on the admissibility of individual and interstate communications. If the matter is not referred to the Inter-American Court, the Commission examines the merits of the case, assists in efforts to work out a friendly settlement, and, failing that, makes findings on the merits. If the state party in question has accepted the jurisdiction of the Court, the Commission or an interested state may refer the case to the Court. Individuals have no standing to do so. Nevertheless, since 2001, once a case has been referred to the Court, individuals have been permitted to appear before it to plead their case.[44] While in the early years of the Court's existence, the Commission tended to refer cases to it rarely, this situation changed in 2001 when it adopted new Rules of Procedure,[45] which provide, with some minor exceptions, for referral to the Court of all cases of noncompliance by states with the Commission's recommendations.[46]

Today the Inter-American Court of Human Rights, which has both contentious and advisory jurisdiction, plays an ever more important role in the inter-American human rights system. Most of the states that have ratified the Convention to date have now also accepted the Court's contentious jurisdiction. The American Convention, moreover, allows OAS member states, whether or not they have ratified the Convention, and all OAS organs to request advisory opinions from the Court, seeking the interpretation of the Convention or of other human rights treaties of the inter-American system. Advisory opinions may also be sought on the compatibility with the Convention of national legislation.[47] Because the Court's case law has grown significantly since the adoption of the Commission's 2001 Rules of Procedure, states find it increasingly necessary to bring their national legislation and judicial practice into conformity with the Convention to avoid being held in violation of it.

The inter-American human rights system still lags behind its European counterpart in protecting human rights. The American continent continues to suffer from widespread poverty, corruption, discrimination, and illiteracy, not to mention archaic judicial systems that are badly in need of reform. The United States and Canada, as well as some of the Commonwealth Caribbean nations, have not yet ratified the Convention. Their absence has had a detrimental effect on the system, which it deprives of the participation of states with strong legal traditions in the human rights field. Although some national courts in the Americas have also been taking a long time to familiarize themselves with the practice of the Convention institutions and to give domestic legal effect to the rulings of the Court, that situation has improved. Moreover, notwithstanding the problems the region faces, substantial progress has undeniably been made over the years in the protection of human rights in the Americas.

The African Human Rights System

The African human rights system evolved in two distinct stages in a manner somewhat similar to that of its inter-American counterpart. The first stage consisted of the adoption in 1981 by the Organization of African Unity, now the African Union, of the African Charter on Human and Peoples' Rights. It entered into force in 1986 and in the meantime has been ratified by all fifty-three member states of the African Union. The Charter created an African Commission on Human and Peoples' Rights, but not a court. The African Court of Human and Peoples' Rights was established later by means of a separate protocol that came into force in 2004. The Court was formally inaugurated only in 2006.

The catalog of rights that the African Charter guarantees differs from its European and inter-American counterparts in several important respects. The Charter proclaims not only rights but also duties, and it guarantees both individual and peoples' rights. In addition to civil and political rights, the African Charter sets out a series of economic and social rights. The Charter permits the states parties to impose more extensive restrictions and limitations on the exercise of the rights it proclaims than the European and inter-American human rights instruments. It also does not contain a derogation clause, which leaves the question open whether all rights in the African Charter are derogable. The Charter's catalog of rights was heavily influenced by the rights proclaimed in the Universal Declaration of Human Rights and the two International Covenants on Human Rights. African historical traditions and customs are also reflected in some provisions of the Charter, particularly those dealing with duties of individuals and family matters.[48]

The Commission's mandate is "to promote human and peoples' rights and ensure their protection in Africa."[49] It is composed of eleven elected members who serve in their individual capacities. The Commission has promotional and quasi-judicial powers. It discharges its promotional functions by preparing studies, convening conferences and workshops, disseminating information, and collaborating with NGOs. The Commission has the power to make recommendations to governments, calling on them to address human rights problems that have come to its attention from its review of the periodic country reports the states parties are required to submit to it, as well as from other sources, including its own on-site visits and country studies.

The Commission is also empowered to render interpretive opinions and to deal with interstate and individual complaints. The states parties, the African Union, and intergovernmental African organizations recognized by the latter may request advisory opinions from the Commission regarding interpretation of the African Charter on Human and Peoples' Rights.[50] These advisory powers acquire a special significance in light of two Charter provisions. One of these is Article 60, which reads as follows:

> The Commission shall draw inspiration from international law on human and peoples' rights, particularly from the provisions of various African instruments on human and peoples' rights, the Charter of the United Nations, the Charter of the [African Union], the Universal Declaration of Human Rights, other instruments adopted by the United Nations and by African countries in the field of human and peoples' rights as well as from the provisions of various instruments adopted within the Specialized Agencies of the United Nations of which the parties to the present Charter are members.[51]

The other provision is Article 61. It contains the following language:

> The Commission shall also take into consideration, as subsidiary measures to determine the principles of law, other general or special international conventions, laying down rules expressly recognized by member states of the [African Union], African practices consistent with international norms on human and peoples' rights, customs generally accepted as law, general principles of law recognized by African states as well as legal precedents and doctrine.[52]

These interesting and unique provisions provide the Commission with a valuable legislative tool capable of ensuring that its interpretations of the African Charter keep pace with developments in the international human rights field in general. Through the years, the Commission has increasingly relied on these provisions with a view to strengthening the normative contents of the African Charter.[53]

The powers of the African Commission to deal with interstate and individual communications are much more limited than those conferred by the European and inter-American human rights treaties. The Commission is so constrained in part because its findings with regard to the communications it receives cannot be made public without the permission of the African Union's Assembly of Heads of State and Government, a political body that has traditionally not been inclined to take strong action against serious violators of human rights. The Commission's power to deal with individual petitions is limited, furthermore, to "cases which reveal the existence of a series of serious or massive violations of human and peoples' rights."[54] Thus, what we have here is not really a mechanism for individual petitions as it exists in the two other regional human rights systems. It is, rather, a procedure that permits individuals to file petitions charging massive or persistent violations of human rights, but not individual violations of one or the other right guaranteed by the African Charter. It is worth noting, though, that in the past the African Commission found ways around this problem by hearing claims that on their face may not have met the strict requirements of the above provision.

The new African Court of Human and Peoples' Rights, whose function it is to "complement the protective mandate" of the African Commission,[55] has contentious and advisory jurisdiction. Its contentious jurisdiction is broader than that of the European and inter-American Courts; it extends to disputes arising not only under the Charter and the Protocol establishing the Court, but also "under any other relevant Human Rights instrument ratified by the States concerned."[56] On its face, this broad language would permit the Court to adjudicate disputes between African states even with regard to non-African human rights instruments to which they are parties. The Court's contentious jurisdiction covers cases filed by the African Commission, states parties that are applicants and respondents in cases heard before the Commission, states parties whose citizens are victims of human rights violations, and African intergovernmental organizations. NGOs with observer status before the Commission and individuals as such may also institute proceedings before the Court, provided the state party against which the case is filed previously recognized that right in a separate declaration.[57]

The Court also has extensive advisory jurisdiction powers.[58] These are spelled out in Article 4(1) of the Protocol, which reads as follows:

> At the request of a Member State of the [African Union], the [AU], any of its organs, or any African organization recognized by the [AU], the Court may provide an opinion on any legal matter relating to the Charter or any other relevant human rights instruments, provided that the subject matter of the opinion is not related to a matter being examined by the Commission.[59]

It remains to be seen how the Court will interpret the phrase "any other relevant human rights instruments" in dealing with requests for advisory opinions. This open-ended language might be read to permit the Court to render advisory opinions relating to any human rights instruments whatsoever. It might also be argued that the reference to "relevant" instruments was intended to indicate that Article 4(1) referred only to human rights instruments relevant to the interpretation of the Charter.

Since the African Court came into being only in 2006, we cannot know how it will interpret the important powers the Protocol confers on it or how long it will take for it to make a significant contribution to the protection of human and peoples' rights in Africa. The future of the Court has been further complicated by the African Union's conclusion of yet another Protocol that calls for the establishment of an African Court of Justice.[60] When this Protocol enters into force, the new court is supposed to be merged with the African Court of Human and Peoples' Rights. What impact such a merger will have on the latter Court's role is still too early to say. Moreover, the political, economic, and social problems Africa faces are much more severe than the comparable problems that plague the Americas or Europe. In addition to severe poverty and corruption, the African continent continues to be the victim of wars and internal armed conflicts that have killed millions of human beings, while AIDS is ravaging the entire populations of some countries. Africa has also not been able to rid itself of authoritarian regimes, some of which still hold power. It will therefore not be easy in the short term for the African Court and Commission to create an effective regional human rights system.

Other Developments

The Charter of the United Nations and the human rights instruments and machinery it has spawned, together with the three regional human rights institutions described in the preceding sections, mark the centerpiece of the contemporary international human rights system. But there is much more to that system.[61] It comprises, inter alia, the human rights instruments and protection mechanisms adopted by various specialized agencies of the United Nations, among them in particular the International Labour Organization and the United Nations Educational, Scientific and Cultural Organization. Other intergovernmental organizations, notably the Organization for Security and Co-operation in Europe, have also made significant contributions to the protection of human rights in recent decades. Developments in the human rights field that deserve special mention include the continuing normative and institutional efforts to strengthen the enjoyment of internationally proclaimed economic, social, and cultural rights and the protection of minorities and other vulnerable groups, among them internally displaced persons and indigenous populations. As the contents of the Declaration and Programme of Action adopted at the 1993 World Conference on Human Rights in Vienna demonstrated, the contemporary international human rights agenda is an ever-expanding work in progress. This fact is also readily apparent from the recent developments described below.

International Criminal Tribunal

In the 1990s, following the Rwandan genocide and the horrendous crimes that were then being committed in the Balkan conflict, the international community finally realized that existing human rights mechanisms were not effective in dealing with such crimes and that the creation of international tribunals with jurisdiction to try the individuals responsible for those crimes was essential. As a result, the UN Security Council established the International Criminal Tribunal for the Former Yugoslavia and the International Criminal Tribunal for Rwanda, the first such international criminal courts to come into being in more than half a century after the Nuremberg and Tokyo war crimes tribunals. In addition, the need to establish these tribunals on an ad hoc basis in the absence of a permanent international criminal court revived long-dormant efforts to create such a court, which bore fruit in 2002 with the entry into force of the Rome Statute of the International Criminal Court. Today some hundred states are parties to the Rome Statute.

The establishment of these three tribunals, as well as other ad hoc international criminal tribunals, constitutes a further important step in the long struggle to protect human rights. The earlier focus on developing and strengthening the legal norms and institutions that would hold states responsible for the human rights violations by their governments frequently proved to be ineffective in getting at the root of the problem, for it failed to provide adequate mechanisms to punish the individuals who had ordered or committed large-scale violations of human rights. As a rule, the governments that were held liable for the violations had come to power when the culpable regimes were no longer in charge. Moreover, the former leaders who had oppressed the people, and frequently also impoverished the country while enriching themselves, were often living in opulent retirement. All these considerations compelled the conclusion that the traditional remedy needed to be reinforced with international judicial mechanisms allowing the criminal prosecution of the individuals responsible for serious human rights violations that amounted to offenses under international criminal law. This is the mandate of the permanent International Criminal Court, which has its seat in The Hague, Netherlands.

Truth Commissions

Truth commissions are another type of institution that has come into being in recent decades: ad hoc bodies that fit somewhere between traditional human rights institutions and international criminal tribunals. Truth commissions are usually set up to investigate large-scale violations of human rights committed in a country during a protracted civil war or following the demise of a particularly brutal regime.[62] In addition to investigating these events, truth commissions are frequently charged with recommending measures for national reconciliation, including the preparation of impartial accounts of the causes that led to a given conflict. The composition of truth commissions has tended to vary from country to country. Some have been national commissions, others have been mixed, consisting of nationals and foreign members, while still others have been international in that they were composed entirely of foreigners. The best-known national truth and reconciliation commissions were those established in Argentina and South Africa. The truth commission in Guatemala, for example, was mixed, whereas the United Nations Truth Commission for El Salvador was composed entirely of foreign nationals. The establishment of the Guatemalan and Salvadoran truth commissions was provided for in the UN-sponsored peace agreements that the insurgents in those two countries concluded with their respective governments.

Nongovernmental Organizations

Another important and relatively recent development can be seen in the phenomenal growth of human rights NGOs.[63] As UN and regional human rights institutions have multiplied, so have NGOs that monitor, promote, and criticize their activities. Some of them were created to advance the protection of human rights in general or in various organizations, such as the United Nations; others concern themselves only with the regional human rights bodies or institutions, for example, the Organization for Security and Co-operation in Europe. Some NGOs are international in character and have offices or links in different regions of the world; others work only at the national level. Depending upon their charters, these organizations perform a variety of functions. They represent petitioners before international judicial and quasi-judicial human rights institutions; they lobby national and international political bodies on human rights issues; and they publicize human rights violations in their own countries or abroad. Some of them focus on one specific issue, such as health; others deal with a whole range of issues. A few NGOs prepare reports on human rights conditions in specific countries. They frequently submit these reports to UN human rights rapporteurs and to members of UN human rights treaty bodies to challenge the claims governments make in their official periodic human rights reports. Similar NGO reports may also be presented to international and national aid agencies that take human rights conditions into account in making country-finding decisions. NGOs regularly advocate the ratification of human rights conventions, the conclusion of additional human rights treaties, and the creation of new human rights mechanisms. Powerful coalitions of NGOs also contributed significantly to garnering governmental support for the establishment of the International Criminal Court and the ratification of its Statute.

As a group, the human rights NGOs have been playing an ever more important role in helping to transform the conglomerate of weak institutions that constitute the international human rights system into an institutional machinery that will make it increasingly more difficult for states to give mere lip service to their international human rights obligations. In this connection, it is worth remembering that the adoption of the large number of international and regional human rights instruments now on the books not only internationalized the subject of human rights; it also legitimated the activities of NGOs in promoting these rights and thus contributed to their growth. Some states still try to characterize their national or some international NGOs as subversive institutions or seek to outlaw them for a variety of other reasons, but these efforts are often hampered by the growing political status and influence of the organizations. Taken together, NGOs have become a powerful pressure group in the service of international human rights.

Human Rights in Domestic Legal Orders

The proliferation of human rights treaties and the emergence of international and regional human rights tribunals with jurisdiction to interpret and apply these treaties have prompted an increasing number of states to accord human rights treaties a special status in their national constitutions. That status facilitates the domestic implementation of the decisions of these tribunals. It also contributes to a legal and political climate in the countries concerned that enables their judiciaries and legislatures to take international and regional human rights obligations into account without having to face some of the constitutional obstacles that have traditionally impeded effective domestic compliance with international judicial and quasi-judicial decisions.

Various countries in Europe and the Americas have pioneered these constitutional changes, influenced in part by their past experience with dictatorial regimes and the emergence in those regions of strong human rights systems, which were created in part to prevent the return to power of such regimes. One of the most interesting constitutional provisions in this regard is Article 10(2) of the Spanish Constitution of 1978, which reads as follows: "The norms relative to basic rights and liberties which are recognized by the Constitution shall be interpreted in conformity with the Universal Declaration of Human Rights and the international treaties and agreements on those matters ratified by Spain." In complying with this provision, Spanish courts have looked not only to the language of the Universal Declaration and the human rights treaties to which Spain is a party, but also to the case law of international tribunals interpreting these treaties, in particular the judgments of the European Court of Human Rights. As a practical matter, this approach has had the effect of transforming the European Court's judgments into Spanish constitutional jurisprudence. Other countries, among them Argentina, have conferred constitutional rank on human rights treaties. Argentina did so when it amended its Constitution in 1994 and adopted a new Article 75(22). That provision confers constitutional rank on various international human rights instruments, including the American Convention on Human Rights and the two International Covenants on Human Rights. Also included in that list are the Universal Declaration of Human Rights and the American Declaration of the Rights and Duties of Man. The reference to the latter two instruments, both adopted in the form of nonbinding resolutions, no doubt reflects the view of some states that these declarations have acquired a normative character.[64] Another constitutional development worth noting is the amendment by Costa Rica of its Constitution in 1989, which established a constitutional chamber within the Supreme Court. The legislation implementing the amendment granted the new chamber the power, inter alia, to issue writs of habeas corpus and *amparo* to protect individuals claiming the denial of rights guaranteed them under both the Costa Rican Constitution and any human rights treaty ratified by that state. In this regard, it is also noteworthy that the Austrian law ratifying the European Convention on Human Rights declared the treaty to have the normative rank of a constitutional law.

A large number of countries, particularly in Europe and Latin America, consider many provisions of various human rights treaties, especially those guaranteeing civil and political rights such as the European and American Conventions and the International Covenant on Civil and Political Rights to be self-executing in character. As such, they become directly applicable domestic law. In other countries, incorporating legislation is required to make a treaty provision directly applicable. The United Kingdom, for example, promulgated such a law in 1998 with respect to the European Convention on Human Rights. Some other countries have adopted similar measures.[65]

The foregoing national constitutional developments hold great importance for the protection of human rights. They make it possible for international human rights treaties and the decisions of international tribunals applying these instruments to have a direct impact on the domestic administration of justice. That, in the long run, is the best way to ensure the effective implementation of internationally guaranteed human rights.

Human Rights in International Relations

The activities of international and regional human rights institutions, as well as the work of human rights NGOs, have gradually changed governmental perceptions of the role human rights play in contemporary international relations. The decision of the Carter administration to elevate human rights to a high-priority item on the foreign policy agenda of the United States not only reflected the political importance it attached to the protection of human rights. The decision had a domino effect, leading some other governments to take similar positions and helping to transform a subject that had been treated as generally irrelevant from the point of view of Realpolitik into an issue that gradually gained substantial international political significance. As a result, more and more human rights issues began to appear on the agendas of intergovernmental conferences and bilateral diplomatic meetings. As international human rights gained currency, an increasing number of governments established special bureaus in their foreign or justice ministries to deal with such matters, giving the subject domestic bureaucratic relevance and policymaking clout it had not previously enjoyed.

All these recent developments have obviously not put an end to the many violations of human rights that are still victimizing millions of human beings in different parts of the world. It would be a mistake not to recognize, however, that with each passing day states find it politically more costly to engage in or tolerate massive violations of human rights. That phenomenon, in turn, has doubtless influenced many a government and its leaders to desist from pursuing policies likely to have serious economic and political consequences for them. Some of these consequences may consist of the loss of financial assistance from multinational or national funding agencies that today make their grants dependent on a country's human rights policies and practices. Other economic consequences may involve a reluctance of foreign corporations to invest in countries with poor human rights records. Similar considerations may also keep a country out of intergovernmental organizations or groupings, such as the Council of Europe and the European Union, that demand strict adherence to human rights standards by applicant countries. Increasingly, too, countries that blatantly disregard their human rights obligations are coming to be seen as international pariahs, a status that invariably hurts their economic development, leads to political isolation, and may result in the imposition of economic sanctions.

Conclusion

As this overview of the evolution of the contemporary international human rights system demonstrates, this branch of international law has experienced phenomenal growth over the past one hundred years. When the first volume of the *American Journal of International Law* was published in 1907, human beings qua human beings had no rights under international law. Today international law accords individuals a plethora of internationally guaranteed human rights. But because so much international human rights law has come into force and so many intergovernmental institutions have been created to give effect to it, one might be led to believe that the system as a whole is functioning well and that it is effective in protecting rights of human beings the world over. That is certainly not true! Although the international human rights system as it exists today is undeniably functioning better than many would have believed possible twenty or thirty years ago, it has not prevented the massive violations that have been, and continue to be, committed in many parts of the world. Equally, though, the system in place today—and here I refer not only to the formal institutions and legal norms, but also to the work being done by NGOs and various human rights bureaucracies both national and intergovernmental—has saved lives, improved the human rights conditions in many countries, and is succeeding in forcing an increasing number of governments to take their human rights obligations more seriously than before. That is progress regardless of how one defines it.

One phenomenon above all others has been a major contributing factor to the growing political impact of human rights on the conduct of international relations and the behavior of governments: the ever more pervasive and readily observable conviction of human beings around the world that they are entitled to the enjoyment of human rights. This phenomenon, I would argue, has taken on almost universal proportions and is attributable to several factors. First is the massive corpus of human rights legislation that the United Nations, its specialized agencies, and various regional organizations have promulgated and publicized over the years. Of equal impact is the growing importance the international community has come to attach to human rights as a priority item on the agendas of international diplomatic conferences and in bilateral and multilateral relations. This development grew out of the decades-long efforts by various NGOs and a handful of governments to call attention to human rights violations, to stigmatize the violators, and, in general, to make international human rights law more effective. Not to be overlooked, finally, is the global electronic communications explosion. It has played and continues to play an important role in focusing the world's attention almost instantaneously on violations of human rights no matter where they occur. While over the years some government leaders in various countries and different extremist political groups have sought in a variety of ways to undermine these developments, their efforts have on the whole been unsuccessful. They have been unable to halt what has become a worldwide movement that has captured the imagination of human beings yearning to be treated humanely and with dignity.

Notes

1. *See* Philip Marshall Brown, *The Individual and International Law,* 18 AJIL 532(1924); André N. Mandelstam, *La protection internationale des droits & l'homme,* 38 RECUEIL DES COURS 125 (1931 IV).

2. The authoritative French text is reproduced in 2 ANNUAIRE DE L'INSTITUT DE DROIT INTERNATIONAL 298 (1929), and reprinted in part in James Brown Scott, Editorial Comment: Nationality, 24 AJIL 556, 560 (1930). An unofficial English translation can be found in George A. Finch, *The International Rights of Man,* 35 AJIL 662, 663–64 (1941) [hereinafter Declaration]. In that Editorial Comment, Finch claims that President Franklin D. Roosevelt's 1941 "Four Freedoms" speech was influenced by the Declaration.

3. Declaration, *supra* note 2, pmbl., & Arts. I, II.

4. Philip Marshall Brown, *The New York Session of the Institut de Droit International* 24 AJIL 126, 127 (1930).

5. *Id.*

6. *Id.*

7. 1 L. OPPENHEIM, INTERNATIONAL LAW: A TREATISE 509 n.4 (Hersch Laucerpacht ed., 5th ed 1937).

8. *See, e.g.,* Minority Schools in Albania, Advisory Opinion, 1935 PCIJ (ser. A/B) No. 64 (Apr. 6); Questions Relating to Settlers of German Origin in Poland, Advisory Opinion, 1923 PCI (set. B) No. 6 (Sept. 10). See also the fascinating advisory opinion Consistency of Certain Danzig Legislative Decrees with the Constitution of the Free City, 1935 PCIJ (ser. A/B) No.65 (Dec. 4). *See generally* PABLO DE AZCÁRATE, LEAGUE OF NATIONS AND NATIONAL MINORITIES (1945); TENNENT H. BAGLEY, INTERNATIONAL PROTECTION OF NATIONAL MINORITIES (1950).

9. On the role of NGOs at the San Francisco Conference, see WILLIAM KOREY, NGOs AND THE UNIVERSAL DECLARATION OF HUMAN RIGHTS: "A CURIOUS GRAPEVINE" 29(1998).

10. For the reasons motivating these powers, see Thomas Buergenthal, *The Normative and Institutional Evolution of International Human Rights,* 19 HUM. RTS. Q. 703, 706–07 (1997).

11. In addition to these provisions, the Charter contains Articles 13(1), 62(2), and 68, which authorize the General Assembly and the Economic and Social Council to initiate human rights studies and make recommendations in the human rights field. Note that, in this connection, Article 68 authorized ECOSOC to set up "commissions in economic and social fields and for the promotion of human rights." This mandate was implemented as soon as the United Nations came into being, with the establishment of the UN Human Rights Commission.

12. Article 2(7) reads as follows:

Nothing contained in the present Charter shall authorize the United Nations to intervene in matters which are essentially within the domestic jurisdiction of any state or shall require the Members to submit such matters to settlement under the present Charter; but this principle shall not prejudice the application of enforcement measures under Chapter VII.

13. For an analysis of these arguments, see Thomas Buergenthal, *Domestic Jurisdiction, Intervention, and Human Rights: The International Law Perspective, in* HUMAN RIGHTS AND U.S. FOREIGN POLICY: PRINCIPLES AND APPLICATIONS 111 (Peter Brown & Douglas MacLean eds., 1977); Felix Ermacora, *Human Rights and Domestic Jurisdiction (Article 7, para. 7 of the Charter),* 124 RECUEIL DES COURS 371(1968II); Louis Henkin, *Domestic Jurisdiction, in* HUMAN RIGHTS, INTERNATIONAL LAW AND DOMESTIC JURISDICTION 21 (Thomas Buergenthal ed., 1977).

14. For the relevant UN practice under Articles 55(c) and 56, see 2 THE CHARTER OF THE UNITED NATIONS: A COMMENTARY 897–943 (Bruno

Simma ed., 2002). *See also* LA CHARTE DES NATIONS UNIES 865–93 (Jean-Pierre Cot & Alain Pellet eds., 2d ed. 1991); Hurst Hannum, *Human Rights, in* UNITED NATIONS LEGAL ORDER 319 (Oscar Schachter & Christopher C. Joyner eds., 1995).

15. Universal Declaration of Human Rights, GA Res. 217A (III), UN Doc. A/810, at 71(1948); *see* John Humphrey, *The Universal Declaration of Human Rights: Its History, Impact and Juridical Character, in* HUMAN RIGHTS: THIRTY YEARS AFTER THE UNIVERSAL DECLARATION 21 (Bertrand Ramcharan ed., 1979).

16. *See* GA Res. 60/251 (Mar. 15, 2006) (establishing the Council).

17. ECOSOC Res. 1235 (XLII), para. 3 (June 6, 1967).

18. ECOSOC Res. 1503 (XLVIII), para. 1 (May 27, 1970).

19. *See* Nigel Rodley, *United Nations Non-Treaty Procedures for Dealing with Human Rights Violations, in* GUIDE TO INTERNATIONAL HUMAN RIGHTS PRACTICE 70 (Hurst Hannum ed., 3d ed. 1999). See also BEATE RUDOLF, DIE THEMATISCHEN BERICHT-ERSTAYER UND ARBEITSGRUPPEN DER UN-MENSCHENRECHTSKOMMISSION (2000).

20. *See* HOWARD B. TOLLEY JR., THE U.N. COMMISSION ON HUMAN RIGHTS (1987); Philip Alston, *The Commission on Human Rights, in* THE UNITED NATIONS AND HUMAN RIGHTS: A CRITICAL APPRAISAL 126, 138 (Philip Alston ed., 1992) [hereinafter A CRITICAL APPRAISAL]; Asbjørn Eide, *The Sub-Commission on Prevention of Discrimination and Protection of Minorities, in id.* at 211.

21. See the multivolume, periodically updated UN publication, HUMAN RIGHTS: A COMPILATION OF INTERNATIONAL INSTRUMENTS, UN Doc. ST/HR/1/Rev.6, UN Sales No. E.02.XIV.4 (2002).

22. ECOSOC Res. 17 (May 28, 1985); *see* Philip Alston, *The Committee on Economic, Social and Cultural Rights,* in A CRITICAL APPRAISAL, *supra* note 20, at 473; *see generally* THE UN HUMAN RIGHTS TREATY SYSTEM IN THE 21ST CENTURY (Anne F. Bayefsky ed., 2000).

23. *See, e.g.,* Legal Consequences of the Construction of a Wall in the Occupied Palestinian Territory, Advisory Opinion, 2004 ICJ REP. 136 (July 9); Pratt & Morgan v. Attorney Gen. for Jam., [1994] 2 App. Cas. (P.C. 1993) (appeal taken from Ct. App. Jam.).

24. *See generally* LOUIS B. SOHN, RIGHTS IN CONFLICT: THE UNITED NATIONS & SOUTH AFRICA (1994).

25. For a thorough analysis of the subject, see THEODOR MERON, THE HUMANIZATION OF HUMAN RIGHTS 510–17(2006). See also Mariano Aznar-Gómez, *A Decade of Human Rights Protection by the Security Council: A Sketch of Deregulation?* 13 EUR. J. INT'L L. 223 (2002); Christopher Le Mon & Rachel Taylor, *Security Council Action in the Name of Human Rights: From Rhodesia to the Congo,* 10 U.C. DAVIS J. INT'L L. & POL'Y 198 (2004).

26. *See* Hillel C. Neuer, *So Far, a Profound Disappointment; UN Human Rights Council,* INT'L HERALD TRIB., Sept. 8, 2006, at 8.

27. For the political reasons prompting this action by the Council of Europe, see ARTHUR H. ROBERTSON & JOHN C. MERRILLS, HUMAN RIGHTS IN EUROPE: A STUDY OF THE EUROPEAN CONVENTION ON HUMAN RIGHTS (4th ed. 2001).

28. European Convention for the Protection of Human Rights and Fundamental Freedoms, pmbl., Nov. 4, 1950, 213 UNTS 221 [hereinafter European Convention].

29. Various categories of economic and social rights are protected in a separate Council of Europe treaty, the European Social Charter, which entered into force in 1964. *See generally* DAVID HARRIS & JOHN DARCY, THE EUROPEAN SOCIAL CHARTER (2d ed. 2001).

30. Under Article 24 of the Convention, the Commission had automatic jurisdiction to deal with any case referred to it by one state party against another state party. But Article 25 authorized individuals to bring cases to the Commission against a state party only if the state had filed a declaration with the Commission recognizing the right of private petition to do so.

31. For the Court to have jurisdiction to hear any case referred to it by either the Commission or a state party required a prior declaration by the state party accepting the Court's jurisdiction under the Article 46 that was then in force.

32. *Sec* Christian Walter, Die Europäische Menschenrechtskonvention als Konstitutionalisierungsprozess, 59 HEIDELBERG J. INT'L. L. 961 (1999).

33. Jörg Polakiewicz & Valerie Jacob-Foltzer, *The European Human Rights Convention in Domestic Law: The Impact of Strasbourg Case-Law in States where Direct Effect Is Given to the Convention,* 12 HUM. RTS. L. J. 65, 125 (1991).

34. The caseload is staggering. In 2005 Lord Henry Woolf reported that in 2004, 44,100 new applications were lodged and that the number of pending cases before the Court—82,100 in 2005—would rise to 250,000 by the year 2010. Lord Woolf, *Review of the Working Methods of the European Court of Human Rights,* 26 HUM. RTS. L. J. 447 (2005).

35. Protocol No. 14 to the Convention for the Protection of Human Rights and Fundamental Freedoms, Amending the Control System of the Convention, May 13, 2004, 26 HUM. RTS. L. J. 88 (2005), *available at* <http://conventions.coe.int/Treaty/en/Treaties/Html/194.htm>.

36. *See* Philip Leach, Access to the European Court of Human Rights—From a Legal Entitlement to a Lottery? 27 HUM. RTS. L. J. 11 (2006).

37. M. Eaton & J. Schokkernbroek, *Reforming the Human Rights Protection System Established by the European Convention on Human Rights,* 26 HUM. RTS. L. J. 1(2005).

38. On the inter-American human rights system in general, see HECTOR FAUNDEZ-LEDESMA, EL SISTEMA INTERAMERICANO DE PROTECCIÓN DE LOS DERECHOS HUMANOS: ASPECTOS INSTITUCIONALES Y PROCESALES (2d ed. 1999); THOMAS BUERGENTHAL & DINAH SHELTON, PROTECTING HUMAN RIGHTS IN THE AMERICAS: CASES AND MATERIALS (4th ed. 1995).

39. OAS Charter, *as amended,* Arts. 51, 112(1), now Arts. 53, 106(1), available at<http://www.oas.org/main/english/>; *see generally* Thomas Buergenthal, The Revised OAS Charter and the Protection of Human Rights, 69 AJIL 828 (1975).

40. These first reports are reproduced in OAS SECRETARIAT, THE ORGANIZATION OF AMERICAN STATES AND HUMAN RIGHTS: 1960–1967, pt. III (1972).

41. Inter-Am. Comm'n on Human Rights. Report on the Situation of Human Rights in Argentina, OEA/Ser.L/V/II.49, doc. 19, corr. 1 (1980).

42. Economic, social, and cultural rights are dealt with in a parallel treaty of the Organization of American States, namely, the Additional Protocol to the American Convention on Human Rights in the Area of Economic, Social and Cultural Rights—the "Protocol of San Salvador"—which entered into force on November 16, 1999. For a review of the various inter-American instruments relating to these rights and the relevant practice under them, see Fabián Salvioli, *La protec-*

ción de los derechos económicos, sociales y culturales en el sistema interamericano & derechos humanos REVISTA IIDH, Jan.–June 2004, at 101.

43. American Convention on Human Rights, Art. 4(1), Nov.22, 1969, 1144 UNTS 123 [hereinafter American Convention]; *see also id.*, Art. 14 (Right of Reply), Art. 7(6) (Right to Personal Liberty). The latter provision proclaims a kind of anticipatory habeas corpus right.

44. Inter-Am. Court of Human Rights, Rules of Procedure, Art. 23, Inter-Am. C.H.R. (ser. A) No. 17 (2003).

45. Dinah Shelton, *New Rules of Procedure for the inter-American Commission on Human Rights,* 22 HUM. RTS. L.J. 169 (2001); see also Thomas Buergenthal, *Remembering the Early Years of the Inter-American Court of Human Rights,* 37 N.Y.U. J. INT'L L. & POL. 259, 269–73 (2005).

46. Inter-Am. Comm'n on Human Rights, Rules of Procedure, Art. 44, *available at* <http://www.iachr.org/Basicos/basicl6.htm>. These rules also give individuals an opportunity to be heard by the Commission on the question of referral of the case to the Court. *Id.*, Art. 43.

47. See generally JO M. PASQUALUCCI, THE PRACTICE AND PROCEDURE OF THE INTER-AMERICAN COURT OF HUMAN RIGHTS (2003).

48. *See* African Charter on Human and Peoples' Rights. pmbl., June 27, 1981, 21 ILM 58(1982) [hereinafter African Charter]; *see also* Frans Viljoen, *The African Charter on Human and Peoples' Rights: The Travaux Preparatoires in the Light of Its Subsequent Practice,* 25 HUM. RTS. L.J. 313, 319 (2004).

49. African Charter, *supra* note 48, Art. 30; *see generally* RACHEL MURRAY, THE AFRICAN COMMISSION ON HUMAN AND PEOPLES' RIGHTS (2000).

50. African Charter, *supra* note 48, Art. 45

51. *Id.*, Art. 60.

52. *Id.*, Art. 61.

53. For an analysis of this practice, see Viljoen, *supra* note 480, at 323–24.

54. African Charter, *supra* note 48, Art. 58(1). Note that this language is quite similar to the language of ECOSOC Resolution 1503, *supra* note 18.

55. Protocol to the African Charter on Human and Peoples' Rights on the Establishment of an African Court on Human and Peoples' Rights, Art. 2, June 10, 1998, *available at* <http://www.africa-union.org/root/au/Documents/Treaties/treaties.htm> [hereinafter Protocol].

56. *Id.*, Art.3.

57. *Id.*, Arts. 5, 34(6).

58. Anne Pieter van der Mei, *The Advisory Jurisdiction of the African Court on Human and Peoples' Rights,* 5 AFR. HUM. RTS. L.J. 27(2005).

59. Protocol, *supra* note 55, Art. 4(1).

60. Protocol of the Court of Justice of the African Union, July 11, 2003, *available at* <http://www.africa-union.org/root/au/Documents/Treaties/treaties.htm>.

61. For a comprehensive overview, see MERON, *supra* note 25.

62. PRISCILLA B. HAYNER, UNSPEAKABLE TRUTHS: FACING THE CHALLENGES OF TRUTH COMMISSIONS (2001). See also the three-volume TRANSITIONAL JUSTICE: HOW EMERGING DEMOCRACIES RECKON WITH FORMER REGIMES (Neil Kritz ed., 1995).

63. *See generally* HENRY STEINER, DIVERSE PARTNERS: NON-GOVERNMENTAL ORGANIZATIONS IN THE HUMAN RIGHTS MOVEMENT (1991). For NGOs in general, see the centennial essay by Steve Charnovitz, *Nongovernmental Organizations and International Law,* 100 AJIL 348 (2006).

64. The Inter-American Court of Human Rights reached the same conclusion

with regard to the American Declaration in its Advisory Opinion OC-10/89, *Interpretation of the American Declaration of the Rights and Duties of Man Within the Framework of Article 64 of the American Convention on Human Rights*, Inter-Am. Cr. H.R (ser. A) No. 10 (1989).

65. The United States Senate, by contrast, has declared the provisions of all major human rights treaties ratified by the United States, including the International Covenant on Civil and Political Rights, to be non-self-executing. As a result, American courts are denied the opportunity to apply international human rights treaties to which the United States is a party. This position of the United States, as we have seen, runs counter to the contemporary approach of many countries, among them some leading democratic countries. For an eloquent critique of the U.S. position toward human rights treaties by an eminent American scholar on the subject, see Louis Henkin, *U.S. Ratification of Human Rights Conventions: The Ghost of Senator Bricker*, 89 AJIL 341 (1995).

CHAPTER 16

The Responsibility to Protect: Humanitarian Concern and the Lawfulness of Armed Intervention

Christopher C. Joyner

DURING THE TWENTIETH CENTURY, AT LEAST 170 MILLION deaths resulted from internal state conflicts, mostly by tyrannical regimes killing their own citizens.[1] According to scholar Rudolph Rummel, this incredible number of people slaughtered by "democide"[2] exceeds by nearly five times the thirty-five million military casualties killed during the same period by the armies of governments fighting in interstate wars.[3] These statistics indicating innocent people killed by their own governments are of such a magnitude that it is difficult to relate to or appreciate their meaning. In fact, it remains an irony of psychology that all too often it is easier to evoke pathos over the plight of a single individual's death than over the fate of many millions of victims.

When one looks back into recent history, such human catastrophes all too frequently happen: In a civil war driven by ethnic hatred between 1966 and 1979, as many as 565,000 people died in Nigeria;[4] as many as 1,365,000 persons might have perished in Indonesia between 1965 and 1987;[5] as many as 500,000 humans were butchered under Idi Amin in Uganda between 1971 and 1979;[6] and some three million people were executed under the Pol Pot regime in Cambodia during 1975 to 1979.[7] How should the international community deal with such egregious atrocities? Surely international law cannot condone under any circumstances such massive butchery of a people by its government.

The puzzle is how best to legally reconcile respect for the preeminent principle of state sovereignty with the critical human rights necessity of protecting municipal populations from their own governments. What is the solution to this legal incongruity? The answer lies in the concept of the

---

Reprinted with permission of the *Virginia Journal of International Law.*

"responsibility to protect." The key is to rethink the fundamental meaning of sovereignty, which should be conceived as the preeminent requirement for the government of a state to exercise responsibility for, not merely control over, its actions. In addition, this responsibility must be motivated by the supreme duty of a government to protect its population, without a legal license to kill massive numbers of that population.

This article examines the legality of armed intervention by putting into context the role of governmental responsibility as it relates to national sovereignty. Part I examines the concept of humanitarian intervention and the criticism of its use as a legal rationale for international interference into another state's internal affairs. Part II deals with the UN Charter framework and sets out the legal premises on which contemporary international intervention may be permissible. Part III treats sovereignty as a legal principle that explicitly requires a state to exercise responsibility as an ingredient necessary for its governance to be considered legitimate. To this end, Part IV identifies certain criteria that ought to be weighed in the event an international intervention to halt genocide or ethnic cleansing is contemplated. Finally, a number of reflections are proffered on how the growth of human rights law has impacted the evolution of the "responsibility to protect" as a norm, as well as the prospects for mobilizing international political will for converting moral rhetoric into legal opportunity.

Humanitarian Intervention

An important debate arose in the international legal community over the permissibility of outside actors using armed force to halt humanitarian atrocities. Primarily beginning in the 1970s and culminating in the 1990s, the dilemma of states employing armed intervention to halt such massacres was critically proclaimed and discussed.[8] Known as humanitarian intervention, the concept involved an armed intervention into another state, without the agreement of that state, to address the threat or actual infliction of grave and large-scale violations of fundamental human rights.[9] The main question centered on whether it was ever lawful for a state or group of states to take military action against a sovereign state in order to protect that state's citizens from their government.[10]

As a polemical legal issue, humanitarian intervention became the subject of increasingly acrimonious academic debate during the 1990s.[11] During this period, several government-instigated human rights atrocities spotlighted the killing fields and the failure, apathy, or incompetence of the international community to respond. There was the debacle of the United States–led armed intervention into and withdrawal from Somalia in 1993;[12] the pitifully inadequate international response to the horrific genocide of

800,000 Tutsis in Rwanda in 1994;[13] the shameful unwillingness of UN peacekeeping forces to prevent the murderous ethnic cleansing of 7,000 to 8,000 Muslim men and boys in Srebrenica in Bosnia in July 1995;[14] the ethnic cleansing in Kosovo of Kosovar Albanians, which left 700,000 persons displaced and thousands killed.[15] Today, as the world continues to look on and do little, a reprehensible genocide is being perpetrated in Darfur, leaving perhaps as many as 400,000 persons dead and 2.5 million displaced.[16] None of these cases was well handled, and the sense of acute failure to do anything compounded frustration over the capability and responsibility of the United Nations, when set against the impenetrable nature and limits of state sovereignty. Other cases involving large-scale human rights violence further aggravated that concern: the desperate plight of the Kurds in northern Iraq, and murderous civil strife in Liberia, Haiti, Sierra Leone, and East Timor. To be sure, intractable tensions between the exigent need to intervene militarily in horrendous human rights situations versus unimpeachable state sovereignty in all circumstances, made the issue of humanitarian intervention legally, politically, morally, and ethically contentious. Humanitarian intervention was deemed by many to be an impermissible assault on state sovereignty.[17] If that indeed is the case, how can the United Nations or the international community successfully halt pervasively violent abuses of human rights and massive carnage? For any real policy to proceed, common sense must prevail to square this contradiction.

The fact is, however, that these conceptual questions are not new,[18] and they require answers to determine what actions states are permitted to take when confronted with real or perceived attacks on their territory or against their own nationals, as authorized by the principle of self-defense as set out in Article 51 of the UN Charter or through the authority of the Security Council "to maintain international peace and security" under provisions in Chapter VII. While enormously important in international law, these questions remain distinct from the issues posed by the debate over the lawful permissibility of humanitarian intervention. Whereas the former pertain to conflicts between states, the latter is concerned with the justification for external actors intervening militarily into intrastate conflicts, an issue on which the UN Charter is conspicuously silent.

Most governments and jurists are reluctant to endorse unilateral humanitarian military intervention under modern international law because of the potential that powerful states will abuse such a doctrine. The history of humanitarian military intervention is replete with examples of powerful states or coalitions invoking a humanitarian doctrine to conceal their own geopolitical interests.[19] In very few cases, if any, has the right to intervene for humanitarian purposes been declared under circumstances that were actually humanitarian, rather than motivated or driven by self-interest and power-seeking. To be sure, the doctrine of forcible intervention in the name of international justice usually gave rise to serious abuses, and was reserved for the most powerful states.

The UN Charter Framework

Under the UN Charter framework, three principal goals are proclaimed: the preservation of peace, the protection of human rights, and the promotion of self-determination. The Charter system, however, creates a tension between these goals, with peace upheld as predominant among them. "Justice"—the pursuit of human rights, self-determination, and other goals such as economic development and the correction of past wrongs—was to be sought, but not at the expense of "peace." Given the experience of two world wars, the framers of the Charter believed that force was too dangerous to be seen as a legitimate means of altering the political or territorial status quo. Under the Charter, other mechanisms were established to allow states the means to seek justice peacefully.[20]

The cornerstone of the Charter framework for recourse to force is Article 2, paragraph 4. This Article provides that "[a]ll Members [of the United Nations] shall refrain in their international relations from the threat or use of force against the territorial integrity or political independence of any state, or in any other manner inconsistent with the Purposes of the United Nations."[21] Article 2(4), therefore, constitutes a basic proscription on the use and even the threat of force that in some manner violates the territorial integrity or political independence of states, or that in some other way transgresses the purposes of the United Nations. In the Charter, there are only two explicit exceptions to this prohibition that are still applicable: (1) force undertaken in self-defense and (2) force authorized by the Security Council. First, under Article 51 of the Charter, states maintain "an inherent right of individual" and "collective self-defense if an armed attack occurs . . . until the Security Council has taken measures necessary to maintain international peace and security."[22] Hence, if one state commits an armed attack against another state, the aggrieved state may use force to repel the attack until such time as the Security Council acts. Moreover, the victim state may call upon other states to assist it in collective self-defense. Second, under Article 39, the Security Council is empowered to determine if there is a "threat to the peace, breach of the peace, or act of aggression."[23] If the Council so determines, it is permitted under Article 42 to authorize the use of military force against the offending state.[24] Under Chapter VIII of the Charter, regional organizations are allowed to deal with "matters relating to the maintenance of international peace and security,"[25] but those organizations cannot undertake an "enforcement action"[26] absent authorization by the Security Council.

Under UN Charter law, for armed force to be a permissible remedy for a humanitarian crisis, the Security Council must first determine under Chapter VII provisions that massive violations of human rights are occurring, or are about to occur. Additionally, it must then conclude that such an event actually constitutes a threat to international peace, and finally, it must authorize an enforcement action to prevent or halt those violations. In the absence of such Security Council consent, resort by other governments to military means for compelling a state not to perpetrate, or even not to tolerate, human rights atrocities within its territory would constitute a breach of Article 2(4) of the Charter. Accordingly, that situation would be considered unlawful. In addition, as long as that humanitarian crisis did not spill over national borders and give rise to armed attacks against other states, recourse to Article 51 as a justification would not be available.

Human rights law aims to promote and protect the dignity and worth of the human person. The UN Charter in fact makes promotion of human rights a fundamental purpose of the United Nations, and asserts so in the Charter's preamble. Articles 55[27] and 56[28] of the Charter obligate each UN member to "take joint and separate action" to ensure the "universal respect for, and observance of human rights and fundamental freedoms." Thus a conflict arises in the UN Charter between the core objectives of ensuring human rights and preserving state sovereignty when a regime deprives its citizens of fundamental human rights. Vital questions are raised for diplomats and policymakers: Do certain acts, even if they are the most heinous crimes imaginable, remain within the sovereign prerogatives and jurisdiction of that state? Do they pose any actual military threat to world peace? If not, is the United Nations still empowered to act? But, what if the Security Council should opt, for whatever reason, not to act? Must tens of thousands or even millions of people die from violence, starvation, and disease for the sake of sovereignty? International legal commentators are divided on such key issues underlying the concept of humanitarian intervention. The focal problem is the legal principle of state sovereignty and the explicit command within it concerning nonintervention.

Rethinking Sovereignty as Responsibility

Since the mid-seventeenth century, sovereignty, supported by the prerogatives of authority and control, has underpinned the Westphalian state system of international relations. It is said that sovereignty endows a government with the lawful capability to make authoritative decisions concerning the people and use of resources within the territory of its state.[29] The traditional view is that international law empowers a sovereign state to exercise exclusive, absolute jurisdiction within its territorial borders, and that other states and multilateral actors have the corresponding duty not to interfere in a state's internal affairs. Since the end of the Second World War, gaining membership in the United Nations became viewed as symbolic attainment of independent sovereign statehood and lawful acceptance into the community of states. Moreover, the United Nations was deemed to be a world organization dedicated to maintaining interstate peace and security, as it functioned largely to protect the territorial integrity, political independence, and national sovereignty of its member states.

Over the past six decades, however, the character of the international system and its conflicts has changed. Whereas originally only fifty-one polities were members of the United Nations, the process of decolonization has produced at least 192 states today. Moreover, since 1945, a spate of new actors have entered the international scene and gained status as subjects under international law. Nonstate actors have proliferated on the international scene. Intergovernmental organizations, nongovernmental organizations, multinational corporations, and even the individual person have all acquired recognized status under international law.[30] Relatedly, certain subnational groups—terrorists, crime syndicates, and narco-traffickers, inter alia—operate transnationally in carrying out their unlawful activities. Perhaps more significantly, no longer do armed conflicts primarily occur between states. The vast majority of armed conflicts today are internal wars—uncivil wars—that leave mainly innocent civilians, not soldiers, as casualties and victims. Thus, as new realities and challenges emerged since the end of the Second World War, so too have new expectations for action and new standards of behavior arisen in national and international relations.

As a concept, the responsibility to protect evolved from mere aspirations voiced by Secretary-General Kofi Annan to the status of a norm in process of becoming a legal principle. At the United Nations General Assembly in 1999,[31] and again as a pillar of UN reform in his Millennium address in 2000,[32] Secretary-General Annan made compelling appeals to the international community to find international consensus for resolving the dilemma of humanitarian intervention. In his 2000 address before the Millennium Summit, he tersely and soberly presented the question to the critics of humanitarian intervention: "[I]f humanitarian intervention is, indeed, an unacceptable assault on sovereignty, how should we respond to a Rwanda, to a Srebrenica—to gross and systematic violations of human rights that offend every precept of our common humanity?"[33] This question summed up the essential dilemma confounding the lawful permissibility of humanitarian intervention.

In response to the Secretary-General's challenge, in September 2000, the Canadian Government established an International Commission on Intervention and State Sovereignty. Chaired by Gareth Evans and Mohamed Sahnoun, this ten-member commission issued its report, The Responsibility to Protect, in December 2001.[34] Since then, the notion was formally endorsed by and recommended in two prominent UN Secretary-General reports,[35] as well as by a study commissioned by U.S. Institute of Peace entitled *American Interests and UN Reform*.[36]

Conceiving sovereignty in terms of governmental responsibility fosters certain implications. First, it suggests that state officials are responsible for policies that ensure the protection of their citizens and the promotion of their welfare.[37] Secondly, it implies that governments are obligated to their own nationals and to the international community.[38] Third, sovereignty as responsibility means that government officials are responsible for their own policy decisions and are accountable for their own actions.[39]

The rationale for conceiving sovereignty in terms of responsibility is increasingly being justified by the escalating influence that human rights norms exert as they are accepted as genuine components of human security. In this regard, the equation of sovereignty as governmental responsibility is increasingly being codified in international human rights instruments and recognized in state practice. Since 1948, the adoption of several salient international human rights instruments have established legal benchmarks for state conduct and erected the global legal regime that mandates national and international protection for and promotion of individual human rights.

No less important is that, during the last two decades, a salient shift occurred in thinking about security as a national concept. The traditional view held that security pertained preeminently to states, their borders, and their ability to protect themselves from external aggression. Today, the conceptualization of security has broadened considerably beyond the physical defense of states to include the welfare of their populations—their citizens' physical safety, socio-economic wellbeing, and safeguarding their basic human rights and freedoms.[40] At the same time, it has become recognized that the basic elements of human security—the safety of people against threats to life, liberty, health, personal wellbeing, and human dignity—can be imperiled not only by external aggression, but also by circumstances and forces within a state, including actions by its military and police forces.[41] Here again, emphasis is placed not so much on what governments are permitted to do under the guise of sovereignty, as what they are not permitted to do in carrying out legal responsibilities to their own people.

During the past six decades, disparities have widened between the presumed lawful conduct of sovereign states as defined in the UN Charter and actual state behavior in international relations as justified under the pretext of sovereign rights. It seems evident that the United Nations' founders never intended for the Charter to justify government officials possessing unrestrained power to do whatever they wanted to their own citizens. Rather, the Charter and UN practice both indicate that sovereignty entails a dual responsibility: On the one hand, sovereignty implies the duty to respect the sovereignty of other states and to refrain from interfering in their internal affairs. On the other hand, sovereignty summons the concomitant duty of the government to respect the fundamental rights of all peoples within the state and take action to protect them.[42] The point here is clear. By construing sovereignty as a principle of state responsibility, relations between states can proceed with less conflict and greater cooperation. At the same time, however, the basic rights of persons within states can be guaranteed under internationally agreed upon legal standards.

Use of "responsibility to protect," instead of the more proverbial "right to intervene," furnishes greater worth to the humanitarian issues in question. It adds a positive, more humane context to what is clearly a terrifying situation inside a state. The puzzle here is how best to legally reconcile respect for the preeminent principle of state sovereignty with the critical human rights necessity of protecting municipal populations from their own governments. What must be done to fix this legal incongruity? The answer lies in the concept of the "responsibility to protect." The key is to rethink the fundamental meaning of sovereignty. The notion of sovereignty should be conceived as the preeminent need for the government of a state to exercise responsibility, not merely control over its actions. In addition, this responsibility must be motivated by the supreme duty of a government to protect its population without any alleged legal license to kill massively selected members within it. The Charter of the United Nations establishes international obligations for states in their international relations.[43] Among these duties are to refrain from the threat or use of force, to settle disputes peacefully, to promote human rights and self-determination, to respect the sovereign equality of states, to respect the territorial sovereignty and political independence of states, and to conform with general principles of international law. There are other advantages as to why the term "responsibility to protect" should be heralded as a normative principle for guiding international behavior. For one, the responsibility to protect invites consideration of the issues from the perspective of those who urgently need help, as opposed to governments that might undertake a military intervention.[44] "The responsibility to protect" casts international attention where concern should fall: on the obligation to protect people from mass murder, women from systematic rape, and children from starvation.[45] For another, the responsibility to protect underscores the crucial role for the government concerned to assert the paramount duty to protect its citizens.[46] If that government is unable or unwilling to perform that protective role, or if it itself is the perpetrator of massive human rights crimes, then the responsibility devolves to the international community to act in its place. Finally, the responsibility to protect is multidimensional, as it entails not merely a responsibility to react, but also the responsibilities to prevent and rebuild. The responsibility to prevent means taking action to curtail internal discontent and the roots of violence that put populations at risk.[47] This requires use of the toolbox of measures available, including political means, diplomatic initiatives, legal processes, economic strategies, and, if necessary, military force. Indeed, the single most important feature of the responsibility to protect is prevention. To prevent harm from occurring is to exercise the responsibility to protect against harm.

The responsibility to rebuild connotes reconstructing civil order in a state in the aftermath of an intervention.[48] Reconstruction involves facilitating the recovery of a society from violent upheaval and the reconciliation of its people into a civil society. This means full assistance with recovery, reconstruction, and reconciliation after the military intervention. There must be genuine commitment to build both a durable peace and a society under legitimate authority, governed by the rule of law.

As might be expected, the most critical aspect of the responsibility to protect, as well as the most difficult to implement conceptually and politically, is the requisite responsibility to react.[49] This means responding to situations of compelling human need with appropriate measures, including armed force, if necessary. At its core, the responsibility to protect inculcates the responsibility to take action in response to extreme situations in which there is a compelling need for protecting against threats to innocent persons. When preventive efforts fail to check or constrain internal violence and the government is unable or unwilling to remedy the state of affairs, then measures of coercive intercession by other members of the international community may be necessary. Such coercive means might involve the use of political, economic, or judicial remedies, and in extraordinary and extreme situations, they could necessitate the use of armed force. But herein lies a critical obstacle that must be overcome, namely what precisely entails an "extreme" case?[50] What threshold must be reached for violations of human rights to trigger action that amounts to legitimate military intervention? What conditions are applicable for determining whether intervention should occur? Perhaps thorniest of all, who makes these determinations? Who retains the ultimate authority to decide whether, when, where, and how intervention involving deadly force on a possibly massive scale should proceed? The answers to these critical questions rest in the identification of criteria that must be considered in weighing a decision to intervene. To that end, six threshold criteria are suggested under the principle of the responsibility to protect. These criteria can be weighed and factored into the calculus for deciding whether to intervene militarily into a state. They are just cause, legitimate intention, last resort, proportionality, reasonable prospects, and legitimate authority.[51]

The Threshold of Just Cause

Resort to the use of armed force must be taken only when the cause is just and when circumstances reach extreme conditions.[52] Extreme conditions fall into two categories of internal situations. The first occurs when a massive loss of life, real or potential, with or without genocidal intent, results from either deliberate government action or the inability of the government to exercise the responsibility to protect its own citizens.[53] The second involves a situation in which massive or "large-scale" ethnic cleansing is being or might be perpetrated, regardless of whether it is carried out by mass murder, forced depopulation, extensive evictions, premeditated acts of terror, or premeditated strategies of using rape pervasively as an instrument of war. While the adjectives "massive" or "large-scale" are used as qualifiers for determining the need for a military intervention, neither concept can be precisely quantified. Nor should they have to be. If the responsibility to protect is to have any legal credibility or political integrity, military action must be legitimized in anticipation of the onslaught of pervasive killings or ethnic cleansing in a society. Genuine protection demands the here and now. The international community does not have to wait until genocidal atrocities commence before initiating forceful action to stop them from occurring in a state.[54]

It must be understood, however, that certain situations involving human rights deprivations are excluded from the just cause threshold because they fall short of being genocide or ethnic cleansing. Accordingly, such cases that would not justify military action for protection purposes include those earmarked by political oppression or methodical racial discrimination, the overthrow of a democratically-elected government, or the rescue by a government of its own nationals in a foreign state. These latter circumstances do not attain the threshold of just cause.

The Threshold of Rightful Intention

The primary purpose motivating a "responsibility to protect" action must be to stop or prevent human suffering.[55] That is, if military intervention is undertaken, the preeminent motivation for that action must be the clear and present protection of endangered persons.[56] This stipulation might seem reasonable enough, but it is difficult to gauge with compelling precision. In any event, intervention taken to protect must be carried out so as to ensure respect for the general rule of law and not to pursue the realization of any government's individual advantage. In effect, under the responsibility to protect, governments act as trustees and defenders of the law of humanity when that law is violated in some state. Intervening governments must not use the law to prosecute their own self-interested ends under the guise of humanitarian concerns.

A legacy of past large-scale atrocities can furnish a legitimate prerequisite for exercising preemptively the responsibility to protect. If the government of a state has a history of killing, torturing, or creating conditions of intolerable suffering for large numbers of its own citizens, then intervention taken under the responsibility to protect may be a viable prospect in the future. The right to life is a fundamental human right that civilized governments are supposed to protect through due process, not take away *en masse* through genocidal acts.[57]

The Threshold of Last Resort

Before using force to execute the responsibility to protect, governments are legally bound to pursue all reasonable peaceful means available to resolve the situation.[58] These means might include diplomatic protests, appeals to the UN Security Council, and even economic sanctions. Even so, the time available for resort to these peaceful means remains contingent upon the situation in the delict state. If human rights conditions worsen, or the threats to the security of persons in that state escalate, the lawful justification—and need—for military intervention will rise correspondingly. The prerequisite requirement to undertake peaceful means of dispute settlement dissipates as human rights conditions deteriorate in the offending state. It makes no sense to say that the search for means to restore domestic peace in a state must go forward while thousands of innocent persons in that state are killed. In such circumstances, the procedural search for conflict resolution must give way to the responsibility to protect potential victims through preemptive armed intervention. To do otherwise could prompt the perpetrators to start killing, and might instigate the slaughter of innocents on a massive scale.

In any event, clear and compelling evidence must indicate that gross and egregious violations of human rights involving the deaths of hundreds or even thousands of innocent people are actually going to occur in the territory of a sovereign state.[59] The threat of these atrocities, which would amount to genocide or crimes against humanity, is made real either with the complicity or support of the governmental authorities, or because those authorities are unable or unwilling to prevent them. The bottom line is this: The responsibility to react with military force can only be justified if the responsibility to prevent through means of peaceful dispute settlement has been attempted to a reasonable degree of effort.

The Threshold of Proportionate Means

The magnitude, duration, and power of the military intervention used for human rights protection must be limited to the minimum level necessary to halt impending human rights violations.[60] The intervening state or states must plan and carry out the military action carefully so as not to inflict more harm, death, or injury than is sought to be prevented. Generally, the authority structure of the offending state should not be overthrown, nor should the domestic political process of that state be permanently altered.[61] If, however, the government of an offending state is responsible for planning or committing massive human rights abuses, it does so at the risk of being removed by an intervening humanitarian force, but only if necessary to halt the loss of life. An action undertaken on grounds of responsibility to protect must also be limited in duration to the time that is necessary to stop the atrocities from taking place or to halt their execution. Upholding the right to protect innocent persons cannot be a rationale for military occupation of some state, nor is it acceptable as a justification for annexation or integration of territory by another state.

The armed force taken should be used exclusively for the limited purpose of preventing or halting the atrocities and restoring respect for human rights. Such humanitarian coercion must be stopped as soon as the purpose of the intervention is secured. The use of force, moreover, must be proportionate to the threat that it seeks to address.

The critical point remains that human rights have evolved such that the rights of all people merit protection under international law. International law should be directed at protecting the sovereignty inherent in people, not merely the legal polity known as the state. That is, sovereignty resides in the citizens of the state, not in the government as sovereign, particularly when that government by commission or omission fails to halt brutal depredations of human rights, or is actually engaged in perpetrating them against its own citizens. The bottom line here is this: If force is used consistently with other principles in the UN Charter without being directed against the territorial integrity or political independence of another state, it may well be held as commendable rather than condemnable under the UN Charter.[62]

The Threshold of Reasonable Prospects for Success

Resort to military invention can only be legitimized if it has a realistic chance of successfully stopping or preventing large-scale atrocities or suffering.[63] Armed intervention cannot be justified if actual protection cannot be achieved, or if the action appears likely to produce adverse consequences or suffering greater than if there were no intervention at all. Here is an important point: A military action taken for human protection should not be justified if in the process it touches off a more deadly conflict.

This observation obviously poses an inherently troublesome question relating to the Great Powers on the Security Council. Given their relative superior military might, an armed intervention into their territories would likely spark a major conflict, with little chance for ultimate success. Here again, the issue of double standards arises, as interventions might not be possible in every case where genuine reason exists to do so.

The Threshold of Legitimate Authority

When authorization is needed for human protection purposes, the first stop must be the UN Security Council.[64] The United Nations was created to be the primary instrument for determining legitimate action and, accordingly, the link between authority and state recourse to force. Under the UN Charter framework, it is the Security Council that first and foremost bears responsibility for dealing with issues concerning the maintenance of international peace and security, including violently brutal anarchic situations within states. But what if the Security Council is unwilling or unable to take coercive action to prevent or halt massacres or massive human rights atrocities in some country? Such UN inaction could originate from disagreement among permanent members on the council, or from one of them casting a veto, or simply from that body opting to adopt a resolution condemning the situation and admonishing the state in question to refrain from any massive atrocities, rather than taking any effective preventive action aimed at stopping human rights atrocities. The decisive question then becomes, should this impasse be the last stop for the international community in its efforts to avert large-scale human carnage?

The answer must be a resounding no. The United Nations undoubtedly remains a vital institution for constructing, securing, and applying international legal authority. It was founded to provide a foundation for world order and international stability. It was to serve as the structure within which governments could negotiate legal agreements to resolve problems of global import, while establishing norms for the appropriate behavior of states that might foster peace and security, as opposed to conflict or confrontation. Thus the United Nations was viewed as the forum for mediating great power rivalries, for overseeing political adjustments within the international community, for promulgating new legal norms, and for bestowing the imprimatur of international legitimacy. In that regard, the authority of the United Nations rests not on any power of armed force, but rather on its ability to confer legitimacy on interstate actions.

Other legitimate options are available under the emerging norm of the responsibility to protect. For one, the United Nations General Assembly could convene in an Emergency Special Session under the "Uniting for Peace" procedure that furnished the legitimizing authority for operations in Korea (1950), Egypt (1956), and the Congo (1960).[65] It seems likely that if serious efforts had been made by major powers to use the Uniting for Peace Resolution to deal with the situations in Rwanda (1994) and Kosovo (1998), the General Assembly may well have authorized emergency protective action.[66] For another, there is the option to take action with regional organizations under Chapter VIII of the UN Charter, subject to their seeking authorization from the Security Council. Again, this alternative also is susceptible to being frustrated by political paralysis in the Security Council.

It is clear that armed interventions by a state, or even ad hoc coalitions of states, that are undertaken without the umbrella of legitimacy furnished by Security Council or General Assembly authorization are viewed as highly suspect by the international community.

Reflections

A cardinal principle of contemporary international law is state sovereignty. The condition of sovereignty identifies the state as a legitimate actor entitled to protection under international law. Possession of sovereignty imbues the government of a state with supremacy over its territory and independence in international relations. In principle, however, such independence is neither absolute nor unlimited.

In light of recent developments, there is clearly a fundamental tension between the concept of state sovereignty and the concern for human rights. If intervention is permitted by any and all states to protect human rights in some other state, then an invitation is issued for widespread abuse of military intervention and disruption of international stability. On the other hand, if a flat prohibition is placed on the use of any forcible intervention under any circumstances, including genocide, massacres, pervasive torture, or other human rights atrocities, then the principle of nonintervention takes on an immoral character. An international law founded to promote justice for all peoples is sacrificed on the altar of national sovereignty by the principle of nonintervention.

Little gratification comes from field reports and political rhetoric when massive human suffering is evident. If all people have the fundamental right to life and are equally entitled to protection from evildoers in their government, then words of warning must be matched with reality, and principle to act must be mirrored by practice. If there is to be a civil international society, then governments must work together to preserve that civility—not only in their own states, but in every state. There must be no more Holocausts, no more Cambodias, no more Srebrenicas, and no more Rwandas. Marshalling the political will to implement the responsibility to protect as a functional legal norm promises to make considerable progress toward attaining that lofty but clearly necessary goal in twenty-first century international relations. This will not be easy. Moreover, much will depend upon the degree of leadership, commitment, and cooperation from the Great

Powers. In the long term, attaining that political cooperation may be the greatest challenge of all.

Notes

1. R.J. RUMMEL, DEATH BY GOVERNMENT 9–12 (1994).

2. *Id.* at 31 (defining democide as "[t]he murder of any person or people by a government, including genocide, politicide, and mass murder").

3. R.J. Rummel, Editorial, *War Isn't This Century's Biggest Killer,* WALL ST. J., July 7, 1986, at A10, *available at* http://www.hawaii.edu/powerkills/WSJ.ART.HTM.

4. R.J. RUMMEL, STATISTICS OF DEMOCIDE 353 (1997). *See generally* W. Michael Reisman with Myres S. McDougal, *Humanitarian Intervention to Protect the Ibos, in* HUMANITARIAN INTERVENTION AND THE UNITED NATIONS 167 (Richard B. Lillich ed., 1973) (stating that the 1967–70 Biafra secession, civil war, and humanitarian disaster in Nigeria were candidates for humanitarian intervention).

5. RUMMEL, *supra* note 4, at 352. *See generally* Roger S. Clark, *East Timor, Indonesia, and the International Community,* 14 TEMP. INT'L & COMP. L.J. 75 (2000).

6. RUMMEL, *supra* note 4, at 354. *See generally* Farooq Hassan, *Realpolitik in International Law: After Tanzanian-Ugandan Conflict: "Humanitarian Intervention" Reexamined,* 17 WILLAMETTE L. REV. 859 (1980–81); S.K. Chatterjee, *Some Legal Problems of Support Role in International Law: Tanzania and Uganda,* 30 INT'L & COMP. L.Q. 755 (1981).

7. RUMMEL, *supra* note 4, at 351. *See generally,* ELIZABETH BECKER, WHEN THE WAR WAS OVER: THE VOICES OF CAMBODIA'S REVOLUTION AND ITS PEOPLE (1986); NAYAN CHANDA, BROTHER ENEMY: THE WAR AFTER THE WAR (1986); MICHAEL VICKERY, CAMBODIA: 1975–1982 (1984); Michael J. Bazyler, *Reexamining the Doctrine of Humanitarian Intervention in Light of the Atrocities in Kampuchea and Ethiopia,* 23 STAN. J. INT'L L. 547, 550–53 (1987); Hurst Hannum, *International Law and Cambodian Genocide: The Sounds of Silence,* 11 HUM. RTS. Q. 82, 85–91 (1989); Kenneth M. Quinn, *The Pattern and Scope of Violence, in* CAMBODIA 1975–1978: RENDEZVOUS WITH DEATH 179 (Karl D. Jackson ed., 1989) (detailing the atrocities of the Khmer Rouge regime).

8. *See, e.g.,* PHILIP JESSUP, A MODERN LAW OF NATIONS 172–74 (1948); Ian Brownlie, *Humanitarian Intervention, in* LAW AND CIVIL WAR IN THE MODERN WORLD 217 (John N. Moore ed., 1974); Ian Brownlie, *The Principle of Non-Use of Force in Contemporary International Law, in* THE NON-USE OF FORCE IN INTERNATIONAL LAW 17 (W.E. Butler ed., 1989); Richard Lillich, *Forcible Self Help Under International Law, in* 62 READINGS IN INTERNATIONAL LAW FROM THE NAVAL WAR COLLEGE REVIEW 129, 133–38 (Richard Lillich & John N. Moore eds., 1980).

9. *See generally* FERNANDO TESON, HUMANITARIAN INTERVENTION: AN INQUIRY INTO LAW AND MORALITY 5 (1997).

10. Contending scholars fell into two broad categories: "restrictionists" and "counter-restrictionists." *See* Anthony Clark Arend & Robert J. Beck, INTERNATIONAL LAW AND THE USE OF FORCE: BEYOND THE UN CHARTER PAR-

ADIGM 131–35 (1993) (introducing the terms "restrictionist" and "counter-restrictionist"). Restrictionists argued that Article 2(4) of the United Nations Charter should be interpreted as a general proscription on the use of force against states. Consequently, absent a clear case of an actual armed attack or the explicit authorization of the Security Council, states could not lawfully use force, even for humanitarian purposes. On the other hand, counter-restrictionists advanced a series of arguments supporting the lawfulness of humanitarian intervention. Their contention was that humanitarian intervention should be regarded as permissible because it fell below the Article 2(4) threshold. That is, humanitarian intervention is not unlawful because it does not constitute a use of force against the territorial integrity or political independence of states, nor does it transgress the purposes of the United Nations. It does not violate the territorial integrity of a state, since the purpose of such intervention is not to gain territory or alter an existing border. It does not violate the political independence of states because it does not seek to subject the recalcitrant state to the political domination of the intervening state. Moreover, humanitarian intervention is not inconsistent with the purposes of the United Nations; in fact, it is in consonance with the United Nations Charter goals of promoting human rights and self-determination.

11. The theoretical debates over humanitarian intervention are summarized in TESON, *supra* note 9.

12. *See* Sean D. Murphy, *Nation-Building: A Look at Somalia*, 3 TUL. J. INT'L & COMP. L. 19, 24–33 (1995).

13. The Secretary-General, *Report of the Secretary-General on the Situation in Rwanda*, ¶ 8, *delivered to the Security Council*, U.N. Doc. S/1994/924 (Aug. 3, 1994); The Secretary-General, *Final Report of the Commission of Experts Established Pursuant to Security Council Resolution 935 (1994)*, ¶¶ 61–72, *delivered to the President of the Security Council*, U.N. Doc. S/1994/1405 (Dec. 9, 1994); *see also* Human Rights Watch/Africa, *Genocide in Rwanda: April–May 1994*, at 3 (1994); Dorinda Lea Peacock, *"It Happened and It Can Happen Again": The International Response to Genocide in Rwanda*, 22 N.C. J. INT'L L. & COM. REG. 899 (1995); Yogesh K. Tyagi, *The Concept of Humanitarian Intervention Revisited*, 16 MICH. J. INT'L L. 883 (1995).

14. *See also* Prosecutor v. Krstic, Case No. IT-98-33-T, Judgment, ¶ 84 (Aug. 2, 2001); Katherine G. Southwick *Srebrenica as Genocide? The Krstic Decision and the Language of the Unspeakable*, 8 YALE HUM. RTS. & DEV. L.J. 188 (2005).

15. *See* Sean D. Murphy, *Contemporary Practice of the United States Relating to International Law, Humanitarian Intervention in Kosovo*, 93 AM. J. INT'L L. 161, 167–68 (1999); Laura Geissler, *The Law of Humanitarian Intervention and the Kosovo Crisis*, 23 HAMLINE L. REV. 323, 336 (2000).

16. Genocide Intervention Network, *Background on Darfur*, http://www.genocideintervention.net/educate/darfurinfo (last visited Apr. 25, 2006). The statistics on the genocide vary widely, depending upon the source. *See also* Human Rights watch, *Ensuring Protection in Darfur: The UN Mandate* (Apr. 2006), http://hrw.org/backgrounder/afnca/sudan0406/1.htm.

17. *See generally supra* note 10.

18. *See* Malvina Halberstam, *The Legality of Humanitarian Intervention*, 3 CARDOZO J. INT'L & COMP. L. 1,2 (1995) (asserting that references to principles of humanitarian intervention originated as early as 1579).

19. Arend and Beck examined eleven cases of alleged humanitarian intervention (among them the Congo by the Belgians in 1960, the Dominican Republic by the United States in 1965, East Pakistan by India in 1971, Kampucha by Vietnam in

1978, Uganda by Tanzania in 1979, and Grenada by the United States in 1983). Their conclusion in each case was that ulterior political motives superseded humanitarian concerns. *See* Arend & Beck, *supra* note 10, at 112–27.

20. U.N. Charter ch.VI.

21. *Id.* art. 2, para. 4.

22. *Id.* art. 51.

23. *Id.* art. 39.

24. *Id.* art. 42. Article 42 provides:

> Should the Security Council consider that measures provided for in Article 41 [(diplomatic and economic sanctions)] would be inadequate or have proved to be inadequate, it may take such action by air, sea, or land forces as may be necessary to maintain or restore international peace and security. Such action may include demonstrations, blockade, and other operations by air, sea, or land forces of Members of the United Nations.

25. *Id.* art 52.

26. *Id.* art. 53. Article 53 provides in part: "The Security Council shall, where appropriate, utilize such regional arrangements or agencies for enforcement action under its authority. But no enforcement action shall be taken under regional arrangements or by regional agencies without the authorization of the Security Council." *Id.* Article 53 did provide an exception. Security Council approval was not required for "measures against any enemy state [of World War II]" or when undertaken by "regional arrangements directed-against-renewal of aggressive policy on the part of any such state, until such time as the Organization [(the United Nations)] may, on request of the Governments concerned, be charged with the responsibility for preventing further aggression by such a state." *Id.* Most commentators conclude that this special exception is no longer applicable.

27. Article 55 provides that "the United Nations shall promote . . . universal respect for, and observance of, human rights and fundamental freedoms for all without distinction as to race, sex, language, or religion." *Id.* art. 55(c).

28. Article 56 asserts: "All Members pledge themselves to take joint and separate action in co-operation with the Organization for the achievement of the purposes set forth in Article 55." *Id.* art. 56.

29. In the UN Charter, the principle of sovereign equality of all states is preserved in Article 2(1), which is bolstered in Article 2(4) with the corresponding norm of nonintervention by states, and in Article 2(7) nonintervention by the Organization.

30. *See* CHRISTOPHER C. JOYNER, INTERNATIONAL LAW IN THE 21ST CENTURY: RULES FOR GLOBAL GOVERNANCE 24–28 (2005). Among transnational actors in 2006, there are at least 6,400 intergovernmental organizations, 44,000 international nongovernmental organizations, 500,000 multinational corporations and foreign affiliates, and 6.4 billion persons. *Id.*

31. In his September 20, 1999, address to the General Assembly, Secretary-General Annan declared:

> In the case of Kosovo . . . the inability of the international community to reconcile the question of the legitimacy of an action taken by a regional organization without a United Nations mandate, and the universally accepted imperative of effectively halting gross and systematic violations

> of human rights, could only be viewed as a tragedy. It had revealed the core challenge to the Security Council and the United Nations as whole in the next century: to forge unity behind the principle that massive, systematic violations of human rights—wherever they might take place—should not be allowed to stand.

Press Release, General Assembly, Implications of International Response to Events in Rwanda, Kosovo Examined by Secretary-General, in Address to General Assembly, U.N. Doc. GA/9595 (Sept. 20, 1999), *available at* http://www.un.org/News/Press/docs/1999/19990920.ga9595.html.

32. KOFI ANNAN, "WE THE PEOPLES": THE ROLE OF THE UNITED NATIONS IN THE 21ST CENTURY, U.N. Sales No. E.00.I.16 (2000), *available at* http://www.un.org/millennium/sg/report/full.htm.

33. *Id.* at 48.

34. INTERNATIONAL COMMISSION ON INTERVENTION AND STATE SOVEREIGNTY, THE RESPONSIBILITY TO PROTECT: REPORT OF THE INTERNATIONAL COMMISSION ON INTERVENTION AND STATE SOVEREIGNTY (2001), *available at* http://www.iciss.ca/report-en.asp [hereinafter RESPONSIBILITY TO PROTECT REPORT].

35. THE SECRETARY-GENERAL'S HIGH-LEVEL PANEL ON THREATS, CHALLENGES AND CHANGE, A MORE SECURE WORLD: OUR SHARED RESPONSIBILITY 65–66 (2004), *available at* http://www.un.org/secureworld ("The principle of non-intervention in internal affairs cannot be used to protect genocidal acts or . . . large-scale violations of international humanitarian law or large-scale ethnic cleansing."). The report concludes that a norm is emerging that holds "there is a collective international responsibility to protect, exercisable by the Security Council authorizing military intervention as a last resort, in the event of genocide and other large-scale killing, ethnic cleansing or serious violations of international humanitarian law which sovereign Governments have proved powerless or unwilling to prevent." *Id.* at 66.

36. TASK FORCE ON THE UNITED NATIONS, AMERICAN INTERESTS AND U.N. REFORM 28–39 (2005), *available* at http://www.usip.org/un/report/index.html. The report recommended that, "*The United States should endorse and call on the UN Security Council and General Assembly to affirm a responsibility of every sovereign government to protect its own citizenry and those within its borders from genocide, mass killing, and massive and sustained human rights violations.*" *Id.* at 28 (emphasis in original).

37. *See* RESPONSIBILITY TO PROTECT REPORT, *supra* note 34, at 13.

38. *Id.*

39. *Id.*

40. RESPONSIBILITY TO PROTECT REPORT, *supra* note 34, at 15.

41. *Id.*

42. RESPONSIBILITY TO PROTECT REPORT, *supra* note 34, at 17.

43. The Charter of the United Nations is a legally binding international instrument, which conveys in each of its provisions legally binding obligations for member states. *See* U.N. Charter.

44. RESPONSIBILITY TO PROTECT REPORT, *supra* note 34, at 17.

45. *Id.* at 18.

46. *Id.*

47. *See id.* at 19–27.

48. *See id.* at 39–45.

49. *See id.* at 29–37.

50. *Id.* at 31.

51. *Id.* at 32. These criteria in the Commission Report are described as "precautionary principles" to underscore the need for "prudence or precaution to the decision making equation." *Id.* at 29.

52. RESPONSIBILITY TO PROTECT REPORT, *supra* note 34, at 32–35.

53. *Id.* at 32. The Report uses the terms "large-scale" loss of life and "large-scale" ethnic cleansing without explaining how those thresholds are precisely determined. *Id.*

54. *Id* at 33.

55. *Id.* at 35.

56. *See* Bazyler, *supra* note 7, at 601–02.

57. Article 3 of the Universal Declaration of Human Rights tersely avers, "Everyone has the right to life, liberty and security of person. . . ." Universal Declaration of Human Rights, G.A. Res. 217A, at 71, U.N. GAOR, 3d Sess. 1st plen. mtg., U.N. Doc A/810 (Dec. 12, 1948). The International Covenant on Civil and Political Rights affirms in Article 6 that, "Every human being has the inherent right to life. This right shall be protected by law. No one shall be arbitrarily deprived of his life." International Covenant on Civil and Political Rights an. 6, *opened for signature* Dec. 16, 1966, 999 U.N.T.S. 171, S. Exec. Doc. E, 95–2 (1978), 6 I.L.M. 368 (1967) (entered into force on Mar. 23, 1976), *available at* http://www.ohchr.org/english/law/ccpr.htm.

58. RESPONSIBILITY TO PROTECT REPORT, *supra* note 34, at 36.

59. Such evidence could be gleaned from independent human rights organizations, United Nations observers, international media reports, eyewitness accounts of refugees, and national embassy and diplomatic assessments in the country. *Id.* at 34–35.

60. *Id.* at 37. Obviously, the concept of "minimum" is fraught with difficulties, since such a threshold will depend upon different circumstances in different situations. The force must be necessary to prevent human rights atrocities, but at the same time protect the troops being sent to accomplish that mission.

61. This point is critical to allay international suspicions about ulterior political motivations of the governments deploying intervening troops. There is great likelihood that the government of such a state will in fact undergo transition in the aftermath of a large-scale armed intervention.

62. JULIUS STONE, AGGRESSION AND WORLD ORDER: A CRITIQUE OF UNITED NATIONS THEORIES OF AGGRESSION 43 (1958).

63. RESPONSIBILITY TO PROTECT REPORT, *supra* note 34, at 37.

64. *Id.*. at 47–52.

65. Uniting for Peace Resolution, G.A. Res. 377(V), at 10, U.N. GAOR, 5th Sess., U.N. Doc. A/1775 (Nov. 3, 1950); RESPONSIBILITY TO PROTECT REPORT, *supra* note 34, at 53. The Uniting for Peace Resolution empowers the General Assembly to call up peacekeeping troops when the Security Council is blocked. Because keeping the peace is the UN's basic mission, the General Assembly can call on members within twenty-four hours" to take effective collective measures for the prevention . . . of acts of aggression."

66. RESPONSIBILITY TO PROTECT REPORT, *supra* note 34, at 53.

PART 2.3

International Law as Normative System: For the Protection of the Environment

CHAPTER 17

International Environmental Agreements: A Survey of Their Features, Formation, and Effects

Ronald Mitchell

SINCE AT LEAST THE LATE 1800s AND WITH INCREASING REGULARITY in the past half century, countries have negotiated hundreds of international legal agreements to address environmental problems they cannot resolve alone. Conventions addressing ozone depletion, climate change, and biodiversity are well-known, but governments have also concluded global, regional, and bilateral agreements to mitigate pollution of oceans, regional seas, rivers, and lakes; reduce over-exploitation of numerous species of fish, birds, and land and marine mammals; and slow the degradation of wetlands, deserts, and other habitats. This review surveys the landscape of such agreements, offering a description of over 700 multilateral environmental agreements (MEAs) of three or more member countries and more than 1,000 bilateral treaties, conventions, protocols, and amendments (BEAs) designed to protect the environment.

Describing the Population of International Environmental Agreements

Multilateral Agreements

The list of international environmental agreements (IEAs) allows relatively confident claims to be made about MEAs. At least 729 MEAs fit the IEA definition, far more than UNEP's 1996 listing of 216 or Burhenne's listing through 1998 of 474 (26, 40). This accounting is larger, in part, because it more systematically identifies protocols and amendments. Only half of the MEAs, 357, were original agreements, with 20 percent protocols and 30

Reprinted with permission of the *Annual Review of Environmental Resources*.

percent amendments. Several MEAs were signed but never (or have not yet) entered into force, and over 50 have been replaced by other agreements or terminated. As implied by the discussion of original agreements and modifications above, this does not mean there are 700 fully distinct and separate multilateral commitments. Rather, it means that three or more governments have agreed on legally binding environmental commitments over 700 times; some are quite distinct from previous commitments, and others involve minor changes to previous commitments.

Connections Among Multilateral Agreements: Lineages and Secretariats

These 729 MEAs are not all independent but are linked to each other in various ways. Much recent scholarship has sought to capture these connections through the concept of international environmental regimes (41, 42). The term *regime* is usually defined broadly as "implicit or explicit principles, norms, rules, and decision-making procedures around which actors' expectations converge" (43, p. 2). This broad definition recognizes that state behaviors can be influenced by informal, nonbinding understandings as well as by formal legal agreements and that, even where legal agreements exist, the interpretation and implementation of those agreements and their impacts on state behavior often reflect numerous extra-legal factors related to ideas, norms, and the actors mobilized on the issue (44). This broad definition allows the *marine pollution protection regime* to be defined as including only those IMO conventions addressing global marine pollution or, alternatively, as including all international efforts addressing marine pollution, which include these IMO conventions but also include regional seas conventions, bilateral agreements, and related ministerial declarations. Although such breadth is useful for some analytic purposes, it would introduce unnecessary ambiguity into the present effort to clarify, classify, count, and describe IEAs.

Therefore, to group legally related agreements, the term *lineage* is used to refer to one or more legally linked instruments. A lineage is any set of agreements, protocols, and amendments that modify, extend, replace, or explicitly derive from one or more original agreements. For example, the marine pollution (MARPOL) lineage includes a 1954 agreement with 4 amendments replaced by a 1973 agreement and integral 1978 protocol that have been modified by another protocol and 36 amendments. Such lineages are distinct from but often form the basis of regimes. This definition groups the 729 MEAs into approximately 250 lineages. Over 40 percent of all agreements cluster into the largest twenty lineages, each of which has at least 8 instruments. Another 30 percent cluster in 50 lineages of 3 to 7 instruments each. The remaining 30 percent are split; 13 percent belong to 50 lineages that involve an initial agreement and a single modifying protocol or amendment, and 128 agreements (or 17 percent) have never been legally modified.

The larger lineages tend to consist of either frequently modified original agreements or sets of linked agreements. Rivaling the MARPOL lineage in number of agreements, the whaling lineage includes 2 early conventions and 4 protocols, the currently operative 1946 convention that replaced those, more than 50 annual binding amendments of the agreement's schedule of catch quotas, a 1956 protocol, a 1963 agreement on international observers, and several related bilateral agreements. The UN's Mediterranean Action Plan (MEDPLAN) generated an original agreement, eight protocols, and three amendments, and the 1979 LRTAP [Long-range Transboundary Air Pollution] Convention has eight protocols covering various air pollutants. Members of the 1991 Convention Concerning the Protection of the Alps have negotiated 10 protocols in 10 years addressing, inter alia, sustainable development, nature protection, forestry, agriculture, tourism, soils, energy, and transportation. The 1979 Convention on the Conservation of Migratory Species of Wild Animals (CMS) has been amended three times, but it has also facilitated negotiation of six new agreements on seals, cetaceans, albatrosses and petrels, waterbirds, and bats (the last of which has been amended twice) and six nonbinding memorandums of understanding (MOUs) on other species.

Although multi-agreement lineages usually indicate considerable international activity on an issue, the absence of a long stream of legal instruments does not imply a lack of activity. Regimes need not develop only through binding agreements. Most fisheries set catch limits through resolutions, presumably to avoid ratification delays if such limits were made binding. Although the 1949 Convention for the Establishment of an Inter-American Tropical Tuna Commission has been legally modified only once, the Commission has adopted over 40 resolutions in the last 5 years alone, limiting, inter alia, catch, gear, bycatch, and fishing by nonparties. The 1971 Convention on Wetlands of International Importance has only one protocol and one amendment, but annual Conferences of the Parties have adopted numerous recommendations and worked closely with member states to improve protection of wetlands.

As already noted, an agreement's legal designation provides only limited insight into its substantive importance. The choice to establish a convention or treaty as a new original agreement, to negotiate a protocol, or to pass an amendment appears to be driven either by legal requirements in earlier agreements or facets of institutional culture. For example, most agreements admit new members without legal action, but new members have also been admitted through conventions, protocols, and amendments. Enforcement efforts have been codified both in original agreements and in protocols. By contrast, at least one very significant and controversial change, the commercial whaling moratorium, was adopted by amendment. The CMS agreement has used both binding agreements and nonbinding MOUs to protect endangered species. Notably, the two longest lineages (whaling with 70 instruments and MARPOL with 44) both rely on *tacit acceptance* procedures that allow particular types of amendments to enter into force on a given date unless a certain number of parties object rather than when a certain number of parties accept. Agreements that require explicit acceptance (with corresponding ratification delays) for an amendment to enter into force either deter otherwise desirable changes or channel reform efforts into mechanisms that are not legally binding.

Many IEAs that are not part of the same lineage are connected by having been negotiated under a common organization's auspices. Almost 200 agreements have been negotiated under the auspices of UN organizations. The UNEP Governing Council established a Regional Seas Programme in 1974 that has produced over 40 agreements covering 10 regional seas (15). The IMO has fostered not only 44 MARPOL agreements but 10 instruments on oil pollution compensation, 9 on dumping of wastes, and 6 on oil pollution accidents and response. The UN Economic Commission for Europe facilitated nine LRTAP agreements but also five MEAs addressing transboundary environmental issues and numerous nonbinding regulations on motor vehicles (45). Fifteen agreements with 25 amendments have been concluded under the FAO Constitution (Article XIV), and numerous other IEAs have been concluded through the FAO's regional fisheries bodies and plant protection commissions (19, 46). The Council of Europe, the Benelux Economic Union, and the Association of Southeast Asian Nations (ASEAN) have also promoted development of various environmental agreements.

Most MEAs are managed through a policy-making body of member state representatives (e.g., a Conference of the Parties) and an administrative secretariat that coordinates the efforts of member states. Indeed, the primary goal of many agreements is to establish an organization to manage an environmental problem rather than to promulgate regulations that do so directly. Over 150 secretariats have been established to help manage agreements; some have large staffs actively engaged in formulating and implementing policies, yet others exist in name only [a list of these secretariats is available at (31)]. Many agreements also establish subsidiary bodies, such as the UNFCCC's Subsidiary Bodies for Implementation and for Scientific and Technological Advice or the International Whaling Commission's Scientific Committee.

Substantive and Temporal Patterns in Multilateral Agreements

Given the number of MEAs, it is not surprising that they cover a range of environmental problems. To categorize them involves, by necessity, creating groupings that reflect the perspective of the person categorizing and that cannot be mutually exclusive because many agreements address themselves to multiple environmental issues [for an alternative categorization, see (38)]. Thus, many individual agreements appear in multiple categories in the descriptive summary that follows. Almost half, 348, of all MEAs attempt to protect species or manage human impacts on those species. More than one third of the species-related instruments, 124, relate directly to fisheries and fish protection and management (with 72 original agreements and 52 protocols and amendments), and another 87 agreements, protocols, and amendments relate to other marine animals including whales, other cetaceans, turtles, and fur seals. Other species-specific agreements target polar bears, bats, vicuña (a South American camelid), birds, or wildlife generally. Over time, MEAs have come to focus more on pollution with a recent increase in agreements addressing habitat. Until 1972, less than 20 percent of MEAs, 39 of 221, were pollution related and 67 percent (149) were species related; since then, the adoption rate has been almost exactly even (199 on species, 203 on pollution). More than half of all pollution agreements, 126, address marine pollution, but many address lake and river pollution (a balance that is probably quite different among BEAs). Nuclear pollution from energy production and nuclear weapons has been explicitly addressed in 39 agreements. Although highly visible, MEAs addressing atmospheric pollutants have numbered only 20; these included climate change, acid rain, ozone protection, and air pollution from ships. Although habitat protection was addressed in agreements in 1900, 1933, and 1940, it has been an infrequent target of MEAs and constituted only about 3 percent of the total (22 agreements).

Although international environmental activity has increased recently, states began cooperating on what we would now consider environmental issues in the nineteenth century. By 1910, three agreements addressing the invasive species of *Phylloxera vastatrix* (a North American insect that devastated the French wine industry), five on European fisheries, two on transport of environmentally harmful materials on the Rhine, one on birds, and one on species and habitat conservation in Africa had been negotiated. Between 1911 and 1945, 21 MEAs were negotiated addressing protection of North Pacific fur seals and whales; fisheries in the Baltic and the Atlantic; and various agricultural issues (including formation of the FAO, locusts, and contagious animal diseases). A 1933 convention calling on governments to establish national parks listed more and less severely threatened species in separate annexes that foreshadowed the approach of the Convention on International Trade in Endangered Species (CITES) 40 years later. After World War II, MEAs were adopted with increasing speed. A prewar rate of an agreement every two years became a rate of seven agreements per year between 1946 and 1972, the year of the UN Conference on the Human Environment (UNCHE). That rate has continued to increase with 319 agreements completed in the 20 years from UNCHE to the 1992 UN Conference on Environment and Development (16 agreements per year), and 189 agreements completed from 1993 through 2002 (19 agreements per year).

Bilateral Agreements

Developing a comprehensive list of BEAs proves more difficult because they often are documented and known about only within the two signatory countries. Listings are generated less frequently than for multilaterals, often by foreign ministries that generally do not make them readily available, separate environmental from nonenvironmental agreements, or, understandably, reproduce them in languages other than those of the signatory states. Thus, a definitive description of BEAs, and hence of IEAs as a whole, must await a more concerted, resource-intensive effort than any yet undertaken. That said, the IEA database has made a significant effort in this direction that makes some description of the population of BEAs possible.

Although this project's IEA database focused initially on identifying multilaterals, it has since identified over 1,040 BEAs. This number represents a lower bound of BEAs. An estimate for an upper bound can be arrived at by noting that BEAs exist in approximately a 3-to-1 ratio to MEAs in FAO's FAOLEX database and in work reported by Jacobson & Brown Weiss (47, 48, p. 1). Assuming this ratio holds for the population of IEAs, then the 700 MEAs identified here suggest an upper bound of 2,100 BEAs, a number that could be refined through a more systematic accounting. Of the BEAs identified, only 100 (10 percent) are protocols or amendments, a much lower proportion than among MEAs; governments appear to replace BEAs more often than they modify them. Of the BEAs identified, about 30 percent address fisheries; 25 percent address freshwater management; 10 percent address environmental protection generally; and 10 percent address plant, animal, and agricultural issues. Time trends in BEAs parallel those of MEAs. Already by 1900, 29 had been negotiated, almost exclusively among European states to address river or fisheries management. The 74 BEAs signed from 1901 to 1945 (a rate of 1.5 per year) ramped up quickly to 227 being signed from 1946 to 1972 (8 per year), 389 from 1973 to 1992 (20 per year), and 314 from 1993 to 2002 (32 per year). Even this incomplete dataset of BEAs demonstrates that they play an important and increasing role in global environmental governance, one that has not yet received the same scholarly interest as, and seems likely to differ from, the role of MEAs.

Negotiating International Environmental Agreements: Why We Have Those We Have

Investigating the causes of, and conditions that foster, negotiation of international agreements, including environmental ones, has been a major focus of international relations research for some time. This discussion switches to discussing environmental regimes to reflect the fact that research on their formation and research on their effects (described in the next section) generally are interested in understanding regimes in the broad sense defined above rather than in the narrower sense of formal legal agreements (49). Much research has focused on why the international community takes up (or ignores) a particular environmental issue at the time and in the form it does (50, 51, 52, 53, 54, 55). Neither scientific nor public consensus about a problem's existence, importance, or causes nor efforts by those concerned about a problem are enough to produce international action. Indeed, there appear to be many necessary (or at least facilitative) conditions for the negotiation of IEAs but very few, if any, sufficient conditions. The timing and content of IEAs are influenced by the strength of states' interests in environmental protection relative to other concerns and their power to promote those interests, the knowledge and discourse that structure perceptions of environmental problems and their solutions, and the efforts of individuals and groups in proposing solutions and pressing governments to accept agreements that are on the table.

Interests, Power, and Discourse

Refining more general arguments from international relations, scholars of international environmental politics have sought to understand how the array of interests among states influences the ability to negotiate, and the design of, international agreements. They have proposed various typologies to explain why nations have formed regimes quickly in response to some environmental problems, more slowly in response to others, and not at all in response to yet others (42, 56, 57, 58, 59). Despite differences, these typologies all see the ease or difficulty of regime formation as a function of conflicts between the political, economic, and environmental interests of relevant countries. In some environmental problems, the obstacles to agreement stem from a tragedy of the commons in which all countries have mixed motives, i.e., all want the problem resolved but none want to contribute to its resolution (60). Yet, the obstacles to agreement can be even greater in unidirectional or "upstream/downstream" problems in which upstream perpetrators lack any incentives to restrain their pollution levels, and downstream victims have no credible threats with which to induce such restraint (61). Likewise, problems involving fundamental conflicts over the environmental goal (as in current negotiations on whaling and climate change) tend to resist resolution more than those involving conflicts on the means of achieving a shared goal (as in negotiations to reduce acid precipitants through common targets or differentiated critical loads) (62).

These problem typologies help explain the content, as well as the likelihood, of agreement. In mixed motive problems, any agreement must address the ongoing incentives of members to cheat, i.e., the desire all members have to encourage others to contribute to the problem's remedy while, secretly, not contributing themselves. In contrast, agreements to harmonize environmental policies among states already committed to environmental protection (say, for domestic political reasons) need only identify the policies members should harmonize to, because the agreement is not addressing members' incentives to violate but only their need for a rule about how to comply (56, 63). Thus, agreements addressing overexploitation of fisheries (a mixed motive problem) usually have more stringent enforcement provisions than those among, for example, European states to harmonize national environmental policies to facilitate international trade. Further, agreements addressing mixed motive problems usually can rely on reciprocal behavioral commitments (e.g., all countries reducing pollution levels or fish harvests by specified amounts). Such commitments will not resolve upstream/downstream problems: Upstream countries do not benefit from downstream countries reducing their pollution and must be offered side payments or rewards to join and comply (61).

Features beyond the underlying politics of a problem also affect whether agreements are concluded. Highly visible, immediate, and dramatic environmental damage that actors in powerful states care about tend to receive international attention. Thus, marine pollution agreements have addressed oil pollution more often than less visible pollutants, such as chemicals, garbage, or sewage; the relative rarity of agreements on air pollution may reflect the diffuse, difficult to identify, and chronic nature of air pollution's effects. As the domestic policy literature notes, policy shifts more easily after accidents and crises or during moments of windows of opportunity (64, 65, 110, 111, 112, 113). Although crises "are not driving forces like material conditions, interests, or ideas," they can prompt international action if deeper forces make conditions ripe (53, p. 77). Environmental disasters, such as the Chernobyl nuclear accident and chemical spills on the Rhine, raise public awareness of a problem, produce calls for action, and clear political "space for the consideration of new ideas on how to explain and solve problems" (66, p. 185). Scientific breakthroughs, like discovery of the stratospheric ozone hole, can serve a similar function (67; 68, p. 27; 69). And, when one country or region comes to see an environmental problem as a crisis, other countries also tend to see that problem in crisis terms, which makes international action easier than would have been possible even months before (54). However, the often chronic environmental problems of developing countries that have long ago been remedied in industrialized countries, such as poor water quality, often receive little international attention (70). Indeed, major oil spills off Europe and North America have often prompted negotiations on marine pollution, yet those off Africa and Latin America have not (71, 72).

Astute politicians and institutions, of course, do not wait for catalytic events but expend "political capital in an effort to persuade others to recognize [certain] issues as priority agenda items" (53, p. 7; 64). Scientists (and the "epistemic communities" they compose) clarify environmental impacts and propose solutions (73, p. 224). Although the legitimacy accorded to science gives global environmental assessments considerable influence, as evident with the Intergovernmental Panel on Climate Change's reports, many still "sink without a trace" (69). International organizations develop expertise and focus resources on certain issues, as with UNEP's Regional Seas efforts and IMO's efforts on marine pollution. And, often, international cooperation on one pollutant or species fosters cooperation in related areas. NGOs provide information, conduct research, and propose and evaluate policies, actions that introduce both ideas and political pressure into negotiations (74, 75). Corporations and other interest groups in agenda-setting states often internationalize domestic issues to avoid the costs of unilateral action by their governments (76). Although domestic political pressures can predispose certain governments to be leaders, leadership in any given case usually reflects an interplay between those pressures and characteristics of the environmental problem (53, p. 7; 54, 76).

Whether these factors produce agreement depends on how governments perceive their political interests and preferences. States become supportive "leaders" or oppositional "laggards" based on an interplay of the environmental "facts" (e.g., whether a state is upwind or downwind), the economic impacts of action and of inaction, and the way these factors are perceived by domestic political audiences (77, p. 78; 78). These basic preferences are influenced, in turn, by policy styles, party politics, bureaucratic structures, and transnational linkages (76, 79, 80). If interests and preferences vary from state to state, the constellations of interests among states also vary from environmental issue to environmental issue, with many involving multiple, overlapping types of problems. Thus, states concerned about a particular pollutant may face a tragedy of the commons problem among themselves and an upstream/downstream problem with polluting states that do not share their concern (62, 81).

States' goals for negotiations also influence how quickly they succeed. Framework conventions, cooperative research programs, or nonbinding resolutions may reflect universally low concern, an inability to resolve conflict between concerned and unconcerned states, or high concern but uncertainty about how best to address the problem. Disputes over the solutions proposed can cause as much resistance to agreement as disputes about whether the problem needs resolution. Even efforts that are relatively unambitious ecologically may be strongly opposed if they impose high costs on powerful states or influential economic actors. Thus, the climate convention has met considerable resistance because of the costs it requires states to incur, despite the fact that its emission targets fall far short of what climate experts consider necessary to avert climate change.

Although states have no obligation to join any agreement, membership is not always fully voluntary. A powerful state, or group of states, can impose regimes or make membership more attractive than non-membership (82, pp. 84, 85, 86; 83). Over the past quarter century, a combination of threats of American economic sanctions and public outcries have caused many whaling states, often reluctantly, to join the whaling convention, to reduce their opposition to a moratorium on commercial whaling, and to remain members of an agreement many view as increasingly ignoring their interests (84, 85). Power may reflect general economic or military power or more issue-specific power from the ability to influence outcomes if no agreement is reached or from voting and bargaining strength within a regime (86). Thus, China and India refused to join the ozone regime until industrialized states codified financial transfers (87). Brazil can block progress on tropical rainforest protection, as Botswana, Namibia, and Zimbabwe can on elephants. In contrast, if states responsible for a problem share a desire to resolve it, spontaneous patterns of social practice may make legal agreements unnecessary (82, pp. 84, 85, 86).

Although interests matter, IEAs are not simply aggregations of states' "well-developed conceptions of their own interests" (53, p. 97). Preferences can be unclear and unstable in environmental arenas in which knowledge is uncertain, issues are complex, and material interests are "weakly or ambiguously affected" (88, pp. 132–133). High levels of uncertainty can make interests and preferences hard to identify, sometimes hindering and sometimes facilitating agreement (63). Bargaining persuades as well as communicates interests, threats, and promises, and it alters perceived interests and whether and what type of regimes form (63). Framing a problem as global gives "every participant in the negotiation process real bargaining leverage" and veto power (53, p. 14). Framing the problem as regional may facilitate evolutionary progress, as evident in UNEP regional seas agreements and regional plant protection agreements. In short, how things are discussed, not just what is discussed, matters.

Actors and Processes

Within the constraints of interests, power, and discourse, actors and processes still influence when and what agreements get signed. Although different scholars have focused on states, secretariats, epistemic communities, NGOs, domestic political constituencies, and individual leaders, the similarities in their lists of how these different groups influence the negotiation process suggest functional distinctions may be more useful (75, 89, 90, p. 18; 91). Those who understand environmental trends and their causes can motivate negotiators by causing them to reestimate the costs of reaching, or failing to reach, agreement. When claims by other governments are suspect, policymakers often seek advice from scientists, international organizations, and NGOs they perceive as more impartial (75, p. 727; 90, p. 12). Indeed, many NGOs seek out resources and expertise to supplement traditional advocacy with impartial information provision. NGOs also provide negotiators' insight into, and influence on, various constituencies' perceptions of environmental issues (74, p. 217).

At local, national, and international levels, NGOs, industry trade groups, and even scientists lobby, promote media coverage, campaign, protest, or engage in ecosabotage to raise issue salience. By providing information on the progress of international negotiations to constituencies, environmental NGOs and corporations create pressure to succeed in environmental negotiations (6, 7). States grant NGOs (e.g., the Earth Negotiations Bulletin) access to negotiations to get detailed daily reporting but accept, in exchange, dissemination of that reporting, which can increase public and NGO pressure for agreement (75, p. 730).

Agreement design is intimately connected with the negotiation progress. The desire to negotiate, sign, and ratify an agreement depends on the current terms of debate. States often reject substantive restrictions on their behavior only to sign framework conventions that require ongoing collective decisionmaking that is likely to produce similar, if not more stringent, restrictions. Incorporating financial mechanisms makes potential donors less likely to join but potential recipients more likely to join. Particular decision-making rules, proscriptions, prescriptions, implementation provisions, and withdrawal and renegotiation clauses can all become deal breakers or deal makers. This setting rewards "deft diplomats" who can "add and subtract issues to facilitate the bargaining process, craft the terms of negotiating texts, and broker the deals needed to achieve consensus" (53, p. 23). Although material resources are certainly helpful, high-ranking international, domestic, and nonstate representatives can foster agreement without such resources often simply by tabling compelling proposals (53, p. 23; 74, 75, p. 727; 91, p. 67).

Particularly when exogenous forces make reaching agreement difficult, maintaining political momentum becomes crucial (53, pp. 87; 88). Indeed, the many agreements in certain lineages noted above illustrates how secretariats or individual entrepreneurial leaders can develop, or keep alive, proposals and propose them when conditions become conducive (92). Thus, UNEP Executive Director, Mostafa Tolba, played a crucial role in fostering progress in the ozone negotiations by his careful drafting and introduction of texts at crucial points in the negotiating process (53, p. 119; 68, p. 26). Even the act of holding a meeting can promote agreement because ending the meeting without agreement is so often construed as failure.

As noted, protecting the international environment does not require international law. Indeed, circumventing the state may be quicker, easier, and more open to innovation (93). States sometimes act unilaterally to protect the global environment, funding environmental projects in other countries or sanctioning countries for violating domestic or international environmental standards (76, 94). NGOs and transnational issue networks can engage in world civic politics, using rhetorical persuasion to directly influence the values and behaviors of individuals and corporations (6, 7). Governments, NGOs, and trade groups (and partnerships among them) promote ecolabeling and voluntary codes of conduct, fund debt for nature swaps, and promote consumer boycotts and buy green campaigns that directly shape corporate incentives (6, 91, p. 66; 95, 96, 97).

Making International Environmental Agreements Effective: Why Some Work and Others Do Not

Ultimately, the value of IEAs is evident not in their negotiation but in their influence on human behaviors that harm the environment. Some environmental problems have improved since relevant IEAs were signed, but others have changed little or become worse. Global production of ozone depleting substances and European and North American emissions of acid precipitants have declined since treaties were signed while many marine ecosystems and fish stocks have deteriorated despite regional and global efforts. Yet, a simple interpretation of this variation (that the former agreements outperformed the latter) is likely to be wrong. It is tempting to interpret continuing environmental decline as failure and environmental improvement as success, to attribute improvements as caused by particular features of relevant agreements, and to promote those features as models for other environmental arenas. And these conclusions may be correct. But they often misinterpret the evidence. First, improvement is preferable to decline, but pressures for environmental degradation are often so strong that success may often only be evident in slower rates of degradation. Second, an IEA's influence requires comparing observed outcomes to what would have happened without the treaty rather than to what did happen before the treaty. Environmental quality and behavior are functions of numerous factors, and improvements often arise from fortuitous economic or technological changes unrelated to a treaty. Third, variation in effectiveness may reflect differences in the problems being addressed, the international context, or other factors that have little to do with the agreements themselves. Identical treaties would reduce ozone depletion and acid rain more than overfishing and marine pollution if the former proved more susceptible to regulation or had conditions that were more favorable than in the latter cases.

Work on the implementation, compliance, effects, and effectiveness of IEAs has been dominated by the study of regimes. During the 1990s, individuals and teams representing differing disciplines, countries, and theoretical approaches examined numerous cases to produce a remarkably coherent research program. By themselves, English-language edited volumes directly evaluating environmental regime effectiveness identify a plethora of factors and forces considered influential (41, 42, 94, 98, 99, 100, 101).

Identifying the Effects of Regimes

Identifying an appropriate scale for evaluating regimes proves difficult because regime effects can be so varied. Most work on regime impacts has focused on whether regimes achieve their desired objectives in relatively direct ways. However, agreements can have indirect, nonobvious, and nonimmediate effects, such as when agreements improve scientific knowledge of a problem and thereby cause governments, corporate actors, and individuals to reassess their interests and adopt less environmentally harmful behaviors. They can have external effects in arenas beyond those targeted by the agreement (41). Indeed, any environmental agreement that causes environmental improvements will also cause corresponding economic changes. The ozone regime all but eliminated a flourishing chlorofluorocarbon (CFC) industry, and many IEAs that establish nature reserves or specially protected areas dramatically alter the lives of nearby residents. Effects can also be characterized as positive or negative (41, pp. 14, 15). Recent conflicts within CITES reflect, in part, concerns that a ban on ivory sales would have been negatively effective and undercut elephant protection by blocking revenues from ivory sales that range state governments could use to prevent poaching and preserve elephant habitat.

Starting with environmental quality, an agreement's explicit environmental goals serve as a useful metrics for evaluating how much a regime helped resolve "the problem that led to its formation" (102, p. 109; 103, p. 366). These environmental goals are useful metrics at times but are often unclear, are hortatory rather than realistic, or may change as scientific understanding improves (102, p. 109). Equally important, analysts may want to evaluate progress toward goals that differ from, or are more ambitious than, those held by the parties (81, 104). Thus, although the whaling convention sought "to provide for the proper conservation of whale stocks and thus make possible the orderly development of the whaling industry," some may want to know whether it has promoted a norm of a whale's right to life (105).

Much research to date has focused on changes in behavior rather than environmental improvements. This reflects a recognition that the latter requires the former and that our ability to estimate counterfactuals regarding environmental quality (a product of natural variation, human behavior, and myriad other factors) is even more limited than our ability to estimate counterfactuals regarding human behavior (41, 42, 101, 154). Legal compliance provides a useful initial metric but misses overcompliance and good faith noncompliance that also constitute evidence of regime influence (106). For example, LRTAP's influence was more evident in the otherwise-unlikely 10 percent reductions in Hungarian sulfur emissions than from Nordic reductions that far surpassed the 30 percent requirement but would have occurred anyway (78). The problem, of course, is that regimes may induce significant behavioral change that falls far short of the environmental goals of regime negotiators, let alone the goals held by interested scientists, analysts, or environmental advocates (81, p. 4).

Beyond identifying a scale for evaluation, the analyst must identify a reference point on the scale chosen. Two basic types of reference points have been identified: relative improvement and goal achievement (81, p. 5). The first compares observed outcomes to a no-agreement or no-regime baseline. The second compares them to the desired value, as defined by regime negotiators (goal achievement) or an independent analyst (collective optimum) (81, p. 6). These standards are complementary: The former, glass half full, criterion asks how far have we come; the latter, glass half empty, criterion asks how far have we yet to go. Several scholars have sought to combine these criteria in a measure of progress that calculates observed improvement from a no-regime baseline as a fraction of total possible improvement from that baseline, a strategy that moves us beyond claims that a regime made a difference toward claims that a regime achieved (or fell short of) its potential (81, 104).

Several additional aspects of regime effects research deserve comment. Research that compares one regime's performance to another's (rather than evaluating a single regime's performance) has begun but faces obstacles in convincingly accounting for differences in how hard problems are to resolve and comparing progress made in noncomparable realms (107). Questions of efficiency, cost-effectiveness, and equity also remain under studied. The plethora of claims regarding what features improve performance under what conditions have still to be carefully evaluated against the empirical evidence (81, p. 8; 102, p. 116; 103, p. 374). And efforts to answer these questions still rely excessively on case studies without sufficient use of other analytic techniques (108).

A Summary of the Effects of Environmental Agreements

A summary of existing analyses clarifies (a) that major obstacles exist to analyzing agreement effects accurately, (b) that only a relatively small subset of agreements have been analyzed, (c) that data exists on a significantly broader range of agreements, and (d) that more careful and systematic comparison of IEA effects is needed. Scholars have analyzed only a small fraction of extant IEAs, in part because the number of IEAs has been consistently underestimated but more because relevant data on behaviors or environmental quality are not readily available. First, finding effects data is difficult because, although some agreements have a single, unambiguous, and obvious behavioral indicator (e.g., the 1973 Agreement on the Conservation of Polar Bears or the 1976 Convention on the Protection of the Rhine Against Pollution by Chlorides), many others target multiple environmental problems (e.g., CITES addresses numerous species, and MARPOL addresses myriad ocean pollutants) or address behaviors that are not readily quantified (e.g., the Wetlands Convention requires countries to "promote the conservation [and] wise use of wetlands"). Second, agreements negotiated in the past 5–10 years are too recent to have had effects that can be evaluated. Third, data useful for distinguishing the influence of regimes from other factors often do not exist or exist but are not well known or readily available. In many cases, data collection begins only after agreements are signed, precluding pre-post analysis. In others, data is not systematically collected with the quality or precision needed. Data relevant to many older agreements may be buried as appendices in obscure reports that prove increasingly difficult to find in an electronic information age. Fourth, relevant data that do exist often are formatted in ways that discourage analysis. For example, FAO has an extensive database of fish catch (FISHSTAT) broken down by country, year, species, region where caught, and gear used (109). However, using that data to analyze any of the scores of extant fisheries agreements requires identifying which species were regulated in which regions in which years for which countries so that regulated catch can be compared to unregulated catch.

Despite these problems, available data would allow analysis of far more agreements than scholars usually assume. Many IEAs identified here probably do not have the quality and quantity of data needed to support rigorous analysis. But, several hundred agreements could be analyzed using data that exist or that could be developed readily by combining various data sources. FISHSTAT offers opportunities for evaluating the myriad fishery agreements and amendments and for comparing their binding requirements to their many nonbinding recommendations and regulations. Detailed multi-country, multi-year datasets also exist with data relevant to IEAs that address several endangered species, e.g., whales, polar bears, North Pacific fur seals, acid rain and ozone depleting substances, and various marine and river pollutants. Useful datasets are often available from treaty secretariats; other international, governmental, and nongovernmental organizations; scientists; doctoral dissertations; and published sources. Careful combination and compilation of data from such sources as well as efforts to adopt techniques that would make better and more innovative use of the historical record could provide data useful to analyzing an even larger subset of all environmental agreements (110). Efforts to develop such datasets and analyze them using quantitative techniques have only recently begun (107).

A brief and incomplete summary gives some sense of how the effects of agreements, and assessments of those effects, vary. Most scholars credit the ozone agreements with rapidly reducing production and consumption of CFCs by industrialized countries, despite debate over whether this reflects regulatory, scientific, economic, or political dynamics and despite concern that the effects on developing countries may be less dramatic (87, 111, 112). A 1911 convention to protect fur seals is credited with dramatically reducing harvest and recovering seal stocks (113, 114). One recent analysis has argued that the whaling regime, until 1984, demonstrated "the impotence of . . . IEAs" (115, p. 17); another has argued that the whaling regime has become "quite effective" recently (85, p. 380). Assessments of the LRTAP protocols and pollution of the Rhine suggest they had some influence on behaviors but that many environmental improvements could be better accounted for by factors other than the agreement (78, 116, 117, 118, 119, 120). The many MEDPLAN agreements are generally judged as having done little to reduce Mediterranean pollution (73, 121). There are so many fisheries regimes with such different regulatory approaches that, not surprisingly, some appear to have performed quite well, and others appear to have actually made matters worse (122, 123, 124). The reader of these and many other assessments is generally left with the sense that evaluating a single agreement well requires sensitivity to complexity and variation and that regimes often have effects that change over time due to institutional change. Change in exogenous factors may influence one behavior or set of actors, but have no influence on other behaviors or actors (125).

This dynamic and multifaceted character of effects has been highlighted by projects that explicitly have tried to compare the effects of different regimes and the responses of different countries to different regimes (41, 42, 98, 101, 126, 154). A study led by Brown Weiss & Jacobson of five regimes concluded that the regimes related to ozone protection and ocean dumping of radioactive wastes (the London Dumping Convention) were more effective than those related to the 1972 World Heritage Convention and the 1982 International Tropical Timber Agreement (127, pp. 515, 516). Another study led by Miles & Underdal examined 14 regimes (each composed of multiple agreements) and found that more than half achieved significant or major behavioral improvements relative to the no-regime counterfactual during one or more time periods. They also found, however, that almost 60 percent were not particularly effective in "accomplishment of functionally optimal solutions" (128, p. 435). Like Brown Weiss & Jacobson, they deemed the regimes on ozone protection and ocean dumping of radioactive waste to be quite effective and had similar evaluations of the regional regimes protecting the North Sea from dumping by ships and aircraft and managing tuna fisheries in the Central and Southwest Pacific Ocean (42). They also found that the MEDPLAN, MARPOL, the whaling regime, and the 1980 Convention on the Conservation of Antarctic Marine Living Resources were not particularly effective at inducing behavioral change. Regimes related to LRTAP, protection of the North Sea from land-based pollution, and management of salmon in the North Pacific were found to have produced mixed results. Although both these studies judged CITES as being less effective than other agreements, several more detailed evaluations have judged its impacts quite favorably (128A, p. 26; 128B). The judgments made by these researchers, and particularly conflicting judgments such as those regarding CITES or the whaling regime, highlight (a) the difficulty of assessing agreement impacts, (b) the difficulty of comparing impacts, and (c) how much those impacts depend on the standard used by the analyst (117, p. 233). They also suggest that summary claims about regime effects may be less valuable than more nuanced claims about particular effects of interest during particular regime stages. That said, the literature as a whole suggests that some regimes fail quite miserably, others do reasonably well, but very few fully and permanently resolve the problems they address (128, p. 435).

The Determinants of Regime Effects

To say that IEA effects are evident in changes in behavior or environmental quality is not to say that they are the only sources of such changes. Any behavior that can be influenced by an agreement is also subject to many other influences. Changes in treaty-regulated behaviors are often due to factors other than the treaty. Even the strongest supporter of international environmental law would recognize that agreements, however well designed, are not always the cause of good outcomes.

The political science literature to date has focused on how regimes influence the environmental behaviors of states, but it could benefit by framing the question as what explains variation in the environmental behavior of states. This subtle shift directs our attention to the many nonlegal drivers of environmental behaviors that are often arrayed against international environmental agreements but sometimes facilitate their efforts. Environmental economists have done considerable research into factors that explain variation in pollution across countries, factors that have often been ignored when evaluating IEA effects (129). Including economic, technological, political, and other drivers of behavior as explanatory variables in an analysis allows their use as control variables and demonstrates that covariation between an IEA and some outcome persists even after controlling for other factors. This also allows assessment of whether an IEA's influence depends on, and is large or small relative to, these other influences. The plethora of factors hypothesized as driving environmental degradation can be categorized into four groups: characteristics of the country, the international context, the environmental problem, and the agreement (127). Cutting across these categories run distinctions between domestic and international factors and among economic, political, social, and demographic factors.

Both theoretical considerations and empirical evidence suggest that characteristics of the environmental problem explain the likely effects of an agreement on a given behavior but also explain variation in those behaviors (over time, across actors, and across problems) that have nothing to do with agreements (127, p. 521). At the simplest level, countries that are ecologically vulnerable and have low adjustment costs tend to be more responsive to agreements while those that are not affected ecologically or have high adjustment costs tend to be more recalcitrant (77). Problems whose resolution requires new behaviors tend to face violations owing to incentives and incapacity, whereas those that require restraint tend to face only violations owing to incentives. Environmental problems differ in how willing and able relevant actors are to alter their behavior and, hence, how difficult it will be to induce conformance with regime rules (42; 81, p. 1; 101; 102, p. 117). Market structures can reinforce or undercut regulatory efforts—the recovery of fur seals in response to the 1911 agreement owed much to the ease of monitoring that stemmed from London being the only major market for skins (113). Marine pollution agreements benefit from the incentives shipbuilders and ship insurers have to monitor and enforce them, but international endangered species agreements create shortages and price increases that encourage smuggling that undermines their effectiveness (71; 127, p. 521). The major threats to agreements that address tragedy of the commons situations involve efforts to cheat clandestinely; the success of such agreements often requires stringent compliance monitoring to identify cheating. The major threats to agreements that address upstream/downstream situations involve perpetrating states threatening victims with violations unless they receive more compensation for their cooperation; such extortion attempts are, by definition, public and so compliance monitoring is less crucial to these agreements (130).

Other important problem characteristics include the number of actors contributing to a problem, levels of uncertainty about the problem or its resolution, the role and position of corporations, and the concentration of the activity being regulated (127, figure 15.2). Variation in these factors can cause changes in behaviors independent of any agreement. New knowledge of a behavior's environmental impacts will, even without an agreement, reduce such behaviors if their damage imposes large and immediate costs on those engaged in the behavior or on others who have influence over those who engage in the behavior. Polluting behaviors often decline if environmentally friendly technologies become economically attractive, whereas extractive behaviors (e.g., fishing or whaling) tend to be less responsive to technological developments because environmental damage is more inherent to those behaviors. Social and cultural commitments to an activity and economic inertia can create resistance to change, as evident in the difficulty of reducing whaling by countries with cultural commitments to it, such as Norway, or reducing dependence on fossil fuels in most developed states.

Country characteristics explain why countries vary in their environmental degradation and in their responsiveness to agreements. Indeed, economic research has sought to explain pollution levels by reference to country characteristics, such as economic indicators, political and policy indicators, and demographic and social indicators (129, 131, 132, 133). Political scientists note the importance of relatively stable forces, such as history and culture, geographic size and heterogeneity, resource endowments, and the number of neighbors; more variable factors, such as level of development, type of government, the role of environmental parties, and attitudes and values; and quite immediate drivers, such as changes in administrative and financial capacity, leadership, NGO activities, and knowledge and information (127, p. 535; 134, 135, 136, 137). These factors drive environmental behaviors independent of agreements but also influence the ability and willingness of states to implement international commitments. Marine pollution agreements had little influence on tanker owners and operators when their flag states were the only ones with enforcement rights; they became far more effective after amendments extended enforcement rights to port states that were both more concerned and more able to enforce them (71). Incapacity has been shown to be a major reason that many countries, particularly developing ones, fail to fulfill their environmental commitments (98, 127). And, incapacity problems are worse for agreements that must invoke positive expenditures of resources rather than simple requirements of restraint.

Characteristics of the international context tend to explain major shifts in environmental practices (127, p. 528). The end of the Cold War, the start of the war on terrorism, global economic booms or recessions, large-scale shifts toward democratic governance, and development of new technologies can alter how, and how much, countries protect the environment. Globalization can both encourage environmental protection and hasten environmental degradation (138). The increasing attention of global media and the public to environmental problems has led individuals, corporations, and countries to adopt behaviors and design technologies that produce less environmental harm. That attention is promoted by international conferences, such as the 1972 UN Conference on the Human Environment, the 1992 UN Conference on Environment and Development, and the 2002

World Summit on Sustainable Development, and by major scientific reports on such problems as climate change, biodiversity, or ozone loss (69). NGOs, such as Worldwide Fund for Nature and Greenpeace, and intergovernmental organizations, such as UNEP and the World Bank, have led countries to focus on environmental problems and provided financial and informational resources to address them. These forces also overlap and interplay with agreement features (139, 140). Indeed, although the increasing density of environmental agreements may foster the ability of each to achieve its objectives, there are competing views about whether integrating all environmental agreements into a global environmental organization would facilitate or impede environmental progress (141, 142).

Characteristics of the agreement constitute the influences on environmental behaviors of most interest (127, p. 523). Were realist theory always correct, then characteristics of the problem, countries, and international context would determine behavioral outcomes (143, 144). Institutionalists have shown, however, that regime design and problem-solving capacity also influence outcomes (81, p. 1; 145). Indeed, the time spent negotiating IEAs reflects the assumption that the outcomes achieved depend on agreement design, not just the exogenous factors just delineated. What follows attempts to make sense of the "plethora of propositions as to which types of institutions are likely to be more effective" (103, p. 374).

The social and political process of defining the problem, and the strategies and aggressiveness with which it is addressed, condition an agreement's effects because they determine the costs, obstacles, and resistance to achieving it (54, 146). Aggressive goals may motivate significant behavior change by those who try yet fail to meet them, or they may be ignored as unachievable (54, 147). More realistic goals may achieve visible results quickly but may provide few incentives for actors to do more. The means chosen also surely matter, but even simple questions, such as whether binding agreements induce more change than nonbinding resolutions, remain open (34). Clear regulatory rules may seem crucial to behavioral change, but we do not yet know how regulatory regimes compare to procedural regimes that facilitate recurring collective choice, programmatic regimes that pool resources toward collective goals, or generative regimes that develop new norms (53, p. 145; 102, p. 24). The conditions for success of regulatory regimes have been more fully specified, however, if only because their explicitness makes measuring their effects easier.

Regulatory regimes induce compliance through primary rule systems, information systems, and response systems (106). Effective regimes design these systems so they fit the environmental and behavioral demands of the problem. Regime designers must choose among behavioral prescriptions and proscriptions. Deciding which activity to regulate dictates which actors with what interests and capacities must change their behavior, how large and costly those changes will be, and whether other factors will reinforce or undercut compliance incentives. Designing more specific rules clarifies what is expected for those predisposed to comply and removes the opportunity to claim inadvertence or misinterpretation for those predisposed to violate (148). Even perceptions regarding the fairness of rules can influence their effects (127).

Regimes can increase their effects through choices regarding information systems. Regulating highly transparent activities or those that involve transactions between actors can reassure each actor that others are complying and allow them to protect their interests if they are not. Although most regimes rely on self-reporting systems, those that supply incentives and build the capacity to report appear to work better than others that sanction nonreporting or fail to address practical obstacles to reporting (149). Intrusive monitoring systems have been authorized in several environmental agreements, and rising environmental concern may make them more common.

A regime's influence also depends on how it responds to compliance and violation. In trade and arms control treaties, strategies of direct tit-for-tat reciprocity are likely to be both used and effective: Member states have incentives to raise tariffs on states that violate tariff rules and to build more missiles if other states violate a weapons limitation, and those responses, if carried out, are costly enough to deter many violations (150). In environmental realms, such strategies are less useful because regime supporters are generally unwilling to harm the environment in retaliation for a violation, and even if they did so, such actions would have little influence on those unconcerned about the environment. Recognizing this, many have stressed the need for treaties to couple economic sanctions with careful monitoring and verification mechanisms to trigger them (103, p. 363; 151, 152). Chayes and Chayes argue that such enforcement is less effective than compliance management using diplomacy, norms, and rewards (148). Empirical research has yet to resolve whether enforcement trumps management and, if so, under what conditions (152). Systems of implementation review, sunshine methods, eco-certification, and prior informed consent have also been used by various IEAs to induce behavior changes (127, 101). Norms unsupported by sanctions or rewards, e.g., the Wetland Convention's "wise use" requirement, can foster dialogue and discussion, which in turn may alter perceptions of (and engagement in) appropriate and inappropriate behaviors (153). Crucial questions remain regarding which of these (and other) strategies work best in which circumstances, once the analyst has controlled for characteristics of the issue area, international context, and actors.

The Endogeneity Problem

Evaluating IEA influence not only requires evaluating these competing explanations but poses a final, challenging endogeneity problem: The factors that drive environmental behaviors also determine the agreements that states negotiate as well as which states join agreements once they are concluded. Such factors offer a rival explanation for any purported IEA influence. Agreements are signed only by those states that are ready to limit environmental harm—and only when they are ready to do so. Therefore, by definition, but for reasons unrelated to IEAs, the activities of member states will differ both from their prior behavior and from that of nonmember states. Cases where different treaty provisions correlate with behaviors or environmental quality may be mere reflections of underlying differences in the problem being addressed or other factors. Thus, changes in economic interests may produce pressures to negotiate an agreement and to change behaviors. Highly interdependent (e.g., European) states may adopt more ambitious agreements and change their behavior more readily than less interdependent states. Empirical research on IEA effects faces several such obstacles that require careful theorizing and the use of analytic techniques that are available but are only beginning to be applied to the task.

Conclusion

If an IEA is defined as an intergovernmental document intended as legally binding (whether an original agreement or a modification thereto) with a primary stated purpose of managing or preventing human impacts on natural resources, over 700 multilateral IEAs can be identified. Although more difficult to identify, there are more than 1,000 and perhaps as many as 2,100 BEAs. MEAs break down into about 250 lineages of legally linked agreements, though almost 40 percent of agreements fall into only 20 distinct lineages with many other lineages consisting of only 1 or 2 agreements. Several IEAs were already signed by 1900, and agreement adoption has increased steadily to the point that currently an average of over 20 MEAs and 30 BEAs are signed each year. Among MEAs, an initial focus on species protection has increasingly been balanced by concern with pollutants and, more recently, with habitat protection.

Whether governments are willing to negotiate and join IEAs depends on a range of factors, including the magnitude, likelihood, and distribution of the consequences of an environmental problem; the environmental, economic, social, and political effects of taking or not taking action on the problem; the way those effects are distributed across countries; the way different sectors within those countries perceive the costs and benefits of those effects; each country's inclinations regarding whether and how to respond to such threats; and the general and issue-specific power countries have to promote or restrain international agreement. Crises involving environmental disasters or breakthroughs in scientific understanding can foster agreement where it might otherwise be unlikely. In understanding global efforts on climate change, regional efforts on air pollution and fisheries, or bilateral efforts on river and lake pollutants, these and related factors go far to explain both the positions of individual governments and the ebb and flow in the success and failure of negotiations.

Deciphering whether IEAs, once signed, change the behaviors of governments, corporations, and individuals in ways that improve the environment also poses challenging analytic tasks. The effects and effectiveness of most environmental agreements have yet to be carefully analyzed, but research to date has identified considerable variation in their effectiveness. Agreements on stratospheric ozone depletion, dumping of wastes in the North Sea, and dumping of radioactive wastes globally are some of those that have been judged as quite influential; those addressing the world's natural and cultural heritage, tropical timber, and many fisheries have usually been judged as less effective (42, 124, 154). But such judgments of these and other agreements depend considerably on the criteria used to evaluate effectiveness and on the analyst's skills in estimating what would have happened without the agreement. Research to date has demonstrated that, although the inclusion of specific design features in particular IEAs can sometimes make them more effective, whether any particular IEA design is effective also will depend on a wide range of other variables and parameters including characteristics of the countries involved, the environmental problem being addressed, and the international context (127).

Treaties, conventions, and other legal agreements among governments will be important features of global environmental governance for the foreseeable future. Policymakers will want to develop IEAs to address new environmental problems in the future and redesign existing IEAs that are performing poorly in the present. Scholars have begun to address these policy needs; they have shed light on the factors that foster and hinder intergovernmental negotiation and that lead some IEAs, once concluded, to perform well and others to perform poorly. But greater efforts to answer existing questions and pose new ones, to employ a broader range of methodologies, and to use evidence from more of the extant MEAs and BEAs than have been studied to date will allow researchers to advise policymakers more confidently and more effectively in the future.

Literature Cited

1. UN Glob. Compact Netw. 2002. *The Global Compact.* http://www.unglobalcompact.org.

2. Kara J, Quarless D. 2002. *Guiding Principles for Partnerships for Sustainable Development ('Type 2 Outcomes') to be Elaborated by Interested Parties in the Context of the World Summit on Sustainable Development:*

Explanatory Note by the Vice-Chairs, UN Comm. Sustain. Dev. New York. http://www.un.org/esa/ sustdev/partnerships/guiding.principles7 june2002.

3. Nye JS, Donahue JD, eds. 2000. *Governance in a Globalizing World*. Washington, DC: Brookings Inst.

4. Keck ME, Sikkink K. 1998. *Activists Beyond Borders: Advocacy Networks in International Politics*. Ithaca: Cornell Univ. Press.

5. Costanza R, Low BS, Ostrom E, Wilson J. 2001. *Institutions, Ecosystems, and Sustainability*. New York: Lewis.

6. Wapner P. 1996. *Environmental Activism and World Civic Politics*. Albany, NY: State Univ. New York Press.

7. Lipschutz RD, Mayer J. 1996. *Global Civil Society and Global Environmental Governance: The Politics of Nature From Place to Planet*. Albany, NY: State Univ. New York Press.

8. Board Sustain. Dev. Policy Div., Natl. Res. Counc. 1999. *Our Common Journey: A Transition Toward Sustainability*. Washington, DC: Natl. Acad.

9. Kiss AC, ed. 1983. *Selected Multilateral Treaties in the Field of the Environment*. Vol. 1. Nairobi: UN Environ. Program.

10. Rummel-Bulska I, Osafo S, eds. 1991. *Selected Multilateral Treaties in the Field of the Environment*. Vol. 2. Nairobi: UN Environ. Program.

11. Hohmann H. 1992. *Basic Documents of International Environmental Law*. Boston: Graham & Trotman.

12. Brown Weiss E, Magraw DB, Szasz PC. 1999. *International Environmental Law: Basic Instruments and References, 1992–1999*. Ardsley, NY: Transnational.

12a. Sands P, Tarasofsky R. 1994. *Documents in International Environmental Law*. Manchester, UK: Manchester Univ. Press.

13. Alder J, Lugten G, Kay R, Ferriss B. 2001. Compliance with international fisheries instruments in the North Atlantic. In *Fisheries Impacts on North Atlantic Ecosystems: Evaluations and Policy Exploration*, eds. T Pitcher, UR Sumaila, D Pauly, pp. 55–80. Vancouver: Fish. Cent., Univ. British Columbia.

14. Burns W. 2002. *American Society of International Law Wildlife Interest Group Listing of Treaties and Soft Law Agreements*. http://eelink.net/~asilwildlife/ treaties.shtml.

15. UN Environ. Program. 2002. *Regional Seas Conventions and Protocols*, http://www.unep.ch/seas/main/hconlist.html.

16. UN Environ. Program. 2002. *Legal Agreements Relating to the Marine Environment*. http://www.unep.ch/seas/ main/hlegal.html.

17. Hedley C. 2002. *Oceanlaw's Internet Guide to International Fisheries Law*. http://www.oceanlaw.net.

18. Molitor M, ed. 1991. *International Environmental Law: Primary Materials*. Boston, MA: Kluwer Law Tax.

19. UN Food Agric. Organ. Legal Off. 2002. *Treaties Deposited With FAO*. http:// www.fao.org/Legal/treaties/Treaty-e. htm

20. UN Environ. Program. Div. Environ. Conv. 2002. *Multilateral Environmental Agreements*. http://www.unep.ch/conventions/geclist.htm.

21. Int. Marit. Organ. 2002. *Complete List of Conventions*. http://www.imo. org/Conventions/mainframe.asp?topic_id=260.

22. Can. Dep. Foreign Aff. Int. Trade. 2002. *Database of Canada's International Environmental Commitments*. http://pubx.dfait-maeci.gc.ca/A_Branch/ AES/Env_commitments.nsf/Homepage.

23. Finn. Minist. Environ. 2002. *Finland's International Environmental Agreements*. http://www.vyh.fi/eng/intcoop/ agreem/agree_t.htm.

24. Pace Virtual Environ. Law Libr. 1997. *International Table of Contents*. http://www.pace.edu/lawschool/env/chronologicalorder.html.

25. Fletcher Sch. Law Dipl. 2002. *Multilaterals Project: Multilateral Conventions*. http://fletcher.tufts.edu/multi/chrono.html.

26. Burhenne WE, ed. 1974. *International Environmental Law: Multilateral Treaties*. Bonn: Kluwer Law Int.

27. Rüster B, Simma B, eds. 1975. *International Protection of the Environment: Treaties and Related Documents*. Dobbs Ferry, NY: Oceana.

28. Rüster B, Simma B. 1990. *International Protection of the Environment, Second Series: Treaties and Related Documents*. Dobbs Ferry, NY: Oceana.

29. ECOLEX. 2002. *Multilateral Treaties*. http://www.ecolex.org.

30. Cent. Int. Earth Sci. Inf. Netw. 2001. *ENTRI Treaty Tests: Menu of Treaty Texts*. http://sedac.ciesin.columbia.edu/entri.

31. Mitchell RB. 2003. *International Environmental Agreements Database*. http://darkwing.uoregon.edu/~rmitchel/iea.

32. Aust A. 2000. *Modern Treaty Law and Practice*. Cambridge, UK: Cambridge Univ. Press.

33. Burhenne WE, Jahnke M. 1993. *International Environmental Soft Law: Collection of Relevant Instruments*. Dordrecht: M. Nijhoff.

34. Brown Weiss E, ed. 1997. *International Compliance With Nonbinding Accords*. Washington, DC: Am. Soc. Int. Law.

35. Abbott KW, Snidal D. 2000. Hard and soft law in international governance. *Int. Organ.* 54:421–56.

36. Caldwell LK. 1980. *International Environmental Policy and Law*. Durham, NC: Duke Univ. Press.

37. Birnie PW, Boyle AE. 2002. *International Law and the Environment*. Oxford: Oxford Univ. Press.

38. Hans PM, Sundgren J. 1993. Evolving international environmental law: changing practices of national sovereignty. In *Global Accord: Environmental Challenges and International Responses*, ed. N Choucri, pp.401–29. Cambridge, MA: MIT Press.

39. Daily GC, ed. 1997. *Nature's Services: Societal Dependence on Natural Ecosystems*. Washington, DC: Island.

40. UN Environ. Program. 1996. *Register of International Treaties and Other Agreements in the Field of the Environment*. Nairobi: UN Environ. Program.

41. Young OR, ed. 1999. *Effectiveness of International Environmental Regimes: Causal Connections and Behavioral Mechanisms*. Cambridge, MA: MIT Press.

42. Miles EL, Underdal A, Andresen S, Wettestad J, Skjæseth JB, Carlin EM, eds. 2001. *Environmental Regime Effectiveness: Confronting Theory With Evidence*. Cambridge, MA: MIT Press.

43. Krasner SD. 1983. Structural causes and regime consequences: regimes as intervening variables. See Ref. 155, pp. 1–22.

44. Lipson C. 1991. Why are some international agreements informal? *Int. Organ.* 45:495–538.

45. UN Econ. Comm. Europe. 2002. *UNECE Environment and Human Settlements Division Home Page*. http://www. unece.org/env.

46. UN Food Agric. Organ. 2002. *FAO Regional Fisheries Bodies Home Page*. http://www.fao.org/fi/body/rfb/index.htm.

47. UN Food Agric. Organ. 2002. *FAOLEX database*. http://faolex.fao.org/faolex.

48. Jacobson HK, Brown Weiss E. 1998. A framework for analysis. See Ref. 154, pp. 1–18.

49. Mitchell RB. 2002. International environment. In *Handbook of International Relations*, ed. W Carlsnaes, T Risse, B Simmons, pp. 500–16. Thousand Oaks, CA: Sage.

50. Young OR. 1989. The politics of international regime formation: managing natural resources and the environment. *Int. Organ.* 43:349–76.

51. Lipschutz RD. 1991. Bargaining among nations: culture, history, and perceptions in regime formation. *Eval. Rev.* 15:46–74.

52. Young OR, Osherenko G, eds. 1993. *Polar Politics: Creating International Environmental Regimes*. Ithaca: Cornell Univ. Press.

53. Young OR. 1998. *Creating Regimes: Arctic Accords and International Governance*. Ithaca: Cornell Univ. Press.

54. Soc. Learn. Group, eds. 2001. *Learning to Manage Global Environmental Risks*. Vol.1. *A Comparative History of Social Responses to Climate Change, Ozone Depletion and Acid Rain*. Cambridge: MIT Press.

55. Soc. Learn. Group, ed. 2001. *Learning to Manage Global Environmental Risks*. Vol. 2. *A Functional Analysis of Social Responses to Climate Change, Ozone Depletion and Acid Rain*. Cambridge: MIT Press.

56. Stein AA. 1983. Coordination and collaboration: regimes in an anarchic world. See Ref. 155, pp. 115–40.

57. Martin LL. 1992. Interests, power, and multilateralism. *Int. Organ.* 46:765–92.

58. Barkin JS, Shambaugh G, eds. 1999. *Anarchy and the Environment: The International Relations of Common Pool Resources*. Albany, NY: State Univ. New York Press.

59. Wettestad J. 1999. *Designing Effective Environmental Regimes: The Key Conditions*. Cheltenham, UK: Edward Elgar.

60. Hardin G. 1968. The tragedy of the commons. *Science* 162:1243–48.

61. Mitchell RB, Keilbach P. 2001. Reciprocity, coercion, or exchange: symmetry, asymmetry and power in institutional design. *Int. Organ.* 55:891–917.

62. Hasenclever A, Mayer P, Rittberger V. 1997. *Theories of International Regimes*. Cambridge, UK: Cambridge Univ. Press.

63. Zürn M. 1998. The rise of international environmental politics: a review of current research. *World Polit.* 50:617–49.

64. Kingdon JW. 1984. *Agendas, Alternatives, and Public Policies*. Boston, MA: Little, Brown.

65. Sabatier PA, Jenkins-Smith HC, eds. 1993. *Policy Change and Learning: An Advocacy Coalition Approach*. Boulder, CO: Westview.

66. Litfin KT. 1994. *Ozone Discourses: Science and Politics in Global Environmental Cooperation*. New York: Columbia Univ. Press.

67. Benedick RE. 1998. *Ozone Diplomacy: New Directions in Safeguarding the Planet*. Cambridge, MA: Harvard Univ. Press.

68. Keohane RO. 1996. Analyzing the effectiveness of international environmental institutions. See Ref. 94, pp. 3–27.

69. Clark WC, Mitchell RB, Cash DW, Alcock F. 2002. *Information as influence: how institutions mediate the impact of scientific assessments on global environmental affairs. Rep. Fac. Res. Work. Pap. RWP02-044*, Kennedy Sch. Gov., Harvard Univ., Cambridge, MA.

70. Kammen DM, Dove MR. 1997. The virtues of mundane science. *Environment* 39:10–19.

71. Mitchell RB. 1994. *Intentional Oil Pollution at Sea: Environmental Policy and Treaty Compliance*. Cambridge, MA: MIT Press.

72. M'Gonigle RM, Zacher MW. 1979. *Pollution, Politics, and International Law: Tankers at Sea*. Berkeley, CA: Univ. of Calif. Press.

73. Hans PM. 1990. *Saving the Mediterranean: The Politics of International Environmental Cooperation*. New York: Columbia Univ. Press.

74. Princen T, Finger M. 1994. *Environmental NGOs in World Politics: Linking the Local and the Global*. New York: Routledge.

75. Raustiala K. 1997. States, NGOs, and international environmental institutions. *Int. Stud.* Q. 41:719–40.

76. DeSombre ER. 2000. *Domestic Sources of International Environmental Policy: Industry, Environmentalists, and US. Power*. Cambridge, MA: MIT Press.

77. Sprinz D, Vaahtoranta T. 1994. The interest-based explanation of international environmental policy. *Int. Organ.* 48:77–105.

78. Levy M. 1993. European acid rain: the power of tote-board diplomacy. See Ref. 98, pp. 75–132.

79. O'Neill K. 2000. *Waste Trading Among Rich Nations*. Cambridge, MA: MIT Press.

80. Schreurs MA, Economy E, eds. 1997. *The Internationalization of Environmental Protection*. Oxford: Oxford Univ. Press.

81. Underdal A. 2001. One question, two answers. See Ref. 42, pp. 1–47.

82. Young OR. 1989. *International Cooperation: Building Regimes for Natural Resources and the Environment*. Ithaca, NY: Cornell Univ. Press.

83. Gruber L. 2000. *Ruling the World*. Princeton: Princeton Univ. Press.

84. Caron DD. 1995. The International Whaling Commission and the North Atlantic Marine Mammal Commission: the institutional risks of coercion in consensual structures. *Am. J Int. Law* 89:154–74.

85. Andresen S. 2001. The International Whaling Commission (IWC): more failure than success? See Ref. 42, pp. 379–403.

86. Keohane RU. 1986. Reciprocity in international relations. *Int. Organ.* 40:1–27.

87. Parson EA. 2003. *Protecting the Ozone Layer. Science and Strategy*. Oxford: Oxford Univ. Press.

88. Stokke OS. 1998. Understanding the formation of international environmental regimes: the discursive challenge. See Ref. 156, pp. 129–48.

89. Sandford R. 1996. International environmental treaty secretariats: a case of neglected potential? *Environ. Impact Assess. Rev.* 16:3–12.

90. Hans PM. 1992. Epistemic communities and international policy coordination. *Int. Organ.* 46:1–35.

91. McCormick J. 1999. The role of environmental NGOs in international regimes. In *The Global Environment: Institutions, Law, and Policy*, ed. NJ Vig, RS Axelrod, pp. 52–71. Washington, DC: CQ Press.

92. List M, Rittberger V. 1998. The role of intergovernmental organizations in the formation and evolution of international environmental regimes. See Ref. 156, pp. 67–81.

93. Deudney D. 1990. The case against linking environmental degradation and national security. *Millennium* 19:461–76.

94. Keohane RO, Levy MA, eds. 1996. *Institutions for Environmental Aid: Pitfalls and Promise*. Cambridge, MA: MIT Press.

95. Jakobeit C. 1996. Nonstate actors leading the way: debt-for-nature swaps. See Ref. 94, pp. 127–66.

96. Garcia-Johnson R. 2000. *Exporting Environmentalism: US. Multinational Chemical Corporations in Brazil and Mexico*. Cambridge, MA: MIT Press.

97. Clapp J. 1998. The privatization of global environmental governance: ISO 14000 and the developing world. *Glob. Gov.* 4: 295–316.

98. Haas PM, Keohane RO, Levy MA, eds. 1993. *Institutions for the Earth: Sources of Effective International Environmental Protection.* Cambridge, MA: MIT Press.

99. Cameron J, Werksman J, Roderick P, eds. 1996. *Improving Compliance With International Environmental Law.* London: Earthscan.

100. Deleted in proof.

101. Victor DG, Raustiala K, Skolnikoff EB, eds. 1998. *The Implementation and Effectiveness of International Environmental Commitments: Theory and Practice.* Cambridge, MA: MIT Press.

102. Young OR. 1999. *Governance in World Affairs.* Ithaca, NY: Cornell Univ. Press.

103. Bernauer T. 1995. The effect of international environmental institutions: how we might learn more. *Int. Organ.* 49:351–77.

104. Helm C, Sprinz D. 2000. Measuring the effectiveness of international environmental regimes. *J Confl. Resolut.* 44:630–52.

105. D'Amato A, Chopra SK. 1991. Whales: their emerging right to life. *Am J. Int. Law* 85:21–62.

106. Mitchell RB. 1996. Compliance theory: an overview. See Ref. 99, pp. 3–28.

107. Mitchell RB. 2002. A quantitative approach to evaluating international environmental regimes. *Glob. Environ. Polit.* 2:58–83.

108. Sprinz D, Wolinsky Y, eds. 2004. *Methods of Inquiry in International Politics.* Ann Arbor: Univ. of Mich. Press. In press.

109. UN Food Agric. Organ. 2002. *Fishery Software, FISHSTAT Plus: Universal Software for Fishery Statistical Time Series.* http://www.fao.org/fi/statist/FISOFT/FISHPLUS.asp.

110. Jackson JBC, Kirby MX, Berger WH, Bjorndal KA, Botsford LW, et al. 2001. Historical overfishing and the recent collapse of coastal ecosystems. *Science* 293:629–37.

111. Wettestad J. 2001. The Vienna Convention and Montreal Protocol on ozone-layer depletion. See Ref. 42, pp. 149–70.

112. Greene O. 1998. The system for implementation review in the ozone regime. See Ref. 101, pp. 89–136.

113. Gay JT. 1987. *American Fur Seal Diplomacy: The Alaskan Fur Seal Controversy.* New York: Peter Lang.

114. Dorsey K. 1991. Putting a ceiling on sealing: conservation and cooperation in the international arena, 1909–1911. *Environ. Hist. Rev.* 15:27–45.

115. Schneider V, Pearce D. 2002. *What saved the whales? An economic analysis of 20th century whaling.* Presented at New Zealand Assoc. Econ. Conf. 2002, Wellington.

116. Wettestad J. 2001. The Convention on Long-Range Transboundary Air Pollution (CLRTAP). See Ref. 42, 197–221.

117. Munton D, Soroos M, Nikitina E, Levy MA. 1999. Acid rain in Europe and North America. In *The Effectiveness of International Environmental Regimes: Causal Connections and Behavioral Mechanisms,* ed. OR Young, pp. 155–247. Cambridge, MA: MIT Press.

118. Murdoch JC, Sandler T, Sargent K. 1997. A tale of two collectives: sulphur versus nitrogen oxides emission reduction in Europe. *Economica* 64:281–301.

119. Bernauer T. 1995. The international financing of environmental protec-

tion: lessons from efforts to protect the River Rhine against chloride pollution. *Environ. Polit.* 4:369–90.

120. Bernauer T, Moser P. 1996. Reducing pollution of the Rhine River: the influence of international cooperation. *J Environ. Dev.* 5:391–417.

121. Skjærseth JB. 2001. The effectiveness of the Mediterranean Action Plan. See Ref. 42, pp. 311–30.

122. Miles EL. 2001. The management of tuna fisheries in the west central and southwest Pacific. See Ref. 42, pp. 117–48.

123. Stokke OS, Anderson LG, Mirovitskaya N. 1999. The Barents Sea fisheries. See Ref. 117, pp. 91–154.

124. Peterson MJ. 1993. International fisheries management. See Ref. 98, pp. 249–308.

125. Gehring T. 1994. *Dynamic International Regimes: Institutions for International Environmental Governance*. Frankfurt am Main: P. Lang.

126. Breitmeier H. 1999. *International Regimes Database*. http://www.ifs.tudarmstadt.de/pg/ird_home.htm.

127. Jacobson HK, Brown Weiss E. 1998. Assessing the record and designing strategies to engage countries. See Ref. 154, pp. 511–54.

128. Underdal A. 2001. Conclusions: patterns of regime effectiveness. See Ref. 42, pp. 433–65.

128a. Sand PH. 1997. Commodity or taboo? International regulation of trade in endangered species. In *Green Globe Yearbook of International Co-operation on Environment and Development 1997*, ed. HO Bergesen, G Parmann, pp. 19–36. New York: Oxford Univ. Press.

128b. Sand PH. 2001. A century of green lessons: the contribution of nature conservation regimes to global environmental governance. *Int. Environ. Agreements: Pol., Law Econ.* 1:33–72.

129. Harbaugh W, Levinson A, Wilson D. 2000. *Re-examining the empirical evidence for an environmental Kuznets curve*. Rep. 7711, Natl. Bur. Econ. Res., Cambridge, MA.

130. Darst RG. 2001. *Smokestack Diplomacy: Cooperation and Conflict in East-West Environmental Politics*. Cambridge, MA: MIT Press.

131. Grossman GM, Krueger AB. 1995. Economic growth and the environment. *Q. J. Econ.* 110:353–77.

132. Selden T, Song D. 1994. Environmental quality and development: Is there a Kuznets curve for air pollution emissions? *J. Environ. Econ. Manag.* 27:147–62.

133. Anderson D, Cavendish W. 2001. Dynamic simulation and environmental policy analysis: beyond comparative statics and the environmental Kuznets curve. *Oxford Econ. Pap.* 53:721–46.

134. Inglehart R. 1990. *Culture Shift in Advanced Industrial Society*. Princeton: Princeton Univ. Press.

135. Dauvergne P. 1997. *Shadows in the Forest: Japan and the Politics of Timber in Southeast Asia*. Cambridge, MA: MIT Press.

136. Ross ML. 2001. *Timber Booms and Institutional Breakdown in Southeast Asia*. Cambridge: Cambridge Univ. Press.

137. Steinberg PF. 2001. *Environmental Leadership in Developing Countries: Transnational Relations and Biodiversity Policy in Costa Rica and Bolivia*. Cambridge, MA: MIT Press.

138. Clark WC. 2000. Environmental globalization. See Ref. 3, pp. 86–108.

139. Young OR. 2002. *The Institutional Dimensions of Environmental Change: Fit, Interplay, and Scale*. Cambridge, MA: MIT Press.

140. Stokke OS. 2001. *Governing High Seas Fisheries: The Interplay of Global and Regional Regimes*. Oxford: Oxford Univ. Press.

141. Biermann F. 2000. The case for a world environment organization. *Environment* 42:23–31.

142. Juma C. 2000. The perils of centralizing global environmental governance. *Environment* 42:44–4.

143. Waltz K. 1979. *Theory of International Politics*. Reading, MA: Addison-Wesley.

144. Strange S. 1983. Cave! Hic dragones: a critique of regime analysis. See Ref. 155, pp. 337–54.

145. Mitchell RB. 1994. Regime design matters: intentional oil pollution and treaty compliance. *Int. Organ.* 48:425–58.

146. Eijndhoven JV, Clark WC, Jäger J. 2001. The long-term development of global environmental risk management: conclusions and implications for the future. See Ref. 55, pp. 181–97.

147. Levy MA, Cavender-Bares J, Clark WC, Dinkelman G, Nikitina E, et al. 2001. Goal and strategy formulation in the management of global environmental risks. See Ref. 55, pp. 87–113.

148. Chayes A, Chayes AH. 1995. *The New Sovereignty: Compliance With International Regulatory Agreements*. Cambridge, MA: Harvard Univ. Press.

149. Mitchell RB. 1998. Sources of transparency: information systems in international regimes. *Int. Stud. Q.* 42:109–30.

150. Axelrod R. 1984. *The Evolution of Cooperation*. New York: Basic Books.

151. Wettestad J. 1995. Science, politics and institutional design: some initial notes on the Long-Range Transboundary Air Pollution Regime. *J. Environ. Dev.* 4:165–83.

152. Downs GW, Rocke DM, Barsoom PN. 1996. Is the good news about compliance good news about cooperation? *Int. Organ.* 50:379–406.

153. Finnemore M. 1996. *National Interests in International Society*. Ithaca: Cornell Univ. Press.

154. Brown Weiss E, Jacobson HK, eds. 1988. *Engaging Countries: Strengthening Compliance With International Environmental Accords*. Cambridge, MA: MIT Press.

155. Krasner SD, eds. 1983. *International Regimes*. Ithaca, NY: Cornell Univ. Press.

156. Underdal A, ed. 1998. *The Politics of International Environmental Management*. Dordrecht: Kluwer Acad.

CHAPTER 18

Responsibility for Biological Diversity Conservation Under International Law

Catherine Tinker

THE INTERNATIONAL LAW ON BIOLOGICAL DIVERSITY HAS developed along with scientific understanding and now embodies an ecosystem approach to the conservation of the variety of life. The ecosystem concept and a basic sense of state responsibility not to harm the environment was formulated in 1972 in the Stockholm Declaration and later, in the World Charter for Nature. Since Principle 21 of the Stockholm Declaration, the concept has crystallized in customary international law, but it did not appear in binding treaty law until the United Nations Convention on Biological Diversity (the Convention or Treaty) entered into force in 1993. Earlier wildlife protection treaties contained some aspects of the approach that was later adopted in the Biodiversity Convention. For example, the Ramsar Convention adopted a habitat and sustainable use approach to the conservation of wetlands; the World Heritage Convention has been a factor in some national development plans that were altered to avoid damage to listed sites.

The nature of state responsibility under Principle 21, which is not to harm the territory of other states or the territory beyond national jurisdiction, is still evolving. One way of implementing the goals contained in Article 3 of the Biodiversity Convention is to apply the precautionary principle, which requires restraint of any human activity that may adversely affect biodiversity. The precautionary principle in international environmental law is one response to the popular recognition that preventive action in the face of scientific uncertainty about future harm is necessary. The precautionary principle lowers the burden of proof required for blocking proposed or existing activities that may have serious long-term harmful

---

Reprinted with permission of the *Vanderbilt Journal of Transnational Law*.

consequences. There is no agreement on the content of the precautionary principle nor is there consensus on whether a principle, rather than an approach, has actually emerged. "Nevertheless, countries have begun to develop precise and useful formulations of the principle in specific contexts."[1]

There is tremendous scientific uncertainty about the loss of biodiversity caused by various human activities, both lawful and unlawful. The numbers and types of life forms that exist as genes, species, sub-species, microorganisms, and bacteria in various ecosystems and habitats are a vast unknown. In the face of this, the precautionary principle requires an even greater degree of restraint in human activity to conserve and sustainably use biodiversity. Perhaps, for now, the precautionary principle should mandate a policy of "no action." Such an interpretation would be consistent with those who have called for a clarification of the notion of responsibility and prevention in environmental concerns. As one author has asserted, "[i]t is no longer sufficient to talk of state responsibility for environmental damage. The context must change to reflect state responsibility for the preservation of global environmental well-being."[2]

Traditional international lawmaking or standard-setting is an inherently slow process. This is particularly true in international environmental law where there is very little consensus surrounding existing norms. Soft law, customary law, and treaties are needed to set standards and define legally-binding duties and obligations based on the precautionary approach. Existing environmental treaties need to be enforced and additional states urged to ratify them. To ensure the highest degree of compliance, the principle of precautionary action to avoid environmental harm must be recognized in international law as a means of fulfilling states' obligations to conserve, sustainably use, and equitably share biodiversity.

The United Nations Convention on Biological Diversity codifies a line of soft law and international custom to create hard law in the treaty. The obligations accepted by states party to the Convention are threefold: conservation of biodiversity; sustainable use of biological diversity; and equitable sharing of biodiversity benefits. States party to the Convention are mandated to establish national legislation and plans. In order to fully comply with the treaty, these internal laws and development plans must take into account the responsibility accepted under the Principle 21 language and the jurisdictional scope article, Article 4. Arguably, to fully comply with the letter and spirit of the Convention, states must apply the precautionary principle in their decision-making processes and whenever they take action under national legislation and development plans.

Full application of the principle of precautionary action may require states to forego the short-term financial opportunities available from resource depletion and loss of biodiversity in order to secure long-term human benefits for the planet and future generations. For those developing countries in which poverty, disease, and starvation make it almost impossible to forego short-term but destructive gains, the Convention offers means of financing biodiversity conservation projects and the transfer of appropriate technology. In the meantime, the Convention requires states to monitor, study, and catalogue the rich storehouse of genetic variety contained in their rainforests, coral reefs, wetlands, deserts, and coastal zones. When greater scientific certainty about the effect of human activity on ecosystems and habitats is achieved, planners, lawyers, and diplomats may be better able to balance conservation and sustainable use of biological diversity. In the meantime, the lack of full scientific certainty should not be used as a reason for postponing measures to avoid or minimize a threat of significant reduction or loss of biological diversity.

International attention should be drawn to formulating global responsibility for biodiversity conservation and sustainable use. The Convention on Biological Diversity echoes Principle 22 of the Stockholm Declaration with a weak reference to the need to study state liability. It may be fruitful for such a study to follow the guidance of two other Stockholm Declaration principles. Principle 4 states that "[humanity] has a special responsibility to safeguard and wisely manage the heritage of wildlife and its habitat, which are now gravely imperiled by a combination of adverse factors. Nature conservation, including wildlife, must therefore receive importance in planning for economic development." Principle 5 states that "[t]he non-renewable resources of the earth must be employed in such a way as to guard against the danger of their future exhaustion and to ensure that benefits from such employment are shared by all [humanity]." The arguments for global conservation of biological diversity are weighted in favor of intangibles: aesthetics or preservation of open space or potential value for generations not yet born, based on equity or fairness.

This article analyzes the legal issues that attend fulfillment of the ambitious objectives of the Convention on Biological Diversity. This article also notes areas of ambiguity in the Convention, which remain to be clarified, and emphasizes responsibility for loss of biodiversity and prevention of that loss. Part II explores the failure of the traditional international law of state responsibility and liability to adequately protect the environment. Part II also reviews the U.N. International Law Commission's work on draft articles that incorporate a preventive or precautionary approach, specifically the draft articles on state responsibility and liability for environmental harm from lawful activities. This article suggests that a more appropriate legal approach is the application of the precautionary principle, which seeks to prevent harm rather than determine liability and damages after harm has occurred.

Part III argues that as greater scientific knowledge is achieved, the precautionary principle should be applied to all proposed human actions that may cause a loss of biodiversity, alter ecosystem and habitats, or affect genetic material. The article concludes that the principle of precautionary action may be seen as the means of enforcing the Biodiversity Convention and used as a procedural test to decide whether a proposed use of biodiversity is sustainable. Ultimately, the real test of the Convention on Biological Diversity will be the extent to which its provisions safeguard the planet's rich biological diversity, and the extent to which humans can undertake development projects without irrevocably destroying their global genetic heritage.

State Responsibility and Liability

Under traditional concepts of international law, the doctrine of state responsibility developed to address the relationship between a given state and citizens of other countries. The concept of state responsibility presupposes a clear legal duty or international plane or an obligation arising under treaty or the customary law. The state-alien example implicates the international principle of nondiscrimination against aliens and treaty obligations involving the treatment of diplomatic persons or the right of innocent passage. In the early 1970s, the concept of state responsibility was broadened to include any internationally wrongful acts.

The problem for international law is to interpret the concept of state responsibility in the environmental context. The U.S. understanding of international law is codified in the *Restatement (Third) of the Foreign Relations Law of the United States,* which states that a nation is obligated to take necessary measures to ensure that activities within the jurisdiction or control of that state conform to "generally accepted" international rules or standards. Even in the absence of an injury, a state is responsible to all other states for any violation of this obligation and for any resultant significant injury to "the environment of another state or to its property, or to persons or property within that state's territory or under its jurisdiction or control." The application of the broad language of Section 601, however, is limited by the state's obligation to take only "such measures as may be necessary, to the extent practicable under the circumstances. . . ."

"Generally accepted" international obligations and rules of conduct related to international environmental law now require, inter alia, the conservation and sustainable use of biological diversity and nonrenewable natural resources. At the same time, pressures for resource development and short-term economic gain encourage a broad range of public and private activities that adversely affect the environment, either now or in the future. In the area of generally accepted international obligations, state responsibility is triggered by the *de minimis* duty to observe the principle of *sic utere tuo ut alienum non laedas.*[3] Thus, states have a general duty to prevent uses of their territory that cause significant harm to other states. A state causing transboundary pollution is obligated to take reasonable measures to protect neighboring states from harm and to compensate them for damage. In addition, there may be obligations *erga omnes;*[4] the *Restatement* contemplated these obligations as they apply to areas beyond national jurisdiction and they are described by the International Court of Justice in the *Barcelona Traction* case.

The International Law Commission's Approach: State Responsibility for Internationally Wrongful Acts

The United Nations International Law Commission (I.L.C.) differentiates internationally wrongful acts from activities not contrary to international law. The first give rise to state responsibility. The second give rise to liability for injurious consequences. It is well established in international law that breach of a rule of international law entails state responsibility for an internationally wrongful act. The I.L.C.'s 1980 Draft on State Responsibility specified: "There is an internationally wrongful act of a State when conduct consisting of an action or omission is attributable to the State under international law; and that conduct constitutes a breach of an international obligation of the State."

The I.L.C. approach to state responsibility is to differentiate between "primary rules" and "secondary rules" of conduct that specify the action or refusal to act, which triggers state responsibility. Primary rules are obligations; secondary rules determine the legal consequences of failure to abide by primary rules. Secondary rules "specifically [deal] with the issues of responsibility and liability, although these issues cannot always actually be separated from the operation of the primary rules."[5] Allott has taken issue with the possibly meaningless distinction between primary and secondary rules and with the amount of time that has been invested over the past four decades in belaboring the point. Allott charges that the resultant delay in the formulation of the I.L.C. draft on state responsibility, "is doing serious long-term damage to international law and international society."[6] Even more seriously, Allott charges that the I.L.C.'s process and states' substantive approach to state responsibility virtually assure that states will not be held accountable for their actions.[7]

Under traditional public international law, three threshold questions are used to determine state responsibility: Was there a duty under international law? Was the duty breached? Can responsibility be attributed to a state for the violation of international law? Acts by nonstate entities, such as a citizen or official for whose acts a state is not responsible, do not give rise to state responsibility. Through the doctrine of attribution, however, a state can be responsible for the acts of its own citizens against another state.

The I.L.C. maintains that state responsibility attaches only to internationally wrongful acts. Although the violation of a clearly-defined treaty obligation or an unequivocally recognized norm of customary law clearly constitutes an internationally wrongful act, the I.L.C. has neither listed nor defined other potentially wrongful acts. Under the I.L.C. rubric, state responsibility is triggered when a state commits an international delict, regardless of whether any injury results. Once a state accepts binding duties, any failure to observe them necessarily amounts to a breach of international obligations. The breach may provoke a variety of responses, ranging from state protests to formal diplomatic expressions of displeasure and censure throughout the world community.

A state may raise a defense to its breach of an international obligation; in I.L.C. parlance, these defenses are known as "conditions precluding wrongfulness." The defenses include necessity, prior consent, self-defense, and *force majeure*. They may be raised in many situations, including a failure to observe the precautionary principle that causes transboundary pollution or degradation of biological diversity. Because the international obligation at issue is one that requires the state to balance competing interests, almost every state can be expected to raise a defense such as necessity. Here the difficulty of defining and applying the precautionary principle becomes apparent. If the precautionary principle is merely a guideline to actions that may accomplish other goals, then it cannot be a primary rule or an obligation for purposes of state responsibility analysis. The application of the precautionary principle may be seen as a consequence of attempting to fulfill a primary obligation.

Although state responsibility does not arise unless there is a breach of an international obligation, the breaching action or inaction must be attributable to the state. Difficulties of attribution are inherent in the concept of objective responsibility, because a state is always liable for the acts of its officials and organs, even when they act *ultra vires.*[8] Brownlie notes that Grotius viewed the *culpa* as the proper basis of state responsibility.[9] Brownlie, however, moved beyond the confines of fault to a more realistic test when he wrote that one "need not qualify responsibility of a state for an internationally wrongful act by the negligence *(culpa)* or intention *(dolus)* of the actor."[10] In the I.L.C.'s consideration of objective state responsibility, negligence or fault is not generally important for determining state responsibility or establishing an internationally wrongful act. After several years of inattention to the topic of state responsibility, in 1993 the I.L.C. formally adopted articles on cessation, reparation, restitution in-kind, compensation, satisfaction and assurances, and guarantees of nonrepetition, and included exceptionally detailed commentaries to the articles.

Consideration of whether to include a draft article on "international crimes" was postponed until the I.L.C.'s 1994 session. International crimes include internationally wrongful acts that are considered "essential for the protection of the fundamental interests of the international community" as a whole.[11] In its list of proposed international crimes, draft Article 19(3)(d) includes the serious breach of an international obligation of essential importance for the safeguarding and preservation of the human environment. Thus, according to the proposal, massive pollution of the atmosphere or of the seas would constitute an international crime. The I.L.C. remains divided on this controversial subject. Some members consider the same serious acts to be wrongful acts or to be violations of *erga omnes* obligations. From this perspective, there is no need to use the label "crimes." In contrast, other I.L.C. members consider the same acts to be crimes and believe that "crimes" is an appropriate label.

The International Law Commission's Approach: Liability of States for Injurious Consequences of Acts Not Contrary to International Law

If an exporting state—or a company within its jurisdiction or control—failed to obtain prior informed consent from the importing state and shipped hazardous biotechnology products, such an activity could be considered an internationally wrongful act, and thus trigger state responsibility regardless of whether any harm occurred. On the other hand, the shipment could be considered an activity not contrary to international law, which could only trigger liability for the exporting state if there were injurious consequences. The need to fit the facts of a given situation into these particular categories—whether the distinction is meaningful or not—arises from the decision of the I.L.C. to split the issue into two separate topics: state responsibility for internationally-wrongful acts, consisting of both primary and secondary obligations; and international liability for injurious consequences of activities not contrary to international law.

On a theoretical level, it is not clear that the conceptual basis on which it—liability for injurious consequences of activities not contrary to international law—is distinguished from state responsibility is either sound or necessary. On a more practical level, it is questionable whether it represents a useful basis for codification and development of existing law and practice relating to environmental harm, the field in which the Commission has mainly located the topic. From either perspective, it is liable to seem at best a questionable exercise in reconceptualising an existing body of law or, at worst, a dangerously retrograde step that may seriously weaken international efforts to secure agreement on effective principles of international environmental law.

The I.L.C. draft on liability for the injurious consequences of activities not contrary to international law states that civil liability will attach when four factors are present. There must be: (1) human activity; (2) the activity must be within the territory or control of a state; (3) the activity must be capable of giving rise to harm; and (4) there must be actual harm to persons or things within the territory or control of another state. Unlike the doctrine of state responsibility, which can attach even in the absence of harm, the concept of liability requires actual harm. Most commentators agree that the harm must be "substantial" or "serious," because state liability should not attach to minor incidents. There are several unanswered questions surrounding the draft. These questions include the draft's intended meaning of "control" and whether the draft applies when a state fails to act to remove a natural danger.

The I.L.C.'s current approach to liability is to "focus on prevention of harm from activities that constitute a particular risk." The I.L.C. begins by clarifying that the scope of the article includes lawful activities that "create a risk of causing significant transboundary harm through their physical consequences." The I.L.C. defines risk to include both "a low probability of causing disastrous harm and a high probability of causing other significant harm." The I.L.C. then goes on to address prior authorization, risk assessment, and measures to minimize risks.

States are most likely to be deterred from causing environmental harm if some standard of liability is imposed. Whether the system is grounded in strict liability or negligence is of considerably less importance. If international law adopts a liability system, states will be liable for environment damage caused by both public and private actors, regardless of whether the harm occurs within another state or beyond the boundaries of national jurisdiction. The liability approach best protects the rights of innocent victims of environmental harm because it shifts the burden of proof and makes it possible to collect prompt, adequate, and effective compensation once injury is established. Of course, the most effective way to protect the rights of the innocent is to prevent the harm or destruction from occurring in the first place.

One of the most difficult issues facing the I.L.C. is whether to impose a strict liability system or a fault-based system. For a number of obvious political and financial reasons, states are reluctant to adopt strict liability and therefore lack the will to negotiate an environmental liability protocol.[12] On the other hand, "the very absence of responsibility or liability provisions may be essential to the success of many environmental protection agreements."[13]

The meaning of strict liability and absolute liability in the context of activities affecting the environment is particularly relevant to hazardous or ultrahazardous activities and has created substantial problems for the I.L.C.

The most visible ultrahazardous activity is nuclear and there is precedent for finding liability in cases where nuclear operations have caused environmental damage. The treaties pertaining to nuclear accidents have adopted a variety of approaches. Other treaties have addressed the harms caused by such specialized problems as objects that fall to earth from outer space.

The I.L.C. has had considerable difficulty addressing ultrahazardous activities. The I.L.C. created a working group and later adopted the group's recommendations. In essence, the I.L.C. is attempting to create consensus within itself on the basic issues of prevention and remediation.[14] If general consensus does develop, the I.L.C. will be able to move on to consideration of the specific mechanisms that should be used to address ultrahazardous risks.[15]

The Precautionary Principle and the International Law of Biological Diversity

Traditional models of international law and state responsibility focus upon ensuring compensation for transboundary damages and do not adequately address the challenges arising in international environmental law. The classic model poses a bilateral conflict between one state as actor and another state as victim, with significant physical harm occurring across national boundaries attributable to the first state. Emerging conflicts over the fundamental assumptions and value choices inherent in the "sustainable development" and "sustainable use" of nonrenewable natural resources located within a given state do not fit the bilateral paradigm. Presently, unless some transboundary damage is implicated, no state may raise a legal objection to the domestic environmental policies of any other state. Within the confines of their own borders, international law permits each state to deplete or injure its natural resources, to destroy its gene pool, species, and habitats, and to otherwise harm its environment. Thus, the traditional model of international environmental law creates a jurisdictional problem.

A second problem is that the long-standing "duty and damages for breach" model is inherently reactive and simply cannot prevent the loss of biological diversity, the despoliation of Antarctica, or the destruction of the ozone layer. Although the reactive model once may have been an appropriate response to transfrontier air or water pollution, today a growing number of environmental problems do not fit the mold of narrowly-defined transfrontier pollution and duties imposed on single states. International relations in the field of environmental protection have developed mostly in multilateral frames.

A new, more preventive model is needed to protect transnational ecosystems and the global commons. Under the new model, proponents of development will bear the burden of proving, before they proceed, that the planned use is sustainable and that no harm will result from proposed development. Only compliance with standards based on the precautionary principle and international cooperation will provide the necessary protection for the planet. Ultimately, achieving conservation and sustainable use of biodiversity and nonrenewable natural resources will require changes in human production and consumption. Certain groups or individuals in society will have to sacrifice short-term gains for long-term benefits and to consider meeting the basic needs of future generations as well as those of the present. International law and state responsibility doctrines must necessarily expand to reflect this new imperative for precautionary approaches to human activity and their regulation.

The Precautionary Principle

The precautionary principle has been defined in two ways. It has been defined as an international application of the German law principle of precautionary action (*vorsorgeprinzip*). It has also been defined as the variety of regulatory approaches adopted by governments to implement the *vorsorgeprinzip* principle; efforts to control emissions at their source by using best available technology are one example of this definition in practice. The precautionary principle can be used as a theory and justification for environmental strict liability; this perspective is rooted in the tort law goal of providing compensation to victims of harm. The precautionary principle also may be understood more broadly as a duty to take precautionary action and to avoid risk. In practice, the precautionary principle informs a substantive duty of care that requires environmental impact assessments or other regulatory investigations prior to permitting given actions.

The phrase "the precautionary principle" has appeared in a number of international instruments. Its meaning varies from "its weakest formulations . . . to its strongest [in which] it can be seen as a reversal of the normal burden of proof, as in the Oslo Convention Prior Justification Procedure."[16] Several recent United Nations documents, including the 1992 Rio Declaration, have articulated the precautionary principle: "In order to protect the environment, the precautionary approach shall be widely applied by States according to their capabilities. Where there are threats of serious or irreversible damage, lack of full scientific certainty shall not be used as a reason for postponing cost-effective measures to prevent environmental degradation." In another formulation, the preamble to the U.N. Convention on Biological Diversity also refers to the precautionary principle, but omits phrases such as "according to their capabilities" and "cost-effective" measures, which qualify the language of the Rio Declaration. The Biodiversity Convention declares its intentions by, "[n]oting also that where there is a threat of significant reduction or loss of biological diversity, lack of full scientific certainty should not be used as a reason for postponing measures to avoid or minimize such a threat." In the Biodiversity Treaty, the language of obligation has been softened by using "should" to replace the mandatory "shall" used in the Rio Declaration. Other references to the precautionary principle appear in recent multilateral treaties, conference declarations, and regional agreements, especially in agreements related to oil pollution of the North Sea. It has been noted that the precautionary principle turns away from the "assimilative capacity" approach to environmental pollution, and recognizes the limitation to scientific knowledge on ecosystems.

Each of these formulations of the precautionary principle gives rise to different applications of the international law of state responsibility and liability. At its strongest, the precautionary principle may be interpreted to prohibit virtually all uses of natural resources and all human activities in certain ecosystems. Such a moratorium could continue indefinitely, until sufficient scientific knowledge developed about the effects of proposed activities or uses. At its weakest, the precautionary principle may be merely hortatory language that is intended to guide states as they adopt national legislation and plans. This permissive approach to resource use and human activity creates a balancing of interests that makes it possible for developmental and quality of life considerations to outweigh the need to conserve biodiversity and take other preventive action. Although the international community may strive to achieve an expansive application of the precautionary principle in the future, the permissive interpretation dominates the status quo.

The precautionary principle has appeared as soft law in numerous conference declarations and other statements of what governments think international law should be. In the absence of strong evidence of state practice and *opinio juris,*[17] such as an explicit statement from a high-level government minister that precautionary measures were adopted because they are mandated under international law, it is difficult to conclude that the precautionary principle is currently customary international law. Examples of national legislation that refer to the precautionary principle or that are implicitly based on such a principle are insufficient to demonstrate a binding international legal obligation.

Apart from any sense of legal obligation under international law, there are many subjective variables that may affect a state's choice of precautionary action. Precautionary actions may save money in several situations: when there is a great likelihood that damages will occur; when damages, while unlikely, will be of great magnitude should they occur; and when a large number of people are likely to be injured if the harm is not prevented. The type or degree of damage contemplated and the ease of adopting precautionary measures may also induce precautionary action, particularly if there is public demand or political support for precautionary action. A state may act voluntarily based on a moral or ethical imperative. It may also voluntarily adopt a precautionary course for economic reasons. Sometimes it is more cost-efficient to prevent damage than to wait for damage to occur and pay the resulting costs.

It is never easy to say precisely when a rule crystallizes into customary international law. There is no convenient bright line test or formula to apply; the number of years that have elapsed since the original articulation of the principle and the number of times the principle has been quoted in soft law documents are not dispositive. To find the *opinio juris,* it is always necessary to locate the reasons for state practice. Similarly, if states adopt the language of international instruments that are neither binding nor intended to be binding upon the parties, then the mere fact that states have adopted that language is insufficient to prove that a customary rule of international law exists.

If a state happens to follow such a nonbinding principle, it may not necessarily believe that it was under a legal compulsion to do so and may not accept that it could be liable for breach under international law for failing to follow the law. To structure the definition of customary international law otherwise would be to erase the difference between nonbinding and binding international law, and to eliminate the incentive for states to join the soft law declarations from which international environmental law frequently evolves. For purposes of this article, it is not necessary to definitively state whether the precautionary principle is or is not customary law. Rather, the question is whether the precautionary principle affects the international law of state responsibility and liability when the principle is or becomes law, either through treaty obligations or through the future development of customary international law.

The relationship between state responsibility and the precautionary principle has yet to be fully defined. The first element of state responsibility is the existence of a clear legal duty or obligation that gives rise to the concept of an "internationally wrongful act." The second element is a breach of the legal duty. The next step is evaluation of possible defenses to the breach. Finally, compensation for victims of the breach must be determined.

The first element is the crux of the relationship between the precautionary principle and state responsibility. If the precautionary principle has not yet risen to the level of a legal duty or obligation, then it is difficult or even impossible to move on to the problems of breach, defenses, and compensation. Certainly, it may also be impossible to deter harmful behavior.[18] Because the concept of environmental harm is relatively new international law, there are few clearly-defined internationally wrongful acts that could trigger state responsibility. As principles of international environmental law become recognized as binding law through customary law and treaty law, more obligations will exist. Breach of those obligations may then lead to state responsibility. At present, a state's failure to follow the precautionary principle is not an internationally wrongful act that can trigger state responsibility. Even when a state is obligated by treaty to observe the precautionary principle, an internationally wrongful act has not necessarily occurred. It is necessary to examine the precise language of the treaty obligation. If the treaty says "should" instead of "shall," the offending state is not bound. Similarly, state obligations are often conditioned by phrases such as "to the extent practicable" and "according to their capabilities." Treaties frequently require adoption of only those preventive measures that are "cost-effective." Another problem in the relationship between the precautionary principle and the law of state responsibility is that some treaties referring to the precautionary principle are quite new and have not entered into force. In such situations, it is impossible to gauge the extent of compliance to be expected from states parties, or to imagine extending the obligation to states not party to the treaty. If the treaty is regional, it is difficult to draw out a clear rule of international law with "global applicability." Furthermore, the problem remains: how to determine what action must be taken to fulfill the obligation.

One starting point is to consider the relationship between the precautionary principle and Principle 21 of the Stockholm Declaration. It may be possible to achieve compliance with Principle 21 through observation of the precautionary principle. Principle 21 of the Stockholm Declaration is an example of an international environmental text containing the principle of state responsibility. It states that all nations have a responsibility to ensure that activities under their jurisdiction or control do not cause damage to the environment of other states or to areas beyond national jurisdiction. Principle 21 should be read in conjunction with Principle 22, which calls for the development of international law "regarding liability and compensation for the victims of pollution and other environmental damage. . ."

The Stockholm Declaration can also be read as a policy shift. Some developed nations addressed newly-recognized global environmental problems and, at the same time, some developing nations asserted sovereignty over their own natural resources. The broadening of the responsibility concept can be seen both in the second clause of Principle 21 and in the World Charter for Nature, in which states accepted the responsibility principle in relation both to other states and to nature itself. Perhaps the notion of state responsibility to nature will be further extended in the future to include a state's responsibility to international civil society. The foregoing discussion demonstrates that the principle of precautionary action may be considered a secondary obligation or a consequence of the states' primary responsibility not to harm the territory of another state or the territory beyond national jurisdiction. It remains to be seen whether Principle 21 applies to harms that occur within a state's own territory.

Efforts to link Principle 21 to states' responsibility not to breach international obligations are supported by the recommendations of the World Commission on Environment and Development. The Brundtland Report noted that "recognition by states of their responsibility to ensure an adequate environment for present as well as future generations is an important step toward sustainable development." The Brundtland Report defined international environmental obligations the breach of which triggers the duty to pay compensation by saying that states have a responsibility toward their own citizens and to other states. While the Brundtland Report provides a road map for the future development of general principles of international environmental law, it is not a source of binding legal duties or obligations for states.

The Brundtland Commission convened a group of legal experts that drafted one obligation on state responsibility and a second obligation on "liability for transboundary environmental interferences resulting from lawful activities"; the International Law Commission divided consideration of the two subjects in a similar manner. The main object of the liability article clearly is payment of compensation for transboundary environmental harm. Indeed, the article seems to assume that the cost of preventing harm or reducing the risk is so great that prevention is realistically impossible. In Article 11, the state responsibility article of the Brundtland Commission's legal experts group report, the mandate is much broader than in Article 21. Under Article 11, the state must cease the internationally wrongful act and restore the *status quo ante* as far as possible. Where appropriate, the state must give satisfaction and pay compensation for harm caused by its breach of international obligations.

In order to identify the possible impact of the precautionary principle upon the international law of state responsibility, it is necessary to examine the nature of the obligations that the precautionary principle as international law would create. Given the uncertainty over the scope and meaning of the precautionary principle and the extent to which it obligates a state to act, violation of the precautionary principle presently does not constitute a breach of international law. This section suggests that the precautionary principle may develop into its own treaty and customary norm. If this occurs, the precautionary principle will be analytically similar to the duty to warn and the duty to mitigate; through these duties a link will be forged between state responsibility and the obligation not to harm the territory of another state or the territory beyond national jurisdiction.

The Precautionary Principle and Biological Diversity

International biodiversity law and policy objectives are strongly affected by ideas concerning the value of biodiversity and the root causes of biodiversity loss. These same value judgments affect related national and regional policies and laws. Valuing biodiversity is difficult because little is understood about genes, species, and ecosystems. First, biodiversity has direct economic value from products derived from biodiversity, such as medicines or new breeds of animals or plants. Second, biodiversity has indirect value, such as ecotourism.

Third, biodiversity possesses options value, because it offers uses not yet known but of value to future generations. Fourth, biodiversity possesses existence value, which is drawn from the mere continuance of life forms in and of themselves, without regard for their economic utility. In addition to these economic, aesthetic, and ethical values, biodiversity has ecological and scientific value, because it is a storehouse of genes and micro-organisms that may permit organisms and ecosystems to recover from various afflictions. The World Charter for Nature recognized humanity's powerful impact upon the environment, the benefits of biodiversity, and the causes of biodiversity destruction.

Given the potential transboundary impact of the loss of biodiversity and the attendant mitigation costs, loss of biodiversity is clearly a matter of international concern. Furthermore, human activity is undeniably responsible for the accelerating loss of global biodiversity. Human activity is rapidly altering both terrestrial and aquatic ecosystems at an unprecedented and alarming rate. Human impact far exceeds the impact of catastrophic natural events, such as periodic fires, floods, and pestilence, that have occurred since prehistoric times. Although the planet possesses a remarkable ability to recuperate from natural disasters and even some human-made disasters, many authorities agree that the planet has reached the limits of its endurance.

Conditions of poverty are the impetus for the governments of developing countries to seek an improved quality of life for their citizens. This legitimate and worthy goal must be counterbalanced by the need to prevent further loss of biodiversity or, at the least, to make informed choices reflecting both long-term and short-term costs and benefits. Importantly, the Rio Declaration repeated the World Charter for Nature's concern for unsustainable consumption and production patterns.

The Convention on Biological Diversity requires party states to draw up national plans and legislation to achieve the Convention's objectives. If a state produces a plan claiming to address the conservation and sustainable use of biological diversity, that state has fulfilled its Convention obligations. At present, no mechanism exists to assess the substantive adequacy and consistency of national plans with the goals of the Convention. Without this important oversight mechanism, it is nearly impossible to charge a state party with breach of its Convention obligations. Similarly, until clear international standards of sustainability are developed, it is impossible to gauge the effects of a state's plan or a proposed activity on the long-term conservation and sustainable use of biological diversity.

The Convention also failed to explain its relationship to other treaties, such as the Convention on International Trade in Endangered Species and the Ramsar Convention. Under the specific language of the treaty, the general "last in time rule"[19] of treaty interpretation and preemption does not apply. Determining the effect of an action taken under multiple international instruments is difficult. The Law of the Sea Treaty clearly trumps the Biodiversity Convention according to the Convention itself. But under earlier conservation and wildlife treaties, it is much less certain whether a decision from the Conference of the Parties (COP) overrides a decision by the treaty body of a different instrument. The interrelationship and overlapping jurisdiction of various U.N. bodies also creates problems. For example, the location of the forests issue is being debated in numerous fora including the COP to the Convention on Biological Diversity; the U.N. Commission on Sustainable Development (CSD); the Global Environment Facility (GEF); the U.N. Food and Agriculture Organization (FAO); and other treaty bodies. Although this may be a salutory multi-fora approach to a complicated problem, it may also permit special interests to "forum-shop" for a receptive audience.

New treaties and soft law declarations of the past two decades and states' increasingly serious reports on their environmental protection activities have created an international environmental law that is strong and growing. The goals of conservation, sustainable use, and equitable benefit-sharing have at last elicited common efforts at the local, national, and international levels that are mutually reinforcing, as will be seen in the next subsection's examination of the international law on biodiversity.

"Soft Law," Customary International Law, and Treaty Law Related to Responsibility for Biodiversity

Commentators frequently refer to international conference statements that represent international consensus or aspiration as "soft law,"[20] a legal form that is not actually binding on states. Soft law is the newest and most common form of law-making in the international system; it frequently appears in new areas of international law-making in which obligations are not dependent upon custom. International soft law states global goals and public expectations. Once the expectations are stated, they may lead to increased public pressure, and ultimately states may recognize the soft law goals as enforceable international prohibitions. Examples of soft law include declarations and resolutions by conferences on the ministerial level or head of state level, multi-disciplinary meetings of scholars or professionals, and U.N. General Assembly resolutions. Even if soft law declarations are not initially binding, they indicate the direction in which the international community is interested in moving and how far states are willing to go.

The U.N. World Charter for Nature, adopted by the General Assembly in 1982, is a good illustration of a "soft law" that formulated a rule and caused some countries to follow the rule as a matter of policy. The General Assembly "expressed its conviction that the benefits which could be obtained from nature depended on the maintenance of natural processes and on the diversity of life forms and that those benefits were jeopardized by the excessive exploitation and the destruction of natural habitats." The General Assembly also "solemnly invited Member States, in the exercise of their permanent sovereignty over their natural resources, to conduct their activities in recognition of the supreme importance of protecting natural systems, maintaining the balance and quality of nature and conserving natural resources, in the interests of present and future generations."

The World Charter for Nature was adopted against this background as a statement of aspirations. The Charter contained a number of far-reaching significant statements regarding the relationship of human beings to other forms of life and the consequences of human activity for natural resources. Some of these statements were dropped or altered significantly in the UNCED documents and in the Biodiversity Treaty ten years later. The general principles in the World Charter for Nature included respect for nature, preservation of global genetic resources, global conservation, and sustainable use.

Customary international law is another recognized method of international lawmaking. The central problem in customary international law is determining whether and when a rule has reached the point of universality and legality. Although the traditional two-pronged test of customary international law searches for evidence of state practice and evidence of *opinio juris*, the test does not necessarily provide a simple answer. Principle 21 of the Stockholm Conference on the Human Environment provides a useful case study of the long road leading to becoming customary international law. Principle 21 provides that "[s]tates have . . . the sovereign right to exploit their own resources pursuant to their own environmental policies, and the responsibility to ensure that activities within their jurisdiction or control do not cause damage to the environment of other states or of areas beyond the limits of national jurisdiction." This statement is the result of a long progression that began with the appearance of the general idea of the principle in the *Trail Smelter* arbitration, a decision with no precedential value in any judicial forum. *Trail Smelter*'s principle was repeated in a decision of the International Court of Justice in the *Corfu Channel* case, and later included as part of the declaration of the 1972 Stockholm Conference. The principle was repeated more strongly in the "soft law" World Charter for Nature resolution. Each of these steps was evidence that at some point,

Principle 21 had become customary law. Finally, the principle became hard law when it was included in the U.N. Convention on Biological Diversity.

The language that became Principle 21, and later Article 3 of the Convention on Biological Diversity, changed slightly through its various incarnations. The *Trail Smelter* arbitration decision said that no state has the right "to use or permit the use of its territory in such a manner as to cause injury by fumes in or to the territory of another or the properties or persons therein, when the case is of serious consequences and the injury is established by clear and convincing evidence." The *Corfu Channel* case expanded the general principle to recognize every state's obligation not to knowingly allow its territory to be used for acts contrary to the rights of other states. The Stockholm Declaration was much more specific and prohibited states from activities that, "cause damage to the environment of other States or of areas beyond the limits of national jurisdiction." The U.N. General Assembly revised the principle's language somewhat. The "soft law" World Charter for Nature appeared and announced that "[s]tates and, to the extent they are able, other public authorities, international organizations, individuals, groups and corporations shall . . . [e]nsure that activities within their jurisdictions or control do not cause damage to the natural systems located within other States or in the areas beyond the limits of national jurisdiction. . . ."

Although the World Charter for Nature changed the term "environment" to "natural systems," it still limited the prohibition against harm to areas "within other States or in the areas beyond the limits of national jurisdiction." This jurisdictional scope limitation persisted in later formulations, including the Biodiversity Treaty. The addition of a phrase referring to both nations' developmental and environmental policies emphasizes the concern for sustainable development that was articulated first, and most effectively, in the Brundtland Report. This concern for sustainability characterized the UNCED documents, including the Rio Declaration, Agenda 21, and the U.N. Convention on Biological Diversity.

In its next incarnation, Principle 21 appeared in the Rio Declaration, and said:

> States have, in accordance with the Charter of the United Nations and the principles of international law, the sovereign right to exploit their own resources pursuant to their own environmental and developmental policies, and the responsibility to ensure that activities within their jurisdiction or control do not cause damage to the environment of other States or of areas beyond the limits of national jurisdiction.

The recognized test for whether Stockholm Principle 21 has become customary law is the traditional inquiry of evidence of both state practice and *opinio juris.* Evidence of state practice can be found in the presence of statements made by governments since 1972 that support Principle 21; in the inclusion of the principle in other treaties or formal declarations; and in the decisions of arbitral panels and judicial bodies that cite or rely on the principle. *Opinio juris* is evidenced by the writing of jurists who claim to have found an acceptance of Principle 21 in major legal systems around the world, as well as by a number of bilateral and regional agreements that have referred specifically to the Stockholm Declaration in their texts. Each of these documents establishes that states are following Principle 21 in practice and believe themselves to be obligated.

Statements and declarations by the U.N. General Assembly and other multilateral conferences that include the text of Principle 21 can also be cited as proof that the principle has indeed crystallized into customary law. Principle 21's language has been copied countless times in other declarations and resolutions. Moreover, when Principle 21 was codified in the Biodiversity Treaty, it earned international acceptance. Once codified in a treaty, Principle 21 is separately binding on all parties to the treaty, regardless of whether it is customary law.

Since Principle 21 was codified in the Biodiversity Treaty, it becomes necessary to define the meaning of Principle 21 in that context. The existence of states' rights implies that states have a corresponding moral, ethical, and increasingly legal responsibility. The principle of sovereignty guarantees the right of a state to act. Principle 21 balances that right with a state's duty to protect the environment within its jurisdiction or control and to prevent transboundary harm. This responsibility necessarily limits a state's right to use its natural resources with unfettered discretion. Similarly, international law restricts a state's right to use force at will through the requirements of necessity and proportionality. States' absolute sovereignty is already restricted by the global imperative to survive in the face of grave threats to the planet's soil, water, and air. Absolute freedom of consumption without regard for environment costs and nonsustainable means of production are also becoming the target of restrictions under international law and policy.

States may find themselves increasingly under prohibitions regarding the protection or sharing of scarce natural resources, under both permissive and prohibitive systems of laws. As described above, in a permissive system, everything that is not prohibited is permitted and states' sovereignty is absolute. In a prohibitive system, everything not explicitly permitted is assumed prohibited unless clear pension can be found from some supranational source. Principle 21 as binding customary law appears to be a permissive system, tempering states' absolute rights with only the responsibility not to harm the territory of another or territory beyond national jurisdiction. Both the precautionary principle and Principle 21 of the Stockholm Declaration as contained verbatim in the Biodiversity Convention embody the concept of responsibility and need to consider sustainability.

The shift toward prevention and responsibility, and away from the notion of liability and compensation after harm occurs, is a crucial step in accepting the fundamental concept of international biological diversity. Once the basic premises of responsibility and sharing are accepted, resources can be redirected to find the means to achieve these ends. Some possible solutions include transfer of environmentally-sound technology, access to genetic resources, and distribution of some of the royalties from successful genetically-derived products to the source countries and local communities. Greater international cooperation will benefit those who participate; countries may choose not to share, but they will be denied access to valuable resources.

Protection of biological diversity requires more than species preservation. Scientists have discovered the importance of ecosystems; they act both as corridors between habitats that support endangered species and as rich depositories of unidentified organisms. It is inadequate to measure the value of an ecosystem by reference to its utility for human beings, because it is impossible to value uses that have not yet been imagined. Utility valuation also fails to account for the intrinsic value of ecosystems and life forms. The degree of environmental harm and the true cost of biodiversity loss are important in decision-making and risk analysis; they also have implications for any future liability and compensation regime. Given the present inability to accurately value biodiversity, it is best to adopt a preventive approach rather than to risk unknown harm. The precautionary principle does not require absolute scientific certainty as a prerequisite to preservation of an area or species that may be irreparably harmed before it is fully understood.

The new United Nations Convention on Biological Diversity attempts to balance interests on a global level and represents a general commitment to the conservation and sustainable use of biodiversity. In an effort to clarify the interests being balanced, the Convention carefully defines biological diversity, biological resources, and biotechnology. Although the Convention codifies Principle 21, it does not resolve the problem of liability for the loss of biodiversity.

The parties to the Biodiversity Convention accepted a binding obligation to conserve biodiversity and received an affirmation of their sovereign right to use forests, wetlands, and other ecosystems for development, tempered by the requirement of sustainable use. This obligation was a new departure for developing countries. In return for guaranteed access to the genetic resources located in genetically rich developing countries, developed countries accepted an obligation to share the benefits of biotechnology. The final compromise, then, endorsed both the conservation of biodiversity and its sustainable use. To some, this trade-off has ominous overtones. The Third World Network, an Indian nongovernmental organization, fears that the North is attempting to preserve its access to the South's genetic resources. Thus, the South would supply the "raw material for the [North's] next industrial revolution," in the North's privately-held biotechnology industry.

International law does not yet possess state responsibility or means of calculating appropriate damages for the accidental or willful destruction of biodiversity. Nevertheless, since the Convention on Biological Diversity entered into force in December 1993, it is plausible that the international law of precautionary action may rise to the level of a duty, which can trigger state responsibility when breached. The breach may occur when states fail to regulate activities within their jurisdiction or control or cause damage in areas beyond national jurisdiction. In order to achieve the conservation and sustainable use of biological diversity, it may be necessary to use the international legal system to regulate or restrict development patterns in accordance with the precautionary principle.

When a state breaches its duty to uphold the precautionary principle, Article 3 of the Convention on Biological Diversity offers a basis for assessing the state's responsibility. Although the duty applies only to extraterritorial harm, the Convention's article on jurisdictional scope may give rise to responsibility for a state's activities, regardless of where the effect occurs. The Convention's jurisdiction varies somewhat. The Convention's jurisdiction over components of biodiversity is consistent with Principle 21 and extends only to harms caused in the territory of other states or in the territory beyond national jurisdiction. The Convention's jurisdiction over processes and activities is considerably broader and leaves room for further interpretation of responsibility beyond the transborder context. Such an extension of jurisdictional scope is inherently necessary to the conservation of biological diversity.

New principles of international environmental law have developed quickly in recent years in response to global imperatives for sustainable development; nowhere is that trend more noticeable than in the formation of international law on biodiversity. The United Nations Convention on Biological Diversity, which entered into force as binding international law on December 29, 1993, has been ratified by 127 nations. The first Conference of the Parties took place in late 1994, formally adopting many of the interim institutional and financial mechanisms for the operation of the treaty established when the treaty was opened for signature during the United Nations Conference on Environment and Development in June, 1992. A declaration adopted at the close of the first COP noted that states party to the Convention on Biological Diversity regard it "as much more than just a set of rights and obligations: it is a global partnership with new approaches to multilateral cooperation for conservation and development. . . ."

The U.N. Convention on Biological Diversity represents a new style of treaty negotiation, in that the Convention's subject matter is very broad and the Convention was negotiated with unusual speed and openness. Other features also contribute to the treaty's uniqueness. First, the treaty pioneers an ecosystem approach to conservation that moves beyond the species-specific or habitat-specific approaches of earlier conservation treaties, including those on migratory birds, wetlands, and trade in endangered species. Second, both the preamble and the body of the treaty emphasize the participation of women, local communities, and nongovernmental organizations (NGOs) in biodiversity protection. This language is a significant departure from most other multilateral instruments, which address only the role of the states party to the treaty. The Convention's identification of nonstate actors is a recognition that successful implementation of the treaty will require cooperation from many sectors.

Third, the initial formulation of the treaty was marked by the initiative and contributions of NGOs; indeed, the first draft of the treaty was prepared by an NGO. Fourth, the Biodiversity Treaty is unique, because the text of Stockholm Principle 21 appears verbatim as Article 3, marking the first time this language has appeared in binding international law, rather than in "customary law" or "soft law." The idea of national sovereignty over resources is balanced or tempered to some degree by the requirement that each state accept its responsibility not to harm the territory of any other state or the territory beyond its own national jurisdiction. Finally, the treaty represents a trade-off of mutually beneficial goods, a trade-off that is possible because both developing and developed states have something of value that the other group wants.

Although it is too early to tell how effectively the treaty will be implemented, there is cause for some optimism. The Convention calls for the study of the creation of a Clearinghouse Mechanism for Technical and Scientific Cooperation, which would share knowledge on biological diversity and promote cooperation. In addition, the Convention establishes the Subsidiary Body on Scientific, Technical, and Technological Advice (SBSTTA). On-going discussions at the two meetings of the Intergovernmental Committee on the Convention on Biological Diversity and at the first COP centered on the institutional and organizational entities needed to implement the Convention, as well as on related concerns such as financial mechanisms, intellectual property rights, and biosafety. Most of the NGOs in attendance at the meetings on the Convention in 1993 and 1994 called for efforts to address the relationships between poverty, unsustainable production and consumption, unequal trade relations, and biodiversity; the discussions did not, however, directly address these underlying causes of biodiversity loss.

By the end of the first COP, many of the organizational issues required to set up a new treaty were resolved. The United Nations Environment Programme (UNEP) was designated the appropriate institutional body to function as the Secretariat, and the rules of procedure were established. Finally, the work of the next three years was divided into topics and compiled as the Medium Term Programme of Work of the Conference of the Parties 1995–1997. Despite progress at the first COP, many aspects of the Biodiversity Treaty remain open to interpretation. These gray areas include: state responsibility for prevention of loss of biodiversity; the meaning of "sustainable use" of biological diversity; the extent of a party's obligations to enforce the treaty's objectives through domestic laws; the relationship of the Convention to other wildlife and habitat treaties; and the relationship of the COP and Secretariat to other U.N. bodies whose mandates include aspects of biodiversity.

Conclusion

New international environmental law principles, including sustainable development and recognition of serious human threats to the global environment, have created new applications for the doctrines of state responsibility and liability, although states' environmental obligations under international law remain ill-defined. It is difficult to reconcile most activities threatening loss of biological diversity with the I.L.C.'s language on state responsibility for "primary" and "secondary" obligations and "internationally wrongful acts." Furthermore, the concept of "injurious consequences arising from acts not contrary to international law" appears to be of limited use when only ultrahazardous activities are examined. The concept's use is limited, because biodiversity loss most frequently occurs through the accumulation of ordinary human activities that affect an ecosystem.

Principle 21's concept of state responsibility links sovereign power and privilege with general obligations not to harm the territory of another state or the area beyond national jurisdiction. The legal principles relevant to air, space, aircraft, and maritime boundary disputes are considerably less relevant to problems involving micro-organisms and migratory species. Similarly, territorially-based concepts are not very useful in assessing states' responsibility when they fail to regulate multinational commercial entities that destroy or unsustainably exploit biodiversity resources. One option is to define such commercial activities as internationally wrongful or otherwise prohibited under international law. Unfortunately, this step is unlikely to occur. Another option is to recognize the precautionary principle as a means to comply with state responsibility not to harm the environment. Failure to adopt national plans or procedures incorporating a precautionary approach may then trigger international responsibility or liability.

In other words, a state's duty to take precautionary action may be seen as one of a cluster of procedural norms similar to the duties to warn other states, to mitigate damages, and to assist in case of emergency. For example, the Rio Declaration reaffirms a state's obligation to provide early notification in an emergency and when activities may have a significant transboundary impact. The Rio Declaration also affirms a state's obligation to assist in the event of such emergencies. Moreover, some states are required by treaty to provide both early notification of risk to other states and assistance to other states in the event of a nuclear accident. The goal of these procedural norms is to make information widely available to local communities and to the international community so that states can make informed choices and undertake appropriate responses. A state wishing to comply with the principle of precautionary action may do so by incorporating environmental impact assessment procedures in national planning and legislation.

At the 1992 United Nations Conference on Environment and Development (UNCED), participating states affirmed the importance of environmental impact assessment (EIA) procedures as an integral part of the development process. Currently, more than fifty nations require EIA as a matter of domestic law; and sixteen states of the United States have adopted laws that are more substantive than the National Environmental Protection Act (NEPA). In addition, international organizations, such as the World Bank, have adopted EIA procedures as part of their decision-making process. The popularity of EIAs is due in large measure to their proven effectiveness in anticipating and mitigating the adverse environmental impacts of development projects, and their usefulness in providing environmental information to decision-makers. Moreover, EIA procedures often give potentially affected local communities an opportunity to participate in the decision-making process.

The widespread acceptance of environmental impact assessments is demonstrated by the passage of the Espoo Convention on Environmental Impact Assessment in a Transboundary Context, which was opened for signature in 1991. As of mid-1995, twenty-eight states have signed the convention; a majority of Western and Eastern European states, the United States, and Canada are among the signatories. The Convention requires parties to "take all appropriate and effective measures to prevent, reduce, and control significant adverse transboundary environmental impact from proposed activities." To comply with the Convention, states must notify potentially affected states of environmental dangers, and must consult with affected states to reduce or eliminate adverse environmental effects. The use of EIAs, then, may be one way to implement the precautionary principle in national and international law and policy. It is an approach with particular relevance to the conservation and sustainable use of biological diversity.

Another conceptual way to approach the goal of biodiversity conservation under international law, as explored *supra* in Part II, is through state responsibility and liability. The current limitation of obligations not to harm territory within the jurisdiction of another state or beyond the national jurisdiction does not fully protect global biodiverse resources, for states may still destroy such resources within their territorial boundaries under existing international law. What is needed in the future, then, is to extend responsibility to all states to conserve and sustainably use such resources as a global storehouse of genetic information or medicine chest, separate and apart from claims of sovereign rights, unless subject to the balances and tradeoffs negotiated in the Convention on Biological Diversity.

Applying the principle of state responsibility in areas beyond national jurisdiction, such as Antarctica and the high seas, creates an opportunity to apply the doctrine of state responsibility in a context free from the claims of sovereign rights. The U.N. Convention on the Law of the Sea (LOS) offers a plan that is tailored for the maximum preservation of humanity's common heritage. Similarly, Antarctica offers the chance to preserve a unique ecosystem of "enormous scientific, ecological, spiritual, and aesthetic importance."[21] The Madrid Protocol to the Antarctic Treaty "implicitly adopts the precautionary principle of environmental planning."[22] In the concept of pollution on the high seas, "[d]octrine and practice . . . now evidence the existence of a parallel obligation to prevent harm to the shared resource of the high seas environment. . . . The 1982 LOS Convention [codifies a duty] as the obligation to act with 'due regard' for other states."[23]

The concept of "internationally wrongful act" creates problems for the application of traditional notions of state responsibility for environmental damage. Because clear norms of international environmental law have not yet been fully and universally recognized, the application of the doctrine of state responsibility is not particularly useful at this time. Thus, "[i]t may be concluded that, with respect to transfrontier pollution, the principle of state responsibility is undergoing a process of development and consolidation, but it is not yet to be considered to have hardened into a rule of international law."[24] As discussed by the I.L.C., much serious environmental harm can result from activities that are not "wrongful" in themselves, but whose cumulative effect is disastrous. The international system still awaits the development of an international law on liability and compensation for victims and a broader concept of state environmental responsibility. Obviously, the best strategy for a state that is mindful of its responsibility is to avoid a breach of international obligations entirely or to adopt preventive measures. It is the duty of the international community to develop a full understanding of those obligations.

The creation of international environmental law has led to the recognition of certain legal obligations, such as states' responsibility not to harm the territory of another state and the territory beyond national jurisdiction. This responsibility should be expanded to address threats to global resources and biodiversity even when the threats occur within the territory of individual states. The new international environmental legal system should encourage states to observe their obligations to conserve and sustainably use the environment. In cases where it is difficult to know whether an activity is sustainable the best course for legislators and policy makers is to apply the precautionary approach and prevent environment harm. States that take their environmental responsibilities seriously, comply with their treaty obligations, and strengthen their national regulatory systems need not fear the establishment of international standards and an extended notion of state environmental responsibility. The international community soon must formulate a clear understanding of state environmental responsibility that is proactive and designed to minimize risk. The duty to take precautionary action is becoming customary international law. As such, it offers one way for states to undertake sustainable development, to uphold Stockholm Principle 21, to conserve and sustainably use biological diversity, to protect areas beyond national jurisdiction, and to meet other global obligations. In the process, states' and citizens' self-interest in adopting precautionary measures will become apparent as the Biodiversity Convention is implemented and other sources of international law develop.

Notes

1. Edith Brown Weiss, *International Environmental Law: Contemporary Issues and the Emergence of a New World Order,* 81 Geo. L.J. 675, 690 (1993).

2. Susan H. Bragdon, *National Sovereignty and Global Environmental Responsibility: Can the Tension Be Reconciled for the Conservation of Biological Diversity?,* 33 Harv. Int'l L.J. 381, 391 (1992).

3. This phrase is roughly translated as a form of the golden rule or good neighborliness—an injunction to use one's property in a manner that does not injure another's property. It is related to the civil law concept of "abuse of rights." One classic example of the principle is the idea that neighbors may not build "spite fences" to separate themselves from one another.

National laws also contain "the doctrine that makes an otherwise proper exercise of one's property rights wrongful unless the use [sic] compensates the person who is injured by the use." Louis Henkin et al., International Law: Cases and Materials 1380 (3d ed. 1993). *See also* James Barros & Douglas M. Johnston, The International Law of Pollution 74–76 (1974).

4. *Erga omnes* obligations are obligations owed to the international community as a whole, rather than just to another state.

5. Francisco O. Vicuña, *State Responsibility, Liability, and Remedial Measures Under International Law: New Criteria for Environmental Protection,* in Environmental Change and International Law 124, 128 (Edith Brown Weiss ed., 1992).

6. Philip Allott, *State Responsibility and the Unmaking of International Law,* 29 Harv. Int'l L.J. 1, 1 (1988).

7. *Id.* at 16.

8. [T]he public law analogy of the *ultra vires* act is more realistic than a seeking for subjective *culpa* in specific natural persons who may, or may not, 'represent'

the legal person (the state) in terms of wrongdoing. . . . the state also bears an international responsibility for all acts committed by its officials or its organs which are delictual according to international law, regardless of whether the official organ has acted within the limits of his competency or has exceeded those limits." Ian Brownlie, Principles of Public International Law 437–40 (4th ed. 1990) (citing Estate of Jean-Baptiste Caire v. United Mexican States, 5 R.I.A.A. 516, 529–31 [1929]).

[T]here is no need to show fault in the sense of malicious intent or negligence on the part of the state officials responsible for the action of inaction. . . . [O]pinions of eminent authorities such as Lauterpacht, Verdross and Eagleton . . . have favoured the Grotian view that State responsibility rests on "the conception of States as moral entities accountable for their acts and omissions in proportion to the *mens rea* of their agents, the real addressees of international duties. . . ."

Oscar Schachter, International Law in Theory and Practice 203 (1991) (quoting Hersh Lauterpacht, Private Law Sources and Analogies 173 [1970]).

9. Brownlie, *supra* note 8, at 437.

10. *Id.* at 437–39. Negligence and fault are, however, pertinent when determining reparations. *Id.*

11. *Report of the International Law Commission on the Work of Its Twenty-Eighth Session,* U.N. GAOR, 28th Sess., Supp. No. 10, U.N. Doc. A/28/10 (1976), *reprinted in* 2 Y.B. Int'l L. Comm'n 95, U.N. Doc. A/CN.4/SER.A/1976/Add.1 (pt. 2) (1976).

12. In fear of possible liability for environmental harm from their own activities, no state is leading the charge to impose international liability. For example, following the Chernobyl accident, one might have expected states such as Sweden to bring a case against the U.S.S.R. at the International Court of Justice for damage suffered within their state. In reality, no such case was brought. This suggests Sweden is concerned that it too could be subject to third party claims, such as those resulting from acid rain pollution damage.

13. Jutta Brunnée, *The Responsibility of States for Environmental Harm in a Multinational Context—Problems and Trends*, 34 Les Cahiers de Droit [C. de D.] 827, 845 n.96 (citing A. Rest, *New Tendencies in Environmental Liability/Responsibility Law,* 21 envtl. Pol'y & L. 135 [1991] [supporting the adoption of instruments of legal responsibility and liability]).

14. In other words, the Commission will focus first on preventive measures in respect of activities creating a substantial risk of harm, and then on remedial measures after harm has occurred. The goal is to create, in this manner, agreement in the Commission on basic elements of its work on the topic.

15. It remains to be seen whether this procedure will enable the Commission to free itself of the difficulties it has faced. If so, the Commission may be able to focus on various approaches, including insurance schemes of the type contained in the International Convention on Civil Liability for Oil Pollution Damage and the 1971 International Convention on the Establishment of an International Fund for Compensation for Oil Pollution Damage. These instruments reflect a market-oriented socialization of the risk with regard to one class of undeniably useful, indeed essential, activities known to be ultrahazardous in terms of their potential damage.

16. David Freestone, *The Precautionary Principle*, in International Law and Climate Change 21, 30 (Robin Churchill & David Freestone eds., 1991).

17. The *opinio juris communis,* or expression of a legal obligation, relates to a nation's perception of its duties. Proof of obligation can be found in decisions of national courts, and in statements by leaders and jurists as to the legal effect of a declaration, etc.

18. Deterrence theory posits that a change in behavior will occur when the

threatened consequences of an act become too painful or expensive, and when it is clear that such consequences will occur. Deterrence works only if the consequences are sufficiently unpleasant.

19. The "last in time rule" provides that in the case of a direct conflict between a treaty and a federal statute, the last in time will prevail.

20. Alexandre C. Kiss, Survey of Current Developments in International environmental Law 23 (1976) (citing Rene J. Dupuy, *Droit déclaratoire dt Droit Programmatoire: de la Coutume Sauvage à la Soft Law, in* l'élaboration Du Droit International Public 132 (1975)). See also Christine M. Chinkin, *The Challenge of Soft Law: Development and Change in International Law,* 38 Int'l & Comp. L.Q. 850 (1989); Panel, *A Hard Look at Soft Law,* 82 Proc. Am. Soc'y Int'l L. 317 (1988).

21. David J. Bederman, *The Antarctic and Southern Ocean Coalition's Convention on Antarctic Conservation,* 4 Geo. Int'l Envtl. L. Re. 47, 47 (1991).

22. Bederman, *supra* note 21, at 49.

23. *See* Brian D. Smith, State Responsibility and the Marine Environment: the rules of Decision (1988), at 89.

24. Jutta Brunnée, Acid Rain and Ozone Layer Depletion: International Law and Regulation (1986) at 113 (citing Lothar Gündling, *Verantwortlichkeit der Staaten für grezüberschreitende Umweltbeeintäctigungen,* 45 Zeitschrift Fur Auslandisches Offentliches Recht und Volkerrecht [Zaörv] 265, 273 [1985]).

PART 2.4

International Law as Normative System: Managing the Commons

CHAPTER 19

The Territorial Temptation: A Siren Song at Sea

Bernard Oxman

THE HISTORY OF INTERNATIONAL LAW SINCE THE PEACE OF Westphalia is in significant measure an account of the territorial temptation.[1] The bonds of family, clan, tribe, nation, and faith; the need to explore, to trade, and to migrate; the hope for broader cooperation to confront common challenges—all in time came to be subordinated in the international legal order to the insistent quest for supremacy of the territorial state. At least in theory. At least on land.

The sea yields a different story. It wasn't always so. And perhaps it isn't necessarily so. But in fact the law of the land and the law of the sea developed in very different ways. If the history of the international law of the land can be characterized by the progressive triumph of the territorial temptation, the history of the international law of the sea can be characterized by the obverse; namely, the progressive triumph of Grotius's thesis of *mare liberum* and its concomitant prohibition on claims of territorial sovereignty.[2] That triumph reflected not only the transitory nature of human activity at sea, but a rational conclusion that the interests of states in unrestricted access to the rest of the world outweighed their interests in restricting the access of others at sea.

The Territorial Temptation Turns Seaward

The mid-twentieth century was a watershed for the international law of the sea. At the same time that the territorial temptation ran up against increasingly important legal constraints on land—often in response to the values of

---

facilitation of trade, communication, and cooperation, which had traditionally informed the law of the sea—the obverse again occurred at sea. The territorial temptation thrust seaward with a speed and geographic scope that would be the envy of the most ambitious conquerors in human history. The effective start of this process—President Truman's claim to the continental shelf in 1945[3]—was so quickly accepted and emulated by other coastal states[4] that the emergence of the regime of the continental shelf, in derogation of the principle of *mare liberum*,[5] has been cited as an example of instant customary law.[6] The Truman Proclamation unleashed a quarter-century of territorial and quasi-territorial claims to the high seas so vast that, at the dawn of the Third United Nations Conference on the Law of the Sea, the leader of the Canadian delegation, Ambassador J. Alan Beesley, could quip that he comes to bury Grotius, not to praise him.

The Geneva Conventions of 1958

To be sure, the International Law Commission had made an earnest effort to codify the traditional law of the sea as one of its earliest undertakings in the 1950s, as had the first Conference on the Law of the Sea, which followed in 1958. The 1958 Convention on the High Seas, the only one of the four adopted at Geneva to declare itself a codification, elaborated the Grotian regime and its application with admirable attention to principle and important detail; its text survived largely unchanged as Part VII of the 1982 United Nations Convention on the Law of the Sea.

The High Seas Convention defined the high seas as "all parts of the sea that are not included in the territorial sea or in the internal waters of a State."[7] While the classic 3-mile limit was defended well into the twentieth century,[8] the Hague Codification Conference, the International Law Commission, and the 1958 Convention on the Territorial Sea and the Contiguous Zone failed to prescribe the maximum permissible breadth of the territorial sea, and accordingly the limits of the free high seas. In addition, the 1958 Convention on the Continental Shelf failed to specify a definitive seaward limit for the coastal state's sovereign rights over seabed resources beyond the territorial sea, and accordingly the landward limit of any "international" seabed area.[9]

Moreover, the 1958 Convention on Fishing and Conservation of the Living Resources of the High Seas failed to provide an effective means for avoiding the "tragedy of the commons," namely, a solution to the allocation problem and attendant conservation problem that arise when exploitation of a stock by multiple users approaches or exceeds its sustainable yield. This increasing threat prompted political pressure on coastal states to find ways to protect local fishing industries facing foreign competition for a limited resource. That pressure contributed to some claims to control the sea out to 200 miles[10] or beyond that had already appeared in Latin America when the International Law Commission began its work.

While in retrospect one can imagine that the 1958 Conventions might have done more to redirect the way that governments approached problems posed by the high seas regime, the inability of the Conventions to identify precisely where that regime applies is a symptom of the reemergence of the territorial temptation at sea. Key provisions of the Conventions reflect the disagreements and confusion occasioned by that reemergence; they do not explain it and did not cause it.

Choices

The response that emerged with full force following World War II to the systemic problems posed by the insistent demand by the territorial state for substantive discretion on land was to elaborate reciprocal international and regional instruments and mechanisms of restraint and cooperation through which each state could influence the acts and omissions of other states and, through the intermediation of those states, influence human behavior beyond its territorial reach. That enterprise embraces the bulk of the international law agenda at the dawn of the twenty-first century, whether the object is trade and investment, environmental protection, human rights, or indeed the maintenance of international peace and security.

Then why not the sea? If the approach to the problems posed by the range of discretion of the territorial state is to work on the basis of that framework to shape international agreements and mechanisms to achieve desired levels of mutual restraint and cooperation, why not take the same instrumental approach to the problems posed by the range of discretion of the flag state (or state of nationality) in a nonterritorial system and work on the basis of that framework? To some extent the response to flag state discretion at sea has been the same as the response to the territorial state's discretion on land—a system of international agreements and mechanisms to restrain the scope of discretion, especially with respect to navigation and communications, Grotius's primary concern. This response is augmented, however, by significant port state and coastal state powers discussed later in this essay.

As for natural resources, the triumph of the territorial temptation with respect to almost all of the commercial fisheries and hydrocarbons in and beneath the sea resulted from a variety of factors. They include political and bureaucratic ambition, the lure of tax revenues and other economic rent, protection against competition,[11] impatience, frustration with international organizations, and, yes, domino effects and a dash of xenophobia. Once past the public rhetoric,[12] there may be some considerations behind the successful push to territorialize the ocean's resources that one would not necessarily wish to flaunt before Heaven's gatekeeper, even one with a degree in economics.

Except for one thing. Was there a better plausible alternative?

Perhaps those who conceived the outcomes at Bretton Woods and Chicago in 1944 and San Francisco in 1945 might have come up with something different from the Truman Proclamation had their attention been directed to the issue. Perhaps they would have wondered why it was proposed that the world's largest consumer of energy, and one of the few sources of the necessary capital and technology at the time, cede control over perhaps 90 percent of the world's exploitable undersea hydrocarbons to foreign states, including some that might not provide a hospitable investment climate for Americans or others.[13] Even if investment in oil and gas development depends on a system of exclusive private rights to exploit a site that in turn requires a recognized public grantor,[14] and also depends on the cooperation of a nearby state to fulfill a variety of practical needs, extension of coastal state jurisdiction is an obvious way, but not necessarily the only way, to accommodate those needs. Still, it is not clear how one might deflect concerns, exaggerated or not, about a fixed offshore installation under the control of a foreign power.

As for fisheries, a system of international negotiation and regulation had actually been tried on a bilateral and regional basis, before and after World War II. It was found wanting. In critical areas, durable solutions to the allocation problem eluded negotiators, the expedient tendency to agree on an allowable catch large enough to accommodate competing allocation demands was self-defeating, and the problems of monitoring and enforcement posed abiding difficulties. There was no reason to believe that a global organization, even if politically plausible, could have done better.

The UN Convention on the Law of the Sea

The real challenge faced by the Third United Nations Conference on the Law of the Sea, then, was to find ways to accommodate the territorial temptation in the context of an overall system that promised the degree of stability, predictability, and measured change one expects from law. The response to the territorial temptation was to define and circumscribe both its geographic and its substantive reach. To that extent it mirrors the modern response to the territorial temptation on land. The difference is that the limitations in the Law of the Sea Convention are much more extensive and at times more innovative.

The geography of the accommodation is familiar. Sovereignty is limited to internal waters, archipelagic waters of an archipelagic state, and the territorial sea. The territorial sea has a precise maximum limit of 12 miles, measured from the normal baseline along the low-water mark or from straight baselines enclosing internal or archipelagic waters.[15]

Three zones of functional jurisdiction extend seaward from the outer limit of the territorial sea, and therefore overlap to some extent:

- the contiguous zone, whose maximum limit is 24 miles from the coastal baselines, and where the coastal state may prevent and punish infringement of its customs, fiscal, immigration, or sanitary laws in its territory or territorial sea;[16]
- the exclusive economic zone (EEZ), whose maximum limit is 200 miles from the coastal baselines, and where the coastal state has sovereign rights over the exploration and exploitation of the natural resources of the waters and the seabed and subsoil, and certain other specific competences;[17] and
- the continental shelf, whose maximum limit is the outer edge of the continental margin or 200 miles from the coastal baselines if the continental margin does not extend up to that distance, and where the coastal state exercises sovereign rights over the exploration and exploitation of the natural resources of the seabed and subsoil and certain other specific competences.[18]

The sovereignty of the coastal state in the territorial sea and in internal waters created by straight baselines is qualified by the right of innocent passage for ships of all states[19] and, in straits used for international navigation between two parts of the high seas or an EEZ, by the more liberal right of transit passage for ships and aircraft of all states.[20] Similar qualifications apply to archipelagic waters.[21]

"High seas" is not defined in geographic terms as such. The freedoms of the high seas preserved in the EEZ are navigation, overflight, the laying of submarine cables and pipelines, and other internationally lawful uses of the sea related to these freedoms, while those beyond the EEZ are more extensive and open-ended.[22] Apart from this difference, the regime of the high seas applies both seaward of the EEZ and, except with respect to living resources, within the EEZ to the extent not incompatible with other provisions regarding the zone.[23]

Is the System Stable?

The basic question is whether this system is stable. The territorial temptation received much to digest from the Law of the Sea Convention and the coastal state claims preceding it. But the temptation has far from disappeared. Will it continue to restructure the law of the sea? If so, will it do so within the current conventional framework or occasion its collapse?

The latter may be the more important question. The underlying significance of the Law of the Sea Convention, evident in its very existence, as well as in its regulatory and institutional structures, is global multilateralism: to discipline the prior unilateralist system by subjecting the territorial temptation to organized international scrutiny and decision. In a multilateral forum, states are more likely to measure and balance their own overall long-term interests. For example, multilateral negotiation is more likely to reflect the reality that the majority of coastal states, even those with large coastlines, are either entirely or in significant measure dependent for their access to the rest of the world upon navigation and overflight through the EEZs of their neighbors and other states as well as straits bordered by those states.

Geographic Limits

The pressures on the geographic limits of the accommodation continue, but those limits appear to be holding. The textual indeterminacy inherited from the generalization in the 1958 Territorial Sea Convention of the International Court of Justice's decision in the *Anglo-Norwegian Fisheries* case renders squabbles about straight baselines inevitable.[24] Their impact, while important, seems to be confined.

The International Tribunal for the Law of the Sea has been careful to keep the competences of the coastal state in the 24-mile contiguous zone confined to that area, and to resist open-ended assertions of similar competence beyond that limit.

The 200-mile limit came under almost immediate pressure from coastal states concerned about high seas fishing adjacent to the EEZ. Argentina, Canada, and Chile made temporary or indeterminate claims of right with respect to fishing beyond the 200-mile line, and threatening noises were heard from Russia and the United States. Some of the underlying pressure apparently is being relieved by formal adherence to, and practical application of, the 1995 UN agreement on the implementation of the relevant fisheries provisions of the Convention, which increases protection for coastal state interests in stocks that straddle or migrate across the 200-mile line, and by regional agreements. But the problem persists. So long as states resort to negotiations and international tribunals to resolve the matter, there is reason to hope that a solution will be found that strengthens the underlying structure.

The Commission on the Limits of the Continental Shelf is receiving an increasing number of submissions from broad-margin states that, if approved, will permit those states to establish the definitive limits of their respective continental shelves beyond 200 miles and, accordingly, the limits of the international seabed "Area."[25] Although the commission faces a task of enormous magnitude, and its operations could benefit from greater transparency and public attention, the key point again is the international setting in which the territorial pressures are being considered.

The Substantive Balance

A more difficult question is whether the substantive balance within the specified limits can be maintained against a persistent territorial temptation. The classic debate in the law of the sea between *mare liberum* and *mare clausum* has shifted, at least for now, from an argument about geographic limits to an argument about substantive limits. In this respect, the real issue concerns the EEZ and the concomitant right of transit passage of straits connecting two parts of the EEZ. At heart, however, the issue remains the same as it has always been; territorializing the EEZ is simply another way of expanding the limits of the territorial sea.

The EEZ embraces about a third of the marine environment. All of the important seas and gulfs of the world are composed entirely, or mainly, of waters within 200 miles of the coast of some state.

The essence of the EEZ is its substantive balance. That balance is particularly vulnerable to the territorial temptation because the EEZ is already perceived in quasi-territorial terms. In this regard, we need to consider that, after all is said and done, what really separates the EEZ from the territorial sea is that the former embraces freedom of navigation, overflight, and communications, and is not in principle subject to comprehensive coastal state jurisdiction, while the latter is subject to comprehensive coastal state jurisdiction and, outside of straits, includes only a very limited, and suspendable, right of innocent passage that is subject to both important qualifications and unilateral coastal state regulation.

In an early assault on the substantive balance in an institutional setting, a very few states that clung to claims to a 200-mile territorial sea attempted to persuade the International Civil Aviation Organization to cast doubt on the continued application to the EEZ of the provisions regarding overflight of the high seas in the Convention on International Civil Aviation. That effort failed.

A better organized assault on that balance in an institutional setting occurred in the United Nations Educational, Scientific and Cultural Organization, from which emerged a controversial UNESCO convention that purports to expand the authority of coastal states in the EEZ and on the continental shelf to embrace marine archaeology.[26] In itself, this matter may have little impact on the balance of the EEZ. The problem is that it reflects a view of the EEZ as an appropriate vessel for accumulating additional coastal state competences. And each such move increases the territorial perception of the EEZ, which in turn facilitates further territorialization.

Be that as it may, a frontal assault on freedom of navigation itself in the EEZ, if successful, would undeniably go a long way toward creating a functional 200-mile territorial sea. Two main sources for such an assault are likely to command attention for some time: national security and protection of the marine environment. Both reflect important values that should be advanced. Both attract committed adherents who believe that other values must be subordinated to their efforts.

National security. The law of the sea in general, and the regime of the EEZ in particular, accommodate two different types of security interests. Most states share both in some measure. One is global mobility; high seas freedoms constitute its legal manifestation. The other is coastal security; coastal state sovereignty and jurisdiction constitute its legal manifestation.

The interest in global mobility seeks to avoid impediments to the deployment of forces by sea anywhere in the world. This interest is ordinarily associated with naval powers. In fact, the security of almost every state depends in some measure upon the mobility of the forces of naval powers for the maintenance of stability and security in its region.

Global mobility is a predicate of the international security system as it exists at present and for the foreseeable future. Both collective self-defense and collective security under the United Nations Charter, including enforcement, peacekeeping, and humanitarian operations, continue to rest on the assumption of global mobility, which means under current law that naval and air forces enjoy the freedoms of the seas in EEZs, as well as the concomitant right of transit passage through straits connecting EEZs.[27]

While the nature of security threats may change, the underlying interest in global mobility of forces does not. It is as pertinent to the threats of today as it was to those during the Cold War. The right at stake is the freedom to get to the sources of the threat. Absent that freedom, a right to act once there—such as the right to board and inspect, one aspect of the so-called proliferation security initiative[28]—is of no avail. If the right to board and inspect is rooted in flag state consent and flag state duties of cooperation derived from high seas principles, it protects the global mobility essential to the achievement of the purposes of that system. Yielding to the territorial temptation and utilizing the EEZ and its 200-mile limit as the basis for boarding rights would have exactly the contrary effect: it would in all but name breach the essence of the distinction between the territorial sea and the EEZ for security purposes. The amendments to Chapter V of the regulations annexed to the International Convention for the Safety of Life at Sea regarding long-range identification and tracking of ships provide for notification to the coastal state when a ship is within 1,000 miles of the coast. From the perspective of both coastal security and global mobility, use of the 200-mile figure, as some delegates suggested, would have been a mistake, providing less useful information and entailing further territorialization of the EEZ.[29] The temptation to impose new security controls in the 200-mile zone nevertheless remains a serious problem as states consider other measures to deal with the terrorist threat from the sea.

The territorial sea is the most obvious manifestation of the influence of the territorial temptation in the law of the sea and its association with coastal security concerns.[30] This influence is reflected not only in the sovereignty of the coastal state over the territorial sea, but in its right, except for straits, to suspend innocent passage temporarily "if such suspension is essential for the protection of its security."[31] But accommodation of coastal security concerns is not limited to the territorial sea. The EEZ and continental shelf regimes respond to such concerns as well by placing most offshore installations and structures, apart from submarine cables and pipelines, under coastal state jurisdiction.[32] In addition, the elaborate requirements regarding scientific research in the EEZ and on the continental shelf, while primarily a response to economic concerns, were adopted in some measure in reaction to coastal security concerns.[33]

As a result, the EEZ regime is designed to protect both types of security concerns, according each priority with respect to different types of activity. Global mobility prevails with respect to navigation, overflight, submarine cables, and activities related to those freedoms. Coastal security concerns prevail with respect to most fixed installations.

The accommodation in the territorial sea, while real, is much different. The right of innocent passage is a limited one. Only with respect to transit passage of straits does the accommodation approach that in the EEZ, and even then transit passage applies only to ships and aircraft in continuous and expeditious transit, and does not embrace the range of the high seas freedoms preserved in the EEZ.

The balance of the EEZ regime with respect to security interests appears to be stable for now.[34] It nevertheless remains subject to both direct and indirect challenge. The strongest one might well be the environmental challenge discussed below. But others might emerge alone or in combination with the environmental challenge. Regionalism could be one vehicle. Although the Law of the Sea Convention mandates cooperation between coastal states that border an enclosed and semienclosed sea, it does not augment coastal state rights or subject the freedoms and rights of all states to special regimes in such seas.[35] Yet the fact that the access of states outside the region may be a check on the ambitions of major regional powers has not escaped the latter's notice. And the fact that the manifestation may be regional makes the role of the territorial temptation no less real.

Protection and preservation of the marine environment. One of the distinguishing features of the LOS Convention is the attention it devotes to environmental protection. It remains "the strongest comprehensive environmental treaty now in existence or likely to emerge for quite some time."[36] It contains elaborate and complex provisions that seek to accommodate the navigational rights and freedoms of all states with the need to ensure effective protection for the environment. Many of these provisions relate to, and qualify, freedom of navigation in the EEZ.[37]

A significant aspect of these provisions is that they are self-adjusting. The obligation of the flag state to apply to its ships "generally accepted" standards,[38] like the coastal state's right to enforce generally accepted international standards regarding operational discharges in the EEZ,[39] evolves with the standards. Moreover, the flag state is subject to compulsory arbitration or adjudication, including provisional measures, for breach of its navigational and environmental obligations.[40] In addition, the Convention permits the coastal state to seek approval from the International Maritime Organization to adopt and enforce additional standards regarding discharges or navigational practices in its EEZ.[41] States also have the increasingly important option of seeking new IMO regulations under existing conventions with liberal tacit acceptance amendment provisions regarding the entry into force of new technical requirements, including those with respect to particularly sensitive sea areas. And, of course, the IMO remains a responsive forum for the negotiation of new instruments that implement the provisions of the LOS Convention, such as the International Convention for the Control and Management of Ships' Ballast Water and Sediments, adopted on February 13, 2004.[42]

The LOS Convention contains no res riction on the right of a state to establish port entry requirements, including those regarding the construction, manning, equipment, or design of ships.[43] Acting either alone, or in concert with other states,[44] a state can therefore use port entry restrictions to control the construction, manning, equipment, or design of ships operating off its coast that are headed to or from its own ports or those of a state with similar entry requirements.[45] In the case of the United States, for example, such control now effectively applies to the overwhelming majority of ships operating off its coast.

The balance of a system rooted in port state and coastal state enforcement of evolving international standards, coupled with port state unilateral control of port entry requirements, need not be an impediment to the pursuit of new environmental objectives with respect to the EEZ. In most instances this balance turns on procedural rather than substantive constraints, and the IMO is showing itself to be very responsive in its procedural role in this connection. But procedural constraints do mean that some of the factors previously identified as influencing the reemergence of the territorial temptation with respect to the natural resources of the sea might remain pertinent here as well. From that list, one might recall, for example, political and bureaucratic ambition, impatience, and frustration with international organizations.

Nevertheless, that environmentalists in particular would embrace the territorial temptation is curious since their essential goal, especially with respect to the oceans, is to achieve global protection. That goal can best be realized through strong and effective international measures that states are obliged and empowered to enforce.

If experience teaches us the difficulties of overcoming states' resistance to restraints on the discretion that accompanies territorial sovereignty, and the power of emotional appeals to territorial sovereignty by those who would resist international restraints, why allow the territorial temptation to expand its reach in the sea? The need for common ground rules and cooperation by users in an area open to all is self-evident; it is an indispensable concomitant of a regime of freedom of action itself; as demonstrated by the basic principle that high seas freedoms "shall be exercised by all States with due regard for the interests of other States in their exercise of the freedom of the high seas."[46] Even though yielding to the territorial temptation with respect to a particular environmental problem may promise some short-term or tactical benefit, doing so may augment the difficulties of achieving a desired level of international regulation of environmental problems in that area and elsewhere.

There is ample evidence that states more readily accept international regulation of activities that relate exclusively or principally to areas that are not subject to territorial sovereignty than to areas that are. The environmental calculus is difficult. The serious literature makes clear that we have gone beyond the easy part of Manichaean norms, and must mediate between competing goods as best we can.[47] To do so, we must confront the complex choices and enforcement challenges that attend almost every environmental decision.

Let us take, for example, the transport of radioactive nuclear materials for reprocessing. Obviously, such an activity requires careful regulation: the LOS Convention and other treaties provide the substantive foundation for doing so, and both the IMO and the International Atomic Energy Agency offer competent venues. Also obviously, fear of an accident is likely to trigger negative reactions by coastal states. Up to a point, those reactions are useful: they indicate that a special problem exists, and can help gain the attention necessary to spur productive international negotiation. But does the substantive solution reside in yielding to the territorial temptation?

Regardless of one's view of the appropriate elements of a solution to this problem, an outcome in the general interest that accommodates the relevant concerns, including the desire both to minimize proliferation of nuclear reprocessing capability and to protect the oceans and coastal areas, is more likely to emerge from international negotiations. Left to their own devices, coastal state politicians are prone to respond to local pressures simply to keep the ships away.

One marvels that the emerging political hub of the world's historic and still dominant global maritime shipping countries identifies maritime traffic of noncoastal origin as a problem without referring to countervailing interests in global navigation rights and freedoms in the EEZ and straits. It would be ironic if the territorial temptation were to administer its coup de grace in the very place where the Grotian system first emerged.

A further type of challenge to the system of functional allocation of competence in the EEZ is found in the increasing pressure, especially from environmentalists, for "spatial planning." The underlying idea of coordinated or integrated management can be expected to promise similar benefits and pose similar problems to those on land. The difficulties are compounded at sea by the decidedly territorial focus and the coastal state's selection of and control over the planners. In the context of the exercise of coastal state jurisdiction over most activities requiring coordination, the need to deal with foreign ministries, not to mention foreign governments and international organizations, regarding navigation or submarine telecommunications cables seems nettlesome indeed, a pest to be swatted the next time an accident arouses public concern. And lest aviators think themselves immune, they might recall that it is the legal status of the surface of the earth that determines the legal status of the airspace.

Quite apart from its provisions on pollution from ships and coastal state rights in that regard, the Law of the Sea Convention imposes significant environmental obligations on coastal states with respect to their own offshore activities.[48] Many of these and other limitations on the territorial temptation in the LOS Convention were achievable because they were negotiated in the context of substantial disagreement over the nature and extent of coastal state jurisdiction itself. That is no longer the case.[49]

The experience with fishing may illustrate the point. Lured by the hopeful prospect of sound management by a few coastal states whose citizens tend to dominate international nongovernmental organizations, conservationists were largely content to accept the argument that coastal state control of fishing in the EEZ would yield desirable results. Some were skeptical but, in vivid contrast to the hard obligations achieved with respect to environmental and pollution matters in general, the coastal state conservation obligations they settled for in the EEZ are not easy to violate and are not subject to compulsory arbitration or adjudication.[50]

That the alliance between coastal fishing industries and conservationists with respect to fisheries management was largely a marriage of rhetorical convenience became clear once the coastal fishing industries, having embraced the territorial temptation and achieved subordination or expulsion of their foreign competitors in the EEZ, became more wary of conservation restraints notwithstanding their long-range interests in maintaining a renewable resource. The result is evident in the troubling statistics on the state of the world's ocean fisheries, even though some 90 percent of them have been placed under the largely discretionary control of coastal states by virtue of the regime of the EEZ.

Of course, the outcome probably would not have been any better absent the advent of the EEZ. But the puzzlement in this story is the failure of some environmentalists to realize that they made a mistake not only in assuming that territorialization in itself would solve conservation problems, at least in most places, but also in failing to exact a higher price for accommodating the territorial temptation before it consolidated its grasp on the living resources of the EEZ. When interested coastal states engaged environmentalists in efforts to launch the negotiations that led to the 1995 UN implementing agreement on stocks that straddle or migrate across the 200-mile line, a few individuals who did appreciate the problem hoped the negotiations would afford an opportunity to add new normative, organizational, or dispute settlement obligations regarding conservation within the EEZ. But such hopes were dashed.[51] The coastal states regarded their existing range of discretion in the EEZ, including their right to determine the total allowable catch and to take as much of it as their harvesting capacity would permit, as vested rights.[52] To protect those rights, they focused on the acquisition of means to reduce competition from foreign high seas fishing. Fortunately, at least beyond 200 miles, a stronger model for an international conservation regime responded both to environmental values and to the allocational objectives of coastal fishing industries.

The link between environmentalism and the territorial temptation remains real. It is worth considering its origin. Canada was the first to dramatize a conflict between environmental protection and freedom of navigation. Its 1970 claim to a 100-mile zone in which it asserted unilateral control over navigation,[53] complemented by a reservation to its acceptance of the compulsory jurisdiction of the International Court of Justice, evoked considerable controversy.[54] Much of that controversy was expected to subside with the settlement reached in the LOS Convention, including both its general provisions regarding pollution from ships and a special provision regarding ice-covered areas.[55] But, as was foreseen at the time the claim was first made, the real object was sovereignty.[56] Canada has since established baselines around its Arctic islands and taken the position that the waters thereby enclosed are sovereign historic waters.

Conclusion

International law at any given time represents an equilibrium between opposing pressures. Whether or not rooted in a tendency to extend historical trend lines into the future, the territorial temptation evidently continues to influence proposals to change the law of the sea. Although one would normally expect the maritime powers to be the main source of resistance to such a trend, some facts suggest otherwise.

• While the U.S. Department of State is careful to monitor and protest coastal state claims that it believes to be inconsistent with the LOS Convention, and the U.S. Navy tries to devote adequate resources to a program entailing the global exercise of rights designed to demonstrate nonacquiescence in such claims, the effectiveness of these efforts is impaired by perceptions of a lack of will rooted in at least two factors: (1) the U.S. political system is as yet unequal to the task of formally embracing the only plausible basis for disciplining the evolution of the law of the sea, the United Nations Convention on the Law of the Sea; and (2) the Departments of State and Defense face a constant struggle with unilateralist territorialist sentiments percolating at any given moment in one or another U.S. domestic agency concerned with marine resources, environmental protection, or law enforcement, not to mention such sentiments in Congress and the states.

• The European Community and its member states seem on the verge of leading a new wave of territorialization against navigation itself in the name of environmental protection.

• The existing and emerging maritime powers of Asia—China, India, Japan, and South Korea—have shown little disposition to assume global leadership on these issues. Some need to liberate themselves from legal perspectives ill suited to their status and expectations.

Whatever one's projection may be, the critical issue is how the law of the sea will change in response to old pressures and new perceptions. The question of multilateralism lies at the center of that inquiry and arises at two levels. The first is whether the allocation of powers of governance derives from a multilateral process: will multilateral treaty negotiation rooted in consensus under UN General Assembly auspices, building on the LOS Convention and perhaps using additional implementing agreements, become established as the source of legitimacy at sea, and displace a costly and occasionally bloody unilateralism? The second is whether the powers of governance are themselves allocated to individual flag states or individual coastal states, or to global multilateral institutions, including the novel system rooted in the navigational and environmental provisions of the LOS Convention; namely, a shared coastal state/IMO legislative competence paired with flag state enforcement obligations and supplementary port state and coastal state enforcement powers, all kept in check by compulsory dispute settlement procedures.

The outcome will depend in some measure on how governments behave in the multilateral regulatory system through which the LOS

Convention effects its implementation, be it in a global organization like the IMO or in a regional fishery management organization. Making such a system work requires some accommodation of substantive preferences to the broader interests in the success of the multilateral process that is the key to stability and ordered change in the law of the sea.

Reflexive negativism in multilateral institutions is likely to yield perverse effects. It weakens confidence in those institutions and poses a long-term risk of provoking unilateral action, which may entail substantive losses on the issue at hand and strengthen the territorial temptation. That is a high price to pay for buying time or avoiding responsibility for difficult decisions.

Activist constituencies might bear in mind that, measured carefully against the benefits of a universal law of the sea rooted in the substantive and institutional provisions of the UN Convention on the Law of the Sea and global multilateral implementing agreements that provide a clear and workable basis for protecting coastal and environmental interests, the territorial temptation is best recognized today for what it is: a unilateralist impulse often born of narrow agendas, impatience, frustration, or political and bureaucratic ambition. It tends to confuse substance with inspiring rhetoric and useful tactics. If locally successful, it may simply export environmental problems elsewhere.[57] Most important, it entails systemic costs that may ultimately imperil the existing and future foundation for strong international measures necessary to protect the global marine environment and provide a rational global order for the oceans.

Louis Henkin summed it up this way:

> [I]f those favored by the old law court catastrophe if they merely sit on ancient rights, coastal states are hardly likely to make the law that is needed by unilateral assertion. For the issue is not in fact between *laissez-faire* for shippers and *laissez-faire* for coastal states. The seas—all the seas—cry for regulation as a veritable *res communis omnium*.[58]

Notes

1. The phrase borrows from the title of Jean-François Revel's essay, *La tentation totalitaire*, published three decades before his death on April 30, 2006; that essay was first brought to the author's attention during the negotiation of the United Nations Convention on the Law of the Sea by the late Jorge Castañeda y Alvarez de la Rosa, who went on to serve as Mexico's foreign secretary from 1979 to 1982. It can be found in JEAN FRANÇOIS REVEL, NI MARX NI JÉSUS; LA TENTATION TOTALITAIRE; LA GRÂCE DE L'ETAT; COMMENT LES DÉMOCRATIES FINISSENT (rev. ed. 1986). For the source of the epigraph to this essay by René-Jean Dupuy, see *La mer sous compétence nationale*, *in* TRAITÉ DU

NOUVEAU DROIT DE LA MER 219, 219 (René-Jean Dupuy & Daniel Vignes eds., 1985).

2. "[T]he concept of community interests," including the freedom of the seas, "is pre-Grotian" and "appeared in the writings of Suárez and figured prominently in those of its true progenitor, the earlier Gentili." Theodor Meron, *Common Rights of Mankind in Gentili, Grotius and Suárez,* 85 AJIL 110, 113–14 (1991). With respect to the status of the sea as *res communis* in Roman law, see Percy Thomas Fenn Jr., *Justinian and the Freedom of the Sea,* 19 AJIL 716 (1925).

3. Presidential Proclamation No. 2667, Policy of the United States with Respect to the Natural Resources of the Subsoil and Sea Bed of the Continental Shelf, 10 Fed. Reg. 12,303 (1945) [hereinafter Truman Proclamation].

4. The process, including new claims to the waters of the high seas, was already discerned in 1948. *See* Richard Young, *Recent Developments with Respect to the Continental Shelf* 42 AJIL 849 (1948).

5. Some apologists argued that high seas law did not apply to the seabed and subsoil in 1945, as its resources remained to be developed. Leaving aside the fact that at that time sailors dropped anchor, oysters yielded pearls, salvors raised wrecks, and cables linked continents, for purposes of the present analysis the most important response is that the claim of exclusive rights to the resources of the continental shelf was not consistent with the principle of the freedom of the seas. An ironic twist occurred some decades later when, in the face of a widespread view among developing countries that the high seas regime did not apply to the yet-to-be-exploited mineral resources of the seabed and subsoil beyond the continental shelf, the United States Congress expressly asserted that the regime of the high seas did apply to those resources. Deep Seabed Hard Mineral Resources Act, 30 U.S.C. §S1401(a)(12), 1402(a) (2000).

6. RESTATEMENT (THIRD) OF THE FOREIGN RELATIONS LAW OF THE UNITED STATES § 102 reporters' note 2 (1987); *see* David J. Bederman, *Congress Enacts Increased Protections for Sunken Military Craft,* 100 AJIL 649, 663 n.91 (2006).

7. Convention on the High Seas, Art. 1, Apr. 29, 1958, 13 UST 2312, 450 UNTS 82.

8. "Diplomatists seldom or never question it; professors occasionally do." Thomas Baty, *The Three-Mile Limit,* 22 AJIL 503, 503 (1928).

9. Convention on the Continental Shelf, Apr. 29, 1958, 15 UST 471, 499 UNTS 311. Article 1 of the Convention provides that the term "continental shelf" refers "to the seabed and subsoil of the submarine areas adjacent to the coast but outside the area of the territorial sea, to a depth of 200 metres or, beyond that limit, to where the depth of the superjacent waters admits of the exploitation of the natural resources of the said areas." It has been called "one of the most disastrous clauses ever inserted in a treaty of vital importance to mankind." Wolfgang Friedinann, *Selden* Redivivus—*Towards a Partition of the Seas?* 65 AJIL 757, 759 (1971). Its history was traced by this author in *The Preparation of Article One of the Convention on the Continental Shelf* 3 J. MARITIME L. & COM. 245, 445 (1972).

10. It has been asserted that the 200-mile claims "found their origin in the concerns of a weak whaling industry to protect its exclusive access to a resource." Ann L. Hollick, *The Origins of 200-Mile Offshore Zones,* 71 AJIL 494, 500 (1977).

11. Although widely mentioned in this context, conservation is not listed here as a separate independent factor because the primary motivation for extension of jurisdiction over living resources, at least at the time it occurred, was economic: protection of local fishing industries from foreign competition and perhaps collection of

economic rent. Conservation, of course, was, and remains, essential to sustained realization of both goals.

12. For example, the allocation of ocean resources resulting from extended coastal state jurisdiction cannot be squared with the rhetoric of distributive justice that infused some of the debate on the subject. Landlocked countries, most of which are not prosperous, get no allocation. As among coastal states, both area and, more important, resources are very unevenly distributed.

13. But some might. It may be of interest to note that the International Law Commission's commentary explicitly identifies the seabed and subsoil of the Persian Gulf as coming within its definition of the continental shelf. Report of the International Law Commission Covering the Work of Its Eighth Session, [1956] 2 Y.B. Int'l L. Comm'n, Art. 67 Commentary, para. 7, at 253, UN Doc. A/CN.4/SERA/1956/Add. 1 (1956).

14. One might also consider that taxation of income from oil and gas development, including depletion allowances, foreign tax credits, and other tax relief, was itself rooted in such a system.

15. LOS Convention, *See* United Nations Convention on the Law of the Sea, *opened for signature* Dec. 10, 1982, Art. 153(6), Annex III, Arts. 3(4), 16, 1833 UNTS 397 [hereinafter LOS Convention], Arts. 2–11, 13–14, 16, 47–50. A minor exception to the 12-mile limit is that roadsteads "which would otherwise be situated wholly or partly outside the outer limit of the territorial sea, are included in the territorial sea." *Id.*, Art. 12. With respect to baselines, see *infra* note 23.

16. LOS Convention, *supra* note 15, Art. 33 (contiguous zone). For an early discussion of the idea of a contiguous zone of up to four leagues (12 miles) from the baseline, see Editorial Comment, *International Law Involved in the Seizure of the Tatsu Maru,* 2 AJIL 391 (1908).

17. LOS Convention, *supra* note 15, *Arts.* 56–75, 208, 210, 211(5) & (6), 214, 216, 220, 246–53, 258. The rights of the coastal state in the exclusive economic zone that relate to the seabed and subsoil are exercised in accordance with the provisions regarding the continental shelf. *Id.,* Art. 56(3).

18. *Id.*, Arts. 76–81, 142, 208, 210, 214, 216, 246–53, 258. The rules concerning the determination of the outer limit of the continental shelf where it extends beyond 200 miles are complex, and engage review by an expert Commission on the Limits of the Continental Shelf established by the Convention. *Id.,* Art. 76, Annex II. *See* text at notes 29 *infra.* For an attempt by this author to explain and diagram Article 76, see *The Third United Nations Conference on the Law of the Sea: The Ninth Session,* 75 AJIL 211, 227–31 (1981).

19. LOS Convention, *supra* note 15, Arts. 8(2), 17–32, 45, 211(4), 220, 223–27, 230–33.

20. *Id.*, Arts. 34–44, 233; *see* Hugo Caminos, *The Legal Régime of Straits in the 1982 United Nations Convention on the Law of the Sea,* 205 RECUEIL DES COURS 9, 123 (1987 V); John Norton Moore, *The Regime of Straits and the Third United Nations Conference on the Law of the Sea,* 74 AJIL 77(1980); S. N. Nandan & D. H. Anderson, *Straits Used for International Navigation: A Commentary on Part III of the UN Convention on the Law of the Sea 1982,* 1989 BRIT. Y.B. INT'L L. 159.

21. LOS Convention, *supra* note 15, Arts. 52–54.

22. LOS Convention, *supra* note 15, Arts. 58(1), 87(1); *see id.*, Arts. 136, 141.

23. *Id.*, Arts. 58(2), 86.

24. Fisheries (UK v. Nor.), 1951 ICJ REP. 116 (Dec. 18); Convention on the Territorial Sea and the Contiguous Zone, Arc. 4, Apr. 29, 1958, 15 UST 1606, 516

UNTS 205; LOS Convention, *supra* note 15, Art. 7; *see* Jens Evensen, *The* Anglo-Norwegian Fisheries *Case and Its Legal Consequences,* 46 AJIL 609 (1952). The underlying idea has now been extended in a different way to vast "archipelagic waters" of independent island states, but with some, albeit quite liberal, mathematical discipline. *See* LOS Convention, *supra,* Arts. 46–54.

25. *See* LOS Convention, *supra* note 15, Arts. 1(1)(1), 76(8), 134, & Annex II. In this regard, the influence of the territorial temptation is demonstrated by the Commission's decision to permit coastal states with claims of sovereignty or sovereign rights in the immediate vicinity to comment on a submission, but its implicit disregard of the legal interests of all states in the integrity and limits of the international seabed area protected by the principle of the common heritage of mankind by ordering that the technical comments submitted by other states are not to be considered. This position casts an unnecessary cloud over the legitimacy of the carefully constructed system for permitting the coastal state to establish final and binding limits of the continental shelf beyond 200 miles. Its underlying infirmity soon became evident when Australia submitted limits for the continental shelf off that part of Antarctica claimed by Australia, and states from other regions complained that they did not recognize that claim.

26. Convention on the Protection of the Underwater Cultural Heritage, Arts. 9, 10, Nov. 2, 2001, 41 ILM 40 (2002), *available at* <http://www.unesco.org>. The LOS Convention effectively accorded jurisdiction over marine archaeology to the coastal state in the 24-mile contiguous zone. LOS Convention, *supra* note 15, Art. 303(2).

27. Chapter VII of the UN Charter assumes that air, sea, or land forces acting pursuant to a Security Council decision under Article 41 or 42 would enjoy global access. That assumption is presumably based on the international law of the sea, in particular the freedoms of the high seas and concomitant passage rights through the territorial sea. It would be implausible to root the effectiveness of Chapter VII in either the general reference to mutual assistance in Article 49 or the specific reference to rights of passage in Article 43, which contemplates special agreements that have yet to be concluded. Absent global mobility guaranteed by the international law of the sea, conducting any significant collective security operations is hard to imagine.

28. *See* Michael Byers, *Policing the High Seas: The Proliferation Security Initiative,* 98 AJIL 526 (2004); Rüdiger Wolfrum, *Fighting Terrorism at Sea: Options and Limitations Under International Law, in* VERHANDELN FÜR DEN FRIEDEN—NEGOTIATING FOR PEACE: LIBER AMICORUM TONO EITEL 649 (Jochen Abr. Frowein et al. eds., 2003).

29. *See* Proposed Regulation 19-1, para. 8.1.3, IMO Doc. MSC/81/WP.5/Add. 1, at 4 (2006). For the Convention, Nov. 1, 1974, see 32 UST 47, 1184 UNTS 277.

30. How much actual security is thereby achieved is a different matter. The choice between being able to see those who may threaten, and inconveniencing them by forcing them to act covertly or from a distance, is not a question ordinarily addressed in the law of the sea literature, except with respect to law enforcement strategies regarding such problems as smuggling, where economic disincentives and threats of punishment may play a greater role than in questions of state security and intelligence.

31. LOS Convention, *supra* note 15, Art. 25(3).

32. Freedom to lay and maintain submarine cables and pipelines is protected, subject to certain coastal state environmental rights with respect to pipelines. LOS Convention, *supra* note 15, Arts. 58, 79, 87. Apart from submarine cables and pipelines, the LOS Convention places artificial islands, economic installations and

structures, and other installations and structures "which may interfere with the exercise of the rights of the coastal State in the zone" under the jurisdiction of the coastal state in the exclusive economic zone and on the continental shelf. *Id.*, Arts. 60, 80; see *Id.*, Art. 258.

33. *See* LOS Convention, *supra* note 15, Arts. 246, 248, 249, 253.

34. A few verbal skirmishes regarding naval exercises and installations in the EEZ are evident in some of the declarations made by states in their instruments accepting the LOS Convention, and in the response to those declarations. *See* United Nations, Declarations Made upon Signature, Ratification, Accession or Succession or Anytime Thereafter (Aug. 29, 2006), *at* <http://www.un.org/Depts/los/convention_agreements/convention_declarations. htm>.

35. LOS Convention, *supra* note 15, Art. 123.

36. John R. Stevenson & Bernard H. Oxman, *The Future of the United Nations Convention on the Law of the Sea*, 88 AJIL 488,496(1994). Secretary of State Christopher offered the same appraisal in his Letter of Submittal of the Convention of September 23, 1994. S. TREATY DOC. NO. 103-39, at V, VI–VII (1994).

37. *See* LOS Convention, *supra* note 15, Arts. 56(1) (b)(iii), 58(3), 194(5), 210, 211, 216–21, 234.

38. *Id.*, Arts. 94(5), 211(2).

39. *Id.*, Arts. 211(5), 220.

40. *Id.*, Arts. 286, 297(1) (b).

41. LOS Convention, *supra* note 15, Art. 211(6). Moreover, the ability of the straits states to implement and enforce international pollution standards, and to secure IMO approval for the adoption and enforcement of specific safety and traffic regulations, appears to be providing a flexible mechanism that can adapt to new needs and be tailored to specific requirements in a particular strait. *Id.*, Arts. 41, 42, 233. In this regard, the question of whether particular regulations are desirable should be distinguished from the question of the availability of the mixed coastal state/IMO approval procedure for adopting a wide range of binding regulations. All concerned, straits states and maritime states alike, have an interest in the effective functioning and responsiveness of such a "mixed" regulatory system. Given the difficulty of achieving express agreement with all possible flag states, the effect of a narrow construction of that regulatory option is to invite unilateral coastal state action to fill the regulatory vacuum.

42. *See id.*, Art. 196. Brief discussions of the extensive use of tacit acceptance amendment procedures in IMO conventions can be found in IMO, Conventions (n.d.), at <http://www.imo.org>, and of the IMO process for designating particularly sensitive sea areas in Particularly Sensitive Sea Areas (n.d.), <http://www.oceansatlas.com/ unatlas/issues/pollutiondegradation/special_areas/sensitive_sea_areas.htm> (maintained by IMO).

43. The existence of this right is reflected in notice provisions regarding port entry requirements for environmental purposes, and its exercise may even qualify innocent passage in the territorial sea. *Id.*, Arts. 25(2), 211(3).

44. The LOS Convention expressly contemplates such concerted action by port states. *Id.*, Art. 211(3).

45. "The exercise of this right by even a small number of states could have a widespread effect, for many oil tankers depend for their trade on a limited number of major ports." Oscar Schachter & Daniel Serwer, *Marine Pollution Problems and Remedies*, 65 AJIL 84, 93 (1971).

46. LOS Convention, *supra* note 15, Art. 87(2); *accord* Convention on the High Seas, *supra* note 7, Art. 2.

47. For an examination of the role of normative hierarchy in such a process,

see the centennial essay by Dinah Shelton, *Normative Hierarchy in International Law,* 100 AJIL 291(2006).

48. LOS Convention, *supra* note 15, Arts. 192, 193, 194(2), 198, 199, 204–06, 208, 210, 212.

49. Most coastal states have adopted legislation implementing their jurisdictional entitlements under the Convention. Not surprisingly, many of the statutes conveniently omit mentioning a large number of the concomitant limitations and obligations, including those regarding environmental protection.

50. *See* LOS Convention, *supra* note 15, Arts. 61, 68, 297(3).

51. A modest strengthening of conservation measures with respect to highly migratory species within the EEZ was easier to achieve because the LOS Convention itself, in response to the need to manage such stocks throughout their migratory range, imposed stronger cooperative obligations on the coastal state with respect to highly migratory species as part of the original jurisdictional settlement. LOS Convention, *supra* note 15, Art. 64.

52. *See id.,* Arts. 61(1), 62(2).

53. Arctic Waters Pollution Prevention Act of 1970, R.S.C., ch. A–12 (1985), *reprinted in* 9 ILM 543 (1970).

54. Canada, Declaration Concerning Compulsory Jurisdiction of the International Court of Justice, Apr. 7, 1970, 724 UNTS 63,9 ILM 598(1970); *see* Louis Henkin, *Arctic Anti-Pollution: Does Canada Make—or Break— International Law?* 65 AJIL 131 (1971).

55. *See* LOS Convention, *supra* note 15, Art. 234 (ice-covered areas).

56. At the time, Prime Minister Pierre Elliott Trudeau all but admitted this motive when he responded to domestic criticism of the failure to claim full sovereignty by noting that one starts by doing something reasonable. Canadians were doubtless aware of Soviet pretensions to sovereignty over Arctic waters first adumbrated many years earlier. *See* W. Lakhtine, *Rights over the Arctic,* 27 AJIL 703 (1930).

57. "States shall act so as not to transfer, directly or indirectly, damage or hazards from one area to another or transform one type of pollution into another." LOS Convention, *supra* note 15, Art. 195.

58. Henkin, *supra* note 54, at 136.

CHAPTER 20

Towards a New Regime for the Protection of Outer Space as a Province of All Mankind

David Tan

THE NOTION OF STATES SHARING A COMMON INTEREST IN THE exploration and use of outer space has led the international community to declare outer space to be the "province of all mankind."[1] There is a preponderance of literature largely preoccupied with the freedom of exploration and use of outer space[2] and comparatively little on the need to protect it from environmental damage.[3] The concept of outer space as the "province of all mankind" is not confined merely to the prohibition on national appropriation of resources in outer space or the sharing of benefits derived from exploitation of the space environment. Despite criticisms of its amorphous and ideologically abstract nature, the "province of all mankind" has the potential to acquire a legal prescription within a new regime that requires states to conserve and preserve the outer-space environment for all of humanity—for present and future generations. However, this will not be achieved by resorting to hard law, like conventional rules, customary norms, or principles of *jus cogens*. On the contrary, the solution may be found in a softer but more sophisticated regime formation and elaboration process with a clear goal of environmental orientation. . . .

Article I of the Outer Space Treaty declares outer space to be the "province of all mankind" without endowing that phrase with a precise definition,[4] while Article III requires that states conduct their space programs "in accordance with international law."[5] [This essay] will advance the proposition that the concept of the "province of all mankind" limits the freedom of exploration and use of outer space, drawing support from the

---

Reprinted with permission from David Tan, "Towards a New Regime for the Protection of Outer Space as the Province of All Mankind." *Yale Journal of International Law* 25 (2000).

notions of common interest and *res communis*. . . . A new regime will only emerge after decades of information-building, clarification, elaboration, refinement, and international cooperation. An essential first step is to make the notions of sustainable development and intergenerational responsibility applicable to the outer-space environment, and to clarify the meaning of the "province of all mankind" in order to provide a new language for dialogue within a regime building framework.

The conclusion will demonstrate that, while the precise definition of the "province of all mankind" may be unclear, the very nature of the outer-space environment demands special recognition by the international community as a whole—that it must be transmitted in a substantially unimpaired state to future generations. The common interest of states and the freedom of exploration and use of outer space will be jeopardized unless the international community takes immediate steps to protect the space environment from pollution. In balancing delicate political and economic interests, the protection of the outer-space environment from pollution would best be achieved by the adoption of a Framework Convention on the Protection of the Space Environment and the establishment of an International Space Agency. . . .

Understanding Pollution in the Outer-Space Environment

The issues of pollution in outer space are more complex than environmental pollution on Earth, and may appear to many as far-fetched or too insignificant to merit the attention of international lawyers and jurists. This article argues that space pollution is a problem that deserves closer scrutiny, both under the classical international law approach (focusing on sources and hard-law obligations), as well as under a soft-law regime (focusing on the role of institutions, non-governmental organizations, and the active management of compliance). But first, we need a better understanding of the *sui generi* character of pollution in the outer-space environment.

Nuclear Power Sources

The use of nuclear power sources (NPS) in outer space is aimed at providing electric power for spacecraft sub-systems such as altitude control, communications, and command, as well as for the operations of various equipment on board. There are two types of NPS presently in use in outer space. The first is the isotopic source in which energy is obtained from the decay of a radioactive isotope like plutonium-238. The second is the nuclear reactor, which derives its thermal energy from a controlled fission process. The advantages of NPS over other non-nuclear sources of power, such as long life, compactability, and the ability to operate independently of solar radiation, seem to entrench its position as a preferred technical choice for space missions. The escalating use of nuclear energy to power an increasingly wide variety of spacecraft is perhaps inevitable, and the trend continues unabated.[6] However, the hazards associated with the increasing utilization of NPS have raised widespread concern in the international community. The interconnectedness of the Earth's environment and outer space means that any damage or harm to the space environment is likely to have a spillover effect on Earth.[7] This is evidenced by the Cosmos-954 incident in 1978, where a nuclear-powered satellite disintegrated upon re-entry, scattering a significant amount of highly radioactive debris across Canadian territory. Similarly, in 1983, Cosmos-1402, carrying 45 kilograms of uranium-235, malfunctioned and broke into three parts upon re-entry.[8] The hazards to humankind from NPS in outer space will primarily be radiological, arising from radiation exposure through "both direct external radiation and internal radiation from inhalation or ingestion."[9] The freedom of exploration and use of outer space must be "for the benefit and in the interests of all countries."[10] It is in the interest of states that the space environment be free from the radioactive pollution caused by NPS since any radiological contamination of outer space is likely to have an adverse effect on the Earth's environment. The problem is exacerbated by the direct effect the increasing use of NPS has on the accumulation of space debris. Upon the malfunctioning of a nuclear-powered-satellite usually stationed in the geostationary orbit, not only do the component parts contribute to the space debris, but the radioactive materials pose an additional hazard to human life, in particular to manned space stations.

In view of such possible dangers, the Scientific and Technical Sub Committee of COPUOS has discussed the possibility of establishing international standards and safety regulations governing the use of NPS in the outer-space environment.[11] The efforts of this Committee are paralleled by studies of legal implications by the Legal Sub-Committee of COPUOS.[12] After repeated discussions and informal consultations, the Legal Sub-Committee has developed a proposal containing seven draft principles on the use of NPS in outer space.[13] Unfortunately, the consensual approach adopted by COPUOS fails to address the problems in a satisfactory and expedient manner; after almost two decades, many issues still remain unresolved.[14]

Space Debris

In recent years, man-made space debris or space refuse has been an environmental hazard whose seriousness is a shared concern of many scientists and policy-makers in the international community.[15] The deployment of an ever-increasing number of man-made objects into outer space has created a potential for malfunctioning and decay. It has also resulted in a concomitant rise in the number of defunct, damaged, or abandoned objects, which, together with other debris caused by explosions and collisions, has fast become a threat to space activities. It has been estimated that there are over 7,000 trackable man-made objects in space and a substantially larger number of untrackable objects.[16] Most of the trackable objects are located in low-earth-orbit (LEO) with a significant number in geosynchronous orbit (GEO)—an area of intense space activity.[17] The limited empirical data reveal that objects of sizes between 0.01 and 1 centimeter can cause significant damage upon impact. Objects larger than 1 centimeter can produce catastrophic effects.[18] Present spacecraft systems are particularly vulnerable as they have not been designed with these threats in mind.[19] If the growth in numbers is permitted to continue without adequate measures to safeguard active space objects from damage caused by explosion, collision, or harmful radiation, it could easily result in serious accidents involving the loss of human lives or substantial property damage. Collision and interference are the major risks space debris poses to human life and active payloads. Perhaps the most serious consequence of collisions with space debris is the cascade effect: (1) As the number of space objects in earth-orbit increases, the probability of collisions between them also increases; (2) collisions would produce new orbiting fragments (secondary debris), each of which would heighten the risk of further collisions; (3) collisions and any ensuing cascading would lead to an exponential increase of debris flux and could lead to the formation of a debris belt around the Earth by the end of this century; and (4) the near-earth environment could become so populated with space debris that portions of LEO would be unusable.[20] Moreover the majority of NPS satellites reside in the most densely populated regions of LEO, thereby enhancing the danger of collision with space debris.[21] The impact of a spent NPS fuel core colliding with a space station could cause devastating radioactive contamination in addition to structural damage, because the half-life of uranium-235 is in excess of 700,000 years. Russia, as successor state to the Soviet Union, has unofficially acknowledged that space debris poses a hazard to the outer-space environment.[22] . . . Ironically, the abandonment in 1999 of Mir, the "rust-stained, raffling, 13-year-old Russian space station,"[23] will only exacerbate this problem. . . .

Since as early as 1987, it has been noted in COPUOS that increased pollution of the outer-space environment resulting from the proliferation of NPS and space debris is creating a global hazard.[24] In COPUOS's Fifteenth Scientific-Legal Roundtable, held on October 20, 1993, on the "Scientific and Legal Aspects of Space Debris,[25] various well-known experts in this area advocated that policy-makers should support an international legal regime that has as its principal purpose the minimization of the presence of man-made debris." Although a completely accurate picture of the dangers posed by space debris is currently unavailable, there are already compelling scientific data available to ascertain the emerging threat of identifiable space debris.[26] It is with these environmental hazards in mind that we next assess the adequacy of the existing principles in international law in the protection of the space environment.

An Overview of the Principles of the Law of Outer Space

. . . Many skeptics question what role legal rules really play in a highly politicized international arena.[27] An international treaty or convention is the most basic multilateral document that attempts to secure agreement among sovereign nations to act in a particular manner, or to refrain from certain behavior. The closest parallels to the treaties relating to outer space are those that regulate the use of the Earth's environment and resources. The reasons why states ratify and comply with environmental treaties generally fall into three categories: (a) because the signatory states have a "genuine concern for the issue or a stake in the regulated industry and want to influence treaty rulemaking";[28] (b) because the cost of compliance is relatively low compared to the higher cost of noncompliance;[29] and (c) because of fear of the consequences of noncompliance.[30] In the case of the negotiation and ratification of the space treaties from the late 1950s to the 1970s, the spacefaring nations were competing to optimize the use and exploration of outer space, while the nonspacefaring states were concerned with influencing rulemaking to constrain the activities of those states and to protect their own future interests. Perhaps it is true that the incentive to deploy weapons in outer space was originally low, but it was not inconceivable that in the absence of these treaties, one or the other superpower would have begun experimenting with such deployments. These fascinating geopolitical forces resulted in the birth of five space treaties. . . .

A Brief History of the International Space Treaties

The Ad Hoc Committee on the Peaceful Uses of Outer Space was established by the U.N. General Assembly at its thirteenth session in 1958,[31] and was replaced a year later by a permanent body.[32] The preliminary work of COPUOS resulted in the adoption of the 1963 Declaration of Legal Principles Governing the Activities of States in the Exploration and Use of Outer Space.[33] This declaration formed the basis for the 1967 Outer Space Treaty,[34] which introduced many fundamental principles of outer-space law and has been regarded by numerous scholars as the "Magna Charta" of outer space.[35]

The 1967 Outer Space Treaty laid down broad fundamental principles pertaining to the exploration and use of outer space.[36] It was understood that further conventions would have to be negotiated to provide more specific rules. Thus, the impetus provided by the Outer Space Treaty led to the successful conclusion of four other major international conventions, which provide the international legal framework regulating the conduct of space activities. They are:

1. the 1968 Agreement on the Rescue of Astronauts, the Return of Astronauts, and the Return of Objects Launched into Outer Space;[37]
2. the 1976 Convention on the Registration of Objects Launched into Outer Space;[38]
3. the 1977 Convention on the International Liability for Damage Caused by Space Objects;[39] and
4. the 1979 Agreement Governing the Activities of States on the Moon and Other Celestial Bodies.[40]

None of the five major space treaties deals with the protection of either the space environment or the Earth's environment in a satisfactory fashion. Any protection of the environment appears to be incidental. Other treaties that govern space activities and have some bearing on environmental protection are the 1963 Partial Nuclear Test Ban Treaty,[41] the 1972 ABM Treaty,[42] and the 1977 ENMOD Convention.[43]

In broad terms, international space law enables a kaleidoscope of activities to be conducted in the space environment. They include the launch of satellites, the performance of scientific research and experiments, and the operation of commercial telecommunication services. . . . The five space treaties were not formulated to address, and did not foresee, the complex problems of space pollution we face in the twenty-first century. The next section illustrates the underlying inadequacies and the need for a new approach to treaty-making and regime building that allows states to take account of longer-term consequences.

The Space Treaties

The 1967 Outer Space Treaty. In addition to proclaiming outer space to be the "province of all mankind," article I of the Outer Space Treaty also declares that outer space is "free for exploration and use by all states without discrimination of any kind, on a basis of equality," and that "[t]here shall be free access to all areas of celestial bodies."[44] Article II states that outer space, including the Moon and other celestial bodies, is not subject to national appropriation "by claim of sovereignty, by means of use or occupation, or by any other means."[45] States are thus barred from extending to outer space, and exercising within it, those rights that constitute attributes of territorial sovereignty. Although Article II prohibits national appropriation, states are allowed free access to all areas of celestial bodies; this access includes the collection of mineral samples, scientific research, and the exploitation of geostationary orbits.[46] Article VII imposes international liability on states for damage caused by an object launched into space, while Article IX makes no direct reference to the need to protect the space environment against harm, requiring only that space activity be undertaken "with due regard to the corresponding interests of all other States Parties to the Treaty."[47] Finally, apart from the freedom of exploration, another fundamental principle is laid down in Article III—the exploration and use of outer space shall be governed by international law and the U.N. Charter. This is not a simple question of applying existing norms of international law to this new environment in toto. The *sui generis* space environment demands the revision and adaptation of numerous principles of transboundary harm and state responsibility, and inevitably in many situations, new principles, destined purely for outer space, must be created. The content of international law in this area is difficult to determine with any useful clarity. . . .

The 1968 Astronaut Agreement. The 1968 Astronaut Agreement establishes specific procedures to provide assistance to distressed astronauts who may be victims of environmental or other adversities.[48] Moreover, Article 5(4) of the Astronaut Agreement stipulates that if a state party "has reason to believe that a space object or its component parts discovered in territory under its jurisdiction, or recovered by it elsewhere, is of a hazardous or deleterious nature,"[49] it may so notify the launching authority, which is immediately required to take effective measures to eliminate possible danger of harm.[50]

The 1972 Liability Convention. The 1972 Liability Convention provides specific rules as an elaboration of Article VII of the Outer Space Treaty and determines liability for damage caused by a space object.[51] The definition of "space object"[52] is controversial; a major issue is whether a space object remains a space object after its breakup, deterioration, loss, or abandonment, or whether it becomes space debris. Moreover, the "damage" as defined by the Convention may involve loss of life, personal injury, or damage to property, but no mention is made of damage to the environment.[53]

The 1976 Registration Convention. The primary purpose of the Registration Convention is to facilitate the identification of the space object causing damage. The launching state party is required to maintain a national registry and enter into it each object launched into space.[54] Furthermore, information must be furnished to the U.N. Secretary-General on each space object launched for the purposes of international registration.[55] Notice must also be given regarding objects on which information has previously been provided and which have been but are no longer in earth-orbit.[56]

The 1979 Moon Agreement. The Moon Agreement is intended to supplement the 1967 Outer Space Treaty. It is not intended to derogate from or restrict the provisions of the Outer Space Treaty; the Outer Space Treaty will continue to apply where the Moon Agreement does not enunciate more specific provisions.[57] Although Article IX of the Outer Space Treaty already provides for the protection of the environment, both in space and on Earth, Article VII of the Moon Agreement further requires states parties to take measures to prevent the "disruption of the existing balance" of the celestial bodies and avoid harm to the environment of the Earth.[58] The Moon Agreement also refers to the applicability of international law and the U.N. Charter in Articles 2, 6(1), and 11(4). In addition to the prohibition on national appropriation by occupation in Article 11(2), the Moon Agreement further requires an "equitable sharing" by all states parties in the benefits derived from the resources, taking into account the interests and needs of developing countries as well as the contributions made by the developed nations in their operational activities.[59] The possibility of establishing a new international legal regime designed to facilitate exploitative and sharing activities when such exploitation becomes feasible is recognized in Article 11(5).

The Outer Space Treaty and the Moon Agreement are far more concerned with the exploration and use of the outer-space environment than with its preservation in a substantially unimpaired condition for future generations. The non-renewable resources of outer space should be protected from abuse by the developed nations; international law must "maximize the interests and values of all peoples."[60] The question is how we determine the "interests and values of all peoples." Is there such a thing as "common interest"? Is the concept of the "province of all mankind" in Article I of the Outer Space Treaty predicated on the "common interest"?

The Meaning of "Common Interest" and the "Province of All Mankind" in International Law

The concept of common interest becomes relevant when one considers claims to resources located in areas outside territorial sovereignty or beyond national jurisdictions.[61] The *res nullius* concept was associated with the view that no national sovereignty existed in certain areas and that states had the right to assert sovereignty. The alternative view is that some resources, like airspace, the deep sea-bed, solar energy, and radio spectra, are commonly needed by humanity as a condition of survival and are to be used for the common benefit *(res communis);* such resources cannot be subject to private ownership or state sovereignty.[62] In pursuit of the common benefit, the members of the international community are able to determine the conditions under which the exploitation or use of such resources is to take place. . . . Such a theory assumes that states share a common interest in the exploitation and use of the indicated commons.

The notion of *res communis humanitatis* was introduced by Aldo Armando Cocca. It is based upon the rights of mankind and is derived from "the community of interests and benefits recognized in favour of mankind in outer space and celestial bodies."[63] The *res communis liumanitatis* principle was refined to the CHM, which proposes that certain common areas and their resources are open to inclusive use and that there may not be exclusive uses. Furthermore it asserts that the benefits and values so derived must be shared. CHM is defined in the Moon Agreement; according to Article XI(1) of the Moon Agreement, "the Moon and its natural resources are the common heritage of mankind,"[64] and the CHM principle has been interpreted to have limited spatial coverage—it applies only to the Moon and the Moon's orbits and intrajectories, but not to the outer-space environment generally.[65]

On the other hand, the exploration and use of outer space as the "province of all mankind" in Article 1(1) of the Outer Space Treaty is not defined by the Treaty but is, according to Article III, governed by "international law and the Charter of the United Nations."[66] Does the "province of all mankind" then have a particular meaning in international law? First it may be argued that "mankind" in Article 1(1) of the Outer Space Treaty may be understood to be a beneficiary of space exploration and may be considered a new legal subject of international law. There are numerous statements on the definition of "mankind," but only Professor Stephen Gorove has come close to a working definition of the term:

> [M]ankind as a concept should be distinguished from that of man in general. The former refers to a collective body of people, whereas the latter stands for individuals making up that body. Therefore, the rights of mankind should be distinguished, for instance, from the so-called human rights. Human rights are rights to which individuals are entitled on the basis of their belonging to the human race, whereas the rights of mankind relate to the rights of the collective entity and would not be analogous with the rights of the individuals making up that entity.[67]

In contrast, there has been no attempt to define the word "province"; this has made the task of discovering the meaning of the phrase the "province of all mankind" an uphill battle. Some have argued that the CHM principle is designed to replace the abstract "province of all mankind" with a more meaningful legal framework,[68] but the remarkably poor ratification of the Moon Agreement by only ten states and the specificity of various provisions in the Agreement weigh against this conclusion. . . .

The meaning that may have been ascribed to the phrase in 1967 may be different from the understanding that should be accorded to it today. The Outer Space Treaty was concluded over thirty years ago in a political climate dominated by a superpower arms race and a great ideological divide, where both spacefaring and non-spacefaring nations alike were determined not to allow any state to colonize space for strategic weapons deployment or commercial exploitation. It was thus agreed that space was the "province of all mankind" and could not be subverted under the exclusive sovereignty of any state. In the new millennium, while these same nations are now cooperating on the ISS and various space initiatives and scientific research, the "province of all mankind" must mean something different. The lofty aspirations of the expression as understood in 1967—the freedom of use and exploration for the benefit of all nations—must be brought down to Earth.[69]

The meaning of the "province of all mankind" should include the concept of sustainable development. Our exploration and use of the outer-space environment should leave it in a substantially unimpaired condition for the enjoyment and benefit of future generations. The purpose of the existing space treaties was to ensure that no state would arrogate exclusive rights to itself or use them at the expense of others. The freedom of action of states in outer space or on celestial bodies is neither unlimited, absolute, or unqualified, but is determined by the rights and interests of other states and all humanity: "The freedom to use outer space which is granted to everyone must find its limits in the freedom of others."[70] Perhaps this limit is found in Article III of the Outer Space Treaty, which requires that the exploration and use of outer space be "in accordance with international law."[71]

The Protection of the Space Environment: An Analysis of Conventional Law and Customary International Law

In theory, the role of legal norms—whether conventional or customary—in classical international law appears to be a fairly straightforward one. To put it succinctly, they are prescriptions for action in situations of choice, carrying a sense of obligation that they ought to be followed. Where the conduct in question is in an area governed by a treaty or custom, the choice of governing principle may be simplified, though it will not necessarily be clear. Even then, there is no precise linear path that dictates the application of a norm to a specific conduct. As Chayes and Chayes so aptly stated, "the need to operate in a multifaceted, interacting, and interdependent international environment with relatively diffuse power tends to lengthen the time horizon of states and lead them to take account of longer-term."[72]

The Adequacy of the Existing Space Treaties in the Control of Space Pollution

Article VI of the Outer Space Treaty states:

> States Parties to the Treaty shall bear international responsibility for national activities in outer space, including the moon and other celestial bodies, whether such activities are carried on by governmental agencies or by non-governmental entities, and for assuring that national activities are carried out in conformity with the provisions set forth in the present Treaty.[73]

The general terms of Article VI resulted in the 1972 Liability Convention and the 1975 Registration Convention. However, both treaties fail to refer directly to the problem of space debris or nuclear power sources. In orbit, situations endangering property and life may be brought about by the overcrowding of space objects in a particular area, the close proximity of two or more space objects, the conduct of military maneuvers and weapons testing, and the release of harmful radiation from NPS.

Nuclear Power Sources

Article IV of the Outer Space Treaty specifically forbids *only the stationing of nuclear weapons or any other weapons of mass destruction* in outer space. It does not regulate the use of NPS. It provides: "States Parties to the Treaty undertake not to place in orbit around the Earth any objects carrying nuclear weapons or any other kinds of weapons of mass destruction, install such weapons on celestial bodies, or station such weapons in outer space in any other manner."[74] Similarly, Article III of the Moon Agreement carries the same prohibition relating to the Moon and other celestial bodies.[75] Regrettably, the restrictions in the Outer Space Treaty apply only to space objects in orbit and to the stationing of identified kinds of weapons in space.[76] Furthermore, although Articles IV and IX of the Outer Space Treaty and Articles III and VII of the Moon Agreement require states parties to avoid the harmful contamination of outer space and the Moon environment and forbid the deployment of nuclear weapons, they do not require states to transfer space objects with NPS on board to a nuclear-safe orbit (NSO).

Other treaties that are not strictly part of the current space treaties framework can also impose some control on radioactive pollution in space. For example, the testing and deployment of a space-based anti-missile system envisioned by the Strategic Defense Initiative (SDI) program would certainly violate the provisions of the U.S.-Soviet ABM Treaty.[77] Russia has put a series of proposals before the United Nations that have the effect of imposing a prohibition on the testing, deployment, and use of space weapons.[78] Such an effort to demilitarize the space environment is commendable. But because NPS is usually used for non-military purposes in communication satellites and in space stations, where research and manufacturing take place, the regulation of its use falls outside the ambit of the various space weapons treaties. Satellite remote sensing is continuing to make valuable contributions to environmental monitoring, planning sustainable development, water-resource development, monitoring crop conditions, and predicting and assessing drought. Meteorological and atmospheric research satellites are similarly important to the study of global climate change, the greenhouse effect, the degradation of the ozone layer, and other oceanic and global environmental processes.[79] Studies of human and animal psychology conducted in space led to important advances in medical knowledge, in such areas as "blood circulation, hypertension, osteoporosis, cardiovascular physiology, sensory perception, immunology, and the effects of cosmic radiation."[80] Hence the threat to the outer-space environment from nuclear power sources remains largely unchecked, perhaps masked by the significant advances that NPS has made possible.

Space Debris

The specificity of damage, the requirement of fault, and the difficulty of identification all contribute to the impotence of the Liability Convention and the Registration Convention in the protection of the outer-space environment from debris pollution.

In order to ascertain whether the present space treaties are applicable to space debris, a determination must be made whether space debris can be classified as a space object. Under the 1972 Liability Convention, in order for liability to arise, there must be "damage" caused by a "space object." Without damage, there can be no state liability for environmental risks, much as there is no liability if damage is not caused by a space object. "Damage," as defined in Article 1(a), is limited to physical and direct damage, and does not cover indirect damage or non-physical damage, i.e., it does not deal with environmental dangers created by space activities, particularly radioactive hazards presented by NPS. The term "damage" means loss of life, personal injury, or other impairment of health; loss of or damage to property of states or of persons, natural or juridical; or damage to property of international intergovernmental organizations.[81] If damage is to the elements of the space environment that are not property of states, persons, or international intergovernmental organizations, for example, radioactive leakage from nuclear reactors in space, there appears to be no legitimate recourse under the Liability Convention.

Under Article II of the Liability Convention, the absolute liability of the launching state is limited to damage caused by the fall of a space object "on the surface of the Earth or to aircraft in flight."[82] There is no absolute liability for any damage to objects in the outer-space environment; fault must be proved by the state seeking compensation.[83] This requirement of fault for damage caused in outer space presents a significant impediment to a successful claim under the Liability Convention. Moreover, the potential recovery for damage caused by space debris is often seriously hampered by the identification of the launching state associated with the space object.[84] Arguably, Articles VI, VII, and XI of the Outer Space Treaty, Articles IV and VI of the Registration Convention, and Article 5 of the Astronaut Agreement all contribute in varying degrees to the imposition of international responsibility for dangers created by space debris. But the identification problem remains an insurmountable hurdle to any compensation claim.[85]

Many of the treaty provisions are outdated and incapable of coping adequately with the emerging threats of space debris. For example, under a strict interpretation of Article XI of the Outer Space Treaty, if the space activity results in space debris, the launching state is required to inform the U.N. Secretary-General and the international scientific community of the debris resulting from the activity.[86] Provisions of the Registration Convention require the state of registry to give notice of objects that are no longer in earth-orbit and to assist in the identification of hazardous or deleterious space objects.[87] These existing treaty provisions unfortunately are not preventive in character: There is no system of obligatory safety assessment prior to launching, and no appropriate quality-control program in place. Finally, piecemeal treaty provisions relevant to environmental protection in outer space are present in the Partial Nuclear Test Ban Treaty, the ENMOD Convention, and the International Telecommunication Convention.[88] These treaties, however, do not protect the outer-space environment per se, and their provisions only apply to the few signatory states. The inadequacies of the existing multilateral treaty regime in the regulation of pollution in space should be ameliorated by the adoption of a framework convention that deals specifically with the pollution of the space environment. Part VI will provide the outline of such a convention.

Customary International Law—and Its Problems

International Custom in Relation to the Space Environment

The principle of the "province of all mankind" as a limitation on the freedom of exploration appears to lack the requisite *opinio juris* to attain the status of a customary norm. It does not "constitute a principle sufficiently normative in character that it becomes capable of generating specific legal effects or enhancing particular value expectations."[89]

According to Jonathan Charney's criteria,[90] one could contend that the preservation of the outer-space environment has merited international attention and generalized concern as evidenced in the numerous U.N. General Assembly declarations and the formation of COPUOS and its integral role in the making of international space treaties. However, none of the treaty obligations under the framework of the present space treaties contains a discrete, well-defined customary rule that imposes a duty on states to avoid harm to the space environment.

Nevertheless, the generalized concern for the protection of the space environment is reflected in the Sixty-Sixth Conference of the TLA, which adopted the Buenos Aires International Instrument on the Protection of the Environment from Damage Caused by Space Debris,[91] and in the Scientific Subcommittee of COPUOS. It appears that protection of the space environment is currently a pressing issue on the agenda of many expert groups and international bodies. As discussed above, existing treaty rules and custom do not impose concrete obligations on states to prevent pollution to the space environment. Is there some other way that the outer-space environment may be protected from pollution by NPS or debris?

The International Law Commission took the view that "[i]t is not the form of a general rule of international law but the particular nature of the subject-matter with which it deals that may . . . give it the character of *jus cogens*."[92] This statement seems to suggest that the very nature of a subject matter, independent of any reference to custom, may qualify it as a norm of *jus cogens*. What the current literature fails to address is whether the protection and conservation of the outer-space environment as the "province of all mankind" qualifies as a norm of *jus cogens*.[93] Discussions center around the application of the "province of all mankind" and the CHM principles to the use and exploitation of outer space, and rarely address environmental concerns specific to the preservation of the outer-space environment. The notion of *jus cogens* is supported by the view that the satisfaction of the higher interest of the entire community should prevail over often contradictory national preference.[94]

It appears from the foregoing analysis that international law presently does not recognize the "province of all mankind" as possessing any legal prescription pertaining to the protection of the space environment from pollution flowing from space activities. However, it is in the common interest of all states that the exploration and use of outer space should, at the bare minimum, be "sustainable."

The Emerging Norm of Sustainable Development

Concern for future generations figured prominently in the 1972 Stockholm Declaration of the U.N. Conference on the Human Environment, which was adopted by the U.N. General Assembly by 112 votes in favor and none against (with ten abstentions).[95] Principle 1 of the Declaration declares that we have a "solemn responsibility to protect and improve the environment for present and future generations."[96] Since the Declaration, about 300 multilateral agreements and 900 bilateral treaties have been concluded on the environment.[97] On October 29, 1982, the U.N. General Assembly—with 111 votes in favor and 1 against (the United States)—proclaimed the World Charter for Nature, which explicitly states that governments have a duty to pass on humanity's natural heritage to future generations.[98] In 1987 the World Commission on Environment and Development (WCED) published its report on environment and sustainable development, known as the "Brundtland Report."[99] The main guidelines of the Report were unanimously endorsed by the U.N. General Assembly in 1987 as a framework for future environmental cooperation.[100] Unfortunately, the contours of many concepts are blurred and the precise contents of the customary rules are unclear.[101]

Two decades after the Stockholm Declaration, over 170 countries gathered at the Rio Convention to reaffirm their commitment to the protection of the environment for present and future generations, and to implement the goals of sustainable development.[102] Although such international declarations were focused primarily on the protection of the Earth's environment, the theoretical justifications for intergenerational responsibility and sustainable development that underpin the U.N. declarations relating to the human environment are no different from the concept of the transmission of the outer-space environment substantially unimpaired to future generations under the "province of all mankind" principle. Hence such environmental policies should apply equally to the outer-space environment.

Edith Brown Weiss has advanced the theory of "intergenerational equity," which provides for generational rights and obligations.[103] Her thesis consists of a normative framework of intersecting theories of intergenerational and intragenerational equity that are derived from an underlying planetary trust, embodying the notion that generations act as stewards to sustain the welfare and well-being of all generations. . . . Unfortunately, Weiss's model generally rests upon an intertemporal human rights model for preserving the global environment. This presents *many* problems, ranging from the questionable existence of the right to a decent environment to the issue of remedies in respect of claims made by future generations against present generations.[104]

Whether the global awareness of the harm to our sense of intergenerational identity, as evidenced by the various U.N. General Assembly resolutions and numerous international conventions, will be sufficient to mobilize the implementation and enforcement of effective legal measures on behalf of future generations is doubtful. But more importantly, the notions of intergenerational identity and sustainable development will prove to be invaluable concepts in framing the discussion in Part VI. Current literature has concentrated on the notion of sustainable development as involving the integration of economic and environmental considerations at all levels of decision-making.[105] But the outer-space environment has been largely ignored, as if it were simply economic development on Earth that must be environmentally sound. There is no reason, however, why the precautionary principles that emerge from the concept of sustainable development in the Stockholm Declaration, the Rio Declaration, and the World Charter for Nature should not apply equally to the outer-space environment. One might even ultimately find that the uniqueness and vulnerability of the outer-space environment demand that the international community as a whole recognize sustainable development as a "global ethic"[106] that transcends terrestrial boundaries, as a peremptory norm that prohibits "policies and practices that support current living standards by depleting the productive base, including natural resources, and that leaves future generations with poorer prospects and greater risks than our own."[107]

We should not confine our actions to those we are now able to determine as directly or indirectly benefiting ourselves or our descendants. On the contrary, we should "cultivate our natural sense of obligation not to act wastefully or wantonly even when we cannot calculate how such acts would make any present or future persons worse off."[108] It seems impossible to find universally agreed-upon limits on the freedom of exploration and use of outer space. Rather than focus on indeterminate rules of custom-formation, we should concentrate on establishing fair and workable arrangements and institutions that can successfully accommodate the competing interests of all nations. With these guidelines in mind, we will now examine new methods of treaty-making that will enhance the willingness of states to participate in an environmental program that seeks to achieve an acceptable balance between pollution control and freedom of space exploration.

Some Proposals: New Principles of International Environmental Law-Making

Soft Law and a Regime-Building Approach

Environmental regimes are not static structures. Like human rights treaty regimes, they evolve along a continuum from dialogue to the sharing of information and expertise, to more defined framework conventions for cooperation, to more precise binding legal norms contained in protocols. . . . This continuum of regime formation, in both a substantive and a procedural sense, is not always linear, as it allows for "overlapping cycles of cooperation and competition."[109] A space environment regime must include the concepts of sustainable development and intergenerational equity and, at the same time, respect the sovereign interests of states. The regime is like a living organism: When a regime is established through practice and a convergence of interests and expectations around that practice, its interests and expectations may persist even after the forces that shaped its evolution have changed.[110]

In order for the space environment regime to be successful, we must emphasize implementation as a measure of effectiveness and overcome our obsession with mechanisms of dispute settlement. The traditional rhetoric of enforcement will not ensure compliance. Instead, the framework-protocol approach is the best model for the protection and preservation of the space environment, and is well tested in international environmental law.[111] . . . Thus it is important to concentrate on finding the right balance between political exigencies and the need for precise legal wording that imposes obligations on signatory states. The acceptable balance may be found in "soft law."

Soft law, "where international law and international politics combine to build new norms,"[112] has become a fashionable phrase in international environmental law, as it acknowledges the inextricability of law and politics. Treaty-making in an environmental context goes beyond the consideration of traditional treaty-making techniques and cannot be viewed in isolation from international declarations and recommendations that have not yet attained the binding force of international law, but which embody a certain degree of political commitment and hence give rise to expectations for future behavior.[113] The advantages of soft law include range, flexibility, and frequent adherence by the governments that made such declarations. Its shortcomings include the lack of precision in such political commitments and the absence of enforceable legal sanctions.[114] . . . Yet in the absence of *lex lata*, soft law may succeed.[115] Soft-law instruments have been said to include the Stockholm[116] and Rio Declarations,[117] and the 1989 Hague Declaration on the Environment,[118] where the establishment of a comprehensive regulatory regime is contemplated. These should be distinguished from "soft provisions" of treaties, where the treaty in its final form imposes vague and imprecise obligations.[119]

Perhaps one can avoid the rule of unanimous consent by adopting a Framework Convention on the Protection of the Outer Space Environment (the Space Environment Framework Convention or SEFC), much like the 1985 Vienna Convention for the Protection of the Ozone Layer,[120] which established general obligations to cooperate. The Vienna Convention paved the road toward the 1987 Montreal Protocol on Substances that Deplete the Ozone Layer,[121] the 1989 Helsinki Declaration on the Protection of the Ozone Layer,[122] and the 1990 London Amendments,[123] each adding an element of specificity to the general obligations contained in the framework Ozone Layer Convention. This successful regime-building approach has its genesis in a contextual framework and then moves effectively through the continuum to eventuate in a legally binding regime with a convergence of interests. . . .

The process begins with political consensus in multilateral fora, leading to the formation of soft-law obligations. The constellation of political interests are then accommodated in a framework convention that expresses the commitment of signatory states to cooperate in knowledge sharing in a setting in which binding normativity can emerge. Subsequent protocols would supplement and elucidate the content of the fundamental norms in the framework convention.[124] Protocols represent the real operational part of such a regime, and are undoubtedly the cornerstone of the proposed Space Environment Framework Convention. By ratifying the SEFC, states would express their commitment to the protection and preservation of the space environment as the "province of all mankind." These declarations would reflect political commitments toward a common interest that may at some later stage, through the development of specific protocols, acquire the full force of law.

The current configuration of space treaties does not contemplate such a regime-building approach in relation to the protection of the space environment from pollution. The regime-building approach as understood in international relations theory is most conducive to furnishing the fundamental building blocks for the ultimate grand architecture of a more specific holistic regime with binding legal obligations.[125] To facilitate the drafting of the Protocols—the next point in the regime-building continuum after establishing the framework convention—scientific and technical issues relating to the threats posed by space debris and nuclear power sources must be worked out over time by an International Space Agency comprising experts from both spacefaring and non-spacefaring nations. Indeed, this approach allows a framework embodying general aspirations and principles to come into force in a cooperative regime where the consensus necessary for a more detailed agreement is immediately lacking. However, it requires repeated negotiation and identification of protocols, and can only succeed with centralized active management.

A Framework Convention on the Protection of the Space Environment

The SEFC must be grounded in a cooperative paradigm where the focus is on sharing the exploration and use of the "province of all mankind." The

SEFC must aim to secure a dynamic universal cooperation and must resist the allure of succumbing to any attempts to impose a normative code of conduct from the outset. In this regime-building approach, in order to acknowledge the unique nature of the outer-space environment, the SEFC must first encompass all states whose activities can affect or be affected by, in the present or future, the exploration and use of outer space. It should also emphasize the "common interest" of all states in the protection and preservation of the space environment for the common benefit, rather than their competing sovereign interests. It must also speak the new rhetoric of "compliance" and avoid the offensive language of "breach" and "dispute settlement."

In order for the regime to be effective, the SEFC must be able to grow in both the substantive and the procedural sense. At the bare minimum, states should also undertake, in accordance with the means at their disposal and their capabilities, to

1. cooperate by means of systematic observations, research, and information exchange in order better to understand and assess the short-term and long-term effects of human activities on the outer-space environment through epistemic communities coordinated by a central agency;[126]
2. be guided by the emerging principles of sustainable development, intergenerational equity, equitable allocation, and the precautionary principle in their dialogues and in the formulation of agreed measures, procedures, and standards for more precise implementation of the SEFC through the adoption of future protocols;[127] and
3. identify and develop implementation, compliance, and dispute-avoidance mechanisms.[128]

As the emphasis shifts from state interests to common environmental interests in the sharing of knowledge and identification of problems by the epistemic communities,[129] the resulting depoliticization can lead to important substantive evolution of the regime into normative frameworks of law.[130] In the formulation of more concrete binding obligations in future protocols, it is possible to involve different parties in issues of especial concern to them. As protocols are usually focused on relatively narrow issues, each has the capacity to flesh out the broad principles embodied in the SEFC and can crystallize into custom. The main strength of this framework-protocols regime lies in its intrinsic ability to involve both contextual and normative aspects in a creative synergy from formation to maturation at all points in its dynamic continuum.[131] The three broad working principles proposed above provide a wide ambit for procedural cooperation and ample room for epistemic communities to interact and flourish.

Experience may be gleaned from the regime-building approach to climate change, which began with the 1992 U.N. Framework Convention on Climate Change (FCCC).[132] Further elaboration of rules and guidelines through intergovernmental cooperation moved the regime along the continuum that adequately addresses the problem of global climate change, resulting in the adoption of the Kyoto Protocol by over 160 parties to the FCCC in December 1997.[133] The FCCC was designed as a first step in dealing with the threat of anthropogenic climate change, explicitly recognizing that countries have "common but differentiated responsibilities."[134] In the same manner, both spacefaring and non-spacefaring nations have the common responsibility of conserving, protecting, and restoring the integrity of the outer-space environment. The policies that each state adopts—for example, reporting, communication, research, and mitigation measures—will vary depending on their individual space capabilities. . . .

Critics of the Kyoto Protocol may argue that it has no effective compliance regime because it affords member states too much flexibility with respect to how it implements its obligations, at both the national and international levels. Indeed, one of the hallmarks of the regime-building approach—and its ultimate success in securing "compliance"—is this very flexibility. An authoritarian uniform treaty rule that fails to recognize the uniqueness of each member state is destined only for obsolescence. When the framework convention and its subsequent protocols are all driven by a single vision—in the case of the SEFC, the protection of the outer-space environment as the "province of all mankind"—each state party can still comply with its obligations when each designs its own approach in light of its unique economic, technological, social, and political situation. The Antarctic Treaty system is another unusual international regime that has experienced great success in maintaining a balance between international interests and national interests in Antarctica. While once believed to be impossible, the Protocol on Environmental Protection to the Antarctic Treaty is now a reality.[135]

Like the FCCC and the 1992 Convention on Biological Diversity,[136] the SEFC should also contain provisions for funds to finance capacity-building and "compliance."[137] It should specifically require that the commitments of states parties developing space capabilities are contingent on the provision of resources by present spacefaring nations to meet the full agreed incremental costs of compliance. At the same time, in order to secure regime transparency, verification and monitoring functions should be actively managed by a central organization like the International Space Agency.

The aim of the SEFC will be to protect and preserve the outer-space environment as the "province of all mankind," and all subsequent protocols should build upon the structural and institutional components of the SEFC, beginning with reporting and review requirements and potentially culminating in binding implementation norms. While one would not expect substantive obligations to be present in the SEFC, nevertheless the Preamble should begin with a firm commitment by signatory states:

> While we recognize our freedom of the use and exploration of outer space as stated in Article I of the Outer Space Treaty, we also acknowledge our responsibility for conserving the outer-space environment and for using its resources in a sustainable manner for the benefit of present and future generations. . . .

Coercive enforcement of a hegemony of norms is as misguided as it is costly, as we are faced with varying degrees of capability and priority. At the most fundamental level, the new regime assumes a primary managerial role at its genesis and a secondary regulatory role as it matures. The management of this new regime must:

1. ensure transparency in the generation and dissemination of information about the requirements of the SEFC and the parties' performance under it;
2. coordinate the scientific research and data reporting of epistemic communities, national governments, and international organizations;
3. assist in capacity-building by coordinating technical assistance for enabling countries; and
4. establish a multilateral consultative process and dispute-resolution procedure that focuses more on fulfilling the spirit of the SEFC (through mediation, negotiation, or compulsory conciliation) than on sanctions and fault attribution.

These guiding principles are by no means exhaustive, but could provide a fertile ground for further debate and action in the new millennium. The success of this regime-building approach will depend much on the level of collective political will, and the efforts of bureaucratic alliances and interdisciplinary cooperation.

The Need for an International Space Agency

At present, regional and interregional coordination of space science and technical assistance for developing countries is coordinated by the U.N. Programme on Space Applications, through its Office for Outer Space Affairs.[138] However, the Programme's main focus is in making the benefits of space technology available to all countries by such cooperative activities as sharing payloads, ensuring compatibility of space systems, educating in remote sensing, and providing access to launch capabilities.[139] The Programme pays scant attention to the conservation of the space environment. In spite of the establishment of the U.N. Conference on Environment and Development (UNCED) and the U.N. Environment Program (UNEP), the United Nations still lacks any coherent institutional mechanism for dealing effectively with environmental issues. At present, environmental responsibilities are divided among numerous international organizations, but the existing institutions suffer from poor coordination and the lack of real power and authority. In order to offer any credible protection to the outer-space environment a U.N. International Space Agency (UNISA) should be established, and should be managed by COPUOS. NASA (United States), CNES (France), BNSC (United Kingdom), NASDA (Japan), ASI (Italy), DARA (Germany), RKA (Russia), the International Telecommunication Union (ITU), the International Astronomical Federation (IAF), and other international space organizations should be brought under UNISA's umbrella.[140] The presence of one single international agency to coordinate international negotiations on the regulation of space activities is crucial to the success of any program that has the goal of the protection and preservation of the space environment as the "province of all mankind."

A truly inter-disciplinary approach must be undertaken under the auspices of the proposed UNISA. The role of UNISA would be to coordinate the Scientific and Technical Subcommittee and the Legal Subcommittee of COPUOS, and the participation of experts from the areas of science, technology, economics, health, national security, law, and other fields. The contribution of these "communities of shared knowledge" or "epistemic communities"[141] plays a crucial role in influencing the space regime formation, particularly in identifying and developing policy options. . . . The proposed UNISA would also be the international agency in charge of making recommendations to the United Nations to adopt internationally binding norms and enforceable regulations in appropriate international agreements, in the form of protocols to the proposed Space Environment Framework Convention. In order to promote the protection of the space environment and the associated earth environment, states parties should be obliged to arrange for members of UNISA to have access to all parts of stations, installations, equipment, and spacecraft for the purpose of inspection to ensure effective implementation of the Space Environment Framework Convention and its subsequent protocols.

The proposed UNISA is crucial to the success of the regime-building approach to be adopted in the formation of the Space Environment Framework Convention. The following guidelines are instrumental to the effectiveness and success of UNISA as a strategic manager:

1. the formulation of a clear mission, agreed to by the signatories to the SEFC;

2. the acceptance of the role of UNISA in an organizational structure that reflects the interest, power, and capabilities of member states;
3. the minimization of bureaucratic inefficiency through the establishment of an able and professional Secretariat within UNISA to coordinate transnational scientific, technical, technological, and legal matters, maintaining at all times an apolitical agenda;
4. the authority to engage in research on the effects of all space activities on both the outer-space environment and the Earth's environment;
5. the authority to recommend, from time to time and without the need to achieve consensus, relevant principles to be included in a protocol to the Space Environment Framework Convention; and
6. the guarantee of funding from the United Nations.

We have to recognize that UNISA, like all international organizations, will ultimately be a political institution. Like all politics, there will be a fair share of political bargaining and power-brokering. But as long as we have an active management strategy in place—which is as much a part of the bargaining process—commitments will eventuate and performance will ensue. Efforts are already underway to establish regional centers for space science and technology education, led by the U.N. Programme on Space Applications.[142] As mentioned earlier, the establishment of UNISA would harmonize the myriad initiatives and programs undertaken by the spectrum of organizations and agencies involved in the exploration and use of outer space.[143] It will be in a better position to coordinate uniform policies among the many states to implement SEFC rules for the protection of the "province of all mankind." UNISA will draw together COPUOS, its Legal as well as its Scientific and Technical Subcommittees, and the administrators of the U.N. Programme on Space Applications, to work more closely with the governments of member states at the policy-making level. The above criteria may seem like a millennial wish list, but the fact is they have been surfacing as agenda items at numerous meetings, colloquia, conferences, and symposia.

Conclusions

Any attempt to establish a new space order can only be successful if it is based on a realistic assessment of the existing power structures within the international community.[144] Experience indicates that, when the developing countries that lack spacefaring capabilities but possess numerical superiority in the General Assembly attempt to control the process of hard-law formation, the result is a farrago of impractical propositions and vague obligations in multilateral conventions. For example, the CHM regime declared in Article XI of the Moon Agreement finds few supporters, particularly amongst the developed nations, and appears condemned to a philosophical existence.[145] The ephemeral notions of "equitable access" and "equitable distribution" require a delicate balance of the special needs of developing nations with the largely commercial and military interests of the spacefaring states. On the other hand, the protection of the outer-space environment as the "province of all mankind" transcends the politics of technological and economic asymmetry—it affects all individuals, present and future.

As discussed . . . , the current space treaties regime fails to offer satisfactory protection to the space environment. Customary international law can hardly be said to possess adequate content or scope to prevent damage and furnish sufficient sanctions to be directed against the perpetrators when damage to the outer-space environment occurs. It is "not a regulatory system and cannot be turned into one."[146] A unique Space Environment Framework Convention, created within a regime-building approach, still recognize[s] the prohibition on damage or harm to the outer-space environment and overcome[s] "the tyranny of realism"[147] to protect the "province of all mankind." The desirability of this recommendation is supported by the principle of sustainable development as recognized by the international community in the Stockholm Declaration, the Rio Declaration, and various multilateral international fora; it is also grounded in the jurisprudential notions of intergenerational equity and responsibility. The proposals on the possibility of negotiating the Framework Convention on the Protection of the Outer Space Environment and the establishment of a U.N. International Space Agency should be considered seriously. Commitments made within an organizational framework regime as such, no matter how insignificant the skeptics may lead one to believe they are, are visible to the participants and part of the kaleidoscope of favors, promises, and patronage exchanged over time.[148] It has been said that the notion of the outer-space environment as the "province of all mankind" was adopted as a result of "concrete political interests and social or economic requirements involved in the struggle and cooperation of states in pursuit of solutions to compelling problems of the moment."[149] The compelling problems of space debris and the increasing use of nuclear power sources must be addressed immediately. The protection of the space environment in the new millennium is in the interest of all states, developing and developed, and it is in the interest of all human beings, present and future.

Notes

1. Treaty on Principles Governing the Activities of States in the Exploration and Use of Outer Space, Including the Moon and Other Celestial Bodies, Jan. 27, 1967, art. 1, 18 U.S.T. 2410, 610 U.N.T.S. 205 [hereinafter Outer Space Treaty].

2. *See, e.g.*, Bin Cheng, *The 1967 Space Treaty*, 95 Journal Du Droit International [3.Droit- Int'l] 532 (1968); Stephen Gorove, *Property Rights in Outer Space: Focus on the Proposed Moon Treaty*, 2 J. Space L. 27 (1974); He Qizhi, *Certain Legal Aspects of Commercialization of Space Activities*, 15 Annals Air & Space L. 333 (1990); Vladimir Kopal, *The Question of Defining Outer Space*, 8 J. Space L. 154 (1980); H. A. Wassenbergh, *Speculations on the Law Governing Space Resources*, 5 Annals Air & Space L. 611 (1980).

3. . . . *See, e.g.*, Albert Gore, Jr., *Outer Space, the Global Environment, and International Law: Into the Next Century*, 57 Tenn. L. Rev. 329 (1990); Nicolas Mateesco Matte, *Environmental Implications and Responsibilities in the Use of Outer Space*, 14 Annals Air & Space L. 419 (1989); D. E. Reibel, *Environmental Regulation of Space Activity: The Case of Orbital Debris*, 10 Stan. Envt'l. L. J. 97 (1991).

4. *See* Outer Space Treaty, art. I, 18 U.S.T. at 2410, 610 U.N.T.S. at 205.

5. Id. art. III, 18 U.S.T. at 2413, 610 U.N.T.S. at 208.

6. . . . *See* Warren E. Leary, *String of Rocket Mishaps Worries Industry*, N.Y. Times, May 12, 1999, at Al.

7. *See generally* P. U. R. Abeyratne, *The Use of Nuclear Power Sources in Outer Space and Its Effect on Environmental Protection*, 25 J. Space L. 17 (1997) . . . and Stanley B. Rosenfield, *Where Air Space Ends and Outer Space Begins*, 7 J. Space. L. 137 (1979). . . .

8. *See* Abeyratne, *The Use of Nuclear Power Sources*, at 17; He Qizhi, *Towards a New Legal Regime for the Use of Nuclear Power Sources in Outer Space*, 14 J. Space. L. 95, 97 (1986).

9. *Question Relating to the Use of Nuclear Power Sources in Outer Space*, U.N. GAOR, COPUOS, 15th Sess., at 14, U.N. Doc. AIAC.1051220 (1978).

10. Outer Space Treaty, art. I, 18 U.S.T. at 2412, 610 U.N.T.S. at 207.

11. *See Summary Record of the 188th Meeting*, U.N. GAOR, COPUOS, 15th Sess., at 6, U.N. Doc. AJAC.IOSIC.115R188 (1978); *Proposed Terms of Reference for Ad Hoc Working Group of Scientific and Technical Sub-Committee on "Questions Relating to the Uses of Nuclear Power Sources in Outer Space,"* U.N. GAOR, COPUOS, 15th Sess., U.N. Doc. AIAC.105/C.l/L.103 (1978). . . .

12. *See Use of Nuclear Power in Outer Space*, U.N. GAOR, COPUOS, 15th Sess. U.N. Doc. A/AC.105/C.2iL.115 (1978).

13. *See The Elaboration of Draft Principles Relevant to the Use of Nuclear Power Sources in Outer Space*, U.N. GAOR, COPUOS, 26th Sess., U.N. Doc. A/AC.1051C.21L.154 Rev. 2 (1987) [hereinafter *NPS Principles*]. . . .

14. *See* Howard A. Baker, Space Debris: Legal and Policy Implications 107 (1989). . . .

15. *See, e.g.*, Howard A. Baker, *Current Space Debris Policy and Its Implications*, in Proceedings of The Thirty-Second Colloquium on The Law of Outer Space 59 (1990); Howard A. Baker, *The Sci-Lab Perception: Its Impact on Protection of the Outer Space Environment*, in Proceedings of The Thirtieth Colloquium of The Law of Outer Space 121 (1988); Nicholas L. Johnson, *Hazards of the Artificial Space Environment*, in Proceedings of The Thirtieth Colloquium of The Law of Outer Space at 482. The International Aeronautical Federation recognized in a 1984 study that space debris was a "particularly serious" and "real" problem in the low-earth-orbit (LEO) and that international action was "imperative" in order to resolve the problem. *Implications to International Cooperation of Large-Scale Space Systems*, U.N. GAOR, COPUOS, at 19, U.N. Doc. AIAC.1051349 (1984).

16. *See* Stephen Gorove, Developments in Space Law: Issues and Policies 156, 164 (1991).

17. The term "geosynchronous" applies to all orbits having a period of rotation corresponding to that of Earth (about 23 hours, 56 minutes). It is a unique natural resource of vital importance for myriad space activities, including communications, meteorology, broadcasting, remote sensing, data relay, and tracking. Presently the entire civil telecommunication satellite industry is located in GEO. The presence of space debris makes GEO an "endless shooting gallery"; active payloads, otherwise known as functioning space objects, are "sitting ducks." David H. Suddeth, *Debris in the Geostationary Orbit Ring: "The Endless Shooting Gallery"—The Necessity for a Disposal Policy,* in Orbital Debris 349, 356 (Donald J. Kessler & Shin-Yi Su eds., 1985).

18. . . . *See* D. M. Wanland, *Hazards to Navigation in Outer Space: Legal Remedies and Salvage Law* 8979 (research prepared for the NASA-AMES/University Consortium for Astrolaw Research, Hastings College of Law, University of California), cited in Baker, Space Debris: Legal and Policy Implications at 127 nn. 104 & 106. . . .

19. *See* Craig Fishman, *Space Salvage: A Proposed Treaty Amendment to the Agreement on the Rescue of Astronauts, the Return of Astronauts and the Return of Objects Launched into Space,* 26 Va. J. Intl'l. 965, 995 (1986).

20. *See* Baker, Space Debris: Legal and Policy Implications at 13 and . . . Vladimir Bogomolov, *Prevention of an Arms Race in Outer Space—Developments in the Conference on Disarmament in 1994,* 235. Space L. 43, 46 (1995).

21. *See* Baker, Space Debris: Legal and Policy Implications at 23–24, 35–37.

22. U.N. Press Release, *Outer Space Committee Considers Agenda of Legal Sub-Committee,* 05/1259 (Jun. 11, 1986) 3, cited in Baker, Space Debris: Legal and Policy Implications at 146 n. 482.

23. *Last Full Crew Leave Mir, To Be Abandoned After 13 Years,* N.Y. Times, Aug. 28, 1999, at A6.

24. *See Thirtieth Session of the Committee on the Peaceful Uses of Outer Space,* U.N. GAOR, COPUOS, para. 18, U.N. Doc. A/AC.1OS/5R.294 (1987) (remarks by the Pakistani representative on the effects of NPS and space debris).

25. *See* Gorove, Space Debris Issues at 178 (summarizing Carl Christol, *Scientific and Legal Aspects of Space Debris*).

26. . . . *See Draft Technical Report on Space Debris of the Scientific and Technical Subcommittee,* U.N. GAOR, COPUOS, 35th Sess., U.N. Doc. AIAC.105/707 (1998); *Report of the Scientific and Technical Subcommittee on the Work of Its Thirty-Fifth Section,* U.N. GAOR, COPUOS, U.N. Doc. IAC.1051697 (1998); *Report of the Scientific and Technical Subcommittee on the Work of Its Thirty-Fourth Session,* U.N. GAOR, COPUOS, U.N. Doc. AIAC.1051672 (1997). In 1999, the final draft technical report on space debris was adopted by the Subcommittee at its 36th Session in Vienna. *See Report of the Scientific and Technical Subcommittee on the Work of Its Thirty-Sixth Session. See also Thirtieth Session of the Committee on the Peaceful Uses of Outer Space,* U.N. GAOR, COPUOS, U.N. Doc. A/AC.1OS/5R.294 (1987) para. 35.

27. For a brief account of how legal norms work in the international arena, are Abram Chayes & Antonia Handler Chayes, The New Sovereignty: Compliance with International Regulatory Agreements 112–24 (1995).

28. Daniel Vice, *Implementation of Biodiversity Treaties: Monitoring, Fact-Finding, and Dispute Resolution,* 29 N.Y.U. 3. Int'l L. & Pol. 577, 631 (1997).

29. *See* Vice, *Implementation of Biodiversity Treaties* at 632.

30. *See* Vice, *Implementation of Biodiversity Treaties.*

31. *See Question of the Peaceful Use of Outer Space,* G.A. Res. 1348, U.N. GAOR, 13th Sess., 792 plen. mtg., U.N. Doc. AIRES 11348 (1958).

32. *See International Co-operation in the Peaceful Uses of Outer Space,* G.A. Res. 1472, U.N. GAOR, 14th Sess., 856th plen. mtg., U.N. Doc. AIRES/1472 (1959).

33. G.A. Res. 1962, U.N. GAOR, 18th Sess., 1280th plen. mtg., U.N. Doc. AIRES/1962 (963); *see also* G.A. Res. 1721, U.N. GAOR, 16th Sess., 1085th plen. mtg., U.N. Doc. AIRES/1721(1961) (setting expectations and reviewing progress of COPUOS); G.A. Res. 1802, U.N. GAOR, 17th Sess., plen. mtg., U.N. Doc. AIRE5II8O2 (1962) (same); G.A. Res. 1884, U.N. GAOR, 18th Sess, 1244th plen. mtg., U.N. Doc. A1RES/1884 (1963) (calling upon states not to deploy weapons of mass destruction in outer space).

34. The Outer Space Treaty has entered into force for over 90 states, including the United States, Russia, and the People's Republic of China. It has been signed but not yet ratified by about 30 countries. See 18 U.S.T. at 2410, 610 U.N.T.S. at 205.

35. *See* Walter W. C. de Vries, *The Creation of a Concept of the Law of Outer Space,* in Space Law: Views of the Future, 21, 29 (Tanja Zwaan et al. eds., 1988) [hereinafter Views of the Future].

36. These consist of, inter alia, the freedom of exploration and use of outer space in accordance with the fundamental principles of international law, including the Charter of the United Nations. *See* Ida Bagus R. Supaneana, *The Contribution of the Developing Countries to the Legal Formulation of Future Space Law,* in de Vries, Views of the Future at 113, 117.

37. Apr. 22, 1968, 19 U.S.T. 7570, 672 U.N.T.S. 119 (entered into force Dec. 3, 1968) [hereinafter Astronaut Agreement]. It has entered into force for over 75 countries. The European Space Agency is also a party.

38. Opened for signature Jan. 14, 1975, 28 U.S.T. 695, 1023 U.N.T.S. 15 (entered into force Sept. 15, 1976) [hereinafter Registration Convention]. It has been ratified by 37 states.

39. Mar. 29, 1972, 24 U.S.T. 2389, 961 U.N.T.S. 187 (entered into force Oct. 9, 1973) [hereinafter Liability Convention]. It is presently binding in over 70 countries.

40. Opened for signature Dec. 18, 1979, 1363 U.N.T.S. 3 (registered *ex officio* July 11, 1984) [hereinafter Moon Agreement]. The Moon Agreement has been ratified by Austria, Australia, Chile, the Netherlands, Pakistan, the Philippines, and Uruguay; it has also been signed by France, Guatemala, India, Morocco, Peru, and Romania. It is perhaps unsurprising that the Moon Agreement has not been ratified by the major developed states, namely, Canada, France, Germany, Japan, Russia, the United Kingdom, and the United States. Because they possess the technological capabilities to engage in ongoing space activities, the regime of equitable sharing and distribution as proposed in the Agreement remains highly unsatisfactory to the spacefaring nations.

41. Treaty Banning Nuclear Weapon Tests in the Atmosphere, in Outer Space and Under Water, Aug. 5, 1963, 14 U.S.T. 1313, 480 U.N.T.S. 43 (entered into force Oct. 10, 1963) [hereinafter Partial Nuclear Test Ban Treaty].

42. Treaty on the Limitation of Anti-Ballistic Missile Systems, May 26, 1972, U.S.-U.S.S.R., 23 U.S.T. 3435 (entered into force Oct. 3, 1972) [hereinafter ABM Treaty].

43. Convention on the Prohibition of Military or Any Other Hostile Use of Environmental Modification Techniques, May 18, 1977, 31 U.S.T. 333, 1108 U.N.T.S. 151 (entered into force Jan. 17, 1980) [hereinafter ENMOD Convention].

44. Outer Space Treaty, art. I, 15 U.S.T. at 2413, 610 U.N.T.S. at 207–08.

45. Id., art II, 18 U.S.T. at 2413, 610 U.N.T.S. at 208.

46. *See* Bogota Declaration, Dec. 3, 1976, reprinted in 6 J. Space L. 193 (1978).

47. Outer Space Treaty, art. IX, 18 U.S.T. at 2416, 610 U.N.T.S. at 210.

48. *See* Astronaut Agreement, arts. 1975, 19 U.S.T. at 75739775, 672 U.N.T.S. at 121–23.

49. Id., art. 5(4), 19 U.S.T. at 7575, 672 U.N.T.S. at 123.

50. Outer Space Treaty, art. V, 18 U.S.T. at 2414, 610 U.N.T.S. at 209.

51. *See* Liability Convention, art. 11, 24 U.S.T. at 2392, 961 U.N.T.S. at 189.

52. "Space object" is defined as "component parts as well as the launch vehicle and parts thereof." Id., art. I.

53. Id.

54. *See* Registration Convention, art. 11, 28 U.S.T. at 698–99, 1023 U.N.T.S. at 17.

55. *See* id., art. IV(1), 28 U.S.T. at 699, 1023 U.N.T.S. at 17.

56. *See* id., art. IV(3), 28 U.S.T. at 700, 1023 U.N.T.S. at 17.

57. *See* H. A. Wassenbergh, Speculations on the Law Governing Space Resources, 5 *Annals Air & Space L.* (1998) at 617.

58. Moon Agreement, art. 7, 1363 U.N.T.S. at 24.

59. *See* id., art. 11(2), 1363 U.N.T.S. at *25.*

60. Carl Christol, Space Law: Past, Present, and Future 347 (1991).

61. *See* G.A. Res. 1348, U.N. GAOR 13th Sess. (recognizing "the common interest of mankind in outer space"); *see also* G.A. Res. 1472, U.N. GAOR 14th Sess. (calling for international cooperation in the peaceful use of outer space); G.A. Res. 1721, U.N. GAOR, 16th Sess., 1085th plen. mtg., U.N. Doc. AIRES/1721 (1961) (asserting that the use and exploration of outer space should be "for the benefit of mankind").

62. See A. O. Adede, *The System for the Exploitation of the "Common Heritage of Mankind"at the Caracas Conference,* 69 Am. J. Int'l. L. 31(1975). *See also* Declaration of Principles Governing the Sea-Bed and the Ocean Floor, and the Subsoil Thereof, Beyond the Limits of National Jurisdiction, G.A. Res. 2749, U.N. GAOR, 25th Sess., 1933 plen. mtg., U.N. Doc. 1RE512749 (1970). . . .

63. Aldo Armando Cocca, *The Principle of the "Common Heritage of All Mankind" as Applied to Natural Resources from Outer Space and Celestial Bodies,* in Proceedings of the Sixteenth Colloquium on the Law of Outer Space 172, 174 (1974) (quoting the Conclusion of the VITA Hispano-Luso-American Congress on International Law, Buenos Aires, 1969); *see also* Ernst Fasan, "The Meaning of the Term 'Mankind' in Space Legal Language," 2 J. Space L. (1974) at 129.

64. . . . Moon Agreement, art. 11(1), 1363 U.N.T.S. at 25. . . . *See* id., art. 11(5), 1363 U.N.T.S. at 25.

65. *See* Christol, Space Law: Past, Present, and Future, at 406–26.

66. Outer Space Treaty, art. III, 18 U.S.T. at 2413, 610 U.N.T.S. at 208.

67. Stephen Gorove, *The Concept of "Common Heritage of Mankind": A Political, Moral or Legal Innovation?* 9 San Diego L. Rev. 390, 393 (1972).

68. *See* Aldo Armando Cocca, *The Advances in International Law Through the Law of Outer Space,* 9 J. Space L. 13, 16 (1981). . . .

69. . . . Richard H. Fallon, Jr., *Reflections on Dworkin and the Two Faces of Law,* 67 Notre Dame L. Rev. 553, 554 (1992); *see also* Friedrich V. Kratochwil, Rules, Norms and Decisions: On the Conditions of Practical and Legal Reasoning in International Relations and Domestic Affairs 97 (1989) ("The prescriptive force of norms appears then as a claim to validity which is mediated by language and which can be validated discursively.").

70. Ogunsola Ogunbanwo, International Law and Outer Space Activities 66 (1975).

71. Outer Space Treaty, 18 U.S.T. at 2413, 610 U.N.T.S. at 208. *But see* Shyom Brown et al., Regimes for the Ocean, Outer Space and Weather 130 (1977), *quoted in* Young, Law and Policy in the Space Station's Era at 193. . . .

72. Chayes & Chayes, The New Sovereignty: Compliance with International Regulatory Agreements at 124.

73. Outer Space Treaty, art. VI, 18 U.S.T. at 2415, 610 U.N.T.S. at 209.

74. Id., art. IV, 18 U.S.T. at 2413, 610 U.N.T.S. at 208.

75. *See* Moon Agreement, art. 3, 1363 U.N.T.S. at 23. . . .

76. *See* Christol, Space Law: Past, Present, and Future at 471–72. Such restrictions are on weapons systems that can be classified as nuclear weapons or weapons of mass destruction. *See* Gennady Danilenko, *The Progressive Development of Space Law: New Opportunities and Restraints*, in de Vries, *The Creation of a Concept of the Law of Outer Space* at 99, 109.

77. For a discussion of the effect of the ARM Treaty on the SDI, see V. S. Vereshehetin, *"Strategic Defense Initiative" and International Law,* in Proceedings of the Twenty-Ninth Colloquium on the Law of Outer Space (1987).

78. *See, e.g., Draft Treaty on the Prohibition of the Stationing of Weapons of Any Kind in Outer Space,* U.N. GAOR, 36th Sess., Annex, U.N. Doc. A/36/192/Annex (1981) (annex to a request for the inclusion of a supplementary item on the agenda); *Draft Treaty on the Prohibition of the Use of Force in Outer Space and From Space Against the Earth,* U.N. GAOR, 38th Sess., Annex, U.N. Doc. A/38/194/Annex (1983) (same).

79. *See Report of the Scientific and Technical Subcommittee on the Work of Its Thirty-Fifth Session,* U.N. Doc. IAC 1051697 (1998), paras. 126–27.

80. Id., para 131.

81. *See* Liability Convention, art. 1(a), 24 U.S.T. at 2397, 961 U.N.T.S. at 189. Damage may be caused on the surface of the Earth, *see* id., art 11, 24 U.S.T. at 2392, 961 U.N.T.S. at 189, to aircraft in flight, *see* id., or elsewhere other than on the surface of the Earth, *see* id., arts. III and IV, 24 U.S.T. at 23929793, 91 U.N.T.S. at 189–90.

82. Id., art. 11, 24 U.S.T. at 2392, 961 U.N.T.S. at 189.

83. *See* id., art. 111, 24 U.S.T. at 2392, 961 U.N.T.S. at 190.

84. *See* Gorove, Developments in Space Law: Issues and Policies at 154.

85. The Registration Convention does not even provide for any obligatory marking of space objects. *See* Vladimir Kopal, *Some Considerations on the Legal Status of Aerospace Systems,* 22, 3. Space L. 57, 62 (1994).

86. *See* Outer Space Treaty, art. XI, 18 U.S.T. at 2418, 610 U.N.T.S. at 210.

87. *See* Registration Convention, 28 U.S.T. at 700–01, 1023 U.N.T.S. at 17–18.

88. *See* Partial Nuclear Test Ban Treaty, ENMOD Convention, International Telecommunication Convention, Oct. 25, 1973, 28 U.S.T. 2495, 1209 U.N.T.S. 32.

89. Christopher Joyner, *Legal Implications of the Concept of the Common Heritage of Mankind,* 35 Int'l. & Comp. L. Q. 190, 197 (1986).

90. *See* Jonathan I. Charney, *Universal International Law* 87 Am. J. Int'l L. at 543–47.

91. *See* Buenos Aires International Instrument at 112.

92. *Reports of the Commission to the General Assembly,* U.N. Doc. A/6309/Rev.1 (1966), reprinted in [1966] 2 Y.B. Int'l L. Comm'n. 169, 248, U.N. Doc. A/CN.4/5ER.A/1966/Add.1.

93. *See, e.g.,* Christol, Space Law: Past, Present, and Future at 443.

94. *See* Alfred von Verdross, *Forbidden Treaties in International Law,* 31 Am. J. Int'l L. 571, 574 (1937).

95. *See* G.A. Res. 2994, U.N. GAOR, 27th Sess., 2112 plen. mtg., U.N. Doc. A/RE5/2994 (1972).

96. United Nations Conference on the Environment: Final Documents, U.N. Doc. AICONF.45114, reprinted in 11 I.L.M. 1416, 1418 (1972).

97. *See* Veit Koester, From *Stockholm to Brundtland,* 20 Envt'l. Pol'y & L. 14, 15 (1990).

98. *See* G.A. Res. 3717, U.N. GAOR, 37th Sess., 48th plen. mtg., U.N. Doc. A/RES/37/7 (1982).

99. World Comm'n on Env't and Dev, Our Common Future, (1987).

100. *See* G.A. Res. 42/186, U.N. GAOR, 42d Sess., U.N. Doc. AIRE5142/186 (1988); G.A. Res. 42/18⁷, U.N. GAOR, 42d Sess., 96th plen. mtg., U.N. Doc. A/RES/42/187 (1988).

101. *See* Gunther Handl, *Environmental Security and Global Change: The Challenge to International Law,* 1 Y.B. Int'l. Envt'l. L. 3, 3974 (1990); Louis Sohn, *The Stockholm Declaration on the Human Environment,* 14 Harv. Int'l. L. J. 423 (1973).

102. *See* Rio Declaration on Environment and Development, adopted June 14, 1992, U.N. Doc. A/CONF/15 1/26, vol. I, reprinted in 31 I.L.M. 874 (1992) [hereinafter Rio Declaration].

103. *See generally* Edith Erown Weiss, In Fairness to Future Generations at 17–46 (arguing that each generation is obliged to conserve the planet in trust for the next). An alternative theory of our responsibility to future generations was recently put forward in Christopher Stone, Earth and Other Ethics: The·Case for Moral Pluralism 84–91 (1987) and was further developed in Gary P. Supanich, *The Legal Basis of Intergenerational Responsibility: An Alternative View—The Sense of Intergenerational Identity,* 3 Y.B. Int'l. Envt'l. L. 94, 99–105 (1992). . . .

104. *See, e.g.,* Christopher Stone, Earth and Other Ethics: The Case for Moral Pluralism (1987) at 85–89; Philip Alston, A Third Generation of Solidarity Rights: Progressive Development or Obfuscation of International Human Rights Law?, 29 Num. Int'l. L. Rev. 307 (1982); Brian Bany, Justice Between Generations, in Law, Morality and Society 270–76 (P. Hacker & J. Raz eds., 1977). . . .

105. *See, e.g.,* Patricia Birnie & Alan Boyle, International Law and the Environment 119 (1992) ("The protection of common spaces . . . is thus a complex issue in which scientific, moral, ethical, political, economic, social, and technological issues are inextricably intertwined and on which these interests do not always coincide."); *see also* Alexandre S. Timosbenko, *From Stockholm to Rio: The Institutionalization of Sustainable Development,* in Sustainable Development and International Law 143 (Winfried Lang ed., 1995) (chronicling the development and legitimization of the notion of sustainable development beginning with the Stockholm Conference in 1972).

106. Gary P. Supanich, *The Legal Basis of Intergenerational Responsibility: An Alternative View—The Sense of Intergenerational Identity,* 3 Y.B. Int'l. Envt'l. L. (1992) at 107.

107. Robert Repetto, World Enough and Time: Successful Strategies for Resource 15 (1986), quoted in Supanich, *The Legal Basis of Intergenerational Responsibility* at 107.

108. Anthony D'Amato, *Do We Owe a Duty to Future Generations to Preserve the Global Environment?* 84 Am. J. Int'l. L. 190, 198 (1990).

109. Jutta Brunnee & Stephen Toope, Environmental Security and Freshwater Resources: Ecosystem Regime Building, 91 Am. J. Int'l. L. (1997) at 28. . . .

110. *See* Stephen D. Krasner, *Regimes and the Limits of Realism: Regimes as Autonomous Variables,* 36 Int'l. Org. 497, 500 (1982).

111. A detailed examination of the various approaches to treaty-making is beyond the scope of this article. For a comprehensive treatise on the merits of different approaches to treaty-making, see Chayes & Chayes, The New Sovereignty: Compliance with International Regulatory Agreements (1995).

112. Geoffrey Palmer, New Ways to Make International Environmental Law (1992) at 269; *see also* John Gerard Ruggie, *International Regimes, Transactions, and Change: Embedded Liberalism in the Postwar Economic Order,* 36 Int'l. Org. 379, 382 (1982). . . .

113. *See* Military and Paramilitary Activities (Nicar. v. U.S.), 1986 I.C.J. 14, 99 (June 27); Alexandra Kiss & Dinah Shelton, *Systems Analysis of International Law: A Methodological Inquiry,* 17 Neth. Y.B. Int'l. L. 45, 67 (1986).

114. *See* C. M. Chinkin, *The Challenge of Soft Law: Development and Change in International Law,* 38 Int'l. & Comp. L. Q. 850, 859–62 (1989) (commenting on the choice of soft-law forms); Blaine Sloan, *General Assembly Resolutions Revisited (Four Years Later),* 58 Brit. Y.B. Int'l. L. (1987) at 106–25 (analyzing the difficulties of measuring or even categorizing the force of a given norm, as well as the problems involved in attempting to measure its effects). . . .

115. *See, e.g.,* the 1989 Langkawi Declaration on the Environment, in which the Commonwealth heads of government committed themselves to a program of action that stresses the need to promote "economic growth and sustainable development, including the eradication of poverty." Reprinted in 5 Am. U. I. Int'l. L. & Poly 589, 589 (1990). . . .

116. *See* G.A. Res. 2994, U.N. GAOR, 27th Sess., 2112 plen. mtg., U.N. Doc. A/RES/2994 (1972).

117. *See* Rio Declaration on Environment and Development, adopted June 14, 1992, U.N. Doc. A/CONF/151/26m vol. I, reprinted in 31 I.L.M. 874 (1992).

118. The Hague Declaration was signed by 24 nations at the International Summit on the Protection of the Global Atmosphere, March 11, 1989. *See* Hague Declaration on the Environment, 28 I.L.M. 1308 (1989).

119. *See* Winfried Lang, *Diplomacy and International Environmental Law-Making: Some Observations,* 3 Y.B. Int'l. Envt'l. L. (1992) at 109, 116 [hereinafter *Diplomacy and International Environmental Law-Making*]. Examples of soft obligations include articles 2 and 6 of the 1979 Convention on Long-Range Transboundary Air Pollution, Nov. 13, 1979, 34 U.S.T. 3043, 3046–47, 18 I.L.M. 1442, 1443–44 (1979).

120. Ozone Layer Convention.

121. Sept. 16, 1987, S. Treaty Doc. No. 100–10, 26 I.L.M. 1541 (1987) (entered into force Jan. 1, 1989) [hereinafter Montreal Protocol].

122. May 2, 1989, 28 I.L.M. 1335 (1989).

123. Adjustments to the Montreal Protocol on Substances that Deplete the Ozone Layer, June 29, 1990, S. Treaty Doc. No. 102–4, 30 I.L.M. 537 (1991) [hereinafter London Amendments].

124. Such an approach to international environmental law-making has the support of Abram Chayes & Antonia Handler Chayes, The New Sovereignty Compliance with International Regulatory Agreements (1995) at 225–27; Lang, *Diplomacy and International Environmental Law-Making* at 117–22; Palmer, *New Ways to Make International Environmental Law* at 273–78; and Donald Rothwell, *International Law and the Protection of the Arctic Environment,* 44 Int'l. & Comp. L. Q. 280, 308 (1995).

125. *See, e.g.,* Keohane, *The Demand for International Regimes* at 334. . . .

126. *See, e.g.*, Alan E. Boyle, Saving the World? Implementation and Enforcement of International Environmental Law Through International Institutions, 3 J. Envm. L. 229, 231 (1991); Katharina Kummer, Providing Incentives to Comply with Multilateral Environmental Agreements: An Alternative to Sanctions?, 3 Eur. Envn'l. L. Rev. 256, 257 (1994). . . .

127. *See, e.g.*, UNCLOS, art. 192, 21 I.L.M. at 1308, 1315 ("States have the obligation to protect and preserve the marine environment."); id., art. 235(1) ("States are responsible for the fulfillment of their international obligations concerning the protection and preservation of the marine environment. They shall be liable in accordance with international law."); *see also* Elizabeth P. Barratt Brown, *Building a Monitoring and Compliance Regime Under the Montreal Protocol,* 16 Yale Int'l. L. 519, 544–70 (1991). . . .

128. *See, e.g.*, Andronico Adede, *Management of Environmental Disputes: Avoidance Versus Settlement,* in Sustainable Development and International Law at 115 (distinguishing between "dispute avoidance" and "dispute settlement"); Martti Koskenniemi, *Breach of Treaty or Non-Compliance? Reflections on the Enforcement of the Montreal Protocol,* 3 Y.B. Int'l. Envt'l. L. 123, 150–55 (1992) (assessing the effectiveness of the Meeting of the Parties under the Montreal Protocol). . . .

129. *See, e.g.*, Oran R. Young & Gail Osherenko, Polar Politics: Creating International Environmental Regimes (1993); Peter M. Haas, *Do Regimes Matter? Epistemic Communities and Mediterranean Pollution Control,* 43 Int'l. Org. (1989).

130. This effect was observed by the Intergovernmental Panel on Climate Change. *See* Oran R. Young, International Governance: Protecting the Environment in a Stateless Society 41–42 (1994); Daniel B. Bodansky, *The Emerging Climate Change Regime,* 20 Ann. Rev. Energy & Env't. 425, 443–44 (1995); Brunnee & Toope, *Environmental Security and Freshwater Resources* at 43 n A02.

131. At the 66th Conference of the International Law Association in Buenos Aires, Aug. 20, 1994, the Buenos Aires International Instrument on the Protection of the Environment from Damage Caused by Space Debris was adopted by consensus. *See* Maureen Williams, *The ILA Finalizes Its International Instrument on Space Debris in Buenos Aires, August 1994* Space L. (1995) at 77. . . .

132. United Nations Framework Convention on Climate Change, opened for signature June 4, 1992, S. Treaty Doc. No. 102–38 (1992), 31 I.L.M. 849 (1992) (entered into force Mar. 21, 1994) [hereinafter FCCC].

133. Kyoto Protocol to the FCCC, Conference of the Parties, 3d Sess., U.N. Doc. FCCC/CP/19971L.7/Add.l (1998), reprinted in 37 I.L.M. 22 (1998) [hereinafter Kyoto Protocol].

134. FCCC, art. 3(1), 31 I.L.M. 854. . . .

135. *See* Rodney R. McColloch, *Protocol on Environmental Protection to the Antarctic Treaty—The Antarctic Treaty—Antarctic Minerals Convention—Wellington Convention—Convention on the Regulations of Antarctic Mineral Resource Activities,* 22 G.A. 3. Int'l. & Comp. L. 211, 231 (1992). . . .

136. The Biodiversity Convention, June 5, 1992, 31 I.L.M. 818 (1992) [hereinafter Biodiversity Convention], signed at the U.N. Conference on Environment and Development (UNCED) by 153 states and the European Community, is aimed at conserving and protecting ecosystems and biodiversity. . . .

137. *See* FCCC, art. 11, 31 I.L.M. at 864–65; Biodiversity Convention, arts. 209721, 31 I.L.M. at 830–32.

138. *See Report of the Scientific and Technical Subcommittee on the Work of Its Thirty-Sixth Session,* paras. 65–76.

139. *See* id.

140. Extending the activities of the International Atomic Energy Agency (IAEA) to safeguarding the use of NPS in outer space has also been suggested. *See Report of the Legal Subcommittee on the Work of Its Twenty-Third Session (19 March–April 1984)*, U.N. GAOR, COPUOS, at 26, U.N. Doc. AIAC.1051337 (1934); *see also* Hilary F. French, *Reforming the United Nations to Ensure Environmentally Sustainable Development*, 4 Transnat'l. L. & Contemp. Probs. 559, 586 (1994). . . .

141. *See, e.g.*, Oran R. Young & Gail Osherenko, Polar Politics: Creating International Environmental Regimes 245 (1993); Peter M. Haas, *Do Regimes Matter? Epistemic Communities and Mediterranean Pollution Control*, 43 Int'l. Org. 377, 380, 384 (1989). . . .

142. *See Report of the Scientific and Technical Subcommittee on the Work of Its Thirty-Sixth Session*, U.N. GAOR, COPUOS, U.N. Doc. A1AC,105/719 (1999).

143. Similar principles, but in relation to the equitable sharing of benefits from the exploitation of outer space, have been highlighted in Christol, Space Law: Past, Present, and Future (1991) at 440–42.

144. . . . *See* Suzanne C. Massey, *Global Warming—International Environmental Agreements—The 1992 United Nations Conference on the Environment and Development Most Likely Will Not Culminate in a Successfully Preventive Global Warming Treaty Without the United States' Support*, 22 G.A. 3. Int'l. & Comp. L. 175, 208 (1992).

145. *See* Douglas Barritt, *A "Reasonable" Approach to Resource Development in Outer Space*, 12 Loy. L.A. Int'l. & Comp. L. 615, 627–35 (1990); Barbara Ellen Heiin, *Exploring the Last Frontiers for Mineral Resources: A Comparison of International Law Regarding the Deep Seabed, Outer Space and Antarctica*, 23 Vano. 3. Transnational, 819, 834–35 (1990); *see also* Carl Q. Christol, *The 1979 Moon Agreement: Where Is It Today?*, 27 J. Space L. . . .

146. Palmer, *New Ways to Make International Environmental Law* at 266.

147. Don B. Kash, The Politics of Space Cooperation 126, 130–31 (1967) ("Given the weight of evidence put forward by our present reality one could hardly expect the government generally or a government agency to accept the innovative approach."). In the new millennium, a different reality of international cooperation faces us. *See, e.g.*, Aldo Armando Cocca, *Prospective Space Law*, 26 J. Space L. 51 (1998). . . .

148. *See* Lisa L. Martin, *Credibility, Costs and Institutions: Cooperation on Economic Sanctions*, 45 World Pol. 406, 418 (1993).

149. Merlin M. Magallona, *The Concept of* Jus Cogens *in the Vienna Convention on the Law of the Treaties*, 51 Phil. L. J. 521, 526 (1976).

PART 3

The Future of International Law

CHAPTER 21

The Yahoo Case and Conflict of Laws in the Cyberage

Mathias Reimann

TWO FRENCH PUBLIC INTEREST GROUPS, LA LIGUE CONTRE LE Racisme et L'Antisemitisme (LICRA) and L'Union des Etudiants Juifs De France (UEJF), sued Yahoo! Inc., a Delaware corporation headquartered near Santa Barbara, California, in the Tribunal de Grande Instance in Paris. The undisputed facts underlying the complaint were that: Yahoo! Inc. operated, inter alia, an auction website on which various Nazi memorabilia (such as flags, stamps, and military souvenirs) were offered for sale; the respective Yahoo! Inc. website was accessible in France; and the display of the Nazi memorabilia was illegal under French law. The French plaintiffs sought an order prohibiting Yahoo! Inc. from displaying the memorabilia in France. The lawsuit triggered a drama in two acts, the first of which took place in France while the second was played out in California.

In Paris, the French tribunal found that it had (personal) jurisdiction in this case because Yahoo! Inc. had committed a wrong (under section R.645-2 of the French Criminal Code), and caused harm, in France. Applying French law, the court gave short shrift to Yahoo! Inc.'s argument that the website message was speech protected under the First Amendment to the U.S. Constitution. Most importantly, the court rejected Yahoo! Inc.'s argument that compliance with French law would require the complete elimination of the respective website worldwide. After consulting an international team of experts, the tribunal concluded that it was technically possible for Yahoo! Inc. to block access to surfers in France with a 90 percent success rate. It also found Yahoo! Inc.'s impossibility argument undermined by the fact that on its website, Yahoo! Inc. greeted French users with advertisement banners in French. The court thus ordered Yahoo! Inc. "to take such meas-

---

Reprinted with permission of the *Michigan Journal of International Law.*

ures as will dissuade and render impossible any and all consultation on Yahoo.com of the auction service of Nazi objects as well as any other site or service which makes apologies of Nazism or questions the existence of Nazi crimes." It gave Yahoo! Inc. three months to comply with the order and imposed a daily fine *(astreinte)* of FF100,000 (US$13,300) in case of non-compliance.[1] In January 2001, Yahoo! Inc. banned Nazi memorabilia from its U.S. auction sites, claiming, however, that it was not acting in response to the French court order.[2]

Instead of pursuing an appeal in France, Yahoo! Inc. turned around and promptly sued the French plaintiffs in the United States District for the Northern District of California. Although the plaintiffs had made no effort to enforce the French order in California, Yahoo! Inc. sought a declaratory judgment that the French decision could not be recognized in the United States.[3] On June 7, 2001, the District Court found that it had personal jurisdiction over LICRA and UEJF because they had intentionally targeted a California party and purposefully availed themselves of California (and federal) law when they served Yahoo! Inc. with process.[4] Five months later, the court granted summary judgment on the merits in favor of Yahoo! Inc. Judge Fogel held that enforcing the French decision would be incompatible with Yahoo! Inc.'s First Amendment rights and thus violate U.S. public policy.[5] The French defendants appealed the jurisdictional ruling to the United States Court of Appeals for the Ninth Circuit.

Cyberage Conflicts: First Generation Issues

The Yahoo! litigation strikingly exemplifies three major private international law issues that arose right at the dawn of the cyberage. While these issues are best considered separately, they are closely interrelated. The second can be viewed as a subset of the first, and the third as a subset of the first and second.

The first issue is the most general: Should cyberspace be considered a realm unto its own, beyond the reach of governments, or does it still belong to the real world of territorial sovereigns and their regulatory power? This question was the object of an intense scholarly debate in the mid- to late 1990s. One camp viewed cyberspace as transcending the sphere of traditional governmental power; accordingly, its regulation by States was not only ineffective, but undesirable as well.[6] The opposite camp emphasized that even virtual events and transactions have anchors in real (territorial) space: they involve real people, cause real harm, and trigger real State interests; thus cyberspace can, will, and should be regulated by governments.[7] Since the height of this debate, the development of law has by and large validated the second position. Governments increasingly do regulate cyberspace activities and the idea of a laissez-faire virtual world has turned out to be a pipe dream or, depending on one's views, a largely groundless nightmare.[8] The Yahoo! case illustrates the victory of the proregulation advocates. Neither the French tribunal, nor, for that matter, the United States District Court, seriously entertained the idea that Yahoo! Inc.'s activities were beyond the reach of established French or American law. Without doubt, Yahoo! Inc.'s website was subject to real space regulation, enacted and enforced by real territorial sovereigns.

The second issue pertains more specifically to the interstate or international nature of (many) cyberspace cases: if cyberspace is being regulated by territorial sovereigns, can its transboundary dimensions be handled by the traditional conflict-of-laws instruments? Again, two fundamentally different views were proffered. The regulation skeptics cited above also doubted that traditional approaches to jurisdiction and choice of law can work in cyberspace. Since the Internet completely ignores state and national boundaries, so they argued, it renders obsolete our State-centered notions of jurisdiction and applicable law.[9] Most conflicts scholars, however, came to the opposite conclusion. While they did not deny the increased quantity and complexity of conflicts issues in cyberspace, they believed that established approaches to jurisdiction and choice of law can work quite well, at least if appropriately adjusted to the properties of the Internet.[10] In the last few years, the traditionalists have won this battle as well. Most courts have by and large managed to resolve cyberspace cases with the established tools, albeit occasionally in somewhat modified form. The Yahoo! case fits that pattern. The Tribunal de Grande Instance found jurisdiction because the defendant had committed a wrong in France, and it applied French law because the harmful effects had occurred in its territory. The United States District Court essentially accepted these conclusions. Both are indeed traditional grounds and firmly established in American (and foreign) conflicts law.

The third major issue is the most particular: it concerns the protection of free speech in transboundary disputes. Since the Internet is all about information, it is largely about speech, and First Amendment concerns loom large at every turn. In international cases, these concerns raise a particularly thorny question: Who gets to define the freedom of speech on the Internet—the country of the information provider or the country (or countries) of the recipient(s)? Needless to say, reasonable people can and do differ about this issue as well. One position is that the provider State's law must govern: information put on the Internet can flow practically anywhere in the world; yet, so the argument goes, it is well-nigh impossible, or at least excessively burdensome, for the provider to comply with the laws of virtually every country in the world. To put it differently: if the recipient State's law governs, every country can censor the Internet as a whole. The opposite position is that the recipient State sets the limits. According to this view, every country has the right to insist that those entering it comply with its laws. This is true even if the entry occurs electronically and even if the law restricts speech.[11] As with regard to the previous two issues, it seems that this second, more traditional, view reflects the emerging majority opinion, both among scholars and in the courts.[12] The French Yahoo! judgment points in the same direction. It decided the free speech issue in favor of the recipient country's law when it insisted that Yahoo! Inc. comply with French prohibitions. The United States Federal District Court did not deny the French tribunal's right to so insist in France; it simply refused to recognize the result in the United States.

The Yahoo! case is fast becoming a classic of early twenty-first century international conflicts law. At its core, the case vividly demonstrates the primary dilemma of Internet information providers: they need (or at least want) to operate on a worldwide basis but find themselves caught between conflicting national policies and regulatory regimes. It is no surprise that disputes triggered by this dilemma arise in countries all over the world. As Judge Fogel put it in his summary judgment for Yahoo! Inc.: "The implications go far beyond the facts of this case."[13]

The Yahoo! Case Reconsidered: Second Generation Issues

The first development is that technology has advanced to the point where effective geographic filtering of information is becoming possible. Horatia Muir Watt, a leading French conflicts scholar, points out how this has changed the nature of the game.[14] The unbridled flow of information on the Internet, she shows, was never a natural principle but a result of the Internet's original architecture which itself reflects the American preference for freedom of speech and, one might add, for laissez faire more generally. As technology has changed, however, such free dissemination is no longer a necessity but has become a matter of choice. After all, the French court order was based on the finding that Yahoo! Inc. could block access to its website in France quite effectively without having to shut it down worldwide. On the one hand, the new technology thus solves an old dilemma: If service providers can increasingly channel the flow of information, they can also increasingly comply with individual nation's laws and still operate on a worldwide level. On the other hand, the new technology immediately raises a follow-up issue: Who should bear the (technological and financial) burden of developing, implementing, and monitoring geographic filters—the sender or the receiving country? Professor Muir Watt acknowledges that it seems only fair to impose that burden, with the French tribunal, on the service provider as the cause of the problem. Yet, she argues, there is actually much to be said for putting the burden on the State that wants to protect itself. After all, that State may be in a better position to determine the desired level of regulation, to implement it, and to monitor its enforcement. Thus the answer to the question of cost distribution may depend on considerations familiar from the economic analysis of law.

A second development is that with the proliferation of cyberspace related lawsuits, judgments against Internet service providers have become routine even in transboundary cases. In a sense, this renders obsolete the older debate whether States can regulate cyberactivity at all and whether conflicts law can handle cyberage issues. In another sense, however, it just pushes the issue of effective regulation to another level—that of judgment recognition. In the domestic context, such recognition is, of course, straightforward under the full faith and credit clause,[15] but in international cases, where the clause does not apply, it presents a serious issue.[16] To be sure, if the service provider has assets in the forum State, judgments can be enforced locally. In all other cases, however, effective enforcement depends on their recognition in the defendant's home country. Thus international judgment recognition becomes a core issue of effective cyberspace regulation. The American side of the Yahoo! litigation drives this point home. In particular, it raises the question whether the United States should deny the recognition of a foreign judgment against an American service provider on free speech grounds. Professor Van Houweling finds the U.S. court's decision unsatisfactory for at least two reasons.[17] First, the opinion presumes that the enforcement of a foreign judgment amounts to a limitation of speech by the recipient State's government, appropriately triggering First Amendment protection. Such a proposition is hardly self-evident, and the opinion does little to explain it. Second, it assumes, but again fails to clarify, whether the First Amendment should apply extraterritorially, that is, to speech to foreigners in foreign countries. The more salient free speech concerns, Professor Van Houweling points out, may actually lie beyond the court's reasoning and may depend on the quality of available geographic filtering technology. Where such technology is relatively unreliable or too expensive for small-time users, information providers may worry about unintended overspill into foreign jurisdictions; the resulting fear of liability abroad can then chill their speech even at home. Reliable and readily available technology, however, may lead information providers strictly to limit the reach of their speech to the United States; this, in turn, could unduly impoverish the discourse on the international level. At the end of the day, a solid analysis of First Amendment issues in this context requires a more careful consideration of the technological state of the art than the district court provided.

Finally, as Internet access becomes widely available worldwide and international disputes arising from its use proliferate, the need to seek solutions through international cooperation becomes ever more obvious. Already in 2000, the European Union responded to this need when it enacted the so-called E-Commerce Directive.[18] The Directive is a regulatory regime governing cyberspace transactions among EU Member States.[19] It resolves the choice-of-law question principally in favor of the service provider's State but it also provides for a conflict resolution mechanism where other States are unwilling to accept this solution. Mark Kightlinger explores the question whether the EC Directive can serve as a model for a broader international agreement.[20] Drawing on his extensive practical experience as counsel for major American clients in Europe, especially before the EC institutions in Brussels, Kightlinger points out both the inherent difficulties and the benefits of adopting such an agreement. In the end, he is guardedly optimistic that an accord might be possible and worth the effort. While Kightlinger consistently tests his hypothesis against the Yahoo! case, his article actually points beyond that dispute: it is not about how to resolve Yahoo!

Notes

1. For the original order, see LICRA & UEJF v. Yahoo! Inc., T.GL Paris, May 22, 2000, *available at* http://www.lapres.net/yahen.html (Daniel Lapres trans.), *reprinted in* LEA BRILMAYER & JACK GOLDSMITH, CONFLICT OF LAWS: CASES AND MATERIALS 851–53 (5th ed. 2002). The final order, issued after the consultation of the expert team, is dated November 20, 2000. See LICRA et UEJF v. Yahoo! Inc., Ordonnance Référé, T.G.I. Paris, Nov. 20, 2000, *available at* http://www.lapres.net/yahenll.html (Daniel Lapres trans.). For a summary of the decision, see BRILMAYER & GOLDSMITH, *supra,* at 853–54 (falsely dating the decision November 22). *See also* Margaret Khayat Bratt & Norbert F. Kugele, *Who's in Charge?* 80 MICH. BAR J. 43 (July 2001).

2. See BRILMAYER & GOLDSMITH, *supra* note 1, at 854.

3. It is questionable whether the French plaintiffs would ever have tried to get the judgment enforced in the United States, and, had they tried, whether they ever stood a chance to succeed. Thus one may question whether Yahoo! Inc. felt seriously threatened or whether its action was rather a public relations move.

4. Yahoo! Inc. v. La Ligue Contre le Racisme et L'Antisemitisme, 145 F. Supp. 2d 1168 (N.D. Cal. 2001).

5. Yahoo! Inc. v. La Ligue Contre le Racisme et L'Antisemitisme, 169 F. Supp. 2d 1181 (N.D. Cal. 2001).

6. *See especially* David R. Johnson & David G. Post, *Law and Borders—The Rise of Law in Cyberspace,* 48 STAN. L. REV. 1367 (1996) [hereinafter Johnson & Post, *The Rise of Law in Cyberspace*]; David R. Johnson & David G. Post, *The Rise of Law on the Global Network, in* BORDERS IN CYBERSPACE 3 (Brian Kahjn & Charles Nesson eds., 1997).

7. *See especially* Jack Goldsmith, *Against Cyberanarchy,* 65 U. CHI. L. REV. 1199 (1998); Lawrence Lessig, *The Zones of Cyberspace,* 48 STAN. L. REV. 1403 (1996). *See generally* LAWRENCE LESSIG, CODE AND OTHER LAWS OF CYBERSPACE (1999).

8. This is particularly obvious in the area of e-commerce, as the burgeoning literature on this field demonstrates. *See, e.g.*, RONALD MANN & JANE K. WINN, ELECTRONIC COMMERCE (2002); J. CARL POINDEXTER & DAVID L. BAUMER, CYBERLAW AND E-COMMERCE (2001); SUSAN SINGLETON, ECOMMERCE: A PRACTICAL GUIDE TO THE LAW (2001); BARRY B. SOOKMAN, COMPUTER, INTERNET, AND ELECTRONIC COMMERCE LAW (2000); JANE K. WINN & BENJAMIN WRIGHT, THE LAW OF ELECTRONIC COMMERCE (2000); Gregory E. Maggs, *Regulating Electronic Commerce*, 50 AM. J. COMP. L. 665 (2002). On cyberlaw more generally, see RALPH D. CLIFFORD, COMPUTER AND CYBERLAW (1999); RAYMOND S.R. KU ET AL., CYBERSPACE LAW (2002).

9. *See, e.g.*, Johnson & Post, *The Rise of Law in Cyberspace*, *supra* note 6, at 1370–75, 1376 ("Because events on the Net occur everywhere but nowhere in particular . . . no physical jurisdiction has a more compelling claim than any other to subject these events exclusively to its laws.").

10. *See generally, e.g.*, Goldsmith, *supra* note 7; Allan R. Stein, *The Unexceptional Problem of Jurisdiction in Cyberspace*, 32 INT'L LAW. 1167 (1998).

11. Joel R. Reidenberg, *Yahoo and Democracy on the Internet*, 42 JURIMETRICS J. 261 (2002); Jack Goldsmith, *Yahoo! Brought to Earth*, FIN. TIMES, Nov. 26, 2000, *available at* http://news.ft.com/ft/ gx.cgi/ftc?pagename=View&c-Article&cid-FT3W85A41GC&liv.

12. Jack Goldsmith, Oral Presentation at the Meeting of the AALS Conflicts Section (Jan. 3, 2003) (transcript on file with author). Several courts in the United States have approved restrictions under local law on Internet service providers operating in foreign countries with more permissive rules. *See, e.g.*, People v. World Interactive Gaming Corp., 714 N.Y.S.2d 844 (N.Y. Sup. Ct. 1999) (applying New York law to gambling offered on a website operated in Antigua). For further cases, see Reidenberg, supra note 11, at 269–71.

13. Yahoo! Inc. v. La Ligue Contre le Racisme et L'Antisemitisme, 169 F. Supp. 2d 1181, 1186 (N.D. Cal. 2001).

14. Horatia Muir Watt, Yahoo! *Cyber-Collision of Cultures: Who Regulates?* 24 MICH. J. INT'L L. 673 (2003).

15. U.S. CONST. art. IV, § 1.

16. *See* Henry H. Perritt, *Will the Judgment-Proof Own Cyberspace?* 32 INT'L LAW. 1121, 1123 (1998) (arguing that in transnational cyberspace cases, the main problem "is one of enforcement, not jurisdiction"). As Peter Swire has pointed out, enforcement problems will depend on the size and nature of the defendant. Large corporations, like elephants, can put up a tough fight but they cannot hide, while small-time players, like mice, may be easily defeated but they are hard to track down and eradicate. Peter P. Swire, *Of Elephants, Mice, and Privacy: International Choice of Law and the Internet*, 32 INT'L LAW. 991,993 *passim* (1998).

17. Molly S. Van Houweling, *Enforcement of Foreign Judgments, the First Amendment, and Internet Speech: Notes for the Next Yahoo! v. LICRA*, 24 MICH. J. INT'L L. 697 (2003).

18. Council and Parliament Directive 2000/31/EC of 8 June 2000 on Certain Legal Aspects of Information Society Services, in Particular Electronic Commerce, in the Internal Market, 2000 OJ. (L 178) 1–15.

19. For a brief description, see also Saul Litvinoff, *The European Union and Electronic Commerce*, 62 LA. L. REV. 1221 (2002).

20. Mark F. Kightlinger, *A Solution to the Yahoo! Problem? The EC E-Commerce Directive as a Model for International Cooperation on Internet Choice of Law*, 24 MICH. J. INT'L L. 719 (2003).

CHAPTER 22

The Future of International Law Is Domestic (or, The European Way of Law)

Anne-Marie Slaughter and William Burke-White

INTERNATIONAL LAW HAS TRADITIONALLY BEEN JUST THAT—international. Consisting of a largely separate set of legal rules and institutions,[1] international law has long governed relationships among states. Under the traditional rules of international law, the claims of individuals could reach the international plane only when a state exercised diplomatic protection and espoused the claims of its nationals in an international forum.[2] More recently, international law has penetrated the once exclusive zone of domestic affairs to regulate the relationships between governments and their own citizens, particularly through the growing bodies of human rights law and international criminal law.[3] But even in these examples, international law has recognized a clear demarcation between domestic and international politics.

The classic model of international law as separate from the domestic realm reflects the traditional problems the international legal system sought to address, namely the facilitation of state-to-state cooperation and the treatment of one state's nationals by another state. Whether regulating the immunities of diplomats or the rights of ships on the high seas, the traditional purposes of international law have been interstate, not intrastate.

This foundation of international law reflects the principles of Westphalian sovereignty, often seemingly made up of equal parts myth and rhetoric. In this conception, the state is a defined physical territory "within which domestic political authorities are the sole arbiters of legitimate behavior."[4] States can be part of the international legal system to the degree they choose by consenting to particular rules. Likewise, they can choose to remain apart, asserting their own sovereignty and eschewing international involvement. Formally, Westphalian sovereignty is the right to be left alone, to exclude, to be free from any external meddling or interference. But it is also the right to be recognized as an autonomous agent in the international system, capable of interacting with other states and entering into international agreements. With these background understandings of sovereignty, an international legal system, consisting of states and limited by the principle of state consent, emerged.

Today, however, the challenges facing states and the international community alike demand very different responses from and thus new roles for the international legal system. The presses of globalization and the emergence of new transnational threats have fundamentally changed the nature of governance and the necessary purposes of international law in the past few years. From cross-border pollution to terrorist training camps, from refugee flows to weapons proliferation, international problems have domestic roots that an interstate legal system is often powerless to address. To offer an effective response to these new challenges, the international legal system must be able to influence the domestic policies of states and harness national institutions in pursuit of global objectives. To create desirable conditions in the international system, from peace to health to prosperity, international law must address the capacity and the will of domestic governments to respond to these issues at their sources. In turn, the primary terrain of international law must shift—and is already shifting in many instances—from independent regulation above the national state to direct engagement with domestic institutions. The three principal forms of such engagement are strengthening domestic institutions, backstopping them, and compelling them to act.

The most striking feature of this conception of international law is a direct emphasis on shaping or influencing political outcomes within sovereign states in accordance with international legal rules. Even in 1945, the drafters of the U.N. Charter still maintained the classical position that international law and institutions shall not "intervene in matters which are essentially within the domestic jurisdiction of any state."[5] Today, however, the objectives of international law and the very stability of the international system itself depend critically on domestic choices previously left to the determination of national political processes—whether to enforce particular rules, establish institutions, or even engage in effective governance. By ensuring that national governments actually function in pursuit of collective aims, international law is starting to play a far more active role in shaping these national political choices. Assuming that current political, economic, and technological trends continue, the future effectiveness of international law will turn on its ability to influence and alter domestic politics.

These functions of international law are already well known to the members of the European Union ("EU"). Indeed, in extending membership to ten new countries over the course of the past decade, the EU has relied on EU law as its primary tool of reform and socialization.[6] Even among the original member states, EU institutions continue to perform the types of backstopping, strengthening, and mandating functions described here. Europeans themselves are coming to recognize these uses of law; a new generation of European policy thinkers has openly proclaimed the virtues of the European way of law.[7]

Some may, of course, argue that these new functions of international law have no applicability outside the European context in which they were first embraced.[8] Yet each of the three means through which international law is coming to influence domestic outcomes—strengthening domestic institutions, backstopping national governance, and compelling domestic action—is spreading beyond the Continent.

To the extent that what we describe as the "European way of law" is already evident both within the EU and now in a growing number of other contexts, this Article describes an important reorganization of the means and mechanisms through which international law operates. Our argument goes further, however, by suggesting that these new mechanisms of international law have the power to make the system as a whole far more effective. We therefore move beyond description and prediction to prescription, suggesting ways that the European way of law should become the future of international law writ large.

We also recognize, however, the potential dangers in current trends. As we emphasize in the conclusion, our vision of the principal future functions of international law assumes an intensive interaction between international law and domestic politics. But domestic politicians can manipulate international legal institutions and mandates to serve their own purposes, such as jailing political dissidents as part of complying with a Security Council resolution requiring domestic action against terrorism. More broadly, the basic positivist foundations of international law, requiring states to freely accept such interference in domestic politics, raise the possibility of manipulation and even imposition of such "acceptance" as a result of power disparities.

Part I of this Article identifies a new set of global threats and actual and potential responses, including the EU's uses of law to transform new members "from the inside out." Part II argues that the future relevance, power, and potential of international law lie in its ability to backstop, strengthen, and compel domestic law and institutions. Part III examines the potential pitfalls and dangers of these new functions of international law. Finally, Part IV contrasts our analysis with other recent efforts to blur the boundaries between the international and domestic spheres, noting that what is distinctive about our claim is not the intermingling of two kinds of law, but rather the impact of international law on domestic politics and vice versa.

New Threats, New Responses

Rules can reflect and embody aspirations for a better world. Alternatively, and equally likely, rules respond to concrete problems. The changing nature of international legal rules today responds to a new generation of worldwide problems. The most striking feature of these problems is that they arise from within states rather than from state actors themselves.

Examples abound: the terrorist attacks of September 11, 2001, were launched by a group of nonstate actors operating from within the territory of Afghanistan; the massive ethnic crimes in Rwanda, Congo, and Sudan are, in large part, the product of rebel forces within states; the most dangerous examples of nuclear proliferation can often be attributed to nonstate criminal networks such as those of A. Q. Kahn. The 2004 Report of the Secretary-General's High-Level Panel on Threats, Challenges and Change identifies problems of intrastate origin such as "poverty, infectious disease and environmental degradation . . . civil war, genocide and other large scale atrocities . . . nuclear, radiological, chemical and biological weapons, terrorism, [and] transnational organized crime" as among the core threats facing the international community today.[9]

More often than not, the origins of these threats can be addressed directly only by domestic governments that have the jurisdictional entitlements, police power, and institutional capability to act directly against them. Arresting criminals or terrorists, securing nuclear materials, and preventing pollution are within the traditional province of domestic law. The result is that the external security of many states depends on the ability of national governments to maintain internal security sufficient to establish and enforce national law.

Where states are strong enough to combat these internal threats directly, international law can and must play a critical coordinating role to ensure that governments cooperate in addressing threats before they span borders. Far too frequently, however, domestic governments lack the will or the capacity to adequately respond to these challenges. Since the early 1990s, the number of states unable to effectively govern their territories has increased.[10] As Francis Fukuyama affirms, "[s]ince the end of the Cold War, weak or failing states have arguably become the single most important problem for the international order . . . Weak or failing states commit human rights abuses, provoke humanitarian disasters, drive massive waves of immigration, and attack their neighbors."[11]

Where national governments are unable or unwilling to address the origins of these threats themselves, international law may step in to help build their capacity or stiffen their will. This use of international law moves well beyond both its classical definition, as "the rights subsisting between nations,"[12] and its more modern conception, as, in part, regulating the conduct of states toward their own citizens.[13] Where human rights law identifies a set of clear prohibitions on government behavior, coupled with a set of positive aspirations toward economic, social, and cultural rights, these new international legal rules seek actively to shape not only domestic law but also the domestic political environment to enable and enhance domestic government action. The result is far more invasive, but also potentially transformative. For many countries, ranging from the United States to Russia, from the countries of the Middle East to those of Africa, this new use of international law is also far more frightening.

This new model springs from a conception of international law spreading outward from Europe. The Treaty of Westphalia, ending the bloody Thirty Years War with the principle of *cuius regio, eius religio,*[14] has given way to the Treaty of Rome, ending a century of bloody intra-European wars with a concept of pooled sovereignty that has steadily expanded and deepened in the contemporary EU. As the EU's legal system has evolved, the prime purpose of the European Court of Justice and even of the Commission has been less to create and impose EU law as international law than to spur national courts and regulatory agencies to embrace and enforce EU law as national law.

Moreover, as Mark Leonard writes in his provocative book Why Europe Will Run the 21st Century, "Europe's weapon is the law."[15] He describes Europe's power in the world as "a transformative power,"[16] rooted in a strategy of democratization that is based on requiring candidate countries to "swallow all 80,000 pages of European laws and adapt their own legislation to accommodate them," as well as then accepting continual monitoring by EU officials to ensure that they are in fact living up to their new commitments.[17] The result has been a "rebuilding [of] these countries from the bottom up."[18] Indeed, "[t]he European model is the political equivalent of the strategy of the Jesuits: if you change the country at the beginning, you have it for life."[19]

Note the precise way that European law works in this equation. For all the 80,000 pages of regulations, the EU Council of Ministers and the EU Commission issue directives that specify ends rather than means. It is up to national legislatures and courts to decide precisely how the member state in question will fulfill a particular directive. Once those laws are passed, EU institutions—the Court and the Commission—look over national shoulders to ensure that they actually do what they commit to do. This European way of law is precisely the role that we postulate for international law generally around the world.

Espen Barth Bide, a former state secretary in the Norwegian Foreign Ministry, writes that the "EU 'soft' intervention in the 'domestic affairs' of EU member states is almost an everyday experience."[20] This is the hallmark of EU-style "post-Westphalian sovereignty," described so memorably by

Robert Cooper, a top aide to Javier Solana, in The Breaking of Nations.[21] Eide and other leading European security strategists openly call for the extension of regional "integrative projects" based on the EU in Africa, Latin America, and Asia. The European Security Strategy, proposed by Javier Solana and passed by the European Council in December 2003, fell short of openly embracing this vision, but recognized that the Association of Southeast Asian Nations ("ASEAN"), the Southern Cone Common Market ("MERCOSUR"), and the African Union "make an important contribution to a more orderly world."[22]

Spreading the European way of law beyond Europe, a process that is already underway, requires a broader rethinking of the functions of international law. As in Europe, the focus of a growing number of international rules is no longer interstate relations; it is increasingly governments' capacity and will to act in prescribed ways toward their own peoples. The result is a growing interaction between international law and domestic politics, in ways that have lasting implications for both.

The Future Functions of International Law

The all-too-often inadequate domestic response to transnational threats has three separate but related causes: a lack of domestic governance capacity, a lack of domestic will to act, and new problems that exceed the ordinary ability of states to address. International law has key leverage points to help improve the response of domestic governments in each of these three ways. International legal rules and institutions can enhance the capacity and effectiveness of domestic institutions. If properly designed and structured they can help backstop domestic political and legal groups trying to comply with international legal obligations. Finally, they can even compel or mandate action at the national level in response to a global threat. The following sections will examine each of these ways that international law can and in some cases is beginning to play a new role in domestic governance.

Strengthening Domestic Institutions

A primary limitation of the international system is the weakness of government institutions in so many states all over the world. Due to violence, poverty, disease, corruption, and limited technology or training, national governments all too often lack the resources, skills, and ability to provide adequate solutions to local and transnational problems. Examples are numerous: state failure in Somalia in the early 1990s, devastation from natural catastrophes like the 2004 tsunami, civil wars such as that in Angola from 1998 to 2003, or the rampant corruption all too evident in Russia in the mid-1990s. A 2004 report of the Commission on Weak States and U.S. National Security highlighted as a key national security concern the need to assist states "whose governments are unable to do the things that their own citizens and the international community expect from them: offer protection from internal and external threats, deliver basic health services and education, and provide institutions that respond to the legitimate demands and needs of the population."[23] Improving the capacity of government officials of all sorts—regulators, judges, and legislators—to actually govern is paramount.[24] Francis Fukuyama observes: "For the post-September 11th period, the chief issue for global politics will not be how to cut back on stateness but how to build it up."[25] International law has an important role to play in this process.

A critically important tool in strengthening the institutions of national governments is the formalization and inclusion of "government networks" as mechanisms of global governance. These largely voluntary networks link together domestic governmental officials from different countries in similar fields or spheres of responsibility. Such networks provide an effective means to harness national regulatory systems in the pursuit of common, international goals. Such networks can help harmonize national policies and can support the efforts of domestic officials vis-à-vis their own governments.

These networks of national government officials of all kinds are already operating across borders to regulate individuals and corporations operating in a global economy, combat global crime, and address common problems on a global scale.[26] They perform a range of functions that enhance the effectiveness of domestic governance. They build trust and establish relationships among their participants that create incentives to establish a good reputation and avoid a bad one. They regularly exchange information about their own activities and develop databases of best practices, or, in the judicial sphere, different approaches to common legal issues. Finally, they offer technical assistance and professional socialization to members—whether regulators, judges, or legislators—from less developed nations.

If their existence and capacities were more widely recognized, government networks could do far more to strengthen domestic governance. Building the basic capacity to govern in countries that often lack sufficient material and human resources to pass, implement, and apply laws effectively is itself an important and valuable consequence of government networks. Regulatory, judicial, and legislative networks all engage in capacity-building directly, through training and technical assistance programs, and indirectly, through their provision of information, coordinated policy solutions, and moral support to their members. In effect, government networks communicate to their members everywhere the message that the Zimbabwean chief justice understood when he was under siege and commented, "I am not alone."[27]

The best examples of transnational networks strengthening domestic governance may be in the area of regulatory export. Kal Raustiala offers a number of examples of regulatory export in the securities, environmental, and antitrust areas. According to one securities regulator he interviewed, a prime outcome of U.S. Securities and Exchange Commission networking is the dissemination of "the 'regulatory gospel' of U.S. securities law," including: "strict insider trading rules; mandatory registration with a governmental agency of public securities issues; a mandatory disclosure system; issuer liability regarding registration statements and offering documents; broad antifraud provisions; and government oversight of brokers, dealers, exchanges, etc."[28] In effect, U.S. regulatory agencies make their own jobs easier by offering technical assistance and training to their foreign counterparts, because strong foreign authorities with compatible securities, environmental, and antitrust regimes will effectively extend the reach of U.S. regulators.

The EU has enjoyed similar advantages through the International Competition Network ("ICN"). As a result, a growing number of countries, particularly in Eastern Europe, are copying the EU approach to competition policy rather than the U.S. model. The opening conference of the ICN, led by the head of the German competition agency, was held in Italy in 2002. The network describes itself as "a project-oriented, consensus-based, informal network of antitrust agencies from developed and developing countries that will address antitrust enforcement and policy issues of common interest and formulate proposals for procedural and substantive convergence through a results oriented agenda and structure."[29]

Other examples of such networks strengthening domestic capacity in the economic arena include the Basel Committee on Banking Supervision and the International Organization of Securities Commissioners, which have been influential in enhancing the ability of national governments to regulate securities and maintain independent central banks. The net result of these networks is twofold: first, convergence toward a set of standardized practices at the national level and, second, the creation of greater domestic regulatory capacity in participating nations.

It should not be assumed that regulatory expertise flows only from developed to developing countries. At least in the judicial arena, European and Canadian courts have learned as much from South African and Indian courts as vice versa.[30] Among regulators, local experience with a wide range of problems can count for a great deal in the exchange of best practices.

Governments can do much more to strengthen domestic governance through government networks. For example: strengthening the International

Network for Environmental Cooperation and Enforcement, composed of environmental officials; expanding the inclusivity and representativeness of global financial and leadership networks (such as expanding the G-8 to the G-20); creating a Global Justice Network of justice ministers; creating a Global Human Rights Network of the government officials responsible for human rights conditions; and bringing networks of legislators together under the auspices of the United Nations and other international institutions. Such networks must be provided with both concrete tasks and the resources to accomplish them, enabling states to work together to strengthen both collective and individual governance capacity.

As the front line of authority, national government officials exercise an army of coercive and persuasive powers largely unmatched by international institutions. National governments, by operating through government networks, can bring these same powers to bear on behalf of international legal obligations. They can coerce, cajole, fine, order, regulate, legislate, horse-trade, bully, or use whatever other methods that produce results within their political system. They are not subject to coercion at the transgovernmental level; on the contrary, they are likely to perceive themselves as choosing a specific course of action freely and deliberately. Yet, having decided, for whatever reasons, to adopt a particular code of best practices, to coordinate policy in a particular way, to accept the decision of a supranational tribunal, or even simply to join what seems to be an emerging international consensus on a particular issue, they can implement that decision within the limits of their own domestic power.

The international legal system could harness the power of transgovernmental networks much more effectively than it does currently. For example, international law could more explicitly recognize the role of such networks and the soft regulations they often produce. Hard legal instruments could mandate or facilitate the creation of transnational networks in a range of areas of critical state weakness such as justice and human rights. Where the weakness of a particular government in a functional area poses a threat to international order, the U.N. Security Council could require state participation in such a network. Government networks offer an important tool to improve state capacity. Actors within the international legal system would be well served to partner with such networks and more directly integrate them into larger international legal frameworks.

Once again, the international legal system would be taking a leaf from the EU's book in this regard. Most EU law gets made and implemented through transgovernmental networks of EU officials, from ministers on down. Indeed, Mark Leonard describes the EU as "a decentralised network that is owned by its member-states."[31] Reaching outside the borders of Europe, the EU has sought to extend the network model to the Middle East and North Africa through the Euro-Mediterranean Partnership.

Beyond government networks, Stephen Krasner suggests that international law and institutions can strengthen state capacity by engaging in processes of shared sovereignty with national governments. Such shared sovereignty "involves the creation of institutions for governing specific issue areas within a state—areas over which external and internal actors voluntarily share authority."[32] Examples of these arrangements include the creation of special hybrid courts in Sierra Leone, East Timor, and, possibly, Cambodia, involving a mix of international and domestic law and judges. Similarly, a proposed oil pipeline agreement between Chad and the World Bank would involve shared control and governance. Such shared sovereignty, Krasner claims, can "gird new political structures with more expertise, better-crafted policies, and guarantees against abuses of power" onto weak or failing states.

Even within a more traditional framework, the international legal system can employ a range of mechanisms to strengthen the hand of domestic governments. Legal instruments and codes of international best practices can set standards to give national governments benchmarks for enhancing their own capability.[33] International institutions can provide aid and assistance specifically targeted for the domestic institutions of the recipient state.

International financial institutions such as the International Monetary Fund ("IMF") and the World Bank may play a particularly powerful role in building domestic capacity. Conditionality requirements give these bodies strong influence over domestic outcomes. The IMF's success in enhancing the capabilities of domestic governments is much debated,[34] but the World Bank may have a better track record.[35] Part of the Bank strategy in Africa has been to "put countries in the driver's seat" with a "platform of strong public capacity: capacity to formulate policies; capacity to build consensus; capacity to implement reform; and capacity to monitor results, learn lessons, and adapt accordingly."[36] Whatever their successes and failures to date, the IMF and the World Bank have significant leverage to enhance domestic government capacity. What they need is far more input from borrower countries, or at least reformers and political activists in borrower countries, about how best to achieve this goal.

Incorporating these types of mechanisms into future legal regimes as a means of promoting domestic capacity-building must be an ongoing priority. These mechanisms include building government networks, providing technical assistance, setting benchmarks and standards, or encouraging other forms of co-operation. Abram and Antonia Chayes have explained how this can be done through a "managerial model" of compliance.[37] According to this model, the task of maximizing compliance with a given set of international rules is a task more of management than of enforcement, ensuring that all parties know what is expected of them, that they have the capacity to comply, and that they receive the necessary assistance. To the degree Chayes and Chayes are correct,[38] formal international legal regimes must recognize and promote the capacity-building needs of domestic governance through government networks, technical assistance, benchmarks and standards, or other forms of cooperation.

More broadly, the success of many policies at the international level depends on political choices at the national level, for example, choices concerning the allocation of resources or the establishment of particular institutions. The effectiveness of international law may thus depend on its ability to shape political outcomes and institutional structures within states. At the same time, however, a feedback loop from domestic to international institutions becomes crucial for both accountability and effectiveness. Thus the various mechanisms canvassed above to strengthen domestic government institutions must be carefully designed.

Backstopping Domestic Government

A second means through which international law can foster more effective domestic governance is by backstopping domestic institutions where they fail to act. In some ways, this idea is not new at all, but rather follows from a long intellectual tradition. Without developed international institutions such as the International Criminal Court ("ICC"), cooperation among the criminal justice mechanisms of states provided a primitive form of backstopping by ensuring that some state would prosecute an accused criminal even if the territorial state of the crime failed to act. Indeed, as early as 1625, Hugo Grotius recognized that the domestic courts of various states could backstop one another. Referring to an early form of the prosecute or extradite requirement, Grotius observed: "[I]t seems reasonable, that the State where the convicted Offender lives or has taken Shelter, should, upon Application being made to it, either punish the demanded person according to his Demerits, or else deliver him up to be treated at the Discretion of the injured party."[39] Centuries later, in the early 1920s, M. Maurice Travers developed the concept of "la superposition des compétences legislatives concurrentes," suggesting that the layering of overlapping jurisdiction of a number of states would allow national courts to reinforce one another.[40] What is new today is that international institutions—rather than the national courts of third states—are making a conscious effort to backstop their national counterparts. Structural rules that explicitly seek to further this backstopping function are now embedded in the very statutes of international tribunals and institutions.

The most obvious example of international law as a backstop is the complementarity provision of the Rome Statute of the International Criminal Court. The ICC is designed to operate only where national courts fail to act as a first line means of prosecution. Article 17 of the Rome

Statute provides that the Court shall determine a case is inadmissible if "the case is being investigated or prosecuted by a State which has jurisdiction over it, unless the State is unwilling or unable genuinely to carry out the investigation or prosecution."[41] The ICC can step in and provide a second line of defense in cases where domestic institutions fail "due to a total or substantial collapse or unavailability of its national judicial system,"[42] or where a state is unwilling to prosecute "independently or impartially."[43] In other words, if the United States or Iraq were a member of the ICC and both states proved unable or unwilling to prosecute fully all members of the military involved in the abuses at Abu Ghraib, the ICC would have jurisdiction.

Other forms of international institutional design may similarly result in a backstopping function. In various human rights courts, the requirement that individuals first exhaust local remedies gives states—and particularly their domestic courts—an incentive to reach conclusions acceptable to the international institution so that the international court need not intervene to review the case.[44] Similarly, the dispute resolution mechanisms of the North American Free Trade Agreement ("NAFTA") have served as an international backstop for domestic resolution of antidumping cases.[45] Under NAFTA, international arbitral panels are given the authority to review domestic administrative decisions and can remand decisions back to the issuing agency with guidance on acceptable outcomes. If the agency issues an acceptable ruling, no further action is taken. Yet, if the panels remain unsatisfied with the agency's response, they can issue a further ruling and remand the case yet again. Like the Rome Statute's complementarity regime, this remand procedure gives domestic institutions within NAFTA countries an incentive to act first and to get it right. Where they fail to do so, the international process provides a backstop.

The actual effect of such backstopping provisions in international institutional design is twofold.[46] First, and most obvious, is the provision of a second line of defense when national institutions fail. Second, and potentially more powerful, is the ability of the international process to catalyze action at the national level. This second effect most often occurs when a domestic legal or political process exists that could be utilized, should the domestic government decide to do so, but government officials, or at least some powerful group of such officials, deem that the political or financial costs of domestic action outweigh the benefits. In such cases the existence of an international tribunal with concurrent jurisdiction can provide structural incentives that shift the cost-benefit calculation and result in the use of a domestic process that would otherwise have been neglected. The political benefits of adjudicating matters domestically rather than giving jurisdiction to an international tribunal over which domestic officials have little or no control creates new incentives to act locally.

The ICC already appears to be having such a catalytic effect in two of the first situations it is investigating: the Democratic Republic of Congo, and the Darfur region of Sudan. In the wake of the ICC Prosecutor's 2003 announcement of an investigation in Congo, a range of efforts were initiated by certain elements within the Congolese government to reform the Congolese judiciary so as to be able to assert primacy over the ICC and undertake national proceedings. Similarly, after the Prosecutor opened an investigation in Darfur, local courts, though of questionable legitimacy, were established to initiate domestic proceedings. The ICC Prosecutor has himself suggested that complementarity may encourage domestic prosecutions. As he argued upon his swearing-in as the Court's first Prosecutor, "the absence of trials before this Court, as a consequence of the regular functioning of national institutions, would be a major success."[47]

International legal institutions operating as a backstop need not be limited to purely international courts. Adjudication in foreign domestic courts may likewise enhance the willingness of national judiciaries in territorial states to act themselves. The recent advances by Chilean courts toward the prosecution of Augusto Pinochet is, in part, due to the international community—acting largely through the Spanish and English judiciaries—getting serious about ensuring accountability for his crimes. The prosecution by Spain and the proceedings in England[48]—though they did not result in a conviction—made clear to the Chileans that other options existed if they themselves refused to prosecute and may have bolstered the willingness of Chilean courts to hold Pinochet accountable.

The backstopping effect of international institutions will take different forms and often be case specific. Sometimes, the international institution will generate incentives for domestic governmental authorities to act at home as an alternative to international prosecution. At other times, particularly where powerful actors within a national government lack the political will to act at home, the international institution may alter the balance in a domestic power struggle, strengthening the hand of those national officials who want to act. Alternatively, where the domestic government truly lacks the capacity to act, the international institution can backstop domestic courts by genuinely providing another forum. In any of these situations the international institution directly affects domestic government decisions, changing the incentives for domestic action and providing a second, international, forum for legal action.[49] It becomes a tacit actor in domestic political processes, pressuring national governments to reach specific political outcomes and helping to create the conditions to make them possible.

Compelling Action by National Governments

The effectiveness of international law in responding to new transnational threats will, to an ever greater degree, require the active cooperation of national institutions. Despite the proliferation of international courts and tribunals, national governments have retained the nearly exclusive use of their instruments of coercive authority. In most cases, national governments alone can use the police power, a national judiciary, or the military—the tools necessary to address transnational threats before they grow and spread. In many cases, backstopping and strengthening domestic institutions will be sufficient to ensure that national governments use their power to address present and potential dangers. At times, however, domestic governments may be unwilling to use these institutions, either due to differing perceptions of national interest, a lack of political will, or infighting within governments themselves. In these cases, international law can be effective only by finding new ways to ensure that national governments actually use the tools at their disposal to address such threats before they spread.

International legal rules have long sought to constrain or mandate the behavior of states toward other states and toward other states' citizens. More recently, international treaties have required national governments to enact domestic legislation of various sorts, such as the domestic criminalization of certain transnational acts.[50] The type of compulsion described here, however, specifically directs domestic government institutions to go about what was formerly purely domestic business in particular ways. And it does so not by specific agreement on particular legal obligations that must then be domestically implemented, but rather by establishing general goals and requiring domestic governments to achieve them through a broad range of measures. EU directives work this way; in U.S. law, however, Congress is specifically prohibited from imposing broad general mandates requiring individual states to devise and pass specific legislation to achieve them.[51]

The use of international law to combat terrorism immediately after September 11, 2001, is a prime example of how specific obligations can be imposed on U.N. member states that they can fulfill only by directing domestic institutions to act in specific ways at the national level. U.N. Security Council Resolution 1373, for example, requires states to "prevent the commission of terrorist acts" and "deny safe haven to those who finance [or] plan terrorist acts."[52] The resolution demands, among other things, the domestic criminalization of the financing of terrorism, freezing of terrorist assets by national authorities, use of domestic courts to bring to justice those involved in terrorist acts, and ratification by domestic authorities of relevant anti-terrorism conventions.[53]

The White House describes Resolution 1373 as setting "new, strict standards for all states to meet in the global war against terrorism."[54] Likewise, the International Convention for the Suppression of the Financing of Terrorism ("Financing Convention") and the International Convention for the Suppression of Terrorist Bombing ("Bombing Convention") require states to take concrete domestic action. The Financing Convention obliges states to "take appropriate measures . . . for the . . . seizure of any funds used or allocated for" the financing of terrorism,[55] while the Bombing Convention requires domestic criminalization of terrorist acts and the affirmative use of national judicial institutions to bring to justice the perpetrators of terrorist acts.[56]

Resolution 1373 links both the compelling and strengthening functions of the international legal system. Beyond merely mandating domestic action, the resolution establishes a Counter-Terrorism Committee that is tasked with monitoring the implementation of the resolution and increasing the "ability of States to fight terrorism."[57] The Committee requires regular reporting by states of steps taken to comply with Resolution 1373 and provides expert advice on issues ranging from legislative drafting to customs requirements and policing.[58] Working jointly with international, regional, and sub-regional organizations, the Committee shares "codes, standards and best practices in their areas of competence."[59] In addition, the Committee makes available a database of technical assistance and a team of expert advisors to assist states in compliance.[60] By April 2005, at least one report had been received from all 191 member states; the Secretary-General has described state cooperation with the Committee to date as "unprecedented and exemplary."[61]

The Security Council's recent initiatives in the area of non-proliferation have imposed similar obligations on national governments and their respective sub-state institutions to take affirmative domestic action. Security Council Resolution 1540, for example, requires states to adopt national legislation prohibiting the manufacture or possession of weapons of mass destruction by nonstate actors and to establish export control regulations and physical protection regimes for weapons and related technologies.[62] While not going as far as the creation of the Counter-Terrorism Committee, the Security Council again recognized the importance of capacity-building in ensuring domestic action and invited states to offer assistance and resources to one another.[63] Likewise, functional international organizations such as the International Atomic Energy Agency ("IAEA") have compelled states to act through their own institutions. IAEA Safeguards Agreements with nuclear states, for example, require a national system of materials controls and the use of particular accounting mechanisms.[64]

Admittedly, these new functions of international law may not always provide sufficient leverage to produce desired outcomes of state behavior or consistent compliance with international legal obligations. Particularly where states have purposefully excluded themselves from international institutions or lack the will to comply (such as is arguably the situation with the alleged Iranian nuclear weapons program in 2006), resort to other methods—ranging from diplomatic isolation to economic sanctions and, in extreme cases, the use of military force—may be needed. In such hard cases, the best hope of international law is simply to push states toward participation in international institutions and the international legal system generally so that the functions of international law identified here can take hold and influence state behavior and outcomes.

To effectively respond to new international threats, international legal rules must penetrate the surface of the sovereign state by requiring governments to take specific domestic actions to meet specified targets. Sometimes simple backstopping of national institutions may be sufficient to accomplish this task. In other circumstances, assistance and the bolstering of weak state capacity may be an essential prerequisite. At yet other times, international law may have to actively compel state action. When it does so, it once again seeks to alter the political choices of national governments and to compel states to utilize their national institutions in new ways.

The most effective approach will often involve some combination of all three functions of international law. Leaders and legislators should then be held accountable by both their peers and their publics for whether and how their governments respond.

The Dangers of Using International Law to Shape and Influence Domestic Politics

On one level, using international law to build the will and capacity of states to act domestically offers great opportunities to enhance the effectiveness of the international legal system. National governments will have new incentives to act. Domestic institutions will grow stronger, and can be harnessed in pursuit of international objectives. States can thus respond to transnational threats more effectively and efficiently.

Yet each of the new functions of the international system suggested here—backstopping, strengthening, and compelling—is a double-edged sword. Backstopping national institutions can be counterproductive to the degree states may defer to an international forum as a less politically and financially costly alternative to national action. Well-intentioned efforts to help, often through NGOs as well as international institutions, can end up weakening local government actors by siphoning off both funds and personnel. The process of strengthening domestic institutions, if not properly designed and implemented, can also squeeze out local domestic capacity.[65] Finally, and most dangerously, by compelling national action, the international legal system may undermine local democratic processes and prevent domestic experimentation with alternate approaches.[66]

The most significant danger inherent in these new functions of international law, however, lies in the potential of national governments to co-opt the force of international law to serve their own objectives. One of the modern limits to Westphalian concepts of sovereignty is the obligations imposed by international law—particularly human rights law—on the conduct of states toward their own citizens. Yet, by strengthening state capacity, international law may actually make states more effective at the very repression and abuse the interference challenge seeks to overcome. Similarly, by compelling state action, international law may give national governments new license to undertake otherwise illegal or unjust policies. Where critical values such as human rights and state security are seen to be in conflict, international legal compulsion of policies that favor one value may come at the expense of the other. This tension is particularly problematic where a repressive regime is able to use compulsion at the international level as a cover or an excuse to undertake its own domestic policies that may undermine legitimate opposition groups and violate citizens' rights.

Nowhere is this danger more apparent than in the legal compulsion of counter-terrorism activity. Mary Robinson, former U.N. high commissioner for human rights, observes: "Repressive new laws and detention practices have been introduced in a significant number of countries, all broadly justified by the new international war on terrorism."[67] Similarly, Kim Scheppele has documented the number of exceptions to international and domestic legal protections that states have invoked under the cover of fighting terrorism.[68] Among the worst offenders, according to Human Rights First, are Tanzania, Indonesia, Russia, Pakistan, and Uzbekistan, each of which has undertaken "draconian anti-terrorism laws" that compromise human rights and strengthen the hand of government vis-à-vis opposition groups.[69]

If these new purposes of international law are to be both effective and just, the goal must be to maximize the benefits of the backstopping, strengthening, and compelling functions while avoiding the dangers evident in the counter-terrorism case. The theoretical base of these new functions of international law is that domestic institutions can be used to further international legal objectives. Yet these same institutions can become sources of abuse by national governments. The challenge, then, is to design rules that will harness the strengths of well-functioning domestic institutions while targeting and restricting the reach of abusive ones.

One way of making such distinctions is for international law to consider directly the quality of domestic institutions. States with robust and independent institutions, strong constitutional frameworks, transparent political processes, and embedded systems of checks and balances are least likely to appropriate international law for their own purposes and engage or abuse their newfound power. In these states, domestic legal protections and other institutions within the national government can prevent abuse or counterbalance the strength of other institutions. Abuses will still occur in states with good institutional frameworks; however, the assumption built into institutions like the ICC is that when abuses do occur in a well-governed state, that state's own domestic system will provide an internal correction mechanism. It is these states with independent and transparent domestic institutions that should be most receptive to the new functions of the international legal system. European states, at least, largely bear out this prediction.

The problem, of course, is that it is often the states that lack institutional independence and embedded checks and balances that are most in need of capacity-building or compulsion to address threats and challenges at home before they spread. Where international law does target such states, international rules, regimes, and institutions will have to be designed to address both the capacity and quality of domestic governance. Checks and balances will have to be embedded into the system itself, pushing not only for particular substantive outcomes, but also for legitimate domestic processes to achieve those goals. Similarly, international regimes themselves will have to balance a range of competing values—such as human rights and national security—rather than focus on one particular goal when compelling state action.

Finally, as is already becoming apparent, both this overall conception of international law and the specific functions described here will meet with fierce resistance from states with very strong domestic legal systems, such as the United States, and from many states with very weak legal systems but strong political rulers. European states, as noted above, are accustomed to daily "soft intervention." Other states, however, will be far less comfortable with such intervention. The United States will not be alone here, but it may well find itself with a number of unsavory bedfellows. On the other hand, many European powers may find it more difficult than they expect to promote an EU-inspired model of pooled sovereignty among wary former colonies.

International Law, Domestic Politics

International lawyers and political scientists alike have long been fascinated with the blurring of the boundaries between domestic and international rules and institutions. In 1956, Philip Jessup made a hegemonic move, claiming for international lawyers not only the classic domain of international law, but also "all law which regulates actions or events that transcend national frontiers," which he dubbed "transnational law."[70] Forty-five years later, then-Justice Sandra Day O'Connor, a relative newcomer to the world of international law, observed: "[I]nternational law is no longer confined in relevance to a few treaties and business agreements. Rather, it . . . regulates actions or events that transcend national frontiers."[71]

In political science, James Rosenau has popularized the concept of the "domestic-foreign frontier."[72] On this frontier, "domestic and foreign issues converge, intermesh, or otherwise become indistinguishable."[73] In his conception, whereas a boundary is an imaginary line, a frontier is "a new and wide political space . . . continuously shifting, widening, and narrowing, simultaneously undergoing erosion with respect to many issues and reinforcement with respect to others[.]"[74] What Rosenau finds striking about relations along this frontier is that individuals work out a wide range of solutions to various problems through a mix of domestic and international rules, rather than "through the nation-state system."[75]

Our proposition is actually a quite different one. We endorse the division between domestic and international affairs, at least conceptually. Although it is quite possible, indeed likely, that international law is expanding to include all sorts of rules and institutions that have a hybrid domestic-international character, as well as domestic rules reaching beyond borders, we suggest that traditional public international law, meaning treaties and custom operating among nations in their mutual relations, has a distinct identity and a distinct set of functions. We simply argue that those functions are changing fast.

Our claim "that the future of international law is domestic" refers not simply to domestic law but to domestic politics. More precisely, the future of international law lies in its ability to affect, influence, bolster, backstop, and even mandate specific actors in domestic politics. International rules and institutions will and should be designed as a set of spurs and checks on domestic political actors to ensure that they do what they should be doing anyway, that is, what they have already committed to do in their domestic constitutions and laws.

In this conception, it is perfectly acceptable to continue to distinguish concretely between an "international" and a "domestic" sphere, even as we recognize that the boundary between them has blurred and that they intersect and even conflict in growing ways. Indeed, it is valuable for domestic political actors—the prosecutors trying to bring a former government official to justice, the judges seeking to resist executive pressure to decide a case a particular way, the parliamentary faction trying to fight global warming—to be able to point to a mandate, consequence, or spur from a distinct and separate political space. The result will be ever more elaborate two-level games,[76] but each game will remain on its own board, no matter how complex and dense the links between them.

What must change profoundly, however, is the legitimacy of allowing the architects of international rules and institutions to look within the domestic political sphere of all states actually and hypothetically subject to the rule or institution in question. This scrutiny cannot be undertaken with reference to specific parties and actors in actual states, but rather must be based on data culled from history and the social sciences about the likely incentives of those parties and actors in varying circumstances. The critical question must be how the content of specific rules and the processes and procedures of institutions are likely to interact with, influence, or even change these incentives.

In consequence, the very concept of sovereignty will have to adapt to embrace, rather than reject, the influence of international rules and institutions on domestic political processes. A harbinger of this shift is the new doctrine of the responsibility to protect. The responsibility to protect first emerged from the International Commission on Intervention and State Sovereignty ("ICISS"), headed by former Australian foreign minister Gareth Evans and Special Advisor to the U.N. Secretary-General Mohamed Sahnoun.[77] In December 2001 the ICISS issued an important and influential report entitled "The Responsibility to Protect," which essentially called for updating the U.N. Charter to incorporate a new understanding of sovereignty.[78]

In the Commission's conception, the core meaning of U.N. membership has shifted from "the final symbol of independent sovereign statehood and thus the seal of acceptance into the community of nations,"[79] to recognition of a state "as a responsible member of the community of nations."[80] Nations are free to choose whether or not to sign the Charter; if they do, however, they must accept the "responsibilities of membership flowing from their signature."[81] According to the ICISS, "[t]here is no transfer or dilution of state sovereignty. But there is a necessary re-characterization involved: from sovereignty as control to sovereignty as responsibility in both internal functions and external duties."[82] Internally, a government has a responsibility to respect the dignity and basic rights of its citizens; externally, it has a responsibility to respect the sovereignty of other states.

Further, the ICISS places the responsibility to protect on both the state and on the international community as a whole. The ICISS insists that an individual state has the primary responsibility to protect the individuals within it.[83] However, where the state fails in that responsibility, a secondary responsibility falls on the international community acting through the United Nations. Thus, "where a population is suffering serious harm, as a result of internal war, insurgency, repression or state failure, and the state in question is unwilling or unable to halt or avert it, the principle of non-intervention yields to the international responsibility to protect."[84]

These shifts may seem dramatic; they are certainly bold. But in the view of a group of leading European policy thinkers asked to consider how the EU should respond to the U.N. Secretary-General's High-Level Panel Report on Threats, Challenges, and Change, EU states should go considerably further. They should "[p]romote 'the Responsibility to Protect,' while also reframing the sovereignty debate to cover a principle of both enhancing effective and legitimate sovereignty of weak states, (through international assistance) and conditioning sovereignty on state behavior."[85]

International law and the international community itself are thus coming to have not only the right but in many cases also the obligation to intervene in and influence what were previously the exclusive jurisdiction and political processes of national governments. By strengthening, backstopping, and compelling action at the national level, the international legal system has powerful tools at its disposal to alter domestic political outcomes. The future of international law ultimately depends on the future of international politics: the problems raised and the aspirations generated. If those problems and aspirations arise from within states rather than between them, international law must follow suit to shape and regulate domestic government institutions. But if it is simultaneously to remain a distinct body of international law, it must develop a whole new set of effective relationships with those institutions and with entire bodies of domestic law. The EU is a great experiment with precisely this type of system, although one underpinned by a unique history and culture generating the necessary domestic political will and economic and social forces. The world is not likely to replicate this experience in terms of actual political and economic integration monitored by coercive supranational institutions. But to the extent that the European way of law uses international law to transform and buttress domestic political institutions, it is a model for how international law can function, and in our view, will and must function to address twenty-first-century international challenges.

Notes

1. This approach is closely linked to the monist view of international law. Monists argue that international law and domestic law are part of the same system, in which international law is hierarchically prior to domestic law. Dualists, in contrast, claim that international and domestic law are part of two distinct systems and that domestic law is generally prior to international law. *See generally* J. G. Starke, Monism and Dualism in the Theory of International Law, 17 BRIT. YB. INT'L. L. 66 (1936). While both of these theories provide important linkages between international law and domestic law, for adherents of either approach the functions and institutions of international law remain largely at the international level.

2. See Mavromatis Palestine Concessions (Greece v. Gr. Brit.), 1924 P.C.I.J. (ser. A) No. 2, at 12 (Aug. 30). Yet the decision of a state to espouse its citizen's claim is one of domestic politics—the state has no obligation to do so. International law does, however, regulate the right of the state to espouse an individual claim, limiting such rights to cases of "close connection," usually in the form of "real and effective nationality" between the state and the citizen. *See, e.g.*, Nottebohm Case (Liech. v. Guat.), 1955 I.C.J. 4 (Apr. 6).

3. *See generally* Anne-Marie Slaughter & William Burke-White, An International Constitutional Moment, 43 Harv. INT'L. J. 1(2002).

4. *See, e.g.*, STEPHEN D. KRASNER, SOVEREIGNTY: ORGANIZED HYPOCRISY 20 (1999).

5. U.N. Charter art. 2, para. 7.

6. *See generally* MARK LEONARD, WHY EUROPE WILL RUN THE 21ST CENTURY 43–46 (2005).

7. *See, e.g., id.;* Gráinne de Búrca, Beyond the Charter: How Enlargement Has Enlarged the Human Rights Policy of the European Union, 27 FORDHAM INT'L. J. 679, 680 (2004) (arguing that a similar role of law is generating a "more general and comprehensive human rights policy" within the EU).

8. *See, e.g.,* Eric Posner & John Yoo, Reply to Heifer and Slaughter, 93 CAL. L. REV. 957, 966 (2005) ("There is no reason to think that a court that works for Europe, where political and legal institutions in most countries are of high quality, would work for a world political community that lacks the same level of cohesion and integration. Whatever one thinks about the EU, it is nothing like the international community.").

9. Secretary-General's High-Level Panel on Threats, Challenges and Change, A More Secure World: Our Shared Responsibility 2, U.N. Doc. A/59/565 (Dec. 2, 2004).

10. *See* JEREMY W. WEINSTEIN ET AL., ON THE BRINK, WEAK STATES AND US NATIONAL SECURITY: A REPORT OF THE COMMISSION FOR WEAK STATES AND US NATIONAL SECURITY 9–12 (2004) (describing recent incidences of state failure).

11. FRANCIS FUKUYAMA, STATE BUILDING: GOVERNANCE AND WORLD ORDER IN THE 21ST CENTURY 92–93 (2004).

12. Emmerich de Vattel described international law in the 1750s as "the rights subsisting between nations or states, and the obligations correspondent to those rights." EMMERICH DE VATTEL, THE LAW OF NATIONS Preliminaries § 3 (Joseph Chitty et al. trans. & ed. 1883) (1758).

13. *See generally* Slaughter & Burke-White, *supra* note 3.

14. "Whose territory, his religion."

15. LEONARD, *supra* note 6, at 35.

16. *Id.* at 5 (quoting Richard Youngs, Engagement: Sharpening European Influence, in GLOBAL EUROPE REPORT 2: NEW TERMS OF ENGAGEMENT 1, 5 (Richard Youngs ed., 2004)).

17. LEONARD, *supra* note 6, at 45.

18. *Id.* Others have suggested that these changes are, at times, imposed instead from the top down, and may be indicative of a democratic deficit in the EU. *See, e.g.,* Giandomenico Majone, Europe's Democratic Deficit: A Question of Standards, 4 EUR. L. J. 5(1998) (observing that the "democratic deficit. . . refers to the legitimacy problems of non-majoritarian institutions, i.e., institutions which by design are not directly accountable to the voters or to their elected representatives"); Jeremy Rabkin, Is EU Policy Eroding the Sovereignty of Non-Member States?, 1 CHI. J. INT'L L. 273, 273 (2000) (arguing that the EU is based on a "systematic program of eroding or reconfiguring national sovereignty"). For a perspective on the EU that rejects the danger of the democratic deficit and accords more closely with our vision, see Andrew Moravcsik, In Defense of the Democratic Deficit: Reassessing Legitimacy in the European Union, 40 J. COMMON MARKET STUD. 603 (2002).

19. LEONARD, *supra* note 6, at 45–46.

20. Espen Barth Eide, Introduction: The Role of the EU in Fostering "Effective Multilateralism" in EFFECTIVE MULTILATERALISM: EUROPE, REGIONAL SECURTY AND A REVITALIZED UN 1, 1–10 (Espen Barth Eide ed., 2004).

21. *See generally* ROBERT COOPER, THE BREAKING OF NATIONS: ORDER AND CHAOS IN THE 21ST CENTURY (2003).

22. JAVIER SOLANA, A SECURE EUROPE IN A BETTER WORLD—THE EUROPEAN SECURITY STRATEGY 9(2003), http://ue.eu.int/uedocs/cmsUpload/78367.pdf.

23. WEINSTEIN ET AL., *supra* note 10, at 6.

24. For a discussion of the importance of building state capacity, *see* PROBLEMATIC SOVEREIGNTY: CONTESTED RULES AND POLITICAL POSSIBILITIES (Stephen Krasner ed., 2001).

25. FUKUYAMA, *supra* note 11, at 120.

26. *See generally* ANNE-MARIE SLAUGHTER, A NEW WORLD ORDER (2004).

27. SLAUGHTER, *supra* note 26, at 99.

28. Kal Raustiala, Rethinking the Sovereignty Debate in International Economic Law, 6 J. INT'L ECON. L. 841, 843 (2003).

29. International Competition Network, Memorandum on the Establishment and Operation of the International Competition Network, http://www.internationalcompetitionnetwork.org/mou.pdf (last visited Feb. 26, 2006).

30. For a general discussion, *see* SLAUGHTER, *supra* note 26, at 65–103.

31. LEONARD, *supra* note 6, at 23 (citing MANUEL CASTELLS, THE END OF MILLENNIUM (2000)).

32. Stephen D. Krasner, Building Democracy After Conflict: The Case for Shared Sovereignty, 16 J. DEMOCRACY, Jan. 2005, at 69, 76.

33. In the field of judicial independence, the International Covenant on Civil and Political Rights provides a set of such benchmarks. *See* International Covenant on Civil and Political Rights arts. 9–11, Dec. 16, 1966, 999 U.N.T.S. 171. Additionally, the Rome Statute of the International Criminal Court offers further clarification and a potential legal testing ground. Rome Statute of the International Criminal Court art. 17, July 17, 1998, 2187 U.N.T.S. 90 [hereinafter Rome Statute].

34. For two sides of this debate, *see* RANDALL STONE, LENDING CREDIBILITY: THE INTERNATIONAL MONETARY FUND AND THE POST-COMMUNIST TRANSITION 233–34 (2002) (arguing that IMF conditionality is appropriate and beneficial) and JAMES VREELAND, THE IMF AND ECONOMIC DEVELOPMENT 160–65 (2003) (suggesting that IMF conditionality may retard domestic development).

35. *See* Poul Engberg-Pedersen & Brian Levy, Building State Capacity in Africa: Learning from Performance and Results, in BUILDING STATE CAPACITY IN AFRICA: NEW APPROACHES, EMERGING LESSONS 87 (Brian Levy & Sahr Kpundeh eds., 2004) (discussing the role of the World Bank in enhancing state capacity in Africa); *see also* Joel D. Barkan et al., Emerging Legislatures: Institutions of Horizontal Accountability, in BUILDING STATE CAPACITY IN AFRICA: NEW APPROACHES, EMERGING LESSONS 233–34 (Brian Levy & Sahr Kpundeh eds., 2004) (discussing increased awareness across anglophone Africa of development in peer legislatures as a possible result of World Bank initiatives).

36. Frannie A. Léautier & Callisto Madavo, Foreword to BUILDING STATE CAPACITY IN AFRICA: NEW APPROACHES, EMERGING LESSONS, at v (Brian Levy & Sahr Kpundeh eds., 2004).

37. ABRAM CHAYES & ANTONIA HANDLER CHAYES, THE NEW SOVEREIGNTY 3(1995).

38. This model is distinct both in underlying assumptions and in the resultant variables that govern state compliance from carrot-and-stick or norm-socialization approaches. *See, e.g.*, George W. Downs et al., ***Is the Good News about Compliance***

Good News about Cooperation? 50 INT'L ORG. 379 (1996) (offering a carrot-and-stick model); Ryan Goodman & Derek Jinks, International Law and State Socialization: Conceptual, Empirical, and Normative Challenges, 54 DUKE L.J. 983 (2005) (linking compliance to state socialization); Harold H. Koh, Transnational Legal Process, 75 NED. L. REV. 181 (1996) (suggesting the importance of norm internalization). These alternate theories of compliance produce considerably different prescriptions for how international law may best alter state behavior.

39. 2 HUGO GROTIUS, THE RIGHTS OF WAR AND PEACE 1062 (Richard Tuck trans., Liberty Fund (2005) (1625).

40. M. MAURICE TRAVERS, LE DROIT PENAL INTERNATIONAL ET SA MISE EN OEUVRE EN TEMPS DE PAIX ET EN TEMPS DE GUERRE (1922). The key to Travers' argument is that concurrent legislative authority could, in turn, empower the judicial institutions of,a number of states to act against any given criminal and thereby create overlapping judicial authority without the need for a formal international tribunal.

41. Rome Statute, *supra* note 45, art. 17 (1).

42. *Id.* art. 17 (3).

43. *Id.* art. 17 (2).

44. Article 35 of the European Convention on Human Rights provides that "[t]he Court may only deal with the matter after all domestic remedies have been exhausted," European Convention for the Protection of Human Rights and Fundamental Freedoms art. 35(1), Nov. 4, 1950, Europ. T.S. No. 5, 213 U.N.T.S. 222; see also Organization of American States, American Convention on Human Rights art. 46, Nov. 22, 1969, O.A.S.T.S. No. 36, 1144 U.N.T.S. 123 (providing, "[a]dmission by the Commission of a petition or communication lodged in accordance with Articles 44 or 45 shall be subject to the following requirements . . . that the remedies under domestic law have been pursued and exhausted in accordance with generally recognized principles of international law").

45. The 1988 Canadian-American Free Trade Agreement and the more recent NAFTA both contain provisions for the creation of international panels to review the legality of administrative decisions with respect to antidumping and countervailing duty obligations.

46. The potential for international institutions to produce these backstopping effects will often depend on the international institution having jurisdiction over the state in question or individuals within that state. After all, these effects then arise as a result of the threat of potential international adjudication. Where national governments have refused to accept the jurisdiction of international courts, such effects will be limited.

47. Louis Moreno-Ocampo, Chief Prosecutor, ICC, Statement at the Ceremony for the Solemn Undertaking of the Chief Prosecutor of the International Criminal Court (June 16, 2003), http://www.icc-cpi.int/library/organs/otp/030616_moreno_ocampo_english_final.pdf.

48. *See* Regina v. Bow St. Metro Stipendiary Magistrate, ex parte Pinochet Ugarte (No. 3), [2000] 1 A.C. 147 (H.L. 1999).

49. Obviously, where the state in question has rejected the authority of the international tribunal or failed to ratify its Statute, such as the U.S. policy toward the ICC, none of these effects may materialize.

50. For example, many treaties in the area of international criminal law require criminalization of certain behavior at the national level. *See, e.g.*, Convention on the Prevention and Punishment of the crime of Genocide art. 5, Dec. 9, 1948,78 U.N.T.S. 277; Convention Against Torture and Other Cruel, Inhuman, or Degrading

Treatment or Punishment art. 4, Dec. 10, 1984, S. Treaty Doc. No. 100-20 (1988), 1465 U.N.T.S. 113.

51. New York v. United States, 505 U.S. 144, 161 (1992) (quoting Hodel v. Virginia Surface Mining & Reclamation Ass'n, 452 U.S. 264, 288 (1981)) (holding Congress may not "commandee[r] the legislative processes of the States by directly compelling them to enact and enforce a federal regulatory program").

52. S.C. Res. 1373, ¶ 2(c)-(d), U.N. Doc. S/RES/1373 (Sept. 28, 2001).

53. *Id.*

54. THE WHITE HOUSE, NATIONAL STRATEGY FOR COMBATING TERRORISM 13 (2003), http://www.whitehouse.gov/news/releases/2003/02/counter_terrorism/counter_terrorism_strategy.pdf.

55. International Convention for the Suppression of the Financing of Terrorism, G.A. Res. 54/109, ¶ 8, U.N. Doc. A/RES/54/109 (Dec. 9, 1999).

56. International Convention for the Suppression of Terrorist Bombings, G.A. Res. 52/164, ¶¶ 5–7, U.N. Doc. A/RES/52/164 (Dec. 15, 1997).

57. Security Council Counter-Terrorism Committee, http://www.un.org/sc/ctc/ (last visited Feb. 26, 2006).

58. CTC: About the CTC—How Does the CTC Work with States?, http://www.un.org/Docs/sc/ committees/1373/work.html (last visited Feb. 26, 2006).

59. CTC: Assistance to States—Working Together to Raise State Capacity, http;//www.un.org/Docs/sc/committees/1373/capacity.html (last visited Feb. 26, 2006).

60. CTC: Assistance to States—How Can the CTC Help States?, http://www.un.org/Docs/sc/committees/1373/help.html (last visited Feb. 26, 2006).

61. *Id.*

62. S.C. Res. 1540, ¶ 2, U.N. Doc. S/RES/1540 (Apr. 28, 2004).

63. *Id.* ¶ 7.

64. *See, e.g.*, Agreement Between the United States of America and the International Atomic Energy Agency for the Application of Safeguards in the United States, Nov. 18, 1977, 32.3 U.S.T. 3059.

65. Fukuyama argues that "[t]he international community, including the vast numbers of NGOs that are an intimate part of it, comes so richly endowed and full of capabilities that it tends to crowd out rather than complement the extremely weak state capacities of the targeted countries." See FUKUYAMA, *supra* note 14, at 103.

66. For a discussion of the importance of such domestic experimentation, see Michael C. Dorf & Charles F. Sabel, A Constitution of Democratic Experimentalism, 98 COLUM. L. REV. 267 (1998).

67. Mary Robinson, Shaping Globalization: The Role of Human Rights, 19 AM. U. INT'L L. REV. 1, 12 (2003).

68. Kim L. Scheppele, Law in a Time of Emergency: States of Exception and the Temptations of 9/11, 6 U. PA. J. CONST. L. 1001 (2000).

69. HUMAN RIGHTS FIRST, IMBALANCE OF POWERS: HOW CHANGES TO U.S. LAW AND POLICY SINCE 9/11 ERODE HUMAN RIGHTS AND CIVIL LIBERTIES 76–79 (2003).

70. PHILLIP JESSUP, TRANSNATIONAL LAW 2 (1956).

71. Sandra Day O'Connor, Keynote Address at the Ninety-Sixth Annual Meeting of the American Society of International Law (Mar. 16, 2002), in 96 AM. SOC'Y INT'L L. PROC. 348, 350 (2002).

72. Rosenau observes that "[d]omestic and foreign affairs have always formed a seamless web . . . [We] can no longer allow the domestic-foreign boundary to confound our understanding of world affairs." JAMES N. ROSENAU, ALONG THE

DOMESTIC-FOREIGN FRONTIER: EXPLORING GOVERNANCE IN A TURBULENT WORLD 4 (1997).

73. *Id.* at 5.

74. *Id.* at 4–5 (emphasis added).

75. *See id.* at 5–6; see also Mathias Albert & Lothar Brock, Debordering the World of States: New Space in International Relations, 35 NEW POL. SCI. 69 (1996).

76. *See generally* Robert Putnam, Diplomacy and Domestic Politics: The Logic of Two-Level Games, 42 INT'L ORG. 427 (1988).

77. In September 1999, Kofi Annan called on all U.N. members at the opening of the General Assembly to "reach consensus—not only on the principle that massive and systematic violations of human rights must be checked, wherever they take place, but also on ways of deciding what action is necessary, and when, and by whom." Kofi Annan, Two Concepts of Sovereignty, Address Before the U.N. General Assembly (Sept. 20, 1999), in KOFI ANNAN, THE QUESTION OF INTERVENTION: STATEMENTS BY THE SECRETARY-GENERAL (1999).

78. INT'L COMM'N ON INTERVENTION AND STATE SOVEREIGNTY, THE RESPONSIBILITY TO PROTECT: REPORT OF THE ICISS (2001). The ICISS began from the premise that "in key respects. . . the mandates and capacity of international institutions have not kept pace with international needs or modern expectations." *Id.* ¶ 1.11. More specifically, the ICISS argued that the intense debate over military protection for humanitarian purposes flowed from a "critical gap" between the immense and unavoidable reality of mass human suffering and the existing rules and mechanisms for managing world order. At the same time, it noted a widening gap between the rules and the principles of the Charter regarding non-interference in the domestic affairs of member nations and actual state practice as it has evolved since 1945. The ICISS frames the "responsibility to protect" as an "emerging principle" of customary international law—not yet existing as law but already supported both by state practice and a wide variety of legal sources. *See id.* ¶¶ 2.24–2.27.

79. *Id.* ¶ 2.11.

80. *Id.* ¶ 2.14.

81. *Id.*

82. *Id.*

83. *See id.* ¶ 2.29.

84. *Id.* @ XI.

85. Eide, *supra* note 20, at 9.

Index

ABM Treaty, 426, 432
Abu Ghraib, 476
Ad Hoc Committee on the Peaceful Uses of Outer Space, 425–426
Afghanistan, 254, 268, 278–279
African Union, 124, 242, 304–306, 470; African Charter on Human and Peoples' Rights, 121, 303–304; Assembly of Heads of State and Government, 303–304
Agreements: administrative capacity and, 150; arms control, 36–38; behavior within, 157; binding, 38; compliance with, 143–159; constraints on policy in, 150; defection from, 157; dispute settlement and, 143; domestic politics and, 149; endogeneity of, 157; international, 43–159; interpretations of, 146; legitimacy of, 149; multilateral, 101, 102; need for, 144; nonbinding, 39; obligations and, 145; precision of, 39; undoing, 41
Air Pollution Convention, Long Range Transboundary, 175
Akehurst, Michael, 66
Alien Tort Claims Act, 94, 170, 175
Al Qaeda, 270, 278–279
American Association for the International Commission of Jurists, 186–187
American Convention on Human Rights, 300–301, 310
American Declaration of the Rights and Duties of Man, 88, 130, 299, 301, 310, 317
Amin, Idi, 319
Amnesties, 189, 196, 198
Angola, 470
Annan, Kofi, 127, 171, 223, 324
Antarctica, 124, 379, 395, 440
Anti-Ballistic Missile Treaty, 426, 432
Anti-Dumping Agreement, 34, 476
Anti-fraud positions, 472
Apartheid, 68, 196, 293–295
Aristotle, 282
Arms control, 27, 36–38, 361
Arms trafficking, 278
Asia-Pacific Economic Cooperation forum (APEC), 27
Association of South East Asian Nations (ASEAN), 344, 470
Austria, 275, 291, 310
Authority: coercive, 478; delegated, 21, 31, 33, 34; interpretive, 24; legal, 11, 25, 34, 117, 147, 292, 331; legitimate, 331–332; moral, 117; political, 253; supranational, 143

Bacteriological Convention, 272
Ballistic missile defense systems, 37
Barcelona Traction case, 92, 375
Basel Committee on Banking Supervision, 472
Belarus, 63
Belgium, 10, 63, 174–175, 207
Biological diversity: conservation of, 372; economic values and, 384–385;

equitable sharing of benefits from, 372; global responsibility for, 373; international laws and, 371–396; liability of states for, 371–379; options values, 385; poverty and, 385; precautionary principle in law of, 379–393; protections of, 16, 390; scientific value, 385; state responsibility for, 371, 374–379; sustainable use of, 372; transboundary impact of loss of, 385
Biological Diversity, Convention on, 373
Bodin, Jean, 219
Bosnia, 1, 208, 321; *Bosnia and Herzegovina v. Serbia and Montenegro Genocide Convention* case, 205; Serb Army of Republika Srpska (VRS), 208
Brazil, 350
Brundtland Commission, 384, 388, 435
Bryan-Chamorro Treaty, 79–80
Buenos Aires International Instrument on Protection of Environment from Space Debris, 434
Burma (Myanmar), 16, 170

Cambodia, 237, 319, 474
Canada, 8, 231, 302, 394, 406, 413
Capital flows, 101
Caribbean nations, 302
Carter administration, 310–311
Chechens, 63
Chemical Weapons Convention, 272
Chernobyl accident, 348
China, 41, 63, 224, 351, 414; Taipei, 224
Civil Liability for Oil Pollution Damage, International Convention on, 397n15
Civil service, 102, 103, 106
Civil society: actors in, 8, 225; elements of, 171; ICC and, 242; intergovernmental groups and, 170; NGOs and, 128, 171, 242; threats to, 172
Climate change, 107, 276, 311; conventions, 341, 440; emission targets, 350; free rider, 83; Helsinki Accords, 6; MEAs and, 345; multilateral regimes, 85; reports on, 360; research on, 432
Coherence, 59, 60
Cold War, 1, 171, 296, 359; European Convention, 298; failing states, 468; peace settlements, 58; UN Charter system, 176
Colombia, 270
Commission on Human Rights, 88, 300–301
Commons, global, 101; benefits of, 16; ecosystems and, 379; exploitation of, 429; laws of, 16; management of, 2, 15; threats to, 101; tragedy of, 347, 349, 358, 402
Commonwealth Secretariat, 276
Communications: and globalization, 5; International Telecommunication Convention, 433; International Telecommunication Union, 442; interstate, 302, 304; and NGOs, 126
Compliance: with arbitration, 153; with authoritative decisions, 146; defining, 145; democracy and, 152; domestic regime-based explanations for, 144; effectiveness and, 145; with environmental accords, 150, 152; first order, 146; identification of, 144; interest-driven approaches, 148; with international agreements, 143–159; international relations theory and, 146–156; meaning of, 145–146; measurement of, 145–146; moral force and, 153; nature of domestic regime and, 151–152; normative approaches to, 144, 152–156; rational functionalism and, 144, 147–149, 154; realist tradition, 144, 146–147; reputation and, 148; second order, 146; selection bias and, 157, 158; with substantive rules, 146; values of, 150
Conference on Security and Cooperation in Europe, 10
Congo, Democratic Republic of the (DRC), 86–87; Mouvement de liberation du Congo, 208; *v. Rwanda,* 211
Conservation: achieving, 380; aesthetics, 373; of African habitat, 345; biological diversity, 371–396; global, 373, 387; goals of, 386; fisheries, 412; polar bears, 355; treaties, 386, 392; whales, 353

Constitutionalism, 102
Constitutions, 3–4, 175, 309, 483
Continental Shelf Convention, 402, 406
Contracting: costs in soft law, 31–33; delegation and, 30; incomplete, 21, 28, 31
Conventions: Against Torture and Other Cruel, Inhuman or Degrading Treatments, 25, 163, 165, 196–199, 206, 271, 294; anti-terrorism, 110; codification, 49; on Fishing and Conservation of the Living Resources of the High Seas, 402; on International Trade in Endangered Species (CITES), 25, 131, 345, 353, 355, 357; on the Protection of the Rhine Against Pollution by Chlorides, 355
Corfu Channel case, 387–388
Costa Rica, 80, 301, 310
Council of Europe, 107, 276, 311; anti-terrorism and, 273; Convention for Protection of National Minorities, 35; environment and, 344; European court and, 299; human rights and, 298
Court of First Instance, 210, 214
Crimes: accountability for, 185; aggression, 195; drug trafficking, 270, 275, 324; genocide, 188, 196; against humanity, 185, 188, 195, 271, 272, 280; impunity for commission of, 185; international, 188; national jurisdiction, 185; organized, 270, 468; against peace, 188, 195; piracy, 188, 195; rape, 120, 241, 270, 326, 328; serious, 188; sexual slavery or violence, 241; slavery, 188, 195; torture, 188, 196; transnational, 274; universal jurisdiction, 185–200. *See also* War crimes
Criminal law: accountability and, 188, 191; amnesties and, 189; dispute settlement, 191; double jeopardy and, 189–190; due process and, 187; extradition and, 187, 190; immunity and, 188, 196, 197; prosecutions, 198–199; protections for accused, 199; statutes of limitations, 185, 197
Cuba, 300
Custom: action and, 50; balancing fit and substance in, 59–60; binding, 50, 54, 62; breaches of, 61; changes in, 60–62; content of, 58; decline of, 7; deductive process in, 50; defense of, 52; defining, 49; dependence on, 51; descriptive approach, 52–56; dinosaur approach, 50–51; dynamo approach, 50–51; emergence of, 62; as evidence of general practice accepted as law, 49; existence of, 58; facilitative, 53–55; fluid nature of, 60–65; integrity as source of law, 51–52; in international law, 49–68; in international organizations, 112; interpretive process and, 52; on interpretive sliding scale, 57–59; intervention and, 64; justifications for, 56; legitimacy of, 50; modern, 49–52; moral, 53–55, 61; multiple interpreters of, 58; normative approach, 52–56; *opinio juris* and, 49, 56, 58, 61, 66; as primitive source of law, 60; as reflective interpretive concept, 59–65; as significant source of law, 49; slow growth of, 61; state practice and, 49, 50, 56, 58, 66; traditional, 49–52, 54
Cyberspace, 16–17; free speech in, 459–460; geographic filtering of, 460–461; interstate and intrastate nature of, 459; lawsuit proliferation, 461–462; sovereignty, 458–459
Czechoslovakia, 291

Darfur, 16, 239, 241, 296, 321, 477
Decisionmaking: collective, 351; fragmentation of, 172; interactions in, 176; participants in, 1, 4, 10; procedures in, 5; regime theory and, 5; supranational, 144
Decolonization, 277
Demandeurs, 28–29
Democide, 319
Democracy: importance for law compliance, 152; international obligations and, 151; liberal, 152; NGOs and, 152
Developing countries: financing biodiversity conservation projects in, 373; lack of resources to deal with interstate cooperation, 275

Development: benefits of, 224; compliance and, 148; economic, 311, 322, 373, 436; GATT and, 224; high seas regime and, 416; institutional, 36, 124, 290–291; interstate cooperation and, 275; national, 371; permanent sovereignty and, 83, 390; poverty and, 385; space and, 428 441; technological, 16, 359. *See also* Sustainable development
Diplomacy, 106, 125
Discourse, 26
Doha Round, 163
Drug trafficking, 270, 275
Dualist concept of law, 249–256

East Pakistan, 63
East Timor, 321, 477
Economic: actors, 349; concessions, 24; development, 311, 322, 373, 436; disincentives, 418; disparity, 15; embargo, 281; globalization, 78, 270; indicators, 359; law, 104; liabilities, 260; policy, 132; regulation, 143, 148; remedies, 327; sanctions, 296, 311, 329, 335, 350, 361; state responsibility, 144; strategies, 327; treaties, 11, 105; violence, 236
Economic and Social Rights, Covenant on, 14
Eichmann, Adolph, 193
Elimination of All Forms of Racial Discrimination, International Covenant on the, 294
Elimination of Discrimination against Women, Convention on, 109
El Salvador, 308
Enterprise in the Law of the Sea Convention, 34, 111
Environment: pollution control, 436; protection of, 54; wet lands, 355, 371. *See also* Conservation
Environmental law: duty and damages for breach model, 379; evolution of, 382; good neighbor principle, 178; jurisdictional issues, 379; legal obligations to, 395; legitimacy and, 128; liability definitions in, 378, 379; NGOs and, 121; norms, 395; principle in, 379–393, 436–438
Erga omnes, 78, 87–88, 91–93, 375, 377
Espoo Convention on Environmental Impact Assessment in a Transboundary Context, 394
EU. *See* European Union
European Community, 212, 224, 227, 414; legislative institutions in, 30; supranational incorporation within, 25
European Convention on Human Rights, 30–31, 174, 207–208, 297, 302, 310; *Al-Adsani* case, 207, 210, 215
European Court of Justice, 25, 143, 210, 469
European Economic Community, 224
European Monetary Union, 150
European System of Human Rights, 105
European Union (EU), 107, 148; E-commerce directive, 462; ICC and, 242; legal institutions of, 25; as solid state, 220; treaties, 107, 173
European way of law, 467–485
Exclusive Economic Zone (EEZ), 34, 405
Extradition, 187, 194

Fishing, driftnet, 170
Food and Agriculture Organization, 7, 232, 386
Force, use of, 54; arbitration of, 147; goals of use, 254; as last resort, 32; legality, 68, 254; military, 13, 166, 176, 250, 253, 322, 327–329; moral, 54, 59, 153–154; post-Charter obligations, 13–14, 176, 292, 322; prohibition on, 53, 64; recourse to, 215, 249, 322; regional, 155; regulation of, 2, 14, 262; rules on, 16; self-defense, 279; unlawful, 254
Framework Convention for Tobacco Control, 170
Framework Convention on Climate Change, 6, 440
France, 63; International Space Agency, 442; intervention in Iraq, 63; trials *in absentia*, 199; WTO, 231; Yahoo lawsuit, 457–460
Free rider, 83
Furundzija case, 84

General Agreement on Tariffs and Trade (GATT), 11, 37, 111, 143, 157, 221–235; *acquis*, 222; Agreement

Establishing the World Trade Organization, 11; compliance and, 149; contracting parties and, 221; dispute resolution and, 143; enforcement of, 149; expansion of trade and, 37; jurisprudence issues, 229–230; provisions of, 149, 229, 231; trade disputes and, 157; Uruguay Round, 105
General Agreement on Trade and Services, 111
Geneva Conventions, 195; application of, 251; basis of, 277; breaches of, 208, 237, 282; high seas law and, 271; torture and, 271; UN Charter and, 258–259; war crimes and, 195
Genocide, 53, 62, 64, 65, 185; in Princeton Principles, 188
Genocide Convention: breaches of, 83, 237; as control test, 208; European Convention and, 298; Germany, 63; ICJ and, 87, 164, 209; NATO and, 62–63; Nazi, 157–158, 237, 277; state regulation and, 271; *strict sensu,* 252; torture and, 270
Global Compact, 101
Global Environmental Facility (GEF), 129–130, 386
Global Human Rights Network, 129–130, 386
Globalization: beginnings of, 270; characteristics of, 270; economics and, 270; environment and, 359; nature of, 106; pressures of, 466; terrorism and, 270, 273; treaty making and, 106; United Nations and, 78
Global Justice Network, 473
Global warming, 38, 483
Greece, 90
Greenhouse gasses, 163, 432
Greenpeace, 360
Grotius, Hugo, 247, 255, 376, 401–403, 475
Grotius de jure belli ac pacis, 247, 255
Guatemala, 89, 308

Hague Conventions, 251–252, 307, 402, 437
Hague Peace Conferences, 125
Hard law: contracting problems and, 21; cost of reneging and, 24; credibility of commitments and, 21, 23–27; dealing with uncertainty and, 37–40; dispute resolution and, 28; enforcement of commitments and, 27–29; incomplete contracting and, 30–31; interaction and, 27, 28; international law, 21–44; legally binding obligations of, 21; modification of political strategies and, 29–30; negotiation and, 28; rationales for, 23–31; reductions of transaction costs in, 21; restrictions of actor behavior and, 22; sovereignty and, 22, 33–37; specialized legal institutions in, 29; transaction costs and, 27–29
Helsinki Accords, 6, 10
Helsinki Declaration, 438
Helsinki Final Act, 39
Helsinki Watch, 171
High Seas Convention, 402
Hijacking, 110–111, 272
Holocausts, 291, 332
Honduras, 80, 278
Humanitarian Military Intervention: authorization for, 331; history of, 321–322; responsibility to protect, 15–16, 253, 320, 324–329, 484; right to intervene, 15, 321, 326; right to rebuild, 253, 327; state sovereignty and, 323–327; success, 330–331; UN Charter framework, 322–332; UN role in, 331
Human Rights, International Covenants on, 293, 303, 310
Human Rights Systems: achievements of, 296–297; African system, 303–306; in domestic legal orders, 309–310; European system, 297–299; human rights machinery in, 290; Inter-American system, 299–303; International Criminal Tribunal and, 306; in international relations, 310–311; NGOs and, 308–309; regional human rights system, 296–297; treaty-based, 294–295; Truth Commission and, 306–307; UN Charter's role, 295–296; UN Security Council's role, 291–293

IAEA. *See* International Atomic Energy Agency

ICC. *See* International Criminal Court
ICJ. *See* International Court of Justice
IMF. *See* International Monetary Fund
Immunity, 188, 196, 197
India: NATO and, 63; ozone regime and, 350; Third World Network, 390–391; use of force by, 63
Individual(s): international legal personality of, 61; responsibility for human rights violations, 301; rights, 2, 17, 209
Indonesia, 222, 319, 481
Information: access to, 150; asymmetric, 30; electronic age of, 355, 460; genetic, 395; technology, 270
Institute of International Law, 289; Declaration of the International Rights of Man, 289
Institutions: arbitral, 25; creation of, 474; crime-fighting, 273; domestic, 27, 29, 150; financial, 8, 25, 270, 474; international, 21, 29, 147, 273–274; judicial, 25; legal, 27, 28; multilateral, 414–415; political, 151
Integration: economic, 436, 485; of territories, 330
Integrity: as international law source, 68; of NGOs, 129; political, 328; sovereign, 84; territorial, 259, 322, 324, 330
Inter-American Commission on Human Rights, 83, 300–301
Inter-American Court of Human Rights, 209, 211, 301, 302
Inter-American human rights system, 299–302
Inter-American Tropical Tuna Commission, 343
Intergovernmental organizations: antiterrorism and, 273–274; civil society and, 170; governance by, 169; human rights and, 306; ICC and, 104; increase in, 101; NGOs and, 169, 172; recognized status of, 324
International Atomic Energy Agency (IAEA), 32, 44, 107, 109, 479
International Chamber of Commerce, 118, 125
International Civil Aviation Organization, 104, 109, 110, 407
International Commission of Jurists, 186–187
International Commission on Intervention and State Sovereignty, 253, 324, 484
International Committee of the Red Cross (ICRC), 120, 122–123, 169
International community: ad hoc tribunals and, 237; challenges of, 466; collective action of, 94; dissenting states and, 55, 92; environment and, 347; genocide and, 328; human rights and, 296, 312, 319–321, 324, 326; international crimes and, 92–93, 377, 468; jurisdiction of, 185; membership in, 54; modern customs of, 54; normative values of, 17, 82, 88–89, 331; outer space and, 421–423, 429, 436, 443; sovereignty, 34, 64; terrorism and, 270; torture and, 163
International Competition Network (ICN), 472
International Convention for the Safety of Life at Sea, 409
International Convention for the Suppression of Terrorist Bombing, 478
International Convention for the Suppression of the Financing of Terrorism, 478–479
International Court of Justice (ICJ): *Anglo-Norwegian Fisheries* case, 406; *Armed Activities on the Territory of the Congo* case, 86; *Arrest Warrant* case, 207, 241; *Avena and Other Mexican Nationals* case, 173, 209; *Barcelona Traction* case, 92, 375; *Bosphorus*, 214–215; *Congo v. Uganda* case, 205, 208; constitutive norms, 12; Consular Convention, 210; contentious activity at, 143; *Corfu Channel* case, 387–388; custom and, 49; International Commission on Intervention and State Sovereignty, 253, 324, 484; *LaGrand* case, 209–210; *Lockerbie* case, 214; *Nicaragua v. USA* case, 207–208; *Nuclear Weapons* case, 127; *Oil Platforms* case, 214–215; self-determination and, 155; statutes of, 49; *Vienna Convention on Consular Relations* case, 173, 209; *Yusuf* case, 214

International courts: ad hoc tribunals and, 164, 237–240, 271; creation of, 10–11; proliferation of, 478. *See also* International Court of Justice; International Criminal Court
International Covenant on Civil and Political Rights, 89, 120, 130, 206, 209, 261, 294, 301, 310
International Criminal Court (ICC): "Elements of Crimes" and, 238; establishment of, 104, 238; future of, 241–243; judicial functions, 11, 238–240; jurisdiction of, 186, 238, 240, 476; jurisdiction, admissibility, applicable law, and, 239–240; Land Mines Convention, 130; NGOs and, 242; provisions of, 280, 475–476; "Rules of Procedure and Evidence" and, 238; treaty making and, 104; victim treatment under, 237–239; WTO, 11. *See also* Rome Statute
International Criminal Police Organization, 273–274
International Criminal Tribunal for Rwanda, 120, 197, 271, 307
International Criminal Tribunal for the Former Yugoslavia (ICTY), 89, 120, 197, 237–239, 271, 307
International Environmental Agreements: actors in, 350; bilateral, 346; effects of, 352–362; endogeneity problem in, 361–362; lineage, 342–344; multilateral, 341–346; patterns in, 344–346; processes of, 350–352; reasons for, 346–352
International Labour Organization (ILO): constituencies of, 107; NGOs and, 127; treaty making and, 105, 107, 119; tripartisanism, 127; and the WTO, 102, 235
International Law Association: Draft Articles on State Responsibility, 221, 260, 373; International Law Commission, 104, 276; Koskenniemi approach to, 213
International legal system: architecture of, 247; capacity of, 10; centralized enforcement in, 25; classification of, 178–179; coherence in, 235; as collective good, 148; complexity of, 93; credibility of commitments and, 23–27; decentralization of, 58, 61, 93; democratic regimes and, 151; due process and, 240; effectiveness of, 48; evolution of, 233; framework of, 165, 474; hard laws and, 23–32; monitoring provisions in, 27; non-European states and, 8; as normative system, 77, 163; participants in, 8, 13, 77, 465, 476; power relationships in, 166; problems with, 465; roles for, 466–467; state sovereignty and, 466; steps in interpretive process, 57–58; uncertainty and, 37–40; undermining democratic processes, 481; violations in, 24
International Liability for Damage Caused by Space Objects, Convention on the, 426, 428
International Maritime Court (Hamburg), 143
International Maritime Organization, 410
International Military Tribunal (Nuremberg), 92, 237–238
International Monetary Fund (IMF) 34, 150, 232, 474
International norms: adoption of, 179; African practices and, 304; compliance pull of, 154, 168; inquiry into, 12; *jus cogens*, 84; protection of, 176; punishment and, 187; purposes of, 174; understanding of, 10; WTO and, 228–229
International organizations: bureaucracies, 105; custom and, 112; development of, 117, 219; environmental responsibilities of, 442; expertise of, 349; financial, 25; frustration with, 403, 411; functions of, 207, 216, 479; ICC and, 242; increase in, 101; institutional cultures and negotiation in, 108; legitimization of rules by, 155; Marrakesh Agreement, 95; NGOs and, 108, 109; normative processes and, 155; role in GATT, 221; participants in, 108; significance of, 176; structural aspects of, 106; treaty making and, 102–112; WTO as, 219–236
International politics: anarchy and, 2; balance of power in, 153; concerns of, 159; functionalist approaches to, 149; future of, 485; influences in,

156, 158; norms in, 153, 437; realm of, 151; rules of, 144
International relations: compliance and, 146–156; environment and, 16; evolution of, 233; formal agreements in, 143–159; human rights and, 310–312; laws governing, 132; legal process in, 147; paradigms in, 144; soft law and, 41; theory of, 145–156; UN Charter and, 325–326; use of force in, 14; Westphalian system, 323–324
International society: evolution of, 224; importance of, 153; power and, 153; reputational effects on, 26; transformation of, 225; values of, 94
International Space Agency, 422, 438, 440–444
International Standards Organization (ISO), 7
International Trade in Endangered Species, Convention on, 25, 131, 345, 386, 392
International Trade Organization, 37, 221
International Tribunal for the Law of the Sea, 120, 406
Internet: architecture of, 460; censorship of, 459; development of, 16; free speech and, 459; jurisdiction of, 459; importance of, 126; international cooperation and, 462; lawsuits and, 459–461; providers and, 460
Intervention: armed, 320, 329–330, 332; without authorization, 28, 63, 209, 254; collective, 64, 65; custom and, 64; disinterest and, 64; forcible, 62, 321–322, 332; humanitarian, 62–65; illegal, 62; justification of, 253; legality of, 320; liberal, 254; military, 321, 326, 329, 332; modern, 253; NATO, 62; precedent-setting, 62, 63; prohibitions on, 64; protests over, 64; resolutions supporting, 63; self-defense and, 63; soft, 469, 482; unilateral, 62, 64, 65
Investment: foreign, 107, 110–111; protection of, 111; relation-specific, 24, 30
Iraq, 63, 90, 275, 442, 472; Coalition Provision Authority (CPA), 252; special tribunal, 252; use of force in, 163
Israel, 10, 174, 282; Eichmann trial in, 193
Italy, 90, 275, 442, 472

Japan, 43, 84, 106, 252, 414, 442
Jus ad bellum: concepts of, 250–252, 257, 261; difference from *jus in bello,* 250, 257; interplay with *jus in bello,* 262; narrative of, 249; rights under, 249; rules of, 250–251
Jus cogens: breaching, 84–85; content of, 83–84, 88; development of, 79–80; free rider concern, 83; future of, 91–93; and Human Rights Committee, 89; ICJ and, 86–87, 90; immoral conduct and, 54; legal consequences of, 84–88; as limitation, 85; morality and, 80; norms of, 61; in practice, 86–91; prohibition of action and, 53; state consent of, 85; theory, 79; Verdross response, 81–81; Vienna Convention and, 81–83, 91; violations of, 87–88
Jus in bello: concepts of, 250–252, 257, 261; difference from *jus ad bellum,* 250, 257; interplay with *jus ad bellum,* 262; narrative of, 249; rights under, 249; rules of, 250–251
Jus necessarium pro omnium, 81

Kadi case, 215
Kahn, A. Q., 468
Kampuchea, 63
Kant, Immanuel, 131, 256
Kellogg-Briand Pact, 249
Kennedy, John F., 252
Korea, 331
Kosovo: ethnic cleansing, 321; intervention in, 62, 249, 254; lack of UN authorization for action in, 331; North Atlantic Treaty Organization and, 62–63
Kuwait, 91
Kyoto Protocol, 163, 440

Land mines, 109, 126, 130
Laos, 278
Latin America, 42, 301, 310, 348, 403, 470

Law: commons, 16; competition, 31; as contract, 22; as covenant, 22; declaratory, 51; domestic, 25; economic, 104; general principles of, 81, 199, 231, 304; as interpretation, 57–58; natural, 13, 81–83, 86, 88, 255; as shield for weak, 42; transnational, 53; treaty, 386–393. *See also* Law of the Seas
Law of the Seas (LOS): challenge of, 404–405; definition, 402; development of, 401; disputes arising from, 143; environmental protection and, 409–413; exclusive economic zone (EEZ), 405, 407–410, 412; fishing and, 412–413; ILC and, 402; limitations of, 404–405; national security and, 408–409; NGOs and, 120; nuclear material and, 411; significance of, 406; sovereignty of, 405; spillover effect from, 111; UN Convention on, 404–413; United States and, 414; zones of jurisdiction, 405–407. *See also* United Nations Convention on the Law of the Sea
League of Arab States, 273
League of Nations, 119, 123, 128, 166, 219, 249, 289–291
Legalization: aid for weak states in, 42; benefits of, 22; bureaucracies of, 26; choice of levels of, 32; compliance pull and, 26; consequences for violations and, 25; contracting costs, 31–33; costs of reneging and, 24; costs of violation through normative channels and, 26; credibility of commitments and, 24; delegation in, 43; dispute resolution and, 28; enforcement capacity and, 24–25; enforcement of commitments and, 28, 29; as form of political bargaining, 44; forms of discourse in, 26; hard/soft, 21–44; in international relations, 21–44; international uncertainty and, 37–40; negotiation and, 28; normative values and, 22; organization of ongoing interactions and, 28
Legal order: definition, 220; WTO as, 219–236
Legal Principles Governing the Activities of States in the Exploration of Space, Declaration of, 425
Lex ferenda, 66–67
Lex lata, 66–67, 191, 437
Lex specialis, 78–79, 206, 213, 226
Liability Convention, 427, 431–433
Liberia, 254, 270, 321
Libya, 276
La Ligue Contre le Racisme et L'antisemitisme (LICRA), 457–458
Lord's Resistance Army, 241
Luxembourg Court of First Instance, 210, 214–215

MARPOL, 342–344, 355, 357
Marrakesh Agreement, 221, 226, 231
Media, 243, 270, 351
Mexico, 209, 210
Military and Paramilitary Activities in and Against Nicaragua, 50, 54, 62
Milosevic, Slobodan, 197
Minorities: protection of, 289, 306; rights of, 251–252, 290–291; self-determination and, 259
Mir station, 424
Money laundering, 36
Montevideo Convention on the Rights and Duties of States, 35
Montreal Protocol on Substances that Deplete the Ozone Layer, 104–105, 110, 438
Morgenthau, Hans, 144, 147
Multilateral Agreement on Investment (MAI), 110
Multinational corporations, 2, 4, 8, 324
Myanmar, 16, 170

NAFTA. *See* North American Free Trade Agreement
Namibia, 63, 91, 350
National Environmental Protection Act, 394
NATO. *See* North Atlantic Treaty Organization
Netherlands, 307
Netherlands Institute of Human Rights, 187
New International Economic Order, 105
New World Order, 180
Nicaragua: Contras, 278; ICJ case, 50, 54, 62, 81, 86, 90, 207, 214; treaty

with Costa Rica, 80; treaty with United States, 79–80; *v. United States* case, 208

Non bis in idem, 189–190, 194, 199

Nongovernmental organizations (NGOs): collective enforcement by, 121–122; as competitors, 125–127; as consultants, 122–124, 129–132; contributions of, 117; democracy and, 152; ECOSOC and, 123–124; environment and, 130; geographic range, 118; human rights and, 130, 152; ICJ and, 120; identity, 118–122; influence on sources of international law, 118, 127; international law and, 119–122, 124–126; international organizations and, 108, 109; legal personality of, 122; legitimacy of, 127–129; monitoring roles, 120–121; nature of, 117; normative processes and, 155; personality of, 122; treaty input of, 106, 108–109; WTO and, 120–121, 126

Nonintervention: custom of, 62; principles of, 14, 35, 42, 65, 332; sovereignty and, 64–65, 323; UN Charter and, 292

Nonstate actors: diversity of, 107; ICC and, 271; NGOs as, 127; terrorism and, 227, 269, 280–281, 468, 479; in tribunals, 212; WTO and, 225

Normative system of International Law: adaptation of, 167–178; commons management, 15; definition, 12; environmental protection in, 15, 16; legal internalization of, 172–175; NGOs and, 168–172; operating system imbalance with, 164–167; political processes in, 175–178; protection of human rights and, 14–15; regulation of force in, 14–15; soft law mechanisms, 177–178

Norms: constitutive, 13; democratic, 152; development of, 6, 169; emerging, 63, 65, 331, 435–436; hierarchy of, 77, 213–216; human rights, 15–16, 89, 172, 325; legal, 22; peremptory, 64, 81, 83; procedural; 77, 91, 213–216; regime, 12; regulative, 5. *See also* International norms; *Jus cogens*

North American Free Trade Agreement (NAFTA), 34, 476; dispute resolution and, 476; environmental regulation and, 40; labor regulation and, 40; *Methanex* case, 120–121; WTO and, 111

North Atlantic Treaty Organization (NATO): delegation of, 36; hard law and, 27; intervention in Kosovo, 62–63; as invalid agreement, 84

Norway, 339

Nuclear Non-Proliferation Treaty, 13, 32, 42–43

Nuclear power: isotopic sources, 422; nuclear reactors and, 422–423; pollution in space from, 422–423, 431–432

Nuclear weapons, 86, 206, 272, 345, 431, 479

Nuremberg Charter, 195–197

Nuremberg Military Tribunal, 237–238

OAS Secretariat, 276

OECD. *See* Organization for Economic Cooperation and Development

Operating System of International Law: adaptation of, 167–178; definition, 12; commons management, 15; environmental protection in, 15, 16; legal internalization of, 172–175; NGOs and, 168–172; normative system imbalance with, 164–167; political processes in, 175–178; protection of human rights and, 14–15; regulation of force in, 14–15; soft law mechanisms, 177–178

Opinio juris, 68, 382, 387; custom and, 49, 58, 59, 61, 66; obligations and, 50; statements of belief in, 49; state practice and, 51, 52, 56; treaty making and, 112

Organization for Economic Cooperation and Development (OECD), 106, 107, 109

Organization for Security and Co-operation in Europe, 306–308

Organization of African Unity, 273, 303

Organization of American States: antiterrorism and, 273; Charter of, 299–303; cooperation by, 242; norms of, 124

Organization of the Islamic Conference, 273
Organizations: codes of conduct in, 7, 352; financial, 107; private, 7, 119, 128, 167–170; regional, 242, 276, 312, 323, 332, 335, 479; transnational, 155; universal, 103. *See* Intergovernmental organizations
Osbaldo Torres v. State of Oklahoma, 173
Oslo Convention Prior Justification Procedure, 380
Ottawa Convention on Land Mines, 168–170; NGOs, 8
Outer space: accidents in, 423; cascade effect in collisions, 424; common interest and, 428–430; conventional law and, 430–431; customary international law and, 433–436; debris in, 423–425, 432–433; geosynchronous orbits in, 424; international law and, 430–431; law of, 425–428; low-earth orbits in, 424; pollution, 422–425, 431–433; protection of, 421–444; as province of all mankind, 421–444; regime-building approach, 436–438; *res communis humanitatis nullius*, 429; *res communis* in, 421; *res nullius* and, 428; Scientific-Legal Subcommittee, 434; soft law and, 436–438
Outer Space Treaty, 421, 425–427, 429–431; Scientific and Technical Sub-Committee for, 423; Scientific-Legal Roundtable, 424
Ozone layer: contributors to destruction of, 352, 355, 379; depletion of, 13, 83, 105, 110, 360, 363, 432; MEAs and, 345; Montreal Protocol, 104–105, 110, 438; negotiations on, 350–351; protection of, 85; stratospheric hole in, 348; Vienna Convention, 38, 111, 437
Ozone Layer Convention, 438

Pacta sum servanda, 26
Pakistan, 481
Palestine, 282
Pan-American Conference, 119
Partial Nuclear Test Ban Treaty, 426, 433
Peace of Westphalia, 401
Permanent Court of International Justice (PCIJ), 79; *Chinn* case, 80; *S.S. Lotus* case, 50
Permanent Sovereignty over Natural Resources, Declaration on, 83
Pinochet, Augusto, 10, 25, 90, 165, 192, 271, 477
Piracy, 188, 195, 272
Policy: economic, 132; national, 35; tax, 36
Political: authority, 254; bargaining, 38, 44, 443; economy, 36, 132; institutions, 25, 151, 179, 443, 485; networks, 169; rights, 290, 298–301, 303, 310; strategies, 21, 29–30
Political and Civil Rights, Covenant on, 14
Politics: domestic, 149–151; law and, 432; low, 148. *See also* International politics
Pollution: air, 175, 345, 348, 363; cross-border, 466; marine, 342, 345, 348–349, 358–359; oil, 344, 348, 381; space, 422, 426, 431; transboundary, 375–376; transfrontier, 379, 395; water, 13, 379
Pol Pot, 319
Positivism, 117
Poverty, 302, 306, 373, 385, 392, 468–469
Precautionary principle: biological diversity and, 384–386; defining, 380–384; in environmental law, 371; formulations of, 381; as guidelines to action, 376; in international law, 379–393; *opinio juris* and, 381
Prevention and Punishment of the Crime of Genocide, Convention on the, 294
Princeton Project on Universal Jurisdiction, 185–200
Privatization, 171
Protection of National Minorities, Convention for, 35

Rainforests, 350, 373
Ramsar Convention, 371, 385–386
Rape, 120, 241, 270, 326–327
Regimes: change in, 277; democratic, 151, 301; dictatorial, 277; domestic, 277; human rights, 25; international,

24; interstate relations and, 151; norms, 12; obligations of, 24; trade, 109; treaty, 103
Regime theory, 5, 14
Registration of Objects Launched into Outer Space, Convention on the, 426
Res communis, 415, 422, 429
Rescue of Astronauts, Agreement on the, 426, 428
Res nullius, 428–429
Revolutionary Armed Forces of Columbia, 270
Rhodesia, 91, 294
Rights, human: atrocities, 320, 323, 331–332; bodily integrity and, 155; compliance monitoring, 104, 121, 167; covenants on, 293, 303, 310; culture-based, 14; European regimes, 24–25; individual, 295, 297, 325; normative content of, 13–14, 304; norms, 320, 323, 331–332; obligations, 49–53, 78–79, 260, 293, 309, 311–312; sovereignty and, 14–15; standards, 155, 194, 311; universal character of, violations of, 12, 65, 163, 175, 292–297, 305–308; vulnerable groups and, 155
Rights of the Child, Convention on the, 294
Rio Conference on Environment and Development, 38, 435; Forest Principles, 38, 178
Risk-sharing, 38
Robinson, Mary, 481
Rome Statute: adoption of, 186, 239, 242; conclusion of, 108; establishment of ICC and, 307, 475
Roosevelt, Franklin, 279, 280
Russia: ABM treaty, 432; corruption in, 470; Council of Europe, 298, human rights abuse and, 481; outer space and, 424, 442
Rwanda: genocide, 1, 87, 237, 321, 468; human rights in, 86, 324; and *jus cogens,* 87; International Criminal Tribunal, 120, 197, 213, 238–239, 271, 306–311

Sanctions: economic, 296, 311, 329, 350, 361; legal, 437; reparations and, 259–260; Security Council–issued, 214, 276, 296; severity of, 149; trade, 227
San Francisco Conference, 123, 292
Saudi Arabia, 43
SEATO, 84
Sector, private, 8–9, 171, 252
Security: collective, 62, 252–253, 260, 408; as national concept, 325
Self-defense: armed attack, 322–323; collective, 155, 322, 408; inherent right of, 279; principle of, 321
Self-determination: ICJ and, 155; internal, 261; notion of, 261; promotion of, 322; sovereignty and, 256; territorial concept of, 259; United Nations and, 85, 258, 292, 322; Vienna Convention and, 258–259
Sharon, Ariel, 10, 174
Sierra Leone, 122, 254, 270, 321, 474
Slavery, 8, 88, 92, 188, 195
Society: global civil, 127; legal commitment in, 24. *See also* Civil society; International society
Soft law: absence of independent judiciary and, 22; advantages of, 23, 31–44; compromise in, 40–41; contracting costs in, 31–33; criticism of, 22; delegation in, 32; destabilization of normative systems and, 22; enforcement power and, 22; escape clauses and, 32; implementation flexibility and, 40; imprecise commitments in, 32; in international law, 21–44; justifications for, 22; processes of learning and, 41; sovereignty costs and, 33–37; sovereignty implications and, 23; in states with different degrees of readiness for legalization, 40; as tool of compromise, 40–44; transaction costs and, 23; uncertainty and, 37–40; varieties of, 22; weakening of legal arrangements and, 221
Solana, Javier, 470
Somalia, 320, 470
Sosa v. Alvarez Machain, 94
South Africa, 68, 91, 198, 294, 308, 472
South Asian Association for Regional Cooperation, 273
Southern Cone Common Market (MERCOSUR), 470

Sovereignty: absolute, 387, 389; concepts of, 33; costs, 33–37, 149, 178; definition of, 320; delegation of, 34, 68, 149; erosion of, 102, 106; hard law and, 22; hard-shell, 15; internal, 35; issue types, 36–37; legal, 33–34, 143; national, 15, 23, 25, 168, 320, 324, 332, 429; pooled, 469, 482; popular, 261; reduction, 37; over resources, 83; as responsibility, 324–333; shared, 474; state, 15–16, 22, 32–35, 64–65, 224, 253, 278, 319–333; territorial, 84, 258, 326, 401–413, 427–428; Westphalian, 34, 465–466, 469
Soviet Union, 298, 424
Space Environment Framework Convention, 437–438, 442–444
Space pollution, 422, 426, 431
S.S. Lotus case, 50
State behavior, 15, 53, 146; analysis of, 153–154; effects on, 146, 171, 342; factors in, 2–3, 480; legal standards and, 156; modifications of, 11; outcomes of, 479; patterns of, 7; predictors of, 53; regulation of, 6–7, 14, 93, 177; sovereignty and, 484
State positivism, 117
State succession, 258
Stockholm Conference on the Human Environment, 371, 373, 383, 387, 389
Stockholm Declaration, 371, 373, 383, 388–389, 435, 436, 444
Strategic Defense Initiative program, 431–432
Sudan, 239, 241, 276, 468, 477
Suppression of Terrorist Bombings, International Convention for, 478
Sustainable development: conflicts over, 379; emerging norm of, 435–436, 439; environmental and, 388, 393; global imperatives of, 391; in international law, 393; intragenerational equity and, 435, 436; NGOs and, 155, 172; outer space and, 422, 430, 434–436; principles of law in, 231; UN Commission on, 386; world summit on, 360; WTO and, 231
Sustainable Development Commission, 155
Switzerland, 275
System, normative: behavioral norms of, 163; description of, 12–17; goals of, 179; international law and, 3; vs. operating system, 5–6, 164–168; soft law and, 22

Tadic, 93, 207, 209
Tanzania, 63, 481
Technology: biodiversity, 373; commercial, 44; environmentally sound, 390; globalization and, 168, 270; internet, 460–461; military, 44; for publicity, 126; regime failure and, 103; space, 441, 443; standards for, 39; transfer, 44, 373
Terrorism: black market accessibility and, 270; as crime against humanity, 272; defining, 269; double standards and, 282; financing, 270; globalization and, 270; international, 269–282; legal control of, 269–282; long existence of, 269; need for value-neutral convention on, 281; networks, 278; organized crime and, 270; state responsibility for prevention, 276–277; weakness of international law in addressing, 270–276; weapons of mass destruction and, 269
Third World Network, 391
Thirty Years' War, 8, 469
Torres, Osbaldo (*Osbaldo Torres v. State of Oklahoma*), 173
Torture: definition of, 196; freedom from, 84; as grounds for extradition, 190, 199; *jus cogens* and, 90–91; prohibition of, 25, 54, 85, 88–90, 332; as war crime, 90
Tourism, 9, 343, 385
Trade: disputes, 28, 157; global, 163, 165; institutionalization, 37; international, 219, 223, 235, 345, 348, 386; restrictions, 25; sovereignty costs and, 37
Trade Related Investment Measures, 111
Trail Smelter case, 387–388
Transnational actors, 10
Transnational Organized Crime, Convention Against, 468
Travaux préparatoires, 210

Treaties: ad hoc conferences for, 103, 107, 109, 112; Anti-Ballistic Missile Treaty, 426, 432; bilateral, 92, 189, 236, 275, 341, 435; on bribery, 107; custom and, 55; economic, 11, 105; endogeneity of, 157, 158; extradition, 275; functionalism and, 101; human rights, 299, 308, 310, 436; implementation of, 145; intellectual property, 109; "last in time rule," 386; multilateral, 101, 102; mutual legal assistance, 275; need for, 107; negotiations for, 112; normative change and, 13–14, 165–166; proliferation of, 101–102; ratification of, 105, 106; sovereign equality and, 102; spillover effects of, 111; trade, 109
Treaty making, 102; constitutionally sanctioned, 105; dispute settlement and, 104–105; diversity of actors in, 106; early, 102, 103; and experts, 103, 104; increased participation in, 108; information available for, 110, 111; managerial forms of, 103, 104; negotiations, 102–103; nesting issues in, 111; NGOs and, 108–109; organizational venues for, 107, 108, 110, 111; organization patterns, 102–112; package deals in, 111; power and, 109, 110; with strings attached, 105; subject codification and, 101; technological drafts and, 104; United Nations and, 101–102, 104
Treaty of Rome, 30, 469
Tropical Timber Agreement, 356, 363
Truman Proclamation, 402, 404
Truth and Reconciliation Commission (South Africa), 198, 260, 308
Turkey, 63, 291

Uganda, 63, 205, 208–209, 241, 319
Uniform Code of Military Justice, 280
L'Union des Etudiants Juifs De France (UEJF), 457–458
United Kingdom, 63
United Nations: Ad Hoc Committee on the Peaceful Uses of Outer Space, 425; administrative roles of specialized agencies, 38; antiterrorism goals of, 110; Centre for International Crime Prevention, 273; Commission on Sustainable Development, 386; Crime Prevention Centre, 275; Environmental Programme, 392; Food and Agriculture Organization, 7, 232, 386; Foreign Relations Law, 374; General Assembly, 105, 107, 435; Global Environment Facility, 129–130, 386; globalization and, 78, 273; humanitarian interventions and, 15, 176, 293, 321–324; Human Rights Commission, 89, 146, 209, 293–294, 297; Human Rights Watch, 167; legitimacy of, 64; peacekeeping and, 321, 408; Secretariat, 392–393; Security Council, 271, 276; self-determination and, 85, 322; Sub-Commission on the Promotion and Protection of Human Rights, 293; treaties and, 101–102, 104; Trusteeship Council, 291; UNEP, 341, 344, 349–351, 360
United Nations Charter, 62, 279
United Nations Conference on Environment and Development, 359, 391, 394, 442
United Nations Conference on the Human Environment (UNCHE), 345, 426–428
United Nations Convention on Biological Diversity, 389; enforcement of, 374; goals of, 371, 380, 390; Law of the Sea and, 386; precautionary measures, 396; wildlife treaties, 371
United Nations Convention on the Law of the Sea: conservation measures, 234; ecosystem concept, 371; EEZ and, 405–410; geographic limits, 406–407; jurisdiction of, 405
United Nations Economic and Social Council (ECOSOC), 122–124, 131, 294–295
United Nations Educational, Scientific and Cultural Organization (UNESCO), 306, 407
United Nations Framework Convention on Climate Change, 6, 440
United Nations General Assembly Declaration on Principles of International Law, 35

United Nations Programme on HIV/AIDS (UNAIDS), 119
United Nations Programme on Space Applications, 441, 443
United Nations Regional Seas Convention, 342
United States: Alien Tort Claims Act, 170, 175; Alien Tort Statute, 91; Al Qaeda, 278–280; Coalition Provision Authority (CPA), 252; coercive tactics of, 28; Commission on Weak States and National Security, 471; concern over ICC jurisdiction, 34, 280; Constitution, First Amendment, 457–459, 461; death penalty, 88–89; Department of State, 414; determination on antidumping duties, 476; efforts to control environmental protections, 394; *Filartiga v. Pena-Irala*, 91; Foreign Corrupt Practices Act, 106; Foreign Relations Law, 374; Gulf War, 43, 215; human rights and, 310; ICJ judgment against, 90; interventions in Iraq, 63; Iraq, 282, 476; Military Commission, 279–280; as NAFTA authority, 34; protection of marine life, 409–413; *Shrimps* dispute, 225, 231; Somalia invasion, 320; substantive balance, 407–408; Supreme Court, 94, 289, 310; territorial temptation and, 404–405; terrorism and, 109–110, 273, 278; treaty network, 101–102; as unilateralist, 101, 273; Vietnam conflict, 278
Universal Declaration of Human Rights, 120, 261, 293–294, 303–304, 309–310
Universal jurisdiction, 185–200; abuse of, 193; amnesties, 189, 196, 198; competing jurisdictions and, 189; development of, 185–200; dispute settlement, 191; domestic law and, 192; double jeopardy and, 189, 194; due process and, 187; establishment of, 192; exercise of, 187, 196–198; extradition and, 190, 194; fundamentals of, 187–188; immunity and, 196, 197; impartiality of judiciary and, 188; international networks of cooperation in, 194; leadership accountability and, 193–194; legitimate exercise of, 194; *non bis in idem* in, 189–190, 194, 199; *opinio juris* and, 192; politically motivated prosecution and, 193; proper exercise of, 186; prosecutions, 193–195, 198–199; protections for accused, 199; seriousness of crime and, 193; statutes of limitations, 189, 197; terrorism and, 200
Urban Morgan Institute for Human Rights, 187

Vienna Convention for the Protection of the Ozone Layer, 111, 437–438
Vienna Convention on Consular Relations case, 173, 209
Vienna Convention on the Law of Treaties, 86–87, 91, 213, 215, 229, 257, 259
Vienna Convention on the Ozone Layer, 38, 111, 437
Vietnam, 63, 278

War: civil, 260, 307, 319, 468–469; erosion of, 248–249; just, 13, 253–256, 258; laws of, 278, 279; as legal institution, 248; legitimacy of, 278, 279; of national liberation, 277; revolutionary, 278
War crimes: Geneva convention and, 195, 235, 271, 282; ICJ and, 5; *jus cogens* and, 90; as serious crime against international law, 195; universal jurisdiction of, 271
Warsaw Pact, 171
Westphalia: legacy of, 3; peace of, 401; sovereignty of, 33, 220, 465–466, 469, 481; state system, 323; treaties of, 219, 469
Wetlands, 341, 343, 355, 371, 373, 390, 392
Whaling Convention, 25, 350, 353
Williams, Jody, 126, 170
World Bank, 34, 121, 129, 232, 360, 394, 474
World Charter for Nature, 371, 383–388, 435–436
World Commission on Environment and Development, 384, 435
World Conservation Union, 119
World Heritage Convention, 356, 371

World Intellectual Property Organization, 106
World Summit, 129, 360
World Trade Organization (WTO): antidumping measures, 34, 476; Appellate Body, 120–121, 216, 223, 225–232; dispute resolution in, 143; Dispute Settlement Body (DSB), 22, 226–228; Dispute Settlement Understanding in, 222, 225–226; *EC-Bananas*, 225–227; *EC-Swordfish* dispute, 233–234; focus on market access, 228–231; GATT and, 221, 226–229, 231, 234–235; human rights and, 78–79; ILO and, 235; *Indonesia-Autos* dispute, 222; International organizations and, 232–233; jurisdiction issues, 226–227; legal institutions of, 228; as legal order, 219–236; legal personality of, 221, 232, 236; Marrakesh Agreement and, 221, 226, 231; membership, 224; Ministerial Conferences, 223; NGOs in, 224–225; Sanitary and Phytosanitary Agreement (SPS), 231; Secretariat, 222, 225, 232–233; sovereignty and, 227; trade disputes and, 157, 228, 230, 234; trade-environment jurisprudence, 234–235; trade openness and, 233; *United States–Section 301*, 222; *United States–Shrimps*, 225, 231; *US-Gasoline*, 229; Vienna Convention and, 229–230
World War I, 119, 166, 289–291
World War II: aggression following, 240; crimes during, 90; human rights after, 62, 289; realist theory after, 153; self-determination after, 261; treaties and, 186; tribunals resulting from, 237–238
Worldwide Fund for Nature, 360
WTO. *See* World Trade Organization

Yahoo, Inc., 16, 457–462
Yugoslavia: Bosnian Serb army and, 208; ICTY and, 89, 120, 197, 237–239, 271, 307; minority rights and, 29; NATO and, 63; NGOs and, 121

About the Book

COVERING SUBJECTS RANGING FROM TREATIES AND DISPUTE resolution to the environment, human rights, and terrorism, this anthology is unique in revealing the influence of international law on political behavior.

The third edition has been updated with thirteen new chapters that discuss emerging actors and structures, address the most pressing current issues, and consider the future evolution of the international legal system.

Charlotte Ku is assistant dean for graduate and international legal studies at the University of Illinois College of Law. Her publications include *Democratic Accountability and the Use of Force in International Law* and other works on subjects of international law and international organizations. **Paul F. Diehl** is Henning Larsen Professor of Political Science at the University of Illinois at Urbana-Champaign. His publications include *Peace Operations*, *War and Peace in International Rivalry*, and *International Peacekeeping*.